Troubleshooting TCP/IP

Mark A. Miller, P.E.

2ND EDITION

D1501871

M&T Books
A Division of MIS:Press, Inc.
A Subsidiary of Henry Holt and Company, Inc.
115 West 18th Street
New York, New York 10011

Library of Congress Cataloging-in-Publication Data

Miller, Mark, 1955-
    Troubleshooting TCP/IP : analyzing the protocols of the Internet /
Mark A. Miller. -- 2nd ed.
      p.   cm.
    Includes bibliographical references and index.
    ISBN 1-55851-450-3
    1. TCP/IP (Computer network protocol) I. Title.
TK5105.585.M56   1996
004.6'2--dc20   96-15271
                                                                   CIP

10 9 8 7 6 5 4 3 2 1

Associate Publisher: Paul Farrell

Managing Editor: Cary Sullivan	Production Editor: Anne Incao
Editor: Debra Williams Cauley	Technical Editor: John Thompson
Copy Edit Manager: Shari Chappell	Copy Editor: Annette S. Devlin

To Buster, for his faithfulness

CONTENTS

Contents

Contents

Contents

TABLE OF ILLUSTRATIONS

Table of Illustrations

Table of Illustrations

Preface

I am pleased that you have added *Troubleshooting TCP/IP, 2nd Edition* to your technical library. Let me provide a brief summary of the revisions from the first edition.

First and foremost, the use of TCP/IP has migrated from the government and education sectors to general business applications. Chapters 1 and 2 illustrate some of the networks and operating systems that provide this application support.

Second, while the core functions of TCP and IP have remained stable for a number of years, a number of supporting protocols have been added or revised since the publication of the first edition. Examples would include support for ATM networks, which is new; revisions to the Routing Information Protocol, known as RIP version 2; updates to the Bootstrap Protocol, BOOTP, known as the Dynamic Host Configuration Protocol, DHCP; and security revisions to the second version of the Simple Network Management Protocol, SNMP. Chapters 3-7 discuss these, and other protocols, that have matured in the last few years.

But most importantly, at the time that the first edition was written, most of industry expected the TCP/IP suite to be eventually replaced with Open Systems Interconnection (OSI)-based protocols. Current marketplace experience invalidates that prediction. Instead, the present Internet Protocol, now known as IP version 4, is in the process of being replaced by a new version, known as IP Next Generation (IPng) or IP version 6 (IPv6). It is expected that the migration from IPv4 to IPv6 will take several years, however these efforts may require extensive planning on the part of network managers. To summarize, if your internetwork presently uses IPv4, at some time in the future, that internetwork will either directly or indirectly be impacted by IPv6. As a result, a brand new Chapter 8 that details the operation of IPv6 replaces the previous discussion on OSI migration.

The appendices have been updated, and in addition, a CD-ROM containing over 1,000 Internet documents has been added for those readers that want to dig deeper into the various subjects.

As was the case in the first edition, a number of individuals contributed to this work. The management and staff at M&T Books, including Paul Farrell, Debra Williams Cauley, Annette Sroka Devlin, Anne Incao and Joe McPartland provided editorial support. The insights of my technical editor, Dr. John Thompson, were especially appreciated. Karen Cope did much of the research on the Appendices, and David Hertzke of Integrated Graphic Communication produced all of the figures.

Several individuals added their expertise to specific case studies and sections. In alphabetical order, these are: Ed Britton, Pat Burns, Brian Clark, Libby Fox, Paul Franchois, Derek Hodovance, Jack Jackson, Allen Kerr, Nick Lopez, Chip Mesec, Don Mulvey, Ken Pappas, Georgann Russo, Steve Stokes, and Ken Volpe.

As before, Holly, Nathan and Nicholas added their support and encouragement, with Boomer and Brutus assisting as always. It is good to be surrounded by such a distinguished support team.

mark@diginet.com

May 1996

Preface to the First Edition

Writing the *Preface* or *Foreword* is something that I always look *forward* to for several reasons. First, it signals the end of numerous long hours, revisions, and telephone calls. Secondly, it provides a mechanism for me to present a road map for the reader, so that your navigation duties will be minimized. Finally, it provides an opportunity to say a few personal words about an otherwise very impersonal subject.

Presenting the Roadmap

This is the fifth volume of *The Network Troubleshooting Library*, and concentrates on the TCP/IP and related protocols. This book was inspired by the research that I did for the fourth volume, *Troubleshooting Internetworks* (M&T Books, 1991). In doing the research for that book, I wrote to a number of users of the Network General Corp. *Sniffer* Analyzer and asked them to contribute any interesting trace files that they may have saved. These submittals became the case studies that were used in the book. As I was surveying the numerous disks that I received, a trend emerged: There were more TCP/IP-related submittals than any other protocol suite—even more than DECnet, SNA, or NetWare. A light came on, and the idea of devoting an entire volume to TCP/IP was born.

This book is structured like the other volumes in that it makes a somewhat orderly progression from the bottom to the top of the protocol architecture. In this case, however, that architecture is the Defense Advanced Research Projects Agency (DARPA) architecture—the architecture out of which these protocols were developed. In Chapter 1 we will look at the place these protocols occupy within the world of internetworking. In Chapter 2 we will survey the support for the protocols among mainframe, minicomputer, LAN, and analyzer manufacturers. In Chapters 3 through 6, we will study the Network Interface, Internet, Host-to-Host, and Application/Process Layers. Each of these chapters will present an overview of the protocols themselves, and then present a number of case studies that illustrate the protocols working (and not working!). Chapter 7 is devoted to the topic of internetwork management, and Chapter 8 concludes with a glimpse into transition strategies for TCP/IP internetworks that may migrate to OSI protocols. Appendices A through H could be described as "useful information"—protocol parameters and documentation that I have needed to look up and that you may find handy as well.

A Few Personal Notes

As always, a number of people behind the scenes contributed to the volume that you are about to read. My editors at M&T Books, Brenda McLaughlin, Sarah

Wadsworth, Tom Woolf, and Cheryl Goldberg spent many long hours to assure that the project would be completed on schedule.

Nancy Wright and Krystal Valdez did the word processing on the manuscript. David Hertzke of Integrated Computer Graphics took my hand-drawn scratchings and turned them into very legible figures. Thanks to the three of you for all your hard work.

On several occasions, specific tests were required to see how the protocols (running on live networks) would perform under "what if" conditions. Eural Authement, Chris Dutchyn, Ross Dunthorne, and Paul Franchois lent their expertise and time for these experiments.

I am indebted to several individuals who added their expertise to individual sections: Jay Allard, John Case, Dan Callahan, Bill Cohn, Michael Howard, Brian Meek, Larry Thomas, Ursula Sinkewicz, plus a host of folks from Banyan Systems Inc. Eural Authement, Paul Franchois, and Carl Shinn read the entire manuscript, making numerous suggestions for improvements. David Menges of the Colorado SuperNet, Inc. assisted with Internet-related questions and support issues.

The real heros and heroines are the network managers throughout the world who shared their experiences via Network General *Sniffer* trace files that became the basis for the 29 case studies that you will read. It is one thing to discuss a protocol from an academic point of view, but something quite different to see those protocols in action. In alphabetical order, these individuals are: Rohit Aggarwal, Gerald Aster, Eural Authement, Joe Bardwell, Ross Dunthorne, Chris Dutchyn, Tony Farrow, Paul Franchois, Dave Heck, Dell Holmes, James Knights, Iwan Lie, Jeff Logullo, Dan Milligan, Tom Morocz, Mark Ryding, Bob Sherman, Mendy Valinsky, and Wayne Veilleux.

Ed Lucente and Bob Bessin of Network General Corporation provided me with a *Sniffer* Analyzer to study the various problems submitted for case studies. Juancho Forlanda located some unusual trace files when my normal sources failed. Their generosity is greatly appreciated.

I am grateful for three friends, Lloyd Boggs, Gordon England, and Marsh Riggs, who provided encouragement during the writing of the manuscript.

Most importantly, Holly, Nicholas, and Nathan provided the supportive environment that makes the undertaking of such a project possible. Boomer helped me get up for an early morning run, Brutus tried real hard not to bark when we did, and Buster was the ever-faithful sentry. Thanks to all of you for your love.

Mark A. Miller

June 1992

Why This Book is for You

This second edition of the fifth volume in *The Network Troubleshooting Library*, discusses one of the most popular internetworking architectures: TCP/IP and the protocols of the Internet. These protocols were developed as a result of requirements defined by the U.S. Government in the mid-1970s. The rigor of these protocols, together with their widespread use among various research universities and defense contractors, brought them to the commercial forefront in the 1980s. The dramatic growth of the Internet strengthens TCP/IP's position as the predominant internetworking protocol solution to this day.

With the popularity of TCP/IP, a key issue for the internetwork manager is: given that TCP/IP is in place (and may be there for some time), how do I analyze these protocols? A second issue is preparing for the migration from the current IP version 4 to the recently-defined IP version 6. The objective of this book is to answer those questions. Major topics of discussion include:

- How various network architectures, including Ethernet and token ring LANs, FDDI and SMDS MANs, and ATM, Frame Relay and X.25 WAN architectures support TCP/IP.
- The various layers of internet addressing, including the hardware, internet, and port addresses, and how they work together to communicate the end-user's application data.
- A layer-by-layer study of the ARPA architectural model, showing how TCP/IP and the related protocols such as ARP, RARP, ICMP, RIP, OSPF, UDP, BOOTP, DHCP, TELNET, FTP, TFTP, SMTP and SNMP fit into that architecture.
- Over 25 case studies, taken from live internetworks such as Ethernet, token ring, Frame Relay and ATM, demonstrate TCP/IP and the related protocols in use, typical problems that may occur, plus solutions.
- Time-saving appendices that present protocol parameters and documentation to assist in troubleshooting.

In addition, the enclosed CD-ROM, which includes over 1,000 Internet RFC, BCP, FYI, IMR, RTR and STD documents, makes your study and analysis of these protocols that much easier.

If TCP/IP is part of your internetwork, this book should be part of your library.

## CHAPTER 1

Using TCP/IP and the Internet Protocols

On the surface, the Transmission Control Protocol/Internet Protocol (TCP/IP) is just another networking buzzword. But dig deeper and we find one of the most popular solutions for internetworking and interoperability ever devised. More than simply two protocols, TCP/IP is an architecture that enables dissimilar hosts, such as a minicomputer from Digital Equipment Corp. (Maynard, Massachusetts) and a workstation from Sun Microsystems Inc. (Mountain View, California), to communicate. This communication could be via Local Area Network (LAN), Metropolitan Area Network (MAN), Wide Area Network (WAN), or some hybrid internetwork technology— TCP/IP supports them all. You might call TCP/IP "the great communicator" or "the interoperability solution."

TCP/IP was developed, refined, and nurtured to meet the needs of the Internet. The Internet provides a worldwide mechanism for user-to-user, computer-to-computer communication that crosses corporate and national boundaries. The same TCP/IP protocols can meet any LAN or WAN connectivity requirements. But that's getting ahead of the story. We'll come back to the TCP/IP protocols in a little while. First, let's take a brief tour of the Internet.

1.1 The Challenge of the Internet

The word *internet* means different things to different people. Some use it as a verb, as in "to internetwork an IBM SNA environment with a Digital DECnet environment." Others use it as a noun to mean a network comprised of two or more dissimilar networks, i.e., an internet (or internetwork) between two Packet Switched Public Data Networks (PSPDNs). It is also a proper noun, the Internet, that refers to a collection of networks located around the world that interconnect for the purposes of user and computer communication.

Just as the word has diverse meanings, the Internet has diverse challenges. Let's assume you're connected to the Internet. Similar to the way you rely on the public telephone network, you depend on the Internet for communicating with your friends and associates. But what happens when there's a system failure? If the telephone network has a problem, you simply contact the Local Exchange Carrier (LEC) or InterExchange Carrier (IXC) responsible for your service. But when there's trouble with the Internet, service restoration is not as straightforward for several reasons. First, the Internet protocols are more complex than the telephone serving your home or business. Second, you're dealing with computer communication, which is more abstract than voice and more difficult to diagnose. Finally, because the Internet is an interconnected matrix of computer networks, identifying and diagnosing the problem is a greater challenge. Moreover, no single entity or procedure (such as dialing "0" for the operator to connect you to telephone repair) is available to address problems. (Granted, end users can pass the problem to the local administrator, who can then contact the Internet service provider, but then the provider is stuck with the problem.) Whoever ends up with the Internet problem will have to test and diagnose it him or herself. In summary, there is no single entity responsible for the end-to-end operation of *your* Internet connection.

That brings us to the purpose of this book. Since the mid-1970s, the TCP/IP suite has been the glue that holds the Internet together. Several ancillary protocols, such as the Address Resolution Protocol (ARP), Internet Control Message Protocol (ICMP), User Datagram Protocol (UDP), Routing Information Protocol (RIP), Open Shortest Path First (OSPF) Protocol, and many others, have also been developed along the way. And in the last few years of the twentieth century, significant enhancements, referred to as *IPng*, for Internet Protocol next generation, are under development and deployment. The resulting mixture can be a challenge to troubleshoot; in many cases, it requires the help of a protocol analyzer. The purpose of this book is to demystify the process of troubleshooting TCP/IP-based internetworks. To do so, we will learn about the topology of the Internet, study the protocols used within the Internet, and examine case studies of actual Internet problems. But before going on to the mechanics, let's begin with a history lesson.

1.2 A Brief History of the Internet

The *Internet* with a capital *I* is one of the world's most interesting achievements of computer science and networking technology. It provides a worldwide mechanism for user-to-user, computer-to-computer communication that spans corporate and national boundaries. This achievement is even more amazing because the Internet is self-governing: it is run by committees comprised largely of volunteers. In the past, many government organizations, such as the U.S. Department of Defense and individual states, have subsidized the basic expenses. Much of the research into the Internet protocols is conducted at major U.S. research universities, such as the University of California, the University of Colorado, the University of Illinois, and the University of Texas. As the Internet has evolved, however, the expenses for Internet connectivity have been passed down to the individual users—those who benefit from access to this public resource. Let's see how this unique system evolved.

Today's Internet was born in 1969 as the Advanced Research Projects Agency Network (ARPANET) and was sponsored by the U.S. Defense Advanced Research Projects Agency (DARPA), now known as ARPA. The purpose of the ARPANET was to test and determine the viability of a communication technology known as *packet switching* [1-1]. The contract to build the original ARPANET was awarded to a firm known as Bolt, Baranek, and Newman (now BBN Communications, Inc., Cambridge, Massachusetts). ARPANET went online in September 1969 at four locations: Stanford Research Institute (SRI), the University of California at Santa Barbara (UCSB), the University of California at Los Angeles (UCLA), and the University of Utah. The original hosts were Honeywell minicomputers, known as *Interface Message Processors* (IMPs).

The initial test was successful, and the ARPANET grew quickly. At the same time, it became apparent that nonmilitary researchers could also benefit from access to a network of this type, so leaders in the university and industrial research communities made proposals to the National Science Foundation (NSF) for a cooperative network of computer science researchers [1-2]. The NSF approved funding for the Computer Science Network (CSNET) in 1981.

In 1984, the ARPANET was split into two different networks: MILNET (for unclassified military traffic) and ARPANET (for nonmilitary traffic and research). In 1984, the NSF established the Office of Advanced Scientific Computing (OASC) to further the development of supercomputers and to make access to them more widely available. The OASC developed the NSFNET to connect six supercomputing centers across the United States, using T-1 lines operating at 1.544 Mbps in 1987, and subsequently upgraded to the T-3 rate (44.736 Mbps) in 1990. NSFNET, with its higher transmission rates, was a resounding success; as a result, the U.S. Department of Defense declared the ARPANET obsolete and dismantled it in June 1990.

In the meantime, NSFNET connections encompassed a system of regional and state networks. The New England Academic and Research Network (NEARNET), the Southeastern Universities Research Association Network (SURAnet), and the California Education and Research Federation Network (CERFnet) were among the family of NSFNET-connected networks. Since these networks were designed, built, and operated, in part, with government funds, regulations called *Acceptable Use Policies*, or AUPs, governed the types of traffic that could traverse these networks. In general, traffic that was for "research or educational purposes" was deemed acceptable; other traffic was either discouraged or prohibited [1-3]. Few, if any, accounts of the "Internet Police" apprehending an AUP violator were recorded, however, again testifying to the self-governing nature of the Internet.

The business community, seeing the new opportunity for electronic commerce, began looking for ways to support general business traffic on the Internet without violating these regulations. As a result of this opportunity, the Commercial Internet Exchange Association (CIX) was formed in 1991 [1-4]. CIX is a nonprofit trade organization of Public Data Network service providers that promote and encourage the development of the public data communications internetworking services. Membership in CIX is open to organizations that offer TCP/IP or OSI public data internetworking services to the general public; there are currently more than100 member networks. CIX provides these service providers with a neutral forum for the discussion and development of legislative, policy, and technology issues. Member networks agree to interconnect with all other CIX members via the CIX router and to exchange traffic. There are no restrictions placed on the traffic routed between member networks. Nor are there "settlements," or traffic-based charges, as a result of these interconnections.

Another outgrowth of the Internet expansion was the founding of the nonprofit Internet Society (ISOC) in 1992. The Internet Society, headquartered in Reston, Virginia [1-5], is an international organization that strives for global cooperation and coordination for the Internet. Members of the ISOC include government agencies, nonprofit research and educational organizations, and for-profit corporations. The charter of the ISOC emphasizes support for the technical evolution of the Internet, educating the user community in the use and application of the Internet, and promoting the benefits of Internet technology for education at all grade levels.

In April 1995, the existing NSFNET backbone was retired and replaced by a new architecture that provides for very high speed connectivity, while allowing for many different network service providers to carry Internet traffic. We will explore this new architecture in Section 1.4.

Lessons learned from the ARPANET have had a significant effect on a number of data communication technologies, such as LANs and packet switching. References [1-6] and [1-7] provide interesting historical information on these early networks. Now, let's open a different history book and study the development of the protocols used for internetwork communication.

1.3 The Protocols of the Internet

For its first decade, the ARPANET grew quickly, adding an average of one new host computer every 20 days [1-8]. The original protocol for internal network communications was known as the *Network Control Program* (NCP). When compared with the seven-layer Open Systems Interconnection Reference Model (OSI-RM), the NCP provided the functions of the third and fourth layers (Network and Transport), managing the flow of messages between host computers and intermediate packet switches. NCP was designed with the assumption that the underlying communication subnetwork (i.e., OSI Physical, Data Link, and Network Layers) provided a perfect communication channel. Given ARPANET's mission to support government and military networks, which could include radio links under battlefield conditions, the assumption of a reliable communication channel needed reconsideration. In January 1973, ARPA made the Transmission Control Protocol (TCP) a standard for the Internet because of its proven performance. The ARPA internetwork architecture (Figure 1-1) consisted of networks connected by gateways [1-9]. (Note that in the OSI sense of the word, these devices were actually routers, operating at the OSI Network Layer. By current definition, gateways may operate at all seven layers of the OSI-RM. In this chapter, we will refer to these connectivity devices as *gateways*, however we will switch to the more appropriate term *router* when we begin our technical study in Chapter 2.) The ARPA model assumed that each network used packet switching technology and could connect to a variety of transmission media (LAN, WAN, radio, and so on).

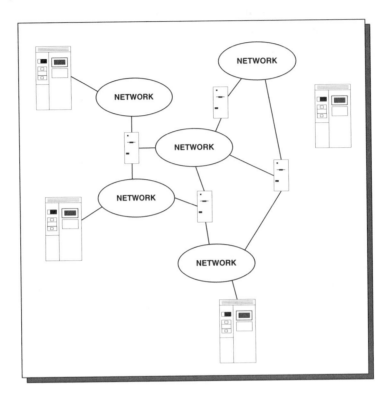

Figure 1-1. Networks connected with Gateways to Form an Internetwork.

The ARPA Internet architecture consisted of four layers (Figure 1-2). The lowest layer was called the *Network Interface Layer* (it is also referred to as the Local Network or Network Access Layer) and comprised the physical link (e.g., LAN) between devices. The Network Interface Layer existed in all devices, including hosts and gateways.

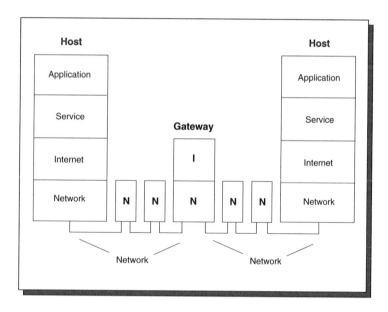

Figure 1-2. ARPA Layered Architecture.

The *Internet Layer* insulated the hosts from network-specific details, such as addressing. The Internet Protocol (IP) was developed to provide end-to-end datagram service for this layer. (Datagram service is analogous to a telegram in which the information is sent as a package.) The Internet Layer (and, therefore, IP) existed only in hosts and gateways.

While the Internet Layer provided end-to-end delivery of datagrams, it did not guarantee their delivery. Therefore, a third layer, known as the *Service Layer* (now called the Host-to-Host Layer), was provided within the hosts. As its name implies, the Service Layer defined the level of service the host applications required. Two protocols were created for the Service Layer: the Transmission Control Protocol (TCP) for applications needing reliable end-to-end service; and the User Datagram Protocol (UDP) for applications with less-stringent reliability requirements. A third protocol, the Internet Control Message Protocol (ICMP), allowed hosts and gateways to exchange monitoring and control information.

The highest ARPA layer, the *Process/Application Layer*, resided only in hosts and supported user-to-host and host-to-host processing or applications. A variety of standard applications were developed. These included the Telecommunications Network (TELNET) for remote terminal access, the File Transfer Protocol (FTP) for file transfer, and the Simple Mail Transfer Protocol (SMTP) for electronic mail.

Figure 1-3 compares the OSI and ARPA architectures. Note that the OSI Physical and Data Link Layers represent the ARPA Network Interface (or Local Network) Layer; the OSI Network Layer corresponds to the Internet Layer; the OSI Transport Layer is functionally equivalent to the Host-to-Host (Service) Layer; and the OSI Session, Presentation, and Application Layers comprise the ARPA Process/Application Layer. References [1-10] through [1-13] describe the development of the ARPANET Reference Model and protocols.

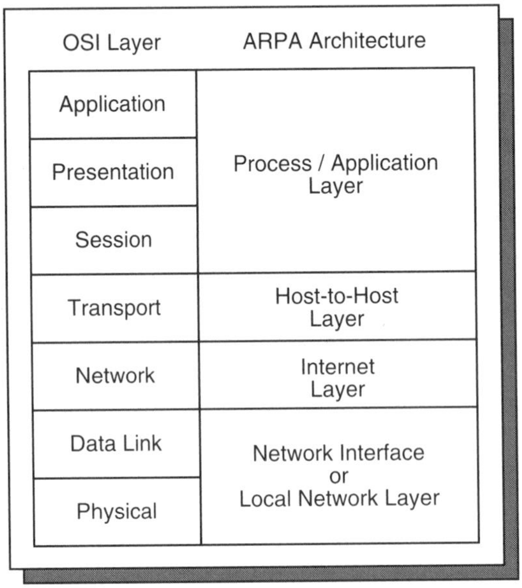

OSI Layer	ARPA Architecture
Application	Process / Application Layer
Presentation	
Session	
Transport	Host-to-Host Layer
Network	Internet Layer
Data Link	Network Interface or Local Network Layer
Physical	

Figure 1-3. Comparing OSI and ARPA Models.

With this background into the development of the IP and TCP protocols, let's look at the family of networks that use these protocols.

1.4 The Internet Family

A number of networks worldwide grew out of the ARPANET research to address nonmilitary requirements. Collectively, they became known as the Internet. The common denominator among these networks was their use of the TCP/IP and related protocols to build the underlying communication infrastructure. According to the organization Network Wizards (URL: http://www.nw.com), approximately 10,000,000 hosts are currently connected. John Quarterman's excellent reference *The Matrix* [1-14] describes these worldwide networks in exacting detail.

As we discussed in Section 1.2, much of the funding for the Internet was derived from U.S. government sources through the NSF. The NSFNET backbone service was operated by Merit Network, Inc., a partnership between ANS, IBM, MCI, and the state of Michigan. In May 1993, NSF proposed a new architecture for national networking, which became operational in April 1995. This architecture consists of four elements: a very high speed Backbone Network Service (vBNS), Network Service Providers (NSPs), Network Access Points (NAPs), and a Routing Arbiter (RA). The vBNS operates at the OC-3 rate (155 Mbps) and is operated by MCI. The Routing Arbiter manages the routing process for the Internet, including topology, connectivity, and routing table information. The RA project is a partnership of Merit Network, Inc., the University of Southern California Information Sciences Institute, IBM, and the University of Michigan. Both the vBNS and RA are funded by NSF. The Network Service Providers include the former regional networks (NEARnet, SURAnet, WESTnet, etc.) and commercial service providers such as Sprint, MCI, and others, and are not funded by the NSF. NAPs are used to interconnect the vBNS with other backbone networks. Four NAPs currently exist: Sprint NAP (Pennsauken, New Jersey), the Pac-Bell NAP (San Francisco, California), the Ameritech Advanced Data Services NAP (Chicago, Illinois), and Metropolitan Fiber Systems (MFS) in Washington, D.C. [1-15].

An example of an NSP is ANSnet, operated by ANS CO+RE Systems, Inc. (Elmsford, New York), and acquired by America Online, Inc., in February 1995. The ANSnet backbone is a mesh of more than 12,000 miles of fiber-optic lines, operating at the DS-3 (44.736 Mbps) rate (Figure 1-4). These lines connect high-speed IP routers located in cities where ANSnet has a point of presence (POP). The connection to ANSnet is via a leased line from the customer's premises to the nearest ANS POP, called the *Core*

Nodal Switching System (CNSS). At the customer's premises, an End Nodal Switching System (ENSS) is connected to this leased line. The ENSS consists of a router from Cisco Systems, Inc., with one serial and one Ethernet, token ring, or FDDI LAN interface; a Channel Service Unit/Data Service Unit (CSU/DSU); and modems for remote access from the ANSnet Network Operations Center (NOC). ANS takes responsibility for the installation, configuration, maintenance, and management of the ENSS, thus allowing its customers to concentrate on its business operations.

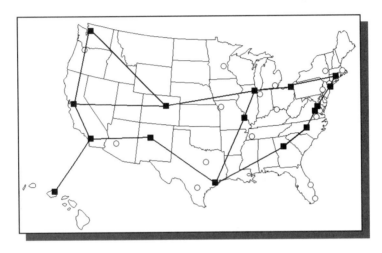

Figure 1-4. ANSnet.
(Courtesy of ANS CO & RE Systems, Inc)

Figure 1-5 shows a more detailed view of WESTnet, which connects the states of Idaho, Utah, Wyoming, Colorado, Arizona, and New Mexico. WESTnet serves a number of educational and commercial organizations and currently offers access at rates of 1.4 Kbps to 10 Mbps. One of the networks connecting to WESTnet is SuperNet, Inc., which serves Colorado (Figure 1-6) and the metropolitan Denver area (Figure 1-7). SuperNet connects a number of the universities, public libraries, and high-technology companies such as Cray Computer Corp., Hewlett-Packard Co., McData Corp., and US West.

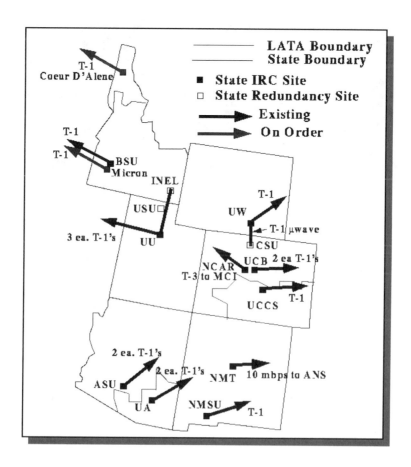

Figure 1-5. WESTnet Inter-Regional Connectivity.
(Courtesy of WESTnet)

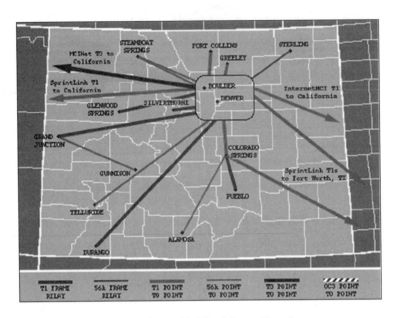

Figure 1-6. SuperNet Backbone Topology.
(Courtesy of SuperNet, Inc.)

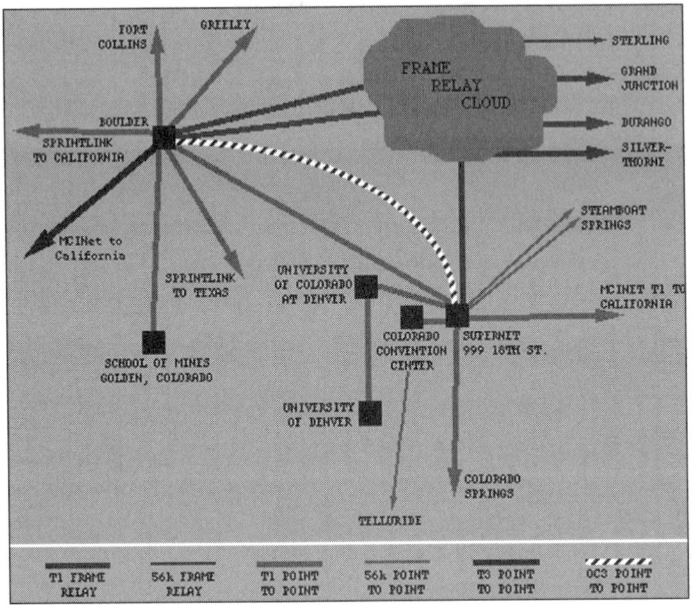

Figure 1-7. Metro Denver Connectivity.
(Courtesy of SuperNet, Inc.)

1.5 Governing and Documenting the Interne

An amazing characteristic of the largely volunteer Internet community is how smoothly this rather avant-garde organization operates. To quote from RFC 1726 [1-16]:

> "A major contributor to the Internet's success is the fact that there is no single, centralized point of control or promulgator of policy for the entire network. This allows individual constituents of the network to tailor their own networks, environments and policies to suit their own needs. The individual constituents must cooperate only to the degree necessary to ensure that they interoperate."

But no organization, avant-garde or not, can operate without some degree of structure. The Internet Society provides some of that structure, and one of the Internet Society's components is the Internet Architecture Board (IAB), chartered in 1992. The IAB consists of 13 members: 12 full members plus the chair of the Internet Engineering Task Force (IETF). The IAB's responsibilities include [1-17]:

- Appointing a chair of the IETF and its subsidiary Internet Engineering Steering Group (IESG)
- Oversight of the architecture for the protocols and procedures used by the Internet
- Oversight of the process used to create Internet standards
- Editorial management and publication of the Request for Comment (RFC) document series and administration of the various Internet assigned numbers
- Representing the interests of the Internet Society to other organizations
- Providing guidance to the Internet Society regarding Internet technologies

Two task forces report to the IAB. The IETF coordinates the technical aspects of the Internet and its protocols and assures that it functions effectively. The Internet Research Task Force (IRTF) researches new technologies.

The IAB produces numerous protocol standards and operational procedures that require dissemination and archiving. Most of these documents are known as *Requests for Comments documents* (RFCs) and are reviewed by the appropriate IETF or IRTF members. Many of the Internet protocols have become U.S. military standards and are assigned a MIL-STD number. For example, the Internet Protocol is described in both RFC 791 and MIL-STD-1777.

Internet documents are published according to two tracks. *Off-track specifications* are labeled with one of four categories: prototype, experimental, informational, or historic. These documents contain information that is useful but not appropriate for an Internet standard. Specifications that are destined to become Internet standards evolve through several levels of testing and revision, known as the *standards track*, described in RFC 1602 [1-18]. Three "maturity levels" are defined. The first level of maturity is called a *Proposed Standard*. This standard is stable, well-understood, has been reviewed by the community, and has sufficient interest to be considered valuable. A *Draft Standard* is one from which at least two independent and interoperable implementations have been developed and for which sufficient operational experience has been obtained. After significant implementation and operational experience is obtained, a Draft Standard may be elevated to an *Internet Standard*.

Two key documents that provide information on Internet standards and parameters, are published on a periodic basis. The Assigned Numbers document (currently RFC 1700 [1-19]) documents protocol parameters, assigned addresses such as port numbers, and many others. This document is prepared by the Internet Assigned Numbers Authority, or IANA (E-mail: iana@isi.edu). The Internet Official Protocol Standards document (currently RFC 1920 [1-20]) describes the standards track process and lists recently published RFCs and the current standardization status of the various protocols. Information on how to obtain Internet documentation is given in Appendix D.

With the explosive growth of the Internet within the last few years, a wealth of information is available. Throughout this text, we will make extensive use of the RFCs and other documents in our study. Readers needing details on the Internet itself could benefit from the following: RFC 1207, "FYI on Questions and Answers—Answers to Commonly Asked 'Experienced Internet User' Questions" [1-21]; RFC 1392, "Internet Users' Glossary" [1-22]; RFC 1402, "There's Gold in Them Thar Networks! Or Searching for Treasure in All the Wrong Places" [1-23]; RFC 1462, "FYI on 'What is the Internet'" [1-24]; RFC 1580, "Guide to Network Resource Tools" [1-25]; RFC 1594, "FYI on Questions and Answers—Answers to Commonly Asked 'New Internet User' Questions" [1-26]; and RFC 1739, "A Primer on Internet and TCP/IP Tools" [1-27].

References [1-28] through [1-32] are excellent resources, available either online or in bookstores, as indicated in Section 1.7. Readers who like suspense will enjoy Cliff Stoll's *The Cuckoo's Egg* [1-33], which describes the author's true experience tracking a hacker through the Internet. Readers needing information on the global growth of the Internet should consult reference [1-34].

1.6 Applying the Technologies of the Internet

In the previous sections of this chapter, we took a short trip down TCP/IP's memory lane. We studied how the U.S. government sponsored the development of these protocols based on the research and development community's requirements. But what if you work for an organization that has nothing to do with research, the U.S. government, or the military? Can your organization benefit from TCP/IP and the Internet protocols? To find out, answer the following questions about your computing environment:

- Do you have a multivendor environment?
- Does your internetwork include LAN and WAN topologies?
- Do your users require file transfer, electronic mail, host terminal emulation, or network management?

The bottom line is that the requirements for most organizations' internetworks do not differ appreciably from those of the 1969-vintage ARPANET. Most of us require a multivendor distributed architecture. We also need proven solutions and are eager to benefit from almost three decades of research and testing.

Even if you have no intention of connecting to the Internet, you can benefit from using TCP/IP. Those who implement these protocols will be in good company, as hundreds of vendors offer products to help configure, install, operate, and manage TCP/IP-based internetworks. (Appendix C lists a number of these vendors, although the list is growing so rapidly that it is impossible to ever be completely up-to-date.)

With this historical background, let's return to the present and take a practical approach. Chapter 2 will discuss the Internet protocols and support for them among Windows, Macintosh, DEC, IBM, and UNIX hosts. Chapters 3 through 7 will examine the Internet protocols, plus troubleshooting and management techniques. Our journey will coincide with the layers of the ARPA internetworking model, beginning with the Network Interface and ending with Process/Application Layers. In Chapter 7 we'll look at strategies for managing TCP/IP-based internetworks, and Chapter 8 will preview the next-generation Internet Protocol—IPng or IPv6. So warm up that protocol analyzer, and let's begin!

1.7 References

[1-1]   Rosner, Roy D. Packet Switching: Tomorrow's Communications Today. Wadsworth, Inc., 1982.

[1-2]   CSNET CIC. "A CSNET Retrospective." CSNET News (Summer 1985): 6–7.

[1-3]   Miller, Mark A. "Get a Grip on Internet Access." Network World (July 19, 1993): 31–37.

[1-4]   Information on the Commercial Internet Exchange may be obtained from:
    CIX Association
    3110 Fairview Park Drive, Suite 590
    Falls Church, VA 22042
    Voice: +1 703 824 9249
    Fax: +1 703 824 1611
    E-mail: info@cix.org
    URL: http://www.cix.com

[1-5]   The Internet Society may be contacted at:
    1895 Preston White Drive, Suite 100
    Reston, VA 22091
    Voice: +1 703 648 9888 or +1 800 468 9507
    Fax: +1 703 648 9887
    E-mail: isoc@isoc.org
    URL: http://www.isoc.org

[1-6]   Quarterman, John S., and Josiah C. Hoskins. "Notable Computer Networks." Communications of the ACM (October 1986):932–971.

[1-7]   Quarterman, John S. "The History of the Internet and the Matrix." ConneXions (April 1995): 13–25.

[1-8]   Dern, Daniel P. "The ARPANET is Twenty: What We Have Learned and the Fun We Had." ConneXions (October 1989): 2–10.

[1-9]   Leiner, B. M., et al. "The ARPA Internet Protocol Suite." RS-85-153, included in the *DDN Protocol Handbook*, Volume 2: 2-27–2-49.

[1-10]   Cerf, V. G. and R. E. Kahn, "A Protocol for Packet Network Intercommunication." *IEEE Transactions on Communications* (May 1974): 637–648.

[1-11]   Padlipsky, M. A. "A Perspective on the ARPANET Reference Model." RFC 871, The Mitre Corp., September 1982.

[1-12]   Cerf, Vinton G., and Edward Cain. "The DoD Internet Architecture Model." *Computer Networks* (October 1983): 307–317.

[1-13]   Cerf, Vint. "Requiem for the ARPANET." *ConneXions* (October 1991): 27.

[1-14]   Quarterman, John S. *The Matrix—Computer Networks and Conferencing Systems Worldwide*. Digital Equipment Corp., 1990.

[1-15]   Merit Network, Inc. "Merit Retires NSFNET Backbone Service." *MichNet News*, Vol. 9, No. 2 (URL: http://www.merit.edu).

[1-16]   Kastenholz, F., and C. Partridge. "Technical Criteria for Choosing IP: The Next Generation." RFC 1726, December 1994.

[1-17]   Huitema, C. "Charter of the Internet Architecture Board." RFC 1601, March 1994.

[1-18]   Internet Architecture Board and Internet Engineering Steering Group. "The Internet Standards Process—Revision 2." RFC 1602, March 1994.

[1-19]   Reynolds, J., and J. Postel. "Assigned Numbers." RFC 1700, October 1994.

[1-20]   Postel, J., Editor. "Internet Official Protocol Standards." RFC 1920, March 1996.

[1-21]   Malkin, G., et al. "FYI on Questions and Answers—Answers to Commonly Asked 'Experienced Internet User' Questions." RFC 1207, February 1991.

[1-22]   Malkin, G., et al. "Internet Users' Glossary." RFC 1392, January 1993.

[1-23]   Martin, J. "There's Gold in Them Thar Networks! Or Searching for Treasure in All the Wrong Places." RFC 1402, January 1993.

[1-24]   Krol, E., and E. Hoffman. "FYI on 'What is the Internet'." RFC 1462, May 1993.

[1-25]   EARN Staff. "Guide to Network Resource Tools." RFC 1580, March 1994.

[1-26]   Marine, A., et al. "FYI on Questions and Answers—Answers to Commonly Asked "New Internet User' Questions." RFC 1594, March 1994.

[1-27]   Kessler, G., and S. Shepard. "A Primer on Internet and TCP/IP Tools." RFC 1739, December 1994.

[1-28]   Spurgeon, Charles. "Network Reading List." The University of Texas at Austin Computation Center. (URL: ftp://ftp.utexas.edu/pub/netinfo/reading-list)

[1-29]   Hedrick, Charles. "Introduction to Internet Protocols." (URL: ftp://nic.merit.edu/introducing.the.internet/intro.to.ip)

[1-30]   Krol, Ed. *The Whole Internet*, User's Guide and Catalog, second edition. O'Reilly & Associates, Inc. (Sebastopol, California), 1994.

[1-31]   Lynch, Daniel C., and Marshall T. Rose. *Internet System Handbook*. Addison-Wesley Publishing Company, Inc. (Reading, Massachusetts), 1993.

[1-32]   LaQuey, Tracy. *Internet Companion*, second edition. Addison-Wesley Publishing Company (Reading, Massachusetts), 1994.

[1-33]   Stoll, Cliff. *The Cuckoo's Egg*. Simon & Schuster (New York, New York), 1989.

[1-34]   Neubarth, Michael, Editor. "The Internet: a Global Look." *Internet World* (November 1995): 94–112.

## CHAPTER 2

Supporting TCP/IP and the Internet Protocols

In Chapter 1, we discussed how TCP/IP and the Internet protocols were developed from requirements set forth by the U.S. government. Various hardware and software vendors have shown a great deal of interest in these protocols for several reasons. First, the U.S. government is a large customer and can generate a great deal of revenue with a single purchase order. Second, as the Internet and the number of connected hosts continues to grow, opportunities for products that support these popular connectivity solutions will increase as well. Finally, TCP/IP and the Internet protocols can serve any organization that needs to connect dissimilar hosts, such as an IBM mainframe to a UNIX workstation, Apple Macintosh, or PC on a LAN.

Of course, anyone who sets up an internet using these protocols is bound to run into problems sooner or later. When you have a problem with your internet connection, you need to first understand the TCP/IP protocols, and then you need a protocol analyzer that supports these protocols.

In this chapter, we'll provide the background you need to understand the TCP/IP protocols, plus various requirements to consider when shopping for an analyzer for your internet. First, we'll provide a general overview of the protocols themselves. Second, we'll discuss how different computing platforms support these protocols. Third, we'll survey the tools available for troubleshooting. We'll defer a detailed discussion of the protocols until Chapter 3.

2.1 The Internet Protocols

TCP/IP and the Internet protocols support the Advanced Research Projects Agency (ARPA) model of internetworking and its four defined layers: Network Interface, Internet, Host-to-Host, and Process/Application (see Figure 2-1). Developed in the early 1970s, this model preceded the Open Systems Interconnection Reference Model

(OSI-RM) by several years. Like ARPA, the OSI-RM was designed to internetwork dissimilar computer systems; however, the two models have different underlying assumptions. The ARPA model was designed to connect hosts serving the academic, research, government, and military populations, primarily in the United States. The OSI-RM was broader in scope. First, the OSI-RM was the product of an international standards body, the International Standards Organization (ISO). Thus, the OSI-RM received input from people in Europe and Asia as well as from North America. Second, it had a much broader charter, the interconnection of Open Systems, and was not constrained by the type of system to be connected (e.g., academic, military, and so forth). To satisfy these two constraints, the ISO developed a seven-layer model in contrast to ARPA's four-layer model. To summarize, the ARPA world was more specific, the OSI world more general. The result was two architectures that are almost, but not quite, parallel. We will study these differences in greater detail in the following chapters. In the meantime, let's take a brief look at the protocols we will be analyzing.

ARPA Layer	Protocol Implementation						OSI Layer
Process / Application	File Transfer	Electronic Mail	Terminal Emulation	File Transfer	Client / Server	Network Management	Application
	File Transfer Protocol (FTP)	Simple Mail Transfer Protocol (SMTP)	TELNET Protocol	Trivial File Transfer Protocol (TFTP)	Sun Microsystems Network File System Protocols (NFS)	Simple Network Management Protocol (SNMP)	Presentation
	MIL-STD-1780 RFC 959	MIL-STD-1781 RFC 821	MIL-STD-1782 RFC 854	RFC 783	RFCs 1014, 1057, and 1094	RFC 1157	Session
Host-to-Host	Transmission Control Protocol (TCP) MIL-STD-1778 RFC 793			User Datagram Protocol (UDP) RFC 768			Transport
Internet	Address Resolution ARP RFC 826 RARP RFC 903		Internet Protocol (IP) MIL-STD-1777 RFC 791		Internet Control Message Protocol (ICMP) RFC 792		Network
Network Interface	Network Interface Cards: Ethernet, Token Ring, ARCNET, MAN and WAN RFC 894, RFC 1042, RFC 1201 and others						Data Link
	Transmission Media: Twisted Pair, Coax, Fiber Optics, Wireless Media, etc.						Physical

Figure 2-1. Comparing ARPA Protocols with OSI and ARPA Architectures.

The first layer of the ARPA model is the Network Interface Layer, sometimes called the Network Access Layer or Local Network Layer; it connects the local host to the local network hardware. As such, it comprises the functions of the OSI Physical and Data Link Layers: it makes the physical connection to the cable system, it accesses the cable at the appropriate time (e.g., using a Carrier Sense Multiple Access with Collision Detection (CSMA/CD) or token passing algorithm), and it places the data into a frame. The *frame* is a package that envelops the data with information, such as the hardware address of the local host and a check sequence to assure data integrity. The frame is defined by the hardware in use, such as an Ethernet LAN or a frame relay interface into a WAN. The ARPA model shows particular strength in this area—it includes a standard for virtually all popular connections to LANs, MANs, and WANs. (Recall that the Internet standards are defined in Request for Comments documents, or RFCs.) These include Ethernet (RFC 894); IEEE 802 LANs (RFC 1042); ARCNET (RFC 1201); Fiber Distributed Data Interface-FDDI (RFC 1103); serial lines using the Serial Line Internet Protocol or SLIP (RFC 1055); PSPDNs (RFC 877); frame relay (RFC 1490); Switched Multimegabit Data Service or SMDS (RFC 1209); and the Asynchronous Transfer Mode (ATM), defined in RFC 1438.

The Internet Layer transfers packets from one host (the computing device which runs application programs) to another host. Note that we said *packet* instead of frame. The packet differs from the frame in that it contains address information to facilitate its journey from one host to another through the internetwork; the address within the frame header gets the frame from host to host on the same local network. The protocol that operates the Internet Layer is known as the Internet Protocol (the IP in TCP/IP). Several other protocols are also required, however.

The *Address Resolution Protocol* (ARP) provides a way to translate between IP addresses and local network addresses, such as Ethernet, and is discussed in RFC 826. The *Reverse Address Resolution Protocol* (RARP), explained in RFC 903, provides the complementary function, translating from the local address (again, such as Ethernet) to IP addresses. (In some architectural drawings, ARP and RARP are shown slightly lower than IP to indicate their close relationship to the Network Interface Layer. In some respects, ARP/RARP overlap the Network Interface and Internet Layers.)

The *Internet Control Message Protocol* (ICMP) provides a way for the IP software on a host or gateway to communicate with its peers on other machines about any problems it might have in routing IP datagrams. ICMP, which is explained in RFC 792, is a required part of the IP implementation. One of the most frequently used ICMP messages is the Echo Request, commonly called the *Ping*, which allows one device to test the communication path to another.

As the datagram traverses the Internet, it may pass through multiple gateways and their associated local network connections. Thus, there's a risk that packets may be lost or that a noisy communication circuit may corrupt data. The Host-to-Host Layer guards against these problems, however remote, and assures the reliable delivery of a datagram sent from the source host to the destination host. (Recall that one of the major objectives of the ARPA project was military communication, which, by definition, must be ultra-reliable.)

The Host-to-Host Layer defines two protocols: the *User Datagram Protocol* (UDP) and the *Transmission Control Protocol* (TCP). The minimum security UDP, described in RFC 768, provides minimal protocol overhead. UDP restricts its involvement to higher-layer port addresses, defining the length, and a checksum. TCP, detailed in RFC 793, defines a much more rigorous error control mechanism. TCP (of the TCP/IP nomenclature) provides much of the strength of the Internet protocol suite. TCP provides reliable datastream transport between two host applications by providing a method of sequentially transferring every octet (8-bit quantity of data) passed between the two applications.

End users interact with the host via the Process/Application Layer. Because of the user interface, a number of protocols have been developed for this layer. As its name implies, the *File Transfer Protocol* (FTP) transfers files between two host systems. FTP is described in RFC 959. To guarantee its reliability, FTP is implemented over TCP. When economy of transmission is desired, you may use a simpler program, the *Trivial File Transfer Protocol* (TFTP), described in RFC 783. TFTP runs on top of UDP to economize the Host-to-Host Layer as well.

Electronic mail and terminal emulation are two of the more frequently used Internet applications. The *Simple Mail Transfer Protocol* (SMTP), given in RFC 821, sends mail messages from one host to another. When accessing a remote host via the Internet, one must emulate the type of terminal the host wishes to see. For example, a Digital host may prefer a VT-100 terminal while an IBM host would rather see a 3278 or 3279 display station. The *Telecommunications Network* (TELNET) protocol provides remote host access and terminal emulation.

As internetworks become more complex, system management requirements increase as well. A large number of vendors, including Hewlett-Packard, IBM, Microsoft, SunSoft, and others have developed network management systems that supply these needs. Common to all of these platforms is the use of a protocol, the *Simple Network Management Protocol* (SNMP), given in RFC 1157, that was originally developed to meet the needs of TCP/IP-based internets. As its name implies, SNMP uses minimal overhead to communicate between the *Manager* (i.e., management console) and the *Agent* (i.e., the device, such as a router, being managed).

With that background into the Internet protocols, let's turn our attention to the host systems that incorporate these protocols, starting with the large systems based upon UNIX, Digital's DECnet, or IBM's SNA.

2.2 Internet Support within UNIX Environments

In the early 1980s, ARPA provided a grant to the University of California at Berkeley to modify the already robust UNIX operating system. One of the changes was support for the Internet protocols. The Berkeley Software Distribution version 4.2 (BSD 4.2) included support for the TCP, IP, SMTP, and ARP protocols. That version proved satisfactory for use on LANs and smaller internetworks.

BSD 4.3 offered support for larger internetworks that included routers and WAN transmission facilities (e.g., 56 Kbps leased lines). The changes included routines for ICMP redirect messages, retransmission algorithms, packet time-to-live parameters, and so on. BSD 4.4 was further enhanced to provide multicasting and other enhancements.

These releases have yielded a variety of implementations from a number of companies, including Hewlett-Packard (HP-UX), IBM (AIX), Novell (UNIXWare), SunSoft (SunOS and Solaris), and the Santa Cruz Operation, or SCO (Xenix). When surveying this marketplace, it is easy to see why Reichard and Johnson in their book *UNIX in Plain English* [2-1] referred to these numerous variants as a "veritable Tower of Babel." Reference [2-2] discusses these UNIX releases from a user's perspective and [2-3] deals with the programming requirements. Roosevelt Giles, in his paper "UNIX and PC Connectivity" [2-4], discusses the various options for connecting UNIX systems and PC networks. Last, John Foley discusses UNIX interoperability issues in reference [2-5].

It should come as no surprise that UNIX environments have strong support for the Internet protocols, since their primary clientele are academic, scientific, and research users. Interest in the business community increased in the mid-1980s, coinciding with the rapid growth in LANs. We'll look at the two key players in the commercial sector, Digital and IBM, next.

2.3 Internet Support within DECnet Environments

Digital Equipment Corp.'s (Maynard, Massachusetts) VAX and Alpha systems have been extremely well-received among the scientific and engineering communities—computer users who have strong interest in the Internet protocols. The Digital Network Architecture, OpenVMS operating system, and Digital's version of UNIX, known as Ultrix, are also popular choices for many internetworks. Solutions are available from both Digital and third-party vendors to integrate OpenVMS, DECnet, and the Internet protocols into one cohesive system.

First, consider the differences between DECnet Phase IV and Digital's DECnet/OSI (formerly called DECnet Phase V). Announced in 1982, DECnet Phase IV provided a proprietary architecture for LAN and WAN connectivity. It supported industry-standard protocols such as Ethernet and ITU-T X.25 at the lower OSI layers, but its upper layer protocols were proprietary. Announced in 1987, DECnet/OSI combines the protocols from DECnet Phase IV and OSI into a merged protocol stack. One stack supports the proprietary DECnet Phase IV, the other the OSI protocols, such as the ISO 10589 (Intermediate Station-to-Intermediate Station, or IS-IS) used at the Network Layer, the OSI 8073 Transport Protocol, and so on. The DECnet/OSI, announced in June 1991, enhances DECnet Phase V by adding a third protocol stack to the architecture—the Internet protocols. Thus, Digital gave users the best of all possible worlds: DECnet proprietary protocols, TCP/IP, and OSI (see references [2-6] and [2-7]).

DECnet Phase IV users who wish to integrate OpenVMS-based systems into a UNIX environment have several options. One is to install a software gateway between the UNIX host and the DECnet host. Digital's TCP/IP Services for VMS is an example of such a gateway. Another common denominator is TCP/IP, which is supported by a number of vendors, including TGV, Inc. (Santa Cruz, California) and the Wollongong Group, Inc. (Palo Alto, California).

Users of DECnet/OSI have several options for TCP/IP connectivity: the Digital architecture's inter-stack communication facilities and Digital's family of multi protocol routers. The most straightforward solution is to take advantage of the communication channels between the three protocol stacks that the Digital architecture provides (see Figure 2-2). The inter-stack communication is designed for either DECnet-to-OSI or TCP/IP-to-OSI channels. From the DECnet side, an internal Data Access Protocol-to-File Transfer and Management (DAP-to-FTAM) gateway provides file transfer between DECnet Phase IV, DECnet/OSI, and OSI systems. An internal FTP-to-FTAM gateway facilitates file transfers from the TCP/IP-to-OSI side. Other gateways between SMTP and X.400 (for electronic mail), and between TELNET and Virtual Terminal Protocol for remote host access are now part of DECnet/OSI. At the Transport Layer, the X/Open Transport Interface (XTI) permits applications to use either TCP or OSI-based transport protocols.

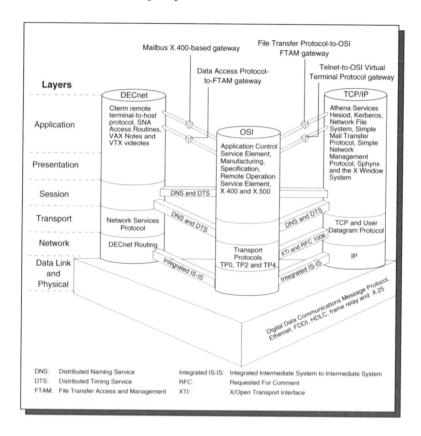

Figure 2-2. Digital's Rearchitected Network Strategy.
(Copyright December 9, 1991 by Network World, Inc., Framingham, NH 01701. Reprinted from Network World. *Source: Digital Equipment Corp., Maynard, MA)*

Digital's networking strategy also includes the WANRouter family of multiprotocol routers that provide WAN support for DECnet, TCP/IP, and OSI. At the high end is a DEC Network Integration Server, a hub device that combines bridging, routing, and ITU-T X.25 packet switching. The server uses a Reduced Instruction Set Computer (RISC) platform to obtain the speed necessary to integrate LANs and WANs. Hardware support includes token ring, FDDI, SMDS, and Frame Relay. Currently available protocols in addition to DECnet include AppleTalk, Novell's IPX, OSI, and TCP/IP. Supported data links include the DDCMP, High-level Data Link Control (HDLC), X.25, and Frame Relay.

A consistent theme of Digital's Networking Strategy is interoperability between DECnet, OSI, and the TCP/IP protocols. This theme runs from the OpenVMS and Digital UNIX operating systems level to the internetworking hardware. References [2-8] and [2-9] evaluate some of these internetworking options. Digital's World Wide Web site [2-10] contains up-to-date information on Digital products and their applications, and Malamud's *Analyzing DECnet/OSI Phase V* presents a detailed study of the protocols [2-11].

2.4 Internet Support within IBM Environments

IBM mainframes, communication controllers, workstations, and minicomputers all support the Internet protocols, including TELNET, FTP, TFTP, NFS, and SMTP as well as lower-layer protocols, such as IP, ICMP, and TCP. (An excellent reference is IBM's *TCP/IP Tutorial and Technical Overview* [2-12].) We'll look at each IBM platform separately.

At the mainframe level, IBM offers products that add support for the Internet protocols within the VM and MVS operating systems. These products are known as TCP/IP for VM and TCP/IP for MVS, respectively. Both products support the client/server nature of the Internet protocols. For example, the TN3270 function allows an IBM PC workstation running TCP/IP to remotely access a VM or MVS host via a LAN. The PC would appear as a client, i.e., IBM 3270-series terminal. Both VM and MVS implement FTP for host-to-host file transfers. The FTP Type command translates data between the mainframe's EBCDIC format and the PC's ASCII format. Both operating systems support SMTP for electronic mail service. IBM also offers an interface to exchange messages between SMTP and the IBM PROFS system. Other higher-layer protocol functions available under VM and MVS include X-Windows, Sun Microsystem's NFS, SNMP, and remote printing.

The IBM 3172 Interconnect Controller, shown in Figure 2-3a, handles the hardware connection between the IBM host and the TCP/IP environment. The 3172 provides a hardware connection between the mainframe channel and Ethernet, FDDI, or token ring LANs, as well as DEC networks, although the DEC connection requires additional gateway software. Software that accompanies the 3172 controls the IBM channel, attached LAN hardware, and the software interface to the TCP/IP functions on the host.

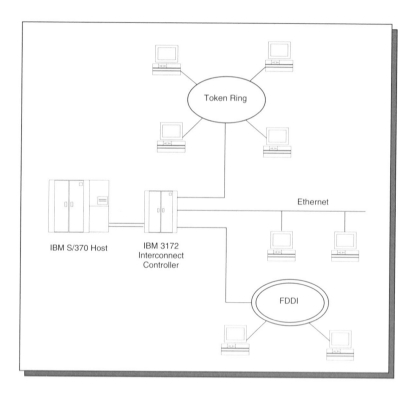

Figure 2-3a. TCP/IP Connections using the IBM 3172 Interconnect Controller.
(Reprinted by permission from TCP/IP Tutorial and Technical Overview
GG24-3376-04 © by International Business Machines Corporation)

In addition to the mainframe environment, IBM supports TCP/IP on a number of other platforms. IBM's version of UNIX, the Advanced Interactive Executive (AIX), runs on hardware, such as the PS/2, RT, RISC System/6000, and 9370. Support among these products for specific protocols varies, however, so consult IBM or Reference [2-12] for complete details. For DOS workstations, the TCP/IP for PC product supports protocols such as TELNET, FTP, and SMTP. OS/2 workstations use the OS/2 TCP/IP product, which adds capabilities such as server functions for TELNET, FTP, and SMTP. IBM provides TCP/IP support for midrange computers such as the AS/400 and System 88 and their operating systems (OS/400 and OS/88, respectively), though not as extensively as for DOS and OS/2 workstations.

As a final example, consider the case in which a number of hosts are connected in a single internetwork that includes a SNA network (see Figure 2-3b). This application is known as *SNAlink*, and it transfers TCP/IP-related information via an SNA backbone. In this example, four hosts running VM, MVS, DOS, and AIX are connected. The DOS machine is connected via an Ethernet and 3172 Interconnect Controller to the MVS host; the AIX and VM host are connected to a token ring. (Conversely, Data Link Switching on the 6611 network processor, a multiprotocol, multiport router and bridge, lets a TCP/IP backbone transport SNA traffic. We will investigate the Data Link Switching protocol in detail in Section 3.7.) A number of applications are possible using IBM's family of TCP/IP software products. Any user can log in to any of the remote hosts using TN3270. Files may be transferred between hosts using FTP or TFTP. Electronic mail may be transferred between any of the users. Finally, a user on the AIX host may use NFS to access files on either the VM or MVS hosts.

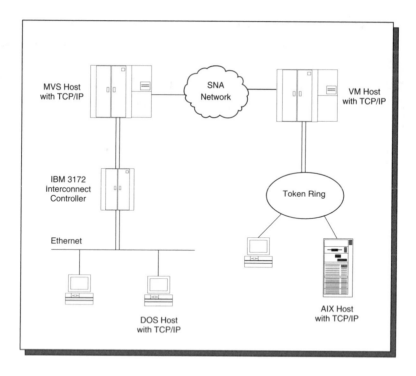

Figure 2-3b. SNAlink Scenario.
(Reprinted by permission from TCP/IP Tutorial and Technical Overview GG24-3376-04
© by International Business Machines Corporation)

2.5 Internet Support within DOS and Windows Environments

Recall from our history lesson in Chapter 1 that the TCP/IP protocols were developed in the early 1960s and that ARPANET came online in 1969. During the 1970s, ARPANET grew because of the addition of mainframe and minicomputer hosts. When the IBM PC was announced in 1981, a new market opened up for TCP/IP software developers—desktop PCs (as long as they were connected to the Internet via a LAN, dial-up link, etc.). Considering the popularity of PCs and the LANs connecting them, it's no wonder that a number of companies have developed TCP/IP connectivity software to support DOS, OS/2, and Microsoft Windows-based workstations. Such vendors include Frontier Technologies Corp. (Mequon, Wisconsin), FTP Software, Inc.

(Andover, Massachusetts), Netmanage, Inc. (Cupertino, California), Novell, Inc. (Provo, Utah), Sunsoft Inc. (Mountain View, California), and The Wollongong Group (Palo Alto, California). References [2-13] through [2-15] discuss some of these desktop requirements and product capabilities. In this section, we will look at the architecture of some sample products and discuss the features to consider when shopping.

Novell's LAN WorkPlace for DOS [2-16] is designed for any DOS-compatible system connected to a TCP/IP-based network (see Figure 2-4). The hardware connection to the LAN is made with an Ethernet, token ring, ARCNET, or other network interface via Novell's Link Support Layer (LSL) and Multiple-Link Interface Driver (MLID). LSL and MLID are components of Novell's Open Data Link Interface (ODI) which we will discuss in Section 2.7. The LSL and MLID provide Data Link Layer functions across a wide variety of Novell products, including the NetWare operating system. The TCP/IP Transport Driver supports the ARP/RARP, IP, ICMP, TCP, and UDP protocols, plus the NetBIOS interface (RFC 1001/1002). The TCP/IP Transport Driver provides a platform for communication services designed for the BSD 4.3 socket and NetBIOS Application Programming Interfaces (APIs). These higher-layer utilities include NetBIOS, third-party DOS socket, TELNET, and Windows 3.1 applications. Thus, the typical LAN user can access applications on remote hosts via IP routers in addition to the usual LAN-based utilities, such as file and print service, multi-user databases, and so forth.

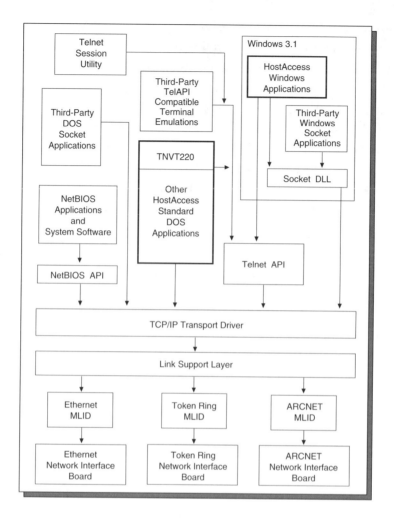

Figure 2-4. LAN Workplace for DOS Archirectural Overview.

(Courtesy of Novell, Inc.)

Another popular TCP/IP implementation for DOS is FTP Software, Inc.'s PC/TCP Network Software for DOS. An extremely flexible product, PC/TCP works with each of the four standard network card interfaces: Novell's ODI, 3Com/Microsoft's Network Driver Interface Specification (NDIS), IBM's Adapter Support Interface (ASI), and the Packet Driver. (There will be more on these LAN interfaces in Section 2.7.) In fact, FTP Software wrote the Packet Driver Specification, which allowed the separation of the driver from the DOS protocol stack, and released it into the public domain in 1987. Using a Packet Driver, PC/TCP can concurrently support its TCP/IP protocol stack and a second stack, such as NetWare, VINES, DECNet, and others.

PC/TCP contains components—such as a driver, a kernel, and programs—that span from the Data Link Layer to the Application Layer of the OSI Reference Model (see Figure 2-5). The components vary, depending on the physical medium and the simultaneous use of other network applications. In its most common configuration, the PC/TCP applications sit above the generic PC/TCP kernel, which in turn sits either on top of a Packet Driver, an NDIS-to-Packet Driver, or an ODI-to-Packet Driver conversion module.

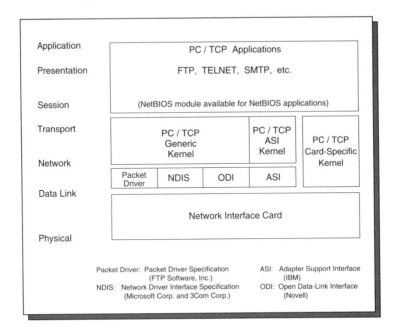

Figure 2-5. PC/TCP for Various Hardware Drivers.
(Courtesy of FTP Software Inc.)

Third-party developers can also use the PC/TCP kernel in their applications for network transport. Developers writing DOS applications can use a Native Mode API or a Berkeley Sockets emulation library, or they can access the TCP, UDP, and other application libraries. Developers writing Windows 3.x applications can use a Sockets Dynamic Link Library (DLL) and a Native Mode DLL. Other options include Remote Procedure Call (RPC) libraries.

Another FTP Software product, OnNet for Windows, is based upon 32-bit Virtual Device Driver (VxD) technology. A VxD implementation is written as a 32-bit module and takes full advantage of the 386/486 architecture. Advantages of the VxD architecture over Terminate and Stay Resident (TSR) or Dynamic Link Library (DLL) implementations include performance improvements and reductions in memory requirements.

The OnNet applications and kernel may be installed together, or the applications can be installed over other industry-standard TCP/IP stacks such as Windows 95 and Windows NT. Some of the key features of the product include: Mail OnNet, an email application which includes support for the Multimedia Internet Mail Extensions (MIME); an advanced Mosaic World Wide Web (WWW) browser; and the KEYview File Viewer, used to view, print, and convert popular file formats. OnNet also features InterDrive 95, an NFS client for Windows 95 which makes it possible to connect from that workstation to Network File System servers for remote file and printer service. The product also includes support for WinISDN, the Microsoft Windows interface which provides for connectivity of 1 or 2 ISDN B channels at 64 Kbps. Over 30 other applications make this a full-featured application package.

Since each network application is different, you should do some hands-on comparison shopping before committing to one of these TCP/IP software products on a company-wide basis. In general, first consider the workstation software platform (e.g., DOS, OS/2, Windows), then the support for your particular LAN hardware (e.g., IBM, 3Com, etc.). A closely related issue is the workstation software and hardware driver's support for your LAN operating system (e.g., VINES or NetWare). Next, look for specific features and the degree to which the product supports them. For file transfers using FTP, consider whether both FTP client and server functions are necessary and available. (Some products support the FTP client function, but not the FTP server.) For remote host access with terminal emulation requirements (TELNET), verify the type of terminal you need to emulate, such as DEC VT-100 or IBM 3278, then check the degree of support. For instance, does it offer a remappable keyboard, non-English characters, and so on. If electronic mail (SMTP) is necessary, look at the client/server capabilities. Most products offer client support, but few provide the host side. Other features that may be important include: developer's kits for writing custom applications; related products from the same manufacturer, such as an OS/2 or Windows version with a similar user interface; and ICMP network testing capabilities, such as the PING function. Table 2-1 provides a brief checklist to use when comparing different TCP/IP software packages.

2.6 Internet Support within Macintosh Workstations

A few years ago, because both the Macintosh and UNIX hosts existed in their own isolated worlds, it would be hard to imagine connecting them. TCP/IP has solved that problem, however.

As Vernon Keenan describes in "From Here to Connectivity" [2-17], there are several ways to connect Macs to UNIX hosts. The first is to install the AppleTalk protocol suite on a UNIX platform. One example of such a product is Pacer Software Inc.'s PacerLink, which is compatible with a variety of UNIX platforms from DEC, Hewlett-Packard, and Sun. A second connectivity solution is to use a Datagram Delivery Protocol (DDP)-to-IP router. Manufacturers such as Cayman Systems, Inc. (Cambridge, Massachusetts), Shiva Corp. (Cambridge, Massachusetts), and the Wollongong Group (Palo Alto, California) provide this connectivity using either LocalTalk or Ethernet hardware.

The third solution involves a combination of several packages: MacTCP from Apple, one from various third-party developers, and the DDP-to-IP router. MacTCP is a software driver written for the Macintosh operating system; it is compatible with all versions including System 7.0, and is bundled with System 7.5 [2-18]. As shown in Figure 2-6, MacTCP provides functionality at the OSI Physical through Transport Layers and relies on third-party products for completion. MacTCP may also rely upon the support of a DDP-to-IP router to send/receive the appropriate DDP packets or IP datagrams. MacTCP implements the following protocols: IP, ICMP, UDP, ARP, RARP, RIP, Bootstrap Protocol (BOOTP), and TCP. These protocols provide the communication services that the higher-layer Session, Presentation, and Application functions require. The product contains interfaces for C and assembly language to facilitate the writing of application programs.

Table 2-1. Workstation Internet Requirements.

Workstation type _____

Workstation operating system _____   version _____

Network interface type _____

Network operating system _____   version _____

File Service Requirements

    FTP client _____

    FTP server _____

    NFS client _____

    NFS server _____

Electronic Mail Requirements

    SMTP client _____

    SMTP server _____

    POP2/POP3 _____

    MIME _____

    Mail reader _____

Remote Host Access Requirements

    TELNET client _____

    TELNET server_____

    DEC emulation _____   Terminal type _____

    IBM emulation _____   Terminal type _____

Network Diagnostic/Management Requirements

    PING _____

    Finger _____

    SNMP agent _____

    SNMP manager _____

Network Interface Requirements

    NDIS _____

    ODI _____

    Packet Driver _____

    SLIP _____

    PPP _____

    X.25 _____

    Frame Relay _____

    ATM _____

    Other _____

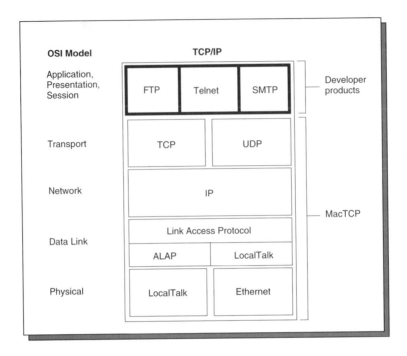

Figure 2-6. Comparing MacTCP with OSI.
(Courtesy of Apple Computer, Inc.)

One vendor that uses MacTCP for a variety of Macintosh connectivity products is Intercon Systems Corp. (Herndon, Virginia). TCP/Connect II is a full-featured workstation package for the Macintosh. It supports TELNET, FTP, SLIP, PPP, SMTP with full MIME support, Gopher client, WWW client for Web browsing, SNMP, and many other protocols. TCP/Connect II offers a number of DEC and IBM terminal emulations for TELNET. It supports both client and server capabilities for FTP. Electronic mail functions are also available, using the Post Office Protocol versions 2 (POP2) and 3 (POP3) for message reception and SMTP for transmission. InterPrint for the Macintosh is an LPR client that allows the Macintosh user to send print requests over a TCP/IP network to any print server that uses the LPR protocol. InterServer Publisher for Macintosh enables Macintosh users to establish Web, FTP, and Gopher servers with a single integrated application. NFS/Share is an NFS client that allows you to mount any NFS server as a local hard drive on your Macintosh desktop. Finally, by using the Planet X package, an X-Window System client for the Macintosh, users of any machine with X-Windows can remotely access and manipulate networked Macintoshes in full color.

Apple's MacTCP driver has opened up the world of the Internet to Macintosh users. Reference [2-19] details some of these possibilities from a user's perspective.

2.7 Internet Support within LAN Operating Systems

Traditionally, LANs have been used for print and file sharing and, occasionally, for remote access to another system. The internetworking capabilities of those systems have only become significant in the last few years, and the TCP/IP protocols have become the solution to many connectivity challenges. Let's see the effect this has had on the software architecture of the LAN.

If we consider the architecture of a typical LAN, we could divide the OSI Reference Model's seven layers into several functional groups (see Figure 2-7). To begin, the typical LAN consists of hardware (Layers 1 and 2) and the operating system (Layers 5 through 7). The Network and Transport layers in between provide internetwork connectivity. These functions include routing the packet through the internetwork (the Network Layer function) and assuring that it gets there reliably (the Transport Layer function). If we only wanted a local network (not internetwork) function, we could design some mechanism to allow the operating system to communicate directly with the hardware. Developers of network operating systems, such as Banyan Systems Inc. (Westboro, Massachusetts), IBM (Austin, Texas), Novell Inc. (Provo, Utah), and Microsoft Corp. (Redmond, Washington), anticipated the need to internetwork LANs and built the required Network and Transport Layer functions into their operating systems. Banyan incorporates the VINES Internet Protocol (VIP) for the Network Layer and either the Sequenced Packet Protocol (SPP) or the VINES Interprocess Communications Protocol (VICP) at the Transport Layer of VINES version 6.0. Novell built the internetworking capabilities of NetWare version 4.1 on the Internetwork Packet Exchange (IPX) Protocol and either the Sequenced Packet Exchange (SPX) or the NetWare Core Protocol (NCP) for the Transport Layer. Microsoft's Windows NT version 3.5 uses the NetBIOS Extended User Interface (NetBEUI) for the Network and Transport Layer functions.

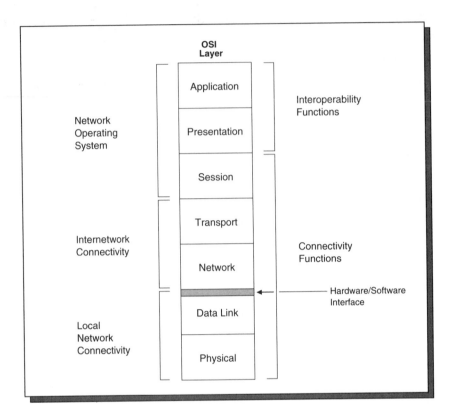

Figure 2-7. LAN and Internetwork Connectivity within the OSI Framework.

To run TCP/IP over a LAN, you can either replace the existing Network/Transport Layer software with TCP/IP or send the TCP/IP information inside existing Network and Transport Layer protocols, a process known as *encapsulation*. If you replace the existing protocols, you must devise a mechanism to allow higher layer protocols to communicate with the LAN hardware, such as the Ethernet board. A software interface that resides at the upper portion of the Data Link Layer provides this link. It also eliminates the need for each higher-layer protocol stack to have its own hardware driver. In other words, the higher layers talk to the driver, and the driver talks to the hardware. Since the driver specifications are published, everyone's work is simpler.

Three such interfaces are widely used. The first is the Packet Drivers, which were originally specified by FTP Software and further developed at Brigham Young University (Provo, Utah), Clarkson University (Potsdam, New York), and Columbia

University (New York, New York), among others. (Reference [2-20] discusses these drivers in detail. Some of these drivers are included in the Crynwr Packet Driver Collection; see reference [2-21] for further information.)

The second interface is the Network Driver Interface Specification (NDIS) developed by 3Com Corp. (Santa Clara, California) and Microsoft and released as part of OS/2 LAN Manager [2-22]. The NDIS contains two components: a Medium Access Control (MAC) driver communicates with the LAN hardware and a protocol driver communicates with the higher layers. The NDIS insulates developers of higher-layer software from the need to write drivers for each type of hardware in use. The third interface, the Open Data Link Interface (ODI), comes from Novell [2-23]. Similar to both the Crynwr drivers and the NDIS, ODI provides a logical link between hardware and software.

Returning to Figure 2-7, note the drivers' function. They reside at the upper portion of the Data Link Layer, providing a way for the Internet protocol stack (i.e., TCP/IP plus applications) or the network operating system (e.g., NetWare) to access the hardware.

The second way to use TCP/IP over a LAN is to use both the native NOS protocols and TCP/IP at the Network and Transport Layers. The NOS protocols (e.g., VINES VIP and VSPP) remain in place and the Internet information (e.g., FTP/TCP/IP) is encapsulated within the VINES packet. This process is known as *tunneling* since the native protocols create a tunnel through which the data from the other protocol stack (i.e., TCP/IP) can pass. This tunnel is created by treating the Internet protocols as data within the packet created by the native network OS protocols. We'll see an example of encapsulation in the next section.

Now that we have a background in the ways in which LAN operating systems support the Internet protocols, let's study Banyan Systems' VINES, IBM's LAN Server, Microsoft's Windows NT and Novell's NetWare in more detail.

2.7.1 Banyan Systems' VINES

Banyan Systems Inc.'s VINES was one of the first network operating systems to incorporate both LAN and WAN protocols (see Figure 2-8a). VINES offers particularly strong support for these protocols at the OSI Physical and Data Link Layers. These layers offer the High-level Data Link Control (HDLC) protocol and ITU-T X.25 for access to Packet Switched Public Data Networks (PSPDNs), plus asychronous transmission. The VINES applications include file access, printing, and electronic mail.

A number of third-party products (shown on the left-hand side of the figure) are also available. VINES version 5.0 added the AppleTalk protocol stack (shown on the right-hand side of the figure). Another integral part of the VINES architecture is support for the Internet protocols, including ARP/RARP, IP, ICMP, TCP, and UDP. VINES also supports the usual applications, such as FTP, TELNET, and so on, using third-party packages. Starting with VINES 6.0, TCP/IP kernels for DOS (TSR), Windows (VxD), and OS/2 are bundled with the base system.

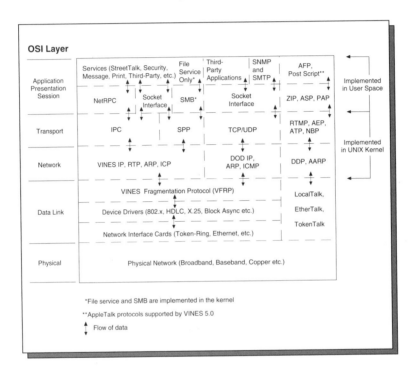

Figure 2-8a. Banyan Elements (Server side)
(Courtesy of Banyan Systems, Inc.)

Banyan offers two alternatives for TCP/IP and VINES integration [2-24]. The first is the TCP/IP Routing Option, which allows the VINES server to route TCP/IP traffic between non-VINES (i.e., foreign) hosts (see Figure 2-8b). In other words, the VINES server is acting as an IP router. In this case, the VINES server contains both the VINES and TCP/IP protocol stacks and participates in the TCP/IP internetwork. To illustrate how this works, we'll trace a message from Host 1 to Host 2. Host 1 generates the message (shown as User Data), adds the appropriate IP and TCP headers, accesses LAN 1, then builds a transmission frame with the appropriate Data Link Layer (DLL) header and trailer. When that frame arrives at VINES Server 1, the server encapsulates the IP datagram within a VINES IP packet by adding the VINES IP header information necessary to route the packet through the VINES network. When the distant server (VINES Server 2) receives the packet, it removes the VINES IP header, and the IP header routes the packet to its destination host.

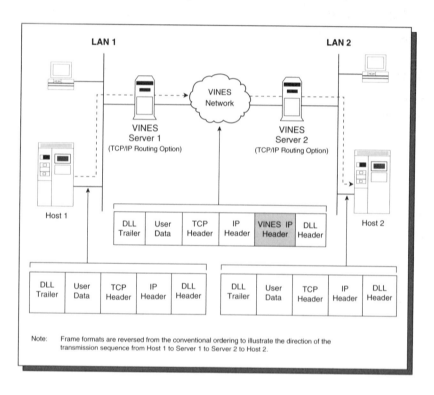

Figure 2-8b. VINES TCP/IP Routing Option Encapsulation.
(Courtesy of Banyan Systems, Inc.)

43

The Routing Option is also capable of routing TCP/IP in and out of the server without any encapsulation. For example, suppose that a VINES server was the gateway to a Cisco Systems router used for access to the Internet. A user wishing to connect to the Internet could access the VINES server, which would communicate across the LAN to the Cisco router, which in turn would connect to the Internet service provider. In this case, all communication is native TCP/IP, and the VINES server is functioning solely as an IP router.

The second alternative is the VINES TCP/IP Server-to-Server option, shown in Figure 2-8c. This option allows VINES and Banyan ENS servers to route VINES traffic through a TCP/IP internetwork. (ENS is Banyan's Enterprise Network Services, which are services that are independent of VINES which run on other operating systems, such as IBM's AIX, Hewlett-Packard's HP-UX, Novell's NetWare, SunSoft's Solaris, and others.) In this case, the VINES server maps the VINES IP address of the desired destination host to an IP address that will allow for packet delivery. A message originating at VINES Server 1 would be in the VINES IP (proprietary) packet format. VINES Server 2 translates the VINES IP destination address to an ARPA IP destination address, adds the IP header, and sends the newly generated IP datagram to the TCP/IP internetwork. Within the TCP/IP internetwork, that IP datagram may pass through a number of other routers. At the end of the TCP/IP internetwork, the VINES server (shown as Server 3) will remove the IP header and deliver the reconstructed VINES packet to its destination, VINES Server 4.

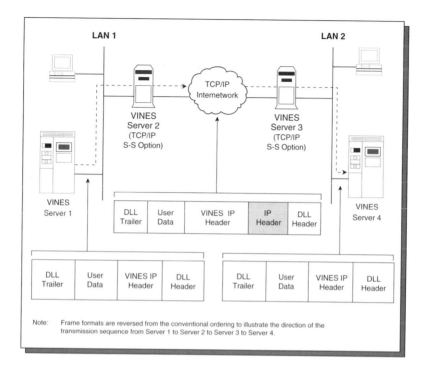

Figure 2-8c. VINES TCP/IP Server-to-Server Option Encapsulation.
(Courtesy of Banyan Systems, Inc.)

Reference [2-25] provides additional details on VINES protocols and their implementation, and reference [2-26] reviews some of the recent VINES enhancements.

2.7.2 IBM's LAN Server and IBM WARP Connect

IBM's LAN Server 4.0 and IBM WARP Connect both provide a TCP/IP protocol stack in a package called Multiple Protocols Transport Services (MPTS), shown in Figure 2-9a. In addition to the TCP/IP protocol, MPTS provides: NetBIOS, IEEE 802.2, LAN Virtual Device Driver (VDD), and NetWare Requester for OS/2 support.

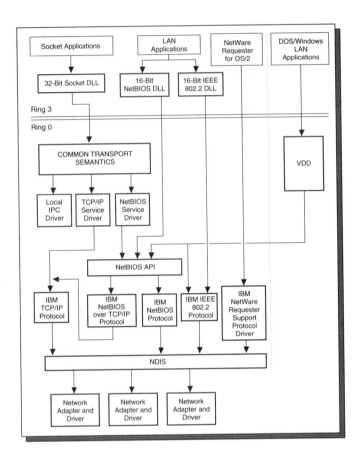

Figure 2-9a. Functional Components of MPTS.
(Reprinted by permission from MPTS Configuration Guide S10H-9693-00
© by International Business Machines Corporation)

MPTS provides a comprehensive solution to interconnecting LANs. The architecture is aimed at providing a general solution for interconnecting network applications by providing a protocol-independent transport interface for network applications, called Common Transport Semantics (CTS), and a hardware independent interface, called Network Driver Interface Specification (NDIS), for transport protocols.

CTS provides an interface so that applications and higher-layer protocols written for a particular transport interface can be carried over another transport protocol with no apparent changes (see Figure 2-9b). This interface is provided via the socket programming interface and allows the socket applications to communicate using Local Inter-Process Communication (LIPC), TCP/IP, or NetBIOS protocols. A comprehensive introduction to MPTN is found in *IBM's Multi-Protocol Transport Networking Architecture, Tutorial and Product Implementations* [2-27].

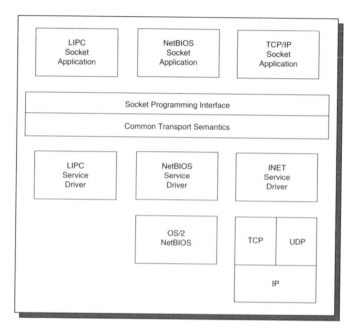

Figure 2-9b. Common Transport Interface.
(Reprinted by permission from MPTS Configuration Guide S10H-9693-00
© by International Business Machines Corporation)

The 3Com Corporation and Microsoft Corporation jointly developed NDIS as an interface that would allow any NDIS-compliant protocol stack to talk to any NDIS-compliant LAN or WAN adapter driver. NDIS has become an industry standard that provides a common open interface, allowing protocol stacks from different manufacturers to communicate with a variety of hardware adapters (review Figure 2-9a). The IBM NetWare Requester Support protocol driver allows an NDIS-compliant adapter driver to communicate with a protocol stack that complies with the Novell Open Data Link Interface (ODI) specification.

The MPTS in LAN Server 4.0 and WARP Connect provides the TCP/IP protocol suite and also those utilities necessary to configure and run TCP/IP applications. You will find TCP, UDP, IP, ARP, RARP, ICMP, and SNMP protocols in MPTS. There is support for SLIP, PPP, and LAN network interface connections. NetBIOS over TCP/IP (RFC 1001, 1002) is supplied by MPTS for running NetBIOS applications across the Internet (see Figure 2-9c). The left-hand portion of that figure shows how NetBIOS is structured. ACSNETB.DLL provides the NetBIOS API for Ring 3 applications. NetBIOS.OS2 processes Ring 3 NetBIOS commands and also provides a Ring 0 interface for device drivers. (The terms Ring 0 and Ring 3 refer to Intel 286 and later CPU security levels, where Ring 0 is the most privileged level and Ring 3 is the least privileged level.) NETBEUI.OS2 is an LM10 (LAN Manager version 1.0) NetBIOS protocol driver, supporting this API and implementing the protocol. The right-hand portion of Figure 2-9c shows how this structure is easily modified to support NetBIOS over TCP/IP. TCPBEUI.OS2 is an LM10 protocol driver that transfers data using sockets rather than binding directly to a MAC driver for data transfers. Since NetBIOS.OS2 can bind to multiple LM10 API protocol drivers, it is an easy matter to configure both NETBEUI.OS2 and TCPBEUI.OS2on your workstation.

TCP/IP Version 3 for OS/2 is a selectable install option in WARP Connect. It provides an integrated phone dialer to assist with attaching to Internet access providers. TCP/IP Version 3 for OS/2 also provides a large portfolio of different TCP/IP tools and programs, including: arp, assist, finger, host, hostname, ifconfig, ifolder, inetcfg, inetver, ipformat, iptrace, linkup, makeidx, netstat, nslookup, ping, ppp, route, sendmail, slattach, slcfg, slip, sliphold, slipkill, slipmsg, slipterm, tracerte and update to name just some of them. FTP, FTPPM, TELNET, TN3270, PMANT, LPR, REXEC, and TFTP are there, and you'll also find more recent Internet applications for navigating and surfing the Web, such as the IBM WEB Explorer, NEWS/Reader, and Gopher. A good reference for all of IBM's TCP/IP suite is Tyson's *Navigating the Internet with OS/2 Warp* [2-28].

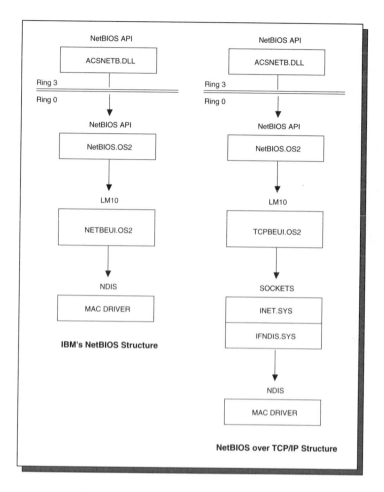

Figure 2-9c. IBM's NetBIOS over TCP/IP.
(Reprinted by permission from MPTS Configuration Guide S10H-9693-00
© by International Business Machines Corporation)

2.7.3 Microsoft's Windows NT

Microsoft Corporation of Redmond, Washington, perhaps best known for its desktop operating systems, has developed a parallel strength in network operating systems. Microsoft included a TCP/IP protocol stack within LAN Manager 2.1 (shipped in 1991), and has continued to support the Internet protocols with the current Windows NT 3.5 Client and Server products.

The Microsoft TCP/IP architecture builds upon the Windows NT networking model which contains two key interfaces (Figure 2-10a). The NDIS interface isolates the network adapter cards or other network hardware from the transport protocols. This interface allows any NDIS-compatible transport protocol stack, such as TCP/IP, IPX/SPX (via Microsoft's NWLink software), or AppleTalk to communicate with a number of LAN or WAN hardware interfaces. Similarly, the Transport Driver Interface (TDI) provides an interface at the Session layer for upper-layer protocols and application communication. Figure 2-10b illustrates how the various TCP/IP components utilize the Network Driver and Transport Device Interfaces for communication.

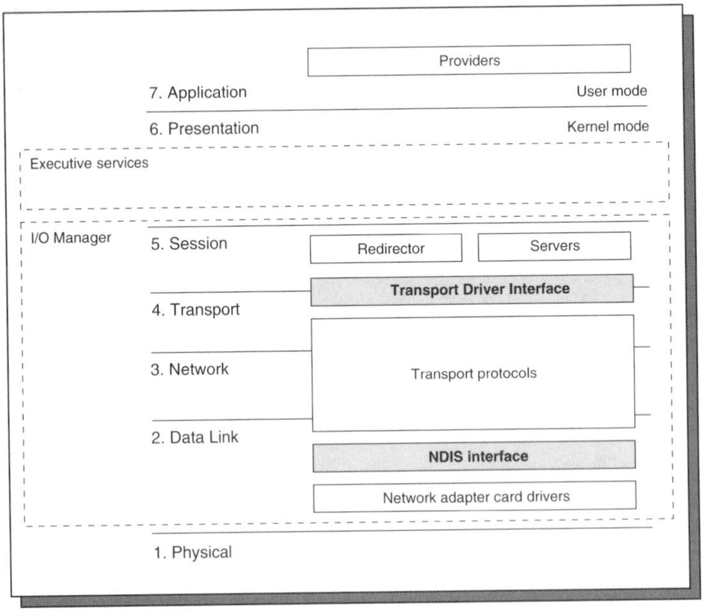

Figure 2-10a. Windows NT Networking Model.
(From Windows NT Networking Guide, Volume 2. Copyright © 1995, Microsoft Corporation. Reprinted with permission of Microsoft Press. All rights reserved.)

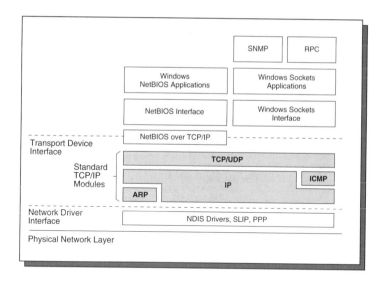

Figure 2-10b. Architectural Model of Windows NT with TCP/IP.
(From Windows NT Networking Guide, Volume 2. Copyright © 1995, Microsoft Corporation. Reprinted with permission of Microsoft Press. All rights reserved.)

The core Microsoft TCP/IP technology includes both integrated applications, and support for third-party add-on components (Figure 2-10c). Internet protocols that are included in the basic architecture include TCP, IP, UDP, ARP, and ICMP. For dial-up applications, the Point-to-Point Protocol (PPP) and Serial Line IP (SLIP) are also included. Support for Application Programming Interfaces (APIs) includes: NetBIOS support over TCP/IP, Network Dynamic Data Exchange (DDE) for document sharing, Remote Procedure Call (RPC) for inter-system communication, and Windows Sockets for network programming. Connectivity services include support for FTP, TFTP, TELNET, FINGER, LPR, RCP, REXEC, and RSH. Diagnostic utilities include ARP, PING, ROUTE, TRACERT, HOSTNAME, IPCONFIG, LPQ, NBSTAT, and NETSTAT. Two other key functions include the Windows Internet Name Service (WINS) and the Dynamic Host Configuration Protocol (DHCP). An SNMP agent is also available to facilitate the management of the Windows NT workstation by a network management console.

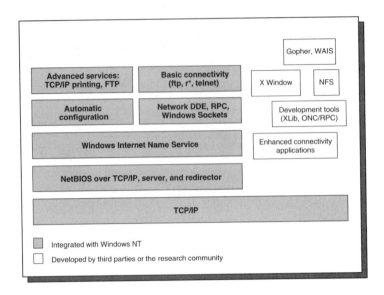

Figure 2-10c. Microsoft TCP/IP Core Technology and Third-party Add-ons.
(From Windows NT Networking Guide, Volume 2. Copyright © 1995, Microsoft Corporation. Reprinted with permission of Microsoft Press. All rights reserved.)

Support for two Windows NT functions, DHCP (defined in RFCs 1533, 1534, 1541, and 1542) and WINS lessens the administrative burdens associated with managing a large TCP/IP-based internet. With DHCP, IP addresses are managed by a server, which leases them to clients for a specified duration of time. When a client workstation boots, it broadcasts a *discover* message on the local network. DHCP servers respond with an *offer* message, which contains the IP address and configuration information. A response from the client to one of the servers acknowledges the address, with the selected server then finalizing the transaction by specifying the lease duration. WINS is also designed for administrative purposes. It provides a distributed database for registering and querying mappings of computer names and IP addresses Thus, administration, allocation, and configuration of IP addresses is more automated, relieving the human network administrator of these tasks.

A great deal of literature has been published detailing the capabilities of Windows NT. References [2-29] and [2-30] are documents that are available from Microsoft, and references [2-31] through [2-33] are recent journal articles that review the capabilities of the operating system.

2.7.4 Novell's NetWare

Novell has greatly increased its support for the Internet protocols since it acquired Excelan in 1989. Excelan developed the Excelan Open System (EXOS) hardware, which dramatically improved the performance of TCP/IP-based workstations by incorporating an Intel 80186 communications processor and the Internet protocol drivers onto an Ethernet network card. Since much of the protocol processing was performed right on the board, it relieved the host's CPU of that task. However, for faster host CPUs (e.g., 80486 platforms), you can achieve faster performance by incorporating the protocols directly into the operating system.

A natural extension to the EXOS line, therefore, was to incorporate the Internet protocols into the NetWare operating system. (See Figure 2-11a. Note the similarity between the LAN WorkPlace for DOS (Figure 2-4) and NetWare architectures at the lower layers.) The TCP/IP implementation built into NetWare version 3.11 is a NetWare Loadable Module (TCPIP/NLM) that acts as a transport subsystem using TCP/IP protocols to transport data. Applications may use one of three APIs to access this NLM. Third parties may write to Novell's Transport Layer Interface (TLI). The second API is NetWare NFS, which supports a Network File System (NFS) server. The third API is a BSD 4.3 socket library. Two applications are included with NetWare 3.11 as additional NLMs: a TCP/IP console (TCPCON) and an SNMP event logger (SNMPLOG). Another included software module, the SNMP NLM, is an SNMP agent for remote clients. Both SNMPLOG and TCPCON are clients of the SNMP agent NLM.

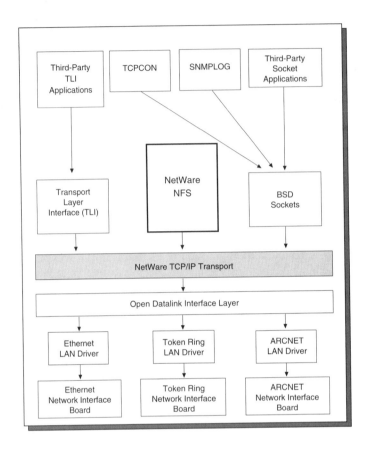

Figure 2-11a. NetWare TCP/IP Transport Architectural Relationships.
(Courtesy of Novell, Inc.)

The IPX/IP Tunnel Module (known as IPTUNNEL.LAN) is of interest to protocol analysts. It allows one IPX-based (NetWare) network to communicate with another IPX network via an IP-based internetwork (see Figure 2-11b). The NetWare server encapsulates the NetWare IPX packet within a UDP packet for transport across the IP internetwork. To the NetWare server, the IP internetwork looks like another LAN that requires another header (UDP/IP) to complete the communication path. Again referring to Figure 2-11b, Server 1 would treat the IPX packet as data and add a UDP and IP header. At the destination, Server 2 would remove the UDP and IP headers, then send the remaining IPX packet into the NetWare network. It is also possible for a client node to use the IPTUNNEL.EXE driver (within the LAN WorkPlace for DOS package) to communicate with a remote NetWare server.

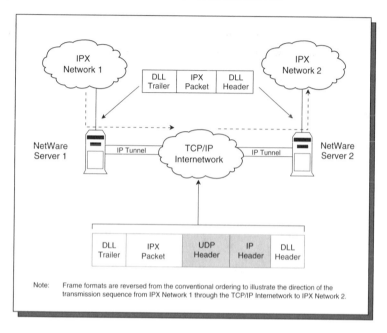

Figure 2-11b. IP Tunnel Connecting Two IPX Networks.
(Courtesy of Novell, Inc.)

An alternative to tunneling NetWare data inside TCP/IP packets is another Novell product, NetWare/IP. This product consists of both client and server software, which allows existing NetWare applications to operate using IP instead of IPX as the communications protocol. Comparing the client architectures illustrates the differences between the two alternatives (see Figure 2-11c and Figure 2-11d). The standard NetWare client includes the IPX protocol stack, which the NetWare applications, libraries, and shell use for the end-to-end transport of data between systems. These upper-layer protocol functions use the Far Call Interface (shown in the center of Figure 2-11c) to access the communication layers. The NetWare/IP client modifies this architecture by replacing the IPX protocol stack with a TCP/IP stack

(Figure 2-11d). Thus, instead of using IPX as the communication protocol, NetWare/IP uses IP and UDP instead. An additional piece of code, called the IPX Far Call Interface Emulation, provides the link between the TCP/IP stack and the IPX Far Call Interface. The NetWare/IP server runs on a NetWare 3.1 or 4.x server, depending on the version. That server may be either local or remote to the client. The NetWare/IP architecture also includes an implementation of the Domain Name System (DNS) server, as well as a Domain SAP Server (DSS). The DSS holds a logical database which contains IPX Service Advertising Protocol (SAP) information, through which the various servers become aware of each other's existence and capabilities.

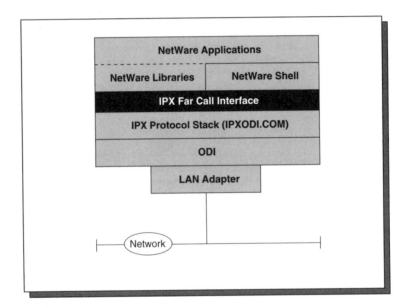

Figure 2-11c. The Standard NetWare Client Architecture.
(Courtesy of Novell, Inc.)

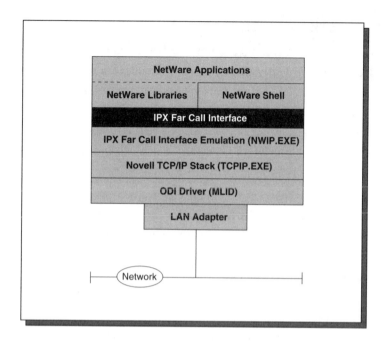

Figure 2-11d. The NetWare/IP Client Architecture.
(Courtesy of Novell, Inc.)

Another alternative for TCP/IP connectivity is the IP Relay product, which ships with the NetWare MultiProtocol 2.x or 3.x router software. The physical configuration is a star topology, with a central server that communicates with all other connected servers via point-to-point links. The central server maintains a table of the IP addresses of all other connected servers for the purpose of routing incoming traffic. Like IP tunneling, this process encapsulates the IPX traffic inside IP packets.

References [2-34] through [2-40] are documents and application notes from Novell that address TCP/IP network applications; reference [2-41] is the location of Novell's World Wide Web site, which contains a wealth of information; and references [2-42] through [2-45] are recent journal articles that describe NetWare features and capabilities.

2.8 Internetwork Analysis Tools

In the previous sections of this chapter, we examined the way networks, such as SNA and DECnet, or LAN operating systems, such as NetWare and VINES, support the Internet protocol suite. From such discussions, we can conclude that we're dealing with complex scenarios, such as encapsulating an IP datagram within a VINES packet and transmitting that packet over an X.25 link to another VINES network. When all goes well, the internetwork manager is a hero. But what happens when something fails?

Internetwork failures call for three things: well-trained analysts, the correct analysis tool, and a quick response. Fortunately, the TCP/IP protocol suite is considered "standard equipment" among analyzer vendors, as testimony to the popularity of these protocols. The key task for the analyst is to review the various products available and select one that satisfies both technical and budgetary constraints. As a starting point, RFC 1470 [2-46] presents a number of these tools for consideration. Readers wishing to solicit bids from various analyzer manufacturers can use Table 2-2 to survey vendors about their support for available LAN, MAN, and WAN interfaces and Internet protocols.

Table 2-2. Evaluating TCP/IP Protocol Analyzers.

Date _____

Vendor _____

Address _____

City, State, Zip _____

Phone _____

Fax _____

Contact Person _____

Model Number _____

Base Price _____

Price as Optioned _____

Interfaces Supported

AppleTalk _____	Frame Relay _____
ARCNET _____	IEEE 802.3 _____
ATM _____	IEEE 802.5 _____
Ethernet _____	SMDS _____
FDDI_____	Other _____

Internet Protocols Supported

ARP/RARP_____	NFS _____
BOOTP _____	OSPF _____
CMIP/CMOT _____	RIP _____
DNS _____	SMTP _____
FTP _____	SNAP _____
IPv4 _____	SNMP _____
IPv6 _____	TCP _____
ICMP _____	TELNET _____
NetBIOS _____	UDP _____

So far, we've surveyed the Internet protocols, studied how different vendors implement them, and looked at analysis tools. In subsequent chapters, we will study the protocols in more depth and will look at case studies of the protocols in use taken from actual internetworks. For consistency, we've detailed all case studies using trace files from the Network General Corp. (Menlo Park, CA) Sniffer protocol analyzer. We will structure our discussion along the lines of the ARPA Internet model. Thus, Chapter 3 will consider the Network Interface Layer, Chapter 4 the Internet Layer, and so on. Now the real work begins.

2.9 References

[2-1]   Reichard, Kevin, and Eric F. Johnson. *UNIX in Plain English*. MIS Press (New York, NY), 1994.

[2-2]   Krol, E. "The Hitchhiker's Guide to the Internet." RFC 1118, September 1989.

[2-3]   Frost, Lyle. "Bridging Networks." *UNIX Review* (May 1991): 46–52.

[2-4]   Giles, Roosevelt. "UNIX and PC Network Connectivity." *Network VAR* (October 1995): 40–46.

[2-5]   Foley, John. "The Unix World." *Information Week* (October 16, 1995): 52–61.

[2-6]   Smalley, Eric. "DEC Crafts Three-Towered Vision of Open Systems." *Network World* (December 9, 1991): 1–37.

[2-7]   Digital Equipment Corporation. *A Guide to Digital Networking*. Document number EC-H5059-93, December 1995.

[2-8]   Gasiewski, Donna. "DECnet, Revised and Revisited." Digital Age (formerly DEC Professional), (May 1995): 24-30.

[2-9]   Cini, Al. "DECnet and TCP/IP: Over Easy." Digital Age (formerly DEC Professional) (April 1995): 37-39.

[2-10]   Current information on Digital products may be found on http://www.digital.com.

[2-11]   Malamud, Carl. *Analyzing DECnet/OSI Phase V*. Van Nostrand Reinhold (New York, NY), 1991.

[2-12]   IBM. *TCP/IP Tutorial and Technical Overview*, Fifth edition, Document number GG24-3376-04. Prentice Hall (Upper Saddle River, NJ), 1995.

[2-13]   Baker, Steven. "Desktop TCP/IP's Destiny." *LAN Magazine* (October 1995): 50–57.

[2-14]   Auerbach, Karl, and Chris Wellens. "Internet Evolution or Revolution?" *LAN Magazine* (October 1995): 60–65.

[2-15]   "TCP/IP Software Product Guide." *LAN Magazine* (October 1995): 67–76.

[2-16] Novell. *LAN WorkPlace for DOS Administrator's Guide*. Publication No. 100-000882-001, 1990.

[2-17] Keenan, Vernon. "From Here to Connectivity." *MacWeek* (September 24, 1991): 20–22.

[2-18] Apple Computer, Inc. *Apple MacTCP Administrator's Guide*, 1989.

[2-19] Snyder, Joel. "TCP/IP for the Mac." *LAN* (May 1992): 93–100.

[2-20] Romkey, John, and Sharon Fisher. "Under the Hood: Packet Drivers." *BYTE* (May 1991): 297–303.

[2-21] For information on the Crynwr packet drivers, contact info@crynwr.com. The packet drivers are archived on URL: ftp://ftp.coast.net/simtel/msdos/pktdrvr, or URL: http://www.coast.net.

[2-22] Richer, Mark. "Who Needs Universal Network Interface Standards?" *Data Communications* (September 21, 1990): 71–72.

[2-23] Breidenbach, Susan. "Network Driver Wars: It's NDIS vs. ODI." *LAN Times* (January 21, 1991): 35.

[2-24] Banyan Systems, Inc. *VINES TCP/IP* Option. Document number 001891, 1992.

[2-25] Banyan Systems, Inc. *VINES Protocol Definition*. Document number 003673, June 1993.

[2-26] Allen, John, et al. "Under the Banyan Tree." *Network World* (September 18, 1995): 55–59.

[2-27] IBM. *Multi-Protocol Transport Networking Architecture, Tutorial and Product Implementations*. Document GG24-4170-00, January 1994.

[2-28] Tyson, Herb. *Navigating the Internet with OS/2 Warp*. SAMS Publishing, 1995.

[2-29] Microsoft Corp. *Windows NT Resource Guide*. Microsoft Press, 1995.

[2-30] Microsoft Corp. *Windows NT Networking Guide*. Microsoft Press, 1995.

[2-31] Redmond Communications, Inc. "Microsoft's BackOffice LAN Connectivity Strategy." *Directions on Microsoft* (March/April 1995): 2–15.

[2-32] Chacon, Michael, and Claude King. "NT: Older and Wiser." *LAN Magazine* (June 1995): 51–56.

[2-33] Robertson, Bruce. "Windows 95: WINevitable." *Network Computing* (September 15, 1995): 53–63.

[2-34] Novell. *NetWare v3.11 TCP/IP Transport Supervisor's Guide*. Publication No. 100-000945-001, 1991.

[2-35] Erwin, Auston, et al. "Installing and Configuring NetWare TCP/IP on a NetWare 3.11 Server." *Novell Application Notes* (March 1993): 23–48.

[2-36] Bautista, Ernesto. "Configuring NetWare Connect with TCP/IP Remote Clients." *Novell Application Notes* (October 1994): 71–90.

[2-37] Mosbuarger, Myron. "Using NetWare IP Over Satellite Networks." *Novell Application Notes* (April 1995): 59–70.

[2-38] Mosbarger, Myron. "Comparing Novell's IPX-to-IP Connectivity Solutions: IP Tunneling, NetWare/IP and IP Relay." *Novell Application Notes* (September 1995): 53–69.

[2-39] Gardner, Dave. "NetWare/IP 2.0: Overview, Planning, Installation and Tuning." *Novell Brainshare 1995 Presentation Book* (Volume 8): 45–49.

[2-40] Meek, Brian. "Novell TCP/IP Technology." *Novell Brainshare 1995 Presentation Book* (Volume 9): 52–54.

[2-41] Much of Novell's documentation is available on URL: http://www.novell.com.

[2-42] Wittman, Art, and James E. Drews. "NetWare 4.1 Puts Novell In the Spotlight." *Network Computing* (January 15, 1995): 50–60.

[2-43] Hurwicz, Mike. "NetWare and Unix United." *LAN Magazine* (June 1995): 59–66.

[2-44] Beurger, David. "Novell Solves Vision Puzzle." *Network World* (September 11, 1995): 54–66.

[2-45]   Kalman, Steve. "Navigating NetWare 4.1." *Interoperability* (April 1995): 8–14.

[2-46]   Enger, R., and J. Reynolds. "FYI on a Network Management Tool Catalog: Tools for Monitoring and Debugging TCP/IP Internets and Interconnected Devices." RFC 1470, June 1993.

## CHAPTER 3

Troubleshooting the Network Interface Connection

We will begin our study of TCP/IP analysis by examining problems that can occur at the ARPA architectural model's Network Interface Layer, which makes the connection to local, metropolitan-area, or wide-area networks (recall our discussion in Section 2.1). The popularity of the Internet protocols has produced Request for Comments (RFC) documents detailing implementations over virtually every type of LAN, MAN, and WAN, including ARCNET, Ethernet, IEEE 802, FDDI, Packet Switched Public Data Networks (PSPDNs) using the ITU-T X.25 protocol, frame relay, Asynchronous Transfer Mode (ATM), and many others.

To connect to LANs, the Network Interface Layer must exist in all hosts and routers, although its implementation may change across the internetwork (see Figure 3-1a). Thus Host A must have a consistent attachment to Router B, but the destination Host Z may be of a different type. In other words, you can start with an Ethernet, traverse a frame relay network, and end with a token ring as long as you maintain pair-wise consistencies.

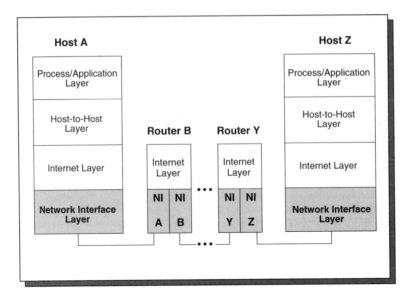

Figure 3-1a. The Network Interface Connection.

Figure 3-1b shows the options for the Network Interface Layer and their supporting RFCs. Recall that the higher-layer information (e.g., IP, TCP, and so on) is treated as data inside the transmitted frame (see Figure 3-1c). The headers and trailers are defined by the particular LAN or WAN in use, e.g., ARCNET, token ring, etc. Immediately following the Local Network header is the IP header, then the TCP header, and, finally, the higher layer Application data, which might be FTP, TELNET, and so forth.

ARPA Layer	Protocol Implementation						OSI Layer
Process / Application	File Transfer	Electronic Mail	Terminal Emulation	File Transfer	Client / Server	Network Management	Application
	File Transfer Protocol (FTP)	Simple Mail Transfer Protocol (SMTP)	TELNET Protocol	Trivial File Transfer Protocol (TFTP)	Sun Microsystems Network File System Protocols (NFS)	Simple Network Management Protocol (SNMP)	Presentation
	MIL-STD-1780 RFC 959	MIL-STD-1781 RFC 821	MIL-STD-1782 RFC 854	RFC 783	RFCs 1014, 1057, and 1094	RFC 1157	Session
Host-to-Host	Transmission Control Protocol (TCP) MIL-STD-1778 RFC 793			User Datagram Protocol (UDP) RFC 768			Transport
Internet	Address Resolution ARP RFC 826 RARP RFC 903		Internet Protocol (IP) MIL-STD-1777 RFC 791		Internet Control Message Protocol (ICMP) RFC 792		Network
Network Interface	Network Interface Cards: Ethernet, Token Ring, ARCNET, MAN and WAN RFC 894, RFC 1042, RFC 1201 and others						Data Link
	Transmission Media: Twisted Pair, Coax, Fiber Optics, Wireless Media, etc.						Physical

Figure 3-1b. ARPA Network Interface Layer Protocols.

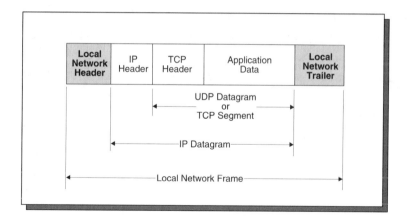

Figure 3-1c. The Internet Transmission Frame.

In summary, the TCP segment comprises the TCP header plus the application data. The IP process treats the TCP segment as data, adds the IP header, and produces the IP datagram. The Local Network process adds the frame header and trailer and transmits that frame on the physical network, such as the Ethernet cable or the X.25 link.

In this chapter, we'll study how various Network Interface Layer options support TCP/IP and the constraints on those implementations when they transmit TCP/IP-related information. The case studies in Section 3.13 will illustrate these protocol interactions in detail. A good reference about support for the Network Interface Layer is RFC 1122, "Requirements for Internet Hosts: Communications Layers" [3-1]. We'll begin by examining how ARCNET networks support TCP/IP.

3.1 ARCNET

ARCNET, which stands for Attached Resource Computer Network, was developed by Datapoint Corp. in 1977. ARCNET is a token passing architecture that supports a number of Physical Layer alternatives, including a linear bus, a star, or a branching tree [3-2]. The original version supported a transmission rate of 2.5 Mbps and up to 255 workstations. It is standardized as ANSI 878.1. An enhancement to the architecture, known as ARCNETPLUS, operates at 20 Mbps.

The Internet standard for ARCNET, RFC 1201 [3-3], suggests methods for encapsulating both IP and ARP datagrams within the ARCNET frame. Three frame formats are available, as shown in Figure 3-2. (Note that this RFC supercedes the older version (RFC 1051) and makes a number of protocol enhancements that have improved TCP/IP support.) The short frame format (Figure 3-2a) limits transmitted client data to 249 octets (an *octet* represents 8 bits of information). The long frame (Figure 3-2b) allows between 253 and 504 octets of client data. An exception frame (Figure 3-2c) is used with frames having between 250 and 252 octets of client data. (Note that Figure 3-2 shows the frame formats that appear in the software buffers; the hardware transmits formats that duplicate the Destination ID (DID), do not send the Unused and Protocol ID fields, and add some hardware framing.)

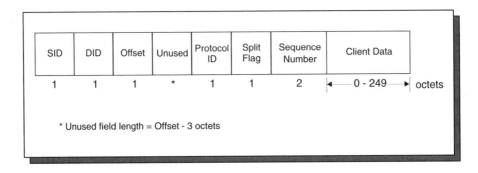

Figure 3-2a. ARCNET Short Frame Format.

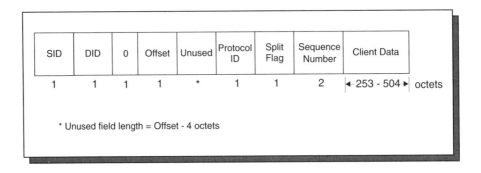

Figure 3-2b. ARCNET Long Frame Format.

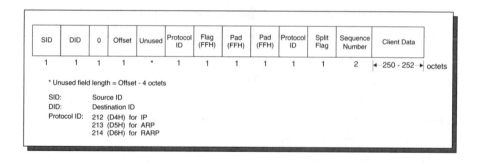

Figure 3-2c. ARCNET Exception Frame Format.

The ARCNET frame may contain up to 512 octets, of which 504 octets may be client data. The sender fragments larger packets, using the Split Flag and Sequence Number fields for identification. The Split Flag takes on one of three values depending on the fragmentation required. Unfragmented packets use Split Flag = 0. The first fragment of a fragmented packet uses Split Flag = ((T-2)*2)+1, where T is the total number of expected fragments. Subsequent fragments use Split Flag = ((N-1)*2), where N is the number of this fragment.

For example, assume that a packet requires eight fragments. The Split Flag values would be:

Fragment	Split Flag (decimal)
1	13
2	2
3	4
4	6
5	8
6	10
7	12
8	14

The ARCNET frame may contain up to 120 fragments, yielding a maximum value of 238 decimal (or EE in hexadecimal; throughout this text, we will use an uppercase h (H) to represent hexadecimal numbers). This allows up to 60,480 octets per packet (120 * 504 = 60,480). All fragments belonging to the same packet use an identical 2-octet sequence number.

Another unique characteristic of ARCNET is the addressing structure it uses to define an 8-bit address field. This structure allows 255 unique hardware addresses, plus a broadcast designation (address = 0). (This address is implemented with an 8-position DIP switch that you set manually on each ARCNET card. An error in duplicating these switch settings can cause a complete network failure, so use caution when setting the address and other options on the ARCNET card.)

To correlate the 8-bit ARCNET address with the 32-bit IP address, RFC 1201 considers three scenarios: Unicast, Broadcast, and Multicast. (Section 4.2 will discuss the IP addresses in detail.) Unicast IP addresses may be mapped to an ARCNET address using the Address Resolution Protocol (ARP), which we will discuss in Section 4.3.1. Broadcast IP addresses are mapped to the ARCNET broadcast address of 0. Multicast IP addresses must also be mapped to the ARCNET broadcast address since ARCNET has no provision for multicasting.

RFC 1201 also discusses the transmission of ARP and Reverse Address Resolution Protocol (RARP) packets that may be required to support the more common IP datagrams. When ARP is used, the ARP packet will indicate ARCNET hardware by setting the ARP Hardware Type = 7. RARP packets are transmitted in a similar fashion.

3.2 Ethernet

Developed by DEC, Intel, and Xerox (known collectively as DIX) in 1973, Ethernet was the first LAN to achieve widespread acceptance. The first version, known as Experimental Ethernet, operated at 3 Mbps and used 8-bit addresses. It was later upgraded to Ethernet version 1 and finally to the Ethernet version 2 that we use today, which transmits at 10 Mbps and uses 48-bit addresses. Much of Ethernet's development coincided with research into the Internet protocols. As a result, many TCP/IP-based internetworks contain Ethernet segments.

A word of caution is in order, however. In the early 1980s, DIX turned over the Ethernet Standard [3-4] to the IEEE as a model for today's IEEE 802.3, Carrier Sense Multiple Access Bus with Collision Detection (CSMA/CD) network. The IEEE made improvements in the DIX version and published IEEE 802.3 in 1983 [3-5]. Thus, the

Ethernet and IEEE 802.3 standards are not identical. Section 3.3 will discuss examples of these differences. In this section we will examine Ethernet, and in Section 3.3 we will discuss IEEE 802.3.

The Ethernet frame format (Figure 3-3) defines a length between 64 and 1,518 octets including the header, data, and trailer. The header consists of Destination and Source addresses that are 6 octets (48 bits) each and a 2-octet field known as the Type (or EtherType) field. ARP or RARP perform any address mapping between the 32-bit IP address and the 48-bit Ethernet address, which we will explore in Section 4.2. The Ethernet-designated Destination Address for Broadcast frames is all ONEs (FFFFFFFFFFFFH). The Type designates the higher-layer protocol in use within the Data field. Appendix E defines and gives a number of these Ethernet protocol types. Examples relevant to the Internet protocols include 0800H (IP), 0805H (X.25 Level 3), and 0806H (ARP).

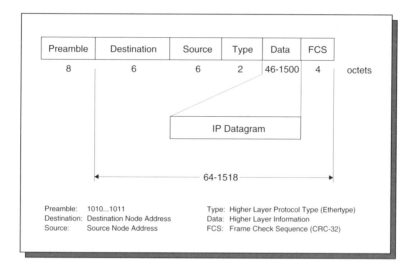

Figure 3-3. Ethernet Frame with IP Datagram.
(Courtesy Digital Equipment Corp.)

The Data field itself must be between 46 and 1,500 octets in length. Should an extremely short IP datagram be transmitted (i.e., fewer than 46 octets), the IP process must pad the Data field with zeros to reach the minimum length. (This padding is not considered part of the IP datagram length and is not counted in the Total Length field within the IP header.) The maximum length of the Ethernet Data field is 1,500 octets, which also constrains the IP datagram length. Recall that the default IP datagram Maximum Transmission Unit (MTU) is 576 octets, which easily fits inside one Ethernet frame. The information within the IP datagram is transmitted as a series of octets in numerical order (i.e., first octet transmitted first, second octet transmitted second, and so on). The Internet Standard for Ethernet networks, RFC 894 [3-6], and Appendix B of the IP specification (RFC 791) provide further details on the specific data formats.

3.3 IEEE 802.3

The IEEE project 802 is concerned with internetworking between LANs and MANs. All of the IEEE 802 series of LANs (802.3, 802.4, and 802.5) are covered by the same Internet standard, RFC 1042 [3-7]. These LANs, therefore, exhibit similar characteristics, notably a common addressing format and the use of the IEEE 802.2 Logical Link Control mechanism, that facilitate their interconnection. The primary differences are in the Medium Access Control (MAC) header formats, which are unique to each transmission frame type as dictated by the requirements of the topology. We will point out these differences and similarities as we proceed through our discussion of the IEEE 802 LANs.

As we discussed in the last section, the IEEE 802.3 standard is similar but not identical to the DIX Ethernet. Figure 3-4 shows the IEEE 802.3 frame format. Several differences between the IEEE 802.3 and the Ethernet frame are readily apparent. First, the IEEE 802.3 Destination and Source address fields may have a length of 2 or 6 octets, although the 6-octet length (matching the Ethernet address lengths) is most common. ARP maps the IP address (32 bits) to the IEEE 802.3 address (48 bits). The ARP hardware code for IEEE 802 networks is 6. Broadcast addresses for both Ethernet and IEEE 802 networks are consistent, however, and use all ones.

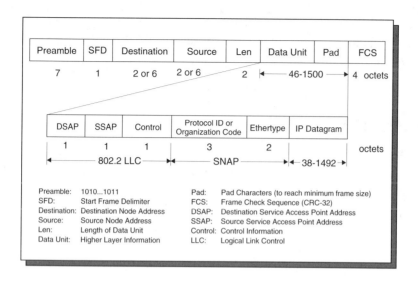

Figure 3-4. IEEE 802.3 Frame Including 802.2 LLC and SNAP Headers, plus IP Datagram
(Courtesy of IEEE)

Next, the IEEE 802.3 frame defines a Length field, which specifies the length of the Data unit. Recall that in the Ethernet frame this position was the Type, indicating the higher-layer protocol in use. These 2 octets (the Type or Length fields) distinguish the frame format—Ethernet or IEEE 802.3, respectively. If the Data Link Layer driver mixes these up, confusion results. For example, a destination host expecting an Ethernet frame with a Type field will be unable to respond to an IEEE 802.3 frame that contains the Length field. This is because the destination host's higher-layer software can recognize only a finite number of Types, such as IP (0800H), ARP (0806H), DEC-net Phase IV (6003H), and DEC LAT (6004H). Suppose that the transmitting host had an IEEE 802.3 driver and the Data field was 1,500 octets (05DCH) long. The transmitting host would insert 05DCH in the Length field, which the destination host would be unable to recognize. We will look at an example of this confusion in Section 3.13.4.

The Data field contains the information from the higher layers, plus two IEEE-defined headers. The first header is the Logical Link Control (LLC) header, defined by IEEE 802.2 [3-8]. The LLC header includes Destination and Source Service Access Point addresses (DSAP and SSAP, respectively) and a Control field. The second header is the Sub-Network Access Protocol (SNAP), described in Reference [3-9]. The SNAP header includes a Protocol ID or Organization Code field (3 octets) and an Ethernet

Type field, or EtherType (2 octets). The combination of the LLC and SNAP headers allows the higher-layer protocol to be identified with both a SAP and a Type designation. The balance of the Data field contains the higher-layer information, such as an IP datagram.

3.4 IEEE 802.5

Another IEEE 802 network of interest is the token ring, described in the IEEE Standard 802.5 [3-10]. The token ring's popularity is due partially to strong support from major networking companies such as Apple, IBM, and Proteon. Its success is also due to its built-in internetworking. This provision is known as Source Routing [3-11]; it uses the Routing Information (RI) field to connect rings via bridges. The RI field specifies the path the frame must take from its source to its destination. The mechanism for determining that path is called Route Discovery. (Chapter 6 of *Troubleshooting Internetworks* [3-12] discusses the Source Routing protocol and gives several internetwork examples.)

Figure 3-5 shows the token ring frame format. An IP datagram occupies the Information field of the token ring frame. Any necessary routing information precedes the Information field. The Information field contains the IEEE 802.2 LLC header (3 octets), SNAP header (5 octets), and the IP datagram. Given a minimum IP datagram header of 20 octets, the protocol overhead (LLC + SNAP + IP) is, thus, 28 octets per IP datagram. The maximum length of the Information field (and, thus, the encapsulated IP datagram) varies, depending on a parameter known as the Token Holding time. This parameter specifies the length of time any one node may hold the token before it must pass the token to its downstream neighbor. RFC 1042 gives an example for a Token Holding time of nine milliseconds that results in a maximum length of the IP header plus datagram of 4,464 octets.

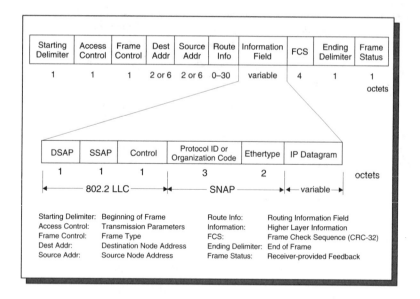

**Figure 3-5. IEEE 802.5 Frame Including IEEE 802.2 LLC
and SNAP Headers, plus IP Datagram.**
(Courtesy of IEEE)

When bridges connect multiple rings, the Largest Frame (LF) parameter within the RI field controls the maximum frame size and, thus, the maximum IP datagram length. The LF parameter assures that a source station does not transmit a frame length that exceeds an intermediate bridge's processing or memory capabilities. If an intermediate bridge cannot handle a particular frame length, all devices along that transmission path must use a shorter frame. Currently defined LF lengths are between 516 and 62,543 octets.

As a final note, RFC 1042 clarifies the differences between the IEEE and Internet procedures for transmitting the data on the cable. The IEEE specifies numbers in bit-wise little-endian order, i.e., the way they are transmitted on the cable [3-9]. The Internet specifies numbers in byte-wise big-endian order. The following table shows examples of commonly used numbers:

Usage	IEEE HEX	IEEE Binary	Internet Binary	Internet Decimal
LLC UI Op Code	C0	11000000	00000011	3
LLC SAP for SNAP	55	01010101	10101010	170
LLC XID	F5	11110101	10101111	175
LLC XID, P	FD	11111101	10111111	191
LLC TEST	C7	11000111	11100011	227
LLC TEST, P	CF	11001111	11110011	243
LLC XID Info	818000			129.1.0

3.5 FDDI

The Fiber Distributed Data Interface (FDDI) is a standard for fiber optic data transmission developed by the American National Standards Institute (ANSI) and defined in Reference [3-13]. FDDI is a token passing ring architecture operating at 100 Mbps. (The actual data rate for FDDI is 125 Mbps, but one out of five bits is used for overhead.) Because of its transmission rate, FDDI may emerge as an important alternative to Ethernet or token ring for local TCP/IP data transport.

The FDDI frame structure (Figure 3-6) is similar to that for IEEE 802.5. The maximum frame size is 4,500 octets (or 9,000 symbols, with 4 bits/symbol). When 6-octet addressing (the most common) is used, the MAC-Layer header (Preamble through Source address) uses 16 octets, and the MAC-Layer trailer uses 6 octets. Subtracting the headers from the maximum frame size leaves 4,478 octets for data. As we saw in the last section, the IEEE 802.2 LLC header requires 3 octets and the SNAP header requires 5 octets. Subtracting these yields the maximum IP datagram length of 4,470 octets.

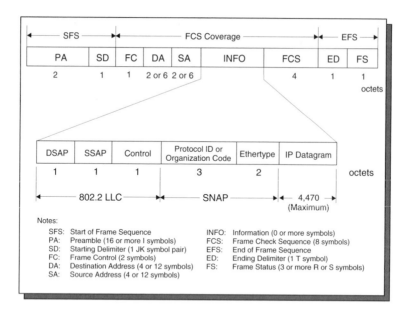

Figure 3-6. FDDI Frame Including IEEE 802.2 LLC and SNAP Headers, plus IP Datagram.
(Courtesy of American National Standards Institute)

Like IEEE 802 networks, FDDI networks use ARP to map the 32-bit Internet addresses to the 48-bit FDDI addresses [3-14]. An ARP Hardware Type = 1 designates the FDDI hardware used to provide interoperability with bridged Ethernet networks. Readers needing further information on FDDI should consult Reference [3-15].

3.6 Serial Lines

For years, digital and analog leased lines have been the mainstay of host-to-host and LAN-to-LAN connections. As TCP/IP-based internets grew larger, leased lines became a natural solution for the WAN connection. Two protocols have been developed to support TCP/IP-based data transmission over those topologies: the Serial Line IP (SLIP) and the Point-to-Point Protocol (PPP).

3.6.1 Serial Line IP

Serial Line IP (SLIP), described in RFC 1055 [3-16], frames IP datagrams on a serial line. SLIP is not an Internet standard, but it is included in BSD 4.3 UNIX. As the RFC describes, SLIP performs no other protocol functions.

SLIP defines two characters: END (C0H or octal 300 or decimal 192) and ESC (DBH or octal 333 or decimal 219). To transmit, the SLIP host begins sending the IP datagram (see Figure 3-7). It replaces any data octet equivalent to the END character with the 2-octet sequence of ESC plus octal 334 (DB DCH). It replaces any octet equal to the ESC character with the 2-octet sequence of ESC plus octal 335 (DB DDH). After completing the datagram transmission, it sends an END character. (Note that the ESC character used with SLIP is not the ASCII escape character.)

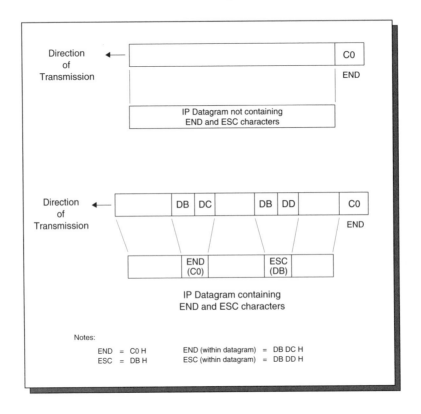

Figure 3-7. Serial Line IP (SLIP) Frame Format.

Because SLIP is nonstandard, it has no maximum packet size. Many systems adhere to the maximum packet size used by the Berkeley UNIX SLIP of 1,006 octets (excluding the SLIP framing characters). Because of its nonstandard status, any SLIP implementation must assure that the packet size is compatible at both ends of the link before transmitting data.

An enhancement to SLIP, known as Compressed SLIP or CSLIP, compresses the TCP/IP header for transmission over low speed serial lines. CSLIP is defined in RFC 1144, and is many times referred to as Van Jacobson header compression. This technique minimizes the protocol overhead being sent, thus partially compensating for the lower speed of the transmission system.

3.6.2 Point-to-Point Protocol

The Point-to-Point Protocol (PPP), described in RFC 1661 [3-17], is the second protocol used for serial line connections. Unlike SLIP, PPP is a standard protocol for use over asynchronous or synchronous serial lines. RFC 1661 describes three main components of PPP: a method of encapsulating multiprotocol datagrams, a Link Control Protocol (LCP), and a family of Network Control Protocols (NCPs). LCP packets initialize the Data Link Layer of the communicating devices. NCP packets negotiate the Network Layer connection between the two endpoints. Once the LCP and NCP configuration is complete, datagrams may be transmitted over the link. Let's look at the PPP frame structure in detail.

The PPP frame is based upon the ISO High Level Data Link Control (HDLC) protocol (known as ISO 3309) which has been implemented by itself and has also been incorporated into many other protocol suites, including X.25, Frame Relay, and ISDN. (The 1979 HDLC standard addresses synchronous environments; the 1984 modification extends the usage to asynchronous environments. When asynchronous transmission is used, all octets are transmitted with 1 start bit, 8 data bits, and 1 stop bit.) The PPP frame (see Figure 3-8a) includes fields for beginning and ending Flags (set to 07H); an Address (set to FFH, the all-stations address); Control (set to 03H, for Unnumbered Information); Protocol (a one- or two-octet field identifying the higher-layer protocol in use); Information (the higher-layer information, with a default maximum length of 1,500 octets); and a Frame Check Sequence (2 octets). RFC 1662 describes the details of the HDLC-like framing.

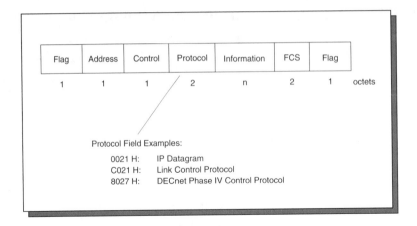

Figure 3-8a. Point-to-Point Protocol Frame.

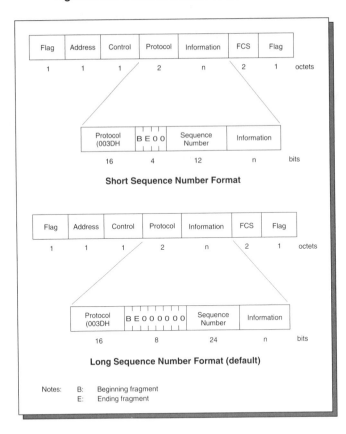

Figure 3-8b. PPP Multilink Frame.

The Protocol field is used to distinguish multiprotocol datagrams, with the value contained in that field identifying the datagram encapsulated in the Information field of the packet. RFC 1661 specifies values for the Protocol field that are reserved; the Assigned Numbers document (currently RFC 1700) contains specific Protocol field assignments.

The Protocol field is 2 octets (or 4 hex characters) in length, with possible values from 0000 - FFFFH. Values in the 0xxx - 3xxx range identify the Network Layer protocol of specific packets, and values in the 8xxx - Bxxx range identify packets belonging to the associated Network Control Protocols (NCPs), if any. Protocol Field values in the 4xxx - 7xxx range are used for protocols wirh low volume traffic which have no associated NCP. Protocol field values in the Cxxx - Fxxx range identify packets as link layer Control Protocols (such as LCP). Examples include:

Value	Protocol
0021H	Internet Protocol (IPv4)
0023	ISO CLNP
0027	DECnet Phase IV
0029	AppleTalk
002B	Novell IPX
0035	Banyan VINES
003D	PPP Multilink
003F	NetBIOS Framing
0201	802.1D Hello Packets
0203	IBM Source Routing BPDUs
C021	Link Control Protocol (LCP)
C023	Password Authentication Protocol
C025	Link Quality Report
C223	Challenge Handshake Authentication Protocol

PPP's second component is the Link Control Protocol (LCP), which deals with Data Link Layer issues. LCP defines five steps for link control. The process begins with the Link Dead phase, which indicates that the Physical Layer is not ready. When the Physical Layer is ready to be used, the process proceeds with the Link Establishment phase. In the Link Establishment phase, the Link Control Protocol (LCP) is used to establish the connection through the exchange of Configure packets between the two ends of the link. The Authentication Phase, which is optional, allows the peer at the other end of the link to authenticate itself prior to exchanging Network Layer protocol packets. In the Network Layer Protocol Phase, each Network Layer in operation, such as IP, Novell's IPX, or AppleTalk, is configured by the Network Control Protocol (NCP). The final step, the Link Termination Phase, uses LCP to close the link.

PPP's third objective is to develop a family of NCPs to transmit Network Layer information. A number of NCPs have been defined, each addressing a particular Network Layer protocol. These include DECnet Phase IV, defined in RFC 1762; Banyan VINES, defined in RFC 1763; and Xerox Network Systems (XNS) Internet Datagram Protocol (IDP), defined in RFC 1764. Each of these protocols would be defined by a distinct value of the Protocol field:

Value (hex)	Protocol
8025	XNS IDP Protocol
8027	DECnet Phase IV Control Protocol
8035	Banyan VINES Control Protocol

Consult the current Assigned Numbers document, under the PPP section, for additional NCP assignments.

3.6.3 PPP Multilink Protocol

In some cases, a WAN may provide multiple logical links available to the end user applications. On example of this is ISDN, in which multiple bearer (or B) channels are provided that carry application data. In the case of an ISDN Primary Rate Interface (PRI) line, the end user sees two B channels, each with a 64 Kbps bandwidth, for a total of 128 Kbps bandwidth. Other WAN architectures that include similar multiplexing capabilities are X.25 and frame relay.

A high speed application can utilize these multiple links if a mechanism for alternating packets delivered to the individual links, plus a mechanism for recombining these individual data streams for delivery to the single receiver, is provided. The goal of the PPP Multilink Protocol (MP), as stated in RFC 1717 [3-18] is to "coordinate multiple independent links between a fixed pair of systems, providing a virtual link with greater bandwidth than any of the constituent members."

That coordination function is accomplished through the addition of a two- or four-octet sequencing header inside the PPP frame. Two formats are defined, supporting either short sequence numbers or long sequence numbers (see Figure 3-8b). Note that for either case, the Protocol field of the PPP frame contains the value 003DH, identifying the PPP Multilink protocol. Both the two- and four-octet sequencing headers contain two single-bit flags that indicate if that fragment begins (B) or ends (E) a PPP packet. When the fragment is the beginning of sequence, B=1, and when the fragment is the end of a sequence, E=1. A 12- or 24-bit sequence number then completes the header. The four-octet header (with a 24-bit sequence number) is the default case, however the four-octet header may be replaced with the two-octet version upon negotiation with the other end of the link. Details regarding this negotiation process, plus implementation specifics, are provided in RFC 1717.

3.7 Data Link Switching

Many internetworks, especially those that support banking, insurance, and other financial business operations, operate as two parallel networks: one internetwork supporting IBM Systems Network Architecture (SNA) functions, and a second supporting TCP/IP. SNA networks are connection-oriented, and are based upon protocols such as the Synchronous Data Link Control (SDLC), IEEE Logical Link Control 2 (LLC2), or Network Basic Input/Output System (NetBIOS). TCP/IP networks, in contrast, are connectionless, and are based upon the Internet Protocol which we will study in Chapter 4.

In many cases these two internetworks operate in parallel, connecting the same locations, which increases the total cost of operation. Tunneling the SNA traffic inside TCP/IP packets would solve the issue of dissimilar protocols; however, the connection-oriented nature of SNA must still be addressed. This connection-orientation, inherent in both the SDLC and LLC2 protocols, requires that data be acknowledged within a certain period of time, or the sender will retransmit. If multiple retransmissions occur, the upper protocol layers conclude that the logical connection (or session) is no longer active, and drop that connection. We know this as a session timeout.

To solve this problem, IBM developed a process known as *Data Link Switching* (abbreviated DLSw), a technique which maintains the connection-oriented nature of the connection while tunneling SNA traffic inside TCP/IP packets. Support for DLSw comes from the Advanced Peer-to-Peer Networking Implementers Workshop (AIW) Data Link Switching Related Interest Group, or AIW DLSw RIG for short. The AIW DLSw RIG has published RFC 1795 [3-19], which defines the methods and procedures for DLSw operation.

As defined in RFC 1795, DLSw is a forwarding mechanism for SNA and NetBIOS protocols. The DLSw Switch-to-Switch Protocol (SSP) defines a method for switching at the Data Link Layer, and then for the encapsulation of that data inside TCP/IP packets. When used within token ringbased LAN internetworks, the Data Link Switch (DLS) appears as a source-routed token ring bridge. Problems associated with bridged internetworks that DLSw is designed to solve include: Data Link Control (DLC) timeouts; DLC acknowledgments over the WAN (which consume scarce bandwidth); flow and congestion control; broadcast control of token ring search (or discovery) frames; and the hop count limits associated with source route bridging environments.

The operation of a DLSw-based internetwork is illustrated in Figure 3-9. Note that the protocol flows are divided into two major sections: interaction between the host and the Data Link Switch and end-to-end control across the TCP/IP internetwork. At the local and remote ends, the DLSs acknowledge the data sent from the connected hosts, without requiring that those acknowledgments traverse the WAN and be returned from the receiving device. A connection-oriented transport protocol, such as TCP or OSI Transport Class 4 (TP4), assures reliable delivery of the data. This technique is known as *spoofing*, as the local host is "spoofed" into thinking that the acknowledgments come from the distant receiver, when in reality they are coming from the other end of that data link. This design limits the LLC2 communication to the local networks, which limits the timeouts and reduces the amount of traffic traversing the WAN link. The DLSs control the broadcast of token ring discovery frames, further limiting the amount of extraneous traffic. In addition, the DLSs can provide flow or congestion control to the host systems as required by the current status of the WAN link.

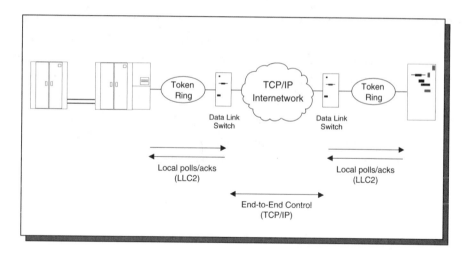

Figure 3-9. Data Link Switching Architecture.

A number of router vendors, including Ascom Timeplex, Bay Networks, Cisco Systems, Hughes Network Systems, IBM, Proteon, and 3Com, have added DLSw capabilities to their products. Further details regarding the DLSw architecture and protocol are found in RFC 1795.

3.8 Public Data Networks Using X.25

Much of the early work that produced TCP/IP and the Internet protocols was also applicable to the development of packet switching technologies. Some of the most popular WANs are Packet Switched Public Data Networks (PSPDNs) that use the X.25 protocol. X.25 can, therefore, be considered a by-product of much of this research and is frequently used in conjunction with the TCP/IP protocols for the WAN element of an internetwork.

The X.25 standard encompasses three layers of protocols for the Physical Layer, the Frame Layer, and the Packet Layer. The Physical Layer defines the X.21 protocol, a digital interface that is primarily used in Europe. In North America, the X.21 bis (equivalent to EIA-232) is used. The Frame (or Data Link) Layer protocol is known as the Link Access Procedure Balanced (LAPB) protocol. The Packet (or Network) Layer protocol is simply called the Packet Layer Protocol (PLP).

In previous sections, we discussed the transmission of IP datagrams within the Data Link Layer frames, such as Ethernet or token ring. The X.25 protocols transmit the IP datagram within a PLP packet, which in turn carries the IP datagram. Figure 3-10 shows the LAPB frame structure, which is identical to the HDLC or Synchronous Data Link Control (SDLC) formats that are familiar to many readers. The LAPB frame begins and ends with a Flag character (01111110 binary or 7EH). It contains separate fields for address and control information and a Frame Check Sequence (FCS). The PLP packet is carried inside the frame's Information field.

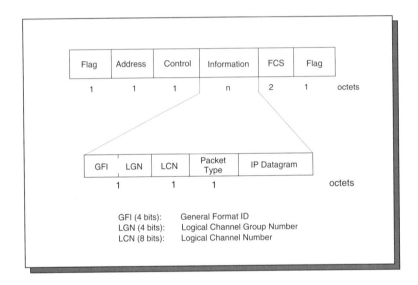

Figure 3-10. X.25 LAPB Frame with IP Datagram.
(Courtesy of ITU-T X.25-1988)

When the virtual circuit (i.e., WAN connection) is first established, the Call Request packet specifies a value of CCH (binary 11001100 or decimal 204) to indicate that IP will be used within the packet. The IP datagram is then placed within a PLP data packet for transmission. A 4-octet PLP header precedes the IP datagram and specifies the General Format ID (GFI) used for control purposes, the Logical Channel Group Number (LGN) and Logical Channel Number (LCN) that identify the logical channel, and a Packet Type field containing packet sequence numbers and flags. The maximum size of the IP datagram transmitted over X.25 is 576 octets, unless both sender and receiver negotiate otherwise. RFC 877 [3-20] specifies additional details. *Inside X.25: A Manager's Guide* [3-21] is an excellent handbook for network administrators.

3.9 Frame Relay

Frame Relay (FR) was developed by the International Telecommunications Union— Telecommunications Standards Sector (ITU-T), and derived from earlier work on Integrated Services Digital Networks (ISDNs). As such, the FR protocol is similar to ISDN's Link Access Protocol for the D-Channel (LAPD). FR is also a packet switching technology, similar to X.25, designed to transport data over a WAN link. FR improves on its X.25 predecessor primarily through its faster processing speed.

FR has cranked up its processing speed by streamlining the way it deals with information. Most protocols, such as X.25, that operate within the communications subnetwork (i.e., the OSI Physical, Data Link, and Network Layers) process information at all three layers: the Physical Layer decodes the bits, the Data Link Layer decodes the frame, and the Network Layer decodes the packet. Both frames and packets perform error checking to assure reliable communication. While this method increases the reliability of the data transmission, it also increases overhead in the number of bits transmitted and in the time required to process the bits. FR eliminates the Network Layer (i.e., packet) processing and performs only a few Data Link Layer functions. For example, FR checks the frame for errors, but it does not automatically request a retransmission if it discovers one. Should an error occur, the processes within the sender and receiver take responsibility for that function.

Note that FR operates under two assumptions. The first is that the underlying communications subnet is more reliable than the networks of years ago. With the trend within telephone networks of replacing copper circuits with fiber optic cable, this is a valid argument. If the communication subnetwork is reliable, why bother with all the rigorous error control? Second, FR technology assumes that if an error does sneak by, the sending and receiving devices are usually computers with the intelligence to diagnose and cure the problem. For example, they can ask for a retransmission and simply try again.

The FR frame structure is shown in Figure 3-11 and resembles the X.25 frame shown in Figure 3-10. You can see the differences in the formats in the first 2 octets following the Flag character. In the X.25 LAPB frame, these 2 octets are used for the Address and Control fields. The Information field would contain the X.25 packet. For FR, the first 2 octets comprise the FR header and are followed by the higher-layer information, such as an IP datagram.

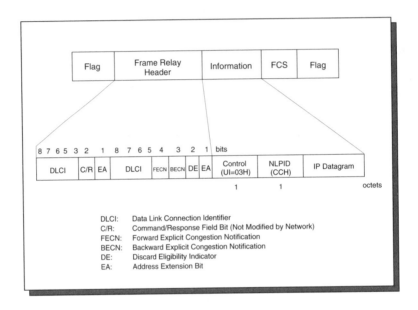

Figure 3-11. Frame Relay Frame with IP Datagram.

The FR header contains a number of subfields. The longest of these is the Data Link Connection Identifier (DLCI), which identifies the virtual circuit used for any particular communication path. (A virtual circuit is a logical communication channel between the end-user equipment, or Data Terminal Equipment (DTE), and the FR network, or Data Circuit-Terminating Equipment (DCE). In most cases, the DTE is called a Frame Relay Access Device, or FRAD, and the DCE is called a Frame Relay Network Device, or FRND. The FR network interface, called the User Network Interface, or UNI, is defined at the physical communication line between the FRAD and the FRND.) Multiple virtual circuits may exist at this interface. For example, if a router is the FRAD, it may serve 50 workstations on a LAN, which could each conceivably have a virtual circuit (identified with the DLCI field) into the FR network. The DLCI field (10 bits in length) allows up to 1,024 virtual circuits, although some are reserved for network diagnostic purposes. These circuits are further defined as Permanent Virtual Circuits (PVCs) and are established when the FRAD is attached to the FR network.

When a frame enters the FR network, the FRND examines the Frame Check Sequence (FCS) at the end of the frame for errors. If an error is present, the frame is discarded. If the FCS passes, the FRND examines the DLCI field and a table lookup determines the correct outgoing link. If a table entry does not exist for a particular frame, the frame is discarded. (By now, you should appreciate why FR is a streamlined protocol—if the frame contains any errors or if there is any confusion over how to process the frame, the frame is simply discarded. The higher-layer protocols within the machines at either end of the link must recover from the problem.)

The FR header contains 3 bits to indicate congestion on the FR network. The first 2 bits are known as Explicit Congestion Notification (ECN) bits. Any node within the FR network can send an ECN bit in two directions: downstream using the Forward ECN (or FECN) bit and upstream using the Backward ECN (or BECN) bit. The third bit used for congestion control is the Discard Eligibility (DE) bit. The DE bit indicates which frames should be discarded to relieve congestion. ANSI T1.617a discusses these congestion management principles.

Returning to Figure 3-11, the Command/Response (C/R) and Extended Address (EA) complete the FR Header. The C/R bit was defined for LAPD, but is not used with FR networks. The EA bits allow the FR Header to extend to 3 or 4 octets in length to accommodate more DLCI addresses.

The Internet standard for frame relay support is RFC 1490 [3-22], which provides specifics for implementing multiprotocol traffic over FR networks. The key word in RFC 1490's title is "multiprotocol" since the FR Information field has several variations. Consistent among all the variants, however, are the Control field and the Network Level Protocol ID (NLPID). The Control field may either specify Unnumbered Information (UI) with a field value of 03H or Exchange Identification (XID) with a field value of AF or BFH. ISO and ITU-T administer the NLPID and identify the type of protocol used within the Information field. RFC 1490 gives the following examples:

NLPID	Usage
00H	Null Network Layer (not used with Frame Relay)
80	SNAP
81	ISO CLNP
82	ISO ESIS
83	ISO ISIS
CC	Internet IP
CE	EtherType (unofficial temporary use)

Of particular interest to Internet designers is NLPID = CCH, which indicates that the frame contains an IP datagram. If a protocol does not have an NLPID, the 1-octet NLPID field is replaced with a 6-octet field. That field includes NLPID = 80H (indicating the SNAP), followed by the 5-octet SNAP header. The EtherType within the SNAP header would then identify the higherlayer protocol in use. An ARP packet is an example of a SNAP-encoded frame. The first 6 octets of the Information field (i.e., NLPID plus SNAP) would contain 80-00-00-00-08-06H. The 80 identifies NLPID = SNAP, the 00-00-00 is the SNAP Organization ID and the 08-06 is the EtherType for ARP. Inverse ARP performs the conversion between DLCIs and protocol addresses, and it is described in RFC 1293 [3-23]. Other formats for routed and bridged frames have been defined as well; consult RFC 1490 for specific details.

A number of carrier and equipment vendors joined together in 1991 to establish the Frame Relay Forum. The purpose of the Forum was to promote FR technology from an implementation and user perspective. On the standards side, ANSI T1.606 [3-24] describes the service; standards such as T1.617, T1.618, and others deal with signaling, core aspects, congestion management, and so on. The Frame Relay Forum publishes a newsletter, provides information on upcoming conferences and the status of standards, and produces implementation agreements which describe agreed-upon methods for implementing the published standards. Reference [3-25] provides contact information for the Frame Relay Forum.

Both users and carriers have demonstrated great interest in FR services. Like other data transport services—and as is especially important when using new technologies—FR networks must be designed with careful consideration for the end-user application.

Users need to understand where FR fits into their WAN strategies along with existing technologies, such as X.25 packet switching, and network technologies, such as ATM. Christine Heckart's *The Guide to Frame Relay Networking* [3-26] provides further details on design constraints. Hume and Seaman's "X.25 and Frame Relay: Packet Switched Technologies for Wide Area Connectivity" [3-27] offers an interesting perspective on WAN connectivity.

3.10 Switched Multimegabit Data Service

The IEEE 802.6 standard describes a network topology known as a Distributed Queue Dual Bus (DQDB) [3-28]. The Switched Multimegabit Data Service (SMDS) is an emerging technology based on the IEEE 802.6 standard. As its name implies, DQDB consists of two buses arranged in a loop topology. It is intended for metropolitan- or wide-area use, such as a loop around metropolitan Denver, CO. (Strictly speaking, SMDS has no distance limitations.) When one organization needs to transmit data to another, it can use SMDS as the connection between the two LANs.

Bell Communication Research, Inc. (Bellcore), the jointly owned research organization, developed SMDS as a data transport standard for use by the Regional Bell Operating Companies (RBOCs). SMDS is a packet switched data transport mechanism that provides connectionless service. Bellcore describes SMDS in Technical Report TR-TSV-000772 [3-29], which defines the Subscriber Network Interface (SNI) and the SMDS Interface Protocol (SIP). The SMDS SNI resembles other network interfaces, such as ISDN or X.25, in that it functions as a point of data ingress and egress between the user and the transmission facility; by conforming to the interface specification, both the user and the network can communicate efficiently.

SIP is a three-layer protocol. SIP Level 1 provides physical data transport and is usually implemented at the DS-1 (1.544 Mbps) or DS-3 (44.736 Mbps) rates. SIP Level 2 defines the frame format, including the header and trailer, for data transmission. Level 2 functions include detecting errors and segmenting and reassembling the variable length SIP Level 3 Protocol Data Unit (PDU). The length of the SIP Level 2 frame is fixed at 53 octets. The Level 3 PDU includes the additional address and control information needed to reliably transfer the user information from source to destination via the SMDS network. The SIP Level 3 PDU may contain up to 9,188 octets of data.

The Bellcore specification [3-29] suggests a scenario for interconnecting TCP/IP end systems using SMDS (see Figure 3-12a). End System A includes the higher layers, TCP, IP, and the MAC layer specific to the attached LAN. End System B also includes the higher TCP and IP layers, but the lower layers connect to the SMDS network using SIP. A router ties together the LAN and SMDS network, connecting to the LAN MAC layer on one side and the SMDS SIP layers on the other.

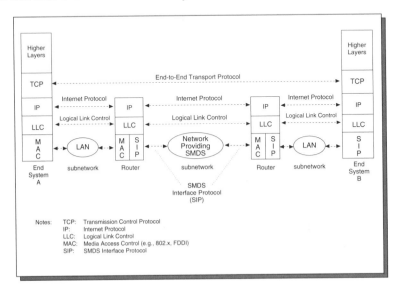

Figure 3-12a. Using SMDS with the Internet Protocols.
(Reprinted with permission from TR-TSV-000772, Copyright © 1991 Bellcore.)

The Internet community has also defined scenarios for internetworking between LANs and SMDS for the transmission of IP and ARP packets [3-30]. The resulting packet structure incorporates the SMDS SIP headers, the IEEE 802.2 header, the SNAP header, and the IP/ARP information (see Figure 3-12b). For efficient transmission on the SMDS network, the Level 3 PDU is segmented into many smaller SIP Level 2 frames. The SIP L3 PDU may contain up to 9,188 octets of data, but the SIP L2 PDU may contain only 44 octets. Thus, one L3 PDU may generate a number of L2 frames. The data structure in Figure 3-12b shows the order of the fields and the IP/ARP data as it would be assembled prior to the fragmentation process that occurs at SIP L2.

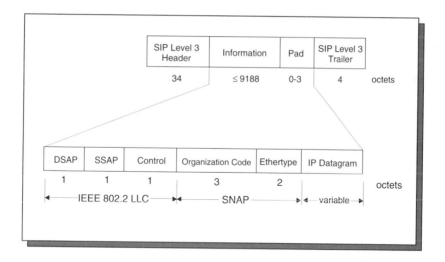

**Figure 3-12b. SMDS SIP Level 3 PDU Including IEEE 802.2 LLC
and SNAP Headers, plus IP Datagram.**
(Reprinted with permission from TR-TSV-000772, Copyright © 1991 Bellcore.)

Within the SIP Level 3 header, the Higher Layer Protocol ID (HLPI) field must be set to a value of 1, indicating IEEE 802.2 LLC. The SMDS Information field then begins with the IEEE 802.2 LLC header, which includes the DSAP and SSAP fields (set to AAH) and the Control field, set to 3 (Type 1 Unnumbered Information). The next fields include the SNAP header, which contains the Organization code (set to zero) and an EtherType. The EtherType for IP packets is 0800H and 0806H for ARP. The total length of the SIP Level 3 PDU may not exceed 9,188 octets, thus allowing an IP datagram to have an MTU of up to 9,180 octets.

SMDS enhances the speed, reliability, and subscriber services for metropolitan-area and wide-area data transport services. These services come out of the addressing features (such as Source and Destination address screening) incorporated in the SMDS standard. One such subscriber benefit is the ability to use the SMDS 8-octet addressing scheme to create Logical IP Subnetworks (LISs), also known as closed user groups. (ARP translates Internet addresses to/from SMDS addresses. The ARP Hardware Address length is eight (HA=8) and the Hardware Type is 14.) Within an LIS, the hosts may communicate with each other directly via the SMDS. When communicating to a host outside of that LIS, an IP router performs the network address translation.

SMDS is a technology that meets the requirements for high-speed data transport, especially within metropolitan areas. More importantly, it provides an excellent transition to the next major level of high speed networking, ATM. Information on the SMDS Interest Group, or SIG, an industry consortium of SMDS users, service providers, and equipment vendors, is noted in reference [3-31].

3.11 Asynchronous Transfer Mode

Asynchronous Transfer Mode, or ATM, is a very high speed transmission technology designed for LAN, MAN, and WAN applications. It operates over a wide range of transmission rates, as currently defined from 1.5 Mbps (DS-1) to 622 Mbps (OC-12). The ATM architecture is connection-oriented, and is based upon high speed switches which direct the 53-octet cells of information from their source to the ultimate destination. ATM technology, which is generally considered to be the next generation of high speed networking, is actively supported by the ATM Forum [3-32], a consortium of users, vendors, and carriers who have joined together to further develop the technology. The principle document from the ATM Forum is known as the User Network Interface [3-33], which defines the interaction between user devices and an ATM network. ATM is based upon a four layer architecture. This includes the Physical Layer, which handles bit timing and transmission-related issues; the ATM layer, responsible for the transfer of the 53-octet cells; the ATM Adaptation layer, which supports the transport of higher layer information by dividing that information into 53-octet cells and incorporating appropriate error control mechanisms; and the Higher layers, containing user information. A thorough study of ATM is beyond the scope of this text. However, readers interested in an in-depth study of ATM and its protocols are referred to a companion text, *Analyzing Broadband Networks* [3-34].

In this section, we will survey three related alternatives for TCP/IP internetworking with ATM: LAN Emulation (LANE), Classical IP and ARP over ATM, and Multiprotocol over ATM (MPOA).

3.11.1 LAN Emulation

LAN Emulation, or LANE as it is commonly known, is a service that allows existing end-user applications to access an ATM network. More importantly, this access appears to the application as if it were using more traditional protocols, such as TCP/IP or Novell's Internetwork Packet Exchange (IPX), and as if it were running over more traditional LANs such as Ethernet or token ring. One of the design constraints is to account for the differences in protocol design—ATM is connection oriented, whereas IP and IPX are connectionless. A number of functions, including setting up the ATM connection and translating LAN to ATM addresses, must be hidden from the upper layers, thus making the application think that it is operating over a traditional network.

The ATM Forum has defined two different interfaces for LAN Emulation: a LAN Emulation User to Network Interface, called LUNI; and a LAN Emulation Network to Network Interface, called LENNI. Current work has focused on the LUNI.

The ATM Forum's LAN Emulation Specification [3-35] defines two scenarios that are applicable. In the first, an ATM network may be used to interconnect Ethernets to Ethernets, an Ethernet to an ATM device, or an ATM device to another ATM device. The second scenario replaces Ethernet LANs with token ring LANs under similar conditions. To make either of these systems operate requires the LAN Emulation protocol stack, shown in Figure 3-13a. Notice that the LAN host and its applications operate over traditional protocols, such as TCP/IP and IPX, and that a driver, such as NDIS or ODI, provides an interface between the upper layer software and the MAC layer hardware. The ATM-to-LAN converter sits at the edge of the network, running dual protocol stacks: one that communicates with the LAN (on the right) and another that communicates with the ATM switch (on the left). Note that this ATM-to-LAN converter is functioning as a bridge, operating independently of the Network and higher layer protocols. The ATM switch (or switches) do not participate in LAN emulation other than to switch the ATM connections, as would be the case with any other ATM-based network scenario. An element of LAN emulation is also active on the ATM host (the left side of Figure 3-13a), masking the ATM functions from the higher layer processes. In summary, the LAN emulation function maps the Ethernet or token ring MAC layer functions into ATM virtual connections, while shielding the application from the connection setup and handshaking functions that the ATM switch requires.

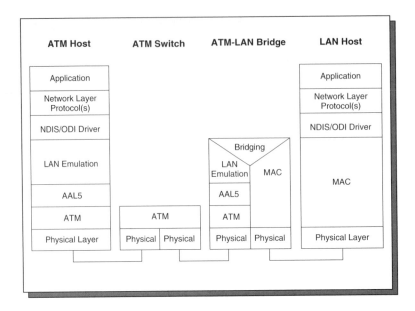

Figure 3-13a. LAN Emulation Architecture.

(From 3TECH. Copyright © 1995. Reprinted with permission of 3Com Corporation. All rights reserved)

The LANE architecture is designed around a client/server paradigm, such that the LAN Emulation Client (LEC) derives information that it needs from one of several servers: the Configuration Server, the LAN Emulation Server (LES), or the Broadcast and Unknown (BUS) Server. The LEC software may be incorporated into workstation drivers, or it could be incorporated into other internetworking devices such as routers or switches.

Several steps are required to establish an emulated LAN connection. The control functions (shown in the upper portion of Figure 3-13b), occur prior to any data transfer (shown in the lower portion of Figure 3-13b). First, the LEC is initialized by learning the ATM address of the LAN Emulation Configuration Server (LECS). (The Configuration Server resides at a well-known address, making this task easier.) The LEC next obtains configuration information, sending the LECS its ATM and MAC addresses, plus the LAN type and frame size requested. The LECS returns the address of the LAN Emulation Server (LES), plus the LAN type and frame size to use. The connection between the LEC and the LECS is transient; once the required information is obtained, the connection is torn down. When the LEC has the required configuration information, it requests to join the emulated LAN by sending a message to the LAN Emulation Server (LES). The LES maps

96

the MAC-to-ATM addresses, allowing a switch (or switches) to establish a connection to the correct destination. The LES may be implemented in a number of devices, including switches, routers, or file servers; however, only one LES is used per configuration. The LES also supplies the LEC with the ATM address of the Broadcast and Unknown Server (BUS), which relays multicast or broadcast frames to all emulated LAN clients. A bidirectional connection is established with the BUS, and then data transfer is allowed.

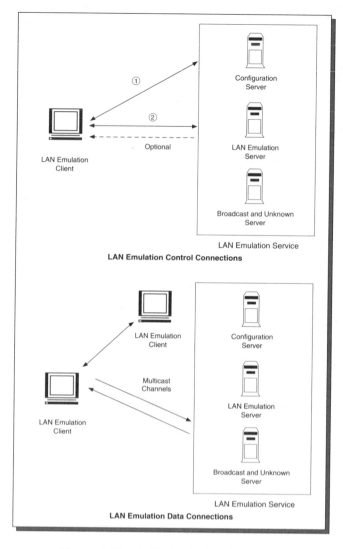

Figure 3-13b. LAN Emulation Operation.

When communication with another LEC is required, the sending LEC will first check its internal address cache to see if the destination address is known. If it is not known, it consults with the LES. After the ATM address is available, a direct connection with the remote LEC is established, streamlining that subsequent communication.

As is evident in Figure 3-13a, LANE is essentially a bridging function, independent of Network or higher layer protocols. Two other techniques—IP over ATM and Multi-Protocol over ATM (or MPOA)—address the routing scenario, and will be investigated next.

3.11.2 IP over ATM

As ATM technology has developed, a number of documents have been written to address the need for sending TCP/IP information over ATM connections. RFC 1483, *Multiprotocol Encapsulation over ATM Adaption Layer 5*, describes two encapsulation techniques for carrying network interconnect traffic over ATM AAL5. The first method provides for the multiplexing of multiple protocols over a single ATM virtual circuit, while the alternative approach sends each protocol over a separate ATM virtual circuit. RFC 1577, "Classical IP and ARP over ATM" [3-36], considers the application of ATM as a direct replacement for the physical transmission technologies (such as cables and routers) that have heretofore been employed.

In this case, the network is assumed to be configured as a Logical IP Subnetwork (LIS). RFC 1577, section 3, defines the following requirements for members of a LIS: all members must have the same IP network/subnet number and address mask; all members within a LIS must be directly connected to the ATM network; all members outside of the LIS must be accessed via a router; all members of the LIS must have a mechanism for resolving IP addresses to ATM addresses using ATMARP; all members must have a mechanism for resolving virtual circuits (VCs) to IP addresses using InATMARP; and all members of a LIS must be able to communicate with all other members of the same LIS using ATM. Each LIS operates and communicates independently of other LISs on the same ATM network. Hosts connected to ATM communicate directly to other hosts within the same LIS. To communicate with a host outside of the local LIS requires an IP router. Figure 3-13c illustrates such a LIS, where all members have a consistent IP network and subnet address [N.S.x] and use a router for communication outside of the LIS.

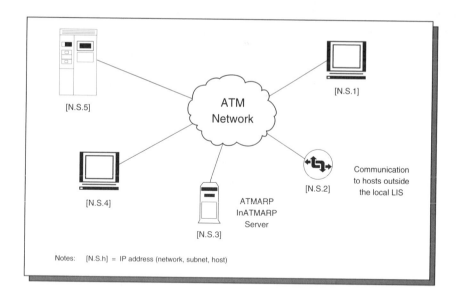

Figure 3-13c. Logical IP Subnetwork.

For two LIS members to communicate, they must know each other's IP and ATM addresses. IP over ATM uses an enhanced version of the Address Resolution Protocol (ARP) called ATMARP to provide translation between ATM and IP addresses. ATMARP runs on a server that exists at an ATM address that all LIS members are aware of. To communicate with another member requires the establishment of an ATM connection using the resources of the ATMARP server (see Figure 3-13d.) As LIS clients are initialized, they register with the ATMARP server, which allows the server to build an address table. If Client A needs to resolve a destination IP address, it sends an ATMARP Request to the server, which responds with an ATMARP Reply containing the needed ATM address. A connection may then be established with remote Client B. A similar process occurs at Client B if it needs the ATM address of Client A. After all addresses have been resolved, Clients A and B communicate directly. We will look at the packet structure of ATMARP in Section 4.3.4.

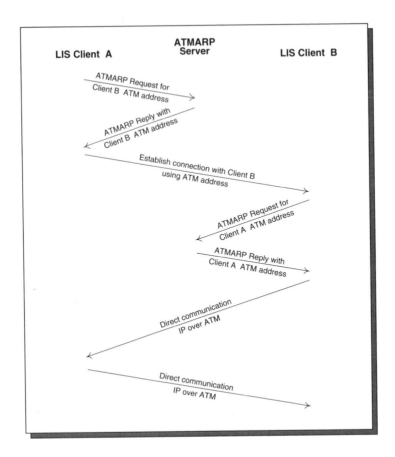

Figure 3-13d. LIS Client/ATMARP Server Operation.

The IP datagram is encapsulated within an ATM Adaptation Layer 5 (AAL5) message, and is then further subdivided into cells for transmission over the ATM network. IEEE 802.2 LLC and SNAP headers precede the IP datagram for higher-layer protocol identification. The default maximum transmission unit (MTU) for the AAL5 PDU is 9,188 octets, which allows 8 octets for the LLC and SNAP headers, and 9,180 octets for the IP datagram, as discussed in RFC 1626, "Default UP MTU for use over ATM AAL5." Further details on IP over ATM are found in RFC 1755, "ATM Signaling Support for IP over ATM."

3.11.3 Multiprotocol over ATM

The ATM Forum has developed a process known as Multi-Protocol over ATM (MPOA), which is an evolution of the LAN Emulation work. While LANE operates at the MAC layer (OSI Data Link Layer), MPOA operates at the OSI Network layer. MPOA is designed to integrate with LAN Emulation, and to support the traditional routing functions of protocol filtering plus enhanced security through firewalls, while handling both Data Link and Network layer operations.

The MPOA architecture consists of three elements: edge devices, route servers, and Internet Address Summarization Groups (IASGs). The edge device is defined as a physical device that can forward packets between legacy LAN interfaces and ATM interfaces. For example, an ATM-attached hub with a number of Ethernet ports would qualify as an edge device. The route server runs Network Layer routing protocols and communicates with other MPOA devices to resolve routing queries. The route server could be implemented in a router or in a separate processor within an ATM switch. Data forwarding functions may also be included in the route server. The IASG organizes the MPOA architecture by dividing hosts into ranges of internetwork layer addresses, such as IP subnets. If a host was running more than one protocol, it could be a member of more than one IASG. In effect, the edge devices provide most of the switching functions, while the route servers supply these edge devices with the routing information required. Taken together, the edge devices and route server form a distributed routing architecture.

The LANE, Classical IP, and MPOA standards are currently in various stages of deployment and development. What is interesting to note is that of all the protocols that the various standards bodies could have selected for their initial research, the Internet protocols were at the top of everyone's list. In the final two sections of this chapter, we will consider some typical problems that occur at the Network Interface Layer, along with solutions.

3.12 Troubleshooting the Network Interface Connection

So far in this chapter, we have explored the hardware configurations upon which a TCP/IP-based internetwork may operate, including options for LANs (Ethernet or token ring), MANs (SMDS), and WANs (serial lines or PSPDNs). The large number of available and documented alternatives attests to the popularity of the protocols.

Reviewing Figure 3-1b, notice that we are still discussing the physical, not the logical, communication path.

If you're like most TCP/IP administrators, you'll spend as much (if not more) time troubleshooting the hardware (i.e., the Network Interface Layer) as the higher-layer software. If a connector is bad or a network interface card is defective, you must troubleshoot and repair those elements before moving up the protocol stack to analyze the TCP/IP protocols. A companion volume to this book, the *LAN Troubleshooting Handbook,* second edition [3-37], discusses LAN hardware troubleshooting in detail. Here are some key points to consider:

- First, check the basic communication path between devices. Broken cables, loose connectors, and so on can cause what appear to be more complex problems.
- Check for compliance with standards. For example, verify that all workstations on an Ethernet are transmitting Ethernet, not IEEE 802.3 frames. Or verify that all segments have the correct cable type, such as the RG58A/U used with IEEE 802.3 10BASE2 networks, not the RG59A/U used with video systems such as VCRs.
- Systematically isolate the problem to a single LAN, MAN, or WAN segment. It is rare for two segments to fail simultaneously.

In our next section, we will examine case studies that demonstrate Network Interface Layer problems typical for TCP/IP-based internetworks.

3.13 Case Studies

In light of our previous discussion of the protocols used at the ARPA Network Interface Layer, let's look at some case studies of actual situations that illustrate the operation of the protocols. For consistency, we captured all data with the Network General Sniffer protocol analyzer.

3.13.1 Initializing a Token Ring Workstation

In our first case study, we'll look at how a workstation becomes an active member of a token ring network, prior to initiating any higher-layer service such as a file transfer using FTP (see Figure 3-14). In general, the workstation must complete two steps before

TCP/IP or any higher-layer protocols can be activated. First, the workstation must make the physical (electrical) connection to the token ring network. Second, it must make the logical connection into the token passing system, assuring its proper standing among its peers. Let's examine these processes in detail.

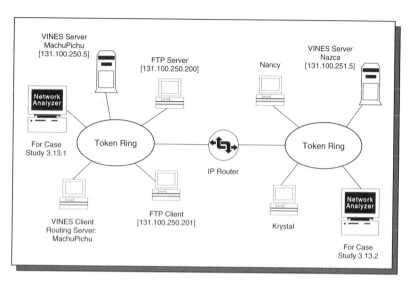

Figure 3-14. IEEE 802.5 Network with Banyan VINES and TCP/IP.

The token ring standard (IEEE 802.5) defines two types of transmission frames. A Logical Link Control (LLC) frame carries user data, such as an electronic mail message. A Medium Access Control (MAC) frame transmits network management information. (These frame types are distinguished by the first two bits of the Frame Control field: 00 = MAC and 01 = LLC.) The MAC frames are always transmitted first (because one of their functions is network initialization), then a combination of MAC and LLC frames may be transmitted. The IEEE 802.5 standard defines a total of 25 MAC frames, which perform a number of network management functions.

Two examples of MAC-related functions are the Active Monitor (AM) and the Standby Monitor (SM). All token ring controller chips (such as Texas Instruments' TMS380) can perform these functions. The AM function observes the overall health of the network, making sure that the token circulates properly, that transmitted frames circle the ring only once, and so on. The workstation with the highest address (the 48-bit address stored in a ROM on the network interface card) is selected to be the

AM. All other workstations assume an SM function and assure the proper operation of the AM. (This is somewhat akin to parents leaving their children with a sitter. The sitter watches the children, but the children also report any unusual actions, such as excessive telephone use, of the sitter.) The AMs and SMs identify themselves by periodically transmitting the Active Monitor Present (AMP) and Standby Monitor Present (SMP) frames.

In this example (see Trace 3.13.1 at the end of this section), a workstation (designated FTP Client) wishes to enter the token ring network on the left-hand side of the TCP/IP Router. The network analyzer is placed on the left-hand ring, network [131.100.250.x] to capture the data. Only the network analyzer and the server (designated FTP Server) are currently active. The server is the AM and transmits an AMP frame approximately every seven seconds. When the TR client is turned on, its NIC actuates the relay connected to its port within the token ring wiring hub, known as the Multistation Access Unit (MSAU). Because the relay actuation momentarily disrupts the signal transmission, the AM transmits a Ring Purge MAC frame to test the transmission path.

Next, the FTP client transmits a frame to itself (see Frame 6, the MAC Duplicate Address Test (DAT)), to determine whether another workstation with the same address is active on the ring. If two identical addresses existed, both stations might respond to a transmission and would confuse the recipient. Thus, if the new station received a response to the DAT frame, it would abort its login.

Each workstation maintains a register containing the address of its nearest upstream neighbor. When this address changes (or is entered for the first time) the workstation reports a change in the Stored Upstream Address (SUA) to the Configuration Report Server (CRS). (The CRS is a functional address that maintains the logical topology of the ring for purposes of network management.) Notice that a second DAT frame is sent in Frame 8, followed by a Report SUA Change in Frame 9. In Frame 11, the server also reports an SUA change. As a passive device, the network analyzer does not participate in these logical ring transmissions.

In Frames 12 through 15 the client requests its parameters from another functional address, the Ring Parameter Server (RPS). The RPS is not active; therefore, the FTP Client uses its default parameters and continues. The AM station has been keeping track of the transmission interruptions caused by the new workstation's MSAU relay actuation and transmits an error report to another functional address, the Ring Error Monitor (REM), in Frame 16.

Finally, the new workstation participates in a Ring Poll, which verifies its status as an SM, since the AM (FTP Server) is already selected. Frames 17 and 18 (AMP then SMP) show this Ring Poll, which repeats every seven seconds (Frames 23-24 and 25-26). The Internet protocols become active in Frame 19, when the FTP Client uses ARP to determine a hardware address that matches internet address 131.100.250.200. ICMP and TCP information is also transmitted (Frames 21-22 and 27-29, respectively) before an FTP session begins in Frame 30. The TCP sequence is known as a three-way handshake, which we will look at in detail in Section 5.5.5.

To summarize, the FTP Client underwent the following MAC-Layer functions to make the physical and logical connection to the token ring network:

Event 1	**The relay actuation triggers the transmission of a Ring Purge frame.**
Event 2	The new node transmits one or two Duplicate Address Test frames.
Event 3	The new node and its downstream neighbor report a Stored Upstream Address change to the Configuration Report server.
Event 4	The new node requests Initialization parameters from Ring Parameter server (maximum 4 tries).
Event 5	The new node's downstream neighbor transmits a Report Error frame.
Event 6	The new node participates in a Ring Poll.

Sniffer Network Analyzer data 16-Jan at 14:54:28, file FTPXCHNG.TRC, Pg 1

SUMMARY	Delta T	Destination	Source	Summary
M 1		LAN Manager	NwkGnlE00E1A	IBMNM Trace Tool Present
2	2.009	Broadcast	FTP Server	MAC Active Monitor Present
3	6.998	Broadcast	FTP Server	MAC Active Monitor Present
4	6.998	Broadcast	FTP Server	MAC Active Monitor Present
5	2.900	Broadcast	FTP Server	MAC Ring Purge
6	0.001	FTP Client	FTP Client	MAC Duplicate Address Test
7	0.000	Broadcast	FTP Server	MAC Active Monitor Present
8	0.001	FTP Client	FTP Client	MAC Duplicate Address Test
9	0.001	Config Srv	FTP Client	MAC Report SUA Change
10	0.017	Broadcast	FTP Client	MAC Standby Monitor Present

11	0.000	Config Srv	FTP Server	MAC Report SUA Change
12	0.000	Param Server	FTP Client	MAC Request Initialization
13	0.000	Param Server	FTP Client	MAC Request Initialization
14	0.000	Param Server	FTP Client	MAC Request Initialization
15	0.000	Param Server	FTP Client	MAC Request Initialization
16	2.166	Error Mon.	FTP Server	MAC Report Soft Error
17	4.798	Broadcast	FTP Server	MAC Active Monitor Present
18	0.017	Broadcast	FTP Client	MAC Standby Monitor Present
19	4.032	Broadcast	FTP Client	ARP C PA=[131.100.250.200] PRO=IP
20	0.003	FTP Client	FTP Server	ARP R PA=[131.100.250.200] HA=10005A2502CE PRO=IP
21	0.003	FTP Server	FTP Client	ICMP Echo
22	0.003	FTP Client	FTP Server	ICMP Echo reply
23	2.937	Broadcast	FTP Server	MAC Active Monitor Present
24	0.016	Broadcast	FTP Client	MAC Standby Monitor Present
25	6.981	Broadcast	FTP Server	MAC Active Monitor Present
26	0.016	Broadcast	FTP Client	MAC Standby Monitor Present
27	0.903	FTP Server	FTP Client	TCP D=21 S=3592 SYN SEQ=82509567 LEN=0 WIN=1800
28	0.005	FTP Client	FTP Server	TCP D=3592 S=21 SYN ACK=82509568 SEQ=48955135 LEN=0 WIN=1800
29	0.003	FTP Server	FTP Client	TCP D=21 S=3592 ACK=48955136 WIN=1800
30	0.042	FTP Client	FTP Server	FTP R PORT=3592 220-hewey PC/TCP 2.0 FTP Server by FTP Software re...
31	0.150	FTP Server	FTP Client	TCP D=21 S=3592 ACK=48955253 WIN=1683
32	3.461	FTP Server	FTP Client	FTP C PORT=3592 USER anonymous<0D><0A>
33	0.003	FTP Client	FTP Server	TCP D=3592 S=21 ACK=82509584 WIN=1784
34	0.032	FTP Client	FTP Server	FTP R PORT=3592 230 User OK, no password<0D><0A>
35	0.125	FTP Server	FTP Client	TCP D=21 S=3592 ACK=48955279 WIN=1774
36	2.252	Broadcast	FTP Server	MAC Active Monitor Present
37	0.015	Broadcast	FTP Client	MAC Standby Monitor Present
38	3.428	FTP Server	FTP Client	FTP C PORT=3592 PWD<0D><0A>

39	0.004	FTP Client	FTP Server	TCP D=3592 S=21
				509589 WIN=1795
40	0.009	FTP Client	FTP Server	FTP R PORT=3592
				250 Current working
				directory is
				C:\MIKES\PCTCP<0D>...

Trace 3.13.1. Token Ring Station Initialization

In our next example, we'll see how information passes from one server to another within an IP tunnel.

3.13.2 Transmitting Banyan VINES Packets Through the Internet

In Section 2.7, we discussed the concept of tunneling or encapsulation. Recall that in this process, a LAN operating system, such as NetWare or VINES, uses the Internet protocols to transmit data over a WAN connection. The process is often referred to as an IP tunnel.

Figure 3-14 illustrates the tunneling process using a VINES internetwork. The VINES client is connected to network 131.100.250.X and must access a server (Nazca) on another network, 131.100.251.X. An IP-based internetwork connects the two rings. Several steps are necessary to complete the connection. First, the client must attach to its routing server (MachuPichu) on the local ring. Next, the local server encapsulates the VINES packets in an IP datagram for transmission on the internetwork. Finally, the distant server (Nazca) receives the token ring frame, strips off the token ring header, IP header, and token ring trailer, and returns the VINES packet to the way it was before encapsulation in the IP datagram. Let's use the analyzer to examine this process.

The placement of the analyzer is vital to understanding the protocol interaction. In this example, we located the analyzer on the distant ring (review Figure 3-14). If the analyzer were on the local ring, it would only be able to see the traffic going into the router; by locating the analyzer on the distant ring you can verify the data coming out of the router and the communication line in between. The analyzer is capturing both VINES and IP packets. The VINES packets represent traffic between the client and the routing server, MachuPichu. The IP packets represent traffic (via the IP Router) between the routing server, MachuPichu, and the server on the client's ring, Nazca.

In Trace 3.13.2a, we observe several interactions, including a MAC AMP frame (sent from IP Router in Frame 4) and the MAC SMP frames sent from the other ring stations (Frames 5 and 6). In Frame 7, the router and server begin exchanging IP packets that come from node 131.100.250.5 (MachuPichu, the client's routing server) to the target server (Nazca), node 131.100.251.5. The IP packets contain the requests from, and the responses to, the client for file service.

Trace 3.13.2b shows the details of Frame 7, the client's request for a file search. (Frame 8 contains the server's reply, which is not shown in Trace 3.13.2b.) Note that the token ring header also contains the SNAP header (IEEE 802.2 LLC plus Ether-Type) shown in Figure 3-5. The SNAP header uses DSAP = AAH, SSAP = AAH, and Control = 03H (Unnumbered Information or UI). The Protocol ID = 000000H (not indicated in the trace file, but available in the hexadecimal decode), with an Ether-Type = 0800H (IP). The 20-octet IP header is transmitted next. It identifies source network address 131.100.250.5 (MachuPichu) and destination network address 131.100.251.5 (Nazca). These addresses confirm the communication between the two VINES servers. Note that IP datagrams in both directions are given an ID number (e.g. 20253 in Frame 7) from the originating node. The final portion of the IP datagram is the VINES packet itself.

We may derive two conclusions from this example. First, the placement of the analyzer has a dramatic effect on the data that is captured during encapsulation. (Move the analyzer to either side of an encapsulating server and observe the results for yourself.) Second, multiple protocols, such as IP and VINES, may exist on an internetwork simultaneously. This requires a number of protocol interpreters within the analyzer. Make sure that your analyzer can analyze all of your protocols.

Sniffer Network Analyzer data 15-Jan at 19:40:38, file TCPTUNEL.TRC Pg 1

SUMMARY	Delta T	Destination	Source	Summary
M 1		Nazca	IP Router	VMATCH Call
				Port=00C0 (Unknown)
				ID=0 Procedure=100
				Arguments=<0006>
2	0.004	Nazca	IP Router	VMATCH Call
				Port=00C0 (Unknown)
				ID=0 Procedure=100
				Arguments=<0007>
3	0.009	Nazca	IP Router	VSTRTK C NewIncome
				IncomeType=Detail

4	2.701	Broadcast	IP Router	MAC Active Monitor Present
5	0.014	Broadcast	IBM 38235C	MAC Standby Monitor Present
6	0.019	Broadcast	Nazca	MAC Standby Monitor Present
7	1.214	Nazca	IP Router	SMB C Search
				\TEMP\????????.???
8	0.013	IP Router	Nazca	SMB R 1 entry found
9	0.081	Nazca	IP Router	SMB C Search
				\TEMP\????????.???
10	0.037	IP Router	Nazca	SMB R 15 entries found
11	0.024	Nazca	IP Router	SMB C Check dir \TEMP
12	0.013	IP Router	Nazca	SMB R OK
13	0.359	Nazca	IP Router	VSPP Ack NS=854 NR=875
				Window=879 RID=0027
				LID=0011
14	0.086	Nazca	IP Router	SMB too short to decode
15	0.012	IP Router	Nazca	SMB R Got Disk Attributes
16	0.341	Nazca	IP Router	VSPP Ack NS=855 NR=876
				Window=880 RID=0027
				LID=0011
17	3.093	Nazca	IP Router	VSTRTK C NewIncome
				IncomeType=Detail
18	1.694	Broadcast	IP Router	MAC Active Monitor Present
19	0.014	Broadcast	IBM 38235C	MAC Standby Monitor Present
20	0.018	Broadcast	Nazca	MAC Standby Monitor Present

Trace 3.13.2a. VINES Packet Tunneling Summary

Sniffer Network Analyzer data 15-Jan at 19:40:38, file TCPTUNEL.TRC Pg 1

- - - - - - - - - - - - - - - - Frame 7 - - - - - - - - - - - - - - - -

DLC: ——- DLC Header ——-
DLC:
DLC: Frame 7 arrived at 19:40:44.533; frame size is 140 (008C hex) bytes.
DLC: AC: Frame priority 0, Reservation priority 0, Monitor count 0
DLC: FC: LLC frame, PCF attention code: None
DLC: FS: Addr recognized indicators: 00, Frame copied indicators: 00
DLC: Destination = Station IBM 11A83D, Nazca
DLC: Source   = Station IBM 39078A, IP Router
DLC:
LLC: ——- LLC Header ——-
LLC:

LLC: DSAP = AA, SSAP = AA, Command, Unnumbered frame: UI
LLC:
SNAP: ——- SNAP Header ——-
SNAP:
SNAP: Type = 0800 (IP)
SNAP:
IP: ——- IP Header ——-
IP:
IP: Version = 4, header length = 20 bytes
IP: Type of service = 00
IP: 000. .... = routine
IP: ...0 .... = normal delay
IP: .... 0... = normal throughput
IP: .... .0.. = normal reliability
IP: Total length = 118 bytes
IP: Identification = 20253
IP: Flags = 0X
IP: .0.. .... = may fragment
IP: ..0. .... = last fragment
IP: Fragment offset = 0 bytes
IP: Time to live = 254 seconds/hops
IP: Protocol = 83 (VINES)
IP: Header checksum = 7143 (correct)
IP: Source address = [131.100.250.5]
IP: Destination address = [131.100.251.5]
IP: No options
IP:
VFRP: ——- VINES FRP Header ——-
VFRP:
VFRP: Fragmentation byte = 03
VFRP: 0000 00.. = Unused
VFRP: .... ..1. = End of packet
VFRP: ....1 = Beginning of packet
VFRP:
VFRP: Sequence number = 186
VFRP:
VIP: ——- VINES IP Header ——-
VIP:
VIP: Checksum = A7D8
VIP: Packet length = 96
VIP:
VIP: Transport control = 5E
VIP: 0... .... = Unused

VIP: .1.. .... = Contains RTP redirect message
VIP: ..0. .... = Do not return metric notification packet
VIP: ...1 .... = Return exception notification packet
VIP: .... 1110 = Hop count remaining (14)
VIP:
VIP: Protocol type = 2 (Sequenced Packet Protocol - VSPP)
VIP:
VIP: Destination network.subnetwork = 0000067A.0001
VIP: Source network.subnetwork   = 00000384.8001
VIP:
VSPP: ———- VINES SPP Header ———-
VSPP:
VSPP: Source port   = 0203
VSPP: Destination port = 0253
VSPP:
VSPP: Packet type = 1 (Data)
VSPP:
VSPP: Control = 60
VSPP: 0... .... = Unused
VSPP: .1.. .... = End of message
VSPP: ..1. .... = Beginning of message
VSPP: ...0 .... = Do not abort current message
VSPP: .... 0000 = Unused
VSPP:
VSPP: Local connection ID = 0011
VSPP: Remote connection ID = 0027
VSPP:
VSPP: Sequence number   = 852
VSPP: Acknowledgment number = 872
VSPP: Window   = 876
VSPP:
SMB: ———- SMB Search Directory Command ———-
SMB:
SMB: Function = 81 (Search Directory)
SMB: Tree id   (TID) = 002A
SMB: Process id   (PID) = 0E67
SMB: File pathname = "\TEMP\????????.???"
SMB: Maximum number of search entries to return = 25
SMB: Attribute flags = 0008
SMB: ....0. .... = File(s) not changed since last archive
SMB: ....0 .... = No directory file(s)
SMB: .... 1... = Volume label info
SMB: .... .0.. = No system file(s)

SMB: ....0. = No hidden file(s)
SMB: ....0 = No read only file(s)
SMB:

Trace 3.13.2b. VINES Packet Tunneling Details

3.13.3 Collisions on an Ethernet

Ethernet and IEEE 802.3 networks operate under a principle known as Carrier Sense, Multiple Access with Collision Detection (CSMA/CD). This means that any station wishing to transmit must first listen to the cable (i.e., carrier sense) to detect whether any other station is transmitting. If the station hears no other signals, it may proceed. Otherwise, it must repeat the carrier sense process later. During periods of heavy traffic, several stations may be waiting for a station to complete its transmission. If those stations make the carrier sense test simultaneously, different stations may conclude that the cable is not in use and that it's OK to proceed. When this happens, signals from the two stations collide, neither transmits data, and precious bandwidth is wasted. In short, everyone loses. Collisions also become self-perpetuating; as more stations collide, more bandwidth is wasted, more stations need to transmit, and so on. These collisions may occur on any Ethernet or 802.3 network, regardless of the higher-layer protocol in use, because they are a hardware or electrical signal phenomenon.

In this case study, an Ethernet is running a mixture of DECnet and Internet protocols, such as TCP (see Trace 3.13.3a). We chose this protocol/hardware combination because when the TCP/IP protocols were developed in the 1970s, Ethernet networks were by far the most common LAN solution; therefore, TCP/IP and Ethernet are frequently associated. Thus, if you have TCP/IP you probably have some Ethernet networks (and vice versa), and you'll probably see collisions.

Let's see how such collisions would appear on a network analyzer. Without warning, frames appear with no identifiable Source or Destination address (see Frames 5, 9, 12, 14, 18, 19, etc.). The network analyzer places question marks (????????????) in place of the normal 12 hexadecimal characters since it cannot decode that information. The summary of the frame (on the right-hand side of the trace) indicates that the highest layer within that frame is the Data Link Control (DLC) Layer. This means that the analyzer was also unable to decode any data from the frame's Information field. Note the BAD FRAME indication in the summary.

The details of Frames 18 and 19 (see Trace 3.13.3b) yield little additional information. Both frames are fragments (less than the required 64 octets in length) and have bad alignment, which indicates that the frame does not contain an integral number of octets. There are two clues, however. The first is in the hexadecimal decode of the Address fields. In Frame 18, the decoded data is all ONEs (FF FF FF. . .), indicating that it may have been a Broadcast frame with the Destination address intended to be FFFFFFFFFFFFH. In Frame 19, part of the Destination address is 01 04 80H. Unfortunately, neither of the fragments contains enough information to decode the Source address. If you know the Source address, you might be able to fix the problem by swapping in a new network interface card (assuming the collisions were caused by a faulty CSMA/CD controller chip on the card). The second clue is the time stamp at the top of the trace file (10:18:08). This indicates that the collisions occurred at 10:18 AM. On most networks, the heavy traffic periods are between 10:00 and 11:00 AM and between 2:00 and 3:00 PM. The network administrator could study the network for several days and determine whether the collisions were more prevalent during these peak periods. If so, the administrator could logically segment the network with a bridge to isolate the traffic between the bridged segments. Such bridging would improve overall network performance and would reduce collisions.

Sniffer Network Analyzer data 26-Jan at 10:18:08, file COLSN.ENC, Pg 1

SUMMARY	Delta T	Destination	Source	Summary
M 1		DECnet002130	DECnet001F30	Ethertype=6007 (DEC LAVC)
2	0.0334	01048003C04D	820D00008000	Ethertype=825E (Unknown)
3	0.0312	Sun 0A508D	3Com02D383	TCP D=3184 S=6000
				ACK=191069101
				SEQ=1600831189
				LEN=32 WIN=11557
4	0.0001	01048003C04D	821100008000	Ethertype=825E (Unknown)
5	0.0318	???????????	???????????	DLC, BAD FRAME, size=8 bytes
6	0.0094	01048003C04D	820A00008000	Ethertype=825E (Unknown)
7	0.0116	3Com 02D383	Sun 0A508D	TCP D=6000 S=3184
				ACK=1600831221
				SEQ=191069101
				LEN=40 WIN=4096
8	0.0014	Sun0A508D	3Com02D383	TCP D=3184 S=6000
				ACK=191069141
				WIN=11517
9	0.0161	???????????	???????????	DLC, BAD FRAME, size=7 bytes

10	0.0087	DECnet000130	0000C9007311	LAT C Data D=9301 S=7E13 NR=92 NS=62 Len=2
11	0.0654	3Com05D2DB	0080D3004852	ATP C ID=2196 LEN=6
12	0.0201	???????????	???????????	DLC, BAD FRAME, size=2 bytes
13	0.0083	3Com 05D2DB	0080D3004852	ATP D ID=2196
14	0.0656	???????????	???????????	DLC, BAD FRAME, size=5 bytes
15	0.0051	0000C9007311	DECnet000130	LAT R Data D=7E13 S=9301 NR=64 NS=95 Len=15
16	0.0758	KinetxA09827	3Com 4DE473	NBP C Request ID=31
17	0.0013	DECnet000130	0000C9007311	LAT C Data D=9301 S=7E13 NR=95 NS=65 Len=3
18	0.0223	???????????	???????????	DLC, BAD FRAME, size=5 bytes
19	0.0292	???????????	???????????	DLC, BAD FRAME, size=3 bytes
20	0.0168	0000C9007311	Cisco 006A04	Telnet R PORT=5112 u
21	0.0051	01048003C04D	820A00008000	Ethertype=825E (Unknown)
22	0.0039	???????????	???????????	RI Invalid length
23	0.0191	A5B191A5B99D	80D0A195818C	Ethertype=BDC9 (Unknown)
24	0.0281	01048003C04D	820A00008000	Ethertype=825E (Unknown)
25	0.0190	Sun0A508D	3Com02D383	TCP D=3184 S=6000 ACK=191069141 SEQ=1600831221 LEN=32 WIN=11557
26	0.0088	Sun0A508D	3Com02D383	TCP D=3184 S=6000 ACK=191069181 WIN=11517
27	0.0054	DECnet000130	0000C9007311	LAT C Data D=9301 S=7E13 NR=97 NS=67 Len=3
28	0.0244	???????????	???????????	DLC, BAD FRAME, size=11 bytes

Trace 3.13.3a. Ethernet Collision Summary

Sniffer Network Analyzer data 26-Jan at 10:18:08, file COLSN.ENC, Pg 1

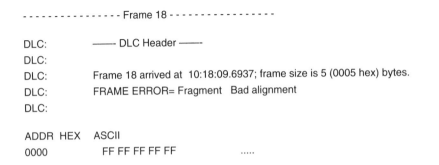

- - - - - - - - - - - - - - - Frame 18 - - - - - - - - - - - - - - - - -

DLC: —— DLC Header ——
DLC:
DLC: Frame 18 arrived at 10:18:09.6937; frame size is 5 (0005 hex) bytes.
DLC: FRAME ERROR= Fragment   Bad alignment
DLC:

ADDR HEX   ASCII
0000   FF FF FF FF FF   .....

```
- - - - - - - - - - - - - - - Frame 19 - - - - - - - - - - - - - - - -

DLC:         ——- DLC Header ——-
DLC:
DLC:         Frame 19 arrived at  10:18:09.7229; frame size is 3 (0003 hex) bytes.
DLC:         FRAME ERROR= Fragment   Bad alignment
DLC:


ADDR HEX    ASCII
0000    01 04 80            ...
```

Trace 3.13.3b. Ethernet Collision Details

3.13.4 Incompatibilities Between Ethernet and IEEE 802.3 Frames

Technical standards assure that all parties involved with a project or procedure can communicate accurately. This "communication" could be a bolt communicating with a nut (adhering to the same number of threads per inch) or a terminal communicating with a host computer (adhering to the same character set, such as ASCII). Unfortunately, the Ethernet world has two separate standards that are both loosely termed "Ethernet." The original Ethernet, last published in 1982 by DEC, Intel, and Xerox, is called the *Blue Book*. The second standard, IEEE 802.3, accommodates elements of the other IEEE LAN standards, such as the IEEE 802.2 Logical Link Control header.

In this case study, a user tries to access some higher-layer TCP/IP functions, TCPCON, but he can't because the lower-layer connection had failed due to the confusion of the two Ethernets on the internet. Let's see what happened.

In Section 2.7.4 we discussed Novell's NetWare operating system and its TCP/IP Transport facility. TCPCON, which is one of TCP/IP's functions, provides SNMP-based management functions through the server's console. To access TCPCON, the user logs into the server from his workstation, executes the remote console (RCONSOLE) command, then loads TCPCON.

The internetwork topology consists of several Ethernet segments that connect a number of devices. The NetWare server doubles as an IP router and connects to both local and remote hosts (see Figure 3-15). The network administrator (David, shown in Trace 3.13.4a) wishes to access TCPCON to check some SNMP statistics at the remote host. He must first log into his NetWare server. Looking for the nearest file server, he broadcasts a NetWare Core Protocol (NCP) packet in Frame 1, then repeats the request every 0.6 seconds. But he receives no response.

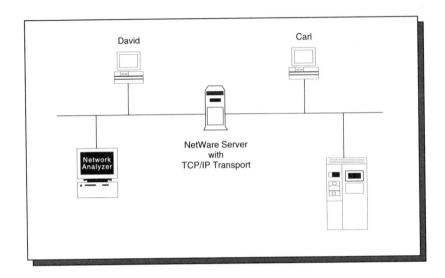

Figure 3-15. IEEE 802.3 Network with Novell NetWare and TCP/IP.

Trace 3.13.4b shows the details of the NCP Nearest Service Query and indicates that David's workstation (address H-P 06CA73) was transmitting an Ethernet frame. We know this because the frame header contains an EtherType (8137H) instead of a Length field. David realizes that the server was configured for IEEE 802.3 framing and speculates that the problem might be a frame incompatibility. He reconfigures the workstation by editing the Protocol.ini file to include a driver (IPXDRV.DOS) that accepts the IEEE 802.3 frame type.

A second attempt (Trace 3.13.4c) proves successful. David's workstation requests the nearest server and receives a response from five servers: NW Svr 2, NW Svr 3, H-P 133A5B, NW Svr 1, and H-P 136A06 (Frames 2 through 6). The NCP algorithm then selects the first responding server (NW Svr 2, shown in Frame 2) and creates a connection to that server in Frame 9. The connection is confirmed and a buffer size accepted in Frames 10 through 12. David is now logged into the server and can finish gathering the SNMP statistics. Trace 3.13.4d examines the NCP Nearest Service Query packet after the workstation reconfiguration. Note that the EtherType field has been replaced with the 802.3 length = 34 octets. All other aspects of the frame are identical. Reviewing Figures 3-3 and 3-4, note that the only difference between the Ethernet and IEEE 802.3 frame formats is the field following the Source Address: Ethernet specifies the Type (the higher-layer protocol type, in this case, NetWare)

116

while IEEE 802.3 counts the length of the Data field (in this example, 34 octets). The receiving station cannot tolerate a mistake in the frame format. If it is expecting a length (0022H) and it receives an EtherType (8137H), it rejects the frame because that frame is outside of the range of valid 802.3 length fields (0000-05DCH or 46-1500 decimal). Now that David has successfully logged into the server, he can complete his business with RCONSOLE and TCPCON. The moral of the story: If a newly configured "Ethernet" workstation cannot communicate with its server (but appears to be functioning otherwise), check the frame format. Until the lower layers can communicate, you cannot transmit or receive any TCP/IP-related information.

Sniffer Network Analyzer data 31-Jan at 4:54:50, file ETHERNET.ENC, Pg 1

SUMMARY	Delta T	Destination	Source	Summary
M 1		Broadcast	David	NCP C Find nearest file server
2	0.5503	Broadcast	David	NCP C Find nearest file server
3	0.6042	Broadcast	David	NCP C Find nearest file server
4	0.6042	Broadcast	David	NCP C Find nearest file server
5	0.6042	Broadcast	David	NCP C Find nearest file server
6	0.6042	Broadcast	David	NCP C Find nearest file server
7	0.6042	Broadcast	David	NCP C Find nearest file server
8	0.6042	Broadcast	David	NCP C Find nearest file server
9	0.6042	Broadcast	David	NCP C Find nearest file server
10	0.6042	Broadcast	David	NCP C Find nearest file server
11	0.6042	Broadcast	David	NCP C Find nearest file server
12	0.6042	Broadcast	David	NCP C Find nearest file server

Trace 3.13.4a. Attempted TCPCON Login Summary

Sniffer Network Analyzer data 31-Jan at 4:54:50 file ETHERNET.ENC, Pg 1

- - - - - - - - - - - - - - - Frame 1 - - - - - - - - - - - - - - - - -

```
DLC:        ——- DLC Header ——
DLC:
DLC:        Frame 1 arrived at  14:54:52.9662; frame size is 60 (003C hex) bytes.
DLC:        Destination = BROADCAST FFFFFFFFFFFF, Broadcast
DLC:        Source    = Station H-P  06CA73, David
DLC:        Ethertype = 8137 (Novell)
DLC:
XNS:        ——- XNS Header ——
```

XNS:	
XNS:	Checksum = FFFF
XNS:	Length = 34
XNS:	Transport control = 00
XNS:	0000 .... = Reserved
XNS:	.... 0000 = Hop count
XNS:	Packet type = 17 (Novell NetWare)
XNS:	
XNS:	Dest net = 00000000, host = FFFFFFFFFFFF,
	socket = 1106 (NetWare Service Advertising)
XNS:	Source net = 00000000, host = 08000906CA73, socket = 16390 (4006)
XNS:	
NCP:	——- NetWare Nearest Service Query ——-
NCP:	
NCP:	Server type = 0004 (file server)

Trace 3.13.4b. Attempted NetWare Server TCPCON Login Details

Sniffer Network Analyzer data 31-Jan at 4:47:46, file IEEE802.ENC, Pg 1

SUMMARY	Delta T	Destination	Source	Summary
M 1		Broadcast	David	NCP C Find nearest file server
2	0.0008	David	NW Svr 2	NCP R ISD
3	0.0003	David	NW Svr 3	NCP R HR
4	0.0004	David	H-P 133A5B	NCP R GL
5	0.0002	David	NW Svr 1	NCP R IC2
6	0.0001	David	H-P 136A06	NCP R ICTEMP
7	0.0018	Broadcast	David	XNS RIP request:
				find 1 network, 00133ADE
8	0.0005	David	NW Svr 2	XNS RIP response:
				1 network, 00133ADE at 1 hop
9	0.0012	NW Svr 2	David	NCP C Create Connection
10	0.0034	David	NW Svr 2	NCP R OK2
11	0.0013	NW Svr 2	David	NCP C Propose buffer size of 1024
12	0.0004	David	NW Svr 2	NCP R OK Accept buffer size of 1024
13	0.0300	David	H-P 11D4BD	NCP R H20
14	0.0016	David	H-P 133A76	NCP R BOOKS
15	0.00272	NW Svr 2	David	NCP C Logout
16	0.0023	David	H-P 133AAA	NCP R OLD
17	0.0008	David	NW Svr 2	NCP R OK
18	0.0012	NW Svr 2	David	NCP R C Get server's clock
19	0.0004	David	NW Svr 2	NCP R OK

Trace 3.13.4c. Successful NetWare Server Login Summary

Sniffer Network Analyzer data 31-Jan at 4:47:46, file IEEE802.ENC, Pg 1

- - - - - - - - - - - - - - - Frame 1 - - - - - - - - - - - - - - - -

```
DLC:        ——- DLC Header ——-
DLC:
DLC:        Frame 1 arrived at  14:48:13.7824; frame size is 60 (003C hex) bytes.
DLC:        Destination = BROADCAST FFFFFFFFFFFF, Broadcast
DLC:        Source     = Station H-P   06CA73, David
DLC:        802.3 length = 34
DLC:
XNS:        ——- XNS Header ——-
XNS:
XNS:        Checksum = FFFF
XNS:        Length = 34
XNS:        Transport control = 00
XNS:             0000 .... = Reserved
XNS:             .... 0000 = Hop count
XNS:        Packet type = 17 (Novell NetWare)
XNS:
XNS:        Dest   net = 00000000, host = FFFFFFFFFFFF,
            socket = 1106 (NetWare Service Advertising)
XNS:        Source net = 00000000, host = 08000906CA73, socket = 16390 (4006)
XNS:
NCP:        ——- NetWare Nearest Service Query ——-
NCP:
NCP:        Server type = 0004 (file server)
```

Trace 3.13.4d. Successful NetWare Server Login Details

3.13.5 Encapsulating IP Packets Inside AppleTalk Packets

In this example, we will discuss another alternative for multiprotocol Internet connectivity: an AppleTalk gateway. As we discussed in Section 2.6, Apple developed the AppleTalk protocol suite, which is described in *Inside AppleTalk* [3-38]. Apple supports the Internet protocols via a product called MacTCP, which supports the Network and Transport Layers over LocalTalk (the 230 Kbps twisted pair network), Ethernet/IEEE 802.3, or token ring. In the internetwork shown in Figure 3-16, a FastPath DDP-to-IP gateway from Shiva Corp. (Cambridge, Massachusetts) connects a LocalTalk and an Ethernet network. The FastPath supports AppleTalk, TCP/IP, and DECnet protocols, plus SNMP network management.

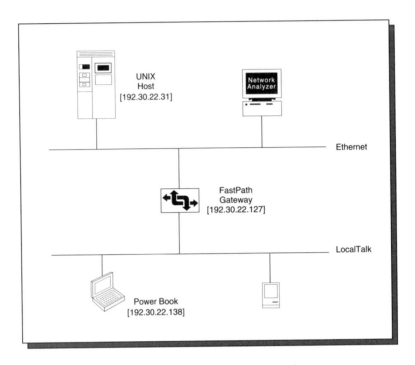

Figure 3-16. AppleTalk to Internet Gateway.

In this case study, a network manager (whom we will call Jeff) is using an Apple PowerBook computer on the LocalTalk network, Apple's MacTCP software, and Intercon's TCP/Connect II application package. Jeff wishes to access a UNIX host on the Ethernet network. The process for the protocols is for Jeff's workstation to communicate with the FastPath using the AppleTalk protocols. The FastPath then converts the AppleTalk to Internet protocols, and then communicates to the UNIX host via the Ethernet network. If we were to place the network analyzer on the LocalTalk side, we would observe LocalTalk frames containing AppleTalk data; with the analyzer on the Ethernet side, we observe Ethernet frames containing TCP/IP data. Let's look and see.

With the analyzer on the Ethernet side, we can capture the communication between the Ethernet network card inside the FastPath and the Ethernet network card inside the UNIX host. Trace 3.13.5a shows a summary of these frames; extraneous traffic on the Ethernet network was filtered out for clarity. Beginning in Frame 9, Jeff initializes a TCP connection to the TELNET port on the remote host. The initialization is a three-way handshake, with Jeff asking for a connection (Frame 9), the host responding (Frame 10), and Jeff confirming the arrangement (Frame 11). Looking at the details of those frames (Trace 3.13.5b), the IP header contains the source of the data (Internet address 192.30.22.138, the PowerBook) and the designated destination (192.30.22.31, the UNIX host). The TCP header addresses the destination process (Destination Port = 23 [TELNET]). The only clue that another protocol suite is in use is in the TCP options contained in Frame 9. Note that the originating station (Jeff) requires a maximum TCP segment size of 536 octets, a constraint imposed by MacTCP. When the TCP segment size is added to the TCP header (20 octets) and the IP header (also 20 octets), a maximum IP datagram size of 576 octets results.

Returning to Trace 3.13.5a, we see the host begin the TELNET options negotiation process, first asking for Jeff's terminal type (Frame 12). Jeff's workstation requests a suppress go-ahead (Frame 15) and responds to the terminal type (Frame 18), plus other parameters (Frames 19 through 26). Jeff then signals the host to log in by hitting the carriage return and linefeed in succession <CR><LF>, which is represented in hexadecimal by <0D><0A> in Frame 29. The Host responds by asking for Jeff's login (Frame 30), and Jeff's workstation responds by sending the login (Guest) one character at a time (Frames 41 through 55). Note that the Host echoes each character (e.g., Frame 42) and that the workstation sends a TCP acknowledgement between each successive character (e.g., Frame 43). Jeff's workstation sends another <CR><LF> in Frame 57, prompting the host to request his password. The password (apple) is transferred one character at a time in Frames 71 through 87, but this time the host does not echo the password characters to the workstation. We only see a TCP acknowledgement from the host to Jeff between password characters. Now that the login and password are validated, Jeff may go about his business on the UNIX host.

Sniffer Network Analyzer data 5-Feb at 16:54:54, file DDPIP.ENC, Pg 1

SUMMARY	Delta T	Destination	Source	Summary
9		UNIX Host	FastPath	TCP D=23 S=28529 SYN SEQ=3613179760 LEN=0 WIN=10843
10	0.0012	FastPath	UNIX Host	TCP D=28529 S=23 SYN ACK=3613179761 SEQ=724864001 LEN=0 WIN=4096
11	0.0170	UNIX Host	FastPath	TCP D=23 S=28529 ACK=724864002 WIN=10843
12	0.0508	FastPath	UNIX Host	Telnet R PORT=28529 IAC Do Terminal type
13	0.0166	UNIX Host	FastPath	TCP D=23 S=28529 ACK=724864005 WIN=10840
15	0.2170	UNIX Host	FastPath	Telnet C PORT=28529 IAC Do Suppress go-ahead
16	0.0013	FastPath	UNIX Host	Telnet R PORT=28529 IAC Will Suppress go-ahead
17	0.0178	UNIX Host	FastPath	TCP D=23 S=28529 ACK=724864008 WIN=10837
18	0.0143	UNIX Host	FastPath	Telnet C PORT=28529 IAC Will Terminal type
19	0.0012	FastPath	UNIX Host	Telnet R PORT=28529 IAC SB ...
20	0.0165	UNIX Host	FastPath	TCP D=23 S=28529 ACK=724864014 WIN=10831
21	0.0809	UNIX Host	FastPath	Telnet C PORT=28529 IAC SB ...
22	0.1126	FastPath	UNIX Host	TCP D=28529 S=23 ACK=3613179782 WIN=4096
23	0.0018	FastPath	UNIX Host	Telnet R PORT=28529 IAC Will Echo
24	0.0233	UNIX Host	FastPath	TCP D=23 S=28529 ACK=724864059 WIN=10798
25	0.0232	UNIX Host	FastPath	Telnet C PORT=28529 IAC Do Echo
26	0.1514	FastPath	UNIX Host	TCP D=28529 S=23 ACK=3613179785 WIN=4096
29	0.6094	UNIX Host	FastPath	Telnet C PORT=28529 <0D><0A>
30	0.0036	FastPath	UNIX Host	Telnet R PORT=28529 <0D><0A>login:
32	0.0193	UNIX Host	FastPath	TCP D=23 S=28529 ACK=724864068 WIN=10834

41	0.5279	UNIX Host	FastPath	Telnet C PORT=28529 G
42	0.0026	FastPath	UNIX Host	Telnet R PORT=28529 G
43	0.0169	UNIX Host	FastPath	TCP D=23 S=28529
				ACK=724864069 WIN=10842
44	0.2052	UNIX Host	FastPath	Telnet C PORT=28529 u
45	0.0025	FastPath	UNIX Host	Telnet R PORT=28529 u
46	0.0171	UNIX Host	FastPath	TCP D=23 S=28529
				ACK=724864070 WIN=10842
47	0.0831	UNIX Host	FastPath	Telnet C PORT=28529 e
48	0.0025	FastPath	UNIX Host	Telnet R PORT=28529 e
49	0.0171	UNIX Host	FastPath	TCP D=23 S=28529
51	0.1882	UNIX Host	FastPath	Telnet C PORT=28529 s
52	0.0026	FastPath	UNIX Host	Telnet R PORT=28529 s
53	0.0170	UNIX Host	FastPath	TCP D=23 S=28529
				ACK=724864072 WIN=10842
54	0.2058	UNIX Host	FastPath	Telnet C PORT=28529 t
55	0.0026	FastPath	UNIX Host	Telnet R PORT=28529 t
56	0.0163	UNIX Host	FastPath	TCP D=23 S=28529
				ACK=724864073 WIN=10842
57	0.3692	UNIX Host	FastPath	Telnet C PORT=28529 <0D><0A>
58	0.0077	FastPath	UNIX Host	Telnet R PORT=28529 <0D><0A>
59	0.0166	UNIX Host	FastPath	TCP D=23 S=28529
				ACK=724864075 WIN=10841
64	0.2520	FastPath	UNIX Host	Telnet R PORT=28529 Password:
65	0.0170	UNIX Host	FastPath	TCP D=23 S=28529
				ACK=724864084 WIN=10834
71	0.3686	UNIX Host	FastPath	Telnet C PORT=28529 a
72	0.0282	FastPath	UNIX Host	TCP D=28529 S=23
				ACK=3613179795 WIN=4096
73	0.1660	UNIX Host	FastPath	Telnet C PORT=28529 p
74	0.0339	FastPath	UNIX Host	TCP D=28529 S=23
				ACK=3613179796 WIN=4096
75	0.1594	UNIX Host	FastPath	Telnet C PORT=28529 p
76	0.0405	FastPath	UNIX Host	TCP D=28529 S=23
				ACK=3613179797 WIN=4096
85	0.1536	UNIX Host	FastPath	Telnet C PORT=28529 l
86	0.0463	FastPath	UNIX Host	TCP D=28529 S=23
				ACK=3613179798 WIN=4096
87	0.1245	UNIX Host	FastPath	Telnet C PORT=28529 e
91	0.0754	FastPath	UNIX Host	TCP D=28529 S=23
				ACK=3613179799 WIN=4096
92	0.0850	UNIX Host	FastPath	Telnet C PORT=28529 <0D><0A>
93	0.0048	FastPath	UNIX Host	Telnet R PORT=28529 <0D><0A>
94	0.0164	UNIX Host	FastPath	TCP D=23 S=28529
				ACK=724864086 WIN=10841

95	0.5532	FastPath	UNIX Host	Telnet R PORT=28529
				<0D><0A>
96	0.0309	UNIX Host	FastPath	TCP D=23 S=28529
				ACK=724864495 WIN=10434
97	0.7618	FastPath	UNIX Host	Telnet R PORT=28529
				TERM = (vt100)
98	0.0172	UNIX Host	FastPath	TCP D=23 S=28529
				ACK=724864510 WIN=10828

Trace 3.13.5a. AppleTalk to Internet Gateway Summary

Sniffer Network Analyzer data 5-Feb at 16:54:54, file DDPIP.ENC, Pg 1

- - - - - - - - - - - - - - - - Frame 9 - - - - - - - - - - - - - - - - -

DLC:	—— DLC Header ——-
DLC:	
DLC:	Frame 9 arrived at 16:54:58.1627; frame size is 60 (003C hex) bytes.
DLC:	Destination = Station 1000E0019B07, UNIX Host
DLC:	Source = Station KinetxA13296, FastPath
DLC:	Ethertype = 0800 (IP)
DLC:	
IP:	—— IP Header ——-
IP:	
IP:	Version = 4, header length = 20 bytes
IP:	Type of service = 00
IP:	000. .... = routine
IP:	...0 .... = normal delay
IP:	.... 0... = normal throughput
IP:	.... .0.. = normal reliability
IP:	Total length = 44 bytes
IP:	Identification = 352
IP:	Flags = 0X
IP:	.0.. .... = may fragment
IP:	..0. .... = last fragment
IP:	Fragment offset = 0 bytes
IP:	Time to live = 59 seconds/hops
IP:	Protocol = 6 (TCP)
IP:	Header checksum = D186 (correct)
IP:	Source address = [192.30.22.138]
IP:	Destination address = [192.30.22.31]
IP:	No options
IP:	
TCP:	——- TCP header ——-

```
TCP:
TCP:           Source port = 28529
TCP:           Destination port = 23 (Telnet)
TCP:           Initial sequence number = 3613179760
TCP:           Data offset = 24 bytes
TCP:           Flags = 02
TCP:           ..0. .... = (No urgent pointer)
TCP:           ...0 .... = (No acknowledgment)
TCP:           .... 0... = (No push)
TCP:           .... .0.. = (No reset)
TCP:           .... ..1. = SYN
TCP:           .... ...0 = (No FIN)
TCP:           Window = 10843
TCP:           Checksum = BE2B (correct)
TCP:
TCP:           Options follow
TCP:           Maximum segment size = 536
TCP:
```

- - - - - - - - - - - - - - - - Frame 10 - - - - - - - - - - - - - - - - -

```
DLC:           ——- DLC Header ——-
DLC:
DLC:           Frame 10 arrived at  16:54:58.1640; frame size is 60 (003C hex) bytes.
DLC:           Destination = Station KinetxA13296, FastPath
DLC:           Source     = Station 1000E0019B07, UNIX Host
DLC:           Ethertype = 0800 (IP)
DLC:
IP:            ——- IP Header ——-
IP:
IP:            Version = 4, header length = 20 bytes
IP:            Type of service = 00
IP:                  000. .... = routine
IP:                  ...0 .... = normal delay
IP:                  .... 0... = normal throughput
IP:                  .... .0.. = normal reliability
IP:            Total length = 44 bytes
IP:            Identification = 2082
IP:            Flags = 0X
IP:            .0.. .... = may fragment
IP:            ..0. .... = last fragment
IP:            Fragment offset = 0 bytes
IP:            Time to live = 30 seconds/hops
IP:            Protocol = 6 (TCP)
```

125

IP:	Header checksum = E7C4 (correct)
IP:	Source address = [192.30.22.31]
IP:	Destination address = [192.30.22.138]
IP:	No options
IP:	
TCP:	——— TCP header ———
TCP:	
TCP:	Source port = 23 (Telnet)
TCP:	Destination port = 28529
TCP:	Initial sequence number = 724864001
TCP:	Acknowledgment number = 3613179761
TCP:	Data offset = 24 bytes
TCP:	Flags = 12
TCP:	..0. .... = (No urgent pointer)
TCP:	...1 .... = Acknowledgment
TCP:	.... 0... = (No push)
TCP:	.... .0.. = (No reset)
TCP:	.... ..1. = SYN
TCP:	....0 = (No FIN)
TCP:	Window = 4096
TCP:	Checksum = 1F58 (correct)
TCP:	
TCP:	Options follow
TCP:	Maximum segment size = 1024
TCP:	

- - - - - - - - - - - - - - - Frame 11 - - - - - - - - - - - - - - - - -

DLC:	——— DLC Header ———
DLC:	
DLC:	Frame 11 arrived at 16:54:58.1810; frame size is 60 (003C hex) bytes.
DLC:	Destination = Station 1000E0019B07, UNIX Host
DLC:	Source = Station KinetxA13296, FastPath
DLC:	Ethertype = 0800 (IP)
DLC:	
IP:	——— IP Header ———
IP:	
IP:	Version = 4, header length = 20 bytes
IP:	Type of service = 00
IP:	000. .... = routine
IP:	...0 .... = normal delay
IP:	.... 0... = normal throughput

IP:	.... .0.. = normal reliability
IP:	Total length = 40 bytes
IP:	Identification = 353
IP:	Flags = 0X
IP:	.0.. .... = may fragment
IP:	..0. .... = last fragment
IP:	Fragment offset = 0 bytes
IP:	Time to live = 59 seconds/hops
IP:	Protocol = 6 (TCP)
IP:	Header checksum = D189 (correct)
IP:	Source address = [192.30.22.138]
IP:	Destination address = [192.30.22.31]
IP:	No options
IP:	
TCP:	——— TCP header ———
TCP:	
TCP:	Source port = 28529
TCP:	Destination port = 23 (Telnet)
TCP:	Sequence number = 3613179761
TCP:	Acknowledgment number = 724864002
TCP:	Data offset = 20 bytes
TCP:	Flags = 10
TCP:	..0. .... = (No urgent pointer)
TCP:	...1 .... = Acknowledgment
TCP:	.... 0... = (No push)
TCP:	.... .0.. = (No reset)
TCP:	.... ..0. = (No SYN)
TCP:	....0 = (No FIN)
TCP:	Window = 10843
TCP:	Checksum = 1B06 (correct)
TCP:	No TCP options
TCP:	

Trace 3.13.5b. AppleTalk to Internet Gateway Details

3.13.6 Transmitting IP Datagrams Over a PSPDN

In Section 3.8, we discussed the principles behind sending IP datagrams over a Packet Switched Public Data Network (PSPDN) using the X.25 protocol. In this case study (see Figure 3-17), we will examine the interactions between TCP/IP and the Internet protocols with the X.25 protocol.

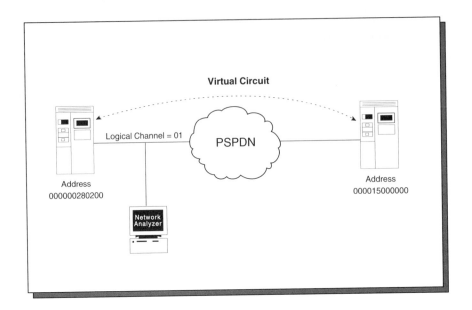

Figure 13-17. Internet Protocols over a PSPDN.

To begin, recall that X.25 defines an interface between a packet mode DTE (the user) and a DCE (the network). To capture the internetwork transmission, you must place the analyzer at the DTE/DCE interface. Before any higher-layer (e.g., IP) data can be transmitted, an X.25 Virtual Call must be established end to end between the two hosts via the network. Trace 3.13.6a reveals that this occurs in Frame 79; it is an X.25 Call Request packet, transmitted on Logical Channel 001 and destined for remote host 000015000000. The X.25 packet, shown in Trace 3.13.6b, contains a Protocol Identification field within the Call User Data field that identifies the higher-layer protocol in use. The value of CCH in the Protocol Identification field tells the destination address (000015000000) that the sender (000000280200) will be using IP. Frame 80 contains a Data Link Layer response. (The response is from LAPB, but is shown as HDLC, in the trace. LAPB is a derivative of HDLC, so the *Sniffer* has given it the generic name.) The destination node's Packet Level response is received in Frame 81 (Call Accepted). The DCE Link Level sends an acknowledgement in Frame 83, and data transfer begins in Frame 84. The data is transmitted on Logical Channel 01 as a single packet (More data bit = 0). Note that the total length of the IP datagram is 46 octets, so it fits completely within the X.25 default packet length of 128 octets. The

128

IP header identifies the protocol within that datagram as the Interior Gateway Protocol (IGP). The internet source address (XXX.YYY.165.2) is broadcasting the IGP information to all hosts on this network (destination address 255.255.255.255). Frame 85 contains a Packet Level acknowledgement (Receive Ready), indicating receipt of the packet at the local X.25 interface. We know that this acknowledgement did not come from the distant host because the Delivery Confirmation bit within the Packet Level header = 0. The value (0) indicates local acknowledgments; a positive value (1) indicates remote (i.e., distant host) acknowledgments.

Returning to the data summary (Trace 3.13.6a), we can observe a communication problem between the Source and Destination hosts. In Frame 87, the local host requests a file using the Trivial File Transfer Protocol (TFTP) described in Chapter 6 (Read Request File = network-confg). Three seconds later, it repeats the request (Frame 89). The DTE process appears to be functioning properly since the packet sequence counter is incrementing correctly (PS = 2 in Frame 87; PS = 3 in Frame 89). The local DCE's Packet Level process acknowledges the request with PR = 4 in Frame 90, but never responds with the requested file. The DTE makes a third and fourth attempts for the file in Frames 92 and 94, with equally disappointing results (Frame 95). Undaunted, the DTE requests a different file (cyg-x1-confg) in Frame 97. Several tries later (Frame 104) this file has also not been received.

The local DTE makes a second Call Request, this time using Logical Channel 002 (Frame 107). By now the local DCE is completely confused and responds with a Clear Request (Frame 109), which is confirmed by the DTE in Frame 111.

The trace file does not identify the exact source of the problem, but it appears to be at the local DTE/DCE interface. The DTE is not the likely culprit since its processes appear to know what they want and have demonstrated patience in their repeated requests. At this point, the network administrator should enlist the aid of the PSPDN analysis center to isolate the problem with the DCE side of the X.25 interface.

Sniffer Network Analyzer data 19-Oct at 15:09:24, file CISX251.SYC Pg 1

SUMMARY	Delta T	From DCE	From DTE
79	6.7309		HDLC R I NR=1 NS=1 P/F=0
			X.25 001 Call Req
			Dst:000015000000
			Src:000000280200 TCP_IP
80	0.0085	HDLC C RR NR=2 P/F=0	

81	0.0099	HDLC R I NR=2 NS=1 P/F=0 X.25 001 Call Acc	

82	0.0583		HDLC R I NR=2 NS=2 P/F=0
			X.25 001 Data PR=0 PS=0
			IP D=[255.255.255.255]
			  S=[131.100.165.2]
			  LEN=26 ID=0

83	0.0086	HDLC C RR NR=3 P/F=0	

84	1.3943		HDLC R I NR=2 NS=3 P/F=0
			X.25 001 Data PR=0 PS=1
			IP D=[255.255.255.255]
			  S=[131.100.165.2]
			  LEN=26 ID=0

85	0.0112	HDLC R I NR=4 NS=2 P/F=0 X.25 001 RR PR=2	
86	0.0087		HDLC C RR NR=3 P/F=0
87	36.4935		HDLC R I NR=3 NS=4 P/F=0 X.25 001 Data PR=0 PS=2 IP D=[255.255.255.255] S=[131.100.165.2] LEN=33 ID=0 UDP D=69 S=28624 LEN=33 TFTP Read request File=network-confg
88	0.0092	HDLC C RR NR=5 P/F=0	

89	3.0128		HDLC R I NR=3 NS=5 P/F=0
			X.25 001 Data PR=0 PS=3
			IP D=[255.255.255.255]
			  S=[131.100.165.2]
			  LEN=33 ID=1
			UDP D=69 S=28624 LEN=33
			TFTP Read request
			File=network-confg

90	0.0122	HDLC R I NR=6 NS=3 P/F=0 X.25 001 RR PR=4	
91	0.0087		HDLC C RR NR=4 P/F=0

92	2.983		HDLC R I NR=4 NS=6 P/F=0
			X.25 001 Data PR=0 PS=4
			IP D=[255.255.255.255]
			  S=[131.108.165.2]
			  LEN=33 ID=2
			UDP D=69 S=28624 LEN=33
			TFTP Read request
			File=network-confg

93	0.0091	HDLC C RR NR=7 P/F=0	
94	2.9939		HDLC R I NR=4 NS=7 P/F=0
			X.25 001 Data PR=0 PS=5
			IP D=[255.255.255.255]
			S=[131.108.165.2]
			LEN=33 ID=3
			UDP D=69 S=28624 LEN=33
			TFTP Read request
			File=network-confg
95	0.0121	HDLC R I NR=0 NS=4 P/F=0	
		X.25 001 RR PR=6	
96	0.0088		HDLC C RR NR=5 P/F=0
97	3.0330		HDLC R I NR=5 NS=0 P/F=0
			X.25 001 Data PR=0 PS=6
			IP D=[255.255.255.255]
			S=[131.108.165.2]
			LEN=32 ID=0
			UDP D=69 S=40712 LEN=32
			TFTP Read request
			File=cyg-x1-confg
98	0.0081	HDLC C RR NR=1 P/F=0	
99	3.0149		HDLC R I NR=5 NS=1 P/F=0
			X.25 001 Data PR=0 PS=7
			IP D=[255.255.255.255]
			S=[131.108.165.2]
			LEN=32 ID=1
			UDP D=69 S=40712 LEN=32
			TFTP Read request
			File=cyg-x1-confg
100	0.0122	HDLC R I NR=2 NS=5 P/F=0	
		X.25 001 RR PR=0	
101	0.0087		HDLC C RR NR=6 P/F=0
102	2.9820		HDLC R I NR=6 NS=2 P/F=0
			X.25 001 Data PR=0 PS=0
			IP D=[255.255.255.255]
			S=[131.108.165.2]
			LEN=32 ID=2
			UDP D=69 S=40712 LEN=32
			TFTP Read request
			File=cyg-x1-confg
103	0.0082	HDLC C RR NR=3 P/F=0	
104	2.9958		HDLC R I NR=6 NS=3 P/F=0
			X.25 001 Data PR=0 PS=1

```
                                                    IP  D=[255.255.255.255]
                                                        S=[131.108.165.2]
                                                        LEN=32 ID=3
                                                    UDP D=69 S=40712 LEN=32
                                                    TFTP Read request
                                                    File=cyg-x1-confg
105      0.0112      HDLC R I  NR=4 NS=6 P/F=0
                        X.25 001 RR  PR=2
106      0.0087                                     HDLC C RR  NR=7    P/F=0
107      35.8026                                    HDLC R I  NR=7 NS=4 P/F=0
                                                        X.25 002 Call Req
                                                        Dst:000015000000
                                                        Src:000000280200 ISO_CLNP
108      0.0082      HDLC C RR  NR=5    P/F=0
109      0.0120      HDLC R I  NR=5 NS=7 P/F=0
                        X.25 002 Clr Req DTE originated
110      0.0087                                     HDLC C RR  NR=0    P/F=0
111      0.0099                                     HDLC R I  NR=0 NS=5 P/F=0
                                                        X.25 002 Clr Conf
```

Trace 3.13.6a. X.25 Call Request and IP Data Transfer

Sniffer Network Analyzer data 19-Oct at 15:09:24 file CISX251.SYC Pg 1

- - - - - - - - - - - - - - - Frame 79 - - - - - - - - - - - - - - - - -

```
DLC:          ——- DLC Header ——-
DLC:
DLC:          Frame 79 arrived at  15:21:44.3950; frame size is 23 (0017 hex) bytes.
DLC:          Destination = DCE
DLC:          Source    = DTE
DLC:
HDLC:         ——- High Level Data Link Control (HDLC) ——-
HDLC:
HDLC:         Address = 03 (Response)
HDLC:         Control field = 22
HDLC:                001. .... = N(R) = 1
HDLC:                ...0 .... = Poll/Final bit
HDLC:                .... 001. = N(S) = 1
HDLC:                .... ...0 = I (Information transfer)
HDLC:
X.25:         ——- X.25 Packet Level —--
```

X.25:
X.25:   General format id = 10
X.25:   .0.. .... = Delivery confirmation bit
X.25:   ..01 .... = Sequence numbering modulo 8
X.25:   .... 0000 = Logical channel group number = 0
X.25:   Logical channel number = 01
X.25:   Packet type identifier = 0B (Call request)
X.25:   Address length field = CC
X.25:   1100 .... = Source length = 12 digits
X.25:   .... 1100 = Destination length = 12 digits
X.25:   Destination address = 000015000000
X.25:   Source address = 000000280200
X.25:   Facility length = 0
X.25:   Protocol identification = CC (TCP_IP)
X.25:
X.25:   [4 bytes of user data = CC000000]
X.25:

- - - - - - - - - - - - - - - - Frame 80 - - - - - - - - - - - - - - - - -

DLC: —— DLC Header ——
DLC:
DLC: Frame 80 arrived at 15:21:44.4036; frame size is 2 (0002 hex) bytes.
DLC: Destination = DTE
DLC: Source   = DCE
DLC:
HDLC: ——- High Level Data Link Control (HDLC) ——
HDLC:
HDLC: Address = 03 (Command)
HDLC: Control field = 41
HDLC: 010. .... = N(R) = 2
HDLC: ...0 .... = Poll/Final bit
HDLC: .... 0001 = RR (Receive ready)
HDLC:

- - - - - - - - - - - - - - - - Frame 81 - - - - - - - - - - - - - - - -

DLC: —— DLC Header ——
DLC:
DLC: Frame 81 arrived at 15:21:44.4135; frame size is 5 (0005 hex) bytes.
DLC: Destination = DTE
DLC: Source   = DCE
DLC:
HDLC: —— High Level Data Link Control (HDLC) ——

HDLC:
HDLC: Address = 01 (Response)
HDLC: Control field = 42
HDLC: 010. .... = N(R) = 2
HDLC: ...0 .... = Poll/Final bit
HDLC: .... 001. = N(S) = 1
HDLC: ....0 = I (Information transfer)
HDLC:
X.25:   ——- X.25 Packet Level ——-
X.25:
X.25:   General format id = 10
X.25:   .0.. .... = Delivery confirmation bit
X.25:   ..01 .... = Sequence numbering modulo 8
X.25:   .... 0000 = Logical channel group number = 0
X.25:   Logical channel number = 01
X.25:   Packet type identifier = 0F (Call accepted)
X.25:

- - - - - - - - - - - - - - - Frame 82 - - - - - - - - - - - - - - - - -

DLC: ——- DLC Header ——-
DLC:
DLC: Frame 82 arrived at 15:21:44.4719; frame size is 51 (0033 hex) bytes.
DLC: Destination = DCE
DLC: Source   = DTE
DLC:
HDLC: ——- High Level Data Link Control (HDLC) ——-
HDLC:
HDLC: Address = 03 (Response)
HDLC: Control field = 44
HDLC: 010. .... = N(R) = 2
HDLC: ...0 .... = Poll/Final bit
HDLC: .... 010. = N(S) = 2
HDLC: ....0 = I (Information transfer)
HDLC:
X.25: ——- X.25 Packet Level ——-
X.25:
X.25: General format id = 10
X.25:   0... .... = Qualifier bit
X.25:   .0.. .... = Delivery confirmation bit
X.25:   ..01 .... = Sequence numbering modulo 8
X.25:   .... 0000 = Logical channel group number = 0
X.25:   Logical channel number = 01

```
X.25:          Data packet info = 00
X.25:                    000. .... = P(R) = 0
X.25:                    ...0 .... = More bit
X.25:                    .... 000. = P(S) = 0
X.25:                    .... ...0 = Packet type identifier (Data)
X.25:
IP:            ——- IP Header ——-
IP:
IP:            Version = 4, header length = 20 bytes
IP:            Type of service = 00
IP:                    000. .... = routine
IP:                    ...0 .... = normal delay
IP:                    .... 0... = normal throughput
IP:                    .... .0.. = normal reliability
IP:            Total length = 46 bytes
IP:            Identification = 0
IP:            Flags = 0X
IP:            .0.. .... = may fragment
IP:            ..0. .... = last fragment
IP:            Fragment offset = 0 bytes
IP:            Time to live = 2 seconds/hops
IP:            Protocol = 9 (IGP)
IP:            Header checksum = 9059 (correct)
IP:            Source address = [131.100.165.2]
IP:            Destination address = [255.255.255.255]
IP:            No options
IP:            [26 byte(s) of data]

- - - - - - - - - - - - - - - - Frame 83 - - - - - - - - - - - - - - - -

DLC:           ——- DLC Header ——-
DLC:
DLC:           Frame 83 arrived at  15:21:44.4805; frame size is 2 (0002 hex) bytes.
DLC:           Destination = DTE
DLC:           Source     = DCE
DLC:
HDLC:          ——- High Level Data Link Control (HDLC) ——-
HDLC:
HDLC:          Address = 03 (Command)
HDLC:          Control field = 61
HDLC:                    011. .... = N(R) = 3
HDLC:                    ...0 .... = Poll/Final bit
HDLC:                    .... 0001 = RR  (Receive ready)
```

135

HDLC:

- - - - - - - - - - - - - - - Frame 84 - - - - - - - - - - - - - - - - -

DLC:	—— DLC Header ——
DLC:	
DLC:	Frame 84 arrived at 15:21:45.8748; frame size is 51 (0033 hex) bytes.
DLC:	Destination = DCE
DLC:	Source = DTE
DLC:	
HDLC:	—— High Level Data Link Control (HDLC) ——
HDLC:	
HDLC:	Address = 03 (Response)
HDLC:	Control field = 46
HDLC:	010. .... = N(R) = 2
HDLC:	...0 .... = Poll/Final bit
HDLC:	.... 011. = N(S) = 3
HDLC:	....0 = I (Information transfer)
HDLC:	
X.25:	—— X.25 Packet Level ——
X.25:	
X.25:	General format id = 10
X.25:	0... .... = Qualifier bit
X.25:	.0.. .... = Delivery confirmation bit
X.25:	..01 .... = Sequence numbering modulo 8
X.25:	.... 0000 = Logical channel group number = 0
X.25:	Logical channel number = 01
X.25:	Data packet info = 02
X.25:	000. .... = P(R) = 0
X.25:	...0 .... = More bit
X.25:	.... 001. = P(S) = 1
X.25:	....0 = Packet type identifier (Data)
X.25:	
IP:	—— IP Header ——
IP:	
IP:	Version = 4, header length = 20 bytes
IP:	Type of service = 00
IP:	000. .... = routine
IP:	...0 .... = normal delay
IP:	.... 0... = normal throughput
IP:	.... .0.. = normal reliability
IP:	Total length = 46 bytes
IP:	Identification = 0

IP:	Flags = 0X
IP:	.0.. .... = may fragment
IP:	..0. .... = last fragment
IP:	Fragment offset = 0 bytes
IP:	Time to live = 2 seconds/hops
IP:	Protocol = 9 (IGP)
IP:	Header checksum = 9059 (correct)
IP:	Source address = [131.100.165.2]
IP:	Destination address = [255.255.255.255]
IP:	No options
IP:	[26 byte(s) of data]

- - - - - - - - - - - - - - - - Frame 85 - - - - - - - - - - - - - - - - -

DLC:	——- DLC Header ——
DLC:	
DLC:	Frame 85 arrived at 15:21:45.8861; frame size is 5 (0005 hex) bytes.
DLC:	Destination = DTE
DLC:	Source = DCE
DLC:	
HDLC:	——- High Level Data Link Control (HDLC) ——
HDLC:	
HDLC:	Address = 01 (Response)
HDLC:	Control field = 84
HDLC:	100. .... = N(R) = 4
HDLC:	...0 .... = Poll/Final bit
HDLC:	.... 010. = N(S) = 2
HDLC:	....0 = I (Information transfer)
HDLC:	
X.25:	—— X.25 Packet Level ——-
X.25:	
X.25:	General format id = 10
X.25:	..01 .... = Sequence numbering modulo 8
X.25:	.... 0000 = Logical channel group number = 0
X.25:	Logical channel number = 01
X.25:	Flow control info = 41
X.25:	010. .... = P(R) = 2
X.25:	...0 0001 = Packet type identifier (Receive ready)
X.25:	

Trace 3.13.6b. X.25 Call Request Details

3.13.7 File Transfers over Frame Relay Networks

Extending our illustration of using TCP/IP over wide-area networks, this example will demonstrate how the File Transfer Protocol operates over a frame relay network. In this case, a user at a branch office needs access to a file that is resident on a host at the headquarters location (see Figure 3-18). A frame relay network connects the various locations, with two permanent virtual connections (PVCs) between the two sites in question. These PVCs operate over a 56 Kbps leased line, transmitting both IPX and IP traffic. The IP traffic is of greatest interest to our discussion; this traffic is carried on the PVC identified by Data Link Connection Identified (DLCI) 140.

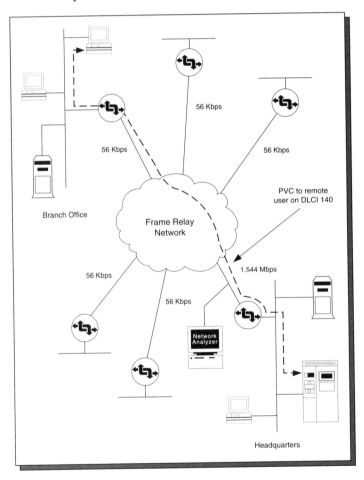

Figure 3-18. TCP/IP over Frame Relay.

Note from Figure 3-18 and Trace 3.13.7a that the data was captured at the host end (or headquarters side) of the connection. As a result, careful attention to the Source/Destination address designations is necessary to avoid confusion. For example, in Frame 1078, the destination specified is the DTE, which is actually the host at headquarters. The source of the data in Frame 1078 is the DCE (the network), which is actually the data coming from the remote user, via the network. (As in previous examples, this trace has been filtered to only show frames relevant to our discussion.)

The remote user initiates the file transfer process in Frame 1078 by entering **TYPE A** at his workstation to indicate to the headquarters host that an ASCII file transfer is being requested. The host confirms the TYPE A transfer in Frame 1079. The ports to be used are defined in Frame 1082 and confirmed in Frame 1083. The user indicates the file to be retrieved in Frame 1088 (Otherlinks.html). The host opens the data connection in Frame 1092, and begins the file transfer in Frame 1093. An acknowledgement from the remote user is seen in Frame 1105, and the host completes the file transfer in Frame 1107.

Sniffer Internetwork Analyzer data from 8-Mar at 12:44:38, file FR1.SYC, Pg 1

SUMMARY	Delta T	Destination	Source	Summary
1078	2.5111	DTE	DCE	FTP C PORT=1214 TYPE A<0D0A>
1079	0.0128	DCE	DTE	FTP R PORT=1214 200 Type set to A.<0D0A>
1082	0.0751	DTE	DCE	FTP C PORT=1214 PORT
				161,69,133,72,4,254<0D0A>
1083	0.0110	DCE	DTE	FTP R PORT=1214 200
				PORT command successful.<0D0A>
1088	0.0491	DTE	DCE	FTP C PORT=1214 RETR Otherlinks.html<0D0A>
1092	0.0552	DCE	DTE	FTP R PORT=1214 150 Opening ASCII
				mode data connection for Oth...
1107	0.2048	DCE	DTE	FTP R PORT=1214 226
				Transfer complete.<0D0A>

Trace 3.13.7a. File Transfer Summary

The details of the file transfer illustrate how FTP operates over frame relay connections (see Trace 3.13.7b). In Frame 1078, note that the frame relay header (the lines designated FRELAY in Trace 3.13.7b) identifies the DLCI in use (140), the absence of any congestion (either forward or backward), and other details. The IP header identifies the protocol inside the IP datagram (Protocol = 6 (TCP)), along with the IP addresses of the source and destination (the remote workstation and the head-quarters host, respectively), indicating that they are on different IP subnetworks. The TCP header defines the host port that will be accessed (Destination Port = 21, the FTP Control port), along with the TCP connection-related information such as sequence and acknowledgement numbers and flags. The FTP layer decode identifies the eight octets of data that were transmitted (TYPE A <0D0A>, where the 0D is a carriage return character, and the 0A is a line feed character).

Readers studying subsequent frames can trace the consistency of the source and destination IP addresses, the orderly progression of the TCP sequence and acknowl-edgement numbers, and the details of the FTP process at both the remote and host ends of the connection. In the following chapters, we will study these protocol intricacies in greater detail.

Sniffer Internetwork Analyzer data 8-Mar at 12:44:38, file FR1.SYC, Pg 1

- - - - - - - - - - - - - - - Frame 1078 - - - - - - - - - - - - - - - - -

```
DLC:  ----- DLC Header -----
DLC:
DLC:  Frame 1078 arrived at  15:07:45.5908; frame size is 52 (0034 hex) bytes.
DLC:  Destination = DTE
DLC:  Source = DCE
DLC:
FRELAY: ----- Frame Relay -----
FRELAY:
FRELAY: Address word = 20C1
FRELAY: 0010 00.. 1100 .... = DLCI 140
FRELAY: .... ..0. .... .... = Response
FRELAY: .... .... .... 0... = No forward congestion
FRELAY: .... .... .... .0.. = No backward congestion
FRELAY: .... .... .... ..0. = Not eligible for discard
FRELAY: .... .... .... ...1 = Not extended address
FRELAY:
ETYPE: Ethertype  = 0800 (IP)
ETYPE:
IP:  ----- IP Header -----
IP:
IP:  Version = 4, header length = 20 bytes
IP:  Type of service = 00
```

```
IP:      000. .... = routine
IP:      ...0 .... = normal delay
IP:      .... 0... = normal throughput
IP:      .... .0.. = normal reliability
IP:   Total length   = 48 bytes
IP:   Identification = 12828
IP:   Flags          = 4X
IP:      .1.. .... = don't fragment
IP:      ..0. .... = last fragment
IP:   Fragment offset = 0 bytes
IP:   Time to live   = 31 seconds/hops
IP:   Protocol       = 6 (TCP)
IP:   Header checksum = F1B8 (correct)
IP:   Source address      = [XXX.YYY.133.72]
IP:   Destination address = [XXX.YYY.81.1]
IP:   No options
IP:
TCP: ——- TCP header ——-
TCP:
TCP:  Source port         = 1214
TCP:  Destination port    = 21 (FTP)
TCP:  Sequence number      = 3275985
TCP:  Acknowledgment number  = 725589307
TCP:  Data offset         = 20 bytes
TCP:  Flags               = 18
TCP:         ..0. .... = (No urgent pointer)
TCP:         ...1 .... = Acknowledgment
TCP:         .... 1... = Push
TCP:         .... .0.. = (No reset)
TCP:         .... ..0. = (No SYN)
TCP:         .... ...0 = (No FIN)
TCP:  Window              = 8065
TCP:  Checksum            = BC15 (correct)
TCP:  No TCP options
TCP:  [8 byte(s) of data]
TCP:
FTP: ——- FTP data ——-
FTP:
FTP: TYPE A<0D0A>
FTP:
```

- - - - - - - - - - - - - - - Frame 1079 - - - - - - - - - - - - - - - -

```
DLC:  ——- DLC Header ——-
DLC:
DLC:  Frame 1079 arrived at  15:07:45.6037; frame size is 64 (0040 hex) bytes.
DLC:  Destination = DCE
DLC:  Source = DTE
DLC:
FRELAY: ——- Frame Relay ——-
FRELAY:
FRELAY: Address word = 20C1
FRELAY: 0010 00.. 1100 .... = DLCI 140
FRELAY: .... ..0. .... .... = Response
FRELAY: .... .... .... 0... = No forward congestion
FRELAY: .... .... .... .0.. = No backward congestion
FRELAY: .... .... .... ..0. = Not eligible for discard
FRELAY: .... .... .... ...1 = Not extended address
FRELAY:
ETYPE: Ethertype  = 0800 (IP)
ETYPE:
IP:  ——- IP Header ——-
IP:
IP:  Version = 4, header length = 20 bytes
IP:  Type of service = 00
IP:      000. .... = routine
IP:      ...0 .... = normal delay
IP:      .... 0... = normal throughput
IP:      .... .0.. = normal reliability
IP:  Total length   = 60 bytes
IP:  Identification  = 7358
IP:  Flags        = 0X
IP:      .0.. .... = may fragment
IP:      ..0. .... = last fragment
IP:  Fragment offset = 0 bytes
IP:  Time to live   = 51 seconds/hops
IP:  Protocol      = 6 (TCP)
IP:  Header checksum = 330B (correct)
IP:  Source address     = [XXX.YYY.81.1]
IP:  Destination address = [XXX.YYY.133.72]
IP:  No options
IP:
TCP: ——- TCP header ——-
TCP:
TCP:  Source port       = 21 (FTP)
TCP:  Destination port     = 1214
```

```
TCP:  Sequence number      = 725589307
TCP:  Acknowledgment number  = 3275993
TCP:  Data offset        = 20 bytes
TCP:  Flags           = 18
TCP:          ..0. .... = (No urgent pointer)
TCP:          ...1 .... = Acknowledgment
TCP:          .... 1... = Push
TCP:          .... .0.. = (No reset)
TCP:          .... ..0. = (No SYN)
TCP:          .... ...0 = (No FIN)
TCP:  Window          = 4096
TCP:  Checksum         = 1289 (correct)
TCP:  No TCP options
TCP:  [20 byte(s) of data]
TCP:
FTP:  —— FTP data ——
FTP:
FTP:  200 Type set to A.<0D0A>
FTP:
```

- - - - - - - - - - - - - - - Frame 1082 - - - - - - - - - - - - - - - -

```
DLC:  —— DLC Header ——
DLC:
DLC:  Frame 1082 arrived at  15:07:45.6787; frame size is 70 (0046 hex) bytes.
DLC:  Destination = DTE
DLC:  Source = DCE
DLC:
FRELAY:  —— Frame Relay ——
FRELAY:
FRELAY: Address word = 20C1
FRELAY: 0010 00.. 1100 .... = DLCI 140
FRELAY: .... ..0. .... .... = Response
FRELAY: .... .... .... 0... = No forward congestion
FRELAY: .... .... .... .0.. = No backward congestion
FRELAY: .... .... .... ..0. = Not eligible for discard
FRELAY: .... .... .... ...1 = Not extended address
FRELAY:
ETYPE: Ethertype  = 0800 (IP)
ETYPE:
IP:  —— IP Header ——
IP:
IP:  Version = 4, header length = 20 bytes
```

```
IP:  Type of service = 00
IP:      000. .... = routine
IP:      ...0 .... = normal delay
IP:      .... 0... = normal throughput
IP:      .... .0.. = normal reliability
IP:  Total length   = 66 bytes
IP:  Identification = 13084
IP:  Flags          = 4X
IP:      .1.. .... = don't fragment
IP:      ..0. .... = last fragment
IP:  Fragment offset = 0 bytes
IP:  Time to live   = 31 seconds/hops
IP:  Protocol       = 6 (TCP)
IP:  Header checksum = F0A6 (correct)
IP:  Source address     = [XXX.YYY.133.72]
IP:  Destination address = [XXX.YYY.81.1]
IP:  No options
IP:
TCP: ——- TCP header ——-
TCP:
TCP: Source port        = 1214
TCP: Destination port       = 21 (FTP)
TCP: Sequence number        = 3275993
TCP: Acknowledgment number   = 725589327
TCP: Data offset        = 20 bytes
TCP: Flags          = 18
TCP:          ..0. .... = (No urgent pointer)
TCP:          ...1 .... = Acknowledgment
TCP:          .... 1... = Push
TCP:          .... .0.. = (No reset)
TCP:          .... ..0. = (No SYN)
TCP:          .... ...0 = (No FIN)
TCP: Window         = 8045
TCP: Checksum       = F946 (correct)
TCP: No TCP options
TCP: [26 byte(s) of data]
TCP:
FTP: ——- FTP data ——-
FTP:
FTP: PORT 161,69,133,72,4,254<0D0A>
FTP:

- - - - - - - - - - - - - - - Frame 1083 - - - - - - - - - - - - - - - -
```

```
DLC: ——- DLC Header ——-
DLC:
DLC: Frame 1083 arrived at  15:07:45.6897; frame size is 74 (004A hex) bytes.
DLC: Destination = DCE
DLC: Source = DTE
DLC:
FRELAY: ——- Frame Relay ——-
FRELAY:
FRELAY: Address word = 20C1
FRELAY: 0010 00.. 1100 .... = DLCI 140
FRELAY: .... ..0. .... .... = Response
FRELAY: .... .... .... 0... = No forward congestion
FRELAY: .... .... .... .0.. = No backward congestion
FRELAY: .... .... .... ..0. = Not eligible for discard
FRELAY: .... .... .... ...1 = Not extended address
FRELAY:
ETYPE: Ethertype  = 0800 (IP)
ETYPE:
IP:  ——- IP Header ——-
IP:
IP:  Version = 4, header length = 20 bytes
IP:  Type of service = 00
IP:      000. .... = routine
IP:      ...0 .... = normal delay
IP:      .... 0... = normal throughput
IP:      .... .0.. = normal reliability
IP:  Total length   = 70 bytes
IP:  Identification = 7396
IP:  Flags          = 0X
IP:      .0.. .... = may fragment
IP:      ..0. .... = last fragment
IP:  Fragment offset = 0 bytes
IP:  Time to live   = 51 seconds/hops
IP:  Protocol       = 6 (TCP)
IP:  Header checksum = 32DB (correct)
IP:  Source address    = [XXX.YYY.81.1]
IP:  Destination address = [XXX.YYY.133.72]
IP:  No options
IP:
TCP: ——- TCP header ——-
TCP:
TCP: Source port       = 21 (FTP)
TCP: Destination port    = 1214
```

TCP: Sequence number   = 725589327
TCP: Acknowledgment number = 3276019
TCP: Data offset   = 20 bytes
TCP: Flags   = 18
TCP: ..0. .... = (No urgent pointer)
TCP: ...1 .... = Acknowledgment
TCP: .... 1... = Push
TCP: .... .0.. = (No reset)
TCP: .... ..0. = (No SYN)
TCP: ....0 = (No FIN)
TCP: Window   = 4096
TCP: Checksum   = E04C (correct)
TCP: No TCP options
TCP: [30 byte(s) of data]
TCP:
FTP: ——- FTP data ——-
FTP:
FTP: 200 PORT command successful.<0D0A>
FTP:

- - - - - - - - - - - - - - - Frame 1088 - - - - - - - - - - - - - - - - -

DLC: ——- DLC Header ——-
DLC:
DLC: Frame 1088 arrived at 15:07:45.7388; frame size is 66 (0042 hex) bytes.
DLC: Destination = DTE
DLC: Source = DCE
DLC:
FRELAY: ——- Frame Relay ——-
FRELAY:
FRELAY: Address word = 20C1
FRELAY: 0010 00.. 1100 .... = DLCI 140
FRELAY: .... ..0. .... = Response
FRELAY: .... 0... = No forward congestion
FRELAY: .... .0.. = No backward congestion
FRELAY: ....0. = Not eligible for discard
FRELAY: ....1 = Not extended address
FRELAY:
ETYPE: Ethertype = 0800 (IP)
ETYPE:
IP: ——- IP Header ——-
IP:
IP: Version = 4, header length = 20 bytes

146

```
IP:  Type of service = 00
IP:      000. .... = routine
IP:      ...0 .... = normal delay
IP:      .... 0... = normal throughput
IP:      .... .0.. = normal reliability
IP:  Total length   = 62 bytes
IP:  Identification = 13340
IP:  Flags          = 4X
IP:      .1.. .... = don't fragment
IP:      ..0. .... = last fragment
IP:  Fragment offset = 0 bytes
IP:  Time to live   = 31 seconds/hops
IP:  Protocol       = 6 (TCP)
IP:  Header checksum = EFAA (correct)
IP:  Source address     = [XXX.YYY.133.72]
IP:  Destination address = [XXX.YYY.81.1]
IP:  No options
IP:
TCP: ——- TCP header ——-
TCP:
TCP: Source port        = 1214
TCP: Destination port   = 21 (FTP)
TCP: Sequence number    = 3276019
TCP: Acknowledgment number = 725589357
TCP: Data offset        = 20 bytes
TCP: Flags              = 18
TCP:          ..0. .... = (No urgent pointer)
TCP:          ...1 .... = Acknowledgment
TCP:          .... 1... = Push
TCP:          .... .0.. = (No reset)
TCP:          .... ..0. = (No SYN)
TCP:          .... ...0 = (No FIN)
TCP: Window             = 8576
TCP: Checksum           = B9EE (correct)
TCP: No TCP options
TCP: [22 byte(s) of data]
TCP:
FTP: ——- FTP data ——-
FTP:
FTP: RETR Otherlinks.html<0D0A>
FTP:
```

- - - - - - - - - - - - - - - Frame 1092 - - - - - - - - - - - - - - - -

```
DLC: ——— DLC Header ———
DLC:
DLC: Frame 1092 arrived at 15:07:45.7940; frame size is 118 (0076 hex) bytes.
DLC: Destination = DCE
DLC: Source = DTE
DLC:
FRELAY: ——— Frame Relay ———
FRELAY:
FRELAY: Address word = 20C1
FRELAY: 0010 00.. 1100 .... = DLCI 140
FRELAY: .... ..0. .... .... = Response
FRELAY: .... .... .... 0... = No forward congestion
FRELAY: .... .... .... .0.. = No backward congestion
FRELAY: .... .... .... ..0. = Not eligible for discard
FRELAY: .... .... .... ...1 = Not extended address
FRELAY:
ETYPE: Ethertype = 0800 (IP)
ETYPE:
IP:  ——— IP Header ———
IP:
IP:  Version = 4, header length = 20 bytes
IP:  Type of service = 00
IP:      000. .... = routine
IP:      ...0 .... = normal delay
IP:      .... 0... = normal throughput
IP:      .... .0.. = normal reliability
IP:  Total length   = 114 bytes
IP:  Identification  = 7442
IP:  Flags        = 0X
IP:      .0.. .... = may fragment
IP:      ..0. .... = last fragment
IP:  Fragment offset = 0 bytes
IP:  Time to live   = 51 seconds/hops
IP:  Protocol     = 6 (TCP)
IP:  Header checksum = 3281 (correct)
IP:  Source address    = [XXX.YYY.81.1]
IP:  Destination address = [XXX.YYY.133.72]
IP:  No options
IP:
TCP: ——— TCP header ———
TCP:
TCP: Source port      = 21 (FTP)
TCP: Destination port   = 1214
```

```
TCP:  Sequence number      = 725589357
TCP:  Acknowledgment number  = 3276041
TCP:  Data offset       = 20 bytes
TCP:  Flags          = 18
TCP:           ..0. .... = (No urgent pointer)
TCP:           ...1 .... = Acknowledgment
TCP:           .... 1... = Push
TCP:           .... .0.. = (No reset)
TCP:           .... ..0. = (No SYN)
TCP:           .... ...0 = (No FIN)
TCP:  Window         = 4096
TCP:  Checksum        = AB7B (correct)
TCP:  No TCP options
TCP:  [74 byte(s) of data]
TCP:
FTP:  ——- FTP data ——-
FTP:
FTP:  150 Opening ASCII mode data connection for Otherlinks.html (1081 bytes).<0D0A>
FTP:


- - - - - - - - - - - - - - - - Frame 1093 - - - - - - - - - - - - - - - - -


DLC:  ——- DLC Header ——-
DLC:
DLC:  Frame 1093 arrived at  15:07:45.8005; frame size is 556 (022C hex) bytes.
DLC:  Destination = DCE
DLC:  Source = DTE
DLC:
FRELAY: ——- Frame Relay ——-
FRELAY:
FRELAY: Address word = 20C1
FRELAY: 0010 00.. 1100 .... = DLCI 140
FRELAY: .... ..0. .... .... = Response
FRELAY: .... .... .... 0... = No forward congestion
FRELAY: .... .... .... .0.. = No backward congestion
FRELAY: .... .... .... ..0. = Not eligible for discard
FRELAY: .... .... .... ...1 = Not extended address
FRELAY:
ETYPE: Ethertype  = 0800 (IP)
ETYPE:
IP:   ——- IP Header ——-
IP:
IP:   Version = 4, header length = 20 bytes
```

```
IP:  Type of service = 00
IP:      000. .... = routine
IP:      ...0 .... = normal delay
IP:      .... 0... = normal throughput
IP:      .... .0.. = normal reliability
IP:  Total length   = 552 bytes
IP:  Identification = 7443
IP:  Flags          = 0X
IP:      .0.. .... = may fragment
IP:      ..0. .... = last fragment
IP:  Fragment offset = 0 bytes
IP:  Time to live   = 51 seconds/hops
IP:  Protocol       = 6 (TCP)
IP:  Header checksum = 30CA (correct)
IP:  Source address    = [XXX.YYY.81.1]
IP:  Destination address = [XXX.YYY.133.72]
IP:  No options
IP:
TCP: ——- TCP header ——-
TCP:
TCP: Source port       = 20 (FTP data)
TCP: Destination port    = 1278
TCP: Sequence number      = 1306944001
TCP: Acknowledgment number  = 4105807
TCP: Data offset        = 20 bytes
TCP: Flags           = 10
TCP:         ..0. .... = (No urgent pointer)
TCP:         ...1 .... = Acknowledgment
TCP:         .... 0... = (No push)
TCP:         .... .0.. = (No reset)
TCP:         .... ..0. = (No SYN)
TCP:         .... ...0 = (No FIN)
TCP: Window          = 4096
TCP: Checksum         = 69D3 (correct)
TCP: No TCP options
TCP: [512 byte(s) of data]
TCP:

- - - - - - - - - - - - - - - Frame 1105 - - - - - - - - - - - - - - - - - -

DLC: ——- DLC Header ——-
DLC:
DLC: Frame 1105 arrived at  15:07:45.9879; frame size is 50 (0032 hex) bytes.
```

```
DLC:  Destination = DTE
DLC:  Source = DCE
DLC:
FRELAY: ——- Frame Relay ——-
FRELAY:
FRELAY: Address word = 20C1
FRELAY:  0010 00..  1100 .... = DLCI 140
FRELAY:  .... ..0.  .... .... = Response
FRELAY:  .... ....  .... 0... = No forward congestion
FRELAY:  .... ....  .... .0.. = No backward congestion
FRELAY:  .... ....  .... ..0. = Not eligible for discard
FRELAY:  .... ....  .... ...1 = Not extended address
FRELAY:
ETYPE: Ethertype  = 0800 (IP)
ETYPE:
IP:  ——- IP Header ——-
IP:
IP:  Version = 4, header length = 20 bytes
IP:  Type of service = 00
IP:      000. .... = routine
IP:      ...0 .... = normal delay
IP:      .... 0... = normal throughput
IP:      .... .0.. = normal reliability
IP:  Total length   = 40 bytes
IP:  Identification = 14108
IP:  Flags        = 4X
IP:      .1.. .... = don't fragment
IP:      ..0. .... = last fragment
IP:  Fragment offset = 0 bytes
IP:  Time to live   = 31 seconds/hops
IP:  Protocol       = 6 (TCP)
IP:  Header checksum = ECC0 (correct)
IP:  Source address     = [XXX.YYY.133.72]
IP:  Destination address = [XXX.YYY.81.1]
IP:  No options
IP:
TCP:  ——- TCP header ——-
TCP:
TCP:  Source port       = 1278
TCP:  Destination port  = 20 (FTP data)
TCP:  Sequence number       = 4105807
TCP:  Acknowledgment number  = 1306944513
TCP:  Data offset       = 20 bytes
```

```
TCP: Flags          = 10
TCP:        ..0. .... = (No urgent pointer)
TCP:        ...1 .... = Acknowledgment
TCP:        .... 0... = (No push)
TCP:        .... .0.. = (No reset)
TCP:        .... ..0. = (No SYN)
TCP:        .... ...0 = (No FIN)
TCP: Window         = 8064
TCP: Checksum       = FAD9 (correct)
TCP: No TCP options
TCP:
```

- - - - - - - - - - - - - - - - Frame 1107 - - - - - - - - - - - - - - - - -

```
DLC: ——— DLC Header ———
DLC:
DLC: Frame 1107 arrived at  15:07:45.9987; frame size is 68 (0044 hex) bytes.
DLC: Destination = DCE
DLC: Source = DTE
DLC:
FRELAY: ——— Frame Relay ———
FRELAY:
FRELAY: Address word = 20C1
FRELAY: 0010 00.. 1100 .... = DLCI 140
FRELAY: .... ..0. .... .... = Response
FRELAY: .... .... .... 0... = No forward congestion
FRELAY: .... .... .... .0.. = No backward congestion
FRELAY: .... .... .... ..0. = Not eligible for discard
FRELAY: .... .... .... ...1 = Not extended address
FRELAY:
ETYPE: Ethertype  = 0800 (IP)
ETYPE:
IP:  ——— IP Header ———
IP:
IP:  Version = 4, header length = 20 bytes
IP:  Type of service = 00
IP:       000. .... = routine
IP:       ...0 .... = normal delay
IP:       .... 0... = normal throughput
IP:       .... .0.. = normal reliability
IP:  Total length   = 64 bytes
IP:  Identification = 7543
IP:  Flags          = 0X
```

```
IP:      .0.. .... = may fragment
IP:      ..0. .... = last fragment
IP:   Fragment offset = 0 bytes
IP:   Time to live   = 51 seconds/hops
IP:   Protocol      = 6 (TCP)
IP:   Header checksum = 324E (correct)
IP:   Source address    = [XXX.YYY.81.1]
IP:   Destination address = [XXX.YYY.133.72]
IP:   No options
IP:
TCP: ——- TCP header ——-
TCP:
TCP:  Source port       = 21 (FTP)
TCP:  Destination port   = 1214
TCP:  Sequence number    = 725589431
TCP:  Acknowledgment number  = 3276041
TCP:  Data offset       = 20 bytes
TCP:  Flags         = 18
TCP:        ..0. .... = (No urgent pointer)
TCP:        ...1 .... = Acknowledgment
TCP:        .... 1... = Push
TCP:        .... .0.. = (No reset)
TCP:        .... ..0. = (No SYN)
TCP:        .... ...0 = (No FIN)
TCP:  Window        = 4096
TCP:  Checksum       = CDC6 (correct)
TCP:  No TCP options
TCP:  [24 byte(s) of data]
TCP:
FTP: ——- FTP data ——-
FTP:
FTP:  226 Transfer complete.<0D0A>
FTP:
```

Trace 3.13.7b. File Transfer Details

In this chapter, we have laid the foundation for internetworking by looking into the many ways that the ARPA Network Interface Layer may be implemented on LANs, MANs, and WANs. In the next chapter, we will study the layer responsible for routing and addressing, the Internet Layer.

3.14 References

[3-1]   Braden, R. "Requirements for Internet Hosts: Communication Layers." RFC 1122, October 1989.

[3-2]   *ARCNET Designer's Handbook,* second edition. Document 61610, Datapoint Corp., 1988.

[3-3]   Provan, D. "Transmitting IP Traffic over ARCNET Networks." RFC 1201, February 1991.

[3-4]   *The Ethernet, A Local Area Network-Data Link Layer and Physical Layer Specification*, version 2.0, November 1982. Published by DEC, Intel, and Xerox, DEC document number AA-K759B-TK.

[3-5]   Institute of Electrical and Electronics Engineers. *Information Technology— Local and Metropolitan Area Networks—Part 3: Carrier sense multiple access with collision detection (CSMA/CD) access method and physical layer specifications.* ISO/IEC 8802-3: 1993 (ANSI/IEEE Std 802.3-1993).

[3-6]   Horning, Charles. "A Standard for the Transmission of IP Datagrams over Ethernet Networks." RFC 894, April 1984.

[3-7]   Postel, J., and J. Reynolds. "A Standard for the Transmission of IP Datagrams over IEEE 802 Networks." RFC 1042, February 1988.

[3-8]   Institute of Electrical and Electronics Engineers. *Information Technology— Telecommunications and information exchange between systems—Local and metropolitan area networks—Specific requirements—Part 2: Logical Link Control.* ISO/IEC 8802-2: 1994 (ANSI/IEEE Std 802.2-1994).

[3-9]   Institute of Electrical and Electronics Engineers. *Standards for Local and Metropolitan Area Networks: Overview and Architecture.* IEEE Std 802-1990, December 1990.

[3-10] Institute of Electrical and Electronics Engineers. *Information Technology —Local and Metropolitan Area Networks—Part 5: token ring access method and physical layer specification.* ISO/IEC 8802-5 (ANSI/IEEE Std 802.5, 1992).

[3-11]   Institute of Electrical and Electronics Engineers. *Information Technology—Telecommunications and information exchange between systems—Local area networks—Media Access Control (MAC) bridges.* ISO/IEC 10038 (ANSI/IEEE Std 802.1D, 1993).

[3-12]   Miller, Mark A. *Troubleshooting Internetworks.* M&T Books, Inc. (New York, NY), 1992.

[3-13]   American National Standards Institute. *Fiber Distributed Data Interface (FDDI)—Token Ring Media Access Control (MAC).* ANSI X3.139 1987.

[3-14]   Katz, D. "A Proposed Standard for the Transmission of IP Datagrams over FDDI Networks." RFC 1188, October 1990.

[3-15]   Sherman, Doug. "Understanding FDDI: Standards, Features, and Applications." *3TECH, the 3Com Technical Journal* (Winter 1992): 18–31.

[3-16]   Romkey, J. "A Nonstandard for Transmission of IP Datagrams Over Serial Lines: SLIP. RFC 1055, June 1988.

[3-17]   Simpson, W., Editor. "The Point-to-Point Protocol (PPP)." RFC 1661, July 1994.

[3-18]   Sklower, K. et. al. "The PPP Multilink Protocol (MP)." RFC 1717, November 1994.

[3-19]   Wells, L., Chair, and A. Bartky, Editor. "Data Link Switching: Switch-to-Switch Protocol AIW DLSw RIG: DLSw Closed Pages, DLSw Standard Version 1.0," RFC 1795, April 1995.

[3-20]   Korb, J. T. "A Standard for the Transmission of IP Datagrams Over Public Data Networks." RFC 877, September 1983.

[3-21]   Schlar, Sherman K. *Inside X.25: A Manager's Guide.* McGraw Hill (New York, NY), 1990.

[3-22]   Bradley, T., et al. "Multiprotocol Interconnect over Frame Relay." RFC 1490, January 1992.

[3-23]   Bradley, T. et al. "Inverse Address Resolution Protocol." RFC 1293, January 1992.

[3-24]   American National Standards Institute. *Integrated Services Digital Network (ISDN)—Architectural Framework and Service Description for Frame-Relaying Bearer Service.* T1.606, 1990.

[3-25]   The Frame Relay Forum may be contacted at:
      Frame Relay Forum North American Office
      303 Vintage Park Drive
      Foster City, CA 94404-1138
      Tel: (415) 578-6980
      Fax: (415) 525-0182
      E-mail: frf@interop.com
      Faxback: (415) 688-4317
      URL: ftp://frame-relay.indiana.edu directory /pub/frame-relay
      URL: http://frame-relay.indiana.edu

[3-26]   Heckart, Christine A. *The Guide to Frame Relay Networking.* Flatiron Publishing, Inc. (New York, NY),1994.

[3-27]   Hume, Sharon, and Alison Seaman. "X.25 and Frame Relay: Packet Switched Technologies for Wide Area Connectivity." *3Tech, the 3Com Technical Journal* (Winter 1992): 33–45.

[3-28]   Institute of Electrical and Electronics Engineers. *Information Technology— Telecommunications and information exchange between systems—Local and metropolitan area networks—Specific requirements—Part 6: Distributed Queue Dual Bus (DQDB) Subnetwork of a Metropolitan Area Network (MAN).* ISO/IEC 8802-6: 1994 (ANSI/IEEE 802.6 1994).

[3-29]   Bell Communications Research, Inc. *Generic System Requirements in Support of Switched Multi-megabit Data Service.* TR-TSV-000772, May 1991.

[3-30]   Piscitello, D., and J. Lawrence. "The Transmission of IP Datagrams over the SMDS Service." RFC 1209, March 1991.

[3-31]   The SMDS Interest Group may be contacted at:
         SMDS Interest Group
         303 Vintage Park Dr.
         Foster City, CA 94404
         (415) 578-6979
         Fax: (415) 525-0182
         E-mail: sig@interop.com
         Faxback: (415) 688-4314
         URL: ftp://ftp.acc.com, directory /pub/protocols/smds

[3-32]   The ATM Forum may be contacted at:
         ATM Forum Worldwide Headquarters
         303 Vintage Park Dr.
         Foster City CA 94404
         Tel: (415) 578-6860
         Fax: (415) 525-0182
         E-mail: info@atmforum.com
         Faxback: (415) 688-4318
         URL: http://www.atmforum.com

[3-33]   The ATM Forum. ATM User-Network Interface Specification Version 3.1, September 1994.

[3-34]   Miller, Mark A. *Analyzing Broadband Networks*. M&T Books, Inc. (New York, NY), 1994.

[3-35]   The ATM Forum. LAN Emulation 1.0 Specification, 1995.

[3-36]   Laubach, M. "Classical IP and ARP over ATM." RFC 1577, January 1994.

[3-37]   Miller, Mark A. *LAN Troubleshooting Handbook*, second edition. M&T Books, Inc., (New York, NY), 1993.

[3-38]   Sidhu, Gursharan, et al. *Inside AppleTalk*, second edition. Addison-Wesley Publishing Company, Inc. (New York, NY), 1990.

CHAPTER 4

Troubleshooting the Internet Connection

In the previous chapter, we discussed the options for the ARPA Network Interface (or Local Network) Layer, ranging from ATM to SMDS. In this chapter, we move up one layer in the ARPA architectural model and explore the Internet Layer. This layer is analogous to the OSI Network Layer and is responsible for delivering a package of data (known as a *datagram*) from its source to its destination via the internetwork. Note that this internetwork may include the Internet, a corporate internet, or any of the LAN and WAN transmission channels that we studied in Chapter 3.

One of the principal functions of the Network Interface Layer is *routing*. Routing gets a data packet from one host to another via the internetwork. Several steps occur during the routing process. First, each device must have a Logical address that uniquely identifies it within the internetwork. This internet address is independent of any Hardware or Physical address, such as the 48-bit Data Link Layer address of an Ethernet or token ring workstation. A mechanism is also necessary to associate the Logical address within the datagram with the Physical address within the LAN, MAN, or WAN frame. The Address Resolution Protocol (ARP) and the Reverse Address Resolution Protocol (RARP) handle this translation.

Second, you may set up the Logical address to identify individual hosts and/or subnetworks (such as LANs) within a network. Third, you must distribute intelligent devices, known as *routers*, throughout the internetwork to guide the packets to their destination. Routers decide on the appropriate path for the packets to take by comparing address information from within the packet with information they have accumulated about the internetwork topology. The Routing Information Protocol (RIP) and the Open Shortest Path First (OSPF) protocol are two of the interior gateway protocols (IGP) that routers use to communicate among themselves. Reference [4-1] is an excellent overview of internetworking hardware; [4-2] discusses routing principles in general, and [4-3] studies IP routing in particular.

Finally, the Internet Control Message Protocol (ICMP) establishes a mechanism for performance feedback and communication within the internetwork. ICMP permits tests, diagnostic procedures, and flow control among various devices. Gerald Mendes' "Top 10 Routing Tips" [4-4] explores the optimization of router-based internetworks. We'll begin our study of the Internet Layer by investigating the current version of the Internet Protocol, IPv4. In Chapter 8 we will study the next-generation Internet Protocol, IPv6.

4.1 Internet Protocol

The Internet Protocol (IP) was developed to "provide the functions necessary to deliver a package of bits (an internet datagram) from a source to a destination over an interconnected system of networks" [4-5]. IP is primarily concerned with delivery of the datagram. Equally important, however, are the issues that IP does not address, such as the end-to-end reliable delivery of data or the sequential delivery of data. IP leaves those issues for the Host-to-Host Layer and the implementations of TCP and UDP that reside there. (As mentioned previously, a new version of IP, called IP Version 6 (IPv6) or IP Next Generation (IPng), has been developed and is being implemented. In this text, we will refer to the older version (IP Version 4 or IPv4) as just IP, and the newer version as IPv6.)

The term datagram refers to a package of data transmitted over a connectionless network. *Connectionless* means that no connection between source and destination is established prior to data transmission. Datagram transmission is analogous to mailing a letter. With both a letter and a datagram, you write a Source and Destination address on the envelope, place the information inside, and drop the package into a mailbox for pickup. But while the post office uses blue or red mailboxes, the Internet uses your network node as the pickup point.

Another type of data transmission is a *virtual circuit connection*, which uses a connection-oriented network. A virtual circuit is analogous to a telephone call, where the Destination address is contacted and a path defined through the network prior to transmitting data. IP is an example of a datagram-based protocol, TCP of a virtual circuit-based protocol.

In the process of delivering datagrams, IP must deal with *addressing* and *fragmentation*. The address assures that the datagram arrives at the correct destination, whether it's across town or across the world. Notice from Figure 4-1a that, unlike the Network Interface Layer, the Internet Layer must be implemented with a consistent

160

protocol, such as the Internet Protocol, on an end-to-end basis for addressing consistency. Figure 4-1b illustrates the protocols implemented at the Internet Layer.

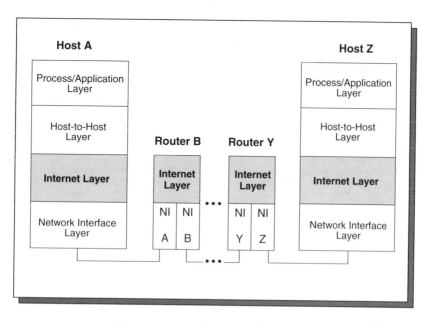

Figure 4-1a. The Internet Connection

ARPA Layer	Protocol Implementation						OSI Layer
Process / Application	File Transfer	Electronic Mail	Terminal Emulation	File Transfer	Client / Server	Network Management	Application
	File Transfer Protocol (FTP)	Simple Mail Transfer Protocol (SMTP)	TELNET Protocol	Trivial File Transfer Protocol (TFTP)	Sun Microsystems Network File System Protocols (NFS)	Simple Network Management Protocol (SNMP)	Presentation
	MIL-STD-1780 RFC 959	MIL-STD-1781 RFC 821	MIL-STD-1782 RFC 854	RFC 783	RFCs 1014, 1057, and 1094	RFC 1157	Session
Host-to-Host	Transmission Control Protocol (TCP) MIL-STD-1778 RFC 793			User Datagram Protocol (UDP) RFC 768			Transport
Internet	Address Resolution ARP RFC 826 RARP RFC 903		Internet Protocol (IP) MIL-STD-1777 RFC 791		Internet Control Message Protocol (ICMP) RFC 792		Network
Network Interface	Network Interface Cards: Ethernet, Token Ring, ARCNET, MAN and WAN RFC 894, RFC 1042, RFC 1201 and others						Data Link
	Transmission Media: Twisted Pair, Coax, Fiber Optics, Wireless Media, etc.						Physical

Figure 4-1b. ARPA Internet Layer Protocols

Fragmentation is necessary because the LANs and WANs that any datagram may traverse can have differing frame sizes, and the IP datagram must always fit within the frame, as shown in Figure 4-1c. (We saw this explicitly in the frame structures illustrated in Chapter 3. For example, an ARCNET frame can accommodate only up to 504 octets of data, while FDDI carries up to 4,470 octets.) Specific fields within the IP header handle the addressing and fragmentation functions (see Figure 4-2). Note from the figure that each horizontal group of bits (called a word) is 32 bits wide.

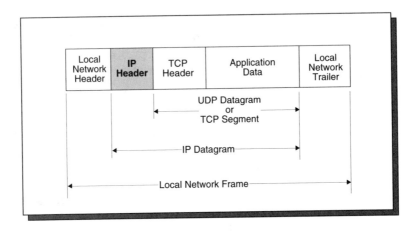

Figure 4-1c. The Internet Transmission Frame and IP Header Position

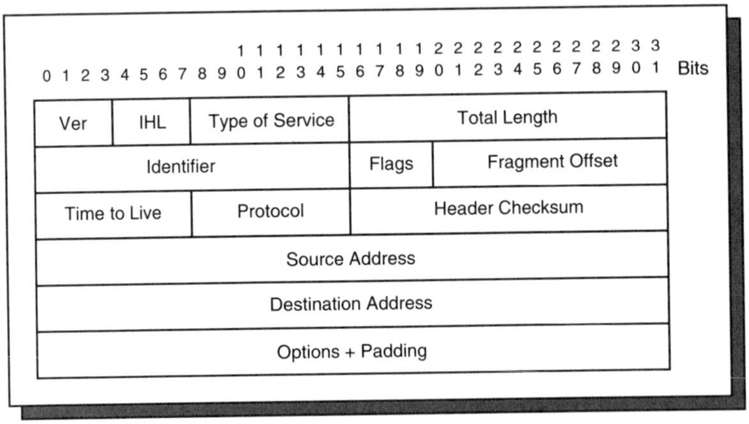

Figure 4-2. Internet Protocol (IPv4) Header Format

The IP header contains a minimum of 20 octets of control information. Version (4 bits) defines the current version of the IP protocol and should equal 4. Internet Header Length (IHL, 4 bits) measures the length of the IP header in 32-bit words. (The minimum value would be five 32-bit words, or 20 octets.) The IHL also provides a measurement (or offset) where the higher-layer information, such as the TCP header, begins within that datagram. The Type of Service (8 bits) indicates the quality of service requested for the datagram. Values include:

Bits 0-2:	Precedence (or relative importance of this datagram)
	111 - Network Control
	110 - Internetwork Control
	101 - CRITIC/ECP
	100 - Flash Override
	011 - Flash
	010 - Immediate
	001 - Priority
	000 - Routine
Bit 3:	Delay, 0=Normal Delay, 1=Low Delay
Bit 4:	Throughput, 0=Normal Throughput, 1=High Throughput
Bit 5:	Reliability, 0=Normal Reliability, 1=High Reliability
Bits 6-7:	Reserved for future use (set to 0)

The Total Length field (16 bits) measures the length, in octets, of the IP datagram (IP header plus higher-layer information). The 16-bit field allows for a datagram of up to 65,535 octets, although all hosts must be able to handle datagrams of at least 576 octets.

The next 32-bit word contains three fields that deal with datagram fragmentation/reassembly. Recall that the IP datagram may be up to 65,535 octets long. What happens if the endpoint of a WAN that handles such a datagram is attached to an IEEE 802.3 LAN with a maximum data field size of 1,500 octets? IP fragments the large IP datagram into smaller pieces (i.e., fragments) that will fit. The Destination node reassembles all the fragments (sort of the antithesis of Humpty Dumpty). The sender assigns the Identification field (16 bits) to help reassemble the fragments into the datagram. Three flags indicate how the fragmentation process will be handled:

Bit 0:	Reserved (set to 0)
Bit 1:	(DF) 0=May fragment, 1-Don't fragment
Bit 2:	(MF) 0=Last fragment, 1-More fragments

The last field in this word is a 13-bit fragment offset, which indicates where a fragment belongs in the complete message. This offset is measured in 64-bit units. The case study in Section 4.8.2 will illustrate the fragmentation process.

The next word in the IP header contains a Time-to-Live (TTL) measurement, which is the maximum amount of time the datagram can live within the internet. When TTL = 0, the datagram is destroyed. This field is a failsafe measure, preventing mis-addressed datagrams from wandering the internet forever. TTL may be measured in either router hops or seconds. If the measurement is in seconds, the maximum is 255 seconds, or 4.25 minutes (a long time to be lost in today's high-speed internetworks). The Assigned Numbers document (currently RFC 1700 [4-6]) specifies a default TTL = 64.

The Protocol field (8 bits) following the IP header identifies the higher-layer protocol in use. Examples include:

Decimal	Keyword	Description
1	ICMP	Internet Control Message Protocol
6	TCP	Transmission Control Protocol
17	UDP	User Datagram Protocol

The Assigned Numbers document (currently RFC 1700 [4-6]) and Appendix F provide a more detailed listing of the protocols defined. A 16-bit header checksum completes the third 32-bit word.

The fourth and fifth words of the IP header contain the Source and Destination addresses, respectively. Recall that we discussed Hardware addresses for the ARPA Network Interface Layer (or OSI Data Link Layer) in Chapter 3. The addresses within the IP header are the Internet Layer (or OSI Network Layer) addresses. The Internet address is a Logical address that gets the IP datagram through the Internet to the correct host and network (LAN, MAN, or WAN). Reference [4-7] is an excellent analysis of addressing schemes used within different LAN and WAN topologies, including X.25, IEEE 802, and IP. In the next section we will study IP addressing in detail.

4.2 Internetwork Addressing

Each 32-bit IP address is divided into Host ID and Network ID sections and may take one of five formats ranging from Class A to Class E, as shown in Figure 4-3. The formats differ in the number of bits they allocate to the Host IDs and Network IDs and are identified by the first 3 bits.

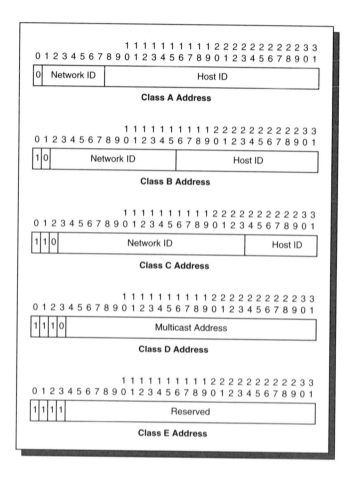

Figure 4-3. IPv4 Address Formats

Class A addresses are designed for very large networks with many hosts. They are identified by Bit 0 = 0. Bits 1 through 7 identify the network, and Bits 8 through 31 identify the host. With a 7-bit Network ID, only 128 Class A network addresses are available. Of these, addresses 0 and 127 are reserved [4-8].

The majority of organizations that have distributed processing systems including LANs and hosts use Class B addresses. Class B addresses are identified with the first 2 bits having a value of 10 (binary). The next 14 bits identify the network. The remaining 16 bits identify the host. A total of 16,384 Class B network addresses are possible; however, addresses 0 and 16,383 are reserved.

Class C addresses are generally used for smaller networks, such as LANs. They begin with a binary 110. The next 21 bits identify the network. The remaining 8 bits identify the host. A total of 2,097,152 Class C network addresses are possible, with addresses 0 and 2,097,151 reserved.

Class D addresses begin with a binary 1110 and are intended for multicasting. Class E addresses begin with a binary 1111 and are reserved for future use.

All IP addresses are written in dotted decimal notation, in which each octet is assigned a decimal number from 0 to 255. For example, network [10.55.31.84] is represented in binary as 00001010 00110111 00011111 1010100. The first bit (0) indicates a Class A address, the next 7 bits (0001010) represent the Network ID (decimal 10), and the last 24 bits (00110111 00011111 1010100) represent the Host ID.

Class A addresses begin with 1-127, Class B with 128-191, Class C with 192-223, and Class D with 224-254. Thus, an address of [150.100.200.5] is easily identified as a Class B address.

As discussed above, the IP addresses are divided into two fields that identify a network and a host. A central authority assigns the Network ID and the local network administrator assigns the Host ID. Routers send packets to a particular network using the Network ID, and that network completes the delivery to the host. If an organization has two networks, it could request two Network ID assignments from the central authority. But this would cause the routing tables within hosts and routers to expand considerably. The popularity of LANs in the mid-1980s, therefore, inspired the Internet community to revise the IP address structure. The new structure allows for an additional field to identify a sub-network within an assigned Network ID. Thus the [Network, Host] address format is replaced with the [Network, Subnetwork, Host] format. The space for the Subnetwork field comes from reducing the Host field. The central authority assigns the Network ID, and the individual organization assigns the Subnetwork IDs and the Host IDs on each subnetwork.

The Address Mask differentiates between various subnetworks. A Subnet Mask is a 32-bit number that has ones in the Network ID and Subnetwork ID fields and zeros in the Host ID field. The router or the host implements a mathematical function that performs a logical AND function between the Subnet Mask and a particular IP address to determine whether a datagram can be delivered on the same subnet, or whether it must go through an IP router to another subnet.

A host or router that needs to make a routing decision uses the Subnet Mask for assistance and the logical AND function to arrive at its conclusion. For example, suppose the Destination address is D and my address is M. Further suppose that the Subnet Mask is [255.255.255.0]. Two calculations are made: Subnet Mask AND Address D, plus Subnet Mask AND Address M. The result of the AND function strips off the host portion of the address, leaving only the network and subnet portions. (Recall that the Host ID field is filled with zeros and that any number AND zero is still zero.) From the calculations, we have two results, each representing a Network ID and a Subnet ID. The two results are then compared and used to make a routing decision. When the two results are identical, Addresses M and D are on the same subnetwork. If Addresses M and D are not equal, the two addresses are on different subnetworks, and the datagram must go to a router for delivery.

If the host doesn't know which Subnet Mask to use, it uses ICMP to discover the right one. The host broadcasts an ICMP Address Mask Request message and waits for an ICMP Address Mask Reply from a neighboring router. If an Address Mask is used improperly and a datagram is sent to a router erroneously, the router that identifies the misdirected packet returns an ICMP Redirect message. We will look at this scenario in Section 4.8.5.

RFC 950, "Internet Standard Subnetting Procedure" [4-9], was written to cover subnet-related issues. Mike Stone's "Guide to TCP/IP Network Addressing" [4-10] and Steve Steinke's "IP Addresses and Subnet Masks" [4-11] discuss the topic from an implementation perspective. RFC 1118, "The Hitchhiker's Guide to the Internet" [4-12], discusses UNIX-related subnetting issues.

Several addresses are reserved to identify special purposes [4-6, page 4], [4-13, Sections 4.2.2.11 and 4.2.3.1]:

Address	Interpretation
[Net = 0, Host = 0]	This host on this network
[Net = 0, Host = H]	Specific Host H on this network (Source address only)
[Net = all ones, Host = all ones]	Limited broadcast (within the source's subnetwork)
[Net = N, Host = all ones]	Directed broadcast to network (Destination address only)
[Net = N, Sub = all ones, Host = all ones]	Directed broadcast to all subnets on Network N (Destination address only)
[Net = N, Sub = S, Host = all ones]	Directed broadcast to all hosts on Subnet S, Network N (Destination address only)
[Net = 127, Host = any]	Internal host loopback address
The following two numbers are used for network numbers, but not IP addresses:	
[Net = N, Host = 0]	Network N, No Host
[Net = N, Sub = S, Host = 0]:	Subnet S, No Host
Abbreviations: Sub = Subnet ID Host = Host ID	Net = Network ID

RFC 1118 [4-12] issues two cautions about IP addresses. First, it notes that BSD 4.2 UNIX systems require additional software for subnetting; BSD 4.3 systems do not. Second, some machines use an IP address of all zeros to specify a broadcast, instead of the more common all ones. BSD 4.3 requires the system administrator to choose the broadcast address. Use caution, since many problems, such as broadcast storms, can result when the broadcast address is not implemented consistently over the network. RFC 1812 [4-13] also discusses cautions in this area.

4.3 Address Translation

In the last two sections, we looked at the differences between the Internet address, used by IP, and the Local address, used by the LAN or WAN hardware. We observed that the IP address was a 32-bit Logical address, but that the Physical address depends on the hardware. For example, ARCNET has an 8-bit and Ethernet a 48-bit Hardware address. Since we may know one of these addresses but not the other, protocols are provided to map the Logical and Physical addresses to each other. Since two translations may be necessary (Logical to Physical and Physical to Logical), two protocols have been developed. The Address Resolution Protocol (ARP) described in RFC 826 [4-14] translates from an IP address to a Hardware address. The Reverse Address Resolution Protocol (RARP) detailed in RFC 903 [4-15] does the opposite, as its name implies. Let's look at these protocols separately.

4.3.1 Address Resolution Protocol

Let's assume that a device, Host X, on an Ethernet wishes to deliver a datagram to another device on the same Ethernet, Host Y. Host X knows Host Y's Destination Protocol (IP) address, but does not know its Hardware (Ethernet) address. It would, therefore, broadcast an ARP packet within an Ethernet frame to determine Host Y's Hardware address. The ARP packet is shown in Figure 4-4a. The packet consists of 28 octets, primarily addresses, which are contained within the Data field of a LAN frame. The sender broadcasts an ARP packet within a LAN frame requesting the information that it lacks. The device that recognizes its own Protocol address responds with the sought-for Hardware address. The individual fields of the ARP message show how the protocol operates.

Figure 4-4a. Address Resolution Protocol (ARP) and Reverse Address Resolution Protocol (RARP) Packet Formats

The first field, Hardware (2 octets), defines the type of hardware in use. Current values are listed in the Assigned Numbers document (currently RFC 1700). Examples include

Hardware = 1 (Ethernet), 6 (IEEE 802 Networks), 7 (ARCNET), 11 (LocalTalk), 14 (SMDS), 15 (Frame Relay), and 16 (ATM). The second field, Protocol (2 octets), identifies the Protocol address in use. For example, protocol = 0800H would identify IP addresses.

The second word allows the ARP packet to be used with a variety of address structures rather than restricting its use to only two, such as IP (32 bits) and IEEE 802 (48 bits). This makes the protocol more adaptive. The Hardware Length (HLEN), 1 octet, and Protocol Length (PLEN), 1 octet, specify the lengths, in octets, of the addresses to be used. Figure 4-4a represents the most common scenario. The Hardware Address (HA) requires 6 octets or 48 bits (HLEN = 6); the Protocol Address (PA) needs 4 octets or 32 bits (PLEN = 4). The Operation field (2 octets) defines an ARP Request = 1 and ARP Reply = 2.

The next fields contain the addresses themselves. With an ARP Request message, the target Hardware address field is unknown and is sent filled with zeros. The ARP Reply packet from the target host will insert the requested address in that field. When it receives the ARP Reply, the originating station records that information in a table, called the ARP cache. The ARP cache reduces internetwork traffic asking to resolve the same address on multiple occasions. Routers' ARP caches have a finite lifetime, which prevents the table from growing too large.

4.3.2 Reverse Address Resolution Protocol

Most hosts on networks are smart enough to remember their own Hardware and Protocol addresses. But diskless workstations rely on the server for much of their intelligence. Such a workstation would know its Hardware address, which is coded into ROM, but the server might assign a Protocol address of which the workstation was unaware. The Reverse Address Resolution Protocol (RARP) can discover an unknown Protocol address given a known Hardware address and a RARP server to supply the answer.

The process of determining an unknown Protocol address is similar to that of finding an unknown Hardware address. The same packet structure is used (review Figure 4-4a) with only minor modifications to the field values. The Operation field adds two new values: 3 (RARP Request) and 4 (RARP Reply). When the RARP Request is made, the Sender Hardware address, Sender Protocol address, and Target Hardware address are transmitted. The RARP Reply contains the sought-after Target Protocol address.

4.3.3 Inverse ARP

ARP allows a Protocol address, such as an IP address, to be associated with a Hardware address, such as Ethernet. In some cases, however, a virtual address identifies the endpoint of the connection, replacing the Hardware address. Two examples of this are frame relay and ATM, where a virtual circuit address identifies the connection endpoint. In the case of frame relay, a permanent or switched virtual circuit (PVC or SVC) is identified by a Data Link Connection Identifier (DLCI) as we studied in Section 3.9. When a new PVC or SVC is provisioned (with its associated DLCI), the end user devices know of the PVC's or SVC's existence, but not the IP address associated with that circuit. For these applications, it is necessary to provide a mechanism to discover the Protocol address associated with that particular virtual circuit. The Inverse Address Resolution Protocol (InARP), defined in RFC 1293 [4-16], provides the details of these protocol operations.

Inverse ARP is an extension to ARP, and therefore uses the same packet format (review Figure 4-4a). The Hardware address field length may be different from the LAN case; for example, frame relay would use a Hardware address length of 2, 3, or 4 octets. Two new operation codes are defined; InARP Request and InArp Reply.

InARP operates in a similar fashion to ARP, with the exception that requests are not broadcast, since the Hardware address (such as a DLCI) of the destination station is already known. Instead, the requesting station fills in the sending and target Hardware addresses plus the sending Protocol address, and sends the InARP Request to the distant station which fills in the missing target Protocol address. For further details on InARP, consult RFC 1293.

4.3.4 ATMARP

Another extension to ARP is provided for IP traffic over ATM-based internetworks, and is defined in RFC 1577, "Classical IP and ARP over ATM" [4-17]. The ATMARP protocol is based upon both ARP (RFC 826) and Inverse ARP (RFC 1293), discussed above. ATMARP provides a mechanism for associating IP and ATM addresses for communication within a Logical IP Subnetwork, or LIS, as we discussed in Section 3.11.2.

The ATMARP packet format expands on the ARP packet format, and is illustrated in Figure 4-4b. The first two fields, Hardware Type (2 octets) and Protocol Type (2 octets), are used identically to the original ARP usage. The Hardware address assigned to the ATM Forum address family is 19 decimal (0013H); however, the Protocol Address field value for IP remains the same (0600H). Four new 1-octet fields define the type and length of the Sender ATM number (SHTL), the Sender ATM subaddress (SSTL), the Target ATM number (THTL), and the Target ATM subaddress (TSTL). The Operation Code (2 octets) defines five operation codes:

Operation Code	Operation
1	ARP Request
2	ARP Reply
8	InARP Request
9	InARP Reply
10	ARP NAK

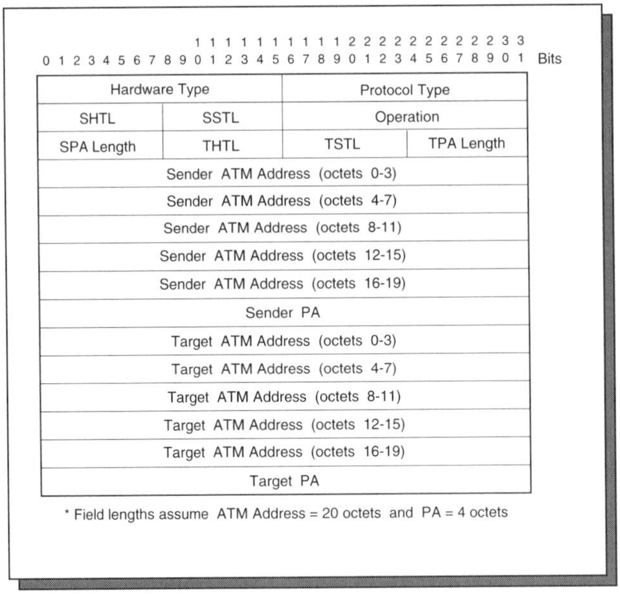

Figure 4-4b. ATM Address Resolution Protocol (ATMARP) and
Inverse ATM Address Resolution Protocol (InATMARP) Packet Formats

172

Two 1-octet fields are also included in the third word which specify the Sender Protocol Address (SPA) length and the Target Protocol Address (TPA) length. The four addresses, Sender ATM, Sender Protocol, Target ATM, and Target Protocol, complete the packet. (Note that the format shown in Figure 4-4b assumes ATM address lengths of 20 octets and a Protocol Address length of 4 octets.) For further details on ATMARP and InATMARP, consult RFC 1577.

4.3.5 Proxy ARP

When IP is run on a LAN, special attention to the addressing scheme is required. In most cases, it is not desirable for each segment to have a distinct network number; instead, subnetting a single network number is the preferred approach for distinguishing individual LAN segments. The details of this subnetted configuration need not be relevant to those outside the LAN, as long as a packet destined for a host on a particular LAN segment can be delivered correctly. RFC 925, "Multi-LAN Address Resolution" [4-18], addresses these issues; it defines a variation on the ARP process, known as Proxy ARP or promiscuous ARP, to handle these operations.

A *proxy* is a person or device that acts on behalf of another person or device. Suppose that two networks use the same IP network address, and that we call these two networks A and B. Router R, running ARP, connects these two networks. Router R will become the proxy device. Now suppose that a host on Network A wishes to communicate with another host on Network B, but doesn't know its Hardware address. The host on Network A would broadcast an ARP Request seeking the Hardware address of the remote host. Router R would intercept the request and reply with HA = R, which would be stored in the host's ARP cache. Subsequent communication between the two hosts would go via R, with Router R using its own lookup table to forward the packet to Network B. In effect, Proxy ARP allows the router to respond to an ARP request that came from one of its attached networks with the information concerning another one of its attached networks. In essence, the router deceives the originating host into thinking that it (i.e. the router) is the correct destination Hardware address. In this way, the outside world is insulated from that LAN's address resolution operation. Black [4-19] and Comer [4-20] discuss the advantages and disadvantages of Proxy ARP in further detail.

4.3.6 Bootstrap Protocol

The Bootstrap Protocol (BOOTP), described in RFC 951 [4-21], is an alternative to ARP/RARP. The protocol gets it name from the fact that it is meant to be contained within a bootstrap ROM. BOOTP is designed for diskless clients that need information from a server, such as their own IP address, the server's IP address, or the name of a file (i.e., the boot file) to be loaded into memory and then executed. The client broadcasts a Boot Request packet, which is answered by a Boot Reply packet from the server.

One of the significant differences between ARP/RARP and BOOTP is the layer of protocol they address. ARP/RARP packets are contained within local network frames and are transmitted on the local network. BOOTP packets are contained within IP datagrams, contain a UDP header, and are transmitted on the internetwork. The designated server can, therefore, be several router hops away from the client. Two reserved port numbers are used: port 67 for the BOOTP Server and port 68 for the BOOTP Client.

The individual fields of the BOOTP packet are shown in Figure 4-5. The OpCode (Op, 1 octet) specifies a BOOTREQUEST (Op = 1) or BOOTREPLY (Op = 2). Hardware address Type (Htype, 1 octet) and Hardware address Length (Hlen, 1 octet) are similar to those fields in the ARP/RARP packet. The Hops field (1 octet) is optional for use in cross-router booting. The Transaction ID (4 octets) correlates the boot requests and responses. The Seconds field (2 octets) allows the client to count the elapsed time since it started the bootup sequence. Two unused octets complete the third word of the BOOTP packet.

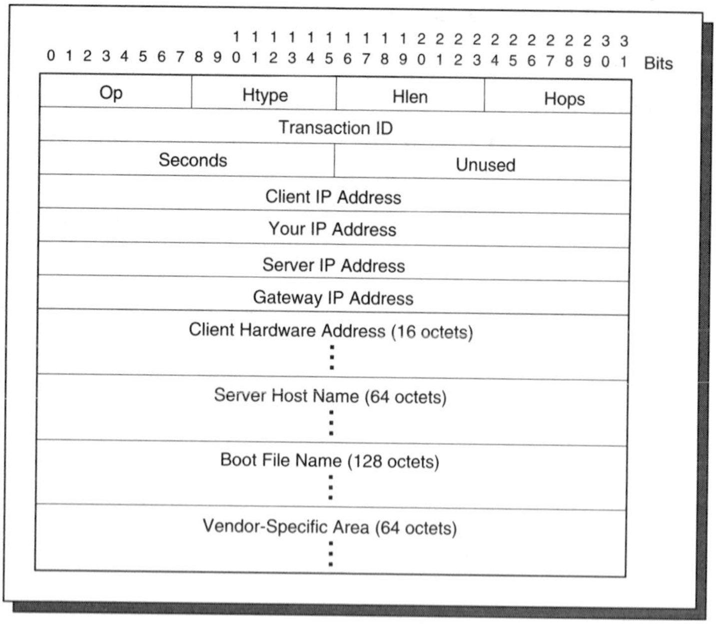

```
                        1 1 1 1 1 1 1 1 1 1 2 2 2 2 2 2 2 2 2 2 3 3
     0 1 2 3 4 5 6 7 8 9 0 1 2 3 4 5 6 7 8 9 0 1 2 3 4 5 6 7 8 9 0 1   Bits
```

Op	Htype	Hlen	Hops

Transaction ID

Seconds	Unused

Client IP Address
Your IP Address
Server IP Address
Gateway IP Address
Client Hardware Address (16 octets)
Server Host Name (64 octets)
Boot File Name (128 octets)
Vendor-Specific Area (64 octets)

Figure 4-5. Bootstrap Protocol (BOOTP) Packet Format

The next four words designate the various IP addresses. The client states the addresses it knows and the server fills in the rest. These include the Client IP address (filled in by client), Your IP address (filled in by the server if the client does not know its own address), Server IP address, and Gateway router IP address. The Client HA (16 octets), Boot File Name (128 octets), and a Vendor-Specific Area (64 octets), containing information to be sent from the server to the client, complete the packet. RFC 1497 discusses implementation of that vendor-specific field. In summary, BOOTP improves on the ARP concept by allowing the address resolution process to occur across routers. Although it uses IP/UDP, it is small enough to fit within a bootstrap ROM on the client workstation.

RFC 1532 [4-22] provides clarifications and extensions to BOOTP, such as its use with IEEE 802.5 token ring networks. RFC 1533 [4-23] discusses extensions to BOOTP, plus a related protocol, the Dynamic Host Configuration Protocol, which will be discussed in further detail in the next section. Jeffrey Mogul's "Booting Diskless Hosts: The BOOTP Protocol" [4-24] describes the client/server interaction in further detail.

4.3.7 Dynamic Host Configuration Protocol

The Dynamic Host Configuration Protocol (DHCP) provides a superset of BOOTP capabilities to include additional configuration options, plus automatic allocation of reusable network addresses. DHCP defines a mechanism to transmit configuration parameters to hosts using the ARPA protocol suite, with a message format based upon the format of BOOTP. DHCP is defined in RFC 1531 [4-25], and the interoperation between DHCP and BOOTP is discussed in RFC 1534 [4-26].

DHCP is built on a client-server model in which the designated DHCP server allocates network addresses and delivers configuration information to the requesting client (another host). Examples of configuration information include: a default TTL, IP address, subnet mask, maximum transmission unit (MTU), list of default routers, list of static routes, ARP cache timeouts, and others. Two components are therefore included in DHCP: a mechanism for allocating network addresses to clients, and a protocol for delivering these host-specific configuration parameters to a dynamically configured host.

Seven types of DHCP messages are defined in RFC 1531:

DHCPDISCOVER: client broadcast to locate available servers.

DHCPOFFER: server to client response to the DHCPDISCOVER message, with an offer of configuration parameters.

DHCPREQUEST: client broadcast to servers requesting offered parameters from one server and implicitly declining offers from all others.

DHCPACK: server to client with configuration parameters, including committed network address.

DHCPNAK: server to client refusing request for configuration parameters.

DHCPDECLINE: client to server indicating configuration parameters invalid.

DHCPRELEASE: client to server relinquishing network address and cancelling remaining lease.

The DHCP message format is based upon the BOOTP message format and is illustrated in Figure 4-6. The first word contains four 1-octet fields: Op, Htype, Hlen, and Hops. The Op Code (Op) defines the message type, with 1 = BOOTREQUEST and 2 = BOOTREPLY. The Hardware Type (Htype) and Hardware Address Length

(Hlen) fields define the hardware type and address, respectively, similar to the fields used in the ARP/RARP messages. The Hops field is optionally used by relay-agents when booting via a relay-agent. A client would set the Hops field to zero. The Transaction ID (also called XID) is a 32-bit random number chosen by the client, which is used by the client and the server to associate messages and responses between a client and a server. The Seconds field (2 octets) is filled in by the client, noting the seconds elapsed since the client started to boot. The Flags field (2 octets) contains a one-bit flag, called the broadcast flag, with all other bits set to zero. Details of the use of this flag are discussed in RFC 1531.

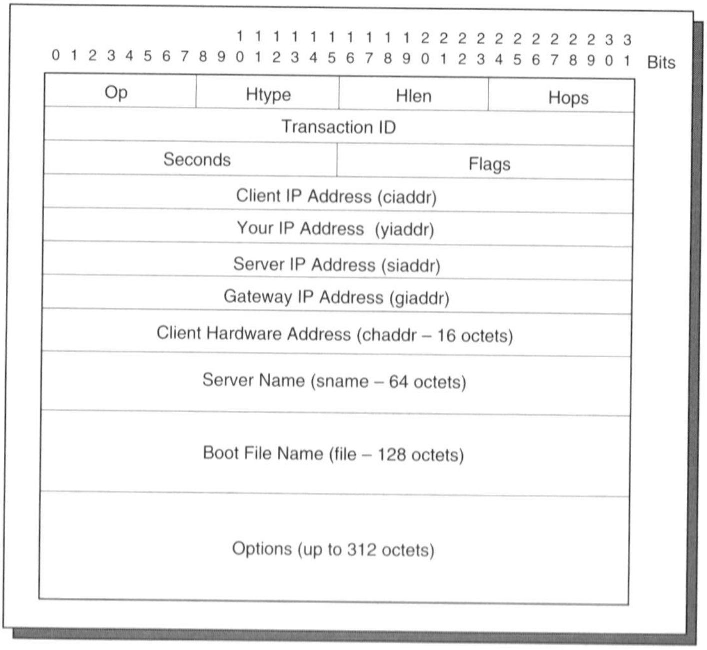

0 1 2 3 4 5 6 7	8 9 0 1 2 3 4 5	6 7 8 9 0 1 2 3	4 5 6 7 8 9 0 1 Bits
Op	Htype	Hlen	Hops
Transaction ID			
Seconds		Flags	
Client IP Address (ciaddr)			
Your IP Address (yiaddr)			
Server IP Address (siaddr)			
Gateway IP Address (giaddr)			
Client Hardware Address (chaddr – 16 octets)			
Server Name (sname – 64 octets)			
Boot File Name (file – 128 octets)			
Options (up to 312 octets)			

Figure 4-6. Dynamic Host Configuration Protocol (DHCP) Message Format

The Client IP address field (4 octets) is set by the client, with its known address or all zeros. The Your IP address field (4 octets) is set by the server if the Client IP address field contains all zeros. The Server IP address field (4 octets) is set by the server, and the Gateway (or router) IP address is set by the relay agent. The Client Hardware Address (16 octets) is set by the client. The Server Name is an optional server host name. The Boot File Name (128 octets) is used by the server to return a fully qualified directory path name to the client. Finally, the Options field (312 octets) may contain DHCP options as defined in RFC 1533.

For further details on DHCP, study RFC 1531 or J. Allard's excellent article entitled "DHCP—TCP/IP Network Configuration Made Easy" [4-27].

4.4 Datagram Routing

So far, we've learned that hosts transmit datagrams and use a 32-bit address to identify the source and destination of the datagram. The host drops the datagram into the internetwork, and the datagram somehow finds its way to its destination. That "somehow" is the work of routers, which examine the Destination address, compare that address with their internal routing tables, and send the datagram on the correct outgoing communication circuit.

Router operation involves several processes [4-2, page 5]. First, the router creates a routing table to gather information from other routers about the optimum path for each packet. This table may be static (i.e., manually built) and fixed for all network conditions, or dynamic (i.e., constructed by the router according to the current topology and conditions). Dynamic routing is considered the better technique because it adapts to changing network conditions. The router uses a metric, or measurement, of the shortest distance between two endpoints to help determine the optimum path. It determines the metric using a number of factors, including the shortest distance, or least cost path, to the destination. The router plugs the metric into one of two algorithms to make a final decision on the correct path. A Distance Vector algorithm makes its choice based upon the distance to a remote node. A Link State algorithm also includes information about the status of the various links connecting the nodes and the topology of the network.

The various routers within the network use the Distance Vector or Link State algorithms to inform each other of their current status. Because routers use them for intranetwork communication, the protocols that make use of these algorithms are referred to as Interior Gateway Protocols (IGPs). The Routing Information Protocol (RIP) is an IGP based upon a Distance Vector algorithm. The Open Shortest Path First (OSPF) protocol is an IGP based on a Link State algorithm. We'll look at these two algorithms separately in the following sections. If one network wishes to communicate routing to another network, it uses an Exterior Gateway Protocol (EGP). An EGP is described in RFC 904 [4-28]; an example of an EGP is the Border Gateway Protocol (BGP), described in RFC 1105. An excellent article on routing is Callon's "Routing in an Internetwork Environment" [4-29].

4.4.1 Routing Information Protocol

The Routing Information Protocol, described in RFC 1058 [4-30], is used for inter-router (or inter-gateway) communications. RIP is based on a Distance Vector algorithm, sometimes referred to as a Ford-Fulkerson algorithm after its developers L. R. Ford, Jr. and D. R. Fulkerson. A Distance Vector algorithm is one in which the routers periodically exchange information from their routing tables. The routing decision is based on the best path between two devices, which is often the path with the fewest hops or router transversals. The Internet standard warns that many LAN operating systems have their own RIP implementations. Therefore, it is important to adhere to the Internet standard to alleviate interoperability problems.

RFC 1058 acknowledges several limitations to RIP. RIP allows a path length of 15 hops, which may be insufficient for large internetworks. Routing loops are possible for internetworks containing hundreds of networks, because of the time required to transmit updated routing table information. Finally, the metrics used to choose the routing path are fixed and do not allow for dynamic conditions, such as a measured delay or a variable traffic load.

RIP assumes that all devices (hosts and routers) contain a routing table. This table contains several entries: the IP address of the destination; the metric, or cost, to get a datagram from the host to the destination; the address of the next router in the path to the destination; a flag indicating whether the routing information has been recently updated; and timers.

Routing information is exchanged via RIP packets, shown in Figure 4-7a, which are transmitted to/from UDP port number 520. The packet begins with a 32-bit header and may contain as many as 25 messages giving details on specific networks. The first field of the header is 1 octet long and specifies a unique command. Values include:

Command	Meaning
1	Request for routing table information
2	Response containing routing table information
3	Traceon (obsolete)
4	Traceoff (obsolete)
5	Reserved for Sun Microsystems

The second octet contains a RIP Version Number. Octets 3 and 4 are set equal to zero. The next 2 octets identify the Address Family being transmitted within that RIP packet; RFC 1058 only defines a value for IP with Address Family ID = 2.

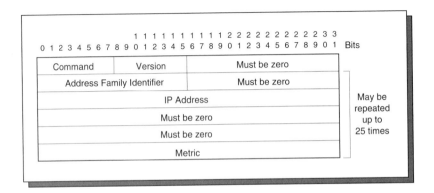

Figure 4-7a. Routing Information Protocol (RIP) Packet Format

The balance of the RIP packet contains entries for routing information. Each entry includes the destination IP address and the metric to reach that destination. Metric values must be between 1 and 15, inclusive. A metric of 16 indicates that the desired destination is unreachable. Up to 25 of these entries (from the Address Family dentifier through the Metric) may be contained within the datagram. We will see an example of RIP in Section 4.8.8.

An extension to the Routing Information Protocol, called RIP version 2, is defined in RFC 1723 [4-31]. This enhancement expands the amount of useful information carried in RIP messages and also adds a measure of security to those messages.

The RIP version 2 packet format is very similar to the original format, containing a four-octet header and up to 25 route entries of 20 octets each in length (see Figure 4-7b).

Within the header, the Command, Address Family Identifier, IP Address, and Metric fields are identical to their counterparts used with the original RIP packet format. The Version field specifies version number 2, and the two-octet unused field (filled with all zeros) is ignored. The Route Tag field carries an attribute assigned to a route which must be preserved and readvertised with a route, such as information defining the routing information's origin (either intra- or inter-network). Within each route entry, the Subnet Mask field (four octets) defines the subnet mask associated with a routing entry. The Next Hop field (also four octets) provides the immediate next hop IP address for the packets specified by this routing entry. The spaces now occupied by the Subnet Mask and Next Hop fields were previously filled with all zeros.

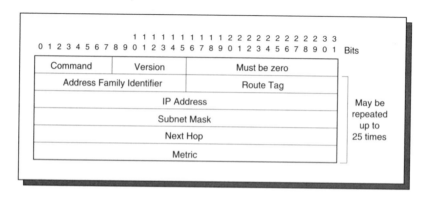

Figure 4-7b. Routing Information Protocol (RIP) Version 2 Packet Format

The first routing entry in a RIP version 2 packet may contain authentication information to identify the origin of the subsequent data. If that authentication information is included in the packet, the maximum number of routing entries is reduced to 24 (from 25). To use this option, the Address Family Identifier is set for FFFFH, the Route Tag field specifies an Authentication Type, and the remaining 16 octets contain the authentication, such as a password.

For further details on RIP version 2, consult RFC 1723 or the companion documents RFC 1721 ("RIP version 2 Protocol Analysis"), RFC 1722 ("RIP version 2 Applicability Statement"), or RFC 1724 (the "RIP version 2 Management Information Base—MIB"). Information on migration from RIP to OSPF is found in Eddie Rabinovitch's paper "Migration to OSPF is not a Luxury" [4-32].

4.4.2 Open Shortest Path First Protocol

The Open Shortest Path First protocol is a Link State algorithm that offers several advantages over RIP's Distance Vector algorithm. These advantages include the ability to configure hierarchical (instead of flat) topologies; to quickly adapt to changes within the internet; to allow for large internetworks; to calculate multiple minimum-cost routes that allow traffic load to be balanced over several paths; to authenticate the exchange of routing table information; and to permit the use of variable-length subnet masks. The protocol uses the IP address and Type of Service field of each datagram (review Figure 4-2) for its operation. An optimum path can be calculated for each Type of Service.

The Internet standard for OSPF version 2 is RFC 1583 [4-33]. OSPF protocol analysis and experience are discussed in RFC 1245 and RFC 1246, respectively. The OSPF version 2 Management Information Base (MIB) is discussed in RFC 1253, and the Applicability Statement for OSPF is found in RFC 1370. References [4-34] through [4-37] are examples of articles that discuss OSPF implementation.

4.4.2.1 Comparing Routing Algorithms

OSPF, a Link State algorithm (LSA), improves on RIP, a Distance Vector algorithm (DVA), in several ways. Before considering the improvements, let's review some of the characteristics of Distance Vector algorithms. First, a DVA routes its packets based upon the distance, measured in router hops, from the source to the destination. With RIP the maximum hop count is 16, which is a possible limitation for large networks. A DVA-based network is a flat network topology, without a defined hierarchy to subdivide the network into smaller, more manageable pieces. In addition, the hop count measurement does not account for other factors in the communication link, such as the speed of that link or its associated cost. Furthermore, RIP broadcasts its complete routing table to every other router every 30 seconds. As we saw in Figure 4-7a, the RIP packet may contain information for up to 25 routes. If a router's table contains more entries, say 100 routes, then transmitting all of these routes would require a total of four RIP packets. This requires considerable overhead at each router for packet processing, and it consumes valuable bandwidth on the WAN links in between these routers.

The improvements obtained with a Link State algorithm come in several areas. First, an LSA is based upon type of service routing, not hop counts. This allows the network manager to define the least-cost path between two network points based upon the actual cost, delay characteristics, reliability factors, and so on. Secondly, OSPF defines a hierarchical, not a flat network topology. This allows the routing information to be distributed to only a relevant subset of the routers in the internetwork instead of to all of the routers. As Eddie Rabinovitch states: "a distance vector algorithm tells all neighbors about the world, while a link state router tells the world about the neighbors" [4-32]. This hierarchical structure reduces both the router processing time and the bandwidth consumed on the WAN links.

An autonomous system (AS), used with an LSA, is defined as a group of routers that exchange routing information via a common routing protocol. The AS is subdivided into areas, which are collections of contiguous routers and hosts that are grouped together, much like the telephone network is divided into area codes. The topology of an area is invisible from outside that area, and routers within a particular area do not know the details of the topology outside of that area. When the AS is partitioned into areas, it is no longer likely (as was the case with a DVA) that all routers in the AS are storing identical topological information in their databases. A router would have a separate topological database for each area it is connected to; however, two routers in the same area would have identical topological databases. A backbone is also defined, which connects the various areas and is used to route a packet between two areas.

Different types of routers are used to connect the various areas. Internal routers operate within a single area, connect to other routers within that area, and maintain information about that area only. An area border router attaches to multiple areas, runs multiple copies of the basic routing algorithm, and condenses the topological information about their attached areas for distribution to the backbone. A backbone router is one which has an interface to the backbone, but it does not have to be an area border router. Lastly, an AS router is one which exchanges information with routers that belong to other Autonomous Systems.

4.4.2.2 OSPF Operation and Packet Formats

The basic routing algorithm for OSPF provides several sequential functions, as defined in RFC 1583, Section 4: discovering a router's neighbors and electing a Designated Router for the network using the OSPF Hello protocol; forming adjacencies between pairs of routers and synchronizing the databases of these adjacent routers; performing calculations of routing tables; and flooding the area with link state advertisements.

These protocol operations are performed using one of five OSPF packets. The OSPF packets are carried within IP datagrams and are designated as IP protocol = 89.

If the datagram requires fragmentation, the IP process handles that function. The five OSPF packet types have a common 24-octet header as shown in Figure 4-8a. The first 32-bit word includes fields defining a Version Number (1 octet), an OSPF Packet Type (1 octet), and a Packet Length (2 octets), which measures the length of the OSPF packet including the header. The five packet types defined are:

Type	Packet Name	Protocol Function
1	Hello	Discover/maintain neighbors
2	Database Description	Summarize database contents
3	Link State Request	Database download
4	Link State Update	Database update
5	Link State Acknowledgment	Flooding acknowledgment

The next two fields define the Router ID of the source of that packet (4 octets) and the Area ID (4 octets) that the packet came from. The balance of the OSPF packet header contains a Checksum (2 octets), an Authentication Type (AuType, 2 octets), and an Authentication field (8 octets), used to validate the packet.

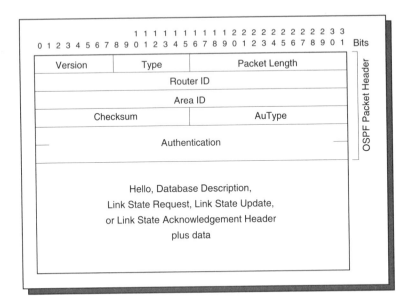

Figure 4-8a. Open Shortest Path First (OSPF) Packet Header Format

Following the OSPF packet header is another header specific to the routing information being conveyed. Hello packets (OSPF Packet Type = 1) are periodic transmissions that convey information about neighboring routers (see Figure 4-8b). Fields within the Hello packet include: a Network Mask (4 octets), the network mask associated with this interface; a Hello Interval (2 octets), the number of seconds between this router's Hello packets; Options (1 octet), this router's optional capabilities, as described in RFC 1583, Section A.2; Router Priority (Rtr Pri, 1 octet), this router's router priority, used in Designated (or backup) router election; Router Dead Interval (4 octets), the number of seconds before declaring a silent router down; Designated Router (4 octets), the identity of the Designated Router for this network; Backup Designated Router (4 octets), the identity of the Backup Designated Router for this network; and Neighbor (4 octets), the Router IDs of each router from whom valid Hello packets have been seen recently (i.e. in the last Router Dead Interval seconds) on the network.

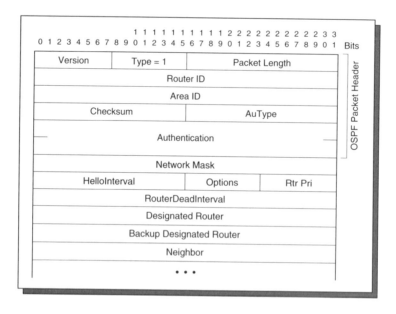

Figure 4-8b. OSPF Hello Packet Formatt

Database Description packets (OSPF Packet Type = 2) convey information needed to initialize the topological databases of adjacent devices (see Figure 4-8c). Fields within the Database Description packet include: Options (1 octet), this router's optional capabilities, as described in RFC 1583, Section A.2; I-bit, the Init bit (when set to one, this packet is the first in the sequence of Database Description packets); M-bit, the More bit (when set to one, it indicates that more Database Description packets are to follow); the MS-bit, the Master/Slave bit (when set to one, it indicates that the router is the master during the Database Exchange process; otherwise the router is the slave); Database Description Sequence Number (DD Sequence Number, 4 octets), used to sequence the collection of Database Description Packets. The remainder of the packet consists of a list of the topological database's pieces. Each link state advertisement in the database is described by its link state advertisement header (described below).

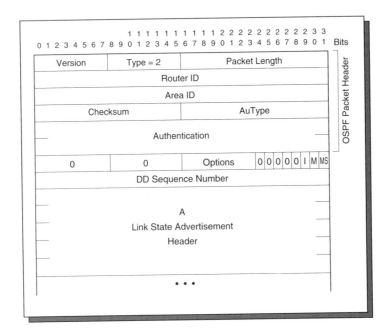

Figure 4-8c. OSPF Database Description Packet Format

Link State Request packets (OSPF Packet Type = 3) obtain current database information from a neighboring router (see Figure 4-8d). Fields within the Link State Request packet include the Link State type (4 octets), which defines the type of the Link State advertisement and is more fully described below. The Link State ID (4 octets) is a unique identification for the advertisement, and the Advertising Router (4 octets) is the identification of the router that originated the link state advertisement.

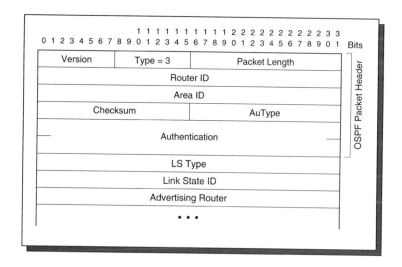

Figure 4-8d. OSPF Link State Request Packet Format

Link State Update packets (OSPF Packet Type = 4) advertise the status of various links within the internet (see Figure 4-8e). Several link state advertisements may be included in a single packet. The Number advertisements field (# Advertisements, 4 octets) defines the number of link state advertisements included in this update. The body of the Link State Update packet consists of a list of link state advertisements. Each of these advertisements begins with a common 20-octet header, followed by one of five link state advertisements:

LS Type	Advertisement Name	Advertisement Description
1	Router link	Describes the states of the router's interfaces to an area
2	Network link	Lists the routers connected to the network
3	Summary link	Describes a route to a network destination outside the area
4	Summary link	Describes a route to an AS boundary router destination outside the area
5	AS external link	Describes a route to a destination in another Autonomous System

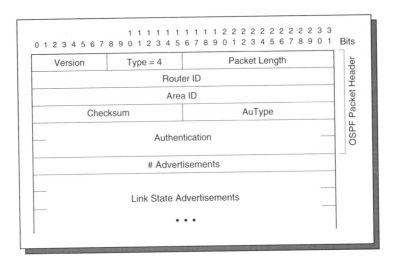

Figure 4-8e. OSPF Link State Update Packet Format

The Link State header contains enough information to uniquely identify the advertisement (see Figure 4-8f). Fields within the Link State header include: Link State Age (LS Age, 2 octets), the time in seconds since the link state advertisement was originated; Options (1 octet), the optional capabilities supported by the described portion of the routing domain and defined in RFC 1583, Section A.2; Link State type (LS Type, 1 octet), the type of link state advertisement, as described in the table above; Link State ID (4 octets), an identifier of the portion of the internet environment that is being described by the advertisement, with the contents of this field dependent on the advertisement's link state type (as above) Advertising Router (4 octets), the Router ID of the router that originated the link state advertisement; Link State Sequence Number (LS Sequence Number, 4 octets), which detects old or duplicate link state advertisements; Link State Checksum (LS Checksum, 2 octets), a checksum for the Link State advertisement; and Length (2 octets), the length, in octets, of the link state advertisement.

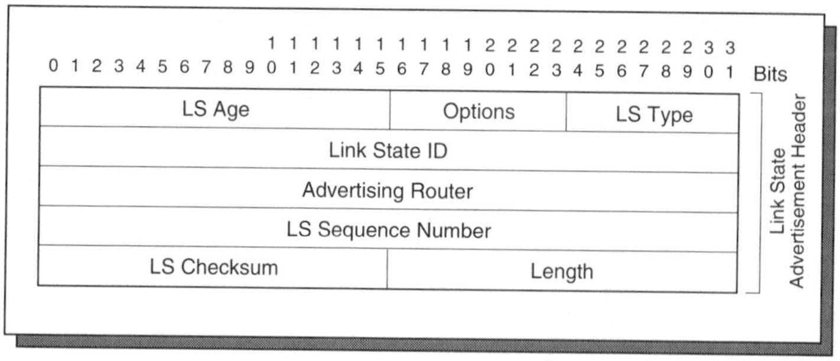

Figure 4-8f. OSPF Link State Advertisement Header Format

The Router Links Advertisements packet (the Type 1 link state advertisement) describes the state and cost of the router's links (or interfaces) to the area (see Figure 4-8g). This packet begins with the Link State advertisement header (20 octets, described above). Other fields within this packet include: V-bit, which, when set, indicates that the router is an endpoint of an active virtual link that is using the described area; E-bit, which, when set, indicates that the router is an external (or AS boundary) router; B-bit, which when set, indicates that the router is an area border router; Number of Links (# Links, 2 octets), the number of router links described by this advertisement.

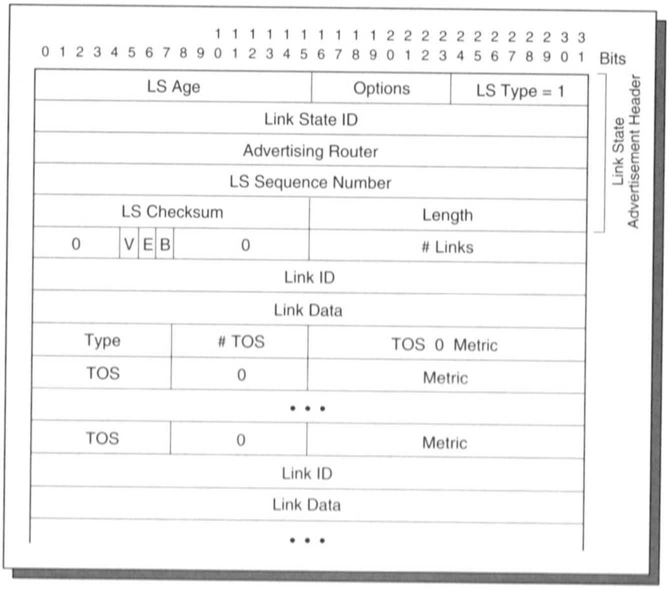

Figure 4-8g. OSPF Router Links Advertisement Packet Format

Seven fields, consuming 16 octets, are then used to describe each router link. The third descriptive field, Type (1 octet), provides a description of the router link, which may be one of the following:

Type	Description
1	Point-to-point connection to another router
2	Connection to a transit network
3	Connection to a stub network
4	Virtual link

The first descriptive field, Link ID (4 octets), identifies the object that this router link connects to; it depends on the link's Type, described above. The values of the Link ID are:

Type	Link ID
1	Neighboring router's Router ID
2	IP address of Designated Router
3	IP network/subnet number
4	Neighboring router's Router ID

The contents of the Link Data field (4 octets) also depend on the Type field. For example, for connections to stub networks, this field specifies the network's IP address mask. For each link, separate metrics may be specified for each Type of Service (TOS). The Number of TOS field (# TOS, 1 octet) provides the number of different TOS metrics given for this link, not counting the required metric for TOS 0. The TOS 0 Metric field (1 octet) provides the cost for using this router link for TOS 0. The Type of Service field (TOS, 1 octet) indicates the IP Type of Service that this metric refers to, while the Metric field (2 octets) indicates the cost of using this outbound router link for traffic of the specified TOS.

The Network Links Advertisements packet (the Type 2 link state advertisement) describes all routers attached to the network, including the Designated Router (see Figure 4-8h). There are two fields in addition to the Link State Advertisement header: Network Mask (4 octets), the IP address mask for the network; and Attached Router (4 octets), the Router IDs of each of the routers attached to the network.

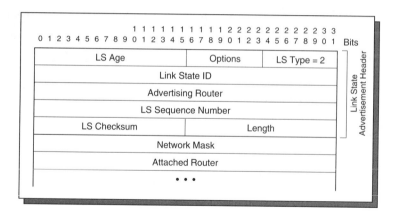

Figure 4-8h. OSPF Network Links Advertisement Packet Format

The Summary Links Advertisements are originated by area border routers and describe destination links outside of the area. Type 3 link state advertisements are used when the destination is an IP network; when the destination is an AS boundary router, a Type 4 Summary Links Advertisement is used (see Figure 4-8i). There are three fields in addition to the Link State Advertisement header: Network Mask (4 octets) indicates the destination network's IP address mask for Type 3, and is not meaningful and is set to zero for Type 4; Type of Service (TOS, 1 octet) indicates the type of service that the following cost concerns; and Metric (3 octets) indicates the cost of this route, expressed in the same units as the interface costs in the Router Links advertisements.

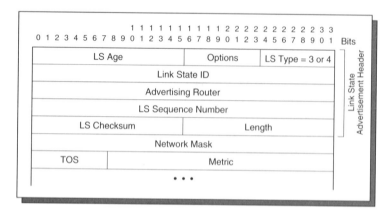

Figure 4-8i. OSPF Summary Link Advertisement Packet Format

AS External Link Advertisements are originated by AS boundary routers and advertise destinations which are external to the AS (see Figure 4-8j). Fields within the AS External Links Advertisement Packet include: Network Mask (4 octets), the IP address mask for the advertised destination; E-bit, which indicates the type of external metric; Type of Service (TOS, 7 bits), the type of service that the following cost concerns; Metric (3 octets), the cost of this route; Forwarding Address (4 octets), which specifies where data traffic for the advertised destination will be forwarded to; and External Route Tag (4 octets), a field attached to each external route, which is not used by the OSPF protocol itself but which may be used to communicate information between AS boundary routers.

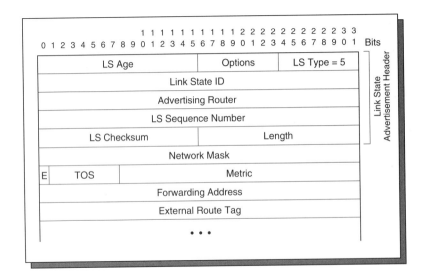

Figure 4-8j. OSPF External Link Advertisement Packet Format

Finally, Link State Acknowledgment packets (OSPF Type = 5) verify the receipt of database information (see Figure 4-8k). The format of this packet is similar to that of the Database Description packet, and contains a list of Link State advertisement headers.

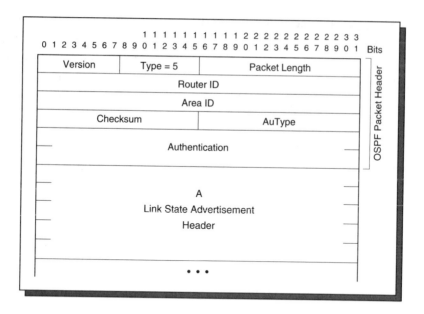

Figure 4-8k. OSPF Link State Acknowledgement Packet Format

4.5 Intra-Network Communications

If the Internet were flawless, it would always route datagrams to their intended destination without errors, excessive delays, or retransmissions. Unfortunately, this is not the case. (If it were, you wouldn't be reading a book on troubleshooting!) As we studied in Section 4.1, IP provides a connectionless service to the attached hosts but requires an additional module, known as the Internet Control Message Protocol (ICMP), to report errors that may have occurred in processing those datagrams. Examples of errors include undeliverable datagrams or incorrect routes. Other uses for the protocol include testing the path to a distant host (known as a PING) or requesting an Address Mask for a particular subnet. ICMP is considered an integral part of IP and must be implemented in IP modules contained in both hosts and routers. The standard for ICMP is RFC 792 [4-38].

ICMP messages are contained within IP datagrams. In other words, ICMP is a user (client) of IP, and the IP header precedes the ICMP message. Thus, the datagram would include the IP header, the ICMP header, and ICMP data. Protocol = 1 identifies ICMP within the IP header. A Type field within the ICMP header further identifies the purpose and format of the ICMP message. Any data required to complete the ICMP message would then follow the ICMP header.

The standard defines thirteen ICMP message formats, each with a specific ICMP header format. Two of these formats (Information Request/Reply) are considered obsolete and several others share a common message structure. The result is six unique message formats, shown in Figure 4-9. The first three fields are common to all headers. The Type field (1 octet) identifies one of the thirteen unique ICMP messages. These include:

Type Code	ICMP Messages
0	Echo Reply
3	Destination Unreachable
4	Source Quench
5	Redirect
8	Echo
11	Time Exceeded
12	Parameter Problem
13	Timestamp
14	Timestamp Reply
15	Information Request (obsolete)
16	Information Reply (obsolete)
17	Address Mask Request
18	Address Mask Reply

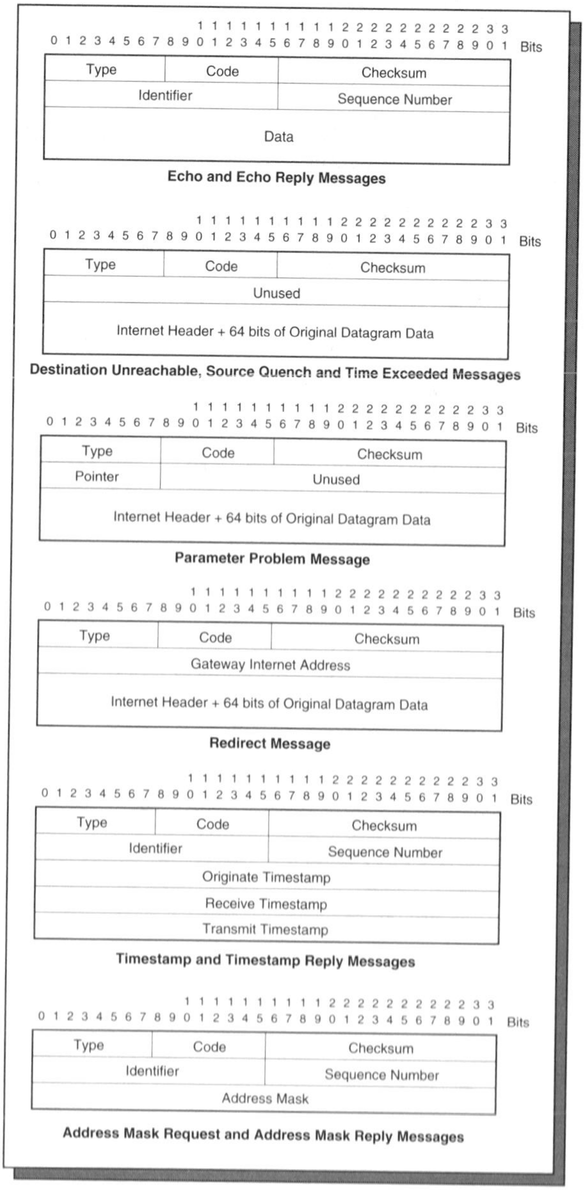

Figure 4-9. Internet Control Message Protocol (ICMP) Message Formats

The second field is labeled Code (1 octet), and it elaborates on specific message types. For example, the Code field for the Destination Unreachable message indicates whether the network, host, protocol, or port was the unreachable entity. The third field is the Checksum (2 octets) on the ICMP message. Because ICMP messages are of great value in internetwork troubleshooting, we will look at all of the ICMP messages in detail. Internet standards describing ICMP formats and usage include the original standard, RFC 792; implementing congestion control, RFC 896 [4-39]; use of source quench messages, RFC 1016 [4-40]; and Subnet Mask Messages, RFC 950 [4-9].

The Echo message (ICMP Type = 8) tests the communication path from a sender to a receiver via the internet. On many hosts, this function is called PING. The sender transmits an Echo message, which may also contain an Identifier (2 octets) and a Sequence Number (2 octets). Data may be sent with the message. When the destination receives the message, it reverses the Source and Destination addresses, recomputes the Checksum, and returns an Echo Reply (ICMP Type = 0). The contents of the Data field (if any) would also be returned to the sender.

The Destination Unreachable message (ICMP Type = 3) is used when the router or host is unable to deliver the datagram. This message is returned to the Source host of the datagram in question and describes the reason for the delivery problem in the Code field:

Code	Meaning
0	Net Unreachable
1	Host Unreachable
2	Protocol Unreachable
3	Port Unreachable
4	Fragmentation Needed and DF Set
5	Source Route Failed

Routers may use codes 0, 1, 4, or 5. Hosts may use codes 2 or 3. For example, when a datagram arrives at a router, it will do a table lookup to determine the outgoing path to use. If the router determines that the Destination network cannot be reached (i.e., a distance of infinite hops away), a Net Unreachable message will be returned. Similarly, if a host cannot process a datagram because the requested protocol or port is inactive, a Protocol Unreachable or Port Unreachable message, respectively, would be returned. Included in the Destination Unreachable message is the IP header plus the first 64 bits (8 octets) of the datagram in question. This returned data should help the host diagnose the failure in the transmission process.

The advantage of connectionless datagram transmission is its simplicity. The disadvantage is its inability to regulate the traffic on the network. (For an analogy, consider the problem that your local post office faces. To handle the maximum number of letters, it should install enough boxes to handle the holiday rush. However, this might be considered wasteful because many of the boxes are only partially used during the summer.) If a router or host gets congested, it may send a Source Quench message (ICMP Type = 4) to the source of the datagrams asking it to reduce its output. This mechanism is similar to traffic signals that regulate the flow of cars onto a freeway. The Source Quench message does not use the second 32-bit word of the ICMP header, but fills it with zeros. The rest of the message contains the IP header and the first 8 octets of the datagram that triggered the request.

Hosts do not always choose the correct Destination address for a particular datagram and occasionally send one to the wrong router. This is most likely to occur when the host is initialized and its routing tables are incomplete. When such a routing mistake occurs, the router that improperly received the datagram will return a Redirect message to the host identifying a better route. The Code field would contain the following information:

Code	Message
0	Redirect datagrams for the network
1	Redirect datagrams for the host
2	Redirect datagrams for the type of service and network
3	Redirect datagrams for the type of service and host

The Redirect message (ICMP Type = 5) contains the correct router (gateway) address to reach the desired destination. In addition, the IP header plus the first 8 octets of the datagram in question are returned to the source host to aid in the diagnostic process.

Another potential problem of connectionless networks is that datagrams can get lost within the network and can wander for an excessive amount of time. Alternatively, congestion could prevent all fragments of a datagram from being reassembled within the host's required time. Either of these situations can trigger an ICMP Time Exceeded message (ICMP Type = 11). The message defines two codes: Time-to-Live Exceeded in Transmit (code = 0) and Fragment Reassembly Time Exceeded (code = 1). The balance of the message has the same format as the Source Quench message: the second word contains all zeros, and the rest of the message contains the IP header and the first 8 octets of the offending datagram.

Higher-layer processes, such as TCP, recognize datagrams that cannot be processed because of errors and discard them, relying upon a higher-layer process to recognize the problem and take corrective action. Parameter problems within an IP datagram header (such as an incorrect Type of Service field) may send an ICMP Parameter Problem message (ICMP Type = 12) to the source of the datagram, identifying the location of the problem. The message contains a pointer that identifies the octet with the error. The rest of the message contains the IP datagram header plus the first 8 octets of data, as before.

The Timestamp Message (ICMP Type = 13) and Timestamp Reply (ICMP Type = 14) measure the round-trip transit time between two machines and synchronize their clocks. The first two words of the Timestamp and Timestamp Reply messages are similar to the Echo and Echo Reply messages. The next three fields contain timestamps measured in milliseconds since midnight, Universal Time (UT). The Timestamp Requester fills in the Originate field upon transmission; the recipient fills in the Receive Time-stamp when it receives the request. The recipient fills in the Transmit Timestamp when it sends the Timestamp Reply message. The Requester may now estimate the remote processing and round-trip transit times. (Note that these are only estimates because network delay is a highly dynamic and variable measurement.) The remote processing time is the Received Timestamp minus the Transmit Timestamp. The round-trip transit time will be the Timestamp Reply message arrival time minus the Originate Timestamp. With these two calculations, the two clocks can be synchronized.

Finally, Address Mask Request (ICMP Type = 17) and Address Mask Reply (ICMP Type = 18) were added to the ICMP message in response to subnetting requirements (RFC 950). It is assumed that the requesting host knows its own Internet address. (If it doesn't, it uses RARP to discover the Internet address.) It then broadcasts the Address Mask Request message to the Destination address [255.255.255.255]. The Address Mask field of the ICMP message would be filled with all zeros. The IP router that knows the correct address mask would respond. For example, the response for a Class B network (without subnetting) would be [255.255.0.0]. A Class B network using an 8-bit subnet field would be [255.255.255.0]. Barry Gerber's article "IP Routing: Learn to Follow the Yellow Brick Road" [4-41] contains additional examples of Subnet Mask usage. Section 4.8.5 will show how an incorrect Subnet Mask can hinder network communication.

4.6 Domain Name System (DNS)

The 32-bit IP addresses and the various classes defined for these addresses provide an extremely efficient way to identify devices on an internetwork. Unfortunately, remembering all of those addresses can be overwhelming. To solve that problem, a system of hierarchical naming known as the *Domain Name System* was developed. DNS is described in RFCs 1034 [4-42] and 1035 [4-43].

DNS is based upon several premises. First, it arranges the names hierarchically, like the numbering plan devised for the telephone network. Just as a telephone number is divided into a country code, an area code, an exchange code, and finally a line number, the DNS root is divided into a number of top-level domains, defined in RFC 920. These are:

Domain	Purpose
MIL	U.S. Military
GOV	Other U.S. Government
EDU	Educational
COM	Commercial
NET	NICs and NOCs
ORG	Non-profit Organizations
CON	Two-letter country code, e.g. US represents the United States, CA represents Canada, and so on.

Specific sites would be under each top-level domain. For example, the University of Ferncliff could use the edu domain designation (using the traditional lower-case letters), and it would be shown as ferncliff.edu. The University could then designate names for its departments, such as cs.ferncliff.edu (Computer Science) or ee.ferncliff.edu (Electrical Engineering). A particular host in the Electrical Engineering department could be named voltage.ee.ferncliff.edu. A user with a login on that host could be identified as boomer@voltage.ee.ferncliff.edu. Note that the @ sign separates the user from the remainder of the Host address.

The second DNS premise is that devices are not expected to remember the IP addresses of remote hosts. Rather, *Name Servers* throughout the internetwork provide this information. The requesting device thus assumes the role of a client, and the Name Server provides the necessary information, known as a *resource record*.

The format for client/server interaction is a DNS message, shown in Figure 4-10. The message header is 12 octets long and describes the type of message. The next four sections provide the details of the query or response.

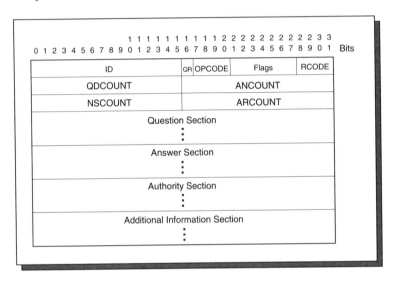

Figure 4-10. Domain Name System (DNS) Message Format

The first field within the header is an Identifier (16 bits) that correlates the queries and responses. The QR bit identifies the message type as a Query (QR = 0) or a Response (QR = 1). An OPCODE field (4 bits) further defines a Query:

OPCODE	Meaning
0	Standard Query (QUERY)
1	Inverse Query (IQUERY)
2	Server Status request (STATUS)
3-15	Reserved

Four Flags are then transmitted to further describe the message:

Bit Number	Meaning
5	Authoritative Answer (AA)
6	Truncation (TC)
7	Recursion Desired (RD)
8	Recursion Available (RA)
9-11	Reserved (set to 0)

A Response Code (RCODE) completes the first word:

Field	Meaning
0	No error
1	Format error
2	Server error
3	Name error
4	Not implemented
5	Refused
6-15	Reserved for future use

The balance of the header contains fields that define the lengths of the remaining four sections:

Field	Meaning
QDCOUNT	Number of Question entries
ANCOUNT	Number of resource records in the Answer section
NSCOUNT	Number of name server resource records in the Authority section
ARCOUNT	Number of resource records in the Additional Records section.

Following the header is the Question section and the Answer sections (Answer, Authority, or Additional Information). We will look at an example of a DNS message in section 4.8.1. A good resource on DNS is Bryan Beecher's article "The Ten Commandments of Domain Name Service" [4-44].

4.7 Troubleshooting the Internetwork Connection

When planning a strategy to diagnose internetwork-related problems, it is important to reconsider the functions of the ARPA Internet Layer discussed in Section 4.1. Recall that its principle function is routing, with the desired result being connectivity between two hosts. Associated with routing are the issues of addressing, subnet assignments, and masks. Because addresses are not always known, protocols such as ARP/RARP and BOOTP may be used. The Domain Name System may also assist in this process.

Intelligent devices known as routers use the addresses to guide the datagram through the internet. Those routers communicate with each other using an IGP, such as RIP or OSPF. Because the routing mechanism doesn't always function properly, another protocol, ICMP, helps the hosts determine what went wrong.

One frequently used test is the ICMP Echo (PING) message, which verifies connectivity between internet devices. The PING can be used in a sequential manner to isolate a problem. For example, first PING a host on your subnet, then PING a router, then PING a host on the other side of that router, and so on until the faulty connection is identified. Another maintenance utility known as *traceroute* is available with some host operating systems. Traceroute uses ICMP messages to verify each segment along a path to a distant host. Traceroute must be used with some caution, however, as it can generate large amounts of internetwork (and/or Internet) traffic.

To summarize, if a problem occurs in the internet and the Network Interface Layer looks healthy (review Section 3.12), look for the significant events at the Internet Layer. These events relate to datagram delivery. The processes of address discovery, address assignment, communication between routers, and notification of router errors may offer clues about the reason for a problem with the delivery of your datagram. Carl Auerbach's paper "Trouble-Busters" [4-45] discusses TCP/IP network troubleshooting and suggests various tools that come in handy. The following case studies will show examples of these clues.

4.8 Case Studies

We have studied a number of protocols in this chapter, including ARP, IP, ICMP, RIP, and OSPF. We have also looked at IP addressing schemes and Subnet Masks. Next, let's look at some case studies that illustrate these protocols in action.

4.8.1 Login to a Remote Host

In our first example, we'll look at the processes necessary to log into a remote host using the UNIX TELNET utility (see Trace 4.8.1a). The network administrator, Paul, resides on an Ethernet segment (Network 132) in one location, and the remote host that he needs to access resides on a different segment (Network 129) in another part of the country (see Figure 4-11).

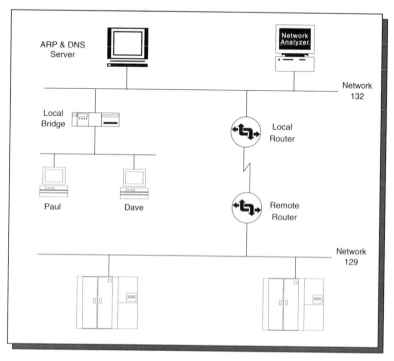

Figure 4-11. Login to Remote Host

First, Paul must find the Domain Name System (DNS) Server. To do so, he broadcasts an ARP Request packet within an Ethernet frame identifying the Protocol Address, PA = [132.XXX.128.1], for the Internet Protocol (IP), but with an unknown Hardware Address (HA = 0) as shown in Frame 1 of Trace 4.8.1b. The Name Server responds in Frame 2, identifying its HA = 08002006B501H. Paul now knows how to reach the Name Server. (Expert analysts will note a subtle difference between the address representations in Frame 2 of Trace 4.8.1a (Summary) and Frame 2 of Trace 4.8.1b (Details). In the Summary trace, the entire hardware address is represented:

HA = 08002006B501. In the Detail trace, the Sniffer decodes the Manufacturer ID portion of the Sender's hardware address (080020) and substitutes the manufacturer's name (Sun). The balance of the address (06B501) remains the same. The substituted name (Name Svr) comes from the Sniffer's manually entered database of node names.)

He next locates the address for the remote host fs1.cam.nist.gov that he wishes to log into. The DNS request is transmitted in Frame 3, with a response given in Frame 4 of Trace 4.8.1c indicating that fs1.cam.nist.gov is located at [129.XXX.80.33]. Recall that Paul is located on Network 132 and the Name Server says that his desired destination is located on another network (Network 129). A router must now spring into action. Paul broadcasts an ARP Request packet looking for the router (address [132.XXX.1.1] in Frame 5 of Trace 4.8.1a). The router responds with its hardware address in Frame 6 (HA = 000093E0807BH).

Paul now has all the information he needs. In Frame 7 he initiates a TCP connection (via a three-way handshake, which we will study in Chapter 5) with the remote host. The details of the Connection Establishment message verify that Paul knows where to find his desired host (see Trace 4.8.1d). In the Data Link Control (DLC, or frame) header, Paul addresses this message to the Proteon router (address ProteonE0807B). We know that this frame is transmitted on a DIX Ethernet (not an IEEE 802.3) LAN, because of the EtherType field identified IP = 0800 H. (Had it been an IEEE 802.3 frame, a Length field would have been shown instead of the EtherType field.) The IP header identifies Paul's workstation as the source of the datagram [132.XXX.129.15], with the destination address of the remote host on a different network [129.XXX.80.33]. The TCP header specifies that the Destination Port = 23 (TELNET). The TCP flags indicate that Paul wants to establish a connection, since the Synchronize flag is set (SYN = 1). Paul also specifies that he can accept a maximum segment size of 512 octets.

In the subsequent frames (8 through 20 of Trace 4.8.1a), Paul's workstation and the remote host negotiate various TELNET parameters, such as the Terminal Type (Frames 10 through 12), Echo (Frames 15 and 16), and Login (Frames 17 through 20). Once Paul is logged in, he can complete his business with the remote host.

To summarize, Paul's workstation undertakes the following steps:

1. Identify DNS Name Server (ARP).
2. Identify remote host address (DNS).

3. Identify required router (ARP).
4. Establish connection with remote host (TCP).
5. Negotiate parameters with remote host (TELNET).
6. Initiate remote terminal session (TELNET).

In the next case study, we will examine how IP fragments long messages.

Sniffer Network Analyzer data 21-Jun at 13:37:00, LOGIN.ENC, Pg 1

SUMMARY M	Delta T	Destination	Source	Summary
1		Broadcast	Paul	ARP C PA=[132.XXX.128.1] PRO=IP
2	0.0006	Paul	Name Svr	ARP R PA=[132.XXX.128.1] HA=08002006B501 PRO=IP
3	0.0016	Name Svr	Paul	DNS C ID=3 OP=QUERY NAME=fs1.cam.nist.gov
4	0.0026	Paul	Name Svr	DNS R ID=3 STAT=OK NAME=fs1.cam.nist.gov
5	0.0088	Broadcast	Paul	ARP C PA=[132.XXX.1.1] PRO=IP
6	0.0010	Paul	Router	ARP R PA=[132.XXX.1.1] HA=000093E0807B PRO=IP
7	0.0016	Router	Paul	TCP D=23 S=3133 SYN SEQ=9947492 LEN=0 WIN=1024
8	0.1081	Paul	Router	TCP D=3133 S=23 SYN ACK=9947493 SEQ=80448000 LEN=0 WIN=4096
9	0.0032	Router	Paul	TCP D=23 S=3133 ACK=80448001 WIN=1024
10	2.1818	Paul	Router	Telnet R PORT=3133 IAC Do Terminal type
11	0.0029	Router	Paul	TCP D=23 S=3133 ACK=80448004 WIN=1021
12	0.0027	Router	Paul	Telnet C PORT=3133 IAC Will Terminal type
13	0.1134	Paul	Router	Telnet R PORT=3133 IAC SB ...
14	0.0070	Router	Paul	Telnet C PORT=3133 IAC SB ...
15	0.1912	Paul	Router	Telnet R PORT=3133 IAC Will Echo
16	0.0053	Router	Paul	Telnet C PORT=3133 IAC Do Echo
17	0.2566	Paul	Router	Telnet R PORT=3133 login:
18	0.0033	Router	Paul	Telnet C PORT=3133 IAC Do Suppress go-ahead

19	0.1113	Paul	Router	Telnet R PORT=3133 IAC
				Don't Echo
20	0.2591	Router	Paul	TCP D=23 S=3133
				ACK=80448057 WIN=968

Trace 4.8.1a. Login to Remote Host Summary

Sniffer Network Analyzer data 21-Jun at 13:37:00, file LOGIN.ENC, Pg 1

- - - - - - - - - - - - - - - - Frame 1 - - - - - - - - - - - - - - - - -

DLC: ——– DLC Header ——-
DLC:
DLC: Frame 1 arrived at 13:37:06.3280; frame size is 60 (003C hex) bytes.
DLC: Destination   = BROADCAST FFFFFFFFFFFF, Broadcast
DLC: Source = Station 3Com 1AB9BE, Paul
DLC: Ethertype   = 0806 (ARP)
DLC:
ARP: ——– ARP/RARP frame ——-
ARP:
ARP: Hardware type = 1 (10Mb Ethernet)
ARP: Protocol type = 0800 (IP)
ARP: Length of hardware address = 6 bytes
ARP: Length of protocol address = 4 bytes
ARP: Opcode 1 (ARP request)
ARP: Sender's hardware address = 3Com 1AB9BE, Paul
ARP: Sender's protocol address = [132.XXX.129.15]
ARP: Target hardware address = 000000000000, 000000000000
ARP: Target protocol address = [132.XXX.128.1]
ARP:

- - - - - - - - - - - - - - - Frame 2 - - - - - - - - - - - - - - - - -

DLC: ——– DLC Header ——-
DLC:
DLC: Frame 2 arrived at 13:37:06.3287; frame size is 60 (003C hex) bytes.
DLC: Destination = Station 3Com 1AB9BE, Paul
DLC: Source   = Station Sun   06B501, Name Svr
DLC: Ethertype = 0806 (ARP)
DLC:
ARP: ——– ARP/RARP frame ——-
ARP:

ARP: Hardware type = 1 (10Mb Ethernet)
ARP: Protocol type = 0800 (IP)
ARP: Length of hardware address = 6 bytes
ARP: Length of protocol address = 4 bytes
ARP: Opcode 2 (ARP reply)
ARP: Sender's hardware address = Sun   06B501, Name Svr
ARP: Sender's protocol address = [132.XXX.128.1]
ARP: Target hardware address = 3Com 1AB9BE, Paul
ARP: Target protocol address = [132.XXX.129.15]
ARP:

Trace 4.8.1b. Login to Remote Host ARP/RARP Details

Sniffer Network Analyzer data 21-Jun at 13:37:00, LOGIN.ENC, Pg 1

- - - - - - - - - - - - - - - - Frame 3 - - - - - - - - - - - - - - - -

DLC: ——— DLC Header ———
DLC:
DLC: Frame 3 arrived at 13:37:06.3304; frame size is 76 (004C hex) bytes.
DLC: Destination = Station Sun   06B501, Name Svr
DLC: Source   = Station 3Com 1AB9BE, Paul
DLC: Ethertype = 0800 (IP)
DLC:
IP: ——— IP Header ———
IP:
IP: Version = 4, header length = 20 bytes
IP: Type of service = 20
IP: 001. .... = priority
IP: ...0 .... = normal delay
IP: .... 0... = normal throughput
IP: .... .0.. = normal reliability
IP: Total length = 62 bytes
IP: Identification = 30
IP: Flags = 0X
IP: .0.. .... = may fragment
IP: ..0. .... = last fragment
IP: Fragment offset = 0 bytes
IP: Time to live = 64 seconds/hops
IP: Protocol = 17 (UDP)
IP: Header checksum = 701A (correct)
IP: Source address = [132.XXX.129.15]

```
IP:  Destination address = [132.XXX.128.1]
IP:  No options
IP:
UDP: ——- UDP Header ——-
UDP:
UDP: Source port = 1116 (Domain)
UDP: Destination port = 53
UDP: Length = 42
UDP: Checksum = 54EF (correct)
UDP:
DNS: ——- Internet Domain Name Service header ——-
DNS:
DNS: ID = 3
DNS: Flags = 01
DNS: 0... .... = Command
DNS: .000 0... = Query
DNS: .... ..0. = Not truncated
DNS: .... ...1 = Recursion desired
DNS: Flags = 0X
DNS: ...0 .... = Unicast packet
DNS: Question count = 1, Answer count = 0
DNS: Authority count = 0, Additional record count = 0
DNS:
DNS: Question section:
DNS:        Name = fs1.cam.nist.gov
DNS:        Type = Host address (A,1)
DNS:        Class = Internet (IN,1)
DNS:
DNS: [Normal end of "Internet Domain Name Service header".]
DNS:

- - - - - - - - - - - - - - - - Frame 4 - - - - - - - - - - - - - - - - -

DLC: ——- DLC Header ——-
DLC:
DLC: Frame 4 arrived at  13:37:06.3330; frame size is 92 (005C hex) bytes.
DLC: Destination = Station 3Com  1AB9BE, Paul
DLC: Source     = Station Sun   06B501, Name Svr
DLC: Ethertype  = 0800 (IP)
DLC:
IP:  ——- IP Header ——-
IP:
IP:  Version = 4, header length = 20 bytes
```

```
IP:   Type of service = 00
IP:               000. .... = routine
IP:               ...0 .... = normal delay
IP:               .... 0... = normal throughput
IP:               .... .0.. = normal reliability
IP:   Total length = 78 bytes
IP:   Identification = 60111
IP:   Flags = 0X
IP:   .0.. .... = may fragment
IP:   ..0. .... = last fragment
IP:   Fragment offset = 0 bytes
IP:   Time to live = 30 seconds/hops
IP:   Protocol = 17 (UDP)
IP:   Header checksum = A778 (correct)
IP:   Source address = [132.XXX.128.1]
IP:   Destination address = [132.XXX.129.15]
IP:   No options
IP:
UDP:  ——- UDP Header ——-
UDP:
UDP:  Source port = 53 (Domain)
UDP:  Destination port = 1116
UDP:  Length = 58
UDP:  No checksum
UDP:
DNS:  ——- Internet Domain Name Service header ——-
DNS:
DNS:  ID = 3
DNS:  Flags = 85
DNS:  1... .... = Response
DNS:  .... .1.. = Authoritative answer
DNS:  .000 0... = Query
DNS:  .... ..0. = Not truncated
DNS:  Flags = 8X
DNS:  ...0 .... = Unicast packet
DNS:  1... .... = Recursion available
DNS:  Response code = OK (0)
DNS:  Question count = 1, Answer count = 1
DNS:  Authority count = 0, Additional record count = 0
DNS:
DNS:  Question section:
DNS:              Name = fs1.cam.nist.gov
```

DNS:	Type = Host address (A,1)
DNS:	Class = Internet (IN,1)
DNS: Answer section:	
DNS:	Name = fs1.cam.nist.gov
DNS:	Type = Host address (A,1)
DNS:	Class = Internet (IN,1)
DNS:	Time-to-live = 2589119 (seconds)
DNS:	Address = [129.XXX.80.33]
DNS:	
DNS:	[Normal end of "Internet Domain Name Service header".]
DNS:	

Trace 4.8.1c. Login to Remote Host DNS Details

Sniffer Network Analyzer data 21-Jun at 13:37:00, LOGIN.ENC, Pg 1

- - - - - - - - - - - - - - - - Frame 7 - - - - - - - - - - - - - - - - -

DLC: ———- DLC Header ———-
DLC:
DLC: Frame 7 arrived at 13:37:06.3445; frame size is 60 (003C hex) bytes.
DLC: Destination = Station PrteonE0807B, Router
DLC: Source   = Station 3Com 1AB9BE, Paul
DLC: Ethertype = 0800 (IP)
DLC:
IP: ———- IP Header ———-
IP:
IP: Version = 4, header length = 20 bytes
IP: Type of service = 00
IP: 000. .... = routine
IP: ...0 .... = normal delay
IP: .... 0... = normal throughput
IP: .... .0.. = normal reliability
IP: Total length = 44 bytes
IP: Identification = 31
IP: Flags = 0X
IP: .0.. .... = may fragment
IP: ..0. .... = last fragment
IP: Fragment offset = 0 bytes
IP: Time to live = 64 seconds/hops
IP: Protocol = 6 (TCP)
IP: Header checksum = A3D3 (correct)

IP: Source address = [132.XXX.129.15]
IP: Destination address = [129.XXX.80.33]
IP: No options
IP:
TCP: ——- TCP header ——-
TCP:
TCP: Source port = 3133
TCP: Destination port = 23 (Telnet)
TCP: Initial sequence number = 9947492
TCP: Data offset = 24 bytes
TCP: Flags = 02
TCP: ..0. .... = (No urgent pointer)
TCP: ...0 .... = (No acknowledgment)
TCP: .... 0... = (No push)
TCP: .... .0.. = (No reset)
TCP: .... ..1. = SYN
TCP: ....0 = (No FIN)
TCP: Window = 1024
TCP: Checksum = EAAF (correct)
TCP:
TCP: Options follow
TCP: Maximum segment size = 512
TCP:

Trace 4.8.1d. Login to Remote Host TCP Details

4.8.2 Fragmenting Long Messages

In this case study, we will investigate how a host fragments a long message into multiple IP datagrams for transmission on a TCP/IP-based internetwork. In this example, the source is a station (DEC 029487) that wishes to send a large SUN RPC file to another station (Intrln 00027C0) on the same LAN. Three frames are needed to transmit the message (see Trace 4.8.2 and Figure 4-12). The message requires a User Datagram Protocol (UDP) header to identify the source and destination ports at the communicating hosts.

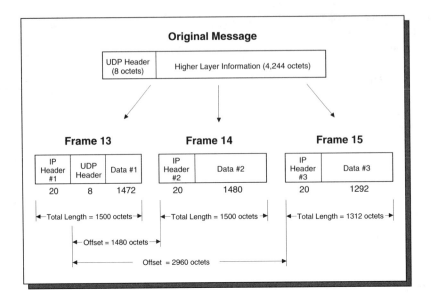

Figure 4-12. IPv4 Fragments

The message contains 4,244 octets of data plus an 8-octet UDP header, for a total of 4,252 octets. The message is divided into three frames, with 1,472, 1,480, and 1,292 octets of data each (Frames 13, 14, and 15, respectively). Frame 13 has a total length of 1,500 octets (matching the maximum Ethernet frame size) and indicates that more fragments, associated with message ID = 59738, are on the way. The next higher-layer protocol within the first fragment is UDP (Protocol = 17, UDP). The Source and Destination addresses [XXX.YYY.0.33] and [XXX.YYY.0.10] identify the network. The UDP header indicates that the total message length is 4,252 octets. This includes the UDP header (8 octets) plus the data (4,244 octets). Thus, the 1,500 octets of Frame 13 consist of the IP header (20 octets), the UDP header (8 octets), and the first data fragment (1,472 octets).

The second frame also contains 1,514 octets of information (14 octets of Ethernet frame header plus 1,500 octets of data). The IP header indicates that this fragment is 1,500 octets in length and that more fragments associated with message ID = 59738 are coming. The fragment offset is 1,480, indicating that the data within Frame 14 starts 1,480 octets after the beginning of the original datagram. Note that the second IP header comprises 20 octets of Frame 14's data, but it does not count in the offset calculation because the IP header is not part of the original message.

212

The third fragment (Frame 15) contains 1,312 octets of information, consisting of a 20-octet IP header and 1,292 octets of data. This third IP header uses the same message ID = 59738 but indicates that no more fragments are coming (the More Fragments bit = 0). This fragment belongs 2,960 octets after the beginning of the original message.

Now let's see if the IP module in the Source host was working properly. The UDP header in Frame 13 says that the total length of this message is 4,252 octets. This is divided into the UDP header (8 octets), Data Fragment 1 (1,472 octets), Data Fragment 2 (1,480 octets), and Data Fragment 3 (1292 octets). Each fragment requires a 20-octet IP header, which does not count in the total. Each frame requires 14 octets of Ethernet header, which also does not count in the total. Reviewing Figure 4-12, we can see that the fragment offsets are also correct: 1,480 (8 + 1,472) for Fragment 2, and 2,960 (8 + 1,472 + 1,480) for Fragment 3. We can therefore conclude that the IP module within station DEC 029487 was functioning properly.

Sniffer Network Analyzer data 10-Dec at 11:20:38, file TCPIP.ENC, Pg 1

- - - - - - - - - - - - - - - Frame 13 - - - - - - - - - - - - - - - - -

SUMMARY	Delta T	Destination	Source	Summary
13	0.0152	IntrIn0027C0	DEC029487	DLC Ethertype=0800,
				size=1514 bytes
				IP D=[XXX.YYY.0.10]
				S=[XXX.YYY.0.33]
				LEN=1480 ID=59738
				UDP D=2049 S=1026 LEN=4252

```
DLC:  ------ DLC Header ------
DLC:
DLC:  Frame 13 arrived at  11:20:35.9514; frame size is 1514 (05EA hex) bytes.
DLC:  Destination = Station IntrIn0027C0
DLC:  Source      = Station DEC   029487
DLC:  Ethertype = 0800 (IP)
DLC:
IP:   ------ IP Header ------
IP:
IP:   Version = 4, header length = 20 bytes
IP:   Type of service = 00
IP:         000. .... = routine
IP:         ...0 .... = normal delay
IP:         .... 0... = normal throughput
```

IP: .... .0.. = normal reliability

IP: Total length = 1500 bytes

IP: Identification = 59738

IP: Flags = 2X

IP: .0.. .... = may fragment

IP: ..1. .... = more fragments

IP: Fragment offset = 0 bytes

IP: Time to live = 255 seconds/hops

IP: Protocol = 17 (UDP)

IP: Header checksum = 6421 (correct)

IP: Source address = [XXX.YYY.0.33]

IP: Destination address = [XXX.YYY.0.10]

IP: No options

IP:

UDP: ——- UDP Header ——-

UDP:

UDP: Source port = 1026

UDP: Destination port = 2049 (Sun RPC)

UDP: Length = 4252 (not all data contained in this fragment)

UDP: No checksum

UDP:

UDP: [1472 byte(s) of data]

UDP:

- - - - - - - - - - - - - - - Frame 14 - - - - - - - - - - - - - - - -

SUMMARY	Delta T	Destination	Source	Summary
14	0.0022	Intrln0027C0	DEC029487	DLC Ethertype=0800,
				size=1514 bytes
				IP D=[XXX.YYY.0.10]
				S=[XXX.YYY.0.33]
				LEN=1480 ID=59738
				UDP continuation ID=59738

DLC: ——- DLC Header ——-

DLC:

DLC: Frame 14 arrived at 11:20:35.9536; frame size is 1514 (05EA hex) bytes.

DLC: Destination = Station Intrln0027C0

DLC: Source   = Station DEC   029487

DLC: Ethertype = 0800 (IP)

DLC:

IP: ——- IP Header ——-

IP:

IP: Version = 4, header length = 20 bytes

214

IP: Type of service = 00
IP: 000. .... = routine
IP: ...0 .... = normal delay
IP: .... 0... = normal throughput
IP: .... .0.. = normal reliability
IP: Total length = 1500 bytes
IP: Identification = 59738
IP: Flags = 2X
IP: .0.. .... = may fragment
IP: ..1. .... = more fragments
IP: Fragment offset = 1480 bytes
IP: Time to live = 255 seconds/hops
IP: Protocol = 17 (UDP)
IP: Header checksum = 6368 (correct)
IP: Source address = [XXX.YYY.0.33]
IP: Destination address = [XXX.YYY.0.10]
IP: No options
IP:
UDP: [1480 byte(s) of data, continuation of IP ident=59738]

- - - - - - - - - - - - - - - - Frame 15 - - - - - - - - - - - - - - - - -

SUMMARY	Delta T	Destination	Source	Summary
15	0.0019	IntrIn0027C0	DEC029487	DLC Ethertype=0800,
				size=1326 bytes
				IP D=[XXX.YYY.0.10]
				S=[XXX.YYY.0.33]
				LEN=1292 ID=59738
				UDP continuation ID=59738

DLC: ——- DLC Header ——-
DLC:
DLC: Frame 15 arrived at 11:20:35.9556; frame size is 1326 (052E hex) bytes.
DLC: Destination = Station IntrIn0027C0
DLC: Source   = Station DEC   029487
DLC: Ethertype = 0800 (IP)
DLC:
IP: ——- IP Header ——-
IP:
IP: Version = 4, header length = 20 bytes
IP: Type of service = 00
IP: 000. .... = routine
IP: ...0 .... = normal delay
IP: .... 0... = normal throughput

IP: .... .0.. = normal reliability
IP: Total length = 1312 bytes
IP: Identification = 59738
IP: Flags = 0X
IP: .0.. .... = may fragment
IP: ..0. .... = last fragment
IP: Fragment offset = 2960 bytes
IP: Time to live = 255 seconds/hops
IP: Protocol = 17 (UDP)
IP: Header checksum = 836B (correct)
IP: Source address = [XXX.YYY.0.33]
IP: Destination address = [XXX.YYY.0.10]
IP: No options
IP:
UDP: [1292 byte(s) of data, continuation of IP ident=59738]

Trace 4.8.2. IP Fragments

4.8.3 Measuring the Aging of ARP Tables

One of the router parameters that network managers must determine is the time period for aging the ARP tables. If the tables age too quickly, the network devices must resend ARP messages to discover the correct Hardware address of an intended destination. Retransmitting ARPs needlessly consumes internetwork bandwidth. Conversely, if the tables age out too slowly (or not at all), the transmission might go to an obsolete (or incorrect) address. Router manufacturers allow the administrator to tailor the ARP table's aging period to respond to local traffic patterns. After you set the time period, it is useful to test the aging with a protocol analyzer to verify proper operation. Let's see how to do this.

First we filter the data to show only the ARP messages (Trace 4.8.3a). From this we see that several devices are active, including Bay Networks Inc.'s Link Node routers (shown as Router LN1 and Router LN2), a Cisco Systems Inc.'s IGS router (shown as Router IGS), and a Sun SPARCstation (shown as Sparcstn). For a consistent test, all of the ARP Request messages ask for a device on the same subnet [192.92.168.X]. The Delta T column gives the time between transmissions in seconds and measures the delay between ARP Requests and Replies.

To determine whether the ARP table of a particular device is operating properly, the analyzer further filters the data to show only the transmission to and from that device. Trace 4.8.3b shows a Bay Networks Link Node router. Frame 4 is set as the baseline for all time measurements. By adding the Delta T measurements, we can determine the time between the transmission of any two frames. Router LN1 broadcasts an ARP message in Frame 4 looking for the Hardware address associated with [192.92.168.3]. Router LN2 responds almost immediately in Frame 6. The next time this Hardware address is requested is almost 158 seconds (about 2.5 minutes) later in Frame 142 (we calculate this by adding the significant Delta T measurements: $11.0 + 1.9 + 14.1 + 130.7 = 157.7$ seconds). Another Bay Networks router responds (Frame 144). The ARP cache timer within the Bay Networks routers was set to age out after two minutes. We note that the ARP Request is retransmitted after 2.5 minutes, thus verifying the proper operation of the timer. From this we can also conclude that the ARP tables in both LN1 and LN2 are functioning properly, since the same values are used for ARP requests and replies on several occasions. Consider implementing a similar test any time you install a new router to verify its proper operation and to eliminate the possibility of excessive traffic due to unnecessary ARP Requests.

Sniffer Network Analyzer data 17-Feb at 13:25:20, ARPTST1.ENC, Pg 1

SUMMARY	Delta T	Destination	Source	Summary
M 4		Broadcast	Router LN1	ARP C PA=[192.92.168.3] PRO=IP
5	0.0001	Broadcast	Router LN1	ARP C PA=[192.92.168.3] PRO=IP
6	0.0005	Router LN1	Router LN2	ARP R PA=[192.92.168.3]
				HA=0000A2009459 PRO=IP
7	0.0010	Router LN1	Router LN2	ARP R PA=[192.92.168.3]
				HA=0000A2009459 PRO=IP
17	11.0782	Broadcast	Router IGS	ARP R PA=[192.92.168.1]
				HA=00000C0079AF PRO=IP
21	1.9512	Broadcast	Router LN2	ARP C PA=[192.92.168.6] PRO=IP
22	0.0002	Broadcast	Router LN2	ARP C PA=[192.92.168.6] PRO=IP
23	0.0001	Router LN2	SparcStn	ARP R PA=[192.92.168.6]
				HA=080020103170 PRO=IP
36	14.1529	Broadcast	Router IGS	ARP C PA=[192.92.168.3] PRO=IP
37	0.0006	Router IGS	Router LN2	ARP R PA=[192.92.168.3]
				HA=0000A2009459 PRO=IP
142	130.7503	Broadcast	Router LN1	ARP C PA=[192.92.168.3] PRO=IP
143	0.0001	Broadcast	Router LN1	ARP C PA=[192.92.168.3] PRO=IP
144	0.0005	Router LN1	Router LN2	ARP R PA=[192.92.168.3]
				HA=0000A2009459 PRO=IP
145	0.0010	Router LN1	Router LN2	ARP R PA=[192.92.168.3]
				HA=0000A2009459 PRO=IP
154	6.2799	Broadcast	Router LN2	ARP C PA=[192.92.168.6] PRO=IP

155	0.0002	Broadcast	Router LN2	ARP C PA=[192.92.168.6] PRO=IP
156	0.0001	Router LN2	SparcStn	ARP R PA=[192.92.168.6] HA=080020103170 PRO=IP
165	7.9092	Broadcast	Router LN2	ARP C PA=[192.92.168.1] PRO=IP
166	0.0001	Broadcast	Router LN2	ARP C PA=[192.92.168.1] PRO=IP
167	0.0015	Router LN2	Router IGS	ARP R PA=[192.92.168.1] HA=00000C0079AF PRO=IP
168	0.0009	Router LN2	Router IGS	ARP R PA=[192.92.168.1] HA=00000C0079AF PRO=IP

Trace 4.8.3a. ARP Messages from Various Routers

Sniffer Network Analyzer data 17-Feb at 13:25:20, ARPTST1.ENC, Pg 1

SUMMARY	Delta T	Rel Time	Destination	Source	Summary
M 4		0.0000	Broadcast	Router LN1	ARP C PA=[192.92.168.3] PRO=IP
5	.0001	0.0001	Broadcast	Router LN1	ARP C PA=[192.92.168.3] PRO=IP
6	0.0005	0.0007	Router LN1	Router LN2	ARP R PA=[192.92.168.3] HA=0000A2009459 PRO=IP
7	0.0010	0.0018	Router LN1	Router LN2	ARP R PA=[192.92.168.3] HA=0000A2009459 PRO=IP
142	157.9338	157.9357	Broadcast	Router LN1	ARP C PA=[192.92.168.3] PRO=IP
143	0.0001	157.9359	Broadcast	Router LN1	ARP C PA=[192.92.168.3] PRO=IP
144	0.0005	157.9365	Router LN1	Router LN2	ARP R PA=[192.92.168.3] HA=0000A2009459 PRO=IP
145	0.0010	157.9375	Router LN1	Router LN2	ARP R PA=[192.92.168.3] HA=0000A2009459 PRO=IP

Trace 4.8.3b. ARP Messages from a Bay Networks Link Node Router

4.8.4 Duplicate IP Addresses

In Section 4.1, we looked at the differences between the Physical (Hardware) address and the Logical (Internet Protocol) address on any internet node. Recall that a ROM on the network interface card (Ethernet, token ring, and so on) normally contains the Physical address, while the network administrator assigns the Logical address. Let's see what happens when human error affects address assignments.

In this scenario, two engineers, Wayne and Benoit, wish to establish TELNET sessions with a router. The router's TELNET capabilities allow administrators to access its configuration files for network management. Wayne establishes his session first (see Trace 4.8.4a). The TCP connection is established in Frames 1 through 3, and the TELNET session initiates beginning in Frame 5. Wayne's session appears to be proceeding normally until Benoit starts to transmit in Frame 43. Benoit sends an ARP broadcast looking for the same router (Frame 43), and the router responds in Frame 44. Benoit then establishes his TCP connection in Frames 45 through 48, and, like Wayne, initiates a TELNET session beginning in Frame 49. Benoit doesn't realize, however, that his presence on the internetwork has caused Wayne's connection to fail. Let's see why.

Details of Wayne's TCP connection message (Frame 1) are shown in Trace 4.8.4b. Note that Wayne is communicating to the router using IP source address [131.195.116.250] on the same Class B network. Wayne is accessing the TELNET port on the router, and is using Sequence Number = 265153482. The router acknowledges the use of this sequence number in its response, shown in Frame 2.

In Trace 4.8.4c, Benoit's TCP connection message looks similar (Frame 45). Benoit claims that his Source Address = [131.195.116.250] (the same as Wayne's) and that the Destination Address = [131.195.116.42]. The TCP header also identifies the same Destination Port (23, for TELNET), but uses a different Sequence Number (73138176).

We can now see why Wayne's TELNET connection failed. When Benoit established a connection with the router using the same IP source address as Wayne's, confusion resulted. The router was examining the IP source address, not the Hardware (Data Link Layer) address. As a result, it was unable to differentiate between the duplicate IP addresses.

We traced the problem to a duplicate entry on the network manager's address database. Unknowingly, he had given both Wayne and Benoit the same IP address for their workstations. After discovering this mistake, Wayne changed his workstation configuration file to incorporate a unique IP address and no further problems occurred.

Sniffer Network Analyzer data 11-Oct at 10:49:04, IPDUPLIC.ENC, Pg 1

SUMMARY	Delta T	Destination	Source	Summary
M 1		Router	Wayne	TCP D=23 S=2588 SYN SEQ=265153482 LEN=0 WIN=1024
2	0.0014	Wayne	Router	TCP D=2588 S=23 SYN ACK=265153483 SEQ=331344504 LEN=0 WIN=0
3	0.0016	Router	Wayne	TCP D=23 S=2588 ACK=331344505 WIN=1024
4	0.0019	Wayne	Router	TCP D=2588 S=23 ACK=265153483 WIN=2144
5	0.0048	Wayne	Router	Telnet R PORT=2588 IAC Will Echo
6	0.0304	Wayne	Router	Telnet R PORT=2588 <0D><0A>
7	0.0896	Router	Wayne	Telnet C PORT=2588 IAC Do Echo
8	0.3010	Wayne	Router	TCP D=2588 S=23 ACK=265153486 WIN=2141
9	0.0312	Router	Wayne	Telnet C PORT=2588 IAC Do Suppress go-ahead
10	0.3005	Wayne	Router	TCP D=2588 S=23 ACK=265153489 WIN=2138
11	0.4320	Router	Wayne	Telnet C PORT=2588 c
12	0.3000	Wayne	Router	TCP D=2588 S=23 ACK=265153490 WIN=2137
13	0.0016	Router	Wayne	Telnet C PORT=2588 d
14	0.2984	Wayne	Router	TCP D=2588 S=23 ACK=265153491 WIN=2136
15	0.0016	Router	Wayne	Telnet C PORT=2588 2
16	0.2985	Wayne	Router	TCP D=2588 S=23 ACK=265153492 WIN=2135
17	0.0016	Router	Wayne	Telnet C PORT=2588 <0D><0A>
18	0.0024	Wayne	Router	Telnet R PORT=2588 <0D><0A>CD_BAS1_2>
19	0.1206	Router	Wayne	TCP D=23 S=2588 ACK=331344857 WIN=1012
20	0.7757	Router	Wayne	Telnet C PORT=2588 s
21	0.0025	Wayne	Router	Telnet R PORT=2588 s

22	0.1552	Router	Wayne	TCP D=23 S=2588
				ACK=331344858 WIN=1023
23	0.1939	Router	Wayne	Telnet C PORT=2588 h
24	0.0030	Wayne	Router	Telnet R PORT=2588 h
25	0.1326	Router	Wayne	TCP D=23 S=2588
				ACK=331344859 WIN=1023
26	0.0158	Router	Wayne	Telnet C PORT=2588
27	0.0030	Wayne	Router	Telnet R PORT=2588
28	0.1458	Router	Wayne	TCP D=23 S=2588
				ACK=331344860 WIN=1023
29	0.0410	Router	Wayne	Telnet C PORT=2588 i
30	0.0026	Wayne	Router	Telnet R PORT=2588 i
31	0.1212	Router	Wayne	TCP D=23 S=2588
				ACK=331344861 WIN=1023
32	0.1134	Router	Wayne	Telnet C PORT=2588 n
33	0.0034	Wayne	Router	Telnet R PORT=2588 n
34	0.1575	Router	Wayne	TCP D=23 S=2588
				ACK=331344862 WIN=1023
35	0.2039	Router	Wayne	Telnet C PORT=2588 t
36	0.0027	Wayne	Router	Telnet R PORT=2588 t
37	0.1229	Router	Wayne	TCP D=23 S=2588
				ACK=331344863 WIN=1023
38	0.1116	Router	Wayne	Telnet C PORT=2588 <0D><0A>
39	0.0332	Wayne	Router	Telnet R PORT=2588
				<0D><0A><0D><0A>Ethernet 0
				line protocol is…
40	0.0026	Router	Wayne	TCP D=23 S=2588
				ACK=331345399 WIN=1024
41	0.0165	Wayne	Router	Telnet R PORT=2588
				ute output rate
				9325 bits/sec,
				2 packets/sec<0D>…
42	0.2203	Router	Wayne	TCP D=23 S=2588
				ACK=331345750 WIN=649
43	41.4005	Broadcast	Benoit	ARP C PA=[131.195.116.42]
				PRO=IP
44	0.0007	Benoit	Router	ARP R PA=[131.195.116.42]
				HA=00000C00A145 PRO=IP
45	0.0013	Router	Benoit	TCP D=23 S=15165 SYN
				SEQ=73138176 LEN=0 WIN=2048
46	0.0015	Benoit	Router	TCP D=15165 S=23 SYN
				ACK=73138177 SEQ=331390708
				LEN=0 WIN=0

47	0.0031	Router	Benoit	TCP D=23 S=15165 ACK=331390709 WIN=2048
48	0.0018	Benoit	Router	TCP D=15165 S=23 ACK=73138177 WIN=2144
49	0.0068	Benoit	Router	Telnet R PORT=15165 IAC Will Echo
50	0.0297	Benoit	Router	Telnet R PORT=15165 <0D><0A>
51	0.2341	Router	Benoit	Telnet C PORT=15165 IAC DoEcho
52	0.2997	Benoit	Router	TCP D=15165 S=23 ACK=73138180 WIN=2141
53	0.0323	Router	Benoit	Telnet C PORT=15165 IAC Do Suppress go-ahead
54	0.2995	Benoit	Router	TCP D=15165 S=23 ACK=73138183 WIN=2138

Trace 4.8.4a. Duplicate IP Address Summary

Sniffer Network Analyzer data 11-Oct at 10:49:04, IPDUPLIC.ENC, Pg 1

- - - - - - - - - - - - - - - - Frame 1 - - - - - - - - - - - - - - - - -

DLC: —— DLC Header ——-
DLC:
DLC: Frame 1 arrived at 10:49:08.4044; frame size is 60 (003C hex) bytes.
DLC: Destination = Station Cisco 00A145, Router
DLC: Source   = Station Intrln06C202, Wayne
DLC: Ethertype = 0800 (IP)
DLC:
IP: —— IP Header ——-
IP:
IP: Version = 4, header length = 20 bytes
IP: Type of service = 00
IP: 000. .... = routine
IP: ...0 .... = normal delay
IP: .... 0... = normal throughput
IP: .... .0.. = normal reliability
IP: Total length = 44 bytes
IP: Identification = 13
IP: Flags = 0X
IP: .0.. .... = may fragment
IP: ..0. .... = last fragment
IP: Fragment offset = 0 bytes
IP: Time to live = 64 seconds/hops
IP: Protocol = 6 (TCP)

```
IP:   Header checksum = 8A14 (correct)
IP:   Source address = [131.195.116.250]
IP:   Destination address = [131.195.116.42]
IP:   No options
IP:
TCP: ——- TCP header ——-
TCP:
TCP:  Source port = 2588
TCP:  Destination port = 23 (Telnet)
TCP:  Initial sequence number = 265153482
TCP:  Data offset = 24 bytes
TCP:  Flags = 02
TCP:  ..0. .... = (No urgent pointer)
TCP:  ...0 .... = (No acknowledgment)
TCP:  .... 0... = (No push)
TCP:  .... .0.. = (No reset)
TCP:  .... ..1. = SYN
TCP:  .... ...0 = (No FIN)
TCP:  Window = 1024
TCP:  Checksum = 9DAF (correct)
TCP:
TCP:  Options follow
TCP:  Maximum segment size = 1460
TCP:

- - - - - - - - - - - - - - - - Frame 2 - - - - - - - - - - - - - - - - -

DLC: ——- DLC Header ——-
DLC:
DLC:  Frame 2 arrived at  10:49:08.4059; frame size is 60 (003C hex) bytes.
DLC:  Destination = Station Intrln06C202, Wayne
DLC:  Source     = Station Cisco 00A145, Router
DLC:  Ethertype  = 0800 (IP)
DLC:
IP:   ——- IP Header ——-
IP:
IP:   Version = 4, header length = 20 bytes
IP:   Type of service = 00
IP:           000. .... = routine
IP:           ...0 .... = normal delay
IP:           .... 0... = normal throughput
IP:           .... .0.. = normal reliability
IP:   Total length = 44 bytes
IP:   Identification = 0
```

IP: Flags = 0X
IP: .0.. .... = may fragment
IP: ..0. .... = last fragment
IP: Fragment offset = 0 bytes
IP: Time to live = 255 seconds/hops
IP: Protocol = 6 (TCP)
IP: Header checksum = CB20 (correct)
IP: Source address = [131.195.116.42]
IP: Destination address = [131.195.116.250]
IP: No options
IP:
TCP: ——- TCP header ——-
TCP:
TCP: Source port = 23 (Telnet)
TCP: Destination port = 2588
TCP: Initial sequence number = 331344504
TCP: Acknowledgment number = 265153483
TCP: Data offset = 24 bytes
TCP: Flags = 12
TCP: ..0. .... = (No urgent pointer)
TCP: ...1 .... = Acknowledgment
TCP: .... 0... = (No push)
TCP: .... .0.. = (No reset)
TCP: .... ..1. = SYN
TCP: ....0 = (No FIN)
TCP: Window = 0
TCP: Checksum = A367 (correct)
TCP:
TCP: Options follow
TCP: Maximum segment size = 1460
TCP:

Trace 4.8.4b. Duplicate IP Address Details (Original station)

Sniffer Network Analyzer data 11-Oct at 10:49:04, IPDUPLIC.ENC, Pg 1

- - - - - - - - - - - - - - - Frame 45 - - - - - - - - - - - - - - - - -

DLC: ——- DLC Header ——-
DLC:
DLC: Frame 45 arrived at 10:49:54.6082; frame size is 60 (003C hex) bytes.
DLC: Destination = Station Cisco 00A145, Router
DLC: Source   = Station Intrln05E253, Benoit

```
DLC: Ethertype = 0800 (IP)
DLC:
IP: ——- IP Header ——-
IP:
IP:   Version = 4, header length = 20 bytes
IP:   Type of service = 10
IP:            000. .... = routine
IP:            ...1 .... = low delay
IP:            .... 0... = normal throughput
IP:            .... .0.. = normal reliability
IP:   Total length = 44 bytes
IP:   Identification = 1
IP:   Flags = 0X
IP:   .0.. .... = may fragment
IP:   ..0. .... = last fragment
IP:   Fragment offset = 0 bytes
IP:   Time to live = 64 seconds/hops
IP:   Protocol = 6 (TCP)
IP:   Header checksum = 8A10 (correct)
IP:   Source address = [131.195.116.250]
IP:   Destination address = [131.195.116.42]
IP:   No options
IP:
TCP: ——- TCP header ——-
TCP:
TCP:  Source port = 15165
TCP:  Destination port = 23 (Telnet)
TCP:  Initial sequence number = 73138176
TCP:  Data offset = 24 bytes
TCP:  Flags = 02
TCP:  ..0. .... = (No urgent pointer)
TCP:  ...0 .... = (No acknowledgment)
TCP:  .... 0... = (No push)
TCP:  .... .0.. = (No reset)
TCP:  .... ..1. = SYN
TCP:  .... ...0 = (No FIN)
TCP:  Window = 2048
TCP:  Checksum = 5FCA (correct)
TCP:
TCP:  Options follow
TCP:  Maximum segment size = 1460
TCP:
```

- - - - - - - - - - - - - - - Frame 46 - - - - - - - - - - - - - - - - -

DLC: ——— DLC Header ———-
DLC:
DLC: Frame 46 arrived at 10:49:54.6097; frame size is 60 (003C hex) bytes.
DLC: Destination = Station Intrln05E253, Benoit
DLC: Source   = Station Cisco 00A145, Router
DLC: Ethertype = 0800 (IP)
DLC:
IP: ——— IP Header ———-
IP:
IP: Version = 4, header length = 20 bytes
IP: Type of service = 00
IP: 000. .... = routine
IP: ...0 .... = normal delay
IP: .... 0... = normal throughput
IP: .... .0.. = normal reliability
IP: Total length = 44 bytes
IP: Identification = 0
IP: Flags = 0X
IP: .0.. .... = may fragment
IP: ..0. .... = last fragment
IP: Fragment offset = 0 bytes
IP: Time to live = 255 seconds/hops
IP: Protocol = 6 (TCP)
IP: Header checksum = CB20 (correct)
IP: Source address = [131.195.116.42]
IP: Destination address = [131.195.116.250]
IP: No options
IP:
TCP: ——— TCP header ———-
TCP:
TCP: Source port = 23 (Telnet)
TCP: Destination port = 15165
TCP: Initial sequence number = 331390708
TCP: Acknowledgment number = 73138177
TCP: Data offset = 24 bytes
TCP: Flags = 12
TCP: ..0. .... = (No urgent pointer)
TCP: ...1 .... = Acknowledgment
TCP: .... 0... = (No push)
TCP: .... .0.. = (No reset)
TCP: .... ..1. = SYN

TCP: ....0 = (No FIN)
TCP: Window = 0
TCP: Checksum = B505 (correct)
TCP:
TCP: Options follow
TCP: Maximum segment size = 1460
TCP:

Trace 4.8.4c. Duplicate IP Address Details (Duplicate station)

4.8.5 Incorrect Address Mask

As discussed in Section 4.2, system implementors can use subnetworks to form a hierarchical routing structure within an internetwork. Subnet addressing works as follows: A 32-bit IP address is comprised of a Network ID plus a Host ID. For example, a Class B network uses 16 bits for the network portion and 16 bits for the host portion. If an internet has multiple physical networks (e.g., LANs), the 16-bit host portion of the address can be further divided into a subnetwork address (representing the particular physical network, such as an Ethernet) and a host address (representing a particular device on that Ethernet). Class B addresses commonly use 8-bit subnetting. This would give a Network ID of 16 bits, a Subnetwork ID of 8 bits, and a Host ID of 8 bits. Thus, it could uniquely identify up to 254 subnetworks (i.e., LANs), each having up to 254 hosts (i.e., workstations, servers, and so on). Recall that the all zeros and all ones addresses are not allowed, thus reducing the theoretical limit of 256 subnetworks and 256 hosts to 254 of each (256 - 2 = 254). The first 16 bits (the Network ID) would deliver the datagram to the access point for the network (the router). The router would then decide which of the 254 subnetworks this datagram was destined for. The router uses a Subnet Mask to make that decision. Subnet Masks are stored within the host and are obtained using the ICMP Address Mask Request message. This case study will show what happens when the host uses an incorrect Subnet Mask.

In this example, a network manager, Paul, wishes to check the status of a host on a different segment but connected via a bridge (see Figure 4-11). Paul's workstation software stores a number of parameters, including the Subnet Mask. The network in question is a Class B network, without subnetting. The Subnet Mask should be set for [255.255.0.0], corresponding with a Network ID of 16 bits and a Host ID of 16 bits. Since subnetting is not used, all datagrams for the local network should be delivered directly, but datagrams destined for another network should go through the router.

Paul uses the ICMP Echo (PING) command to check the status of his host (a Sun 4 Server), but there's a delay in the ICMP Echo Reply. Let's see what happened.

Paul's workstation first broadcasts an ARP message looking for a router (Frames 1-2 in Trace 4.8.5a). This step is unexpected, since a router is not required for this transaction. Next, it attempts an ICMP Echo message (Frame 3). If all systems are functioning properly, an ICMP Echo Reply should follow the ICMP Echo immediately. In Paul's case, however, the ICMP Redirect message in Frame 4 follows the ICMP Echo. The Redirect message (see Trace 4.8.5b) indicates that it is redirecting datagrams for the host (ICMP Code = 1), and that the correct router (gateway) for this operation is [132.XXX.132.12]. Paul's workstation then sends another ARP Request, looking for address [132.XXX.132.12] in Frame 5. The Sun 4 Server responds with HA = 0800200C1DC3H (Frame 6). The ICMP Echo and Echo Reply then proceed as expected in Frames 7 and 8. The question remains: Why did Paul's workstation access the router, causing the ICMP Redirect Message?

The second ICMP Echo (Frame 7) sent from Paul's workstation [132.XXX.129.15] to the Sun 4 Server [132.XXX.132.12] provides a clue. Note that both devices are on the same network [132.XXX]. Since this is a Class B network without subnetting, the Subnet Mask should be [255.255.0.0]. When Paul examined the Subnet Mask in his workstation parameters, he found that it had been set for a Class B network with an 8-bit subnet address field, i.e., [255.255.255.0]. When his workstation calculated the Subnet Mask, it came up with:

```
Subnet Mask            11111111  11111111  11111111  00000000
    AND
Source Address         10000100  XXXXXXXX  10000001  00001111
[132.XXX.129.15]
Result #1              10000100  XXXXXXXX  10000001  00000000


Subnet Mask            11111111  11111111  11111111  00000000
    AND
Destination Address 1000100  XXXXXXXX  10000100  00001100
[132.XXX.132.12]
Result #2              1000100  XXXXXXXX  10000100  00000000
```

Because the workstation found that Result #1 and Result #2 were different, it incorrectly concluded that the two devices were on different subnetworks, requiring the assistance of the router. When Paul reconfigured his workstation's Subnet Mask to [255.255.0.0], the ICMP Echo and Echo Replies proceeded without router intervention.

Sniffer Network Analyzer data 13-Feb at 14:50:26, SUBNETC.ENC, Pg 1

SUMMARY	Delta T	Destination	Source	Summary
M 1		Broadcast	Paul	ARP C PA=[132.XXX.1.1] PRO=IP
2	0.0011	Paul	Router	ARP R PA=[132.XXX.1.1] HA=000093E0A0BF PRO=IP
3	0.0022	Router	Paul	ICMP Echo
4	0.0021	Paul	Router	ICMP Redirect (Redirect datagrams for the host)
5	11.7626	Broadcast	Paul	ARP C PA=[132.XXX.132.12] PRO=IP
6	0.0008	Paul	Sun4Svr	ARP R PA=[132.XXX.132.12] HA=0800200C1DC3 PRO=IP
7	0.0023	Sun4Svr	Paul	ICMP Echo
8	0.0016	Paul	Sun4Svr	ICMP Echo reply

Trace 4.8.5a. Subnet Mask Misconfiguration Summary

Sniffer Network Analyzer data 13-Feb at 14:50:26, SUBNETC.ENC, Pg 1

- - - - - - - - - - - - - - - Frame 3 - - - - - - - - - - - - - - - - -

ICMP: —— ICMP header ——
ICMP:
ICMP: Type = 8 (Echo)
ICMP: Code = 0
ICMP: Checksum = 719E (correct)
ICMP: Identifier = 1315
ICMP: Sequence number = 1
ICMP: [256 bytes of data]
ICMP:
ICMP: [Normal end of "ICMP header".]
ICMP:

- - - - - - - - - - - - - - - Frame 4 - - - - - - - - - - - - - - - - -

ICMP: —— ICMP header ——
ICMP:
ICMP: Type = 5 (Redirect)

ICMP: Code = 1 (Redirect datagrams for the host)

ICMP: Checksum = 738C (correct)

ICMP: Gateway internet address = [132.XXX.132.12]

ICMP: IP header of originating message (description follows)

ICMP:

IP: ——- IP Header ——-

IP:

IP: Version = 4, header length = 20 bytes

IP: Type of service = 00

IP: 000. .... = routine

IP: ...0 .... = normal delay

IP: .... 0... = normal throughput

IP: .... .0.. = normal reliability

IP: Total length = 284 bytes

IP: Identification = 2

IP: Flags = 0X

IP: .0.. .... = may fragment

IP: ..0. .... = last fragment

IP: Fragment offset = 0 bytes

IP: Time to live = 63 seconds/hops

IP: Protocol = 1 (ICMP)

IP: Header checksum = 6C7D (correct)

IP: Source address = [132.XXX.129.15]

IP: Destination address = [132.XXX.132.12]

IP: No options

ICMP:

ICMP: [First 8 byte(s) of data of originating message]

ICMP:

ICMP: [Normal end of "ICMP header".]

ICMP:

- - - - - - - - - - - - - - - - Frame 7 - - - - - - - - - - - - - - - - -

ICMP: ——- ICMP header ——-

ICMP:

ICMP: Type = 8 (Echo)

ICMP: Code = 0

ICMP: Checksum = 4070 (correct)

ICMP: Identifier = 13905

ICMP: Sequence number = 1

ICMP: [256 bytes of data]

ICMP:

ICMP: [Normal end of "ICMP header".]

ICMP:

- - - - - - - - - - - - - - - - Frame 8 - - - - - - - - - - - - - - - -

ICMP: ――― ICMP header ―――
ICMP:
ICMP: Type = 0 (Echo reply)
ICMP: Code = 0
ICMP: Checksum = 4870 (correct)
ICMP: Identifier = 13905
ICMP: Sequence number = 1
ICMP: [256 bytes of data]
ICMP:
ICMP: [Normal end of "ICMP header".]
ICMP:

Trace 4.8.5b. Subnet Mask Misconfiguration ICMP Details

4.8.6 Using ICMP Echo Messages

ICMP messages can answer many questions about the health of the network. The ICMP Echo/Echo Reply messages, commonly known as the PING, are probably the most frequently used. You invoke PING from your host operating system to test the path to a particular host. If all is well, a message will return verifying the existence of the path to the host or network. One caution is in order, however: unpredictable results can occur if you PING an improper destination address. For example, PINGing address [255.255.255.255] (limited broadcast within this subnet) may cause excessive internetwork traffic. Let's look at an example.

One lonely weekend, a network administrator decides to test the paths to some of the hosts on his internet. He has two ways to accomplish this. He could send an ICMP Echo message to each host separately, or he could send a directed broadcast to all hosts on his network and subnetwork. He decides to enter the Destination address [129.99.23.255] that PINGs all of the hosts on Class B network 129.99, subnet 23. Trace 4.8.6a shows the result. Frame 683 is the ICMP Echo (PING); the network administrator receives 27 frames containing ICMP Echo Reply messages. Note that all of the reply messages are directed to the originator of the ICMP Echo message, workstation 020C5D. Also note that the Bay Networks routers on this network did not respond to the PING because their design protects against such a transmission. Other hosts or routers may be designed with such a safeguard in place as well.

Details of the ICMP Echo (Frame 683) and the first ICMP Echo Reply (Frame 684) are given in Trace 4.8.6b. The Echo's Destination address is set for broadcast, and it indicates that the Echo Replies come back to the originating station. As the trace shows, the message originator [129.99.23.146] has specified that all hosts on subnet 23 should respond by setting the Destination address to [129.99.23.255]. The first response (Frame 684) is from device [129.99.23.17], followed by responses from 26 other hosts (Frames 685 through 712). Also note that the ICMP header contains an Identifier (18501) that correlates Echo and Echo Reply messages in case PINGs to/from different hosts occur simultaneously. The 56 octets of data transmitted with the Echo message are returned with the Echo Reply.

We can draw one clear conclusion from this exercise: The ICMP Echo message can be a very valuable troubleshooting tool, but make sure of your destination before you initiate the command. A PING to a broadcast address could have a great impact on the internetwork traffic.

Sniffer Network Analyzer data 17-Feb at 15:31:08, PINGTST4.ENC, Pg 1

SUMMARY	Delta T	Destination	Source	Summary
683		Broadcast	SilGrf 020C5D	ICMP Echo
684	0.0004	SilGrf020C5D	SilGrf 060C44	ICMP Echo reply
685	0.0004	SilGrf020C5D	SilGrf 020FF9	ICMP Echo reply
686	0.0003	SilGrf020C5D	Sun 106604	ICMP Echo reply
687	0.0003	SilGrf020C5D	Sun 0F5DC2	ICMP Echo reply
688	0.0002	SilGrf020C5D	Sun 08FE6B	ICMP Echo reply
689	0.0003	SilGrf020C5D	SilGrf 021193	ICMP Echo reply
690	0.0001	SilGrf020C5D	SilGrf 02137B	ICMP Echo reply
691	0.0004	SilGrf020C5D	Sun 094668	ICMP Echo reply
692	0.0003	SilGrf020C5D	Prteon1064D6	ICMP Echo reply
693	0.0002	SilGrf020C5D	Sun 062A16	ICMP Echo reply
694	0.0002	SilGrf020C5D	Sun 00DAFF	ICMP Echo reply
695	0.0002	SilGrf020C5D	CMC A00666	ICMP Echo reply
696	0.0002	SilGrf020C5D	Sun 00E849	ICMP Echo reply
697	0.0003	SilGrf020C5D	Sun 005513	ICMP Echo reply
698	0.0001	SilGrf020C5D	NSC 010212	ICMP Echo reply
699	0.0002	SilGrf020C5D	00802D0020F8	ICMP Echo reply
700	0.0001	SilGrf020C5D	Exceln 231835	ICMP Echo reply
701	0.0002	SilGrf020C5D	00802D002202	ICMP Echo reply
702	0.0001	SilGrf020C5D	DEC 0A136F	ICMP Echo reply

703	0.0001	SilGrf020C5D	DECnet00F760	ICMP Echo reply
704	0.0001	SilGrf020C5D	Sun 0045AD	ICMP Echo reply
705	0.0001	SilGrf020C5D	Intel 0361A8	ICMP Echo reply
706	0.0001	SilGrf020C5D	Sun 0A73A2	ICMP Echo reply
707	0.0001	SilGrf020C5D	DEC 0D0B05	ICMP Echo reply
708	0.0001	SilGrf020C5D	Sun 00F725	ICMP Echo reply
709	0.0001	SilGrf020C5D	SilGrf 020C38	ICMP Echo reply
712	0.0211	SilGrf020C5D	Intrln 008248	ICMP Echo reply

Trace 4.8.6a. ICMP Echo to IP Address [X.X.X.255] Summary

Sniffer Network Analyzer data 17-Feb at 15:31:08, PINGTST4.ENC, Pg 1

- - - - - - - - - - - - - - - Frame 683 - - - - - - - - - - - - - - - - -

DLC: ——- DLC Header ——-
DLC:
DLC: Frame 683 arrived at 15:31:50.3581; frame size is 102 (0066 hex) bytes.
DLC: Destination = BROADCAST FFFFFFFFFFFF, Broadcast
DLC: Source   = Station SilGrf020C5D
DLC: Ethertype = 0800 (IP)
DLC:
IP: ——- IP Header ——-
IP:
IP: Version = 4, header length = 20 bytes
IP: Type of service = 00
IP: 000. .... = routine
IP: ...0 .... = normal delay
IP: .... 0... = normal throughput
IP: .... .0.. = normal reliability
IP: Total length = 84 bytes
IP: Identification = 16898
IP: Flags = 0X
IP: .0.. .... = may fragment
IP: ..0. .... = last fragment
IP: Fragment offset = 0 bytes
IP: Time to live = 255 seconds/hops
IP: Protocol = 1 (ICMP)
IP: Header checksum = 474F (correct)
IP: Source address = [129.99.23.146]
IP: Destination address = [129.99.23.255]
IP: No options
IP:

```
ICMP:  ——- ICMP header ——-
ICMP:
ICMP:  Type = 8 (Echo)
ICMP:  Code = 0
ICMP:  Checksum = 851E (correct)
ICMP:  Identifier = 18501
ICMP:  Sequence number = 0
ICMP:  [56 bytes of data]
ICMP:
ICMP:  [Normal end of "ICMP header".]
ICMP:
```

```
- - - - - - - - - - - - - - - - Frame 684 - - - - - - - - - - - - - - - - -
```

```
DLC:  ——- DLC Header ——-
DLC:
DLC:  Frame 684 arrived at  15:31:50.3585; frame size is 98 (0062 hex) bytes.
DLC:  Destination = Station SilGrf020C5D
DLC:  Source      = Station SilGrf060C44
DLC:  Ethertype  = 0800 (IP)
DLC:
IP:   ——- IP Header ——-
IP:
IP:   Version = 4, header length = 20 bytes
IP:   Type of service = 00
IP:            000. .... = routine
IP:            ...0 .... = normal delay
IP:            .... 0... = normal throughput
IP:            .... .0.. = normal reliability
IP:   Total length = 84 bytes
IP:   Identification = 985
IP:   Flags = 0X
IP:   .0.. .... = may fragment
IP:   ..0. .... = last fragment
IP:   Fragment offset = 0 bytes
IP:   Time to live = 255 seconds/hops
IP:   Protocol = 1 (ICMP)
IP:   Header checksum = 8666 (correct)
IP:   Source address = [129.99.23.17]
IP:   Destination address = [129.99.23.146]
IP:   No options
IP:
```

234

```
ICMP: ——- ICMP header ——-
ICMP:
ICMP:  Type = 0 (Echo reply)
ICMP:  Code = 0
ICMP:  Checksum = 8D1E (correct)
ICMP:  Identifier = 18501
ICMP:  Sequence number = 0
ICMP:  [56 bytes of data]
ICMP:
ICMP:  [Normal end of "ICMP header".]
ICMP:
```

Trace 4.8.6b. ICMP Echo to IP Address [X.X.X.255] Details

4.8.7 Misdirected Datagrams

In Section 4.5, we studied the operation of the Internet Control Message Protocol (ICMP) and saw how the ICMP Redirect message (ICMP Type = 5) corrects routing problems. A unique code within the ICMP message specifies the datagrams to be redirected (review Figure 4-9).

In this example, a workstation wishes to communicate with a remote host on another subnetwork (see Figure 4-13). Unfortunately, the workstation's configuration file is incorrect, and its initial attempt to communicate with the remote host fails (see Trace 4.8.7a). From out of the internet comes an intelligent router to the rescue! Router 234 (the workstation's default router) recognizes the error and issues an ICMP Redirect in Frame 4. The workstation obliges, switches its transmissions to the correct path (Router 235) in Frame 5, and successfully establishes a TELNET session with the remote host (Frames 6 through 20). Let's look inside the ICMP messages and see what happened (Trace 4.8.7b).

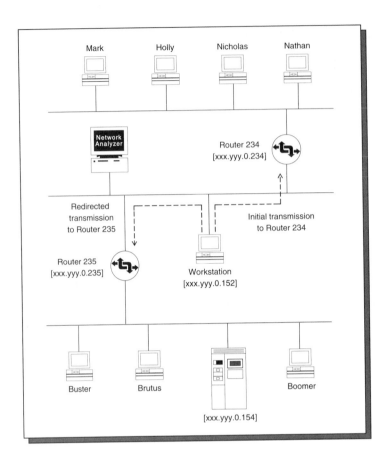

Figure 4-13. Misdirected Datagram Topology

The workstation's initial transmission (Frame 3) is directed to Router 234, with the datagram destined for the remote Host address [XXX.YYY.0.154]. We know that a router will be involved in the communication because the Source address (the workstation address) [XXX.YYY.0.152], and the Host address [XXX.YYY.0.154] are on different subnetworks. Router 234 responds to this initial transmission by issuing an ICMP Redirect in Frame 4. We can now identify the IP address of Router 234 (the Source address [XXX.YYY.0.234] of the ICMP Redirect). The ICMP header indicates a Redirect for the host (ICMP Code = 1) and the correct path, which is via Router 235, address [XXX.YYY.0.235].

The workstation sees the error of its ways and changes the Destination hardware address to be Router 235 (Frame 5). Note that the Source and Destination IP addresses did not change between Frame 3 and Frame 5. In other words, the workstation knew who it wanted to communicate with, it just didn't know how to get there. Frame 6 shows the confirmation of the redirected path; that datagram is a response from the remote host (IP Source address = [XXX.YYY.0.154]).

Upon further study, the network manager discovered that the workstation's default gateway had been set incorrectly. When this parameter was changed to reflect Router 235 (instead of Router 234) the problem did not reoccur.

Sniffer Network Analyzer data 2-Mar at 10:17:44, RICMP.ENC, Pg 1

SUMMARY	Delta T	Destination	Source	Summary
3	0.0162	Router 234	Workstation	Telnet R PORT=2909 <0D><0A>
4	0.0029	Workstation	Router 234	ICMP Redirect (Redirect datagrams for the host)
5	0.0118	Router 235	Workstation	Telnet R PORT=2909 $
6	0.0941	Workstation	Router 235	TCP D=23 S=2909 ACK=813932917 WIN=4096
7	3.7848	Workstation	Router 235	Telnet C PORT=2909 p
8	0.0088	Router 235	Workstation	Telnet R PORT=2909 p
9	0.0065	Workstation	Router 235	TCP D=23 S=2909 ACK=813932918 WIN=4096
10	0.3042	Workstation	Router 235	Telnet C PORT=2909 s
11	0.0082	Router 235	Workstation	Telnet R PORT=2909 s
12	0.0881	Workstation	Router 235	TCP D=23 S=2909 ACK=813932919 WIN=4096
13	0.0053	Workstation	Router 235	Telnet C PORT=2909
14	0.0080	Router 235	Workstation	Telnet R PORT=2909
15	0.1858	Workstation	Router 235	TCP D=23 S=2909 ACK=813932920 WIN=4096
16	0.5343	Workstation	Router 235	Telnet C PORT=2909 -
17	0.0078	Router 235	Workstation	Telnet R PORT=2909 -
18	0.0577	Workstation	Router 235	TCP D=23 S=2909 ACK=813932921 WIN=4096
19	0.1744	Workstation	Router 235	Telnet C PORT=2909 a
20	0.0078	Router 235	Workstation	Telnet R PORT=2909 a

Trace 4.8.7a. Misdirected Datagram Summary

Sniffer Network Analyzer data 2-Mar at 10:17:44, RICMP.ENC, Pg 1

- - - - - - - - - - - - - - - Frame 3 - - - - - - - - - - - - - - - - -

DLC: —— DLC Header ——-

DLC:

DLC: Frame 3 arrived at 10:21:01.5697; frame size is 74 (004A hex) bytes.

DLC: Destination = Station XXXXXX 002461, Router 234

DLC: Source   = Station XXXXXX 01BB41, Workstation

DLC: Ethertype = 0800 (IP)

DLC:

IP: —— IP Header ——-

IP:

IP: Version = 4, header length = 20 bytes

IP: Type of service = 00

IP: 000. .... = routine

IP: ...0 .... = normal delay

IP: .... 0... = normal throughput

IP: .... .0.. = normal reliability

IP: Total length = 42 bytes

IP: Identification = 2931

IP: Flags = 0X

IP: .0.. .... = may fragment

IP: ..0. .... = last fragment

IP: Fragment offset = 0 bytes

IP: Time to live = 30 seconds/hops

IP: Protocol = 6 (TCP)

IP: Header checksum = 31A8 (correct)

IP: Source address = [XXX.YYY.0.152]

IP: Destination address = [XXX.YYY.0.154]

IP: No options

IP:

TCP: —— TCP header ——-

TCP:

TCP: Source port = 23 (Telnet)

TCP: Destination port = 2909

TCP: Sequence number = 813932913

TCP: Acknowledgment number = 63520058

TCP: Data offset = 20 bytes

TCP: Flags = 18

TCP: ..0. .... = (No urgent pointer)

TCP: ...1 .... = Acknowledgment

TCP: .... 1... = Push

TCP: .... .0.. = (No reset)

TCP: .... ..0. = (No SYN)

TCP: ....0 = (No FIN)

TCP: Window = 9116

TCP: Checksum = 0105 (correct)

TCP: No TCP options

TCP: [2 byte(s) of data]

TCP:

Telnet:——— Telnet data ———

Telnet:

Telnet:<0D><0A>

Telnet:

- - - - - - - - - - - - - - - - Frame 4 - - - - - - - - - - - - - - - - -

DLC: ——— DLC Header ———

DLC:

DLC: Frame 4 arrived at 10:21:01.5726; frame size is 70 (0046 hex) bytes.

DLC: Destination = Station XXXXXX 01BB41, Workstation

DLC: Source   = Station XXXXXX 002461, Router 234

DLC: Ethertype = 0800 (IP)

DLC:

IP: ——— IP Header ———

IP:

IP: Version = 4, header length = 20 bytes

IP: Type of service = 00

IP: 000. .... = routine

IP: ...0 .... = normal delay

IP: .... 0... = normal throughput

IP: .... .0.. = normal reliability

IP: Total length = 56 bytes

IP: Identification = 0

IP: Flags = 0X

IP: .0.. .... = may fragment

IP: ..0. .... = last fragment

IP: Fragment offset = 0 bytes

IP: Time to live = 255 seconds/hops

IP: Protocol = 1 (ICMP)

IP: Header checksum = 5CA3 (correct)

IP: Source address = [XXX.YYY.0.234]

IP: Destination address = [XXX.YYY.0.152]

IP: No options

IP:

```
ICMP: ——- ICMP header ——-
ICMP:
ICMP: Type = 5 (Redirect)
ICMP: Code = 1 (Redirect datagrams for the host)
ICMP: Checksum = EE0C (correct)
ICMP: Gateway internet address = [XXX.YYY.0.235]
ICMP: IP header of originating message (description follows)
ICMP:
IP: ——- IP Header ——-
IP:
IP: Version = 4, header length = 20 bytes
IP: Type of service = 00
IP:      000. .... = routine
IP:      ...0 .... = normal delay
IP:      .... 0... = normal throughput
IP:      .... .0.. = normal reliability
IP: Total length = 42 bytes
IP: Identification = 2931
IP: Flags = 0X
IP: .0.. .... = may fragment
IP: ..0. .... = last fragment
IP: Fragment offset = 0 bytes
IP: Time to live = 29 seconds/hops
IP: Protocol = 6 (TCP)
IP: Header checksum = 32A8 (correct)
IP: Source address = [XXX.YYY.0.152]
IP: Destination address = [XXX.YYY.0.154]
IP: No options
ICMP:
ICMP: [First 8 byte(s) of data of originating message]
ICMP:
ICMP: [Normal end of "ICMP header".]
ICMP:

- - - - - - - - - - - - - - - Frame 5 - - - - - - - - - - - - - - - -

DLC: ——- DLC Header ——-
DLC:
DLC: Frame 5 arrived at  10:21:01.5845; frame size is 74 (004A hex) bytes.
DLC: Destination = Station XXXXXX 00244F, Router 235
DLC: Source     = Station XXXXXX 01BB41, Workstation
DLC: Ethertype  = 0800 (IP)
DLC:
```

```
IP:  ——— IP Header ———-
IP:
IP:   Version = 4, header length = 20 bytes
IP:   Type of service = 00
IP:           000. .... = routine
IP:           ...0 .... = normal delay
IP:           .... 0... = normal throughput
IP:           .... .0.. = normal reliability
IP:   Total length = 42 bytes
IP:   Identification = 2932
IP:   Flags = 0X
IP:   .0.. .... = may fragment
IP:   ..0. .... = last fragment
IP:   Fragment offset = 0 bytes
IP:   Time to live = 30 seconds/hops
IP:   Protocol = 6 (TCP)
IP:   Header checksum = 31A7 (correct)
IP:   Source address = [XXX.YYY.0.152]
IP:   Destination address = [XXX.YYY.0.154]
IP:   No options
IP:
TCP:  ——— TCP header ———-
TCP:
TCP:  Source port = 23 (Telnet)
TCP:  Destination port = 2909
TCP:  Sequence number = 813932915
TCP:  Acknowledgment number = 63520058
TCP:  Data offset = 20 bytes
TCP:  Flags = 18
TCP:  ..0. .... = (No urgent pointer)
TCP:  ...1 .... = Acknowledgment
TCP:  .... 1... = Push
TCP:  .... .0.. = (No reset)
TCP:  .... ..0. = (No SYN)
TCP:  .... ...0 = (No FIN)
TCP:  Window = 9116
TCP:  Checksum = E9EC (correct)
TCP:  No TCP options
TCP:  [2 byte(s) of data]
TCP:
Telnet:——— Telnet data ———-
Telnet:
```

Telnet:$

Telnet:

- - - - - - - - - - - - - - - Frame 6 - - - - - - - - - - - - - - - - -

DLC: ——- DLC Header ——-

DLC:

DLC: Frame 6 arrived at 10:21:01.6787; frame size is 60 (003C hex) bytes.

DLC: Destination = Station XXXXXX 01BB41, Workstation

DLC: Source   = Station XXXXXX 00244F, Router 235

DLC: Ethertype = 0800 (IP)

DLC:

IP: ——- IP Header ——-

IP:

IP: Version = 4, header length = 20 bytes

IP: Type of service = 00

IP: 000. .... = routine

IP: ...0 .... = normal delay

IP: .... 0... = normal throughput

IP: .... .0.. = normal reliability

IP: Total length = 40 bytes

IP: Identification = 37695

IP: Flags = 0X

IP: .0.. .... = may fragment

IP: ..0. .... = last fragment

IP: Fragment offset = 0 bytes

IP: Time to live = 58 seconds/hops

IP: Protocol = 6 (TCP)

IP: Header checksum = 8DDD (correct)

IP: Source address = [XXX.YYY.0.154]

IP: Destination address = [XXX.YYY.0.152]

IP: No options

IP:

TCP: ——- TCP header ——-

TCP:

TCP: Source port = 2909

TCP: Destination port = 23 (Telnet)

TCP: Sequence number = 63520058

TCP: Acknowledgment number = 813932917

TCP: Data offset = 20 bytes

TCP: Flags = 10

TCP: ..0. .... = (No urgent pointer)

TCP: ...1 .... = Acknowledgment

TCP: .... 0... = (No push)

TCP: .... .0.. = (No reset)
TCP: .... ..0. = (No SYN)
TCP: ....0 = (No FIN)
TCP: Window = 4096
TCP: Checksum = 21B1 (correct)
TCP: No TCP options
TCP:

Trace 4.8.7b. Misdirected Datagram Details

4.8.8 Confused Routers

For our next example, we'll consider a case of false advertising by a router (see Figure 4-14). This internetwork consists of a number of Ethernet segments and one Apollo token ring connected by routers. Workstations wishing to communicate with other hosts are getting confused because two routers want their datagrams. As a result, the two routers become locked in a battle, with the workstation coming out the loser. Let's see what happened.

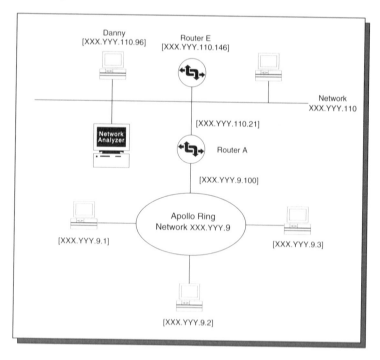

Figure 4-14. Confused Router Topology

In this scenario, a router (designated Router A in Figure 4-14) connects an Ethernet segment and an Apollo token ring. (The Apollo token ring is a proprietary network designed by Apollo Computer, now part of Hewlett-Packard, to connect Apollo workstations.) Confusion occurs between Router A and Router E, which is also connected to the Ethernet segment.

The network manager, Danny, address [XXX.YYY.110.96], has a workstation on the Ethernet segment and wishes to communicate with Router E, address [XXX.YYY.110.146], shown in Trace 4.8.8a. Danny sends an ARP message in Frame 13, and Router E responds in Frame 14 with its Hardware address, 0000A200226CH. Next, Danny initiates a TCP connection in Frame 15 via Router E, asking for a host on an Ethernet 3 hops away. Instead of the expected TCP handshake, Router E tells Danny to redirect his datagrams to Router A (Frame 16), and then passes Danny's TCP connect request to Router A (Frame 17).

Unfortunately, Router A does not agree, and tells Danny to redirect his datagrams back to Router E (Frame 18). Router A then passes the same TCP connect request back to Router E (Frame 19). Router E now disagrees and sends a redirect to Router A, along with the same TCP connect request (Frames 20 and 21). Note the identical Sequence Number in Frames 15, 17, 19, and 21: SEQ = 170068605. The routers are passing the same TCP message back and forth because neither knows what to do with it. The scenario repeats for some time (Frames 22 through 35). Danny's TCP connect request is stuck in a routing loop.

An examination of the RIP broadcasts from both Router A and Router E yields a clue to the problem. Router E's RIPs (Trace 4.8.8b) include 17 routing messages. Danny scrutinized all of the network addresses, along with the number of router hops (the metric) required to reach those other networks. All of the information looked correct except for the Routing data in Frame 16. The IP address of [P.P.9.0] (the Apollo token ring network) showed a metric of 16, or unreachable. This metric was clearly incorrect, since the Apollo network was only one hop away—via Router A. The desired network, however, did not appear in Router E's broadcast.

A similar analysis was then made of Router A's RIP broadcasts (Trace 4.8.8c). A total of 17 Routing data frames were included in the broadcast. Routing data frame 17 correctly identified the Ethernet segment [Q.Q.110.0] as being one hop away. Unfortunately, a number of other networks that could not be reached via Router A were being advertised as reachable. In addition, the target network was not listed in this RIP message either.

The network manager concluded that both Router A and Router E had corrupted routing tables. To correct the problem, he took both routers out of service, reconfigured them, and brought them back up. No further problems were noted—the RIP routing loop had been corrected.

Sniffer Network Analyzer data 15-May at 14:31:02, ATEST.ENC, Pg 1

SUMMARY	Delta T	Destination	Source	Summary
13	1.1843	Broadcast	Danny	ARP C PA=[XXX.YYY.110.146] PRO=IP
14	0.0009	Danny	Router E	ARP R PA=[XXX.YYY.110.146] HA=0000A200226C PRO=IP
15	0.0019	Router E	Danny	TCP D=23 S=14663 SYN SEQ=170068605 LEN=0 WIN=1024
16	0.0008	Danny	Router E	ICMP Redirect (Redirect datagrams for the host)
17	0.0002	Router A	Router E	TCP D=23 S=14663 SYN SEQ=170068605 LEN=0 WIN=1024
18	0.0120	Danny	Router A	ICMP Redirect (Redirect for the network)
19	0.0033	Router E	Router A	TCP D=23 S=14663 SYN SEQ=170068605 LEN=0 WIN=1024
20	0.0008	Router A	Router E	ICMP Redirect (Redirect datagrams for the host)
21		0.0001	Router A	Router E TCP D=23 S=14663 SYN SEQ=170068605 LEN=0 WIN=1024
22	0.0098	Router E	Router A	ICMP Redirect (Redirect datagrams for the network)
23	0.0024	Danny	Router A	ICMP Redirect (Redirect datagrams for the host)
24	0.0098	Danny	Router A	ICMP Redirect (Redirect datagrams for the network)
25	0.0028	Router E	Router A	TCP D=23 S=14663 SYN SEQ=170068605 LEN=0 WIN=1024

26	0.0015	Router A	Router E	ICMP Redirect (Redirect datagrams for the host)
27	0.0001	Router A	Router E	TCP D=23 S=14663 SYN SEQ=170068605 LEN=0 WIN=1024
28	0.0108	Router E	Router A	ICMP Redirect (Redirect datagrams for the network)
29	0.0037	Danny	Router A	ICMP Redirect (Redirect datagrams for the host)
30	0.0084	Danny	Router A	ICMP Redirect (Redirect datagrams for the network)
31	0.0032	Router E	Router A	TCP D=23 S=14663 SYN SEQ=170068605 LEN=0 WIN=1024
32	0.0008	Router A	Router E	ICMP Redirect (Redirect datagrams for the host)
33	0.0001	Router A	Router E	TCP D=23 S=14663 SYN SEQ=170068605 LEN=0 WIN=1024
34	0.0089	Router E	Router A	ICMP Redirect (Redirect datagrams for the network)
35	0.0049	Danny	Router A	ICMP Redirect (Redirect datagrams for the host)

Trace 4.8.8a. Routing Loop Summary

Sniffer Network Analyzer data 15-May at 14:31:02, ERIP.ENC, Pg 1

- - - - - - - - - - - - - - - - Frame 1 - - - - - - - - - - - - - - - - -

DLC: ——- DLC Header ——-
DLC:
DLC: Frame 1 arrived at 14:31:17.3235; frame size is 386 (0182 hex) bytes.
DLC: Destination = BROADCAST FFFFFFFFFFFF, Broadcast
DLC: Source   = Station 0000A200226C, Router E
DLC: Ethertype = 0800 (IP)
DLC:
IP: ——- IP Header ——-
IP:
IP: Version = 4, header length = 20 bytes
IP: Type of service = 00
IP: 000. .... = routine
IP: ...0 .... = normal delay
IP: .... 0... = normal throughput

246

IP: .... .0.. = normal reliability
IP: Total length = 372 bytes
IP: Identification = 35481
IP: Flags = 0X
IP: .0.. .... = may fragment
IP: ..0. .... = last fragment
IP: Fragment offset = 0 bytes
IP: Time to live = 30 seconds/hops
IP: Protocol = 17 (UDP)
IP: Header checksum = B3E4 (correct)
IP: Source address = [XXX.YYY.110.146]
IP: Destination address = [XXX.YYY.110.0]
IP: No options
IP:
UDP: ——- UDP Header ——-
UDP:
UDP: Source port = 520 (Route)
UDP: Destination port = 520
UDP: Length = 352
UDP: Checksum = 157F (correct)
UDP:
RIP: ——- RIP Header ——-
RIP:
RIP: Command = 2 (Response)
RIP: Version = 1
RIP: Unused = 0
RIP:
RIP: Routing data frame 1
RIP: Address family identifier = 2 (IP)
RIP: IP Address = [A.A.0.0]
RIP: Metric = 2
RIP:
RIP: Routing data frame 2
RIP: Address family identifier = 2 (IP)
RIP: IP Address = [B.B.0.0]
RIP: Metric = 3
RIP:
RIP: Routing data frame 3
RIP: Address family identifier = 2 (IP)
RIP: IP Address = [C.C.0.0]
RIP: Metric = 2
RIP:
RIP: Routing data frame 4

RIP: Address family identifier = 2 (IP)
RIP: IP Address = [D.D.0.0]
RIP: Metric   = 2
RIP:
RIP: Routing data frame 5
RIP: Address family identifier = 2 (IP)
RIP: IP Address = [E.E.0.0]
RIP: Metric   = 1
RIP:
RIP: Routing data frame 6
RIP: Address family identifier = 2 (IP)
RIP: IP Address = [F.F.0.0]
RIP: Metric   = 2
RIP:
RIP: Routing data frame 7
RIP: Address family identifier = 2 (IP)
RIP: IP Address = [G.G.0.0]
RIP: Metric   = 2
RIP:
RIP: Routing data frame 8
RIP: Address family identifier = 2 (IP)
RIP: IP Address = [H.H.0.0]
RIP: Metric   = 2
RIP:
RIP: Routing data frame 9
RIP: Address family identifier = 2 (IP)
RIP: IP Address = [I.I.0.0]
RIP: Metric   = 2
RIP:
RIP: Routing data frame 10
RIP: Address family identifier = 2 (IP)
RIP: IP Address = [J.J.0.0]
RIP: Metric   = 4
RIP:
RIP: Routing data frame 11
RIP: Address family identifier = 2 (IP)
RIP: IP Address = [K.K.0.0]
RIP: Metric   = 3
RIP:
RIP: Routing data frame 12
RIP: Address family identifier = 2 (IP)
RIP: IP Address = [L.L.0.0]
RIP: Metric   = 3

```
RIP:
RIP:  Routing data frame 13
RIP:     Address family identifier = 2 (IP)
RIP:     IP Address = [M.M.0.0]
RIP:     Metric    = 1
RIP:
RIP:  Routing data frame 14
RIP:     Address family identifier = 2 (IP)
RIP:     IP Address = [N.N.0.0]
RIP:     Metric    = 3
RIP:
RIP:  Routing data frame 15
RIP:     Address family identifier = 2 (IP)
RIP:     IP Address = [O.O.0.0]
RIP:     Metric    = 3
RIP:
RIP:  Routing data frame 16
RIP:     Address family identifier = 2 (IP)
RIP:     IP Address = [P.P.9.0]
RIP:     Metric    = 16 (Unreachable)
RIP:
RIP:  Routing data frame 17
RIP:     Address family identifier = 2 (IP)
RIP:     IP Address = [Q.Q.0.0]
RIP:     Metric    = 3
RIP:
```

Trace 4.8.8b. Router E RIP Broadcast Message

Sniffer Network Analyzer data 15-May at 14:22:04, ARIP.ENC, Pg 1

- - - - - - - - - - - - - - - - Frame 1 - - - - - - - - - - - - - - - - -

```
DLC:  ——- DLC Header ——-
DLC:
DLC:  Frame 1 arrived at 14:22:30.9929; frame size is 386 (0182 hex) bytes.
DLC:  Destination = BROADCAST FFFFFFFFFFFF, Broadcast
DLC:  Source     = Station 0207010024FB, Router A
DLC:  Ethertype  = 0800 (IP)
DLC:
IP:   ——- IP Header ——-
IP:
IP:   Version = 4, header length = 20 bytes
IP:   Type of service = 08
```

```
IP:              000. .... = routine
IP:              ...0 .... = normal delay
IP:              .... 1... = high throughput
IP:              .... .0.. = normal reliability
IP:   Total length = 372 bytes
IP:   Identification = 47689
IP:   Flags = 0X
IP:   .0.. .... = may fragment
IP:   ..0. .... = last fragment
IP:   Fragment offset = 0 bytes
IP:   Time to live = 10 seconds/hops
IP:   Protocol = 17 (UDP)
IP:   Header checksum = 98A9 (correct)
IP:   Source address = [XXX.YYY.110.21]
IP:   Destination address = [XXX.YYY.110.0]
IP:   No options
IP:
UDP:  ——- UDP Header ——-
UDP:
UDP:  Source port = 520 (Route)
UDP:  Destination port = 520
UDP:  Length = 352
UDP:  Checksum = 14FC (correct)
UDP:
RIP:  ——- RIP Header ——-
RIP:
RIP:  Command = 2 (Response)
RIP:  Version = 1
RIP:  Unused  = 0
RIP:
RIP:  Routing data frame 1
RIP:      Address family identifier = 2 (IP)
RIP:      IP Address = [A.A.111.0]
RIP:      Metric    = 4
RIP:
RIP:  Routing data frame 2
RIP:      Address family identifier = 2 (IP)
RIP:      IP Address = [B.B.112.0]
RIP:      Metric    = 4
RIP:
RIP:  Routing data frame 3
RIP:      Address family identifier = 2 (IP)
RIP:      IP Address = [C.C.0.0]
```

```
RIP:    Metric   = 3
RIP:
RIP: Routing data frame 4
RIP:    Address family identifier = 2 (IP)
RIP:    IP Address = [D.D.113.0]
RIP:    Metric   = 4
RIP:
RIP: Routing data frame 5
RIP:    Address family identifier = 2 (IP)
RIP:    IP Address = [E.E.9.0]
RIP:    Metric   = 1
RIP:
RIP: Routing data frame 6
RIP:    Address family identifier = 2 (IP)
RIP:    IP Address = [F.F.0.0]
RIP:    Metric   = 2
RIP:
RIP: Routing data frame 7
RIP:    Address family identifier = 2 (IP)
RIP:    IP Address = [G.G.90.0]
RIP:    Metric   = 4
RIP:
RIP: Routing data frame 8
RIP:    Address family identifier = 2 (IP)
RIP:    IP Address = [H.H.0.0]
RIP:    Metric   = 3
RIP:
RIP: Routing data frame 9
RIP:    Address family identifier = 2 (IP)
RIP:    IP Address = [I.I.0.0]
RIP:    Metric   = 5
RIP:
RIP: Routing data frame 10
RIP:    Address family identifier = 2 (IP)
RIP:    IP Address = [J.J.0.0]
RIP:    Metric   = 4
RIP:
RIP: Routing data frame 11
RIP:    Address family identifier = 2 (IP)
RIP:    IP Address = [K.K.0.0]
RIP:    Metric   = 3
RIP:
RIP: Routing data frame 12
```

RIP: Address family identifier = 2 (IP)

RIP: IP Address = [L.L.0.0]

RIP: Metric   = 3

RIP:

RIP: Routing data frame 13

RIP: Address family identifier = 2 (IP)

RIP: IP Address = [M.M.0.0]

RIP: Metric   = 3

RIP:

RIP: Routing data frame 14

RIP: Address family identifier = 2 (IP)

RIP: IP Address = [N.N.0.0]

RIP: Metric   = 3

RIP:

RIP: Routing data frame 15

RIP: Address family identifier = 2 (IP)

RIP: IP Address = [O.O.0.0]

RIP: Metric   = 3

RIP:

RIP: Routing data frame 16

RIP: Address family identifier = 2 (IP)

RIP: IP Address = [P.P.0.0]

RIP: Metric   = 4

RIP:

RIP: Routing data frame 17

RIP: Address family identifier = 2 (IP)

RIP: IP Address = [Q.Q.110.0]

RIP: Metric   = 1

RIP:

Trace 4.8.8c. Router A RIP Broadcast Message

4.8.9 Using OSPF

In our final case study, we will look at how OSPF is used within an internetwork to communicate topology information between various routers. The internetwork in question is based upon an FDDI backbone, with four routers extending from that FDDI backbone that connect to various Ethernet and WAN segments (see Figure 4-15). The router in question, called Heathrow, has IP addresses of [132.XXX.2.254] on its FDDI interface, and [132.XXX.10.254] on its Ethernet interface, and communicates with all the other routers using OSPF. (Note that the Sniffer analyzer is on the Ethernet side of this router, and will therefore capture the OSPF broadcasts *from* the router, IP address [132.XXX.10.254]. To capture the OSPF broadcasts *to* the Heathrow router would require a Sniffer attachment on the FDDI side of that router.)

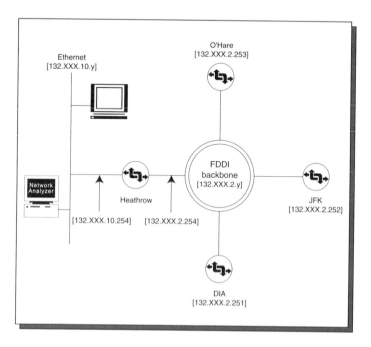

Figure 4-15. Router Communication Using OSPF

A summary of the router communication (filtered to only show the OSPF traffic) is shown in Trace 4.8.9a. Note that the Heathrow router [132.XXX.2.254] is the source of these broadcasts, and that the destination is listed as [224.0.0.5]. This destination address is a special multicast address, as discussed in RFC 1112, "Host Extensions for IP Multicasting" [4-46]. This address is a special case of the family of Class D (multicasting) addresses, which begin with a binary 1110 (or hexadecimal 224). For example, the address [224.0.0.1] is reserved for all systems multicast messages, while the address [224.0.0.5] is reserved for multicast to all OSPF routers. The assigned numbers document (currently RFC 1700) lists these and other multicast addresses under the heading of "Internet Multicast Addresses." Also note that the time (Delta T) between the OSPF Hello messages is approximately 10 seconds, as we will see further in the message details.

Sniffer Network Analyzer data from 15-Dec at 11:05:12, file A:OSPFHELO.ENC, Pg 1

SUMMARY	Delta T	Destination	Source	Summary
3		[224.0.0.5]	[132.XXX.10.254]	OSPF Hello ID=[132.XXX.2.254]
174	10.3129	[224.0.0.5]	[132.XXX.10.254]	OSPF Hello ID=[132.XXX.2.254]
365	10.3129	[224.0.0.5]	[132.XXX.10.254]	OSPF Hello ID=[132.XXX.2.254]

Trace 4.8.9a OSPF Broadcast Summary

The details of the OSPF broadcasts are shown in Trace 4.8.9b. Note that the Destination address at the Data Link layer is also a multicast address (01005E000005), which is then converted into the multicast IP address of [224.0.0.5], according to the procedure outlined in RFC 1112. The Ethertype specifies IP as the next highest layer, and the IP header follows. Within the IP header, note that the next highest protocol specified is OSPF (Protocol = 89), the Source IP address is the address of the Heathrow router [132.XXX.10.254], and the Destination IP address is the multicast address discussed above [254.0.0.5].

The OSPF details are illustrated next. Reviewing Figure 4-8b, note that the router is identified by its IP address [132.XXX.2.254], and the area ID is [0.0.0.0], an area defined by the network manager to encompass all routers attached to the FDDI ring. The Authentication Type = 1 (the simple password type), with a password value of "boulder". Other parameters of interest include the Hello Interval (10 seconds, as verified above), an optional external routing capability, and a Router Dead Interval (40 seconds). Other OSFP messages captured in Frames 174, 365, and so on follow a similar format.

Sniffer Network Analyzer data from 15-Dec at 11:05:12, file A:OSPFHELO.ENC, Pg 1

```
- - - - - - - - - - - - - - - Frame 3 - - - - - - - - - - - - - - - - -

DLC: ----- DLC Header -----
DLC:
DLC: Frame 3 arrived at  11:05:23.1607; frame size is 78 (004E hex) bytes.
DLC: Destination = Multicast 01005E000005
DLC: Source     = Station Prteon10BCDE, Heathrow
DLC: Ethertype  = 0800 (IP)
DLC:
IP:  ----- IP Header -----
IP:
IP:  Version = 4, header length = 20 bytes
IP:  Type of service = 00
```

```
IP:      000. .... = routine
IP:      ...0 .... = normal delay
IP:      .... 0... = normal throughput
IP:      .... .0.. = normal reliability
IP:   Total length = 64 bytes
IP:   Identification = 58761
IP:   Flags = 0X
IP:   .0.. .... = may fragment
IP:   ..0. .... = last fragment
IP:   Fragment offset = 0 bytes
IP:   Time to live = 1 seconds/hops
IP:   Protocol = 89 (OSPF)
IP:   Header checksum = 6435 (correct)
IP:   Source address = [132.XXX.10.254]
IP:   Destination address = [224.0.0.5]
IP:   No options
IP:
OSPF: ——— OSPF Header ———-
OSPF:
OSPF: Version = 2,  Type = 1 (Hello),  Length = 44
OSPF: Router ID      = [132.XXX.2.254]
OSPF: Area ID        = [0.0.0.0]
OSPF: Header checksum = E15A (correct)
OSPF: Authentication: Type = 1 (Simple Password),  Value = boulder
OSPF:
OSPF: Network mask       = [255.255.255.0]
OSPF: Hello interval     = 10 (seconds)
OSPF: Optional capabilities   = X2
OSPF:            .... ..1. = external routing capability
OSPF:            .... ...0 = no Type of Service routing capability
OSPF: Router priority      = 1
OSPF: Router dead interval   = 40 (seconds)
OSPF: Designated router     = [132.XXX.10.254]
OSPF: Backup designated router = [0.0.0.0]
OSPF:
```

Trace 4.8.9b. OSPF Broadcast Details

In this chapter we have covered a number of protocols that work together to deliver datagrams within the internet from one host to another. Since this transmission is based upon the Internet Protocol's connectionless service, guaranteed delivery of those datagrams must be assured by another process, the Host-to-Host Layer. We will study the two protocols that operate at the Host-to-Host Layer, UDP and TCP, in the next chapter.

4.9 References

[4-1]   Roman, Bob. "Making the Big Connection." *3TECH, The 3Com Technical Journal* (Summer 1990): 14–25.

[4-2]   Roman, Bob. "How Routing Works: A Sequel to 'Making the Big Connection.'" *3TECH, The 3Com Technical Journal* (Fall 1991): 5–9.

[4-3]   Ramsay, Clint. "The Fundamentals of IP Routing." *3TECH, The 3Com Technical Journal* (Summer 1990): 26–33.

[4-4]   Mendes, Gerald. "Top 10 Routing Tips." *LAN Magazine* (December 1995): 79–88.

[4-5]   Postel, J. "Internet Protocol." RFC 791, September 1981.

[4-6]   Reynolds, J., and J. Postel, "Assigned Numbers." RFC 1700, October 1994.

[4-7]   White, Gene. *Internetworking and Addressing*. McGraw-Hill, Inc. (New York, NY) 1992.

[4-8]   Kirkpatrick, S., et al. "Internet Numbers." RFC 1166, July 1990.

[4-9]   Mogul, J., et al. "Internet Standard Subnetting Procedure." RFC 950, August 1985.

[4-10]   Stone, Mike. "Guide to TCP/IP Network Addressing." *LAN Technology* (April 1991): 41–46.

[4-11]   Steinke, Steve. "IP Addresses and Subnet Masks." *LAN Magazine* (October 1995): 27–28.

[4-12]   Krol, E., "The Hitchhiker's Guide to the Internet." RFC 1118, September 1989.

[4-13]   Baker, F. Editor. "Requirements for IP Version 4 Routers." RFC 1812, June 1995.

[4-14]   Plummer, D. "An Ethernet Address Resolution Protocol, or Converting Network Protocol Addresses to 48-bit Ethernet Addresses for Transmission on Ethernet Hardware." RFC 826, November 1982.

[4-15]   Finlayson, R., et al. "A Reverse Address Resolution Protocol." RFC 903, June 1984.

[4-16]   Bradley, T., and C. Brown. "Inverse Address Resolution Protocol." RFC 1293, January 1992.

[4-17]   Laubach, M. "Classical IP and ARP over ATM." RFC 1577, January 1994.

[4-18]   Postel, J. "Multi-LAN Address Resolution." RFC 925, October 1984.

[4-19]   Black, Uyless. *TCP/IP and Related Protocols.* McGraw-Hill, Inc. (New York, NY), 1992.

[4-20]   Comer, Douglas E. *Internetworking with TCP/IP.* third edition. Prentice Hall, Inc. (Englewood Cliffs, NJ), 1995.

[4-21]   Gilmore, John. "Bootstrap Protocol (BOOTP)." RFC 951, September 1985.

[4-22]   Wimer, W. "Clarifications and Extensions for the Bootstrap Protocol." RFC 1532, October 1993.

[4-23]   Reynolds, J. "DHCP Options and BOOTP Vendor Extensions." RFC 1533, October 1993.

[4-24]   Mogul, Jeffrey. "Booting Diskless Hosts: The BOOTP Protocol." *ConneXions* (October 1988): 14–18.

[4-25]   Droms, R. "Dynamic Host Configuration Protocol." RFC 1531, October 1993.

[4-26]   Droms, R. "Interoperation Between DHCP and BOOTP." RFC 1534, October 1993.

[4-27]   Allard, J. "DHCP—TCP/IP Network Configuration Made Easy." *ConneXions* (August 1993): 16–24.

[4-28]   Mills, Dave, "Exterior Gateway Protocol Formal Specification." RFC 904, April 1984.

[4-29]   Callon, Ross, et al. "Routing in an Internetwork Environment." *ConneXions* (August 1989): 2–7.

[4-30]   Hedrick, C. "Routing Information Protocol." RFC 1058, June 1988.

[4-31]   Malkin, G. "RIP Version 2 — Carrying Additional Information." RFC 1723, November 1994.

[4-32] Rabinovitch, Eddie. "Migration to OSPF is not a Luxury." ConneXions (November 1995): 20–25.

[4-33] Moy, John, "OSPF Version 2." RFC 1583, March 1994.

[4-34] Moy, John. "OSPF: Next Generation Routing Comes to TCP/IP Networks." *LAN Technology* (April 1990): 71–79.

[4-35] Seifert, William M. "OSPF: The First Wave of Next-Generation Routing Protocols." *Business Communications Review* (July 1991): 31–34.

[4-36] Hume, Sharon. "A Technical Tour of OSPF." *3Tech, The 3Com Technical Journal* (Summer 1991): 44–56.

[4-37] Medin, Milo S. "The Great IGP Debate—Part Two: The Open Shortest Path First (OSPF) Routing Protocol." *ConneXions* (October 1991): 53–61.

[4-38] Postel, J. "Internet Control Message Protocol." RFC 792, September 1981.

[4-39] Nagle, John. "Congestion Control in IP/TCP Internetworks." RFC 896, January 1984.

[4-40] Prue, W., et al. "Something a Host Could Do with Source Quench: The Source Quench Introduced Delay (SQuID)." RFC 1016, July 1987.

[4-41] Gerber, Barry. "IP Routing: Learn to Follow the Yellow Brick Road," *Network Computing* (April 1992): 98–106.

[4-42] Mockapetris, P. "Domain Names: Concepts and Facilities." RFC 1034, November 1987.

[4-43] Mockapetris, P. "Domain Names: Implementation and Specification.", RFC 1035, November 1987.

[4-44] Beecher, Bryan. "The Ten Commandments of Domain Name Service." *ConneXions* (March 1994): 21–27.

[4-45] Auerbach, Carl. "Trouble-Busters." *LAN Magazine* (March 1995): 85–90.

[4-46] Deering, S. "Host Extensions for IP Multicasting." RFC 1112, August 1989.

Troubleshooting the Host-to-Host Connection

Datagrams and virtual circuits both convey information on an end-to-end basis, but each is associated with different benefits and costs. The datagram provides low overhead at the expense of rigorous reliability; the virtual circuit offers high reliability at the cost of high overhead. The choice depends on the reliability necessary for the data being transferred. For example, because humans are involved in sending electronic mail, error detection is built into the transmission process. If a message is lost en route, the intended recipient can simply ask the sender to retransmit the message. An electronic mail message could, therefore, be sent as a datagram. File transfers, on the other hand, demand a high degree of reliability and should employ the connection-oriented virtual circuit.

In this chapter, we will study the two protocols that implement datagrams and virtual circuits: the User Datagram Protocol (UDP) and the Transmission Control Protocol (TCP). Other host-related issues are discussed in RFC 1123, "Requirements for Internet Hosts: Application and Support." The first issue to consider is how UDP and TCP fit into the ARPA architectural model.

5.1 The Host-to-Host Connection

In Chapter 3, we learned that the Network Interface Layer handles the physical connection for the LAN or WAN. In Chapter 4, we explored the Internet Layer, which routes IP datagrams from one device to another on the same network or on a different network via the internetwork. The Internet Layer also administers the 32-bit Internet addresses (used with IP) and takes care of intra-internetwork communication (with ICMP).

Figure 5-1a shows the ARPA architectural model; as you can see, the Host-to-Host Layer is the first layer that operates exclusively within the hosts, not in the routers.

Assuming that the IP datagram has arrived at the Destination host, what issues must the host (and the architect designing the internetwork) deal with in order to establish and use the communication link between the two end points?

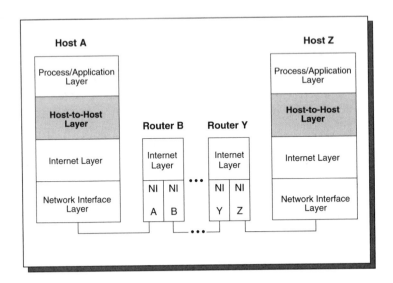

Figure 5-1a. The Host-to-Host Connection

First, we must assume that the host has more than one process at its disposal. Therefore, the datagram will require additional addressing to identify the host process to which it will apply. This additional address is carried within the UDP or TCP header and is known as a Port address (we'll discuss ports in Section 5.2). Another issue to consider is reliability of the datagram; the hosts will want assurance that the datagram arrived correctly. Both the UDP and TCP headers address this concern. A third consideration is the overhead associated with the host-to-host transmission. The overhead directly relates to the type of connection—TCP or UDP—employed. It is the requirements of the Process/Application Layer that determine the choice between TCP and UDP. As shown in Figure 5-1b, the File Transfer Protocol (FTP), Telecommunications Network (TELNET) protocol, and Simple Mail Transfer Protocol (SMTP) run over TCP transport. The Trivial File Transfer Protocol (TFTP), Simple Network Management Protocol (SNMP), and Sun Microsystems Inc.'s Network File System (NFS) protocols work with UDP. We will study these protocols in depth in Chapter 6.

ARPA Layer	Protocol Implementation						OSI Layer
Process / Application	File Transfer	Electronic Mail	Terminal Emulation	File Transfer	Client / Server	Network Management	Application
	File Transfer Protocol (FTP)	Simple Mail Transfer Protocol (SMTP)	TELNET Protocol	Trivial File Transfer Protocol (TFTP)	Sun Microsystems Network File System Protocols (NFS)	Simple Network Management Protocol (SNMP)	Presentation
	MIL-STD-1780 RFC 959	MIL-STD-1781 RFC 821	MIL-STD-1782 RFC 854	RFC 783	RFCs 1014, 1057, and 1094	RFC 1157	Session
Host-to-Host	Transmission Control Protocol (TCP) MIL-STD-1778 RFC 793			User Datagram Protocol (UDP) RFC 768			Transport
Internet	Address Resolution ARP RFC 826 RARP RFC 903		Internet Protocol (IP) MIL-STD-1777 RFC 791		Internet Control Message Protocol (ICMP) RFC 792		Network
Network Interface	Network Interface Cards: Ethernet, Token Ring, ARCNET, MAN and WAN RFC 894, RFC 1042, RFC 1201 and others						Data Link
	Transmission Media: Twisted Pair, Coax, Fiber Optics, Wireless Media, etc.						Physical

Figure 5-1b. ARPA Host-to-Host Layer Protocols

Figure 5-1c shows where the overhead occurs. The Local Network header and trailer delimit the transmission frame and treat the higher-layer information as data inside the frame. The IP header is the first component of overhead, followed by the UDP or TCP header. The UDP header requires 8 octets, and the TCP header requires a minimum of 20 octets. As we will see in the following sections, the overhead relates directly to the rigor of the protocols.

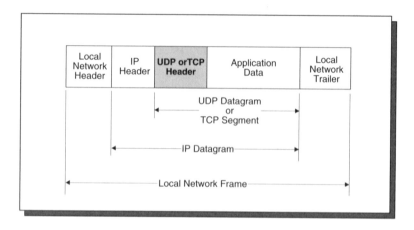

Figure 5-1c. The Internet Transmission Frame and UDP/TCP Header Position

As noted above, both UDP and TCP use Port addresses to identify the incoming data stream and to multiplex it to the appropriate Host process. We'll look at the functions of the Port addresses next.

5.2 Port Addresses

In our tour of the ARPA architectural model, we've encountered addresses for each layer. Let's review these briefly. The Network Interface (or OSI Physical and Data Link) Layer requires a Hardware address. The Hardware address is assigned to the network interface card and is typically a 48-bit number that resides in a ROM on the board itself. The Hardware address uniquely identifies each workstation on the LAN or WAN. Because that address resides in hardware, it remains constant as the device is moved from one network to another.

The Internet (or OSI Network) Layer requires a Logical address, which identifies the network to which a host is attached. As we discussed in Section 4.2, this Internet (or IP) address may be further subdivided into Subnetwork and Host IDs. This address is a 32-bit number that the network administrator assigns to the device. If the device were to be moved from one network to another, a different Internet address would be necessary. The ARP and RARP protocols that we studied in Section 4.4 correlate the Internet Layer and Network Interface Layer addresses.

The third layer of addressing is used at the Host-to-Host (or OSI Transport) Layer and completes the ARPA addressing scheme. This address is known as a *Port address*, and it identifies the user process or application within the host. Each host is presumed to have multiple applications available, such as electronic mail, databases, and so on. An identifier, known as a Port number, specifies the process the user wishes to access. These Port numbers are 16 bits long and are standardized according to their use. Internet administrators assign Port numbers 0–255; other numbers are available for local administration. A complete listing of the assigned ports is available in the Assigned Numbers document (currently RFC 1700). Some examples are given in Tables 5-1a and 5-1b.

Table 5-1a. Port Assignments

Decimal	Keyword	Description
1	tcpmux	TCP Port Service Multiplexer
5	rje	Remote Job Entry
7	echo	Echo
11	systat	Active Users
13	daytime	Daytime
17	qotd	Quote of the Day
18	msp	Message Send Protocol
19	chargen	Character Generator
20	ftp-data	File Transfer Protocol [Default Data]
21	ftp	File Transfer Protocol [Control]
23	telnet	TELNET
25	smtp	Simple Mail Transfer Protocol
33	dsp	Display Support Protocol
37	time	Time
38	rap	Route Access Protocol
42	nameserver	Host Name Server
43	nicname	Who Is
49	login	Login Host Protocol
53	domain	Domain Name Server
67	bootps	Bootstrap Protocol [Server]
68	bootpc	Bootstrap Protocol [Client]
69	tftp	Trivial File Transfer Protocol
70	gopher	Gopher
79	finger	Finger
80	www-http	World Wide Web HTTP
88	kerberos	Kerberos
92	npp	Network Printing Protocol
93	dcp	Device Control Protocol
101	hostname	NIC Host Name Server
102	iso-tsap	ISO-TSAP
107	rtelnet	Remote TELNET Service
109	pop2	Post Office Protocol – v. 2
110	pop3	Post Office Protocol – v. 3
111	sunrpc	SUN Remote Procedure Call

Table 5-1b. Port Assignments (continued)

Decimal	Keyword	Description
115	sftp	Simple File Transfer Protocol
129	pwdgen	Password Generator Protocol
137	netbios-ns	NetBIOS Name Service
138	netbios-dgm	NetBIOS Datagram Service
139	netbios-ssn	NetBIOS Session Service
143	imap2	Interim Mail Access Protocol v.2
144	news	News
146	iso-tp0	ISO-TP0
147	iso-ip	ISO-IP
152	bftp	Background File Transfer Program
153	sgmp	Simple Gateway Monitoring Protocol
160	sgmp-traps	SGMP-TRAPS
161	snmp	Simple Network Management Protocol
162	snmptrap	SNMPTRAP
163	cmip-manage	Common Management Information Protocol/TCP Manager
164	cmip-agent	CMIP/TCP Agent
165	xns-courier	Xerox
179	bgp	Border Gateway Protocol
190	gacp	Gateway Access Control Protocol
193	srmp	Spider Remote Monitoring Protocol
194	irc	Internet Relay Chat Protocol
199	smux	SNMP Multiplexing
201	at-rmtp	AppleTalk Routing Maintenance Protocol
202	at-nbp	AppleTalk Name Binding Protocol
203	at-3	AppleTalk Unused
204	at-echo	AppleTalk Echo Protocol
205	at-5	AppleTalk Unused
206	at-zis	AppleTalk Zone Information
207	at-7	AppleTalk Unused
208	at-8	AppleTalk Unused
209	tam	Trivial Authenticated Mail Protocol
220	imap3	Interactive Mail Access Protocol-v.3
246	dsp3270	Display Systems Protocol

In summary, a message sent from one host to another requires three addresses at the source and the destination to complete the communication path. The Port address (16 bits) identifies the user process (or application) and is contained within the UDP or TCP header. The Internet address (32 bits) identifies the network and host that the process is running on and is located inside the IP header. On some hosts, the combination of the Port address and the IP address is referred to as a *socket*. The Hardware address (usually 48 bits) completes the Data address on the local network. The Hardware address, which is in the Data Link Layer header, is physically configured on the network interface card.

With that background, let's see how UDP and TCP use the Port address to complete the host-to-host connection.

5.3 User Datagram Protocol

As its name implies, the User Datagram Protocol, described in RFC 768 [5-1], provides a connectionless host-to-host communication path. UDP assumes that IP, which is also connectionless, is the underlying (Internet Layer) protocol. Because this service has minimal overhead, UDP has a relatively small header, as shown in Figure 5-2. The resulting message, consisting of the IP header, UDP header, and user data is called a UDP datagram.

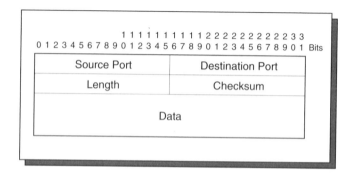

Figure 5-2. User Datagram Protocol (UDP) Header

The first two fields are the Source and Destination Port numbers (each 2 octets long), discussed in Section 5.2. The Source Port field is optional, and when not in use is filled with zeros. The Length field (2 octets) is the length of the UDP datagram, which has a minimum value of 8 octets. The Checksum field (2 octets) is also optional and may be filled with zeros if the Upper-Layer Protocol (ULP) process does not require a checksum. When the checksum is used, it is calculated from the so-called Pseudo header, which includes the Source and Destination addresses, plus the Protocol field from the IP header (see Figure 5-3). By including the IP address in its calculations for the checksum, the Pseudo header assures that the UDP datagram is delivered to the correct Destination network and host. The IP Protocol field within the Pseudo header would equal 17 for UDP.

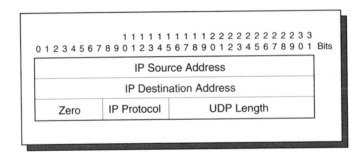

1 1 1 1 1 1 1 1 1 1 2 2 2 2 2 2 2 2 2 2 3 3
0 1 2 3 4 5 6 7 8 9 0 1 2 3 4 5 6 7 8 9 0 1 2 3 4 5 6 7 8 9 0 1 Bits

| IP Source Address |
| IP Destination Address |
| Zero | IP Protocol | UDP Length |

Figure 5-3. UDP Pseudo Header

In summary, the IP Destination address routes the datagram to the correct host on the specified network, then the UDP Port address routes the datagram to the correct host process. Thus, the UDP adds Port addressing capabilities to IP's datagram service. Examples of host processes that use UDP as the host-to-host protocol include the Time protocol, Port number 37; the Domain Name Server (DNS), Port number 53; the Bootstrap Protocol (BOOTP) server and client, Port numbers 67 and 68, respectively; the Trivial File Transfer Protocol (TFTP), Port number 69; and the Sun Microsystems Remote Procedure Call (SunRPC), Port number 111. All of these applications assume that if the host-to-host connection were to fail, a higher-layer function, such as DNS, would recover. Applications that require more reliability in their end-to-end data transmissions use the more rigorous TCP, which we will discuss next.

5.4 Transmission Control Protocol

In Chapter 1, we learned that the Internet protocols were designed to meet U.S. government and military requirements. These requirements dictated that the data communication system be able to endure battlefield conditions. The Internet protocol designed specifically to meet the rigors of the battlefield was the Transmission Control Protocol, described in RFC 793 [5-2]. Unlike UDP, TCP is a connection-oriented protocol that is responsible for reliable communication between two end processes. The unit of data transferred is called a *stream*, which is simply a sequence of octets. The stream originates at the upper layer protocol process and is subsequently divided into TCP segments, IP datagrams, and Local Network frames. RFC 1180, "A TCP/IP Tutorial" [5-3], offers a useful summary of the way the TCP information fits into the related protocols, such as IP, and the Local Network connection, such as Ethernet.

RFC 879, "The TCP Maximum Segment Size and Related Topics" [5-4], describes the relationships between TCP segments and IP datagrams.

TCP handles six functions: basic data transfer, reliability, flow control, multiplexing, connections, and precedence/security. We will discuss these functions in detail in Section 5.5.

The TCP header (see Figure 5-4) has a minimum length of 20 octets. This header contains a number of fields—relating to connection management, data flow control, and reliability—which UDP did not require. The TCP header starts with two Port addresses (2 octets each) to identify the logical host processes at each end of the connection.

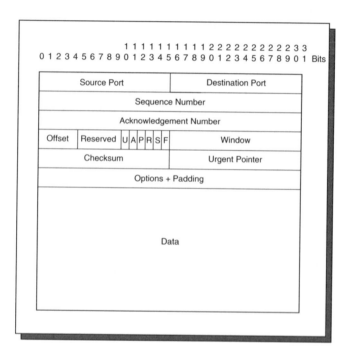

Figure 5-4. Transmission Control Protocol (TCP) Header

The Sequence Number field (4 octets) is the sequence number given to the first octet of data. When the SYN flag bit is set, the sequence number indicates the Initial Sequence Number (ISN) selected. The first data octet sent would then use the next sequence number [ISN+1]. (For example, if ISN = 100, then the data would begin with SEQ = 101. If the sequence number was not advanced by one, the process would end up in an endless loop of transmissions and acknowledgements. More on this in Section 5.5.5.) The sequence number assures the sequentiality of the data stream, which is a fundamental component of reliability.

The Acknowledgement Number field (4 octets) verifies the receipt of data. This protocol process is called Positive Acknowledgement or Retransmission (PAR). The process requires that each unit of data (the octet in the case of TCP) be explicitly acknowledged. If it is not, the sender will time-out and retransmit. The value in the acknowledgement is the next octet (i.e., the next sequence number) expected from the other end of the connection. When the Acknowledgement field is in use (i.e., during a connection), the ACK flag bit is set.

The next 32-bit word (octets 13–16 in the header) contains a number of fields used for control purposes. The Data Offset field (4 bits) measures the number of 32-bit words in the TCP header. Its value indicates where the TCP header ends and the ULP data begins. The Offset field is necessary because the TCP header has a variable, not fixed, length; therefore, the position of the first octet of ULP data may vary. Since the minimum length of the TCP header is 20 octets, the minimum value of the Data Offset field would be five 32-bit words. The next 6 bits are reserved for future use and are set equal to zero.

Six flags that control the connection and data transfer are transmitted next. Each flag has its own 1-bit field. These flags include:

URG:	Urgent Pointer field significant
ACK:	Acknowledgement field significant
PSH:	Push function
RST:	Reset the connection
SYN:	Synchronize Sequence numbers
FIN:	No more data from sender

We will study the use of these flags in greater detail in Section 5.5.

The Window field (2 octets) provides end-to-end flow control. The number in the Window field indicates the quantity of octets, beginning with the one in the Acknowledgement field, that the sender of the segment can accept. Note that, like the Acknowledgement field, the Window field is bi-directional. Since TCP provides a full-duplex communication path, both ends send control information to their peer process at the other end of the connection. In other words, my host provides both an acknowledgement and a window advertisement to your host, and your host does the same for mine. In this manner, both ends provide control information to their remote partner.

The Checksum field (2 octets) is used for error control. The checksum calculation includes a 12-octet Pseudo header, the TCP header, and ULP data. The TCP Pseudo header (shown in Figure 5-5) is similar to the UDP Pseudo header shown in Figure 5-3. Its purpose is to provide error control on the IP header, the TCP header, and the data. The fields included in the TCP Pseudo header include the Source and Destination address, the protocol, and the TCP Length. The TCP Length field includes the TCP header and Upper-Layer Protocol (ULP) data, but not the 12-octet Pseudo header.

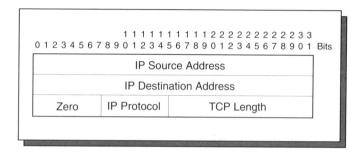

Figure 5-5. TCP Pseudo Header

The Urgent Pointer field (2 octets) allows the position of urgent data within the TCP segment to be identified. This field is used in conjunction with the Urgent (URG) control flag and points to the Sequence number of the octet that follows the urgent data. In other words, the Urgent pointer indicates the beginning of the routine (non-urgent) data.

Options and Padding fields (both variable in length) complete the TCP header. The Options field is an even multiple of octets in length and specifies options required by the TCP process within the host. One option is the maximum TCP segment size, which mandates the amount of data that the sender of the option is willing to accept. We saw this option used by the AppleTalk workstation in Trace 3.13.5. The Padding field contains a variable number of zeros that ensure that the TCP header ends on a 32-bit boundary.

Now that we've explored the fields within the TCP header, we'll see how they provide the six TCP functions: basic data transfer, reliability, flow control, multiplexing, connections, and precedence/security.

5.5 TCP Functions

TCP is a rigorous protocol, rich with the functionality demanded by its government-backed designers. In this section, we'll explore each of the six areas of TCP operation separately, and we'll conclude with a summary of the TCP state diagram. References [5-5] and [5-6] discuss the concepts of the User/TCP interface in greater detail; however, for our troubleshooting purposes, we'll focus on understanding the protocol interactions, not the internal protocol operations.

5.5.1 Basic Data Transfer

A TCP module transfers a series of octets, known as a segment, from one host to another. Data flows in both directions, making for a full-duplex connection. The TCP modules at each end determine the length of the segment and indicate this length in the Options field of the TCP header.

Occasionally, a TCP module requires immediate data delivery and can't wait for the segment to fill completely. An upper-layer process would trigger the Push (PSH) flag within the TCP header and tell the TCP module to immediately forward all of the queued data to the receiver.

5.5.2 Reliability

So far, we've assumed that Host B has received all the data sent from Host A. Unfortunately, there's no such network utopia in the real world. The transmitted data could be lost, inadvertently duplicated, delivered out of order, or damaged. If damage occurs, the checksum will fail, alerting the receiver to the problem. The other conditions are more complex, and TCP must have mechanisms to handle them.

The cornerstones of TCP's reliability are its Sequence and Acknowledgement numbers. The Sequence number is logically attached to each outgoing octet. The receiver uses the Sequence number to determine whether any octets are missing or have been received out of order. TCP is a Positive Acknowledgement with Retransmission (PAR) protocol. This means that if data is received correctly, the receiving TCP module generates an Acknowledgement (ACK) number. If the transmitting TCP module does not receive an acknowledgement within the specified time, it will retransmit. No Negative Acknowledgements (NAKs) are allowed.

One of the design issues for a TCP/IP-based internetwork is optimizing the waiting time before allowing a retransmission to occur. Internetworks, by definition, contain multiple communication paths. Each of these may have a different propagation delay. In addition, the underlying infrastructure is connectionless (using IP); it is possible that a datagram could merely be delayed via a path with a longer propagation time, but not truly lost. In that case, retransmitting too quickly would consume precious bandwidth and cause confusion at the receiver if two identical messages are (eventually) received. On the other hand, if the datagram *is* truly lost, then delaying the retransmission also delays the receiver's ability to reassemble the entire message. An obvious compromise is in order. RFC 793, page 41, discusses the Retransmission Timer, and Comer [5-6] presents an excellent summary of the retransmission and timer issues. Partridge [5-7] discusses how TCP timers affect the protocol's performance, and Karn [5-8] discusses an algorithm known as Karn's Algorithm used to calculate the network Round Trip Time (RTT), which impacts the retransmission timers.

Figure 5-6 illustrates the TCP reliability services. (For simplicity, we'll assume that a large data file is being sent from Host A to Host B.) The first segment (SEQ 101–116) is acknowledged without error. The second segment (SEQ 117–132) is not so fortunate and experiences a transmission error. Since that segment never arrives at Host B, no acknowledgement (ACK = 133) is issued by Host B. The Retransmission Timer in Host A expires and retransmits the second segment (SEQ 117–132). When this segment is received, Host B then issues the acknowledgement.

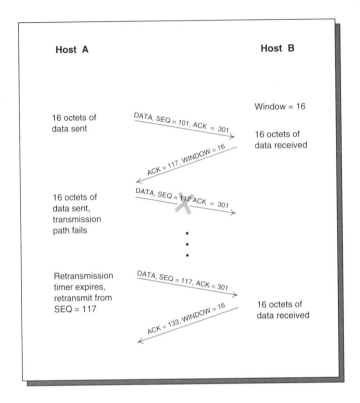

Figure 5-6. TCP Data Retransmissions

5.5.3 Flow Control

Let's begin by reviewing some terms and concepts; then we'll discuss how they relate to the Flow Control mechanism. Recall from the previous section that the Sequence number is attached by the sending device to the TCP segment and counts each octet transmitted. The Acknowledgement number indicates the next expected Sequence number; i.e., the next octet of data expected from the other end of the connection. A third metric, also included within the TCP header, is the Window number. The Window indicates how many more Sequence numbers the sender of the Window is prepared to accept, and is described in RFC 813 [5-9]. The Window controls the flow of data from sender to receiver. Thus, if Host A sends Window = 1024 to Host B, it has much more available buffer space than if Host A sends Window = 10. In the first case, Host A grants Host B permission to transmit 1,024 octets of data past the current Sequence number; in the second case, only 10.

Window = 0 and Window = 1 are two special cases of *sliding window* operations. If a host returns Window = 0, it has shut down communication and will accept no more octets from the other end of the connection. Window = 1 is sometimes known as *stop-and-wait* transmission. The top portion of Figure 5-7 illustrates what happens when Window = 1. (For simplicity, we'll assume that the data is transmitted from Host A to Host B and that acknowledgements go in the opposite direction. In reality, TCP allows full-duplex operation. Therefore, data could also flow from Host B to Host A, with corresponding acknowledgements from Host A to Host B.) Host A has a large, 523K-octet file to send. Host B has set Window = 1, thereby limiting data transmissions to one octet before each acknowledgement. Thus, Host A must wait for Host B's acknowledgement before it can transmit each octet of data. Not very efficient, you might say, and few analysts would disagree.

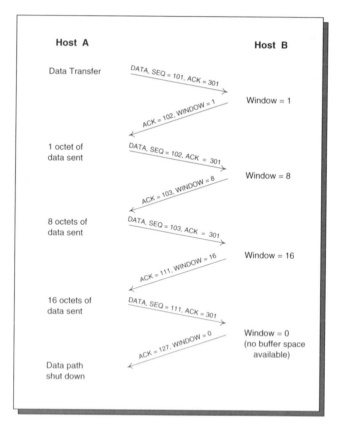

Figure 5-7. TCP Data Transfer (Window Size Varying)

Now suppose that Host B obtains additional buffer space and increases the value to Window = 8. Host A can now send 8 octets of data (SEQ 103–110, inclusive) before requiring an acknowledgement. When the acknowledgement arrives, it indicates the next expected Sequence number (e.g., ACK = 111 would indicate that octets numbered 103–110 arrived correctly and that it is permissible to send 16 more, beginning with SEQ = 111). Similarly, an increase to Window = 32 would allow a corresponding increase in the quantity of data transmitted. We use the term *flow control* to describe the effect of the sliding window operation because you can control the flow of data by adjusting the window value.

The window size is a parameter that requires some optimization. Too many small segments generate needless ACKs, but large segments utilize more buffers. The case study given in Section 5.7.8 provides an example of a window-related problem.

5.5.4 Multiplexing

The TCP module assumes that its associated host may be a multi-function system. Indeed, the host may offer the user an entire menu of applications, and the user may want to use several of them simultaneously. TCP provides a multiplexing function to accommodate these diverse needs. In Section 5.2, we learned that the Port address (16 bits) uniquely identifies an end-user process. The host binds, or associates, a particular port with a process. Some processes, such as the major application protocols FTP, TELNET, and SMTP, have assigned port numbers. Others may be dynamically assigned as the need arises.

A *socket* is the concatenation of the Internet address and the Port address. A *connection* is the association of a pair of sockets, although a socket is not restricted to one connection. For example, if a host has a port assigned to the TELNET protocol—say, Port 23—there's nothing to preclude connections from multiple terminals (i.e., remote sockets) to that port. The host can also have other processes, such as the File Transfer Protocol, operating on another port, such as Port 21. Thus, we can say that TCP provides true multiplexing (the term stems from the Greek noun meaning "many paths") of the data connections into and out of a particular host.

5.5.5 Connections

Because TCP is a connection-oriented protocol, a *logical connection* (known as a virtual circuit) must be established between the two end users before any ULP data can be transmitted. The logical connection is a concatenation of many physical connections, such as Host A to LAN A, connecting to Router 1, connecting via a WAN link to Router 2, and so on. Managing this end-to-end system is much easier if you use a single identifier—the logical connection.

The logical connection is established when the ULP process recognizes the need to communicate with a distant peer and passes an OPEN command across the user/TCP interface to the TCP module in the host. The OPEN command is one of a number of primitives described in the TCP standard, RFC 793. A *primitive* is an event that requests or responds to an action from the other side of the user/TCP interface. The primary TCP primitives include OPEN, SEND, RECEIVE, CLOSE, STATUS, and ABORT. Many parameters traverse the user/TCP interface with the primitive, and therefore more descriptive names such as PASSIVE OPEN or ACTIVE OPEN are often used. Each host operating system may modify these primitives for its particular use.

The OPEN command triggers what is referred to as a *three-way handshake*. The three-way handshake ensures that both ends are prepared to transfer data, reducing the likelihood of data being sent before the distant host can accept it. (If either host becomes confused from an attempted three-way handshake, the confused host sets the Reset (RST) flag, indicating that the segment that arrived was not intended for this connection.) In most cases, one TCP module initiates the connection and another responds. However, it is possible for two TCP modules to request a connection simultaneously; RFC 793 elaborates on this condition.

RFC 793 describes the steps in the three-way handshake as follows:

Host A to Host B: SYN, my sequence number is X
Host B to Host A: ACK, your sequence number is X
Host B to Host A: SYN, my sequence number is Y
Host A to Host B: ACK, your sequence number is Y

In other words, each side of the connection sends it own sequence number to the other end, and receives a confirmation of it in an acknowledgement from the other side. Both sides are then aware of the other's initial sequence number, and reliable communication can proceed. It is possible (and in most cases preferred) for the second and third steps above (from Host B to Host A) to be combined into a single transmission. This combination then yields a total of three transmissions, illustrating the name "three-way handshake."

In Figure 5-8, the initiating module (Host A) generates a TCP segment with the Synchronize (SYN) flag set (SYN = 1) and an initial Sequence number chosen by the module (e.g., ISN = 100). If the connection request was acceptable, the remote TCP module (Host B) would return a TCP segment containing both an acknowledgement for Host A's ISN [ACK = 101], plus its own ISN [SEQ = 300]. Both the Synchronize and Acknowledgement (ACK) flag bits would be set (SYN = 1, ACK = 1) in that response from Host B. Note that the two TCP modules are not required to have the same ISN since these numbers are administered locally. An acknowledgement from the initiating module, Host A, is the third step of the three-way handshake. This TCP segment includes the Sequence number [SEQ = 101] plus an acknowledgement for Host B's desired ISN (ACK = 301).

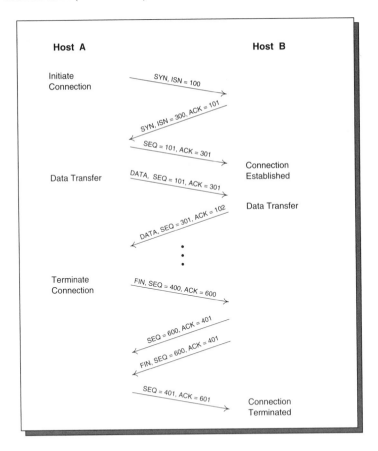

Figure 5-8. TCP Connection Establishment, Data Transfer, and Termination Events

Note that by convention, the ACK in the second TCP segment increments (i.e. ACK = 101) even though no data transfer occurred. Similarly, the ACK in the third segment increments (i.e. ACK = 301) even though no data transfer occurred there either. These exceptions to the normal acknowledgement process occur in order to verify receipt of the other host's ISN segment (which may not contain any data). When data transfer does begin (in the fourth and fifth segments), the same sequence numbers as the previously corresponding ACKs are used (i.e. SEQ = 101 seen in both segments 3 and 4). Another way of saying this is that a segment containing just an ACK (and no data) would not use up a sequence number; the three-way handshake (with the FIN flag set) *does* use a sequence number.

To manage connection-related issues, the TCP module maintains a record known as a *Transmission Control Block* (TCB). The TCB stores a number of variables, including the Local and Remote Socket numbers, the security/precedence of the connection, and pointers to identify incoming and outgoing data streams. Two other TCP functions already discussed, reliability and flow control, manage the data transfer process. The Sequence numbers, acknowledgements, and Window numbers are the mechanisms that the reliability, flow control, and data transfer functions use to ensure their proper operation.

Let's assume the data transfer is complete and the connection is no longer required. Because TCP provides a full-duplex connection, either side may initiate the disconnect. The other end, however, must continue to receive data until the remote module has finished sending it. The TCP connection can be terminated in one of three ways: the local host can initiate the termination, the remote host can initiate it, or both can close the connection simultaneously. The shut-down procedure is the same in all three cases. For example, if the local host has completed its business, it can generate a TCP segment with the Finish (FIN) flag set (FIN = 1). The local host will continue to receive data from the remote end until it receives a TCP segment with FIN = 1 from the remote end. When the second Finish segment is acknowledged, the connection is closed.

The bottom of Figure 5-8 illustrates this scenario. Host A has finished transferring its last data segment and terminates the connection by sending [FIN, SEQ = 400, ACK = 600]. Host B acknowledges receipt of Host A's FIN by sending [SEQ = 600, ACK = 401], and then sends its own FIN [FIN, SEQ = 600, ACK = 401]. Host A acknowledges Host B's FIN with [SEQ = 401, ACK = 601], and the connection is closed.

Make a special note of the sequence and acknowledgement number progression in these last four segments. The first closing segment [FIN, SEQ = 400, ACK = 600] uses the sequence and acknowledgement numbers that were next in line. The second segment is just an acknowledgement for the first [SEQ = 600, ACK = 401], and therefore does not use up a sequence number. The third segment contains a FIN, and again, by convention, uses the same sequence number [SEQ = 600] as was found in the previous ACK. The fourth segment (again, operating by convention) increments the sequence number even though it contains no data ([SEQ = 401], which corresponds with the previous ACK), and also increments the acknowledgement number [ACK = 601]. This verifies receipt of the FIN contained in the third segment. Once again, the connection termination sequence, also called the modified three-way handshake, causes a special condition for the sequence and acknowledgement numbers. This FIN segment (without data) uses a sequence number, much like the case of the SYN flag illustrated previously.

5.5.6 Precedence/Security

As a military application, TCP required precedence and security. Therefore, these two attributes may be assigned for each connection. The IP Type of Service field and security option may be used to define the requirements associated with that connection. Higher-layer protocols, such as TELNET, may specify the attribute required, and the TCP module will then comply on behalf of that ULP.

5.5.7 The TCP Connection State Diagram

Like many computer processes, TCP operation is best summarized with a state diagram, shown in Figure 5-9a and discussed in detail in "TCP Connection Initiation: An Inside Look" [5-10]. TCP operation progresses from one state to another in response to events, including user calls, incoming TCP segments, and timeouts. The *user calls* are commands that cross the User/TCP interface, i.e., the functions that support the communication between user processes. These include OPEN, SEND, RECEIVE, CLOSE, ABORT, and STATUS. When a TCP segment arrives, it must be examined to determine if any of the flags are set, particularly the SYN, ACK, RST, or FIN. The timeouts include the USER TIMEOUT, RETRANSMISSION TIMEOUT, and the TIME-WAIT TIMEOUT.

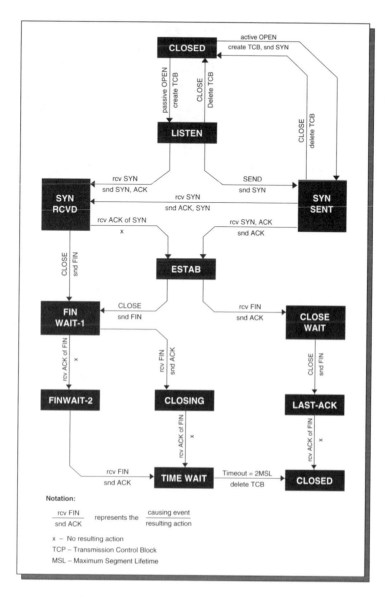

Figure 5-9a. TCP Connection State Diagram

The first state entered by the TCP process is CLOSED, indicating no connection state at all. A passive OPEN creates a Transmission Control Block (TCB), which moves the process to the LISTEN state. It then waits for a connection from a remote TCP and port. If a SYN is received, a SYN, ACK is sent in response. Should another ACK be received, the connection reaches the ESTABLISHED state. When the data transfer is complete at the near end, a CLOSE is issued and a FIN sent, moving to the state FIN-WAIT-1 and subsequently FIN-WAIT-2 or CLOSING. After waiting to confirm that the remote TCP has received the ACK of its FIN, the TCB is deleted and the connection reaches the CLOSED state. In a similar manner, a FIN received from the other end of the connection moves the process to state CLOSE-WAIT, pending the completion of the local user's requirements for that connection. When the ACK of the FIN has been received, the connection once again reaches the CLOSED state. Further explanations of the various states are given in Figure 5-9b.

The meanings of the states are:

LISTEN – represents waiting for a connection request from any remote TCP and port.

SYN-SENT – represents waiting for a matching connection request after having sent a connection request.

SYN-RECEIVED – represents waiting for a confirming connection request acknowledgement after having both received and sent a connection request.

ESTABLISHED – represents an open connection, data received can be delivered to the user. The normal state for the data transfer phase of the connection.

FIN-WAIT-1 – represents waiting for a connection termination request from the remote TCP, or an acknowledgement of the connection termination request previously sent.

FIN-WAIT-2 – represents waiting for a connection termination request from the remote TCP.

CLOSE-WAIT – represents waiting for a connection termination request from the local user.

CLOSING – represents waiting for a connection termination request acknowledgement from the remote TCP.

LAST-ACK – represents waiting for an acknowledgement of the connection termination request previously sent to the remote TCP (which includes an acknowledgement of its connection termination request).

TIME-WAIT – represents waiting for enough time to pass to be sure the remote TCP received the acknowledgement of its connection termination request.

CLOSED – represents no connection state at all.

Figure 5-9b. TCP Connection States

5.6 Troubleshooting the Host-to-Host Connection

In this chapter, we've studied the two protocols that provide end-to-end (or host-to-host) connectivity. We've seen that UDP provides connectionless service and is typically used for applications that need Port identification (or multiplexing) and basic error control. TCP offers connection-oriented service and rigorously maintains Sequence and Acknowledgement numbers to guarantee data delivery. The price for TCP's extensive error control is its additional header overhead (20 vs. 8 octets).

What should you do when the host-to-host connection fails? First, you need to determine the underlying transport protocol—UDP or TCP. If the protocol is UDP, verify that connectionless service is adequate for the application. If it is, then a problem such as multiple retransmissions may result from the upper-layer protocol's assumptions regarding the transport mechanism. For instance, because it has experienced overhead savings all along, the ULP may tolerate an occasional overhead-producing glitch in communications.

TCP is much more complex. In addition to verifying the Port number, look for significant events in the TCP connection. These include the three-way handshake (using the SYN and ACK flags) and the connection termination (using the RST and FIN flags). During the data transfer phase, verify that the Sequence numbers, Acknowledgements, and Window sizes are appropriate for the application, and remember that Window = 0 will close the communication path in the opposite direction.

In short, determine whether the transmitted data is reaching its destination. If it's not, study the Internet Layer for problems, as discussed in Chapter 4. If it is, examine the UDP and TCP headers to determine the source of the delivery problem. RFC 816, "Fault Isolation and Recovery" [5-11], contains interesting thoughts on internet vs. host analysis.

Now that we're steeped in the theory behind UDP and TCP operation, let's examine some case studies that demonstrate how these protocols operate (and where they might fail).

5.7 Case Studies

The case studies in this section concentrate on issues that demonstrate the host-to-host connection. We'll start with examples that use the datagram-based UDP, then we'll move to more complex examples that require the connection-oriented TCP.

5.7.1 Using BOOTP with UDP Transport

The Bootstrap Protocol (BOOTP), described in RFC 951 [5-12] and RFC 1533 [5-13], allows a client device to obtain its bootup parameters from a server. BOOTP runs over the UDP transport and uses two defined ports: Port 67 (BOOTP Server) and Port 68 (BOOTP Client). Because it uses the connectionless UDP as the transport, the connection depends on the end-user processes for reliability. The BOOTP message has a standard format (review Figure 4-5) for both client requests and server replies, which adds to the protocol's simplicity.

Once the client locates its server and boot file, it uses the Trivial File Transfer Protocol (TFTP) to obtain the actual file, as described in references [5-14] and [5-15]. Let's look at what happens when the client can't find its server.

In this example, a Retix bridge is configured to obtain its SNMP parameters from a Sun workstation located on another segment (see Figure 5-10). Upon power-up, the bridge broadcasts a BOOTP request, looking for the BOOTP server (see Trace 5.7.1a). Unfortunately, the administrator of the Sun workstation has not loaded the BOOTP daemon on the Sun workstation, so the BOOTP requests go unanswered. Note that the BOOTP request packets are staggered in time and transmitted at relatively long intervals (2 to 17 seconds apart).

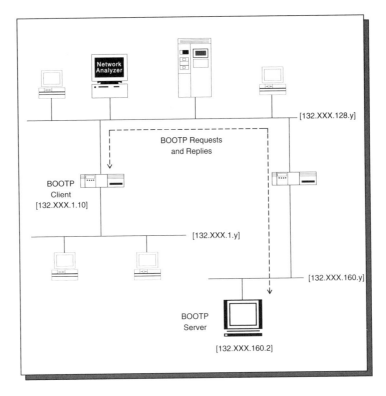

Figure 5-10. Booting Remote Bridge Using BOOTP

When the bridge administrator realizes that his device is not operating properly, he studies the repeated BOOTP requests, theorizing that the BOOTP server is not listening and therefore not responding. His assumption is correct. After the BOOTP daemon is loaded on the Sun workstation, the bridge receives a response (Frame 4 of Trace 5.7.1b). The bridge then requests its boot file from the Sun workstation and receives its information in Frame 6. An acknowledgement from the bridge (Frame 7) completes the transaction.

Details of the scenario (Trace 5.7.1c) show how the BOOTP and TFTP protocols work together. The BOOTP request (Frame 3) contains the boot file name (90034CF1) that the bridge requires. The BOOTP reply (Frame 4) contains a server-assigned IP address for the client [132.XXX.1.10] and the address of the BOOTP server [132.XXX.160.2]. The location of the boot file name (/tftpboot/90034CF1) is also included. Next, the bridge sends a TFTP Read request in Frame 5. The BOOTP server responds with a data packet containing the configuration parameters the bridge requires. A TFTP ACK from the bridge completes the transaction. With the BOOTP daemon properly installed on the Sun workstation, the bridge can receive its configuration parameters and begin initialization.

Sniffer Network Analyzer data 5-Sep at 14:02:52, RETXBOOT.ENC, Pg 1

SUMMARY	Delta T	Destination	Source	Summary
M 1		090077000001	Retix 034CF1	DSAP=80, I frame
2	10.8868	Broadcast	Retix 034CF1	BOOTP Request
3	2.2928	Broadcast	Retix 034CF1	BOOTP Request
4	9.8320	Broadcast	Retix 034CF1	BOOTP Request
5	2.0745	Broadcast	Retix 034CF1	BOOTP Request
6	11.0334	Broadcast	Retix 034CF1	BOOTP Request
7	2.1841	Broadcast	Retix 034CF1	BOOTP Request
8	6.1166	CMC 614107	Retix 034CF1	ARP R PA=[0.0.0.0]
				HA=080090034CF1 PRO=IP
9	7.2104	Broadcast	Retix 034CF	BOOTP Request
10	2.0746	Broadcast	Retix 034CF1	BOOTP Request
11	8.1893	090077000001	Retix 034CF1	DSAP=80, I frame
12	7.2135	Broadcast	Retix 034CF1	BOOTP Request
13	2.2931	Broadcast	Retix 034CF1	BOOTP Request
14	15.4028	Broadcast	Retix 034CF1	BOOTP Request
15	2.0747	Broadcast	Retix 034CF1	BOOTP Request
16	13.2180	Broadcast	Retix 034CF1	BOOTP Request

17	2.2931	Broadcast	Retix 034CF1	BOOTP Request
18	8.7395	Broadcast	Retix 034CF1	BOOTP Request
19	2.0746	Broadcast	Retix 034CF1	BOOTP Request
20	17.6970	Broadcast	Retix 034CF1	BOOTP Request
21	2.1838	Broadcast	Retix 034CF1	BOOTP Request
22	7.7562	Broadcast	Retix 034CF1	BOOTP Request
23	2.0747	Broadcast	Retix 034CF1	BOOTP Request
24	12.1260	Broadcast	Retix 034CF1	BOOTP Request
25	2.1836	Broadcast	Retix 034CF1	BOOTP Request
26	5.4624	Broadcast	Retix 034CF1	BOOTP Request
27	2.0746	Broadcast	Retix 034CF1	BOOTP Request
28	5.4625	Broadcast	Retix 034CF1	BOOTP Request
29	2.2931	Broadcast	Retix 034CF1	BOOTP Request
30	16.4951	Broadcast	Retix 034CF1	BOOTP Request
31	2.0746	Broadcast	Retix 034CF1	BOOTP Request

Trace 5.7.1a. Bridge BOOTP Unanswered Request Summary

Sniffer Network Analyzer data 16-Mar at 09:48:26, BOOTP.ENC, Pg 1

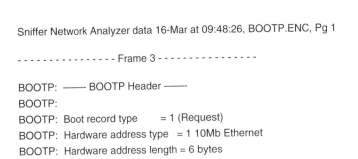

SUMMARY	Delta T	Destination	Source	Summary
M 1		090077000001	Retix 034CF1	DSAP=80, I frame
2	6.6956	090077000001	Retix 034CF1	DSAP=80, I frame
3	4.1908	Broadcast	Retix 034CF1	BOOTP Request
4	0.5307	Retix 034CF1	Sun 0AB646	BOOTP Reply
5	0.0053	Sun 0AB646	Retix 034CF1	TFTP Read request File=/tftpboot/90034CF1
6	0.2037	Retix 034CF1	Sun 0AB646	TFTP Data packet NS=1 (Last)
7	0.0033	Sun 0AB646	Retix 034CF1	TFTP Ack NR=1
8	50.2652	090077000001	Retix 034CF1	DSAP=80, I frame

Trace 5.7.1b. Bridge BOOTP Request/Reply Summary

Sniffer Network Analyzer data 16-Mar at 09:48:26, BOOTP.ENC, Pg 1

- - - - - - - - - - - - - - - - Frame 3 - - - - - - - - - - - - - - - - -

BOOTP: ——- BOOTP Header ——-
BOOTP:
BOOTP: Boot record type   = 1 (Request)
BOOTP: Hardware address type = 1 10Mb Ethernet
BOOTP: Hardware address length = 6 bytes
BOOTP:

BOOTP: Hops = 0
BOOTP: Transaction id = 0000063F
BOOTP: Elapsed boot time = 0 seconds
BOOTP:
BOOTP: Client self-assigned IP address = [0.0.0.0] (Unknown)
BOOTP: Client hardware address   = Retix 034CF1
BOOTP:
BOOTP: Host name   = ""
BOOTP: Boot file name = "90034CF1"
BOOTP:
BOOTP: [Vendor specific information]
BOOTP:

- - - - - - - - - - - - - - - - Frame 4 - - - - - - - - - - - - - - - - -

BOOTP: ——- BOOTP Header ——-
BOOTP:
BOOTP: Boot record type   = 2 (Reply)
BOOTP: Hardware address type = 1 10Mb Ethernet
BOOTP: Hardware address length = 6 bytes
BOOTP:
BOOTP: Hops = 0
BOOTP: Transaction id = 0000063F
BOOTP: Elapsed boot time = 0 seconds
BOOTP:
BOOTP: Client self-assigned IP address = [0.0.0.0] (Unknown)
BOOTP: Client server-assigned IP address = [132.XXX.1.10]
BOOTP: Server IP address   = [132.XXX.160.2]
BOOTP: Gateway IP address   = [132.XXX.160.2]
BOOTP: Client hardware address   = Retix 034CF1
BOOTP:
BOOTP: Host name   = ""
BOOTP: Boot file name = "/tftpboot/90034CF1"
BOOTP:
BOOTP: [Vendor specific information]
BOOTP:

- - - - - - - - - - - - - - - Frame 5 - - - - - - - - - - - - - - - - -

TFTP: ——- Trivial file transfer ——-
TFTP:
TFTP: Opcode = 1 (Read request)
TFTP: File name = "/tftpboot/90034CF1"
TFTP: Mode = "octet"

TFTP:
TFTP: [Normal end of "Trivial file transfer".]
TFTP:

- - - - - - - - - - - - - - - - Frame 6 - - - - - - - - - - - - - - - - -

TFTP: ——- Trivial file transfer ——-
TFTP:
TFTP: Opcode = 3 (Data packet)
TFTP: Block number = 1
TFTP: [160 bytes of data] (Last frame)
TFTP:
TFTP: [Normal end of "Trivial file transfer".]
TFTP:

- - - - - - - - - - - - - - - Frame 7 - - - - - - - - - - - - - - - - -

TFTP: ——- Trivial file transfer ——-
TFTP:
TFTP: Opcode = 4 (Ack)
TFTP: Block number = 1
TFTP:
TFTP: [Normal end of "Trivial file transfer".]
TFTP:

Trace 5.7.1c. Bridge BOOTP Request/Reply Details

5.7.2 Clock Synchronization with UDP

As we've discussed, applications for UDP are not mission critical; that is, the inter-network manager won't get fired if the datagram gets lost and must be retransmitted. One example of such an application is the synchronization of the clocks on all the hosts on the internetwork. The synchronization information is included in a single datagram. Should one of the synchronization datagrams get lost, a retransmission can easily be requested. Besides, it makes little sense to establish a connection using a TCP three-way handshake (which uses three TCP segments), then to send one segment of data, then to use several more segments to close the connection. UDP seems ideal for this application. Let's see how it works.

The protocol selected is the Time protocol, described in RFC 868 [5-16]. Time is a relatively simple protocol that can be used with either UDP or TCP. It uses Port 37 and operates as shown in Figure 5-11. The Time server listens on Port 37 for a Time Request datagram. The user transmits an empty datagram to Port 37, which prompts the server to return a 32-bit number representing the current time. The user receives the Time datagram and uses that information to synchronize its clock with that of the server. The timestamp itself (the 32-bit number) counts the number of seconds that have expired since midnight on January 1, 1900, Greenwich Mean Time (GMT). RFC 868 states that this measurement will be usable until the year 2036. (The network engineer figures he'll be enjoying his retirement in Hawaii by 2036, so he decides to use the Time protocol for his internetwork.)

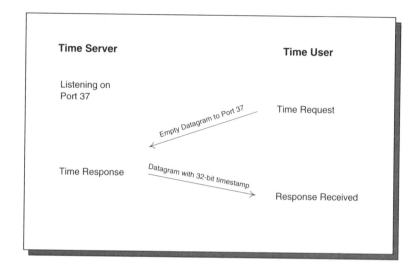

Figure 5-11. Time Protocol Implemented with UDP Transport

The internetwork in question is a series of bridged token ring networks, shown in Figure 5-12. The Time server is a Sun SPARCstation 2 running BSD UNIX 4.3 and attached to network [142.56.20.0]. The user in question is a Sun SPARCstation IPX, also running BSD UNIX 4.3 but attached to network [142.56.17.0].

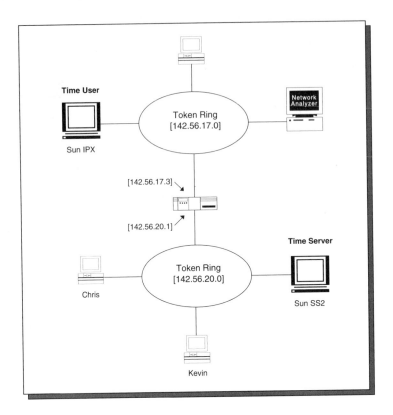

Figure 5-12. Time Service

Although the Time protocol is extremely simple, some confusion occurs. As the network manager discovers, the programmer who wrote the code for the user system (the Sun IPX) used an incorrect Destination Port number. We see the problem in Trace 5.7.2a. In Frame 175, the user sends an empty UDP packet to Port 2057. We know that this packet is empty because its length is only 8 octets, the length of the UDP header (review Figure 5-2). In Frame 176, the Time server (via Bridge 17.3) returns an ICMP Destination Unreachable message, specifying that the selected port is unreachable. A check of the originating message shows a total length of 28 octets, which comprise the IP header (20 octets) and the UDP header (8 octets). Both the Source and Destination addresses are correct and the checksum passes. Clearly, the Destination port (2057) causes the problem; the Time server is listening at Port 37 and does not hear the request for a timestamp.

Once the systems programmer rewrites his code, the time service request succeeds (see Trace 5.7.2b). The Sun IPX transmits an empty UDP packet in Frame 157, and the Sun SPARCstation 2 Time server [142.56.20.16] sends a correct response via the bridge. Both the request and the response are correctly addressed to and from Port 37. In the Time response (Frame 158), note that the message returned is four octets. This data is shown as the last eight hexadecimal characters in the printout, AD 67 8E FD, which corresponds to the appropriate time from the Time server.

This example illustrates two important points: UDP is clearly adequate for many host-to-host applications, but the correct addressing of the host port is vital to the success of the transmission.

Sniffer Network Analyzer data 10-Mar at 12:52:50, TIME_BAD.TRC, Pg 1

```
- - - - - - - - - - - - - - - - Frame 175 - - - - - - - - - - - - - - - - -

UDP: ——- UDP Header ——-
UDP:
UDP:  Source port = 1157
UDP:  Destination port = 2057
UDP:  Length = 8
UDP:  No checksum
UDP:

- - - - - - - - - - - - - - - Frame 176 - - - - - - - - - - - - - - - -

ICMP: ——- ICMP header ——-
ICMP:
ICMP:  Type = 3 (Destination unreachable)
ICMP:  Code = 3 (Port unreachable)
ICMP:  Checksum = F066 (correct)
ICMP:  IP header of originating message (description follows)
ICMP:
IP:  ——- IP Header ——-
IP:
IP:   Version = 4, header length = 20 bytes
IP:   Type of service = 00
IP:           000. .... = routine
IP:           ...0 .... = normal delay
IP:           .... 0... = normal throughput
IP:           .... .0.. = normal reliability
IP:   Total length = 28 bytes
```

IP: Identification = 60919
IP: Flags = 0X
IP: .0.. .... = may fragment
IP: ..0. .... = last fragment
IP: Fragment offset = 0 bytes
IP: Time to live = 59 seconds/hops
IP: Protocol = 17 (UDP)
IP: Header checksum = 5055 (correct)
IP: Source address = [142.56.17.4]
IP: Destination address = [142.56.20.16]
IP: No options
ICMP:
ICMP: [First 8 byte(s) of data of originating message]
ICMP:
ICMP: [Normal end of "ICMP header".]
ICMP:

Trace 5.7.2a. Time Request to Incorrect Port Number

Sniffer Network Analyzer data 10-Mar at 12:40:00, TIME_WRK.TRC, Pg 1

- - - - - - - - - - - - - - - - Frame 157 - - - - - - - - - - - - - - - - -

IP: ——- IP Header ——-
IP:
IP: Version = 4, header length = 20 bytes
IP: Type of service = 00
IP: 000. .... = routine
IP: ...0 .... = normal delay
IP: .... 0... = normal throughput
IP: .... .0.. = normal reliability
IP: Total length = 28 bytes
IP: Identification = 49402
IP: Flags = 0X
IP: .0.. .... = may fragment
IP: ..0. .... = last fragment
IP: Fragment offset = 0 bytes
IP: Time to live = 60 seconds/hops
IP: Protocol = 17 (UDP)
IP: Header checksum = 7C52 (correct)
IP: Source address = [142.56.17.4]
IP: Destination address = [142.56.20.16]
IP: No options
IP:

UDP: ——— UDP Header ———-
UDP:
UDP: Source port = 1141 (Time)
UDP: Destination port = 37
UDP: Length = 8
UDP: No checksum
UDP:

ADDR	HEX		ASCII
0000	10 40 00 00 C9 09 23 4C	08 00 20 0B 8A A7 AA AA	. @ ....#L.. .....
0010	03 00 00 00 08 00 45 00	00 1C C0 FA 00 00 3C 11	......E........<.
0020	7C 52 8E 38 11 04 8E 38	14 10 04 75 00 25 00 08	IR.8...8...u.%..
0030	00 00		

- - - - - - - - - - - - - - - - Frame 158 - - - - - - - - - - - - - - - - -

IP: ——— IP Header ———-
IP:
IP: Version = 4, header length = 20 bytes
IP: Type of service = 00
IP: 000. .... = routine
IP: ...0 .... = normal delay
IP: .... 0... = normal throughput
IP: .... .0.. = normal reliability
IP: Total length = 32 bytes
IP: Identification = 27066
IP: Flags = 0X
IP: .0.. .... = may fragment
IP: ..0. .... = last fragment
IP: Fragment offset = 0 bytes
IP: Time to live = 59 seconds/hops
IP: Protocol = 17 (UDP)
IP: Header checksum = D48E (correct)
IP: Source address = [142.56.20.16]
IP: Destination address = [142.56.17.4]
IP: No options
IP:
UDP: ——— UDP Header ———-
UDP:
UDP: Source port = 37 (Time)
UDP: Destination port = 1141
UDP: Length = 12
UDP: No checksum

UDP:
UDP: [4 byte(s) of data]
UDP:

ADDR	HEX		ASCII
0000	18 40 08 00 20 0B 8A A7	00 00 C9 09 23 4C AA AA	.@.. ....#L..
0010	03 00 00 00 08 00 45 00	00 20 69 BA 00 00 3B 11	......E.. i...;.
0020	D4 8E 8E 38 14 10 8E 38	11 04 00 25 04 75 00 0C	...8...8...%.u..
0030	00 00 AD 67 8E FD		...g..

Trace 5.7.2b. UDP Time Service Details

5.7.3 Establishing and Terminating TCP Connections

In Section 5.5.5, we learned that the TCP connection must be established with a three-way handshake prior to any transmission of data. Once the data has been transferred, a modified three-way handshake terminates the connection. Let's study how these operations function, using a PC and its server as examples.

In this case study, a PC wishes to establish several logical connections to a Sun server via a single Ethernet physical connection. Different Port numbers identify the different logical connections (created using TCP's multiplexing capabilities). Let's follow the steps of one of these logical connections from establishment to data transfer to termination (see Trace 5.7.3a).

A TCP segment identifies the connection establishment with the Synchronize bit set (SYN = 1) and no data in the segment (LEN = 0). We can see this in Frame 706, along with an initial Sequence number, ISN = 1988352000. Also note that the Sun server is initiating this connection and that it is advertising a rather large window size (WIN = 24576). The Source port (S = 20) identifies the File Transfer Protocol (FTP), and the Destination port (D = 1227) is assigned by the Sun server. The PC responds with a similar synchronize segment in Frame 707; the receipt of the server's segment is acknowledged (ACK = 1988352001), the PC's ISN is sent (SEQ = 201331252), but a smaller window size is allowed (WIN = 1024). Note that the Source and Destination port numbers are now reversed, since the original source (the Sun server) has now become the PC's destination. Frame 708 completes the connection establishment, with the server acknowledging the PC's ISN (ACK = 201331253).

The details of the connection establishment are shown in Trace 5.7.3b. Note that one TCP option (the maximum segment size) is used. Maximum segment size = 1460 indicates transmission over an Ethernet/IEEE 802.3 LAN. The Ethernet/IEEE 802.3 can accommodate 1,500 octets of data within the frame. Of these, 20 octets are used for the TCP header and another 20 octets for the IP header, leaving 1,460 octets for the TCP segment. Data transfer may now proceed.

Data transfer begins in Frame 710 with a TCP segment of 1,024 octets (LEN = 1024). (Note that Frame 709 belongs to a previously established FTP connection destined for another port (D = 1219) on the same PC. While Frame 709 illustrates TCP's port multiplexing capabilities, it has nothing to do with the current discussion since it belongs to another logical connection.) The PC acknowledges receipt of the data in Frame 713 by sending ACK = 1988353025 (1988352001 + 1024 = 1988353025). The PC will not permit any more data at this time, and it indicates this by shutting its window (WIN = 0). In Frame 715, the PC's processor has caught up with its backlog (note that it was servicing port 1219 in Frame 714) and restores data flow by sending WIN = 1024. The server responds with another 1,024 octets in Frame 716. This process proceeds normally until the server completes its business.

In Frame 779, the server finishes its business and sends the Finish flag (FIN = 1) along with its last 114 octets of data. The PC responds with an acknowledgement in Frame 780 (ACK = 1988384884), then sends a second segment (Frame 781) containing both an ACK and a FIN. Note that the details in Trace 5.7.3c indicate that the PC does not shut down the connection, but permits up to 910 more octets of data from the other end (Window = 910). The server has said its piece, however; it acknowledges the FIN and closes its end of the connection in Frame 782. Both ends of the logical connection are now closed. In the following example, we'll see what happens when both ends are unable to maintain the connection and the Reset (RST) flag is required.

Sniffer Network Analyzer data 27-Mar at 09:04:54, TCPMEDLY.ENC, Pg 1

SUMMARY	Delta T	Destination	Source	Summary
706	0.0027	PC	Sun Server	TCP D=1227 S=20 SYN
				SEQ=1988352000 LEN=0
				WIN=24576
707	0.0139	Sun Server	PC	TCP D=20 S=1227 SYN
				ACK=1988352001
				SEQ=201331252

				LEN=0 WIN=1024
708	0.0006	PC	Sun Server	TCP D=1227 S=20
				ACK=201331253 WIN=24576
709	0.0007	PC	Sun Server	FTP R PORT=1219
				150 ASCII data connection
710	0.0993	PC	Sun Server	TCP D=1227 S=20
				ACK=201331253
				SEQ=1988352001
				LEN=1024 WIN=24576
711	0.0733	Sun Server	PC	TCP D=21 S=1219
				ACK=1972865105 WIN=951
712	0.0008	PC	Sun Server	FTP R PORT=1219
				226 ASCII Transfer complete
				<0D><0A>
713	0.0529	Sun Server	PC	TCP D=20 S=1227
				ACK=1988353025 WIN=0
714	0.0535	Sun Server	PC	TCP D=21 S=1219
				ACK=1972865135 WIN=956
715	0.0790	Sun Server	PC	TCP D=20 S=1227
				ACK=1988353025 WIN=1024
716	0.0015	PC	Sun Server	TCP D=1227 S=20
				ACK=201331253
				SEQ=1988353025
				LEN=1024 WIN=24576
717	0.1379	Sun Server	PC	TCP D=20 S=1227
				ACK=1988354049 WIN=0
718	0.0644	Sun Server	PC	TCP D=20 S=1227
				ACK=1988354049 WIN=1024
719	0.0015	PC	Sun Server	TCP D=1227 S=20
				ACK=201331253
				SEQ=1988354049
				LEN=1024 WIN=24576
720	0.0553	Sun Server	PC	TCP D=20 S=1227
				ACK=1988355073 WIN=1024
721	0.0015	PC	Sun Server	TCP D=1227 S=20
				ACK=201331253
				SEQ=1988355073
				LEN=1024 WIN=24576
722	0.0575	Sun Server	PC	TCP D=20 S=1227
				ACK=1988356097 WIN=1024

.
.
.

779	0.0008	PC	Sun Server	TCP D=1227 S=20 FIN
				ACK=201331253
				SEQ=1988384769
				LEN=114 WIN=24576
780	0.0204	Sun Server	PC	TCP D=20 S=1227
				ACK=1988384884 WIN=910
781	0.0616	Sun Server	PC	TCP D=20 S=1227 FIN
				ACK=1988384884
				SEQ=201331253
				LEN=0 WIN=910
782	0.0006	PC	Sun Server	TCP D=1227 S=20
				ACK=201331254 WIN=24576

Trace 5.7.3a. TCP Connection Establishment and Termination Summary

Sniffer Network Analyzer data 27-Mar at 09:04:54, TCPMEDLY.ENC, Pg 1

- - - - - - - - - - - - - - - - Frame 706 - - - - - - - - - - - - - - - - -

TCP: ——- TCP header ——-
TCP:
TCP: Source port = 20 (FTP data)
TCP: Destination port = 1227
TCP: Initial sequence number = 1988352000
TCP: Data offset = 24 bytes
TCP: Flags = 02
TCP: ..0. .... = (No urgent pointer)
TCP: ...0 .... = (No acknowledgment)
TCP: .... 0... = (No push)
TCP: .... .0.. = (No reset)
TCP: .... ..1. = SYN
TCP: ....0 = (No FIN)
TCP: Window = 24576
TCP: Checksum = D02F (correct)
TCP:
TCP: Options follow
TCP: Maximum segment size = 1460
TCP:

```
- - - - - - - - - - - - - - - - Frame 707 - - - - - - - - - - - - - - - - -

TCP: ——- TCP header ——-
TCP:
TCP: Source port = 1227
TCP: Destination port = 20 (FTP data)
TCP: Initial sequence number = 201331252
TCP: Acknowledgment number = 1988352001
TCP: Data offset = 24 bytes
TCP: Flags = 12
TCP: ..0. .... = (No urgent pointer)
TCP: ...1 .... = Acknowledgment
TCP: .... 0... = (No push)
TCP: .... .0.. = (No reset)
TCP: .... ..1. = SYN
TCP: .... ...0 = (No FIN)
TCP: Window = 1024
TCP: Checksum = 0DEB (correct)
TCP:
TCP: Options follow
TCP: Maximum segment size = 1460
TCP:

- - - - - - - - - - - - - - - Frame 708 - - - - - - - - - - - - - - - - -

TCP: ——- TCP header ——-
TCP:
TCP: Source port = 20 (FTP data)
TCP: Destination port = 1227
TCP: Sequence number = 1988352001
TCP: Acknowledgment number = 201331253
TCP: Data offset = 20 bytes
TCP: Flags = 10
TCP: ..0. .... = (No urgent pointer)
TCP: ...1 .... = Acknowledgment
TCP: .... 0... = (No push)
TCP: .... .0.. = (No reset)
TCP: .... ..0. = (No SYN)
TCP: .... ...0 = (No FIN)
TCP: Window = 24576
TCP: Checksum = C9A7 (correct)
TCP: No TCP options
TCP:
```

Trace 5.7.3b. TCP Connection Synchronization (SYN) Details

Sniffer Network Analyzer data 27-Mar at 09:04:54, TCPMEDLY.ENC, Pg 1

- - - - - - - - - - - - - - - Frame 779 - - - - - - - - - - - - - - - - -

TCP: —— TCP header ——-
TCP:
TCP: Source port = 20 (FTP data)
TCP: Destination port = 1227
TCP: Sequence number = 1988384769
TCP: Acknowledgment number = 201331253
TCP: Data offset = 20 bytes
TCP: Flags = 19
TCP: ..0. .... = (No urgent pointer)
TCP: ...1 .... = Acknowledgment
TCP: .... 1... = Push
TCP: .... .0.. = (No reset)
TCP: .... ..0. = (No SYN)
TCP: ....1 = FIN
TCP: Window = 24576
TCP: Checksum = 492C (correct)
TCP: No TCP options
TCP: [114 byte(s) of data]
TCP:

- - - - - - - - - - - - - - - Frame 780 - - - - - - - - - - - - - - - - -

TCP: —— TCP header ——-
TCP:
TCP: Source port = 1227
TCP: Destination port = 20 (FTP data)
TCP: Sequence number = 201331253
TCP: Acknowledgment number = 1988384884
TCP: Data offset = 20 bytes
TCP: Flags = 10
TCP: ..0. .... = (No urgent pointer)
TCP: ...1 .... = Acknowledgment
TCP: .... 0... = (No push)
TCP: .... .0.. = (No reset)
TCP: .... ..0. = (No SYN)
TCP: ....0 = (No FIN)
TCP: Window = 910
TCP: Checksum = A5A6 (correct)
TCP: No TCP options
TCP:

```
- - - - - - - - - - - - - - - Frame 781 - - - - - - - - - - - - - - - - -

TCP: ——- TCP header ——-
TCP:
TCP: Source port = 1227
TCP: Destination port = 20 (FTP data)
TCP: Sequence number = 201331253
TCP: Acknowledgment number = 1988384884
TCP: Data offset = 20 bytes
TCP: Flags = 11
TCP: ..0. .... = (No urgent pointer)
TCP: ...1 .... = Acknowledgment
TCP: .... 0... = (No push)
TCP: .... .0.. = (No reset)
TCP: .... ..0. = (No SYN)
TCP: .... ...1 = FIN
TCP: Window = 910
TCP: Checksum = A5A5 (correct)
TCP: No TCP options
TCP:

- - - - - - - - - - - - - - - Frame 782 - - - - - - - - - - - - - - - - -

TCP: ——- TCP header ——-
TCP:
TCP: Source port = 20 (FTP data)
TCP: Destination port = 1227
TCP: Sequence number = 1988384884
TCP: Acknowledgment number = 201331254
TCP: Data offset = 20 bytes
TCP: Flags = 10
TCP: ..0. .... = (No urgent pointer)
TCP: ...1 .... = Acknowledgment
TCP: .... 0... = (No push)
TCP: .... .0.. = (No reset)
TCP: .... ..0. = (No SYN)
TCP: .... ...0 = (No FIN)
TCP: Window = 24576
TCP: Checksum = 4933 (correct)
TCP: No TCP options
TCP:
```

Trace 5.7.3c. TCP Connection Termination (FIN) Details

5.7.4 Reset TCP Connection

The TCP header contains six flags that manage the virtual circuit. In Section 5.7.3, we saw how the Acknowledgement (ACK), Synchronize (SYN), and Finish (FIN) flags are used for connection management and data transfer under normal conditions. One of the remaining flags, known as the Reset (RST) flag, is used when a TCP segment arrives that is not intended for the current connection. The RST flag is also used if a TCP module detects a fatal error or if the application process unilaterally decides to close the connection. One possible scenario is when one TCP module crashes during a session. The term used to describe this condition is a *half-open connection* because one end is maintaining its Sequence numbers and other transmission-related parameters while the other is not. When the crashed host returns to life, its Sequence numbers are unlikely to be the same as those it was using prior to the crash. As a result, it sends unexpected (and thus unacknowledged) Sequence numbers to the host at the other end of the link.

When the crashed host realizes that it has caused this confusion, it sends a Reset to its distant partner, which triggers a three-way handshake to re-establish the connection. Let's see how the Reset flag is used in a failure scenario.

In this case, a Sun workstation is communicating with a remote host located in another part of the country. A TELNET session is in progress over the internet, with the workstation emulating a host terminal. Two routers connect the local and remote Ethernet networks (see Figure 5-13). Without warning, the user loses his response from the host and starts hitting the RETURN key, hoping for a miracle (sound familiar?). We can see his frustration in Trace 5.7.4a. In Frame 3 all appears to be fine, but after almost two minutes of waiting (119.8658 seconds) the Sun sends a carriage return. (Note the <0D> <00> output pattern, indicating that an ASCII Carriage Return <0D> has been transmitted.) The Sun sends these characters (<0D> <00> <0D> <00>...) at increments of 2 seconds apart, then 4 seconds, 8, 16, and so on, attempting to wake up the remote host.

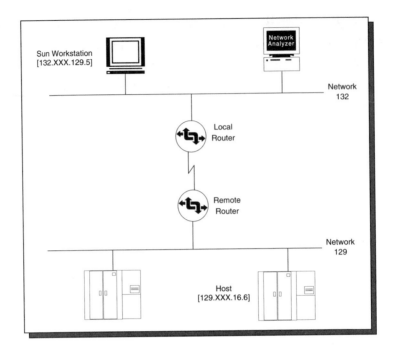

Figure 5-13. TCP Connection Reset

Unfortunately, the efforts are in vain. The remote host gets confused, sends a TCP Reset (RST = 1) in Frame 13, and disables future receptions by setting Window = 0. The Sun resets the connection, but also acknowledges the last data octet that it received in Frame 3 (ACK = 20881447). Clearly, the Sun does not want to end the conversation since it keeps Window = 4096.

The problem is traced to a bad Ethernet card connecting the remote host to its local network. The card's operation is intermittent, working part of the time—such as when the TELNET session was initialized—then failing for no apparent reason. When the failure occurred, it caused a half-open TCP connection, and ultimately the mysterious TCP Reset. When the faulty Ethernet card was replaced, no further problems occurred.

Sniffer Network Analyzer data 14-Sep at 11:43:30, TCPRST.ENC, Pg 1

SUMMARY	Delta T	Destination	Source	Summary
M 1		Router	Sun 01DF5E	TCP D=23 S=1169
				ACK=20881319 WIN=4096
2	5.0808	Sun 01DF5E	Router	Telnet R PORT=1169
				FILE: ROUT (NO CHANGES)
3	0.1189	Router	Sun 01DF5E	TCP D=23 S=1169
				ACK=20881447 WIN=4096
4	119.8658	Router	Sun 01DF5E	Telnet C PORT=1169 <0D><00>...
5	0.8820	Router	Sun 01DF5E	Telnet C PORT=1169 <0D><00>...
6	2.0002	Router	Sun 01DF5E	Telnet C PORT=1169 <0D><00>...
7	4.0001	Router	Sun 01DF5E	Telnet C PORT=1169 <0D><00>...
8	8.0006	Router	Sun 01DF5E	Telnet C PORT=1169 <0D><00>...
9	16.0010	Router	Sun 01DF5E	Telnet C PORT=1169 <0D><00>...
10	32.0020	Router	Sun 01DF5E	Telnet C PORT=1169 <0D><00>...
11	64.0039	Router	Sun 01DF5E	Telnet C PORT=1169 <0D><00>...
12	64.0040	Router	Sun 01DF5E	Telnet C PORT=1169 <0D><00>...
13	0.2722	Sun 01DF5E	Router	TCP D=1169 S=23 RST WIN=0
14	0.0021	Router	Sun 01DF5E	TCP D=23 S=1169 RST
				ACK=20881447 WIN=4096

Trace 5.7.4a. TCP Connection Reset (RST) Summary

Sniffer Network Analyzer data 14-Sep at 11:43:30, TCPRST.ENC, Pg 1

- - - - - - - - - - - - - - - - - Frame 13 - - - - - - - - - - - - - - - - - -

DLC: ——- DLC Header ——-
DLC:
DLC: Frame 13 arrived at 12:24:26.1927; frame size is 60 (003C hex) bytes.
DLC: Destination = Station Sun   01DF5E
DLC: Source   = Station PrteonE0807B, Router
DLC: Ethertype = 0800 (IP)
DLC:
IP: ——- IP Header ——-
IP:
IP: Version = 4, header length = 20 bytes
IP: Type of service = 00
IP: 000. .... = routine
IP: ...0 .... = normal delay
IP: .... 0... = normal throughput
IP: .... .0.. = normal reliability
IP: Total length = 40 bytes

301

IP: Identification = 25254
IP: Flags = 0X
IP: .0.. .... = may fragment
IP: ..0. .... = last fragment
IP: Fragment offset = 0 bytes
IP: Time to live = 19 seconds/hops
IP: Protocol = 6 (TCP)
IP: Header checksum = AE75 (correct)
IP: Source address = [129.XXX.16.6]
IP: Destination address = [132.XXX.129.5]
IP: No options
IP:
TCP: ——- TCP header ——-
TCP:
TCP: Source port = 23 (Telnet)
TCP: Destination port = 1169
TCP: Sequence number = 20881447
TCP: Data offset = 20 bytes
TCP: Flags = 04
TCP: ..0. .... = (No urgent pointer)
TCP: ...0 .... = (No acknowledgment)
TCP: .... 0... = (No push)
TCP: .... .1.. = Reset
TCP: .... ..0. = (No SYN)
TCP: ....0 = (No FIN)
TCP: Window = 0
TCP: Checksum = 25EE (correct)
TCP: No TCP options
TCP:

- - - - - - - - - - - - - - - - Frame 14 - - - - - - - - - - - - - - - - - -

DLC: ——- DLC Header ——-
DLC:
DLC: Frame 14 arrived at 12:24:26.1948; frame size is 60 (003C hex) bytes.
DLC: Destination = Station PrteonE0807B, Router
DLC: Source   = Station Sun   01DF5E
DLC: Ethertype = 0800 (IP)
DLC:
IP: ——- IP Header ——-
IP:
IP: Version = 4, header length = 20 bytes
IP: Type of service = 00

302

```
IP:              000. .... = routine
IP:              ...0 .... = normal delay
IP:              .... 0... = normal throughput
IP:              .... .0.. = normal reliability
IP:   Total length = 40 bytes
IP:   Identification = 25255
IP:   Flags = 0X
IP:   .0.. .... = may fragment
IP:   ..0. .... = last fragment
IP:   Fragment offset = 0 bytes
IP:   Time to live = 30 seconds/hops
IP:   Protocol = 6 (TCP)
IP:   Header checksum = A374 (correct)
IP:   Source address = [132.XXX.129.5]
IP:   Destination address = [129.XXX.16.6]
IP:   No options
IP:
TCP: —— TCP header ——
TCP:
TCP:  Source port = 1169
TCP:  Destination port = 23 (Telnet)
TCP:  Sequence number = 398210404
TCP:  Acknowledgment number = 20881447
TCP:  Data offset = 20 bytes
TCP:  Flags = 14
TCP:  ..0. .... = (No urgent pointer)
TCP:  ...1 .... = Acknowledgment
TCP:  .... 0... = (No push)
TCP:  .... .1.. = Reset
TCP:  .... ..0. = (No SYN)
TCP:  .... ...0 = (No FIN)
TCP:  Window = 4096
TCP:  Checksum = 15EE (correct)
TCP:  No TCP options
TCP:
```

Trace 5.7.4b. TCP Connection Reset (RST) Details

5.7.5 Repeated Host Acknowledgements

TCP is one of a class of PAR protocols that requires a positive acknowledgement within a specified time period, or it will retransmit the data. The acknowledgement mechanism uses the 32-bit Acknowledgement number and sets the Acknowledgement

(ACK) flag. The ACK flag tells the recipient TCP module to process the Acknowledgement field. The Acknowledgement field counts each octet of information received and indicates which octet is expected next. What happens when the receiver does not properly acknowledge incoming data?

In this case, an X-Windows terminal is communicating with a minicomputer. The terminal sends some information, but then seemingly locks up. At first the administrator suspects the terminal, but closer analysis reveals a defect in the host. Let's find out why.

Both the terminal and the host are attached to the same Ethernet, and the protocol analyzer is set to capture all traffic between the two devices. The initial trace reveals a TCP connection between Port 3319 and Port 6000 (the X-Windows port), as seen in Trace 5.7.5a. It is unusual, however, that all communication between host and terminal consists of TCP acknowledgements and that they all flow in one direction—host to terminal. These acknowledgements repeat roughly every millisecond (0.0008 second).

A detailed study of one of the frames reveals the problem (see Trace 5.7.5b). The host's TCP module is stuck in a loop in which it is unable to increment the Acknowledgement number, so each TCP segment contains the same information. The IP datagram contains a total of 40 octets: 20 for the IP header and 20 for the TCP header. No higher-layer data is ever transmitted. The window size is large (WIN = 4096), but the Acknowledgement number never changes (ACK = 28122874). When the terminal receives this segment, it is unable to transmit additional information because the host always asks for the same segment: 4,096 octets beginning at Sequence number 28122874. Since the host prevents the terminal from proceeding, the terminal appears to lock up.

To find the solution, the network administrator contacts the developer of the host software. The developer finds a bug in the TCP module that prevents the Acknowledgement number from incrementing. When the administrator installs a software patch, the terminal-to-host communication works as expected.

Sniffer Network Analyzer data 1-Oct at 11:14:40, HOSTACK.ENC, Pg 1

SUMMARY	Delta T	Destination	Source	Summary
M 1		Terminal	Host	TCP D=6000 S=3319
				ACK=28122874 WIN=4096
2	0.0008	Terminal	Host	TCP D=6000 S=3319
				ACK=28122874 WIN=4096

3	0.0008	Terminal	Host	TCP D=6000 S=3319
				ACK=28122874 WIN=4096
4	0.0008	Terminal	Host	TCP D=6000 S=3319
				ACK=28122874 WIN=4096
5	0.0008	Terminal	Host	TCP D=6000 S=3319
				ACK=28122874 WIN=4096
6	0.0008	Terminal	Host	TCP D=6000 S=3319
				ACK=28122874 WIN=4096
7	0.0008	Terminal	Host	TCP D=6000 S=3319
				ACK=28122874 WIN=4096
8	0.0008	Terminal	Host	TCP D=6000 S=3319
				ACK=28122874 WIN=4096
9	0.0008	Terminal	Host	TCP D=6000 S=3319
				ACK=28122874 WIN=4096
10	0.0008	Terminal	Host	TCP D=6000 S=3319
				ACK=28122874 WIN=4096
11	0.0008	Terminal	Host	TCP D=6000 S=3319
				ACK=28122874 WIN=4096
12	0.0008	Terminal	Host	TCP D=6000 S=3319
				ACK=28122874 WIN=4096
13	0.0008	Terminal	Host	TCP D=6000 S=3319
				ACK=28122874 WIN=4096
14	0.0008	Terminal	Host	TCP D=6000 S=3319
				ACK=28122874 WIN=4096
15	0.0008	Terminal	Host	TCP D=6000 S=3319
				ACK=28122874 WIN=4096
16	0.0008	Terminal	Host	TCP D=6000 S=3319
				ACK=28122874 WIN=4096
17	0.0008	Terminal	Host	TCP D=6000 S=3319
				ACK=28122874 WIN=4096
18	0.0008	Terminal	Host	TCP D=6000 S=3319
				ACK=28122874 WIN=4096
19	0.0008	Terminal	Host	TCP D=6000 S=3319
				ACK=28122874 WIN=4096
20	0.0008	Terminal	Host	TCP D=6000 S=3319
				ACK=28122874 WIN=4096

Trace 5.7.5a. Repeated Host TCP Acknowledgements (Summary)

Sniffer Network Analyzer data 1-Oct at 11:14:40, HOSTACK.ENC, Pg 1

DLC: —— DLC Header ——
DLC:
DLC: Frame 1 arrived at 11:14:41.7541; frame size is 60 (003C hex) bytes.
DLC: Destination = Station XXXXXX 101C43, Terminal
DLC: Source   = Station XXXXXX 032608, Host
DLC: Ethertype = 0800 (IP)
DLC:
IP: —— IP Header ——
IP:
IP: Version = 4, header length = 20 bytes
IP: Type of service = 00
IP: 000. .... = routine
IP: ...0 .... = normal delay
IP: .... 0... = normal throughput
IP: .... .0.. = normal reliability
IP: Total length = 40 bytes
IP: Identification = 17411
IP: Flags = 0X
IP: .0.. .... = may fragment
IP: ..0. .... = last fragment
IP: Fragment offset = 0 bytes
IP: Time to live = 30 seconds/hops
IP: Protocol = 6 (TCP)
IP: Header checksum = F380 (correct)
IP: Source address = [XXX.YYY.1.235]
IP: Destination address = [XXX.YYY.4.98]
IP: No options
IP:
TCP: —— TCP header ——
TCP:
TCP: Source port = 3319
TCP: Destination port = 6000 (X Windows)
TCP: Sequence number = 3524369
TCP: Acknowledgment number = 28122874
TCP: Data offset = 20 bytes
TCP: Flags = 10
TCP: ..0. .... = (No urgent pointer)
TCP: ...1 .... = Acknowledgment
TCP: .... 0... = (No push)
TCP: .... .0.. = (No reset)
TCP: .... ..0. = (No SYN)

```
TCP:  .... ...0 = (No FIN)
TCP:  Window = 4096
TCP:  Checksum = 2E33 (correct)
TCP:  No TCP options
TCP:
```

Trace 5.7.5b. Repeated Host TCP Acknowledgements (Details)

5.7.6 Using the Finger User Information Protocol

In Chapter 4, we discovered that the ICMP Echo (PING) command can test the transmission path between two devices on an internetwork. Another utility, known as the Finger User Information Protocol (Finger) and described in RFC 1288 [5-17], also provides some end-to-end testing. Finger provides an interface to a database of users attached to a particular host, called the Remote User Information Program (RUIP).

Finger consists of a query/response interaction based on TCP transport. To initiate Finger, a TCP connection is established with Port 79 (the Finger port) on the remote host. Then the local host's Finger utility sends a query to RUIP at the remote host. The remote host responds with the information requested. When used in an internet environment, the Finger utility not only checks the end-to-end communication path (like the ICMP Echo), but it also verifies that the remote host knows of the remote user's existence. Let's see how to use the Finger protocol.

The network manager wishes to check on one of his users, Kevin Anderson. From his PC, he establishes a TCP connection with the Sun server to which Kevin is attached (see Trace 5.7.6a). Note that the Destination port requested in the initial TCP connection segment, Frame 801, is the Finger port, 79. The three-way handshake is completed in Frame 803, and the network manager's RUIP sends a query to the server requesting information for the user. The details of the query are shown in Trace 5.7.6b, indicating that the user name or user id (kpa) is sent with the query. Note that the Push (PSH) flag is used to send data on its way immediately.

The Sun server responds with an acknowledgement (Frame 805) followed by the RUIP response (Frame 806). The response contains 174 octets of data that pertain to user kpa. We learn the following about the user:

```
Login name: kpa     In real life: Kevin P. Anderson
Directory: /home/h0008/kpa Shell: /bin/csh
Last login Wed Mar 27 09:22 on ttyp0 from h0009z
```

```
No unread mail
No plan
```

With the answer transmitted, the server's RUIP closes the connection in Frame 807 by setting the Finish (FIN) flag. The PC acknowledges the server's FIN (Frame 808) and sends a FIN of its own (Frame 809). The server acknowledges the final transaction in Frame 810.

In all, it took only 10 frames to learn about user kpa, his directory, shell, last login, and so on. Some of this information may be considered sensitive for security reasons, and network administrators are advised to read the security issues detailed in the Finger standard, RFC 1288. However, if you can surmount these concerns, the Finger protocol can be a valuable addition to your bag of troubleshooting techniques.

Sniffer Network Analyzer data 27-Mar at 09:04:54, TCPMEDLY.ENC, Pg 1

SUMMARY	Delta T	Destination	Source	Summary
801	57.9373	Sun Server	PC	TCP D=79 S=1228 SYN SEQ=134222388 LEN=0 WIN=1024
802	0.0009	PC	Sun Server	TCP D=1228 S=79 SYN ACK=134222389 SEQ=2009792000 LEN=0 WIN=4096
803	0.0130	Sun Server	PC	TCP D=79 S=1228 ACK=2009792001 WIN=1024
804	0.0441	Sun Server	PC	TCP D=79 S=1228 ACK=2009792001 SEQ=134222389 LEN=5 WIN=1024
805	0.1348	PC	Sun Server	TCP D=1228 S=79 ACK=134222394 WIN=4096
806	0.0433	PC	Sun Server	TCP D=1228 S=79 ACK=134222394 SEQ=2009792001 LEN=174 WIN=4096
807	0.0002	PC	Sun Server	TCP D=1228 S=79 FIN ACK=134222394 SEQ=2009792175 LEN=0 WIN=4096

808	0.0225	Sun Server	PC	TCP D=79 S=1228 ACK=2009792176 WIN=850
809	0.4897	Sun Server	PC	TCP D=79 S=1228 FIN ACK=2009792176 SEQ=134222394 LEN=0 WIN=850
810	0.0006	PC	Sun Server	TCP D=1228 S=79 ACK=134222395 WIN=4096

Trace 5.7.6a. Finger User Information Summary

Sniffer Network Analyzer data 27-Mar at 09:04:54, TCPMEDLY.ENC, Pg 1

- - - - - - - - - - - - - - - Frame 804 - - - - - - - - - - - - - - - - -

TCP: —— TCP header ——
TCP:
TCP: Source port = 1228
TCP: Destination port = 79 (Finger)
TCP: Sequence number = 134222389
TCP: Acknowledgment number = 2009792001
TCP: Data offset = 20 bytes
TCP: Flags = 18
TCP: ..0. .... = (No urgent pointer)
TCP: ...1 .... = Acknowledgment
TCP: .... 1... = Push
TCP: .... .0.. = (No reset)
TCP: .... ..0. = (No SYN)
TCP: ....0 = (No FIN)
TCP: Window = 1024
TCP: Checksum = 2B9A (correct)
TCP: No TCP options
TCP: [5 byte(s) of data]
TCP:

ADDR	HEX		ASCII
0000	08 00 20 09 42 A4 00 00	C0 3C 55 17 08 00 45 00	.. .B....<U...E.
0010	00 2D 02 C3 00 00 40 06	63 75 8B B1 FE 5F 8B B1	.-....@.cu..._..
0020	FE D0 04 CC 00 4F 08 00	12 35 77 CA FE 01 50 18	.....O...5w...P.
0030	04 00 2B 9A 00 00 6B 70	61 0D 0A 00	..+...kpa...

- - - - - - - - - - - - - - - Frame 805 - - - - - - - - - - - - - - - - -

TCP: —— TCP header ——

```
TCP:
TCP:  Source port = 79 (Finger)
TCP:  Destination port = 1228
TCP:  Sequence number = 2009792001
TCP:  Acknowledgment number = 134222394
TCP:  Data offset = 20 bytes
TCP:  Flags = 10
TCP:  ..0. .... = (No urgent pointer)
TCP:  ...1 .... = Acknowledgment
TCP:  .... 0... = (No push)
TCP:  .... .0.. = (No reset)
TCP:  .... ..0. = (No SYN)
TCP:  .... ...0 = (No FIN)
TCP:  Window = 4096
TCP:  Checksum = F61F (correct)
TCP:  No TCP options
TCP:
```

ADDR	HEX		ASCII
0000	00 00 C0 3C 55 17 08 00	20 09 42 A4 08 00 45 00	...<U... .B...E.
0010	00 28 D6 EE 00 00 3C 06	93 4E 8B B1 FE D0 8B B1	.(....<..N......
0020	FE 5F 00 4F 04 CC 77 CA	FE 01 08 00 12 3A 50 10	._.O..w.......:P.
0030	10 00 F6 1F 00 00 64 2E	62 79 6E 61	......d.byna

- - - - - - - - - - - - - - - Frame 806 - - - - - - - - - - - - - - - - - -

```
TCP: ——— TCP header ———
TCP:
TCP:  Source port = 79 (Finger)
TCP:  Destination port = 1228
TCP:  Sequence number = 2009792001
TCP:  Acknowledgment number = 134222394
TCP:  Data offset = 20 bytes
TCP:  Flags = 18
TCP:  ..0. .... = (No urgent pointer)
TCP:  ...1 .... = Acknowledgment
TCP:  .... 1... = Push
TCP:  .... .0.. = (No reset)
TCP:  .... ..0. = (No SYN)
TCP:  .... ...0 = (No FIN)
TCP:  Window = 4096
TCP:  Checksum = CAA6 (correct)
TCP:  No TCP options
```

TCP: [174 byte(s) of data]
TCP:

ADDR	HEX		ASCII
0000	00 00 C0 3C 55 17 08 00	20 09 42 A4 08 00 45 00	...<U... .B...E.
0010	00 D6 D6 F3 00 00 3C 06	92 9B 8B B1 FE D0 8B B1	......<.........
0020	FE 5F 00 4F 04 CC 77 CA	FE 01 08 00 12 3A 50 18	._.O..w......:P.
0030	10 00 CA A6 00 00 4C 6F	67 69 6E 20 6E 61 6D 65	......Login name
0040	3A 20 6B 70 61 20 20 20	20 20 20 20 09 09 09 49	: kpa ...I
0050	6E 20 72 65 61 6C 20 6C	69 66 65 3A 20 48 42 4F	n real life:....
0060	0D 0A 44 69 72 65 63 74	6F 72 79 3A 20 2F 68 6F	..Directory: /ho
0070	6D 65 2F 68 30 30 30 38	2F 6B 70 61 20 20 20 20	me/h0008/kpa
0080	20 20 20 20 20 20 09 53	68 65 6C 6C 3A 20 2F 62	.Shell: /b
0090	69 6E 2F 63 73 68 0D 0A	4C 61 73 74 20 6C 6F 67	in/csh..Last log
00A0	69 6E 20 57 65 64 20 4D	61 72 20 32 37 20 30 39	in Wed Mar 27 09
00B0	3A 32 32 20 6F 6E 20 74	74 79 70 30 20 66 72 6F	:22 on ttyp0 fro
00C0	6D 20 68 30 30 30 39 7A	0D 0A 4E 6F 20 75 6E 72	m h0009z..No unr
00D0	65 61 64 20 6D 61 69 6C	0D 0A 4E 6F 20 50 6C 61	ead mail..No Pla...
00E0	6E 2E 0D 0A		n...

Trace 5.7.6b. Finger User Information Details

5.7.7 Tape Backups via an Internetwork

In the last few years, the price of hard disk storage on PCs has dropped to the point where it's not uncommon to have in excess of 1 GB of storage per workstation. But with this increasing storage comes increasing risk: the failure of a large hard disk can have disastrous consequences. To minimize this risk, many users routinely back up their hard disk onto either floppies or a tape drive.

In this case, the network engineer wants to back up his hard disk to a Sun SPARC-station server with an attached tape drive. Software in both the PC and server use TCP as the transport mechanism for the backup via an internetwork (see Figure 5-14). But when the engineer begins the backup procedure on the PC side, the process suddenly fails. Initially he suspects a faulty tape drive, but further analysis reveals another problem.

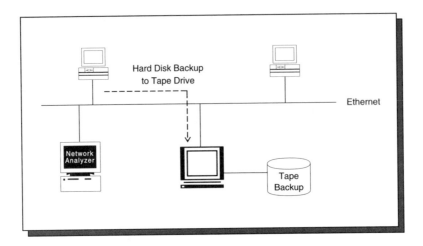

Figure 5-14. PC-to-Server Backup via Ethernet

The analysis begins with the server (shown as SPARCstn in Trace 5.7.7) sending a Window = 4096 in Frame 32 to the PC, then waiting for the data to transfer. The PC begins downloading the backup in Frame 33 and gives the server a Window = 905. The server acknowledges this data with a TCP segment of 35 octets in length (Frame 34). In response, the PC reduces its window size to 870 octets (905 - 35 = 870). Clearly, the PC's window size is more limiting than that of the server. The server, however, abruptly sends a Window = 0 in Frame 37. This segment is repeated in Frames 39 and 41. The server shuts down the communication link from the PC to the tape drive. The engineer theorizes that the server does this so it can process the incoming TCP segment and transfer the data to the tape drive. Unfortunately, the PC software does not know that this delay is necessary. The PC interprets the Window = 0 as a termination command and issues a TCP Reset (RST) command in Frame 42. This is followed by a Finish (FIN) command in Frame 44. The tape backup is aborted, but the hard disk has not been backed up completely.

The solution is to insert some delay into the PC's TCP module. When the tape drive is busy, the Sun workstation instructs its TCP module (on the server) to send Window = 0, preventing the transfer of additional data. As long as the tape drive is busy, it continues to send Window = 0. The TCP module in the PC is rewritten to accept the TCP segment with Window = 0 and then wait 10 seconds for the tape drive to catch up. If it receives two more segments with Window = 0, then the PC resets the connection. Now the backups proceed without a hitch via the internetwork.

Sniffer Network Analyzer data 27-Mar at 09:04:54, TAPEBACK.ENC, Pg 1

SUMMARY	Destination	Source	Summary
32	PC	SPARCstn	TCP D=1022 S=1023
			ACK=694630 SEQ=1839168103
			LEN=17 WIN=4096
33	SPARCstn	PC	TCP D=1023 S=1022
			ACK=1839168120 WIN=905
34	PC	SPARCstn	TCP D=1022 S=1023
			ACK=694630 SEQ=1839168120
			LEN=35 WIN=4096
35	SPARCstn	PC	TCP D=1023 S=1022
			ACK=1839168155 WIN=870
36	SPARCstn	PC	RSHELL C PORT=1023 <00>
37	PC	SPARCstn	TCP D=1023 S=514
			ACK=698772 WIN=0
38	SPARCstn	PC	RSHELL C PORT=1023 <00>
39	PC	SPARCstn	TCP D=1023 S=514
			ACK=698772 WIN=0
40	SPARCstn	PC	RSHELL C PORT=1023 <00>
41	PC	SPARCstn	TCP D=1023 S=514
			ACK=698772 WIN=0
42	SPARCstn	PC	TCP D=514 S=1023 RST
			ACK=1839040002 WIN=1024
43	SPARCstn	PC	TCP D=1023 S=1022
			ACK=1839168155 WIN=1024
44	SPARCstn	PC	TCP D=1023 S=1022 FIN
			ACK=1839168155 SEQ=694630
			LEN=0 WIN=1024
45	PC	SPARCstn	TCP D=1022 S=1023
			ACK=694631 WIN=4096
46	PC	SPARCstn	TCP D=1023 S=514
			ACK=698772 WIN=1536
47	PC	SPARCstn	TCP D=1023 S=514
			ACK=698772 WIN=3072
48	SPARCstn	PC	TCP D=1023 S=1022 RST
			ACK=1839168155 WIN=1024

Trace 5.7.7. Tape Backup with Window = 0

5.7.8 Optimizing the TCP Window Size

The previous case study showed what the receiver's window can do. We saw that when the distant host sends a value of Window = 0, the transmission path to the host effectively shuts down. If you receive a large window (say, Window = 8192), you can transmit a reasonable amount of data. Depending on the application, there should be an optimum window size that won't cause the transmitter to wait for unnecessary acknowledgements (i.e., the window is too small), yet won't overwhelm the receiver with more data than it can handle (i.e., the window is too large). As in "Goldilocks and the Three Bears," you need to find the window size that is "just right."

Two documents provide useful information about optimizing the window size: RFC 879, "The TCP Maximum Segment Size and Related Topics" [5-4], and RFC 813, "Window and Acknowledgement Strategy in TCP" [5-9]. Let's study an internetwork that needs some help in this area.

In the following case study, the internetwork consists of a headquarters location connected to three remote Ethernet segments (see Figure 5-15). Each remote segment contains a UNIX host plus a number of workstations. The remote segments are connected via bridges and 64-Kbps leased lines. The remote hosts contact these peers on a periodic basis to transfer files using a File Transfer Protocol (FTP) facility. In addition, the PC users use TELNET for remote host access. The problem is that while two hosts on the same segment can communicate without a problem, the hosts can't contact other hosts at a remote location without excessive delays and interrupts of the FTP session. Let's see why these problems occur.

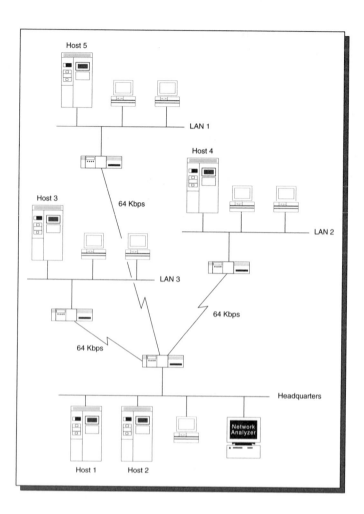

Figure 5-15. Host-to-Host Connections via WAN Bridges

To study the problem, the network engineer captures the data between one host on the headquarters segment (Hdqtr Host) and another host on a remote segment. He places the analyzer on the headquarters segment to capture the information coming to and from the remote host via the bridge (see Trace 5.7.8a). The initial analysis does not reveal any frames with errors. The remote host initiates a TCP connection in Frames 2 through 4, then starts an FTP session. The user identifies himself (Buster, in Frame 9), a password is transmitted (Frame 11), and an account is sent (Frame 15). The login completes in Frame 17, and the user can proceed. The only indication that a problem exists is the delays between frames, shown in Frames 9, 15, 17, and 19. These delays range from 6 to 18 seconds and indicate a transmission problem between the two communicating hosts.

The headquarters host initiates a second TCP data connection beginning in Frame 26. Note that the Destination ports are different—the first connection (Frames 2 through 4) uses Destination port = 21 (FTP Control) and Source Port = 4979. The second connection uses Source port = 20 (FTP data) and Destination Port = 4980. By all appearances, the two hosts should have established a full-duplex connection. Note also that both hosts return Window = 0 in Frames 26 and 27, but subsequently revise that number in Frames 28, 29, and 30.

Data transfer begins in Frame 31 with 512 octets of information. Successive frames convey 512 and 256 octets of data, respectively. An unexpected association of Sequence and Acknowledgement numbers occurs, however, in Trace 5.7.8b:

Frame	Data (octets)	Beginning Sequence	Ending Sequence	Acknowledgement
31	512	55278459	55278970	53214721
32	512	55278971	55279482	53214721
33	256	55279483	55279738	53214721
34	0	53214721	53214721	55278971

Frames 31 through 33 contain data from the headquarters host to the remote host. During this time no data is received in the other direction, since the Acknowledgement number remains constant (ACK = 53214721). Frame 34 contains an acknowledgement from the remote host, but note that it is the acknowledgement for the third previous segment (Frame 31). In other words, Frames 32 and 33 are still en route to the remote host, somewhere in the link between the two bridges.

The data transfer continues for a number of segments until the headquarters host abruptly terminates the connection in Frame 149 via the RST flag (see Trace 5.7.8a). The FTP connection is then closed and no additional data can be transferred. The immediately preceding frames provide the answer:

316

Frame	Sequence	Acknowledgement	Outstanding Data (octets)
144	55310931		
145		55306995	3,936
146	55311373		
147		55306995	4,378

The headquarters host transmits 442 octets of data in Frame 144; the remote host acknowledges a lesser amount (ACK = 55306995), leaving 3,936 octets of data unacknowledged (55310931 - 55306995 = 3,936). The problem worsens in Frames 146 and 147, with 4,378 unacknowledged octets (55311373 - 55306995 = 4,378).

Somewhere between the processing of Frames 144 and 146 a threshold within the host that counts the maximum allowable outstanding octets is crossed, causing the headquarters host to reset the connection. This threshold is half the allowable window size. The host has Window = 8,192, half of which is 4,096. In Frame 145, 3,936 octets are outstanding; in Frame 146 that number increases to 4,378, exceeding the threshold of 4,096.

The reason for the large amount of outstanding data is traced to inadequate I/O buffers on the WAN side of the bridges. Adding I/O buffers improves transmission. A second parameter, the discard threshold, is also increased inside the bridges. The discard threshold determines the maximum number of MAC-level frames that can be queued within the bridge. Setting this parameter to a higher value also improves the internetwork response. With these two bridge parameters adjusted, no further problems occur.

Sniffer Network Analyzer data 23-Jan at 03:10:38, TRACE.ENC, Pg 1

SUMMARY		Delta T	Destination	Source	Summary
M	1		Bridge	Hdqtr Host	ARP R PA=[143.130.1.5]
					HA=08000B001180 PRO=IP
	2	0.0248	Hdqtr Host	Bridge	TCP D=21 S=4979 SYN
					SEQ=44830720 LEN=0 WIN=4096
	3	0.5002	Bridge	Hdqtr Host	TCP D=4979 S=21 SYN
					ACK=44830721 SEQ=55214045
					LEN=0 WIN=8192
	4	0.0258	Hdqtr Host	Bridge	TCP D=21 S=4979
					ACK=55214046 WIN=4096

5	0.2294	Bridge	Hdqtr Host	TCP D=4979 S=21 ACK=44830721 WIN=8192
6	1.1449	Bridge	Hdqtr Host	TCP D=4979 S=21 ACK=44830721 WIN=8192
7	2.7069	Bridge	Hdqtr Host	FTP R PORT=4979 220 1100JD1100 Service ready for new user <0D><0A>
8	0.0635	Hdqtr Host	Bridge	TCP D=21 S=4979 ACK=55214090 WIN=4096
9	14.7769	Hdqtr Host	Bridge	FTP C PORT=4979 USER Buster<0D><0A>
10	0.1605	Bridge	Hdqtr Host	FTP R PORT=4979 331 User name okay, need password.<0D><0A>
11	0.0465	Hdqtr Host	Bridge	FTP C PORT=4979 PASS pass<0D><0A>
12	0.2198	Bridge	Hdqtr Host	TCP D=4979 S=21 ACK=44830745 WIN=8192
13	0.7356	Bridge	Hdqtr Host	FTP R PORT=4979 332 Need account for login. <0D><0A>
14	0.0597	Hdqtr Host	Bridge	TCP D=21 S=4979 ACK=55214155 WIN=4096
15	6.7912	Hdqtr Host	Bridge	FTP C PORT=4979 ACCT Rufus<0D><0A>
16	0.2171	Bridge	Hdqtr Host	TCP D=4979 S=21 ACK=44830761 WIN=8192
17	14.4493	Bridge	Hdqtr Host	FTP R PORT=4979 230 User logged in, proceed <0D><0A>
18	0.1431	Hdqtr Host	Bridge	TCP D=21 S=4979 ACK=55214186 WIN=4096
19	18.7942	Hdqtr Host	Bridge	FTP C PORT=4979 PORT 143,130,2,1,19,116 <0D><0A>
20	0.2157	Bridge	Hdqtr Host	TCP D=4979 S=21 ACK=44830786 WIN=8192
21	0.2449	Bridge	Hdqtr Host	FTP R PORT=4979 200 Command okay.<0D><0A>
22	0.0551	Hdqtr Host	Bridge	FTP C PORT=4979 RETR faithful.jog <0D><0A>

23	0.2195	Bridge	Hdqtr Host	TCP D=4979 S=21 ACK=44830809 WIN=8192
24	2.0346	Bridge	Hdqtr Host	FTP R PORT=4979 150 File status okay; about to open data conn...
25	0.0371	Hdqtr Host	Bridge	TCP D=21 S=4979 ACK=55214259 WIN=4096
26	1.0401	Bridge	Hdqtr Host	TCP D=4980 S=20 SYN SEQ=55278458 LEN=0 WIN=0
27	0.0275	Hdqtr Host	Bridge	TCP D=20 S=4980 SYN ACK=55278459 SEQ=53214720 LEN=0 WIN=0
28	0.2321	Bridge	Hdqtr Host	TCP D=4980 S=20 ACK=53214721 WIN=8192
29	0.0279	Hdqtr Host	Bridge	TCP D=20 S=4980 ACK=55278459 WIN=4096
30	0.0099	Hdqtr Host	Bridge	TCP D=20 S=4980 ACK=55278459 WIN=8192
31	0.9281	Bridge	Hdqtr Host	TCP D=4980 S=20 ACK=53214721 SEQ=55278459 LEN=512 WIN=8192
32	0.0070	Bridge	Hdqtr Host	TCP D=4980 S=20 ACK=53214721 SEQ=55278971 LEN=512 WIN=8192
33	0.0025	Bridge	Hdqtr Host	TCP D=4980 S=20 ACK=53214721 SEQ=55279483 LEN=256 WIN=8192
34	0.3243	Hdqtr Host	Bridge	TCP D=20 S=4980 ACK=55278971 WIN=8192
35	0.0792	Bridge	Hdqtr Host	TCP D=4980 S=20 ACK=53214721 SEQ=55279739 LEN=512 WIN=8192
36	0.0033	Bridge	Hdqtr Host	TCP D=4980 S=20 ACK=53214721 SEQ=55280251 LEN=204 WIN=8192
37	0.0873	Hdqtr Host	Bridge	TCP D=20 S=4980 ACK=55280251 WIN=8192
38	0.0514	Bridge	Hdqtr Host	TCP D=4980 S=20 ACK=53214721 SEQ=55280455 LEN=512 WIN=8192
39	0.0040	Bridge	Hdqtr Host	TCP D=4980 S=20 ACK=53214721 SEQ=55280967 LEN=512 WIN=8192

40	0.0042	Bridge	Hdqtr Host	TCP D=4980 S=20 ACK=53214721 SEQ=55281479 LEN=432 WIN=8192
41	0.1563	Hdqtr Host	Bridge	TCP D=20 S=4980 ACK=55281479 WIN=8192
42	0.0448	Bridge	Hdqtr Host	TCP D=4980 S=20 ACK=53214721 SEQ=55281911 LEN=512 WIN=8192
43	0.0042	Bridge	Hdqtr Host	TCP D=4980 S=20 ACK=53214721 SEQ=55282423 LEN=512 WIN=8192
44	0.0045	Bridge	Hdqtr Host	TCP D=4980 S=20 ACK=53214721 SEQ=55282935 LEN=361 WIN=8192
45	0.1611	Hdqtr Host	Bridge	TCP D=20 S=4980 ACK=55281911 WIN=8192
.				
.				
.				
128	0.0018	Bridge	Hdqtr Host	TCP D=4980 S=20 ACK=53214721 SEQ=55306733 LEN=37 WIN=8192
129	0.2577	Hdqtr Host	Bridge	TCP D=20 S=4980 ACK=55303791 WIN=8192
130	0.0573	Bridge	Hdqtr Host	TCP D=4980 S=20 ACK=53214721 SEQ=55306770 LEN=225 WIN=8192
131	0.0051	Bridge	Hdqtr Host	TCP D=4980 S=20 ACK=53214721 SEQ=55306995 LEN=512 WIN=8192
132	0.0037	Bridge	Hdqtr Host	TCP D=4980 S=20 ACK=53214721 SEQ=55307507 LEN=352 WIN=8192
133	0.0416	Hdqtr Host	Bridge	TCP D=20 S=4980 ACK=55304243 WIN=8192
134	0.0378	Bridge	Hdqtr Host	TCP D=4980 S=20 ACK=53214721 SEQ=55307859 LEN=512 WIN=8192
135	0.0628	Hdqtr Host	Bridge	TCP D=20 S=4980 ACK=55305267 WIN=8192

136	0.0429	Bridge	Hdqtr Host	TCP D=4980 S=20 ACK=53214721 SEQ=55308371 LEN=512 WIN=8192
137	0.0044	Bridge	Hdqtr Host	TCP D=4980 S=20 ACK=53214721 SEQ=55308883 LEN=512 WIN=8192
138	0.0521	Hdqtr Host	Bridge	TCP D=20 S=4980 ACK=55305709 WIN=8192
139	0.0285	Bridge	Hdqtr Host	TCP D=4980 S=20 ACK=53214721 SEQ=55309395 LEN=512 WIN=8192
140	0.1706	Hdqtr Host	Bridge	TCP D=20 S=4980 ACK=55306221 WIN=8192
141	0.0368	Bridge	Hdqtr Host	TCP D=4980 S=20 ACK=53214721 SEQ=55309907 LEN=512 WIN=8192
142	0.1640	Hdqtr Host	Bridge	TCP D=20 S=4980 ACK=55306995 WIN=8192
143	0.0393	Bridge	Hdqtr Host	TCP D=4980 S=20 ACK=53214721 SEQ=55310419 LEN=512 WIN=8192
144	0.0048	Bridge	Hdqtr Host	TCP D=4980 S=20 ACK=53214721 SEQ=55310931 LEN=442 WIN=8192
145	0.1554	Hdqtr Host	Bridge	TCP D=20 S=4980 ACK=55306995 WIN=8192
146	0.0211	Bridge	Hdqtr Host	TCP D=4980 S=20 ACK=53214721 SEQ=55311373 LEN=59 WIN=8192
147	0.1795	Hdqtr Host	Bridge	TCP D=20 S=4980 ACK=55306995 WIN=8192
148	0.1987	Hdqtr Host	Bridge	TCP D=20 S=4980 ACK=55306995 WIN=8192
149	1.4094	Bridge	Hdqtr Host	TCP D=4980 S=20 RST WIN=0
150	0.5261	Bridge	Hdqtr Host	FTP R PORT=4979 426 Connection is closed: A DDP ABORT WAS EXECUTED...
151	0.0648	Hdqtr Host	Bridge	TCP D=21 S=4979 ACK=55214312 WIN=4096

Trace 5.7.8a. TCP Window Management Summary

Chapter 5: Troubleshooting the Host-to-Host Connection

Sniffer Network Analyzer data 23-Jan at 03:10:38, TRACE.ENC, Pg 1

- - - - - - - - - - - - - - - - Frame 31 - - - - - - - - - - - - - - - - -

```
TCP: ------ TCP header ------
TCP:
TCP:  Source port = 20 (FTP data)
TCP:  Destination port = 4980
TCP:  Sequence number = 55278459
TCP:  Acknowledgment number = 53214721
TCP:  Data offset = 20 bytes
TCP:  Flags = 10
TCP:  ..0. .... = (No urgent pointer)
TCP:  ...1 .... = Acknowledgment
TCP:  .... 0... = (No push)
TCP:  .... .0.. = (No reset)
TCP:  .... ..0. = (No SYN)
TCP:  .... ...0 = (No FIN)
TCP:  Window = 8192
TCP:  Checksum = 27AC (correct)
TCP:  No TCP options
TCP:  [512 byte(s) of data]
TCP:
```

- - - - - - - - - - - - - - - Frame 32 - - - - - - - - - - - - - - - - -

```
TCP: ------ TCP header ------
TCP:
TCP:  Source port = 20 (FTP data)
TCP:  Destination port = 4980
TCP:  Sequence number = 55278971
TCP:  Acknowledgment number = 53214721
TCP:  Data offset = 20 bytes
TCP:  Flags = 10
TCP:  ..0. .... = (No urgent pointer)
TCP:  ...1 .... = Acknowledgment
TCP:  .... 0... = (No push)
TCP:  .... .0.. = (No reset)
TCP:  .... ..0. = (No SYN)
TCP:  .... ...0 = (No FIN)
TCP:  Window = 8192
TCP:  Checksum = 16E8 (correct)
TCP:  No TCP options
```

TCP: [512 byte(s) of data]
TCP:

- - - - - - - - - - - - - - - Frame 33 - - - - - - - - - - - - - - - - -

TCP: ——— TCP header ———
TCP:
TCP: Source port = 20 (FTP data)
TCP: Destination port = 4980
TCP: Sequence number = 55279483
TCP: Acknowledgment number = 53214721
TCP: Data offset = 20 bytes
TCP: Flags = 10
TCP: ..0. .... = (No urgent pointer)
TCP: ...1 .... = Acknowledgment
TCP: .... 0... = (No push)
TCP: .... .0.. = (No reset)
TCP: .... ..0. = (No SYN)
TCP: ....0 = (No FIN)
TCP: Window = 8192
TCP: Checksum = 0C2D (correct)
TCP: No TCP options
TCP: [256 byte(s) of data]
TCP:

- - - - - - - - - - - - - - - Frame 34 - - - - - - - - - - - - - - - - -

TCP: ——— TCP header ———
TCP:
TCP: Source port = 4980
TCP: Destination port = 20 (FTP data)
TCP: Sequence number = 53214721
TCP: Acknowledgment number = 55278971
TCP: Data offset = 20 bytes
TCP: Flags = 10
TCP: ..0. .... = (No urgent pointer)
TCP: ...1 .... = Acknowledgment
TCP: .... 0... = (No push)
TCP: .... .0.. = (No reset)
TCP: .... ..0. = (No SYN)
TCP: ....0 = (No FIN)
TCP: Window = 8192
TCP: Checksum = D84E (correct)

TCP: No TCP options
TCP:

Trace 5.7.8b. TCP Window Management Acknowledgements

Sniffer Network Analyzer data 23-Jan at 03:10:38, TRACE.ENC, Pg 1

- - - - - - - - - - - - - - - - Frame 144 - - - - - - - - - - - - - - - - -

TCP: ——- TCP header ——-
TCP:
TCP: Source port = 20 (FTP data)
TCP: Destination port = 4980
TCP: Sequence number = 55310931
TCP: Acknowledgment number = 53214721
TCP: Data offset = 20 bytes
TCP: Flags = 10
TCP: ..0. .... = (No urgent pointer)
TCP: ...1 .... = Acknowledgment
TCP: .... 0... = (No push)
TCP: .... .0.. = (No reset)
TCP: .... ..0. = (No SYN)
TCP: ....0 = (No FIN)
TCP: Window = 8192
TCP: Checksum = 1AD5 (correct)
TCP: No TCP options
TCP: [442 byte(s) of data]
TCP:

- - - - - - - - - - - - - - - Frame 145 - - - - - - - - - - - - - - - - -

TCP: ——- TCP header ——-
TCP:
TCP: Source port = 4980
TCP: Destination port = 20 (FTP data)
TCP: Sequence number = 53214721
TCP: Acknowledgment number = 55306995
TCP: Data offset = 20 bytes
TCP: Flags = 10
TCP: ..0. .... = (No urgent pointer)
TCP: ...1 .... = Acknowledgment
TCP: .... 0... = (No push)
TCP: .... .0.. = (No reset)
TCP: .... ..0. = (No SYN)

TCP: ....0 = (No FIN)
TCP: Window = 8192
TCP: Checksum = 6AD6 (correct)
TCP: No TCP options
TCP:

- - - - - - - - - - - - - - - Frame 146 - - - - - - - - - - - - - - - - -

TCP: ——- TCP header ——-
TCP:
TCP: Source port = 20 (FTP data)
TCP: Destination port = 4980
TCP: Sequence number = 55311373
TCP: Acknowledgment number = 53214721
TCP: Data offset = 20 bytes
TCP: Flags = 10
TCP: ..0. .... = (No urgent pointer)
TCP: ...1 .... = Acknowledgment
TCP: .... 0... = (No push)
TCP: .... .0.. = (No reset)
TCP: .... ..0. = (No SYN)
TCP: ....0 = (No FIN)
TCP: Window = 8192
TCP: Checksum = E735 (correct)
TCP: No TCP options
TCP: [59 byte(s) of data]
TCP:

- - - - - - - - - - - - - - - Frame 147 - - - - - - - - - - - - - - - - -

TCP: ——- TCP header ——-
TCP:
TCP: Source port = 4980
TCP: Destination port = 20 (FTP data)
TCP: Sequence number = 53214721
TCP: Acknowledgment number = 55306995
TCP: Data offset = 20 bytes
TCP: Flags = 10
TCP: ..0. .... = (No urgent pointer)
TCP: ...1 .... = Acknowledgment
TCP: .... 0... = (No push)
TCP: .... .0.. = (No reset)
TCP: .... ..0. = (No SYN)
TCP: ....0 = (No FIN)

TCP: Window = 8192
TCP: Checksum = 6AD6 (correct)
TCP: No TCP options
TCP:

- - - - - - - - - - - - - - - - Frame 148 - - - - - - - - - - - - - - - - -

TCP: ——- TCP header ——-
TCP:
TCP: Source port = 4980
TCP: Destination port = 20 (FTP data)
TCP: Sequence number = 53214721
TCP: Acknowledgment number = 55306995
TCP: Data offset = 20 bytes
TCP: Flags = 10
TCP: ..0. .... = (No urgent pointer)
TCP: ...1 .... = Acknowledgment
TCP: .... 0... = (No push)
TCP: .... .0.. = (No reset)
TCP: .... ..0. = (No SYN)
TCP: ....0 = (No FIN)
TCP: Window = 8192
TCP: Checksum = 6AD6 (correct)
TCP: No TCP options
TCP:

- - - - - - - - - - - - - - - Frame 149 - - - - - - - - - - - - - - - - -

TCP: ——- TCP header ——-
TCP:
TCP: Source port = 20 (FTP data)
TCP: Destination port = 4980
TCP: Sequence number = 55311432
TCP: Data offset = 20 bytes
TCP: Flags = 04
TCP: ..0. .... = (No urgent pointer)
TCP: ...0 .... = (No acknowledgment)
TCP: .... 0... = (No push)
TCP: .... .1.. = Reset
TCP: .... ..0. = (No SYN)
TCP: ....0 = (No FIN)
TCP: Window = 0
TCP: Checksum = 7ABA (correct)

```
TCP:  No TCP options
TCP:

- - - - - - - - - - - - - - - Frame 150 - - - - - - - - - - - - - - - -

FTP:  ——- FTP data ——-
FTP:
FTP:  426 Connection is closed: A DDP ABORT WAS EXECUTED...
FTP:

- - - - - - - - - - - - - - - Frame 151 - - - - - - - - - - - - - - - -

TCP:  ——- TCP header ——-
TCP:
TCP:  Source port = 4979
TCP:  Destination port = 21 (FTP)
TCP:  Sequence number = 44830809
TCP:  Acknowledgment number = 55214312
TCP:  Data offset = 20 bytes
TCP:  Flags = 10
TCP:  ..0. .... = (No urgent pointer)
TCP:  ...1 .... = Acknowledgment
TCP:  .... 0... = (No push)
TCP:  .... .0.. = (No reset)
TCP:  .... ..0. = (No SYN)
TCP:  .... ...0 = (No FIN)
TCP:  Window = 4096
TCP:  Checksum = D30A (correct)
TCP:  No TCP options
TCP:
```

Trace 5.7.8c. TCP Window Management Reset Condition

This chapter marks the three-quarter point in our journey from the bottom to the top of the ARPA protocol stack. We have now made the LAN, MAN, or WAN hardware connection at the Network Interface Layer, transmitted the datagrams at the Internet Layer, and assured the reliability of those datagrams at the Host-to-Host Layer. References [5-18] and [5-19] provide additional insight into the operation of the Host-to-Host layer and TCP. Reference [5-20] discusses why TCP has been more successful than its OSI counterparts.

Now we need some application data to send! We'll discuss these applications in the next chapter by studying protocols for file transfer, electronic mail, and remote host access.

5.8 References

[5-1] Postel, J. "User Datagram Protocol." RFC 768, August 1980.

[5-2] Postel, J., Editor. "Transmission Control Protocol." RFC 793, September 1981.

[5-3] Socolofsky, T., et al. "A TCP/IP Tutorial." RFC 1180, January 1991.

[5-4] Postel, J. "The TCP Maximum Segment Size and Related Topics." RFC 879, November 1983.

[5-5] Black, Uyless. *TCP/IP and Related Protocols*. McGraw-Hill, Inc. (New York, NY), 1992.

[5-6] Comer, Douglas E. *Internetworking with TCP/IP*, third edition. Prentice Hall, Inc. (Englewood Cliffs, NJ), 1995.

[5-7] Partridge, Craig. "Improving Your TCP: Look at the Timers." *ConneXions* (July 1987): 13–14.

[5-8] Karn, Phil. "Improving Your TCP: Karn's Algorithm." *ConneXions* (October 1988): 23.

[5-9] Clark, David D. "Window and Acknowledgement Strategy in TCP." RFC 813, July 1982.

[5-10] Minshall, Greg. "TCP Connection Initiation: An Inside Look." *ConneXions* (July 1988): 2–11.

[5-11] Clark, David D. "Fault Isolation and Recovery." RFC 816, July 1982.

[5-12] Croft, W., et al. "Bootstrap Protocol (BOOTP)." RFC 951, September 1985.

[5-13] Alexander, S., and R. Droms. "DHCP Options and BOOTP Vendor Extensions." RFC 1533, October 1993.

[5-14] Finlayson, Ross. "Bootstrap Loading Using TFTP." RFC 906, June 1984.

[5-15] Mogul, Jeffrey. "Booting Diskless Hosts: The BOOTP Protocol." ConneXions (October 1988): 14–18.

[5-16] Postel, J., et al. "Time Protocol." RFC 868, May 1983.

[5-17] Zimmerman, D. "The Finger User Information Protocol." RFC 1288, December 1991.

[5-18] Stevens, W. Richard. "TCP Keepalives." *ConneXions* (February 1994): 2–7.

[5-19] McCloghrie, Keith, and Marshall T. Rose. "The Internet Transport Layer." *ConneXions* (June 1994): 2–9.

[5-20] Salus, Peter H. "Protocol Wars: Is OSI Finally Dead." *ConneXions* (August 1995): 16–19.

Troubleshooting the Process/Application Connection

In this chapter, we'll study the Process/Application Layer functions. At this layer, the user interacts with the host to perform user functions. These functions may include file transfer using the Trivial File Transfer Protocol (TFTP) or the more complex File Transfer Protocol (FTP); client/server file operations via Sun Microsystems Inc.'s Network File System (NFS); remote host access with the Telecommunications Network (TELNET) protocol; or electronic mail using the Simple Mail Transfer Protocol (SMTP). All of these protocols exhibit their own characteristics and challenges. We'll begin by exploring how they fit into the ARPA architectural model.

6.1 The Process/Application Connection

The Process/Application Layer sits at the very top of the ARPA architectural model. Unlike the Host-to-Host, Internet, and Network Interface Layers, which are transparent to end users, the Process/Application Layer is accessed by users directly via the host's operating system. (Network analysts, of course, must be prepared to troubleshoot problems at any layer!) End users use this layer's functions to perform computer operations such as file transfer, electronic mail, and so on (see Figure 6-1a).

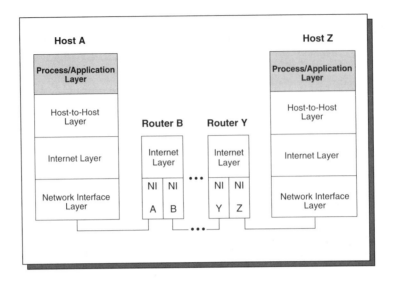

Figure 6-1a. The Process/Application Connection

Figure 6-1b shows examples of the significant Process/Application protocols and the standards that describe them. Since these protocols provide functions that relate to the OSI Session, Presentation, and Application Layers, they are sometimes referred to as Upper-Layer Protocols (ULPs). Figure 6-1c shows the position of the Application (ULP) data within the transmission frame. The lower-layer headers and trailers all serve to reliably transfer the ULP information from one host to another via the internetwork.

ARPA Layer	Protocol Implementation						OSI Layer
	File Transfer	Electronic Mail	Terminal Emulation	File Transfer	Client / Server	Network Management	Application
Process / Application	File Transfer Protocol (FTP)	Simple Mail Transfer Protocol (SMTP)	TELNET Protocol	Trivial File Transfer Protocol (TFTP)	Sun Microsystems Network File System Protocols (NFS)	Simple Network Management Protocol (SNMP)	Presentation
	MIL-STD-1780 RFC 959	MIL-STD-1781 RFC 821	MIL-STD-1782 RFC 854	RFC 783	RFCs 1014, 1057, and 1094	RFC 1157	Session
Host-to-Host	Transmission Control Protocol (TCP) MIL-STD-1778 RFC 793				User Datagram Protocol (UDP) RFC 768		Transport
Internet	Address Resolution ARP RFC 826 RARP RFC 903		Internet Protocol (IP) MIL-STD-1777 RFC 791		Internet Control Message Protocol (ICMP) RFC 792		Network
Network Interface	Network Interface Cards: Ethernet, Token Ring, ARCNET, MAN and WAN RFC 894, RFC 1042, RFC 1201 and others						Data Link
	Transmission Media: Twisted Pair, Coax, Fiber Optics, Wireless Media, etc.						Physical

Figure 6-1b. ARPA Process/Application Layer Protocols

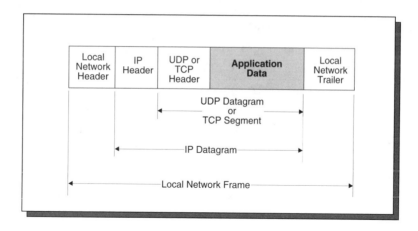

Figure 6-1c. The Internet Transmission Frame and Application Data Position

To complete our tour of the ARPA architectural model, we will study the significant Process/Application protocols, beginning with TFTP. Several references provide details on the protocols discussed in this chapter. Stallings' *Handbook of Computer-Communications Standards, Volume 3, The TCP/IP Protocol Suite* [6-1] contains individual chapters on the common application protocols such as FTP, TELNET, and SMTP. RFC 1123, "Requirements for Internet Hosts: Application and Support" [6-2], details requirements that hosts must provide to properly support file transfer, remote host access, and electronic mail. Specific details and parameters for these protocols are provided in RFC 1700, the "Assigned Numbers" document [6-3]. An excerpt of RFC 1700 is provided in Appendix F for reference.

6.2 Trivial File Transfer Protocol (TFTP)

The Trivial File Transfer Protocol, described in RFC 1350 [6-4], reads and writes files or mail messages from one host to another. It offers no other functions. TFTP's strength is its simplicity. It transfers 512-octet blocks of data without excessive overhead. Because it is implemented on UDP transport, TFTP is one of the easiest ULPs to implement, but it does not guarantee data reliability.

TFTP defines five packet types, which are distinguished by an Opcode (operation code) field (see Figure 6-2):

Opcode	Operation
1	Read Request (RRQ)
2	Write Request (WRQ)
3	Data (DATA)
4	Acknowledgement (ACK)
5	Error (ERROR)

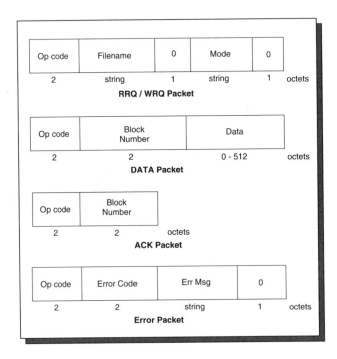

Figure 6-2. Trivial File Transfer (TFTP) Packet Formats

The Read Request (RRQ, Opcode = 1) and Write Request (WRQ, Opcode = 2) packets have the same structure. Following the Opcode (2 octets), a string of netascii characters specifies the filename. (The netascii code is an 8-bit code defined by the ANSI standard X3.4-1968.) An octet containing zero terminates the filename. The Mode field (also a string) specifies which of three data transfer modes are to be used. The choices are netascii, octet (raw 8-bit bytes), and mail. The mail mode is defined as netascii characters destined for a user instead of a host. The Mode field is terminated by an octet containing zero.

The Data packet (Opcode = 3) transfers information. A Block number (2 octets) follows the Opcode and identifies the particular 512-octet block of data being sent. The Data field (0-512 octets in length) carries the actual information. Blocks less than 512 octets in length (i.e., 0-511 octets) indicate the end of an atomic unit of transmission.

The ACK packet (Opcode = 4) is used for acknowledgement. It contains a Block Number field (2 octets) that corresponds to the similar number in the Data packet being acknowledged. For simplicity, TFTP incorporates the lock-step acknowledgement, which requires each data packet to be acknowledged prior to the transmission of another. In other words, because TFTP operates over UDP, not TCP, it has no provisions for a window mechanism, and all packets (except ERROR packets) must be acknowledged. ACK or ERROR packets acknowledge DATA and WRQ packets; DATA or ERROR packets acknowledge RRQ or ACK packets. ERROR packets require no acknowledgement.

The ERROR packet (Opcode = 5) may be used to acknowledge any of the other four packet types. It contains a 2-octet error code that describes the problem:

Value	Meaning
0	Not defined, see error message (if any)
1	File not found
2	Access violation
3	Disk full or allocation exceeded
4	Illegal TFTP operation
5	Unknown transfer ID
6	File already exists
7	No such user

An error message (ErrMsg) consisting of a netascii string followed by a zero completes the packet. When errors occur, an ERROR packet is transmitted and the connection is terminated. Hosts generate ERROR packets for three types of events: when the host cannot satisfy a request such as locating a file; when the host receives a delayed or duplicate packet; or when the host loses access to a resource such as a disk during the transfer.

Figure 6-3 shows TFTP's operation. Host A issues a RRQ or WRQ and receives a response of either DATA (for RRQ) or ACK (for WRQ). Each host initiating a connection chooses a random number between 0 and 65,535 for use as a Transfer

Identifier (TID). The TID passes to UDP, which uses it as a Port address. When the RRQ or WRQ is initially transmitted from Host A, it selects a TID to identify its end of the connection and designates Destination = 69, the TFTP port number. If the connection is accepted, the remote host, Host B, returns its TID B subscript as the source with the TID A subscript as the destination. If a WRQ was the initial transmission, an ACK with Block number = 0 is returned. If the transmission was RRQ, a DATA packet with Block number = 1 is returned. Data transfer then proceeds in 512-octet blocks, with each host identifying the appropriate Source and Destination TIDs with each DATA or ACK packet. The receipt of a DATA packet with less than 512 octets signals the termination of the connection. If errors occur during transmission, they generate an ERROR packet containing the appropriate Error Code. An example of this is provided in Section 6.9.1.

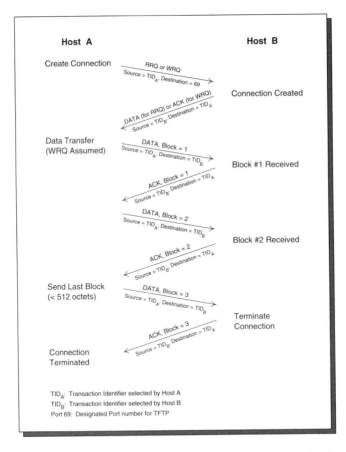

Figure 6-3. TFTP Connection, Data Transfer, and Termination

In addition to RFC 1350, several other documents provide details on TFTP operation. These include: RFC 1782, "TFTP Option Extension;" RFC 1783, "TFTP Blocksize Option;" RFC 1784, "TFTP Timeout Interval and Transfer Size Options;" and RFC 1785, "TFTP Option Negotiation Analysis."

6.3 File Transfer Protocol

One of the most popular Process/Application protocols is the File Transfer Protocol (FTP), described in RFC 959 [6-5]. As its name implies, FTP allows local or remote client and server machines to share files and data using TCP's reliable transport.

The complete FTP service includes a User-FTP and a Server-FTP, as shown in Figure 6-4. The User-FTP includes a User Interface (UI), a User Protocol Interpreter (PI), and a User Data Transfer Process (DTP). The Server-FTP includes a Server-PI and a Server-DTP, but excludes the user interface. The User-PI initiates the logical control connection, which uses the TELNET protocol. The user (or client) uses an internally assigned Port number to connect to Server Port number 21, designated for FTP control. The data to be transferred passes from another self-assigned port on the User-DTP to Port number 20 (designated FTP data) on the Server-DTP. Thus, two Port numbers are used for the two logical communication paths: control and data.

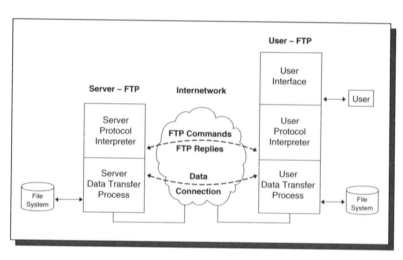

Figure 6-4. File Transfer Protocol (FTP) Model

6.3.1 Data Representation, Data Structures, and Transmission Modes

Three parameters are required to completely specify the data or file to be transferred: the Data Representation, the Data Structure, and the Transmission Mode. The data may be represented in one of four ways: ASCII (the default is 8-bit characters); EBCDIC (8-bit characters); Image (8-bit contiguous bytes), which transfers binary data; and Local, which uses a byte size defined by the local host. Similarly, there are three types of data structures: the File Structure (the default), which is a continuous sequence of data bytes; the Record Structure, which consists of continuous records; and the Page Structure, which is comprised of independent, indexed pages. Three transmission modes are available, including Stream Mode (a transmitted stream of bytes), Block Mode (a header plus a series of data blocks) and Compressed Mode (used for maximizing bandwidth). The proper operation of the data transfer between the User and Server Data Transfer Processes depends on the control commands that go between the User and Server Protocol Interpreters. We'll look at these commands next.

6.3.2 FTP Commands

FTP commands and replies are communicated between the Server and User Protocol Interpreters (review Figure 6-4). These commands are defined in three categories: Access Control, Transfer Parameter, and Service.

6.3.2.1 Access Control Commands

The Access Control commands determine which users may access a particular file; these commands are invoked by the Server-FTP.

Command Code and Argument	Usage
USER <SP> <username> <CRLF>	Identifies the user
PASS <SP> <password> <CRLF>	User's password
ACCT <SP> <account-information> <CRLF>	User's account
CWD <SP> <pathname> <CRLF>	Change working directory
CDUP <CRLF>	Change to Parent directory
SMNT <SP> <pathname> <CRLF>	Structure Mount
REIN <CRLF>	Reinitialize, terminating the user
QUIT <CRLF>	Logout

<SP>	Represents a Space character
<CRLF>	Represents Carriage Return, Line Feed characters

6.3.2.2 Transfer Parameter Commands

The Transfer Parameter commands are used to alter the default parameters used to transfer data on an FTP connection:

Command Code and Argument	Usage
PORT <SP> <host-port> <CRLF>	Specifies the data port to be used
PASV <CRLF>	Requests the Server DTP to listen on a data port
TYPE <SP> <type-code> <CRLF>	Representation type: ASCII, EBCDIC, Image, or Local
STRU <SP> <structure-code> <CRLF>	File structure: File, Record, or Page
MODE <SP> <mode-code> <CRLF>	Transmission mode: Stream, Block, or Compressed

6.3.2.3 Service Commands

Service commands define the file operation requested by the user. The convention for the pathname argument is determined by the FTP Server's local conventions:

Command Code and Argument	Usage
RETR <SP> <pathname> <CRLF>	Retrieve a copy of the file from the other end
STOR <SP> <pathname> <CRLF>	Store data at the Server
STOU <CRLF>	Store Unique
APPE <SP> <pathname> <CRLF>	Append
ALLO <SP> <decimal-integer> [<SP> R <SP> <decimal-integer>] <CRLF>	Allocate storage
REST <SP> <marker> <CRLF>	Restart transfer at checkpoint
RNFR <SP> <pathname> <CRLF>	Rename from
RNTO <SP> <pathname> <CRLF>	Rename to
ABOR <CRLF>	Abort previous service command
DELE <SP> <pathname> <CRLF>	Delete file at Server

RMD <SP> <pathname> <CRLF>	Remove directory
MKD <SP> <pathname> <CRLF>	Make directory
PWD <CRLF>	Print working directory
LIST [<SP> <pathname>] <CRLF>	List files or text
NLST [<SP> <pathname>] <CRLF>	Name list
SITE <SP> <string> <CRLF>	Site parameters
SYST <CRLF>	Determine operating system
STAT [<SP> <pathname>] <CRLF>	Status
HELP [<SP> <string>] <CRLF>	Help information
NOOP <CRLF>	No operation

6.3.3 FTP Replies

An FTP reply consists of a three-digit number and a space, and is followed by one line of text. Each digit of the reply is significant. The first digit (value 1-5) determines whether the response is good, bad, or incomplete. The second and third digits are encoded to provide additional details regarding the reply. The values for the first digit are:

1yz	Positive Preliminary reply
2yz	Positive Completion reply
3yz	Positive Intermediate reply
4yz	Transient Negative Completion reply
5yz	Permanent Negative Completion reply

The values for the second digit are:

x0z	Syntax
x1z	Information
x2z	Connections
x3z	Authentication and accounting
x4z	Unspecified as yet
x5z	File system

The third digit gives a finer definition for each function category specified by the second digit. An example would be:

211: System status
212: Directory status
213: File status
214: Help message

The FTP specification, RFC 959, elaborates in great detail on the states and conditions that trigger these reply messages. Another useful reference is Romkey's "FTP's Tiresome Problems" [6-6], which describes some of the shortcomings of the protocol's implementation under different operating systems.

6.3.4 FTP Operation

A typical scenario in which FTP is used to retrieve a file from a remote host begins when the user initiates a connection to the remote host by entering **FTP [host address]**. For example, to retrieve an RFC, the user would enter *ftp ds.internic.net* to access the Internic's server that contains Internet documentation such as RFCs. The host responds by asking for the username and password. If the desired file is not in the root directory, the user must change to the proper subdirectory. For example, the user would enter cd rfc to change to the subdirectory that contains the RFCs. (Note that some host systems abbreviate certain commands. For example, the CWD command to change the current directory becomes CD. Most systems support the HELP command, which lists the commands or abbreviations accepted by the system.) The third step is for the user to tell the host the action required, such as file transfer. For example, to retrieve an RFC, the command would be get rfcnnnnn.txt, where nnnn represents the number of the desired RFC. If the file transfer requires a different mode (such as binary), the user must specify that mode before invoking the get command. The file transfer would then begin, and the user would terminate the FTP connection (using the FTP **quit** command) when all business was completed. Another example of an FTP session is given in the case study in Section 6.9.2.

6.4 Sun Microsystems Network File System

No discussion about the Application/Process Layer would be complete without mentioning Sun Microsystems Inc.'s Network File System, commonly known as NFS. Sun released NFS in 1985 as part of the Sun Operating System (SunOS) included with Sun workstations. Since then, the NFS protocols have been adopted for a wide variety of computing platforms, including PCs, minicomputers, and large hosts.

NFS is based on a client/server paradigm where the *client* is the local computer that runs the application and the *server* is the computer that manages the file or application program. A LAN or WAN may run between the client and the server. In other words, NFS does not restrict the location of the client or server, and it provides transparent access to files regardless of their location. Any one machine can operate as both a client and a server.

Another advantage of NFS is that it allows the user to access files regardless of the operating system under which they are stored. Therefore, NFS allows directories and files to be shared between, say, an MS-DOS machine and other machines running UNIX, DEC's VMS, IBM's MVS, or Apple Computer's Macintosh operating system. Of course, if all machines are running NFS, NFS assures access to those files.

The foundation for the Sun protocols is the UDP and IP transport protocols, which may operate on a number of LAN/WAN interfaces. As we know, UDP provides a connectionless transport, which is not error-free. The NFS client/server paradigm therefore uses a stateless protocol in which one operation (or state) must complete before another initiates. Thus, after the client makes a request, it must wait for the server's response. If the server does not respond or delays its response, the client repeats its request. A server crash therefore will not impact the client. If the client has received the application file, then the client/server interaction is complete; if the client has not received the file, it will continue to resend the file request until the server is reinitialized. This aspect of the stateless protocol is particularly useful when you add the complexity of an internetwork between client and server.

The protocols that, in aggregate, make up the Sun suite are comprised of three separate modules: the Remote Procedure Call (RPC), the External Data Representation (XDR), and NFS. These three sit on top of UDP and IP (see Figure 6-5). Sun has developed RFCs for each module. The first layer of the Sun protocol stack is the RPC, defined in RFC 1057 [6-7]. The RPC establishes a logical connection between client and server. As with the establishment of a telephone call, the client sends a message to the server and waits for the server's reply. The server's reply includes the results of the requested procedure. The next layer is the XDR, specified in RFC 1014 [6-8].

XDR provides OSI Presentation Layer functions; it describes and encodes the data that is transferred to and from the client and server. The NFS protocol, described in RFC 1094 [6-9], sits at the top of the Sun protocol stack. The NFS protocol defines the file and directory structures and procedures for the client and server. References [6-10] through [6-12] provide excellent background on the Sun protocols and how they compare with other distributed file systems. Reference [6-13] discusses the optimization of NFS network operation.

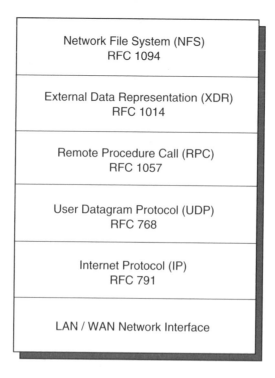

Figure 6-5. Sun Microsystems NFS Protocols

The importance of the Sun protocols lies in their strong ties to the UNIX environment, coupled with the historical tie between UNIX and the Internet protocols. In other words, if you use UNIX, you are likely to also use the TCP/IP and Sun protocols. An in-depth study of these protocols is beyond the scope of this text; refer to Malamud's *Analyzing Sun Networks* [6-14] for further information.

6.5 TELNET

TELNET, which stands for Telecommunications Network, is a protocol that allows a user (or client) at a terminal to access a remote host (or server). TELNET operates with TCP transport using Port number 23, and allows the terminal and host to exchange 8-bit characters of information in a half-duplex manner. The primary standard for TELNET, RFC 854 [6-15], discusses the three objectives of the protocol; RFC 855 [6-16] considers the various TELNET options.

TELNET's first objective is to define the Network Virtual Terminal (NVT). The NVT is a hypothetical representation of a network-standard terminal, also called a *canonical* (or standard) form. When both ends of the connection convert their data representations into the canonical form, they can communicate regardless of whether one end is, say, a DEC VT-100 and the other an SNA Host. The defined NVT format is the 7-bit USASCII code, transmitted in 8-bit octets. Figure 6-6 illustrates the conversion process from the local terminal/host format to the NVT format. The conversion typically occurs inside the devices, although an ancillary device such as a terminal server may perform the conversion for a number of similar devices.

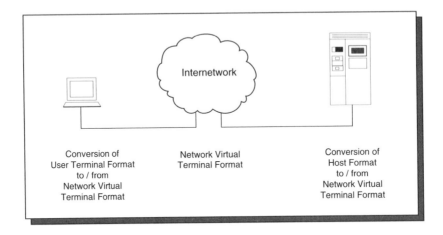

Figure 6-6. TELNET Network Virtual Terminal Operation

The second objective of TELNET is to allow clients and servers to negotiate various options. This feature allows you to use a number of different terminals (some intelligent and some not so intelligent) with equal facility. To begin the negotiation, either

344

or both ends of the connection state their desire to negotiate a particular option. The other end of the connection can accept or reject the proposal. TELNET defines four negotiation options: WILL, WON'T, DO, and DON'T. WILL *XXX* indicates that party's desire (or offer) to begin performing option *XXX*. DO *XXX* or DON'T *XXX* are the returned positive or negative acknowledgements, respectively. DO *XXX* indicates that party's desire (or request) that the other party begin performing option *XXX*. WILL *XXX* and WON'T *XXX* are the returned positive and negative acknowledgements, respectively. For example, suppose the terminal wanted to use binary transmission. It would send a DO Binary Transmission to the remote host. The host could then respond with either a WILL Binary Transmission (a positive acknowledgement) or a WON'T Binary Transmission (a negative acknowledgement). If that terminal does not want its characters echoed across the TELNET connection it would send WON'T Echo; if the remote host agrees that no characters will be echoed it would return DON'T Echo.

The third concept of TELNET is one of symmetry in the negotiation syntax. This symmetry allows either the client or server ends of the connection to request a particular option as required, thus optimizing the service provided by the other party.

TELNET commands consist of a mandatory two-octet sequence and an optional third octet. The first octet is always the Interpret as Command (IAC) character, Code 255. The second octet is the code for one of the commands listed below. The third octet is used when options are to be negotiated, and contains the option number of interest. For example, the command "IAC DO Terminal Type" would be represented by FF FD 18 (hexadecimal), corresponding to the Codes 255 253 24 (which are represented in decimal). RFC 854 defines the following TELNET commands:

Command	Code	Meaning
SE	240	End of subnegotiation parameters
NOP	241	No operation
Data Mark	242	The data stream portion of a Synch. This should always be accompanied by a TCP Urgent notification
Break	243	NVT character BRK
Interrupt Process	244	The function IP
Abort output	245	The function AO
Are You There	246	The function AYT
Erase character	247	The function EC

Erase Line	248	The function EL
Go ahead	249	The GA signal
SB	250	Indicates that what follows is subnegotiation of the indicated option
WILL (option code)	251	Indicates the desire to begin performing, or confirmation that you are now performing, the indicated option
WON'T (option code)	252	Indicates the refusal to perform, or continue performing, the indicated option
DO (option code)	253	Indicates the request that the other party perform, or confirmation that you are expecting the other party to perform, the indicated option
DON'T (option code)	254	Indicates the demand that the other party stop performing, or confirmation that you are no longer expecting the other party to perform, the indicated option
IAC	255	Data Byte 255

RFC 1700 lists the following TELNET options, along with the reference documents that provide further information:

Option	Name	Reference
0	Binary Transmission	RFC 856
1	Echo	RFC 857
2	Reconnection	NIC 50005
3	Suppress Go Ahead	RFC 858
4	Approx Message Size Negotiation	See reference [3-5]
5	Status	RFC 859
6	Timing Mark	RFC 860
7	Remote Controlled Trans and Echo	RFC 726
8	Output Line Width	NIC 50005
9	Output Page Size	NIC 50005
10	Output Carriage-Return Disposition	RFC 652
11	Output Horizontal Tab Stops	RFC 653
12	Output Horizontal Tab Disposition	RFC 654
13	Output Formfeed Disposition	RFC 655

346

14	Output Vertical Tabstops	RFC 656
15	Output Vertical Tab Disposition	RFC 657
16	Output Linefeed Disposition	RFC 658
17	Extended ASCII	RFC 698
18	Logout	RFC 727
19	Byte Macro	RFC 735
20	Data Entry Terminal	RFC 1043
21	SUPDUP	RFC 736
22	SUPDUP Output	RFC 749
23	Send Location	RFC 779
24	Terminal Type	RFC 1091
25	End of Record	RFC 885
26	TACACS User Identification	RFC 927
27	Output Marking	RFC 933
28	Terminal Location Number	RFC 946
29	Telnet 3270 Regime	RFC 1041
30	X.3 PAD	RFC 1053
31	Negotiate About Window Size	RFC 1073
32	Terminal Speed	RFC 1079
33	Remote Flow Control	RFC 1372
34	Linemode	RFC 1184
35	X Display Location	RFC 1096
36	Environment	RFC 1408
37	Authentication	RFC 1409
38	Encryption	N/A
39	New Environment	RFC 1572
255	Extended-Options-List	RFC 861

Note the large number of documents available to describe individual options. Shein's "The TELNET Protocol" [6-17] provides an excellent description of the negotiation processes. The case study in Section 6.9.3 will consider the operation of the Terminal Type option.

6.6 Simple Mail Transfer Protocol

The Simple Mail Transfer Protocol (SMTP) is based on a straightforward model of client/server computing. The model includes a sender and receiver, both of which have access to a file system for message storage. Some type of communication channel links sender and receiver, completing the model. SMTP is intended to be a dependable message delivery system, although it does not provide absolute end-to-end reliability. It is based upon TCP transport, however, which increases its effectiveness. The standard governing the SMTP system is specified in RFC 821 [6-18], while the message format is contained in Standard for the Format of ARPA Internet Text Messages, RFC 822 [6-19]. Reference [6-20] discusses the use of electronic mail over the Internet, while reference [6-21] describes electronic messaging on LANs.

6.6.1 Message Transfer

The transfer of an electronic message can be divided into several distinct stages, all supported by the SMTP model (see Figure 6-7). First, the user provides input to an interface system, known as the user agent, which facilitates the entry of the mail message. Then the message is sent to the Sender-SMTP, which assigns an arbitrary Port number to the process and establishes a TCP connection with Port number 25 on its peer (Receiver-SMTP). While establishing that connection, the receiver identifies itself to the sender. Next, the mail message is transferred using the RFC 822 format (discussed in the following section). Finally, the sender signals its desire to terminate the connection, which is acknowledged by the receiver. After that acknowledgement, the TCP connection is closed.

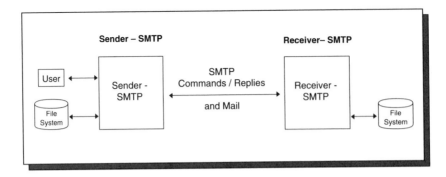

Figure 6-7. Simple Mail Transfer Protocol (SMTP) Model

6.6.2 Message Format

RFC 822 [6-19] defines the message format used with SMTP. The message consists of a header, which contains a number of fields and the message text. A blank line separates the header from the text. Many of the header fields are optional and depend on local implementation; however, some variation of the example below will be present in most systems. The following example of a mail format is taken from Appendix A of RFC 822 and is described as "about as complex as you're going to get."

```
Date        :  27 Aug 76 0932 PDT
From        :  Ken Davis <KDavis@This-Host.This-net>
Subject     :  Re: The Syntax in the RFC
Sender      :  KSecy@Other-Host
Reply-To    :  Sam.Irving@Reg.Organization
To          :  George Jones <Group@Some-Reg.An-Org>,
               Al.Neuman@MAD.Publisher
cc          :  Important folk:
                  Tom Softwood <Balsa@Tree.Root>,
                  "Sam Irving"@Other-Host;,
               Standard Distribution:
                  /main/davis/people/standard@Other-Host,
                  "<Jones>standard.dist.3"@Tops-20-Host>;
Comment     :  Sam is away on business. He asked me to handle
               his mail for him.  He'll be able to provide  a
               more  accurate  explanation  when  he  returns
               next week.
In-Reply-To: <some.string@DBM.Group>, George's message
X-Special-action:  This is a sample of user-defined field-
               names.  There could also be a field-name
               "Special-action", but its name might later be
               preempted
Message-ID: <4231.629.XYzi-What@Other-Host>
```

Note that the header fields are separated from the field contents by a colon. This example shows 11 fields in use, which is certainly more than most host mail systems use.

6.6.3 SMTP Commands

SMTP commands are comprised of a command code and an argument. The command codes are four alphabetic characters in either upper or lower case. The command code is separated from the argument by one or more space characters. Reverse path and forward path arguments are case-sensitive since each host may have a particular convention for mail addresses. The character sequence carriage return-line feed (<CRLF>) ends the argument field. Optional arguments are enclosed within square brackets.

Command Code and Argument	Usage
HELO <SP> <domain> <CRLF>	Identifies Sender-SMTP to Receiver-SMTP
MAIL <SP> FROM:<reverse-path> <CRLF>	Deliver mail data to mailbox(es)
RCPT <SP> TO:<forward-path> <CRLF>	Identify mail data recipient
DATA <CRLF>	The mail data
RSET <CRLF>	Abort current mail transaction
SEND <SP> FROM:<reverse-path> <CRLF>	Deliver mail data to terminal(s)
SOML <SP> FROM:<reverse-path> <CRLF>	Send or Mail
SAML <SP> FROM:<reverse-path> <CRLF>	Send and Mail
VRFY <SP> <string> <CRLF>	Verify that the argument identifies a user
EXPN <SP> <string> <CRLF>	Verify that the argument identifies a mailing list
HELP [<SP> <string>] <CRLF>	Send information
NOOP <CRLF>	No operation
QUIT <CRLF>	Send OK reply, then close channel
TURN <CRLF>	Exchange Sender/Receiver roles

NOTE: <SP> represents a Space character
       <CRLF> represents Carriage Return, Line Feed characters

6.6.4 SMTP Replies

The SMTP Reply messages are three digits long, and each digit has special significance. These replies are similar to the FTP codes in that the first digit is more general, whereas the third digit is more specific. The values for the first digit are:

1yz	Positive Preliminary reply
2yz	Positive Completion reply
3yz	Positive Intermediate reply
4yz	Transient Negative Completion reply
5yz	Permanent Negative Completion reply

The values for the second digit are:

x0z	Syntax
x1z	Information
x2z	Connections
x3z	Unspecified as yet
x4z	Unspecified as yet
x5z	Mail system

The third digit gives a finer definition for each of the function categories specified by the second digit. An example would be:

500: Syntax error, command unrecognized
501: Syntax error in parameters or arguments
502: Command not implemented
503: Bad sequence of commands
504: Command parameter not implemented

If you require more information, turn to RFC 821 for specifics on command usage, state diagrams that detail the command implementation, and command/reply sequences. We will study an example of SMTP in Section 6.9.5.

6.6.5 Multipurpose Internet Mail Extensions

SMTP defined the format for the message headers; however, it made the assumption that the *contents* of that message were ASCII text. In many cases, however, email users wish to transmit other types of messages, such as a graphic or an audio or video clip. The Multipurpose Internet Mail Extensions, or MIME, provides for encoding techniques to allow these other types of messages to be transmitted after the RFC 822 (or SMTP) headers. MIME is specified in two RFCs: "MIME (Multipurpose Internet Mail Extensions) Part One: Mechanisms for Specifying and Describing the Format of Internet Message Bodies," RFC 1521 [6-22], and "Part Two: Message Header Extensions for Non-ASCII Text," RFC 1522 [6-23]. As new media (audio, video, etc.) types are defined, they may be registered according to the procedures outlined in RFC 1590. Another useful reference on the subject is Bruce Robertson's "MIME Speaks Volumes" [6-24].

RFC 1521 defines additional headers that further specify the contents of the electronic message. These headers include:

- **MIME-Version header:** specifies the MIME version for this message.
- **Content-Type header**: specifies the type and subtype of data in the body of the message. Seven data types have been defined:
  - **Text**: textual information in a number of different character sets.
  - **Multipart**: used to combine different types of data into a single message.
  - **Application**: used to transmit application or binary data.
  - **Message**: used for encapsulating another mail message.
  - **Image**: for transmitting still image (or picture) data.
  - **Audio**: for transmitting audio or voice data.
  - **Video**: for transmitting video or moving image data.
- **Content-Transfer Encoding header**: used to specify an auxiliary encoding that was applied to the data in order to allow it to pass through mail transport mechanisms.
- **Content ID and Content Description headers**: further describe the data in the message body.

Below is an example, taken from Appendix C of RFC 1521, which illustrates the use of the above headers.

What follows is the outline of a complex multipart message. This message has five parts to be displayed serially: two introductory plain text parts, an embedded multipart message, a richtext part, and a closing encapsulated text message in a non-ASCII character set. The embedded multipart message has two parts to be displayed in parallel, a picture and an audio fragment.

MIME-Version: 1.0
From: Nathaniel Borenstein <nsb@bellcore.com>
To: Ned Freed <ned@innosoft.com>
Subject: A multipart example
Content-Type: multipart/mixed;
      boundary=unique-boundary-1

This is the preamble area of a multipart message.
Mail readers that understand multipart format
should ignore this preamble.
If you are reading this text, you might want to
consider changing to a mail reader that understands
how to properly display multipart messages.
—unique-boundary-1

    ...Some text appears here...
[Note that the preceding blank line means
no header fields were given and this is text,
with charset US ASCII. It could have been
done with explicit typing as in the next part.]

—unique-boundary-1
Content-type: text/plain; charset=US-ASCII

This could have been part of the previous part,
but illustrates explicit versus implicit
typing of body parts.

—unique-boundary-1
Content-Type: multipart/parallel;
      boundary=unique-boundary-2

—unique-boundary-2
Content-Type: audio/basic

```
Content-Transfer-Encoding: base64

    ... base64-encoded 8000 Hz single-channel
        mu-law-format audio data goes here....

—unique-boundary-2
Content-Type: image/gif
Content-Transfer-Encoding: base64

    ... base64-encoded image data goes here....

—unique-boundary-2—

—unique-boundary-1
Content-type: text/richtext

This is <bold><italic>richtext.</italic></bold>
<smaller>as defined in RFC 1341</smaller>
<nl><nl>Isn't it
<bigger><bigger>cool?</bigger></bigger>

—unique-boundary-1
Content-Type: message/rfc822

From: (mailbox in US-ASCII)
To: (address in US-ASCII)
Subject: (subject in US-ASCII)
Content-Type: Text/plain; charset=ISO-8859-1
Content-Transfer-Encoding: Quoted-printable

    ... Additional text in ISO-8859-1 goes here ...

—unique-boundary-1—
```

As the above example illustrates, MIME provides for a great deal of flexibility for message content specification. Readers needing further technical details should consult RFCs 1521 and 1522.

6.7 NetBIOS

NetBIOS, the <u>Net</u>work <u>B</u>asic <u>I</u>nput <u>O</u>utput <u>S</u>ystem, was developed by IBM and Sytek, Inc. (now Hughes LAN Systems, Inc., Mountain View, California) for use with the IBM PC Network program. Just as ROMBIOS enables a PC's operating system and application programs to access its local I/O devices, NetBIOS provides applications access to network devices. NetBIOS is considered an OSI Session Layer interface and has become a de facto standard. The expansion of LANs into internetworks and the popularity of TCP/IP as the primary internetworking protocol suite have created a need for the NetBIOS interface to operate over the Internet protocols. From an architectural perspective, combining NetBIOS support at the OSI Session Layer with the TCP or UDP protocols at the Transport Layer is a natural way to support the numerous existing LAN applications in a distributed internetwork environment.

Just as different vendors have written ROMBIOS routines specific to their PCs, LAN operating system vendors have also come up with their own implementations of NetBIOS. Haugdahl's *Inside NetBIOS* [6-25] describes some of these variants. RFC 1001 [6-26] and RFC 1002 [6-27] define a standard for NetBIOS support within the Internet community; hopefully, the rigorous detail contained in these RFCs will eliminate the multiple-implementation (semi-proprietary) issue that has crept into LAN environments.

Before delving into the specifics of NetBIOS use within the context of the Internet protocols, you need some background in the operation of NetBIOS. NetBIOS provides four types of primitives: Name Service, Session Service, Datagram Service, and Miscellaneous functions. Application programs use these services to locate network resources, establish and terminate connections, and transfer data.

The Name Service permits you to refer to an application, representing a resource, by a name on the internetwork. The name consists of 16 alphanumeric characters, which may be either exclusive (unique to an application) or shared (used by a group). The application registers the name to ensure that no other applications raise any objections to its use. The Name Service primitives are Add Name, Add Group Name, and Delete Name.

The Session Service is used for the reliable exchange of data between two NetBIOS applications. Each data message may be from 0 to 131,071 octets in length. The Session Service primitives are somewhat analogous to the TCP primitives discussed in Chapter 5 and include: Call, Listen, Hang Up, Send, Receive, and Session Status.

The Datagram Service provides unreliable, non-sequenced, and connectionless data transfer. The data may be transferred in two ways. In one technique, the datagram sender registers a name under which the data will be sent and specifies the name to which it will be sent. The second technique broadcasts the datagram. The Datagram Service primitives are Send Datagram, Send Broadcast Datagram, Receive Datagram, and Receive Broadcast Datagram.

Miscellaneous functions generally control the operation of the network interface and are implementation-dependent. These functions include Reset, Cancel, Adapter Status, Unlink, and Remote Program Load. IBM's token ring implementation added the Find Name primitive, which determines whether a particular name is registered on the network. (Four of the NetBIOS primitives listed above—Reset, Session Status, Unlink, and Remote Program Load—are considered local implementation issues that do not impact interoperability, and are therefore considered outside the scope of the Internet specification.)

RFC 1001 defines three types of NetBIOS end nodes and two NetBIOS support servers. The end nodes include the Broadcast (B), Point-to-Point (P), and Mixed Mode (M) types. Each of these types is specified by the operations it is allowed to perform. The NetBIOS support servers include the NetBIOS Name Server nodes (NBNS) and the NetBIOS Datagram Distribution nodes (NBDD). The NBNS manages and validates names used within the internetwork. NBNS formats the NetBIOS names to be valid Domain Name System (DNS) names and allows the NBNS to function in a fashion similar to the DNS Query service. The NBDD extends the NetBIOS datagram functions to the internet, which does not support multicast or broadcast transmissions. All of the nodes and servers are combined in various topologies of local and interconnected networks; RFC 1001 defines these details.

6.7.1 NetBIOS Name Service

NetBIOS's operation over UDP or TCP transport begins with the NetBIOS Name Service registering the name of the application to be used. The Name Query is the process by which the IP address associated with a NetBIOS name is discovered. Depending on the type of node in use (B, P, or M), the queries are either broadcast or directed to the NBNS. The exact procedures are described in RFC 1001.

NetBIOS Name Service messages use Port number 137 and are compatible with the DNS header format shown in Figure 6-8a. The structure includes a header followed by four entries—the Question section, Answer section, Authority section, and Additional Information section. A typical Name Query message would include the NetBIOS name in the Question section, followed by a Response message that provides details about the name, including its IP address. When an IP address has been found for the target name, either the Session Service (using TCP) or the Datagram Service (using UDP) may be implemented.

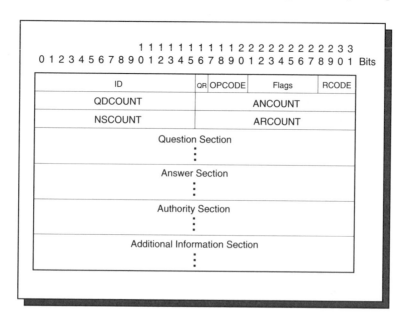

Figure 6-8a. NetBios Name Service Header

6.7.2 NetBIOS Session Service

The NetBIOS Session Service uses Port number 139 and is implemented in three phases: session establishment, steady state, and session close. Session establishment determines the IP address and the TCP port of the called name and establishes a TCP connection with the remote device. Steady state provides data transfer and keep-alive functions. Session close terminates the session and triggers the close of the TCP session. Figure 6-9 illustrates these conditions; note the differences between the TCP and NetBIOS functions.

Figure 6-8b shows the format of the NetBIOS Session Service header. The Session Service header consists of a 4-octet header and a trailer that depends on the type of packet being transmitted. Three fields comprise the header: a Session Type field (1 octet), a Flags field (1 octet), and a Length field (2 octets). Values for the Session Type field are:

Value (hexadecimal)	Packet Type
00	Session message
81	Session request
82	Positive Session response
83	Negative Session response
84	Retarget Session response
85	Session Keep Alive

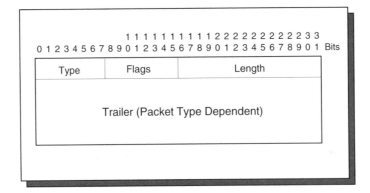

Figure 6-8b. NetBIOS Session Header

The Flags field (1 octet) uses only Bit 7; all others are set to zero. Bit 7 is used as an extension to the Length field (also 1 octet), which specifies the number of octets contained in the trailer (i.e., non-header) fields. When used in combination with the Flag Extension Bit, the cumulative length of the Trailer field(s) has a maximum value of 128K octets.

6.7.3 NetBIOS Datagram Service

NetBIOS datagrams utilize UDP transport with Port number 138. The complete NetBIOS datagram includes the IP header (20 octets), UDP header (8 octets), NetBIOS datagram header (14 octets), and the NetBIOS data. The NetBIOS data consists of the Source and Destination NetBIOS names (255 octets each) and up to 512 octets of NetBIOS user data. The complete NetBIOS datagram can be up to 1,064 octets in length, but it may need fragmentation if the maximum IP datagram length is 576 octets.

NetBIOS datagrams require a Name Query operation to determine the IP address of the destination name. The NetBIOS datagram can then be transmitted within a UDP datagram or multiple UDP datagrams, as required. Three transmission modes are available: unicast, which transmits to a unique NetBIOS name; multicast, which transmits to a group NetBIOS name; and broadcast, which uses the Send Broadcast Datagram primitive.

Figure 6-8c illustrates the NetBIOS Datagram header. The Msg Type field (1 octet) defines the datagram function:

Value (hexadecimal)	Msg_Type
10	Direct_Unique_Datagram
11	Direct_Group Datagram
12	Broadcast datagram
13	Datagram error
14	Datagram Query request
15	Datagram Positive Query response
16	Datagram Negative Query response

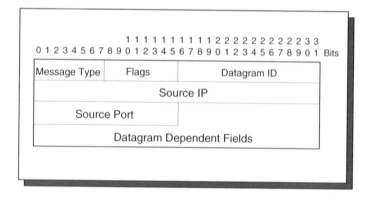

Figure 6-8c. NetBIOs Datagram Header

The flags (1 octet) define the first datagram fragment, whether more fragments will follow, and the type of source node (B, P, or M). The remaining fields support datagram service, with a Datagram ID (2 octets), the Source IP address (4 octets), Source Port (2 octets), Datagram Length (2 octets), and a Packet Offset (2 octets). Datagram-specific user data fields complete each message. We'll see an example of NetBIOS packet operation in Section 6.9.6.

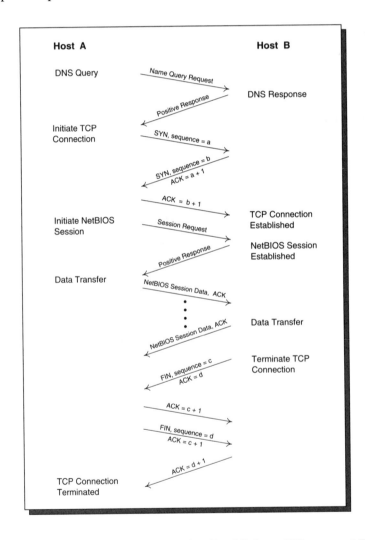

Figure 6-9. TCP and NetBIOs Connection Establishment/Disconnect Events

6.8 Troubleshooting the Process/Application Connection

Upper-layer protocol problems can be challenging to diagnose for several reasons. First, the Application/Process Layer interfaces with the end user. As we know, humans can cause well-ordered computer systems much consternation. Second, the Process/Application Layer must offer numerous options to meet the needs of its diverse clientele (humans). These options may use different file types (options for FTP) or data communication parameters (required to support a particular TELNET connection).

To diagnose these problems, you should begin by determining whether the end-to-end connectivity functions are getting the data to the required destination. If they're not, use the techniques discussed in earlier chapters to determine where in the Network Interface, Internet, or Host-to-Host layers the problem resides, and troubleshoot the failure. If data is getting through, then an upper-layer problem may exist.

Keep in mind that just because data is being received doesn't mean that it is being interpreted properly—if my terminal is transmitting ASCII characters and your host is expecting EBCDIC, we'll exchange bits, but we won't communicate. A logical question to ask, then, is whether the application is being used properly. We've all experienced problems on our PCs that have turned out to be configuration errors. The Process/Application Layer applications are no exception. As long as there's a human element, the probability of error exists. Unfortunately, that probability is higher than any of us care to admit.

A second possibility is that the two application processes are unable to communicate with each other because of internal implementation differences. Even in this day of "open systems" (and the Internet protocols are about as open as you can get), interoperability difficulties should not be eliminated from consideration.

In addition to the protocol analyzer, a number of host-based utilities are available to monitor and diagnose Process/Application Layer problems. An excellent source of information on these utilities is RFC 1470, "FYI on a Network Management Tool Catalog: Tools for Monitoring and Debugging TCP/IP Internets and Interconnected Devices" [6-28]. Many of these tools are devised for UNIX platforms. Examples include:

- *etherfind*—a traffic monitor that runs under the Sun Operating System.
- *Internet Rover*—a network monitor for 4.x BSD UNIX systems that includes modules to test TELNET, FTP, and SMTP.
- *mconnect*—a utility available with 4.x BSD UNIX systems to test SMTP connections.
- *netstat*—a utility available with 4.x BSD UNIX that will report routing table, TCP connections, and traffic statistics.
- *snmpwatch*—a network monitoring utility, compatible with a number of UNIX versions, that reports SNMP variables that have changed in value.

In summary, consult the management utilities included with your operating system and the tools listed in RFC 1470 for assistance with diagnosing upper-layer protocol problems.

6.9 Case Studies

Each of the case studies that follows illustrates the operation of a particular Process/Application Layer protocol. Admittedly, we could write volumes on each of the protocols that we've studied, but space does not permit full elaboration. Keep in mind, however, that the best references are the protocol-specific RFCs themselves, along with several supplements. These include RFC 1700, "Assigned Numbers"; RFC 1122, "Requirements for Internet Hosts: Communication Layers"; and RFC 1123, "Requirements for Internet Hosts—Application and Support," all of which provide details on specific parameters. Given these caveats, let's look at the operation of the upper-layer protocols.

6.9.1 Using TFTP

In our first case study, a Sun workstation (shown as Sun IPX in Trace 6.9.1a) and a PC running TCP/IP workstation software attempt to use TFTP to read and write small source files.

In Frame 1, the Sun IPX initiates a connection to Station XT with a Read Request (RRQ) for file "TFTP_test" in netascii mode. Details of that frame (Trace 6.9.1b) indicate that the Sun IPX has selected Source Transaction ID 1167 (Source port = 1167) with Destination port=69, which is defined as the TFTP port. The connection is accepted in Frame 2. Station XT selects TID 1183 (Source port = 1183) and returns the Sun IPX TID as the destination (Destination port = 1167). The TFTP header indicates a DATA packet, Block number = 1, with 128 octets of data. Frame 3 acknowledges receipt of the data and terminates that connection.

Given that success, Sun IPX next attempts to write the same file using the Write Request (WRQ) from TID = 1167 in Frame 6. Station XT sends an ACK, selecting TID 1184 (Source port = 1184) and designating Block number = 0. The 128 octets of data is successfully written from Port 1167 (Sun IPX) to Port 1184 in Frame 8. An ACK from Station XT is sent in Frame 9, terminating the connection.

The next two operations are not so successful. In Frame 10, the Sun IPX sends an RRQ for file "\test" in netascii mode. Unfortunately, this file does not exist on Station XT. An ERROR packet, indicating an access violation, is returned in Frame 11. The Sun acknowledges its mistake and terminates the connection in Frame 12.

The Sun IPX makes one more attempt in Frame 16, this time a WRQ of the same file ("\test"), which still does not exist. The Sun IPX selects TID = 1167 again, while Station XT assigns TID = 1186 in Frame 17. Note that the ACK sent in response to the WRQ uses Block number = 0 (Frame 17). The Sun IPX then attempts to write the file. But it is empty (nonexistent) and no data is transferred. Station XT acknowledges the previous frame and terminates the connection.

TFTP thus performs as advertised—it transfers files with simplicity. It cannot overcome the faulty memory of the user, however, who can't seem to remember which files do and do not exist!

Sniffer Network Analyzer data 10-Mar at 13:08:44, TFTPTEST.TRC, Pg 1

SUMMARY	Delta T	Destination	Source	Summary
M 1		Station XT	Sun IPX	TFTP Read request
				File=TFTP_test
2	0.108	Sun IPX	Station XT	TFTP Data packet NS=1 (Last)
3	0.001	Station XT	Sun IPX	TFTP Ack NR=1
6	1.236	Station XT	Sun IPX	TFTP Write request
				File=TFTP_test
7	0.109	Sun IPX	Station XT	TFTP Ack NR=0
8	0.002	Station XT	Sun IPX	TFTP Data packet NS=1 (Last)
9	0.021	Sun IPX	Station XT	TFTP Ack NR=1

10	4.024	Station XT	Sun IPX	TFTP Read request File=\test
11	0.432	Sun IPX	Station XT	TFTP Error response
				(Access violation)
12	0.014	Station XT	Sun IPX	TFTP Ack NR=1
16	5.124	Station XT	Sun IPX	TFTP Write request File=\test
17	0.141	Sun IPX	Station XT	TFTP Ack NR=0
18	0.001	Station XT	Sun IPX	TFTP Data packet NS=1 (Last)
19	0.020	Sun IPX	Station XT	TFTP Ack NR=1

Trace 6.9.1a. TFTP Operation Summary

Sniffer Network Analyzer data 10-Mar at 13:08:44, TFTPTEST.TRC, Pg 1

- - - - - - - - - - - - - - - - Frame 1 - - - - - - - - - - - - - - - - -

UDP: ——- UDP Header ——-
UDP:
UDP: Source port = 1167 (TFTP)
UDP: Destination port = 69
UDP: Length = 29
UDP: No checksum
UDP:
TFTP: ——- Trivial file transfer ——-
TFTP:
TFTP: Opcode = 1 (Read request)
TFTP: File name = "TFTP_test"
TFTP: Mode = "netascii"
TFTP:
TFTP: [Normal end of "Trivial file transfer".]
TFTP:

- - - - - - - - - - - - - - - - Frame 2 - - - - - - - - - - - - - - - - -

UDP: ——- UDP Header ——-
UDP:
UDP: Source port = 1183 (TFTP)
UDP: Destination port = 1167
UDP: Length = 140
UDP: Checksum = F0DC (correct)
UDP:
TFTP: ——- Trivial file transfer ——-
TFTP:
TFTP: Opcode = 3 (Data packet)
TFTP: Block number = 1

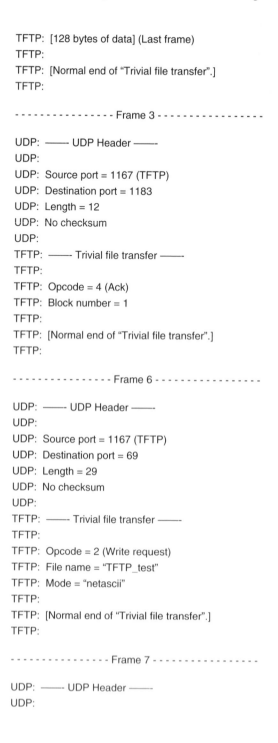

TFTP: [128 bytes of data] (Last frame)
TFTP:
TFTP: [Normal end of "Trivial file transfer".]
TFTP:

- - - - - - - - - - - - - - - Frame 3 - - - - - - - - - - - - - - - - -

UDP: —— UDP Header ——-
UDP:
UDP: Source port = 1167 (TFTP)
UDP: Destination port = 1183
UDP: Length = 12
UDP: No checksum
UDP:
TFTP: ——- Trivial file transfer ——-
TFTP:
TFTP: Opcode = 4 (Ack)
TFTP: Block number = 1
TFTP:
TFTP: [Normal end of "Trivial file transfer".]
TFTP:

- - - - - - - - - - - - - - - Frame 6 - - - - - - - - - - - - - - - - -

UDP: —— UDP Header ——-
UDP:
UDP: Source port = 1167 (TFTP)
UDP: Destination port = 69
UDP: Length = 29
UDP: No checksum
UDP:
TFTP: ——- Trivial file transfer ——-
TFTP:
TFTP: Opcode = 2 (Write request)
TFTP: File name = "TFTP_test"
TFTP: Mode = "netascii"
TFTP:
TFTP: [Normal end of "Trivial file transfer".]
TFTP:

- - - - - - - - - - - - - - - Frame 7 - - - - - - - - - - - - - - - - -

UDP: —— UDP Header ——-
UDP:

365

UDP: Source port = 1184 (TFTP)
UDP: Destination port = 1167
UDP: Length = 12
UDP: Checksum = B7CB (correct)
UDP:
TFTP: ——- Trivial file transfer ——-
TFTP:
TFTP: Opcode = 4 (Ack)
TFTP: Block number = 0
TFTP:
TFTP: [Normal end of "Trivial file transfer".]
TFTP:

- - - - - - - - - - - - - - - Frame 8 - - - - - - - - - - - - - - - -

UDP: ——- UDP Header ——-
UDP:
UDP: Source port = 1167 (TFTP)
UDP: Destination port = 1184
UDP: Length = 140
UDP: No checksum
UDP:
TFTP: ——- Trivial file transfer ——-
TFTP:
TFTP: Opcode = 3 (Data packet)
TFTP: Block number = 1
TFTP: [128 bytes of data] (Last frame)
TFTP:
TFTP: [Normal end of "Trivial file transfer".]
TFTP:

- - - - - - - - - - - - - - Frame 9 - - - - - - - - - - - - - - - -

UDP: ——- UDP Header ——-
UDP:
UDP: Source port = 1184 (TFTP)
UDP: Destination port = 1167
UDP: Length = 12
UDP: Checksum = B7CA (correct)
UDP:
TFTP: ——- Trivial file transfer ——-
TFTP:

TFTP: Opcode = 4 (Ack)
TFTP: Block number = 1
TFTP:
TFTP: [Normal end of "Trivial file transfer".]
TFTP:

- - - - - - - - - - - - - - - Frame 10 - - - - - - - - - - - - - - - - -

UDP: —— UDP Header ——
UDP:
UDP: Source port = 1167 (TFTP)
UDP: Destination port = 69
UDP: Length = 25
UDP: No checksum
UDP:
TFTP: —— Trivial file transfer ——
TFTP:
TFTP: Opcode = 1 (Read request)
TFTP: File name = "\test"
TFTP: Mode = "netascii"
TFTP:
TFTP: [Normal end of "Trivial file transfer".]
TFTP:

- - - - - - - - - - - - - - - Frame 11 - - - - - - - - - - - - - - - - -

UDP: —— UDP Header ——
UDP:
UDP: Source port = 1185 (TFTP)
UDP: Destination port = 1167
UDP: Length = 41
UDP: Checksum = 7497 (correct)
UDP:
TFTP: —— Trivial file transfer ——
TFTP:
TFTP: Opcode = 5 (Error response)
TFTP: Error code = 2 (Access violation)
TFTP: Error message = "unable to open file for read"
TFTP:
TFTP: [Normal end of "Trivial file transfer".]
TFTP:

```
- - - - - - - - - - - - - - - Frame 12 - - - - - - - - - - - - - - - - -

UDP:  ——- UDP Header ——-
UDP:
UDP:  Source port = 1167 (TFTP)
UDP:  Destination port = 1185
UDP:  Length = 12
UDP:  No checksum
UDP:
TFTP:  ——- Trivial file transfer ——-
TFTP:
TFTP:  Opcode = 4 (Ack)
TFTP:  Block number = 1
TFTP:
TFTP:  [Normal end of "Trivial file transfer".]
TFTP:

- - - - - - - - - - - - - - - Frame 16 - - - - - - - - - - - - - - - - -

UDP:  ——- UDP Header ——-
UDP:
UDP:  Source port = 1167 (TFTP)
UDP:  Destination port = 69
UDP:  Length = 25
UDP:  No checksum
UDP:
TFTP:  ——- Trivial file transfer ——-
TFTP:
TFTP:  Opcode = 2 (Write request)
TFTP:  File name = "\test"
TFTP:  Mode = "netascii"
TFTP:
TFTP:  [Normal end of "Trivial file transfer".]
TFTP:

- - - - - - - - - - - - - - - Frame 17 - - - - - - - - - - - - - - - - -

UDP:  ——- UDP Header ——-
UDP:
UDP:  Source port = 1186 (TFTP)
UDP:  Destination port = 1167
UDP:  Length = 12
UDP:  Checksum = B7C9 (correct)
UDP:
```

TFTP: ——- Trivial file transfer ——-
TFTP:
TFTP: Opcode = 4 (Ack)
TFTP: Block number = 0
TFTP:
TFTP: [Normal end of "Trivial file transfer".]
TFTP:

- - - - - - - - - - - - - - - Frame 18 - - - - - - - - - - - - - - - -

UDP: ——- UDP Header ——-
UDP:
UDP: Source port = 1167 (TFTP)
UDP: Destination port = 1186
UDP: Length = 12
UDP: No checksum
UDP:
TFTP: ——- Trivial file transfer ——-
TFTP:
TFTP: Opcode = 3 (Data packet)
TFTP: Block number = 1
TFTP: [0 bytes of data] (Last frame)
TFTP:
TFTP: [Normal end of "Trivial file transfer".]
TFTP:

- - - - - - - - - - - - - - - Frame 19 - - - - - - - - - - - - - - - -

UDP: ——- UDP Header ——-
UDP:
UDP: Source port = 1186 (TFTP)
UDP: Destination port = 1167
UDP: Length = 12
UDP: Checksum = B7C8 (correct)
UDP:
TFTP: ——- Trivial file transfer ——-
TFTP:
TFTP: Opcode = 4 (Ack)
TFTP: Block number = 1
TFTP:
TFTP: [Normal end of "Trivial file transfer".]
TFTP:

Trace 6.9.1b. TFTP Operation Details

6.9.2 Collaborative Efforts of FTP, ARP, and TFTP

In the case study in Section 5.7.1, we examined the process by which a device can obtain its boot and configuration files (known as load and parameter images) from the internetwork. The following case study shows a similar process, using the ARP and TFTP protocols. ARP determines the device's (in this case, a bridge's) Internet (IP) address, and TFTP transfers the load and parameter files to the bridge. We'll also use FTP to transfer a new version of the bridge's load image to the TFTP server prior to the start of the ARP/TFTP sequence. Let's see what happens when these three processes must interact.

The topology of this internetwork consists of local and remote Ethernet segments connected via bridges (see Figure 6-10). The network manager, Ross, has received a new version of the bridge software from the manufacturer on an MS-DOS formatted floppy. Ross uses FTP Software's PC/TCP to transfer the new bridge software from a PC (known as Snoopy) to the TFTP Server, which is a Sun SPARCstation (known as Maestro). Ross establishes a TCP control connection to Port number 21 on Maestro (Frames 2 through 4 of Trace 6.9.2a) and logs in (Frames 5 through 12). Next, Ross stores the new bridge boot image (filename rb1w1.sys) on Maestro in subdirectory /home/tftpboot (Frame 13). Maestro initiates an FTP data connection to Snoopy's Port number 20 in Frames 15 through 17, and the ASCII file transfer begins in Frame 19. Since the file is rather large, it does not complete until Frame 305, at which time both the FTP and TCP connections are terminated (Frames 306 through 314 of Trace 6.9.2b).

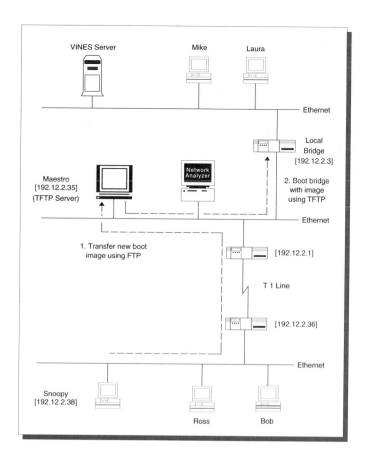

Figure 6-10. File Transfer of Bridge Boot Image

Next, Ross resets the local bridge (known as MX-3510) so that it can obtain and boot from the new load image. The bridges Ross uses are designed to get their boot and configuration files from a number of different servers that might exist on a network. In Frame 315, the bridge broadcasts for a proprietary boot server; in Frame 316, the bridge broadcasts for a BOOTP server; in Frame 317, the bridge broadcasts for a DEC file server using DEC's Maintenance Operations Protocol (MOP); finally, in Frame 318, the bridge broadcasts an ARP message looking for its Internet address. This operation is successful and the bridge uses its IP address to broadcast a TFTP Read request (Frame 320). The SPARCstation (Maestro) responds, triggering the bridge to request a file transfer of the boot image using TFTP (Frame 327). Unfortunately, the file transfer is not successful (see Frame 1393). Details of the error response (Trace 6.9.2c) indicate a Transfer Size Error, with "22 bytes of additional data present." This error message prompts Ross to speculate that the boot image file should have been transferred in FTP Binary mode instead of ASCII mode.

Ross begins again, this time setting the FTP transfer mode to Binary when he loads the file from Snoopy to Maestro. A TCP connection between Snoopy and Maestro is established (Frames 1408 through 1410 of Trace 6.9.2d), and the FTP file transfer begins. But this time the File Type is set for Image (Type I in Frame 1417). The Binary (or Image) data connection is opened in Frame 1426 and completes in Frame 1692 (Trace 6.9.2e). The local bridge is again reset and its boot sequence started (Frames 1696 through 1707). The boot image (filename x004db3.img) is transferred from Maestro to the local bridge, using TFTP in Frames 1708 through 2774. A second file (x004db3.prm) is transferred in Frames 2787 through 2819. The bridge boot sequence is now complete. The lesson learned: check the data representation parameter, or file type, to avoid corrupting the transferred file.

Sniffer Network Analyzer data 30-Aug at 14:07:42, BINARY.ENC, Pg 1

SUMMARY		Delta T	Destination	Source	Summary
M	1		AB0000020000	Local Bridge	MOP	RC System ID Receipt=0
	2	1.2376	Maestro	Snoopy	TCP	D=21 S=20294 SYN SEQ=19468734 LEN=0 WIN=2048
	3	0.0009	Snoopy	Maestro	TCP	D=20294 S=21 SYN ACK=19468735 SEQ=716544001 LEN=0 WIN=4096
	4	0.0016	Maestro	Snoopy	TCP	D=21 S=20294 ACK=716544002 WIN=2048
	5	0.1115	Snoopy	Maestro	FTP	R PORT=20294 220 maestro FTP server (SunOS 4.1) ready.<0D><0A>
	6	0.0374	Maestro	Snoopy	FTP	C PORT=20294 USER root<0D><0A>
	7	0.0073	Snoopy	Maestro	FTP	R PORT=20294 331 Password required for root.<0D><0A>
	8	0.0255	Maestro	Snoopy	FTP	C PORT=20294 PASS bugoff<0D><0A>

9	0.0479	Snoopy	Maestro	FTP	R PORT=20294
					230 User root
					logged in.<0D><0A>
10	0.1621	Maestro	Snoopy	TCP	D=21 S=20294
					ACK=716544104 WIN=1946
11	21.4760	Maestro	Snoopy	FTP	C PORT=20294
					PORT 192,12,2,
					38,79,71<0D><0A>
12	0.0127	Snoopy	Maestro	FTP	R PORT=20294
					200 PORT command successful
					<0D><0A>
13	0.0105	Maestro	Snoopy	FTP	C PORT=20294
					STOR /home/tftpboot
					/rb1w1.sys_v2.0<0D><0A>
14	0.0169	Snoopy	Maestro	TCP	D=20294 S=21
					ACK=19468819 WIN=4096
15	0.0601	Snoopy	Maestro	TCP	D=20295 S=20 SYN
					SEQ=719936001
					LEN=0 WIN=24576
16	0.0020	Maestro	Snoopy	TCP	D=20 S=20295 SYN
					ACK=719936002 SEQ=19468825
					LEN=0 WIN=2048
17	0.0006	Snoopy	Maestro	TCP	D=20295 S=20
					ACK=19468826 WIN=24576
18	0.0018	Snoopy	Maestro	FTP	R PORT=20294 150
					ASCII data connection for
					/home/tftpboot/rb1w1...
19	0.1108	Maestro	Snoopy	TCP	D=20 S=20295
					ACK=719936002 SEQ=19468826
					LEN=1189 WIN=2048
20	0.0065	Maestro	Snoopy	TCP	D=20 S=20295
					ACK=719936002 SEQ=19470015
					LEN=1460 WIN=2048
21	0.0058	Maestro	Snoopy	TCP	D=20 S=20295
					ACK=719936002 SEQ=19471475
					LEN=1460 WIN=2048
22	0.0024	Snoopy	Maestro	TCP	D=20295 S=20
					ACK=19472935 WIN=24576

Trace 6.9.2a. Boot Image Transfer Using FTP ASCII Connection

Sniffer Network Analyzer data 30-Aug at 14:07:42, BINARY.ENC, Pg 1

SUMMARY	Delta T	Destination	Source	Summary	
.					
.					
.					
301	0.0059	Maestro	Snoopy	TCP	D=20 S=20295 ACK=719936002 SEQ=19739400 LEN=1123 WIN=2048
302	0.0053	Maestro	Snoopy	TCP	D=20 S=20295 ACK=719936002 SEQ=19740523 LEN=1460 WIN=2048
303	0.0039	Maestro	Snoopy	TCP	D=20 S=20295 FIN ACK=719936002 SEQ=19741983 LEN=627 WIN=2048
304	0.0007	Snoopy	Maestro	TCP	D=20295 S=20 ACK=19742611 WIN=23949
305	0.0098	Snoopy	Maestro	FTP	R PORT=20294 226 ASCII Transfer complete.<0D><0A>
306	0.0003	Snoopy	Maestro	TCP	D=20295 S=20 FIN ACK=19742611 SEQ=719936002 LEN=0 WIN=24576
307	0.0020	Maestro	Snoopy	TCP	D=21 S=20294 ACK=716544246 WIN=1804
308	0.0015	Maestro	Snoopy	TCP	D=20 S=20295 ACK=719936003 WIN=2048
309	45.9027	Maestro	Snoopy	FTP	C PORT=20294 QUIT<0D><0A>
310	0.0091	Snoopy	Maestro	FTP	R PORT=20294 221 Goodbye.<0D><0A>
311	0.0060	Maestro	Snoopy	TCP	D=21 S=20294 FIN ACK=716544260 SEQ=19468825 LEN=0 WIN=1790
312	0.0006	Snoopy	Maestro	TCP	D=20294 S=21 ACK=19468826 WIN=4096
313	0.0009	Snoopy	Maestro	TCP	D=20294 S=21 FIN ACK=19468826 SEQ=716544260 LEN=0 WIN=4096
314	0.0020	Maestro	Snoopy	TCP	D=21 S=20294 ACK=716544261 WIN=1790
315	9.3205	09008780FFFF	Local Bridge	Ethertype=0889 (Unknown)	

316	4.0209	Broadcast	Local Bridge	BOOTP Request	
317	4.0194	AB0000010000	Local Bridge	MOP	DL Request Program
					Device Type=UNA
					Program Type=System
318	8.0203	Broadcast	Local Bridge	ARP	C HA=080087004DB3 PRO=IP
319	3.0660	Local Bridge	Maestro	ARP	R PA=[192.12.2.3]
					HA=080087004DB3 PRO=IP
320	0.9553	Broadcast	Local Bridge	TFTP Read request	
					File=x004db3.img
321	0.0168	Local Bridge	Maestro	UDP	D=2001 S=1416 LEN=524
322	0.0037	Maestro	Local Bridge	UDP	D=1416 S=2001 LEN=70
323	3.9820	Broadcast	Local Bridge	ARP	C PA=[192.12.2.35] PRO=IP
324	0.0004	Local Bridge	Maestro	ARP	R PA=[192.12.2.35]
					HA=080020103553 PRO=IP
325	7.9964	Maestro	Local Bridge	ARP	C PA=[192.12.2.35] PRO=IP
326	0.0004	Local Bridge	Maestro	ARP	R PA=[192.12.2.35]
					HA=080020103553 PRO=IP
327	0.0010	Maestro	Local Bridge	TFTP Read request	
					File=x004db3.img
328	0.0167	Local Bridge	Maestro	TFTP Data packet NS=1	
329	0.1344	Maestro	Local Bridge	TFTP Ack NR=1	
330	0.0015	Local Bridge	Maestro	TFTP Data packet NS=2	
331	0.0021	Maestro	Local Bridge	TFTP Ack NR=2	
.					
.					
.					
1390	0.0013	Local Bridge	Maestro	TFTP Data packet NS=532	
1391	0.0022	Maestro	Local Bridge	TFTP Ack NR=532	
1392	0.0012	Local Bridge	Maestro	TFTP Data packet NS=533	
1393	0.0012	Maestro	Local Bridge	TFTP Error response	
					(Not defined)
1394	0.0018	Maestro	Local Bridge	TFTP Write request	
					File=loaderr.dmp
1395	3.0193	Local Bridge	Maestro	TFTP Error response	
					(File not found)
1396	0.0047	Broadcast	Local Bridge	TFTP Read request	
					File=type57.img
1397	3.0045	Local Bridge	Maestro	UDP	D=2002 S=1421 LEN=27
1398	0.9889	09008780FFFF	Local Bridge	Ethertype=0889 (Unknown)	

Trace 6.9.2b. ASCII File Transfer Completion and Unsuccessful Bridge Boot

Sniffer Network Analyzer data 30-Aug at 14:07:42, BINARY.ENC, Pg 1

- - - - - - - - - - - - - - - Frame 1393 - - - - - - - - - - - - - - -

DLC: ——- DLC Header ——-
DLC:
DLC: Frame 1393 arrived at 14:09:49.7524; frame size is 88 (0058 hex) bytes.
DLC: Destination = Station Sun 103553, Maestro
DLC: Source   = Station Xyplex004DB3, Local Bridge
DLC: Ethertype = 0800 (IP)
DLC:
IP: ——- IP Header ——-
IP:
IP: Version = 4, header length = 20 bytes
IP: Type of service = 00
IP: 000. .... = routine
IP: ...0 .... = normal delay
IP: .... 0... = normal throughput
IP: .... .0.. = normal reliability
IP: Total length = 74 bytes
IP: Identification = 539
IP: Flags = 0X
IP: .0.. .... = may fragment
IP: ..0. .... = last fragment
IP: Fragment offset = 0 bytes
IP: Time to live = 100 seconds/hops
IP: Protocol = 17 (UDP)
IP: Header checksum = D049 (correct)
IP: Source address = [192.12.2.3]
IP: Destination address = [192.12.2.35]
IP: No options
IP:
UDP: ——- UDP Header ——-
UDP:
UDP: Source port = 2003 (TFTP)
UDP: Destination port = 1417
UDP: Length = 54
UDP: No checksum
UDP:
TFTP: ——- Trivial file transfer ——-
TFTP:
TFTP: Opcode = 5 (Error response)

TFTP: Error code = 0 (Not defined)
TFTP: Error message = "Transfer size error"
TFTP:
TFTP: *** 22 byte(s) of additional data present ***
TFTP:
TFTP: [Abnormal end of "Trivial file transfer".]
TFTP:

Trace 6.9.2c. TFTP Error Response Details

Sniffer Network Analyzer data 30-Aug at 14:07:42, BINARY.ENC, Pg 1

SUMMARY	Delta T	Destination	Source	Summary	
.					
.					
.					
.					
1399	4.0200	Broadcast	Local Bridge	BOOTP Request	
1400	4.0185	AB0000010000	Local Bridge	MOP	DL Request Program
					Device Type=UNA
					Program Type=System
1401	8.0202	Broadcast	Local Bridge	ARP	C HA=080087004DB3 PRO=IP
1402	3.0631	Local Bridge	Maestro	ARP	R PA=[192.12.2.3]
					HA=080087004DB3 PRO=IP
1403	0.9579	Broadcast	Local Bridge	TFTP	Read request
					File=x004db3.img
1404	0.0180	Local Bridge	Maestro	UDP	D=2001 S=1423 LEN=524
1405	0.0037	Maestro	Local Bridge	UDP	D=1423 S=2001 LEN=70
1406	3.9809	Broadcast	Local Bridge	ARP	C PA=[192.12.2.35] PRO=IP
1407	0.0004	Local Bridge	Maestro	ARP	R PA=[192.12.2.35]
					HA=080020103553 PRO=IP
1408	25.2853	Maestro	Snoopy	TCP	D=21 S=20296 SYN
					SEQ=19468830 LEN=0 WIN=2048
1409	0.0010	Snoopy	Maestro	TCP	D=20296 S=21 SYN
					ACK=19468831 SEQ=739648001
					LEN=0 WIN=4096
1410	0.0016	Maestro	Snoopy	TCP	D=21 S=20296
					ACK=739648002 WIN=2048
1411	0.1149	Snoopy	Maestro	FTP	R PORT=20296
					220 maestro FTP server
					(SunOS 4.1) ready.<0D><0A>
1412	0.0377	Maestro	Snoopy	FTP	C PORT=20296
					USER root<0D><0A>

1413	0.0075	Snoopy	Maestro	FTP	R PORT=20296
					331 Password required for
					root.<0D><0A>
1414	0.0249	Maestro	Snoopy	FTP	C PORT=20296
					PASS bugoff<0D><0A>
1415	0.0480	Snoopy	Maestro	FTP	R PORT=20296
					230 User root logged
					in.<0D><0A>
1416	0.1375	Maestro	Snoopy	TCP	D=21 S=20296
					ACK=739648104 WIN=1946
1417	6.2568	Maestro	Snoopy	FTP	C PORT=20296
					TYPE I<0D><0A>
1418	0.0015	Snoopy	Maestro	FTP	R PORT=20296
					200 Type set to I.<0D><0A>
1419	0.1605	Maestro	Snoopy	TCP	D=21 S=20296
					ACK=739648124 WIN=1926
1420	23.3762	Maestro	Snoopy	FTP	C PORT=20296
					PORT 192,12,2,38,
					79,73<0D><0A>
1421	0.0126	Snoopy	Maestro	FTP	R PORT=20296
					200 PORT command successful
					<0D><0A>
1422	0.0118	Maestro	Snoopy	FTP	C PORT=20296
					STOR /home/tftpboot
					/rb1w1.sys_v2.0<0D><0A>
1423	0.0919	Snoopy	Maestro	TCP	D=20297 S=20 SYN
					SEQ=744128001
					LEN=0 WIN=24576
1424	0.0015	Maestro	Snoopy	TCP	D=20 S=20297 SYN
					ACK=744128002 SEQ=19468841
					LEN=0 WIN=2048
1425	0.0006	Snoopy	Maestro	TCP	D=20297 S=20
					ACK=19468842 WIN=24576
1426	0.0018	Snoopy	Maestro	FTP	R PORT=20296
					150 Binary data connection
					for /home/tftpboot/rb1w...
1427	0.1065	Maestro	Snoopy	TCP	D=20 S=20297
					ACK=744128002 SEQ=19468842
					LEN=1460 WIN=2048
1428	0.0031	Maestro	Snoopy	TCP	D=20 S=20297
					ACK=744128002 SEQ=19470302
					LEN=1460 WIN=2048

| 1429 | 0.0013 | Snoopy | Maestro | TCP | D=20297 S=20 |
| | | | | | ACK=19471762 WIN=24576 |

.
.

Trace 6.9.2d. Boot Image Transfer Using FTP Binary Connection

Sniffer Network Analyzer data 30-Aug at 14:07:42, BINARY.ENC, Pg 1

SUMMARY	Delta T	Destination	Source	Summary	
.					
.					
.					
1687	0.0087	Maestro	Snoopy	TCP	D=20 S=20297
					ACK=744128002 SEQ=19738450
					LEN=1460 WIN=2048
1688	0.0031	Maestro	Snoopy	TCP	D=20 S=20297
					ACK=744128002 SEQ=19739910
					LEN=1460 WIN=2048
1689	0.0002	Snoopy	Maestro	TCP	D=20297 S=20
					ACK=19739910 WIN=24576
1690	0.0026	Maestro	Snoopy	TCP	D=20 S=20297 FIN
					ACK=744128002 SEQ=19741370
					LEN=240 WIN=2048
1691	0.0005	Snoopy	Maestro	TCP	D=20297 S=20
					ACK=19741611 WIN=22876
1692	0.0092	Snoopy	Maestro	FTP	R PORT=20296
					226 Binary Transfer
					complete.<0D><0A>
1693	0.0003	Snoopy	Maestro	TCP	D=20297 S=20 FIN
					ACK=19741611 SEQ=744128002
					LEN=0 WIN=24576
1694	0.0020	Maestro	Snoopy	TCP	D=21 S=20296
					ACK=739648268 WIN=1782
1695	0.0008	Maestro	Snoopy	TCP	D=20 S=20297
					ACK=744128003 WIN=2048
1696	31.6613	09008780FFFF	Local Bridge	Ethertype=0889 (Unknown)	
1697	4.0209	Broadcast	Local Bridge	BOOTP Request	
1698	4.0194	AB0000010000	Local Bridge	MOP	DL Request Program
					Device Type=UNA
					Program Type=System
1699	8.0204	Broadcast	Local Bridge	ARP	C HA=080087004DB3 PRO=IP

1700	3.0628	Local Bridge	Maestro	ARP	R PA=[192.12.2.3]
					HA=080087004DB3 PRO=IP
1701	0.9584	Broadcast	Local Bridge	TFTP	Read request
					File=x004db3.img
1702	0.0168	Local Bridge	Maestro	UDP	D=2001 S=1426 LEN=524
1703	0.0037	Maestro	Local Bridge	UDP	D=1426 S=2001 LEN=70
1704	3.9820	Broadcast	Local Bridge	ARP	C PA=[192.12.2.35] PRO=IP
1705	0.0004	Local Bridge	Maestro	ARP	R PA=[192.12.2.35]
					HA=080020103553 PRO=IP
1706	7.9964	Maestro	Local Bridge	ARP	C PA=[192.12.2.35] PRO=IP
1707	0.0004	Local Bridge	Maestro	ARP	R PA=[192.12.2.35]
					HA=080020103553 PRO=IP
1708	0.0010	Maestro	Local Bridge	TFTP	Read request
					File=x004db3.img
1709	0.0168	Local Bridge	Maestro	TFTP	Data packet NS=1
1710	0.1344	Maestro	Local Bridge	TFTP	Ack NR=1
1711	0.0015	Local Bridge	Maestro	TFTP	Data packet NS=2
1712	0.0021	Maestro	Local Bridge	TFTP	Ack NR=2
.					
.					
.					
2771	0.0012	Local Bridge	Maestro	TFTP	Data packet NS=532
2772	0.0022	Maestro	Local Bridge	TFTP	Ack NR=532
2773	0.0011	Local Bridge	Maestro	TFTP	Data packet NS=533 (Last)
2774	0.0019	Maestro	Local Bridge	TFTP	Ack NR=533
2775	11.3936	09008780FFFF	Local Bridge		Ethertype=0889 (Unknown)
2776	4.0129	Broadcast	Local Bridge		BOOTP Request
2777	4.0195	AB0000010000	Local Bridge	MOP	DL Request Program
					Device Type=UNA
					Program Type=System
2778	8.0205	Broadcast	Local Bridge	ARP	C HA=080087004DB3 PRO=IP
2779	3.0610	Local Bridge	Maestro	ARP	R PA=[192.12.2.3]
					HA=080087004DB3 PRO=IP
2780	0.9599	Broadcast	Local Bridge	TFTP	Read request
					File=x004db3.prm
2781	0.0159	Local Bridge	Maestro	UDP	D=2001 S=1440 LEN=524
2782	0.0016	Maestro	Local Bridge	UDP	D=1440 S=2001 LEN=70
2783	3.9846	Broadcast	Local Bridge	ARP	C PA=[192.12.2.35] PRO=IP
2784	0.0004	Local Bridge	Maestro	ARP	R PA=[192.12.2.35]
					HA=080020103553 PRO=IP
2785	7.9971	Maestro	Local Bridge	ARP	C PA=[192.12.2.35] PRO=IP
2786	0.0004	Local Bridge	Maestro	ARP	R PA=[192.12.2.35]
					HA=080020103553 PRO=IP

2787	0.0010	Maestro	Local Bridge	TFTP Read request
				File=x004db3.prm
2788	0.0163	Local Bridge	Maestro	TFTP Data packet NS=1
2789	0.0147	Maestro	Local Bridge	TFTP Ack NR=1
2790	0.0015	Local Bridge	Maestro	TFTP Data packet NS=2
2791	0.0021	Maestro	Local Bridge	TFTP Ack NR=2
.				
.				
.				
2814	0.0012	Local Bridge	Maestro	TFTP Data packet NS=14
2815	0.0021	Maestro	Local Bridge	TFTP Ack NR=14
2816	0.0013	Local Bridge	Maestro	TFTP Data packet NS=15
2817	0.0022	Maestro	Local Bridge	TFTP Ack NR=15
2818	0.0012	Local Bridge	Maestro	TFTP Data packet NS=16 (Last)
2819	0.0021	Maestro	Local Bridge	TFTP Ack NR=16

Trace 6.9.2e. Binary File Transfer Completion and Successful Bridge Boot

6.9.3 Selecting the Proper Terminal Option for TELNET

In Section 6.5 we studied TELNET and discussed a number of options for converting the local terminal/host format into the Network Virtual Terminal format. These options are a common source of TELNET incompatibilities.

In this example, users attached to an Ethernet have two options for communicating with an SNA host (see Figure 6-11). The first option is to use DEC VT-100 terminals through a terminal server connected to the Ethernet. The second option is to use FTP Software Inc.'s popular package PC/TCP on a workstation to connect directly to the Ethernet. The users discover, however, that the terminal server option does not work while the PC/TCP option does. Let's explore why.

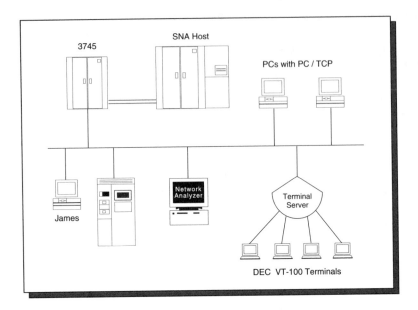

Figure 6-11. TELNET Access to IBM Using TN3270

The first attempt to access the SNA host is via the terminal server, shown in Trace 6.9.3a. The terminal session begins with a TCP connection in Frames 32 through 34 and continues with the TELNET option negotiations. These include the Terminal Type (Frames 36 through 41), End of Record (Frames 42 through 44), Binary Transmission (Frames 45 through 47), and so on. Data transfer from the SNA host begins in Frame 53, but has little success. The terminal server is allowing a rather small window size, ranging from 0 to 256 octets. In Frame 112, the terminal server resets the TCP connection, terminating communication. At this point, the user sees the terminal server prompt on his VT-100 terminal and realizes that the host connection has failed.

To test the process, the network administrator, James, goes to a workstation that has the PC/TCP software package and attempts the same session with the SNA host (see Trace 6.9.3b). Frames 94 through 96 show the TCP connection being established, followed by the same TELNET option negotiation sequence. A significant difference is the window size that the workstation allows (1707-2048 octets) and the orderly termination of the TCP connection in Frames 256 through 259. This time, James is able to log into the host, conduct his business, and properly terminate the connection.

Since this session is successful but the one via the terminal server was not, James decides to check the options negotiated in each case.

Returning to Trace 6.9.3a, the only option open for negotiation is the Terminal Type, beginning in Frame 39, which we know from the Interpret as Command (IAC) Sub-negotiation (SB). Trace 6.9.3c shows the details of that negotiation. The SNA host sends FF FA 18 H, meaning "Interpret as Command, Subnegotiation of option 18H (Terminal Type)." The terminal server responds in Frame 41 with FF FA 18...H, indicating that its terminal type is an IBM-3278-2 (shown in the ASCII decode of Frame 41).

James performs a similar analysis of the trace derived from the workstation's successful connection to the host. Reviewing Trace 6.9.3b, the terminal type negotiation is requested in Frame 97 and occurs in Frames 99 and 100. In Frame 99 of Trace 6.9.3d, the SNA host indicates the negotiation of the terminal type (FF FA 18H), but this time the response is different. The workstation responds with IBM-3278-2-E instead of the IBM-3278-2 which the terminal server sent. This difference suggests to James that the terminal server was not supporting the Extended (E) Attribute set, causing the connection to fail. A check of the defined TELNET terminal types in RFC 1700 and RFC 1091 [6-29] confirms that the two were indeed different. The workstation software supported the IBM-3278-2-E type, allowing the host connection to succeed. The terminal server did not provide support, so that connection failed. What appeared to be a small problem inhibited communication. Readers needing additional details on TN3270 should consult references [6-30] and [6-31].

Sniffer Network Analyzer data 22-Nov at 15:04:36, JK1.ENC, Pg 1

SUMMARY	Delta T	Destination	Source	Summary	
32	38.6694	SNA Host	Term Server	TCP	D=23 S=5029 SYN
					SEQ=159638 LEN=0 WIN=256
33	0.0016	Term Server	SNA Host	TCP	D=5029 S=23 SYN
					ACK=159639 SEQ=849951745
					LEN=0 WIN=4096
34	0.0021	SNA Host	Term Server	TCP	D=23 S=5029
					ACK=849951746 WIN=256
35	0.0020	SNA Host	Term Server	Telnet	C PORT=5029
					IAC Do Echo
36	0.0273	Term Server	SNA Host	Telnet	R PORT=5029
					IAC Do Terminal type

37	0.0032	SNA Host	Term Server	TCP	D=23 S=5029
					ACK=849951749 WIN=253
38	0.0022	SNA Host	Term Server	Telnet C PORT=5029	
					IAC Will Terminal type
39	0.0033	Term Server	SNA Host	Telnet R PORT=5029	
					IAC SB ...
40	0.0023	SNA Host	Term Server	TCP	D=23 S=5029
					ACK=849951755 WIN=250
41	0.0027	SNA Host	Term Server	Telnet C PORT=5029	
					IAC SB ...
42	0.0258	Term Server	SNA Host	Telnet R PORT=5029	
					IAC Do End of record
43	0.0023	SNA Host	Term Server	TCP	D=23 S=5029
					ACK=849951761 WIN=250
44	0.0033	SNA Host	Term Server	Telnet C PORT=5029	
					IAC Will End of record
45	0.0034	Term Server	SNA Host	Telnet R PORT=5029	
					IAC Do Binary transmission
46	0.0022	SNA Host	Term Server	TCP	D=23 S=5029
					ACK=849951767 WIN=250
47	0.0499	SNA Host	Term Server	Telnet C PORT=5029	
					IAC Will Binary transmission
48	0.0041	Term Sun	SNA Host	Telnet R PORT=5029	
					IAC Do Echo
49	0.0027	SNA Host	Term Sun	TCP	D=23 S=5029
					ACK=849951770 WIN=253
50	0.0014	Term Sun	SNA Host	Telnet R PORT=5029	
					IAC Won't Echo
51	0.0017	SNA Host	Term Sun	Telnet C PORT=5029	
					IAC Won't Echo
52	0.0024	SNA Host	Term Sun	TCP	D=23 S=5029
					ACK=849951773 WIN=256
53	0.0029	Term Sun	SNA Host	Telnet R PORT=5029 <05>...	
54	0.0022	SNA Host	Term Sun	TCP	D=23 S=5029
					ACK=849951783 WIN=246
55	0.0602	Term Sun	SNA Host	Telnet R PORT=5029 <05>...	
56	0.0031	SNA Host	Term Sun	TCP	D=23 S=5029
					ACK=849952029 WIN=10
57	0.0018	Term Sun	SNA Host	Telnet R PORT=5029 <11>...	
58	0.0482	SNA Host	Term Sun	TCP	D=23 S=5029
					ACK=849952029 WIN=256
59	0.0146	SNA Host	Term Sun	TCP	D=23 S=5029
					ACK=849952037 WIN=256

60	3.5586	SNA Host	Term Sun	Telnet C PORT=5029 }...
61	0.0662	Term Sun	SNA Host	Telnet R PORT=5029 <05>...
62	0.0024	SNA Host	Term Sun	TCP D=23 S=5029
				ACK=849952083 WIN=210
63	0.0348	SNA Host	Term Sun	TCP D=23 S=5029
				ACK=849952083 WIN=256
64	0.0482	Term Sun	SNA Host	Telnet R PORT=5029 <05>...
65	0.0025	SNA Host	Term Sun	TCP D=23 S=5029
				ACK=849952093 WIN=246
66	0.0573	Term Sun	SNA Host	Telnet R PORT=5029 <05>...
67	0.0031	SNA Host	Term Sun	TCP D=23 S=5029
				ACK=849952339 WIN=10
68	0.0490	SNA Host	Term Sun	TCP D=23 S=5029
				ACK=849952339 WIN=256
69	0.0016	Term Sun	SNA Host	Telnet R PORT=5029 ...
70	0.0031	SNA Host	Term Sun	TCP D=23 S=5029
				ACK=849952595 WIN=0
71	0.0275	SNA Host	Term Sun	TCP D=23 S=5029
				ACK=849952595 WIN=256
72	0.0017	Term Sun	SNA Host	Telnet R PORT=5029 ...
73	0.0031	SNA Host	Term Sun	TCP D=23 S=5029
				ACK=849952851 WIN=0
74	0.0252	SNA Host	Term Sun	TCP D=23 S=5029
				ACK=849952851 WIN=256
75	0.0019	Term Sun	SNA Host	Telnet R PORT=5029 ...
76	0.0032	SNA Host	Term Sun	TCP D=23 S=5029
				ACK=849953107 WIN=0
77	0.0240	SNA Host	Term Sun	TCP D=23 S=5029
				ACK=849953107 WIN=255
78	0.0017	Term Sun	SNA Host	Telnet R PORT=5029 ...
79	0.0044	SNA Host	Term Sun	TCP D=23 S=5029
				ACK=849953362 WIN=0
80	0.0244	SNA Host	Term Sun	TCP D=23 S=5029
				ACK=849953362 WIN=256
81	0.0014	Term Sun	SNA Host	Telnet R PORT=5029
				<00><00><11>[a<\...
82	0.0021	SNA Host	Term Sun	TCP D=23 S=5029
				ACK=849953377 WIN=241
83	8.5150	SNA Host	Term Sun	Telnet C PORT=5029 }\}<11>...
84	0.0670	Term Sun	SNA Host	TCP D=5029 S=23
				ACK=159718 WIN=4096
85	1.0446	Term Sun	SNA Host	Telnet R PORT=5029 <05>...

86	0.0031	SNA Host	Term Sun	TCP	D=23 S=5029
					ACK=849953633 WIN=0
87	0.0505	SNA Host	Term Sun	TCP	D=23 S=5029
					ACK=849953633 WIN=255
88	0.0020	Term Sun	SNA Host	Telnet R PORT=5029 ...	
89	0.0038	SNA Host	Term Sun	TCP	D=23 S=5029
					ACK=849953888 WIN=0
90	0.0250	SNA Host	Term Sun	TCP	D=23 S=5029
					ACK=849953888 WIN=256
91	0.0016	Term Sun	SNA Host	Telnet R PORT=5029 ...	
92	0.0031	SNA Host	Term Sun	TCP	D=23 S=5029
					ACK=849954144 WIN=0
93	0.0260	SNA Host	Term Sun	TCP	D=23 S=5029
					ACK=849954144 WIN=256
94	0.0016	Term Sun	SNA Host	Telnet R PORT=5029 ...	
95	0.0031	SNA Host	Term Sun	TCP	D=23 S=5029
					ACK=849954400 WIN=0
96	0.0259	SNA Host	Term Sun	TCP	D=23 S=5029
					ACK=849954400 WIN=256
97	0.0016	Term Sun	SNA Host	Telnet R PORT=5029 @...	
98	0.0031	SNA Host	Term Sun	TCP	D=23 S=5029
					ACK=849954656 WIN=0
99	0.0258	SNA Host	Term Sun	TCP	D=23 S=5029
					ACK=849954656 WIN=256
100	0.0015	Term Sun	SNA Host	Telnet R PORT=5029 <1D>...	
101	0.0025	SNA Host	Term Sun	TCP	D=23 S=5029
					ACK=849954776 WIN=136
102	0.0384	SNA Host	Term Sun	TCP	D=23 S=5029
					ACK=849954776 WIN=256
103	2.7735	SNA Host	Term Sun	Telnet C PORT=5029	
				}\~<11>\}...	
104	0.0239	Term Sun	SNA Host	Telnet R PORT=5029 <05>...	
105	0.0022	SNA Host	Term Sun	TCP	D=23 S=5029
					ACK=849954780 WIN=252
106	1.9587	Term Sun	SNA Host	Telnet R PORT=5029 <05>...	
107	0.0022	SNA Host	Term Sun	TCP	D=23 S=5029
					ACK=849954790 WIN=246
108	2.2797	Term Sun	SNA Host	Telnet R PORT=5029 <05>...	
109	0.0021	SNA Host	Term Sun	TCP	D=23 S=5029
					ACK=849954800 WIN=246
110	3.2919	Term Sun	SNA Host	Telnet R PORT=5029	
				<11><00><06>@<00>...	

111	0.0025	SNA Host	Term Sun	TCP	D=23 S=5029
					ACK=849954815 WIN=241
112	0.0116	SNA Host	Term Sun	TCP	D=23 S=5029 RST WIN=0

Trace 6.9.3a. Host Access via Terminal Server (Summary)

Sniffer Network Analyzer data 22-Nov at 17:01:38, JK2.ENC, Page 1

SUMMARY	Delta T	Destination	Source	Summary	
94	0.0003	SNA Host	Workstation	TCP	D=23 S=28207 SYN
					SEQ=112068096 LEN=0
					WIN=2048
95	0.0015	Workstation	SNA Host	TCP	D=28207 S=23 SYN
					ACK=112068097
					SEQ=1722719745
					00LEN=0 WIN=4096
96	0.0006	SNA Host	Workstation	TCP	D=23 S=28207
					ACK=1722719746 WIN=2048
97	0.0283	Workstation	SNA Host	Telnet R PORT=28207	
				IAC Do Terminal type	
98	0.0126	SNA Host	Workstation	Telnet C PORT=28207	
				IAC Will Terminal type	
99	0.0045	Workstation	SNA Host	Telnet R PORT=28207 IAC SB ...	
100	0.0013	SNA Host	Workstation	Telnet C PORT=28207 IAC SB ...	
101	0.0262	Workstation	SNA Host	Telnet R PORT=28207	
				IAC Do End of record	
102	0.0015	SNA Host	Workstation	Telnet C PORT=28207	
				IAC Will End of record	
103	0.0034	Workstation	SNA Host	Telnet R PORT=28207	
				IAC Do Binary transmission	
104	0.0014	SNA Host	Workstation	Telnet C PORT=28207	
				IAC Do End of record	
105	0.0754	Workstation	SNA Host	TCP	D=28207 S=23
					ACK=112068124 WIN=4096
106	0.0007	SNA Host	Workstation	Telnet C PORT=28207	
				IAC Will Binary transmission	
107	0.0100	Workstation	SNA Host	Telnet R PORT=28207 <05>...	
108	0.2144	SNA Host	Workstation	TCP	D=23 S=28207
					ACK=1722719777 WIN=2017
109	0.0017	Workstation	SNA Host	Telnet R PORT=28207 <05>...	
110	0.2181	SNA Host	Workstation	TCP	D=23 S=28207
					ACK=1722720031 WIN=1763
140	4.0319	SNA Host	Workstation	Telnet C PORT=28207 }...	

141	0.0862	Workstation	SNA Host	Telnet R PORT=28207 <05>...
142	0.1659	SNA Host	Workstation	TCP D=23 S=28207
				ACK=1722720077 WIN=1717
143	0.6708	Workstation	SNA Host	Telnet R PORT=28207 <05>...
144	0.0008	SNA Host	Workstation	TCP D=23 S=28207
				ACK=1722720087 WIN=1707
145	0.0506	Workstation	SNA Host	Telnet R PORT=28207 <05>...
146	0.0016	SNA Host	Workstation	TCP D=23 S=28207
				ACK=1722721371 WIN=2048
202	17.0982	SNA Host	Workstation	Telnet C PORT=28207 }...
203	0.0559	Workstation	SNA Host	TCP D=28207 S=23
				ACK=112068172 WIN=4096
206	1.7954	Workstation	SNA Host	Telnet R PORT=28207 <05>...
207	0.0016	SNA Host	Workstation	TCP D=23 S=28207
				ACK=1722722830 WIN=2048
216	5.9596	SNA Host	Workstation	Telnet C PORT=28207
				}\~<11>\}...
217	0.0457	Workstation	SNA Host	TCP D=28207 S=23
				ACK=112068181 WIN=4096
218	0.5606	Workstation	SNA Host	Telnet R PORT=28207 <05>...
219	0.0008	SNA Host	Workstation	TCP D=23 S=28207
				ACK=1722722834 WIN=2044
220	1.5828	Workstation	SNA Host	Telnet R PORT=28207 <05>...
221	0.0008	SNA Host	Workstation	TCP D=23 S=28207
				ACK=1722722844 WIN=2034
222	1.3582	Workstation	SNA Host	Telnet R PORT=28207 <05>...
223	0.0007	SNA Host	Workstation	TCP D=23 S=28207
				ACK=1722722854 WIN=2024
224	1.3963	Workstation	SNA Host	Telnet R PORT=28207
				<11><00><06>@<00>...
225	0.0007	SNA Host	Workstation	TCP D=23 S=28207
				ACK=1722722869 WIN=2009
256	16.3941	SNA Host	Workstation	TCP D=23 S=28207 FIN
				ACK=1722722869
				SEQ=112068181
				LEN=0 WIN=2009
257	0.0014	Workstation	SNA Host	TCP D=28207 S=23
				ACK=112068182 WIN=4096
258	0.0058	Workstation	SNA Host	TCP D=28207 S=23 FIN
				ACK=112068182
				SEQ=1722722869
				LEN=0 WIN=4096

259   0.0007   SNA Host   Workstation   TCP   D=23 S=28207
ACK=1722722870 WIN=2009

Trace 6.9.3b. Host Access via PC (Summary)

Sniffer Network Analyzer data 22-Nov at 15:04:36, JK1.ENC, Pg 1

- - - - - - - - - - - - - - - - - Frame 39 - - - - - - - - - - - - - - - - -

Telnet:———- Telnet data ———
Telnet:
Telnet:IAC SB ...

ADDR	HEX		ASCII
0000	08 00 87 00 AA 61 02 60	8C 2E 21 56 08 00 45 00	.....a.`..!V..E.
0010	00 2E F9 11 00 00 1E 06	FE EA 90 48 04 0F 90 48	...........H...H
0020	80 2E 00 17 13 A5 32 A9	3C 05 00 02 6F 9D 50 18	......2.<...o.P.
0030	10 00 F1 01 00 00 FF FA	18 01 FF F0	....

- - - - - - - - - - - - - - - - - Frame 40 - - - - - - - - - - - - - - - - -

TCP: ———- TCP header ———-
TCP:
TCP: Source port = 5029
TCP: Destination port = 23 (Telnet)
TCP: Sequence number = 159645
TCP: Acknowledgment number = 849951755
TCP: Data offset = 20 bytes
TCP: Flags = 10
TCP: ..0. .... = (No urgent pointer)
TCP: ...1 .... = Acknowledgment
TCP: .... 0... = (No push)
TCP: .... .0.. = (No reset)
TCP: .... ..0. = (No SYN)
TCP: ....0 = (No FIN)
TCP: Window = 250
TCP: Checksum = 17FD (correct)
TCP: No TCP options
TCP:

ADDR	HEX		ASCII
0000	02 60 8C 2E 21 56 08 00	87 00 AA 61 08 00 45 00	.`..!V.....a..E.
0010	00 28 00 5D 00 00 40 06	D5 A5 90 48 80 2E 90 48	.(.]..@....H...H

| 0020 | 04 0F 13 A5 00 17 00 02 | 6F 9D 32 A9 3C 0B 50 10 | ....o.2.<.P. |
| 0030 | 00 FA 17 FD 00 00 00 00 | 00 00 00 00 | .... |

- - - - - - - - - - - - - - - Frame 41 - - - - - - - - - - - - - - - -

Telnet:——- Telnet data ——-
Telnet:
Telnet:IAC SB ...

ADDR	HEX		ASCII
0000	02 60 8C 2E 21 56 08 00	87 00 AA 61 08 00 45 00	.`..!V.....a..E.
0010	00 38 00 5E 00 00 40 06	D5 94 90 48 80 2E 90 48	.8.^..@....H...H
0020	04 0F 13 A5 00 17 00 02	6F 9D 32 A9 3C 0B 50 18	........o.2.<.P.
0030	01 00 D1 E6 00 00 FF FA	18 00 49 42 4D 2D 33 32	..........IBM-32
0040	37 38 2D 32 FF F0		78-2..

Trace 6.9.3c. TELNET Parameters from Terminal Server

Sniffer Network Analyzer data 22-Nov at 17:01:38, JK2.ENC, Pg 1

- - - - - - - - - - - - - - - Frame 99 - - - - - - - - - - - - - - - -

Telnet:——- Telnet data ——-
Telnet:
Telnet:IAC SB ...

ADDR	HEX		ASCII
0000	00 00 C0 A6 99 27 02 60	8C 2E 21 56 08 00 45 00	.....'.`..!V..E.
0010	00 2E FE 8B 00 00 1E 06	F9 89 90 48 04 0F 90 48	...........H...H
0020	80 15 00 17 6E 2F 66 AE	9E 05 06 AE 06 04 50 18	....n/f.......P.
0030	10 00 63 78 00 00 FF FA	18 01 FF F0	..cx........

- - - - - - - - - - - - - - - Frame 100 - - - - - - - - - - - - - - - -

Telnet:——- Telnet data ——-
Telnet:
Telnet:IAC SB ...

ADDR	HEX		ASCII
0000	02 60 8C 2E 21 56 00 00	C0 A6 99 27 08 00 45 10	.`..!V.....'..E.
0010	00 3A 00 05 00 00 40 06	D5 F4 90 48 80 15 90 48	.:....@....H...H
0020	04 0F 6E 2F 00 17 06 AE	06 04 66 AE 9E 0B 50 18	..n/......f...P.
0030	07 F7 10 1F 00 00 FF FA	18 00 49 42 4D 2D 33 32	..........IBM-32
0040	37 38 2D 32 2D 45 FF F0		78-2-E..

Trace 6.9.3d. TELNET Parameters from PC

6.9.4 TELNET over ATM

As a second example of TELNET operation, consider the network shown in Figure 6-12, which includes a TELNET client PC attached to a local network, a router, an ATM switch, and a Sun workstation, which is the TELNET server. The client wishes to connect to the Sun server, but must traverse the router and switch to get there. To accomplish this requires that three connections be established: an ATM connection, a TCP connection, and a TELNET connection. Trace 6.9.4a shows the details of these protocol operations. The ATM connection is established in Frames 1-6, the TCP connection is established in frames 7-9, and the TELNET session begins in Frame 13 with the parameter negotiations, login, password, and so on.

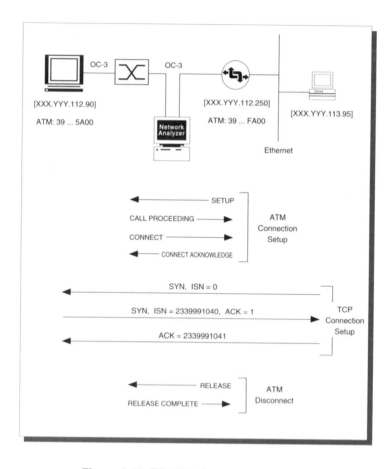

Figure 6-12. TELNET Connection via ATM

Sniffer Network Analyzer data from 23-Jan at 14:46:34, file JIM02.ATC, Pg 1

SUMMARY	Delta T	Destination	Source	Summary
1		ATM Switch	Router	Q2931 Setup
2	0.02720	Router	ATM Switch	Q2931 Call proceeding
3	0.06651	Router	ATM Switch	Q2931 Connect
4	0.00221	[0.0.0.0]	Router	ARP
5	0.00081	ATM Switch	Router	Q2931 Connect acknowledge
6	0.00024	Sun	Router	ARP PRO=IP
7	0.47088	Sun	Client	TCP D=23 S=1405 SYN SEQ=0 LEN=0 WIN=512
8	0.00200	Client	Sun	TCP D=1405 S=23 SYN ACK=1 SEQ=2339991040 LEN=0 WIN=64240
9	0.00273	Sun	Client	TCP D=23 S=1405 ACK=2339991041 WIN=512
10	0.23528	Client	Sun	Telnet R PORT=1405 IAC Do Terminal type
11	0.39640	ATM Switch	Router	SSCOP POLL PDU(Trans Stat Info)
12	0.00393	Router	ATM Switch	SSCOP STAT PDU(Receiver State Info)
13	0.16819	Client	Sun	Telnet R PORT=1405 IAC Do Terminal type
14	0.44008	Sun	Client	TCP D=23 S=1405 ACK=2339991044 WIN=509
15	0.00280	Sun	Client	TCP D=23 S=1405 ACK=2339991044 WIN=512
16	0.00166	Sun	Client	Telnet C PORT=1405 AC Will Terminal type
17	0.00178	Client	Sun	Telnet R PORT=1405 IAC SB ...
18	0.00543	Sun	Client	TCP D=23 S=1405 ACK=2339991050 WIN=512
19	0.00273	Sun	Client	Telnet C PORT=1405 IAC SB ...
20	0.05405	Client	Sun	Telnet R PORT=1405 IAC Will Echo
21	0.05856	Sun	Client	TCP D=23 S=1405 ACK=2339991108 WIN=512
22	0.00154	Sun	Client	Telnet C PORT=1405 IAC Do Echo
23	0.00153	Sun	Client	Telnet C PORT=1405 IAC Do Suppress go-ahead
24	0.00128	Client	Sun	TCP D=1405 S=23 ACK=21 WIN=64240
25	0.00020	Sun	Client	Telnet C PORT=1405 IAC Won't Echo
26	0.00197	Client	Sun	Telnet R PORT=1405 IAC Don't Echo
27	0.04013	Sun	Client	TCP D=23 S=1405 ACK=2339991111 WIN=512

28	0.00123	Client	Sun	Telnet R PORT=1405 login:
29	0.01264	Sun	Client	TCP D=23 S=1405 ACK=2339991118 WIN=512
30	3.57176	Sun	Client	Telnet C PORT=1405 t
31	0.00254	Client	Sun	Telnet R PORT=1405 t
32	0.01943	Sun	Client	TCP D=23 S=1405 ACK=2339991119 WIN=512
33	0.21528	Sun	Client	Telnet C PORT=1405 e
34	0.00258	Client	Sun	Telnet R PORT=1405 e
35	0.02181	Sun	Client	TCP D=23 S=1405 ACK=2339991120 WIN=512
36	0.06454	Sun	Client	Telnet C PORT=1405 s
37	0.00249	Client	Sun	Telnet R PORT=1405 s
38	0.11268	Sun	Client	TCP D=23 S=1405 ACK=2339991121 WIN=512
39	0.08181	Sun	Client	Telnet C PORT=1405 t
40	0.00245	Client	Sun	Telnet R PORT=1405 t
41	0.03649	Sun	Client	TCP D=23 S=1405 ACK=2339991122 WIN=512
42	0.98535	Sun	Client	Telnet C PORT=1405 <0D>
43	0.00265	Client	Sun	Telnet R PORT=1405 <0D0A>
44	0.02949	Sun	Client	TCP D=23 S=1405 ACK=2339991124 WIN=512
45	0.00125	Client	Sun	Telnet R PORT=1405 Password:
46	0.01018	Sun	Client	TCP D=23 S=1405 ACK=2339991134 WIN=512
47	1.37244	Sun	Client	Telnet C PORT=1405 t
48	0.05069	Client	Sun	TCP D=1405 S=23 ACK=30 WIN=64240
49	0.13462	Sun	Client	Telnet C PORT=1405 e
50	0.05406	Client	Sun	TCP D=1405 S=23 ACK=31 WIN=64240
51	0.02487	Sun	Client	Telnet C PORT=1405 s
52	0.05280	Client	Sun	TCP D=1405 S=23 ACK=32 WIN=64240
53	0.14366	Sun	Client	Telnet C PORT=1405 t
54	0.05610	Client	Sun	TCP D=1405 S=23 ACK=33 WIN=64240
55	0.35760	Sun	Client	Telnet C PORT=1405 <0D>
56	0.04223	Client	Sun	Telnet R PORT=1405 <0D0A>
57	0.09575	Sun	Client	TCP D=23 S=1405 ACK=2339991136 WIN=512
58	0.00124	Client	Sun	Telnet R PORT=1405 Last login: Fri Jan 19 15:41:37 on console<0D0A>
59	0.01039	Sun	Client	TCP D=23 S=1405 ACK=2339991180 WIN=512

60	0.31170	Client	Sun	Telnet R PORT=1405
				Sun Microsystems Inc.
				SunOS 5.4 Generi.
61	0.03638	Sun	Client	TCP D=23 S=1405 ACK=2339991239
				WIN=512
62	0.20412	Client	Sun	Telnet R PORT=1405 Arches%
63	0.03536	Sun	Client	TCP D=23 S=1405 ACK=2339991247
				WIN=512

Trace 6.9.4a. TELNET over ATM Summary

The details of the ATM connection setup are shown in Trace 6.9.4b. Recall that ATM is a connection-oriented network and requires that the communication path be established prior to sending any data. This process is somewhat similar to placing a telephone call, in which the initiator (or sender) enters the address (or telephone number) of the desired receiver and then relies on the network to establish a data path to the distant point. The messages that are used to establish, maintain, and terminate the connection are called signalling messages; in the case of ATM, they are defined by an ITU-T standard known as Q.2931. These signalling messages are sent on a pre-assigned virtual connection, VPCI = 0 and VCI = 5.

The connection establishment process begins with a SETUP message transmitted from the router to the ATM switch. Note from Figure 6-12 that the network analyzer is on the right-hand side of the ATM switch, capturing the traffic between the switch and the router. As a result, it cannot capture the traffic on the left-hand side of the switch. This entire call connection process was initiated by communication from the client PC, via the Ethernet LAN, to the router, which in turn sent the SETUP message to the ATM switch. As a result of the analyzer position, we are not able to see this initial client-to-router communication. In response to the client's actions, the router sent the SETUP to the ATM switch, which the Sniffer captured this, and we can see it in this trace.

Returning to Trace 6.9.4b, the ATM Cell Header is shown first, specifying the signalling channel (VPI = 0, VCI = 5) for communication. Next comes the Service Specific Connection Oriented Protocol (SSCOP) header, which provides for the reliable exchange of signalling information across an ATM interface. The Q.2931 signalling message is transmitted next; it includes the message type (SETUP) plus a number of parameters, which are carried within data units called Information Elements, or IEs. These IEs include: an ATM Traffic Descriptor, Broadband Bearer Capability,

Called Party Number, Calling Party Number, Quality of Service, ATM Adaptation Layer Parameters, and Broadband Low Layer Information. Frame 2 shows the CALL PROCEEDING message (from the ATM switch to the router) with a Connection Identifier IE, which identifies the virtual path (VPCI = 0) and virtual channel (VCI = 34), assigned to this call. A CONNECT message from the ATM switch to the router is seen in Frame 3; it also contains a Connection Identifier IE (VPCI = 0, VCI = 34) confirming the channel assignment. A CONNECT ACKNOWLEDGE message is sent from the router in Frame 5, completing the connection establishment process.

Frames 4 and 6 contain address resolution information. In Frame 4, the router sends an Inverse ARP Request (a broadcast) looking for the IP address of the TELNET server. Frame 6 contains the TELNET server's response:

```
ATM: 390000000000000000000000000000000A145705A00,
        corresponds with IP: [XXX.YYY.112.90]
ATM: 390000000000000000000000000000000A14570FA00,
        corresponds with IP: [XXX.YYY.112.250]
```

Sniffer Network Analyzer data from 23-Jan at 14:46:34, file JIM02.ATC, Pg 1

- - - - - - - - - - - - - - - - Frame 1 - - - - - - - - - - - - - - - - -

```
ATM: ——- ATM Cell Header ——-
ATM:
ATM: Frame 1 arrived at  14:48:45.35599 ; frame size is 112 (0070 hex) bytes.
ATM: Link = DTE
ATM: Virtual path id = 0
ATM: Virtual channel id = 5
ATM:
SSCOP: ——- SSCOP trailer ——-
SSCOP:
SSCOP: Sequenced Data PDU
SSCOP: SD send seq num N(S) = 94
SSCOP:
Q2931: ——- UNI 3.x Signalling ——-
Q2931:
Q2931: Protocol discriminator  = 09
Q2931: Length of call reference = 3 bytes
Q2931: Call reference value    = 0003D8
Q2931: Message type          = 05 (Setup)
```

Q2931: Message type Flag/Action = 80

Q2931:   ...0 .... = flag

Q2931:   .... ..00 = action (Clear call)

Q2931: Message Length   = 97

Q2931:

Q2931: Info element id   = 59 (ATM traffic descriptor)

Q2931: Coding Standard/Action = 80

Q2931:   1... .... =   ext

Q2931:   .00. .... =   code stand(ITU-T standardized)

Q2931:   ...0 0000 =   IE field(not significant)

Q2931: Length of info element = 9 byte(s)

Q2931: Forward peak cell rate (CLP = 0+1)

Q2931:   id   = 132

Q2931:   rate   = 1 cells/sec

Q2931:   424 bps

Q2931: Backward peak cell rate (CLP = 0+1)

Q2931:   id   = 133

Q2931:   rate   = 1 cells/sec

Q2931:   424 bps

Q2931: Best effort indicator = 190

Q2931:

Q2931: Info element id   = 5E (Broadband bearer capability)

Q2931: Coding Standard/Action = 80

Q2931:   1... .... =   ext

Q2931:   .00. .... =   code stand(ITU-T standardized)

Q2931:   ...0 0000 =   IE field(not significant)

Q2931: Length of info element = 3 byte(s)

Q2931: Bearer class   = BCOB-X

Q2931: Traffic type   = No indication

Q2931: Timing requirements   = No indication

Q2931: Susceptibility to clipping = Not susceptible to clipping

Q2931: User plane conn config   = Point-to-point

Q2931:

Q2931: Info element id   = 70 (Called party number)

Q2931: Coding Standard/Action = 80

Q2931:   1... .... =   ext

Q2931:   .00. .... =   code stand(ITU-T standardized)

Q2931:   ...0 0000 =   IE field(not significant)

Q2931: Length of info element = 21 byte(s)

Q2931:   1... .... =   ext

Q2931:   .000 .... =   type of num(Unknown)

Q2931:   .... 0010 =   addressing/num plan id(ATM Endsystem Address)

Q2931: Authority and format id = DCC ATM Format

```
Q2931: Data country code  = 0
Q2931: HO_DSP        = 00000000000000000000
Q2931: End system id    = 0000A145705A
Q2931: selector      = 0
Q2931:
Q2931: Info element id     = 6C (Calling party number)
Q2931: Coding Standard/Action = 80
Q2931:         1... .... =       ext
Q2931:         .00. .... =       code stand(ITU-T standardized)
Q2931:         ...0 0000 =       IE field(not significant)
Q2931: Length of info element = 22 byte(s)
Q2931:         0... .... =       ext
Q2931:         .000 .... =       type of num(Unknown)
Q2931:         .... 0010 =       addressing/num plan id(ATM Endsystem Address)
Q2931:         1... .... =       ext
Q2931:         .00. .... =       Presentation indicator (Presentation allowed)
Q2931:         .... ..00 =       Screening indicator (User-provided, not screened)
Q2931: Authority and format id = DCC ATM Format
Q2931: Data country code  = 0
Q2931: HO_DSP        = 00000000000000000000
Q2931: End system id    = 0000A14570FA
Q2931: selector      = 0
Q2931:
Q2931: Info element id     = 5C (Quality of service)
Q2931: Coding Standard/Action = E0
Q2931:         1... .... =       ext
Q2931:         .11. .... =       code stand(Standard defined for network)
Q2931:         ...0 0000 =       IE field(not significant)
Q2931: Length of info element = 2 byte(s)
Q2931: QoS class
Q2931:   forward  = QoS class 0 - Unspecified QoS class
Q2931:   backward  = QoS class 0 - Unspecified QoS class
Q2931:
Q2931: Info element id     = 58 (ATM adaptation layer parameters)
Q2931: Coding Standard/Action = 80
Q2931:         1... .... =       ext
Q2931:         .00. .... =       code stand(ITU-T standardized)
Q2931:         ...0 0000 =       IE field(not significant)
Q2931: Length of info element = 11 byte(s)
Q2931: AAL type       = AAL type 5
Q2931: Forward max CPCS-SDU
Q2931:         id  = 140
Q2931:         size  = 4478
```

Q2931: Backward max CPCS-SDU
Q2931:   id   = 129
Q2931:   size = 4478
Q2931: Mode
Q2931:   id = 131
Q2931:   mode = Message mode
Q2931: UNI 3.0 signalling
Q2931: SSCS type
Q2931:   id = 132
Q2931:   type = Null
Q2931:
Q2931: Info element id   = 5F (Broadband low layer information)
Q2931: Coding Standard/Action = 80
Q2931:   1... .... =   ext
Q2931:   .00. .... =   code stand(ITU-T standardized)
Q2931:   ...0 0000 =   IE field(not significant)
Q2931: Length of info element = 1 byte(s)
Q2931: Layer 2 protocol
Q2931:   1... .... = ext
Q2931:   .10. .... = layer 2 id
Q2931:   ...0 1100 = User info layer 2 protocol(LAN logical link control (ISO 8802/2))
Q2931:

- - - - - - - - - - - - - - - Frame 2 - - - - - - - - - - - - - - - -

ATM: ——- ATM Cell Header ——-
ATM:
ATM: Frame 2 arrived at 14:48:45.38319 ; frame size is 24 (0018 hex) bytes.
ATM: Link = DCE
ATM: Virtual path id = 0
ATM: Virtual channel id = 5
ATM:
SSCOP: ——- SSCOP trailer ——-
SSCOP:
SSCOP: Sequenced Data PDU
SSCOP: SD send seq num N(S) = 94
SSCOP:
Q2931: ——- UNI 3.x Signalling ——-
Q2931:
Q2931: Protocol discriminator = 09
Q2931: Length of call reference = 3 bytes
Q2931: Call reference value   = 8003D8
Q2931: Message type   = 02 (Call proceeding)

398

Q2931: Message type Flag/Action = 80
Q2931:   ...0 .... = flag
Q2931:   .... ..00 = action (Clear call)
Q2931: Message Length   = 9
Q2931:
Q2931: Info element id   = 5A (Connection identifier)
Q2931: Coding Standard/Action = 80
Q2931:   1... .... =   ext
Q2931:   .00. .... =   code stand(ITU-T standardized)
Q2931:   ...0 0000 =   IE field(not significant)
Q2931: Length of info element = 5 byte(s)
Q2931:   1... .... = ext
Q2931:   .00. .... = spare
Q2931:   ...0 1... = VP assoc signalling
Q2931:   .... .000 = Preferred/exclusive
Q2931:   VPCI = 0
Q2931:   VCI = 34
Q2931:

- - - - - - - - - - - - - - - Frame 3 - - - - - - - - - - - - - - - - -

ATM: ——- ATM Cell Header ——-
ATM:
ATM: Frame 3 arrived at 14:48:45.44969 ; frame size is 24 (0018 hex) bytes.
ATM: Link = DCE
ATM: Virtual path id = 0
ATM: Virtual channel id = 5
ATM:
SSCOP: ——- SSCOP trailer ——-
SSCOP:
SSCOP: Sequenced Data PDU
SSCOP: SD send seq num N(S) = 95
SSCOP:
Q2931: ——- UNI 3.x Signalling ——-
Q2931:
Q2931: Protocol discriminator = 09
Q2931: Length of call reference = 3 bytes
Q2931: Call reference value   = 8003D8
Q2931: Message type   = 07 (Connect)
Q2931: Message type Flag/Action = 80
Q2931:   ...0 .... = flag
Q2931:   .... ..00 = action (Clear call)
Q2931: Message Length   = 9

Q2931:

Q2931: Info element id   = 5A (Connection identifier)

Q2931: Coding Standard/Action = 80

Q2931:   1... .... =   ext

Q2931:   .00. .... =   code stand(ITU-T standardized)

Q2931:   ...0 0000 =   IE field(not significant)

Q2931: Length of info element = 5 byte(s)

Q2931:   1... .... = ext

Q2931:   .00. .... = spare

Q2931:   ...0 1... = VP assoc signalling

Q2931:   .... .000 = Preferred/exclusive

Q2931:   VPCI = 0

Q2931:   VCI = 34

Q2931:

- - - - - - - - - - - - - - - - Frame 4 - - - - - - - - - - - - - - - - -

ATM: ——- ATM Cell Header ——-

ATM:

ATM: Frame 4 arrived at 14:48:45.45191 ; frame size is 48 (0030 hex) bytes.

ATM: Link = DTE

ATM: Virtual path id = 0

ATM: Virtual channel id = 34

ATM:

LLC: ——- LLC Header ——-

LLC:

LLC: DSAP Address = AA, DSAP IG Bit = 00 (Individual Address)

LLC: SSAP Address = AA, SSAP CR Bit = 00 (Command)

LLC: Unnumbered frame: UI

LLC:

SNAP: ——- SNAP Header ——-

SNAP:

SNAP: Type = 0806 (ARP)

SNAP:

ARP: ——- ARP/RARP frame ——-

ARP:

ARP: Hardware type = 19 (ATM)

ARP: Protocol type = 0800 (IP)

ARP: Source ATM num

ARP: type = ATM Forum NSAPA format

ARP: length = 20

ARP: Target ATM subaddr

ARP: type = ATM Forum NSAPA format

ARP: length = 0

ARP: Opcode 8 (InARP_REQUEST)
ARP: Length of source prot addr   = 4
ARP: Target ATM num
ARP: type = ATM Forum NSAPA format
ARP: length = 0
ARP: Target ATM num
ARP: type = ATM Forum NSAPA format
ARP: length = 0
ARP: Length of target prot addr   = 4
ARP: source ATM num = 3900000000000000000000000000000A14570FA00
ARP: source prot addr = [XXX.YYY.112.250]
ARP: target prot addr = [0.0.0.0]
ARP:

- - - - - - - - - - - - - - - Frame 5 - - - - - - - - - - - - - - - - -

ATM: ——- ATM Cell Header ——-
ATM:
ATM: Frame 5 arrived at 14:48:45.45272 ; frame size is 16 (0010 hex) bytes.
ATM: Link = DTE
ATM: Virtual path id = 0
ATM: Virtual channel id = 5
ATM:
SSCOP: ——- SSCOP trailer ——-
SSCOP:
SSCOP: Sequenced Data PDU
SSCOP: SD send seq num N(S) = 95
SSCOP:
Q2931: ——- UNI 3.x Signalling ——-
Q2931:
Q2931: Protocol discriminator = 09
Q2931: Length of call reference = 3 bytes
Q2931: Call reference value   = 0003D8
Q2931: Message type   = 0F (Connect acknowledge)
Q2931: Message type Flag/Action = 80
Q2931:   ...0 .... = flag
Q2931:   .... ..00 = action (Clear call)
Q2931: Message Length   = 0

- - - - - - - - - - - - - - - Frame 6 - - - - - - - - - - - - - - - - -

ATM: ——- ATM Cell Header ——-
ATM:
ATM: Frame 6 arrived at 14:48:45.45296 ; frame size is 68 (0044 hex) bytes.

```
ATM:  Link = DCE
ATM:  Virtual path id = 0
ATM:  Virtual channel id = 34
ATM:
LLC:  —— LLC Header ——
LLC:
LLC:  DSAP Address = AA, DSAP IG Bit = 00 (Individual Address)
LLC:  SSAP Address = AA, SSAP CR Bit = 00 (Command)
LLC:  Unnumbered frame: UI
LLC:
SNAP: —— SNAP Header ——
SNAP:
SNAP: Type = 0806 (ARP)
SNAP:
ARP:  —— ARP/RARP frame ——
ARP:
ARP:  Hardware type = 19 (ATM)
ARP:  Protocol type = 0800 (IP)
ARP:  Source ATM num
ARP:      type = ATM Forum NSAPA format
ARP:      length = 20
ARP:  Target ATM subaddr
ARP:      type = ATM Forum NSAPA format
ARP:      length = 0
ARP:  Opcode 9 (InARP_REPLY)
ARP:  Length of source prot addr    = 4
ARP:  Target ATM num
ARP:      type = ATM Forum NSAPA format
ARP:      length = 20
ARP:  Target ATM num
ARP:      type = ATM Forum NSAPA format
ARP:      length = 0
ARP:  Length of target prot addr    = 4
ARP:  source ATM num  = 390000000000000000000000000000A145705A00
ARP:  source prot addr  = [XXX.YYY.112.90]
ARP:  target ATM num  = 390000000000000000000000000000A14570FA00
ARP:  target prot addr  = [XXX.YYY.112.250]
ARP:
```

Trace 6.9.4b TELNET over ATM Connection Setup

Now that the ATM connection is established between the router and the ATM switch, the TCP connection between the TELNET client (the PC) and the TELNET server (the

Sun) may proceed. This communication is illustrated in Frames 7-9 (Trace 6.9.4c). In Frame 7, the client initiates the three-way handshake with SYN, ISN = 0. The Sun responds in Frame 8 with SYN, ISN = 2339991040, ACK = 1. The client then confirms the connection in Frame 9 with ACK, SEQ = 1, ACK = 2339991041. The workstation and server are now logically configured for a connection to port 23 (TELNET). As a final note, look at the ATM Cell Header and observe that the virtual circuit that was established between the ATM switch and the router is now in use (VPI = 0, VCI = 34).

Sniffer Network Analyzer data from 23-Jan at 14:46:34, JIM02.ATC, Pg 1

- - - - - - - - - - - - - - - - Frame 7 - - - - - - - - - - - - - - - - -

```
ATM: ——— ATM Cell Header ——-
ATM:
ATM: Frame 7 arrived at  14:48:45.92383 ; frame size is 52 (0034 hex) bytes.
ATM: Link = DTE
ATM: Virtual path id = 0
ATM: Virtual channel id = 34
ATM:
LLC: ——- LLC Header ——-
LLC:
LLC: DSAP Address = AA, DSAP IG Bit = 00 (Individual Address)
LLC: SSAP Address = AA, SSAP CR Bit = 00 (Command)
LLC: Unnumbered frame: UI
LLC:
SNAP: ——- SNAP Header ——-
SNAP:
SNAP: Type = 0800 (IP)
SNAP:
IP:  ——- IP Header ——-
IP:
IP:  Version = 4, header length = 20 bytes
IP:  Type of service = 00
IP:     000. .... = routine
IP:     ...0 .... = normal delay
IP:     .... 0... = normal throughput
IP:     .... .0.. = normal reliability
IP:  Total length   = 44 bytes
IP:  Identification  = 60067
IP:  Flags      = 0X
IP:     .0.. .... = may fragment
IP:     ..0. .... = last fragment
```

```
IP:  Fragment offset = 0 bytes
IP:  Time to live   = 31 seconds/hops
IP:  Protocol       = 6 (TCP)
IP:  Header checksum = 8CE4 (correct)
IP:  Source address    = [XXX.YYY.113.95]
IP:  Destination address = [XXX.YYY.112.90]
IP:  No options
IP:
TCP: ——— TCP header ———
TCP:
TCP: Source port       = 1405
TCP: Destination port     = 23 (Telnet)
TCP: Initial sequence number = 0
TCP: Data offset        = 24 bytes
TCP: Flags            = 02
TCP:          ..0. .... = (No urgent pointer)
TCP:          ...0 .... = (No acknowledgment)
TCP:          .... 0... = (No push)
TCP:          .... .0.. = (No reset)
TCP:          .... ..1. = SYN
TCP:          .... ...0 = (No FIN)
TCP: Window          = 512
TCP: Checksum         = 6C4E (correct)
TCP:
TCP: Options follow
TCP: Maximum segment size   = 1460
TCP:

- - - - - - - - - - - - - - - - Frame 8 - - - - - - - - - - - - - - - - -

ATM: ——— ATM Cell Header ———
ATM:
ATM: Frame 8 arrived at  14:48:45.92584 ; frame size is 52 (0034 hex) bytes.
ATM: Link = DCE
ATM: Virtual path id = 0
ATM: Virtual channel id = 34
ATM:
LLC: ——— LLC Header ———
LLC:
LLC: DSAP Address = AA, DSAP IG Bit = 00 (Individual Address)
LLC: SSAP Address = AA, SSAP CR Bit = 00 (Command)
LLC: Unnumbered frame: UI
LLC:
SNAP: ——— SNAP Header ———
```

404

```
SNAP:
SNAP: Type = 0800 (IP)
SNAP:
IP: —— IP Header ——
IP:
IP:  Version = 4, header length = 20 bytes
IP:  Type of service = 00
IP:      000. .... = routine
IP:      ...0 .... = normal delay
IP:      .... 0... = normal throughput
IP:      .... .0.. = normal reliability
IP:  Total length   = 44 bytes
IP:  Identification = 22919
IP:  Flags          = 4X
IP:      .1.. .... = don't fragment
IP:      ..0. .... = last fragment
IP:  Fragment offset = 0 bytes
IP:  Time to live   = 255 seconds/hops
IP:  Protocol       = 6 (TCP)
IP:  Header checksum = FDFF (correct)
IP:  Source address     = [XXX.YYY.112.90]
IP:  Destination address = [XXX.YYY.113.95]
IP:  No options
IP:
TCP: —— TCP header ——
TCP:
TCP: Source port        = 23 (Telnet)
TCP: Destination port   = 1405
TCP: Initial sequence number = 2339991040
TCP: Acknowledgment number  = 1
TCP: Data offset        = 24 bytes
TCP: Flags          = 12
TCP:          ..0. .... = (No urgent pointer)
TCP:          ...1 .... = Acknowledgment
TCP:          .... 0... = (No push)
TCP:          .... .0.. = (No reset)
TCP:          .... ..1. = SYN
TCP:          .... ...0 = (No FIN)
TCP: Window         = 64240
TCP: Checksum       = 79D2 (correct)
TCP:
TCP: Options follow
TCP: Maximum segment size   = 1460
```

TCP:

- - - - - - - - - - - - - - - - Frame 9 - - - - - - - - - - - - - - - - -

ATM: ——- ATM Cell Header ——-
ATM:
ATM: Frame 9 arrived at 14:48:45.92857 ; frame size is 54 (0036 hex) bytes.
ATM: Link = DTE
ATM: Virtual path id = 0
ATM: Virtual channel id = 34
ATM:
LLC: ——- LLC Header ——-
LLC:
LLC: DSAP Address = AA, DSAP IG Bit = 00 (Individual Address)
LLC: SSAP Address = AA, SSAP CR Bit = 00 (Command)
LLC: Unnumbered frame: UI
LLC:
SNAP: ——- SNAP Header ——-
SNAP:
SNAP: Type = 0800 (IP)
SNAP:
IP: ——- IP Header ——-
IP:
IP: Version = 4, header length = 20 bytes
IP: Type of service = 00
IP: 000. .... = routine
IP: ...0 .... = normal delay
IP: .... 0... = normal throughput
IP: .... .0.. = normal reliability
IP: Total length   = 40 bytes
IP: Identification = 60068
IP: Flags   = 0X
IP: .0.. .... = may fragment
IP: ..0. .... = last fragment
IP: Fragment offset = 0 bytes
IP: Time to live   = 31 seconds/hops
IP: Protocol   = 6 (TCP)
IP: Header checksum = 8CE7 (correct)
IP: Source address   = [XXX.YYY.113.95]
IP: Destination address = [XXX.YYY.112.90]
IP: No options
IP:
TCP: ——- TCP header ——-
TCP:

406

```
TCP: Source port        = 1405
TCP: Destination port    = 23 (Telnet)
TCP: Sequence number      = 1
TCP: Acknowledgment number  = 2339991041
TCP: Data offset          = 20 bytes
TCP: Flags              = 18
TCP:          ..0. .... = (No urgent pointer)
TCP:          ...1 .... = Acknowledgment
TCP:          .... 1... = Push
TCP:          .... .0.. = (No reset)
TCP:          .... ..0. = (No SYN)
TCP:          .... ...0 = (No FIN)
TCP: Window            = 512
TCP: Checksum          = 8A78 (correct)
TCP: No TCP options
TCP:
```

Trace 6.9.4c. TELNET over ATM TCP Three-Way Handshake

The TELNET session then continues until the end users have completed their business. At that time, the TELNET session is terminated, the TCP connection is also terminated, and the ATM connection is then ready to be taken down. The ATM disconnect sequence is shown in Frames 132 and 135 (Trace 6.9.4d). Note that in Frame 132, the call reference (0003D8) matches the call reference of the initial connection in Frame 1, and that the Q.2931 message type is a RELEASE. A single IE specifies the cause of the release (normal). Frame 135 confirms the release with a RELEASE COMPLETE message. As with the previous frame, this message is sent over the signalling channel (VPI = 0 and VCI = 5.)

In summary, TCP/IP communication over a connection-oriented network such as ATM requires steps for call setup and disconnect that a connectionless network such as an Ethernet does not require. In our next case study, we return to a token ring network example and see how electronic mail communication can present a challenge.

Sniffer Network Analyzer data from 23-Jan at 14:46:34, file JIM02.ATC, Pg 1

- - - - - - - - - - - - - - - - Frame 132 - - - - - - - - - - - - - - - - -

```
ATM: ──── ATM Cell Header ────-
ATM:
ATM: Frame 132 arrived at  14:49:11.93324 ; frame size is 20 (0014 hex) bytes.
ATM: Link = DTE
```

ATM: Virtual path id = 0

ATM: Virtual channel id = 5

ATM:

SSCOP: ——- SSCOP trailer ——-

SSCOP:

SSCOP: Sequenced Data PDU

SSCOP: SD send seq num N(S) = 98

SSCOP:

Q2931: ——- UNI 3.x Signalling ——-

Q2931:

Q2931: Protocol discriminator   = 09

Q2931: Length of call reference = 3 bytes

Q2931: Call reference value   = 0003D8

Q2931: Message type   = 4D (Release)

Q2931: Message type Flag/Action = 80

Q2931:   ...0 .... = flag

Q2931:   .... ..00 = action (Clear call)

Q2931: Message Length   = 6

Q2931:

Q2931: Info element id   = 08 (Cause)

Q2931: Coding Standard/Action = 80

Q2931: 1... .... =   ext

Q2931: .00. .... =   code stand(ITU-T standardized)

Q2931: ...0 0000 =   IE field(not significant)

Q2931: Length of info element = 2 byte(s)

Q2931: Octet 5

Q2931: 1... .... = ext

Q2931: .000 .... = spare

Q2931: .... 0000 = location(User)

Q2931: cause value = normal, unspecified

Q2931:

- - - - - - - - - - - - - - - Frame 135 - - - - - - - - - - - - - - - - -

ATM: ——- ATM Cell Header ——-

ATM:

ATM: Frame 135 arrived at 14:49:11.94152 ; frame size is 20 (0014 hex) bytes.

ATM: Link = DCE

ATM: Virtual path id = 0

ATM: Virtual channel id = 5

ATM:

SSCOP: ——- SSCOP trailer ——-

408

```
SSCOP:
SSCOP: Sequenced Data PDU
SSCOP: SD send seq num N(S) = 98
SSCOP:
Q2931: ——- UNI 3.x Signalling ——-
Q2931:
Q2931: Protocol discriminator   = 09
Q2931: Length of call reference = 3 bytes
Q2931: Call reference value     = 8003D8
Q2931: Message type         = 5A (Release complete)
Q2931: Message type Flag/Action = 80
Q2931:         ...0 .... = flag
Q2931:         .... ..00 = action (Clear call)
Q2931: Message Length        = 6
Q2931:
Q2931: Info element id      = 08 (Cause)
Q2931: Coding Standard/Action = 80
Q2931: 1... .... =       ext
Q2931: .00. .... =       code stand(ITU-T standardized)
Q2931: ...0 0000 =       IE field(not significant)
Q2931: Length of info element = 2 byte(s)
Q2931: Octet 5
Q2931: 1... .... = ext
Q2931: .000 .... = spare
Q2931: .... 0000 = location(User)
Q2931: cause value = normal, unspecified
Q2931:
```

Trace 6.9.4d. TELNET over ATM Connection Release

6.9.5 SMTP Interoperability Problems

One of the premises of any mail system—be it the postal service, voice messaging, or an electronic text system—is that it must be a duplex, not a simplex, operation. Duplex means that if I send you a message, you should be able to reply to me. Let's see what happens when this assumption is invalid.

The network in this case study is a single token ring to which a number of dissimilar workstations are attached (see Figure 6-13). The underlying operating systems are all variants of UNIX running on IBM RS/6000 and Sun SPARCstation II workstations. All of these workstations are implementing an SMTP package and theoretically should be interoperable. Unfortunately, this theory proves incorrect. When the RS/6000 sends a message to the Sun SPARCstation II (SS2), the message is delivered properly. But when the SS2 replies to the message, the delivery fails. The process for each workstation is as follows:

1. The user invokes the workstation's native mail program (Sendmail) to send a message.
2. The Sendmail program invokes SMTP for delivery via the network.
3. The recipient workstation obtains the SMTP message from the network and sends it to its native mail program (also Sendmail in this case).
4. The Sendmail program deposits the message in the recipient user's mailbox.

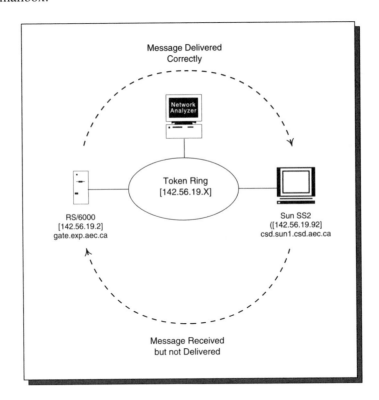

Figure 6-13. Mail Delivery Incompatibilities

The process thus involves two significant operations. One—Steps 1 and 4—is visible to the workstation but invisible to the network, while the other—Steps 2 and 3—is visible to the network but invisible to the workstation.

In Trace 6.9.5, we see the portion that is visible to the network and thus available for capture by the network analyzer (note that this trace was filtered to remove non-SMTP frames, so all frames are not necessarily in sequential order). The first scenario involves the RS/6000 sending a message to the SS2. The following steps are involved:

1. Establishing the SMTP connection:
   HELO <SP> <source mailbox> <CRLF>
   shown in Frames 535-537
2. Identifying the message originator:
   MAIL <SP> FROM: <source mailbox> <CRLF>
   shown in Frames 538-539
3. Identifying the message recipient:
   RCPT <SP> TO: <receiving mailbox> <CRLF>
   shown in Frames 540-541
4. Transferring the text of the message:
   DATA <CRLF>
   shown in Frames 542-548
5. Closing the SMTP connection:
   QUIT <CRLF> shown in Frames 549-550

To verify that the message was delivered, the recipient host (SS2) transmits a "delivering mail..." message in Frame 550. The host process (invisible to the network) then takes over, delivering the mail to the recipient's mailbox. The message appears at the SS2, and all is well.

To verify the connectivity, the SS2 then attempts to reply to the message from the RS/6000. Unfortunately, this operation is unsuccessful and the failure is not readily apparent from the network's point of view. Reviewing Trace 6.9.5, we see a similar mail scenario:

1. Establishing connection: Frames 580-582
2. Identifying originator: Frames 583-594
3. Identifying recipient: Frames 595-597
4. Transferring text: Frames 598-603
5. Closing connection: Frames 604-605

This message was never delivered from the SS2 to the RS/6000, although that isn't readily apparent from the trace file. The clue that a problem existed was found by comparing the acknowledgement messages from the recipients. Recall that the message from the RS/6000 to the SS2 was received and delivered to the end user. The SS2 returned the following message in Frame 548:

```
250 Mail accepted <0D><0A>
```

The message from the SS2 to the RS/6000 was received but not delivered to the end user. The RS/6000 returned the following message in Frame 603:

```
250 Ok <0D><0A>
```

The differences in the two host acknowledgements prompted the network manager, Chris, to check the error log on the RS/6000 host. This is what he found:

```
    —- Transcript of session follows —-
>>> HELO gate.exp.aec.ca
<<< 553 Local configuration error, hostname not recognized as
local
554 <cdutchyn@gate.exp.aec.ca.>... Service unavailable: Bad
file number
    —- Unsent message follows —-
Received: from csd_sun1.csd.aec.ca by gate.exp.aec.ca (AIX
3.1/UCB 5.61/4.03)
          id AA28142; Thu, 16 Apr 92 11:30:44 -0600
Received: by csd_sun1.csd.aec.ca.csd.aec.ca
     id AA00372; Thu, 16 Apr 92 11:37:42 MDT
Date: Thu, 16 Apr 92 11:37:42 MDT
From: cdutchyn@csd.aec.ca (Christopher J. Dutchyn)
Message-Id:
<9204161737.AA00372@csd_sun1.csd.aec.ca.csd.aec.ca>
To: cdutchyn@gate.exp.aec.ca.
Subject: This is a test.
```

```
This is a test response.  If it were a real response, it
would contain more information about what you should know.

Chris
```

The message indicates that the SS2 placed an extra period (.) at the end of the intended recipient's address. Therefore, the recipient was noted as <cdutchyn@gate.exp.aec.ca.> instead of <cdutchyn@gate.exp.aec.ca>. When the address was delivered to the RS/6000 (gate.exp.aec.ca), the RS/6000 was unable to recognize its own address because of the additional period. As a result, the connection failed at the HELO message and the following message was returned:

```
553 Local Configuration error,
    hostname not recognized as local
```

Since this error message occurred in the SMTP process within the RS/6000 host and was never transmitted via the network to the SS2, the message transfer appeared fine from a protocol point of view. Only when the error log of the RS/6000 host was examined did the actual source of the problem (the extraneous period after "ca") surface. Chris then studied the configuration of the SS2 host in greater detail, discovered a configuration error in the name server, and corrected the problem.

Sniffer Network Analyzer data 16-Apr at 10:35:48, file SMTP.TRC, Pg 1

SUMMARY	Delta T	Destination	Source	Summary
535		RS/6000	SUN SS2	SMTP R PORT=2047 220 csd_sun1.csd.aec.ca. csd.aec.ca
536	0.004	SUN SS2	RS/6000	SMTP C PORT=2047 HELO gate.exp.aec.ca <0D><0A>
537	0.007	RS/6000	SUN SS2	SMTP R PORT=2047 250 csd_sun1.csd.aec.ca. csd.aec.ca Hello gate.exp....
538	0.003	SUN SS2	RS/6000	SMTP C PORT=2047 MAIL From:<cdutchyn @gate.exp.aec.ca><0D><0A>

539	0.143	RS/6000	SUN SS2	SMTP R PORT=2047 250 postmaster ... Sender ok<0D><0A>
540	0.012	SUN SS2	RS/6000	SMTP C PORT=2047 RCPT To:<cdutchyn @csd_sun1.csd.aec.ca> <0D><0A>
541	0.111	RS/6000	SUN SS2	SMTP R PORT=2047 250 <cdutchyn @csd_sun1.csd.aec.ca> ... Recipient ok...
542	0.004	SUN SS2	RS/6000	SMTP C PORT=2047 DATA<0D><0A>
543	0.055	RS/6000	SUN SS2	SMTP R PORT=2047 354 Enter mail, end with "." on a line by itself<0D>...
545	0.026	SUN SS2	RS/6000	SMTP C PORT=2047 Received: by gate.exp.aec.ca
547	0.200	SUN SS2	RS/6000	SMTP C PORT=2047 .<0D><0A>
548	0.008	RS/6000	SUN SS2	SMTP R PORT=2047 250 Mail accepted <0D><0A>
549	0.004	SUN SS2	RS/6000	SMTP C PORT=2047 QUIT<0D><0A>
550	0.003	RS/6000	SUN SS2	SMTP R PORT=2047 221 csd_sun1.csd.aec.ca. csd.aec.ca delivering mail...
580	63.636	SUN SS2	RS/6000	SMTP R PORT=1041 220 gate.exp.aec.ca
581	0.006	RS/6000	SUN SS2	SMTP C PORT=1041 HELO csd_sun1.csd.aec.ca. csd.aec.ca<0D><0A>
582	0.007	SUN SS2	RS/6000	SMTP R PORT=1041 250 gate.exp.aec.ca Hello csd_sun1.csd.aec.ca. csd....
583	0.004	RS/6000	SUN SS2	SMTP C PORT=1041 MAIL From:<cdutchyn @csd.aec.ca><0D><0A>

594	1.229	SUN SS2	RS/6000	SMTP R PORT=1041
				250 <cdutchyn
				@csd.aec.ca>...
				Sender ok<0D><0A>
595	0.006	RS/6000	SUN SS2	SMTP C PORT=1041
				RCPT To:<cdutchyn
				@gate.exp.aec.ca.>
				<0D><0A>
597	1.029	SUN SS2	RS/6000	SMTP R PORT=1041
				250 <cdutchyn
				@gate.exp.aec.ca.>
				Recipient ok<0D>...
598	0.004	RS/6000	SUN SS2	SMTP C PORT=1041 DATA<0D><0A>
599	0.018	SUN SS2	RS/6000	SMTP R PORT=1041
				354 Enter mail,
				end with "." on
				a line by itself<0D>...
600	0.016	RS/6000	SUN SS2	SMTP C PORT=1041
				Received: by
				csd_sun1.csd.aec.ca.
				csd.aec.ca.
602	0.035	RS/6000	SUN SS2	SMTP C PORT=1041 .<0D><0A>
603	0.117	SUN SS2	RS/6000	SMTP R PORT=1041
				250 Ok<0D><0A>
604	0.006	RS/6000	SUN SS2	SMTP C PORT=1041 QUIT<0D><0A>
605	0.022	SUN SS2	RS/6000	SMTP R PORT=1041
				221 gate.exp.aec.ca
				closing connection<0D><0A>

Trace 6.9.5. SMTP Mail Service Summary

6.9.6 NetBIOS and TCP Interactions

The following example of NetBIOS service illustrates how all of the ARPA layers must cooperate in order to ensure proper protocol operation. The objective in this case study is for one workstation (shown as Art in Trace 6.9.6a) to use the resources on another workstation, known as Robert. The trace begins with Art broadcasting a NetBIOS Name Service (DNS) Query looking for Robert. Details of the query in Frame 1 of Trace 6.9.6b show a Source port of 275 assigned to NetBIOS service within the UDP header. The query consists of a single question providing the name, type, and class of the object. The response returned in Frame 2 provides necessary details about Robert. These details include the uniqueness of the name and that Robert is a B-type (broadcast) node with an IP address of [XXX.YYY.200.85]. Now that Art knows more about Robert, he can use Robert's resources.

Frames 3-5 show a TCP connection initiated by Art and accepted by Robert. The NetBIOS Session Service begins in Frame 6 and is shown in detail in Trace 6.9.6c. Art begins with a NetBIOS Session Request message (Type = 81) having a length of 74 octets. The data consists of the called and calling names, ROBERT and ARTL, respectively. Robert then responds with a Positive Response (or Session Confirm) message, Type = 82. The logical session is now established.

Art must now negotiate the language he will use to communicate with Robert. To do so, he uses the Server Message Block (SMB) protocol. SMB was developed by Microsoft Corp. to enable a DOS-based client workstation to communicate with its server. SMB information is carried as data inside a NetBIOS message. Speaking in OSI terms, NetBIOS is providing the Session Layer (i.e., logical) connection while SMB information defines the format of the data to be transmitted and thus provides Presentation Layer functions. We see the protocol being negotiated in Frames 9 and 11.

The connection that Art is really after—access to Robert's disk drive—is shown in Frames 13 and 15 (see Trace 6.9.6d). This process is completed in Frame 19. Art may then search the specified directory on Robert's disk (Frame 22), finding one file in Frame 24. A subsequent search (Frame 26) returns ten additional filenames (Frame 28). No more files are noted in Frame 33, prompting Art to his next task: finding the disk attributes (Frames 35 and 38). Finished with his work, Art issues an SMB Disconnection message (Frame 40), which is acknowledged in Frame 42. The TCP connection is then torn down, using the FIN messages from both Art and Robert in Frames 44 and 45, respectively.

Notice the pattern of protocol operation: TCP establishes the end-to-end connection before NetBIOS and SMB undertake the logical session. When there is no longer a need for communication, the higher-layer protocol (SMB) terminates the logical connection and TCP then terminates the end-to-end connection. We will use this process of multi-layer protocol interaction in our final case study, which investigates the operation of a Windows-based workstation.

Sniffer Network Analyzer data 6-Nov at 11:04:32, TCPNETB.ENC, Pg 1

SUMMARY	Delta T	Destination	Source	Summary	
M 1		Broadcast	Art	DNS	C ID=41128
					OP=QUERY NAME=ROBERT
2	0.0018	Art	Robert	DNS	R ID=41128 STAT=OK
3	0.0243	Robert	Art	TCP	D=139 S=257 SYN
					SEQ=172249 LEN=0 WIN=1024
4	0.0028	Art	Robert	TCP	D=257 S=139 SYN
					ACK=172250 SEQ=257461
					LEN=0 WIN=2152
5	0.0160	Robert	Art	TCP	D=139 S=257
					ACK=257462 WIN=1024
6	0.0046	Robert	Art	NETB D=ROBERT S=ARTL<00>
					Session request
7	0.0041	Art	Robert	NETB Session confirm
8	0.0204	Robert	Art	TCP	D=139 S=257
					ACK=257466 WIN=1020
9	0.0106	Robert	Art	SMB C PC NETWORK PROGRAM 1.0
10	0.0043	Art	Robert	TCP	D=257 S=139
					ACK=172391 WIN=2011
11	0.0036	Art	Robert	SMB R Negotiated Protocol 0
12	0.0191	Robert	Art	TCP	D=139 S=257
					ACK=257507 WIN=979
13	0.0096	Robert	Art	SMB C Connect A:\\ROBERT\DISK
14	0.0048	Art	Robert	TCP	D=257 S=139
					ACK=172451 WIN=1951
15	0.0077	Art	Robert	SMB	R T=8F15 Connected
16	0.0138	Robert	Art	TCP	D=139 S=257
					ACK=257550 WIN=936
17	0.0347	Robert	Art	SMB	C End of Process
18	0.0057	Art	Robert	TCP	D=257 S=139
					ACK=172490 WIN=1912
19	0.0057	Art	Robert	SMB	R OK
20	0.0163	Robert	Art	TCP	D=139 S=257
					ACK=257589 WIN=897
21	0.1437	Art	Robert	TCP	D=257 S=139
					ACK=172490 WIN=2152
22	19.4487	Robert	Art	SMB	C Search \????????.???
23	0.0054	Art	Robert	TCP	D=257 S=139
					ACK=172551 WIN=2091
24	0.0157	Art	Robert	SMB	R 1 entry found (done)

25	0.0157	Robert	Art	TCP	D=139 S=257
					ACK=257676 WIN=810
26	0.0676	Robert	Art	SMB	C Search \????????.???
27	0.0054	Art	Robert	TCP	D=257 S=139
					ACK=172612 WIN=2030
28	0.0276	Art	Robert	SMB	R 10 entries found (done)
29	0.0188	Robert	Art	TCP	D=139 S=257
					ACK=258150 WIN=1024
30	0.1490	Art	Robert	TCP	D=257 S=139
					ACK=172612 WIN=2152
31	0.0852	Robert	Art	SMB	C Continue Search
32	0.0052	Art	Robert	TCP	D=257 S=139
					ACK=172681 WIN=2083
33	0.0098	Art	Robert	SMB	R No more files
34	0.0135	Robert	Art	TCP	D=139 S=257
					ACK=258194 WIN=980
35	0.0127	Robert	Art	SMB	C Get Disk Attributes
36	0.0051	Art	Robert	TCP	D=257 S=139
					ACK=172720 WIN=2044
37	0.2589	Art	Robert	TCP	D=257 S=139
					ACK=172720 WIN=2152
38	0.9522	Art	Robert	SMB	R Got Disk Attributes
39	0.0144	Robert	Art	TCP	D=139 S=257
					ACK=258243 WIN=931
40	4.5501	Robert	Art	SMB	C T=8F15 Disconnect
41	0.0059	Art	Robert	TCP	D=257 S=139
					ACK=172759 WIN=2113
42	0.0057	Art	Robert	SMB	R OK
43	0.0173	Robert	Art	TCP	D=139 S=257
					ACK=258282 WIN=892
44	0.0146	Robert	Art	TCP	D=139 S=257 FIN
					ACK=258282 SEQ=172759
					LEN=0 WIN=892
45	0.0029	Art	Robert	TCP	D=257 S=139 FIN
					ACK=172760 SEQ=258282
					LEN=0 WIN=2113
46	0.0116	Robert	Art	TCP	D=139 S=257
					ACK=258283 WIN=892
47	2.5477	Robert	Art	TCP	D=139 S=257
					ACK=258283 WIN=892
48	0.0018	Art	Robert	TCP	D=257 S=139 RST WIN=892

Trace 6.9.6a. NetBIOS over UDP and TCP (Summary)

Sniffer Network Analyzer data 6-Nov at 11:04:32, TCPNETB.ENC, Pg 1

- - - - - - - - - - - - - - - - - Frame 1 - - - - - - - - - - - - - - - - -

DLC: ------ DLC Header ------

DLC:

DLC: Frame 1 arrived at 11:04:51.3527; frame size is 92 (005C hex) bytes.

DLC: Destination = BROADCAST FFFFFFFFFFFF, Broadcast

DLC: Source   = Station Bridge011084, Art

DLC: Ethertype = 0800 (IP)

DLC:

IP: ------ IP Header ------

IP:

IP: Version = 4, header length = 20 bytes

IP: Type of service = 00

IP: 000. .... = routine

IP: ...0 .... = normal delay

IP: .... 0... = normal throughput

IP: .... .0.. = normal reliability

IP: Total length = 78 bytes

IP: Identification = 19

IP: Flags = 0X

IP: .0.. .... = may fragment

IP: ..0. .... = last fragment

IP: Fragment offset = 0 bytes

IP: Time to live = 30 seconds/hops

IP: Protocol = 17 (UDP)

IP: Header checksum = 1420 (correct)

IP: Source address = [XXX.YYY.200.99]

IP: Destination address = [255.255.255.255]

IP: No options

IP:

UDP: ------ UDP Header ------

UDP:

UDP: Source port = 275 (NetBIOS)

UDP: Destination port = 137

UDP: Length = 58

UDP: Checksum = 8153 (correct)

UDP:

DNS: ------ Internet Domain Name Service header ------

DNS:

DNS: ID = 41128

DNS: Flags = 01

DNS: 0... .... = Command

DNS: .000 0... = Query
DNS: .... ..0. = Not truncated
DNS: ....1 = Recursion desired
DNS: Flags = 1X
DNS: ...1 .... = Broadcast packet
DNS: Question count = 1, Answer count = 0
DNS: Authority count = 0, Additional record count = 0
DNS:
DNS: Question section:
DNS: Name = ROBERT
DNS: Type = NetBIOS name service (NetBIOS name,32)
DNS: Class = Internet (IN,1)
DNS:
DNS: [Normal end of "Internet Domain Name Service header".]
DNS:

- - - - - - - - - - - - - - - - Frame 2 - - - - - - - - - - - - - - - - -

DLC: ——- DLC Header ——-
DLC:
DLC: Frame 2 arrived at 11:04:51.3545; frame size is 104 (0068 hex) bytes.
DLC: Destination = Station Bridge011084, Art
DLC: Source   = Station U-B F5D800, Robert
DLC: Ethertype = 0800 (IP)
DLC:
IP: ——- IP Header ——-
IP:
IP: Version = 4, header length = 20 bytes
IP: Type of service = 00
IP: 000. .... = routine
IP: ...0 .... = normal delay
IP: .... 0... = normal throughput
IP: .... .0.. = normal reliability
IP: Total length = 90 bytes
IP: Identification = 18756
IP: Flags = 0X
IP: .0.. .... = may fragment
IP: ..0. .... = last fragment
IP: Fragment offset = 0 bytes
IP: Time to live = 60 seconds/hops

IP: Protocol = 17 (UDP)
IP: Header checksum = 2483 (correct)
IP: Source address = [XXX.YYY.200.85]
IP: Destination address = [XXX.YYY.200.99]
IP: No options
IP:
UDP: ——- UDP Header ——-
UDP:
UDP: Source port = 137 (NetBIOS)
UDP: Destination port = 275
UDP: Length = 70
UDP: Checksum = EC85 (correct)
UDP:
DNS: ——- Internet Domain Name Service header ——-
DNS:
DNS: ID = 41128
DNS: Flags = 85
DNS: 1... .... = Response
DNS: .... .1.. = Authoritative answer
DNS: .000 0... = Query
DNS: .... ..0. = Not truncated
DNS: Flags = 0X
DNS: ...0 .... = Unicast packet
DNS: 0... .... = Recursion not available
DNS: Response code = OK (0)
DNS: Question count = 0, Answer count = 1
DNS: Authority count = 0, Additional record count = 0
DNS: Answer section:
DNS: Name = ROBERT
DNS: Type = NetBIOS name service (NetBIOS name,32)
DNS: Class = Internet (IN,1)
DNS: Time-to-live = 0 (seconds)
DNS: Node flags = 00
DNS: 0... .... = Unique NetBIOS name
DNS: .00. .... = B-type node
DNS: Node address = [XXX.YYY.200.85]
DNS:
DNS: [Normal end of "Internet Domain Name Service header".]
DNS:

Trace 6.9.6b. NetBIOS Name Service Query/Response

Chapter 6: Troubleshooting the Process/Application Connection

Sniffer Network Analyzer data 6-Nov at 11:04:32, TCPNETB.ENC, Pg 1

- - - - - - - - - - - - - - - Frame 6 - - - - - - - - - - - - - - - - -

DLC: ——- DLC Header ——-
DLC:
DLC: Frame 6 arrived at 11:04:51.4023; frame size is 132 (0084 hex) bytes.
DLC: Destination = Station U-B F5D800, Robert
DLC: Source = Station Bridge011084, Art
DLC: Ethertype = 0800 (IP)
DLC:
IP: ——- IP Header ——-
IP:
IP: Version = 4, header length = 20 bytes
IP: Type of service = 00
IP: 000. .... = routine
IP: ...0 .... = normal delay
IP: .... 0... = normal throughput
IP: .... .0.. = normal reliability
IP: Total length = 118 bytes
IP: Identification = 281
IP: Flags = 0X
IP: .0.. .... = may fragment
IP: ..0. .... = last fragment
IP: Fragment offset = 0 bytes
IP: Time to live = 30 seconds/hops
IP: Protocol = 6 (TCP)
IP: Header checksum = 8A9D (correct)
IP: Source address = [XXX.YYY.200.99]
IP: Destination address = [XXX.YYY.200.85]
IP: No options
IP:
TCP: ——- TCP header ——-
TCP:
TCP: Source port = 257
TCP: Destination port = 139
TCP: Sequence number = 172250
TCP: Acknowledgment number = 257462
TCP: Data offset = 20 bytes
TCP: Flags = 10
TCP: ..0. .... = (No urgent pointer)
TCP: ...1 .... = Acknowledgment
TCP: .... 0... = (No push)

422

TCP: .... .0.. = (No reset)
TCP: .... ..0. = (No SYN)
TCP: ....0 = (No FIN)
TCP: Window = 1024
TCP: Checksum = EFCD (correct)
TCP: No TCP options
TCP: [78 byte(s) of data]
TCP:
NETB: ——- NetBIOS Session protocol ——-
NETB:
NETB: Type = 81 (Session request)
NETB: Flags = 00
NETB: Total session packet length = 74
NETB: Called NetBIOS name = ROBERT
NETB: Calling NetBIOS name = ARTL<00>
NETB:

- - - - - - - - - - - - - - - - Frame 7 - - - - - - - - - - - - - - - - -

DLC: ——- DLC Header ——-
DLC:
DLC: Frame 7 arrived at 11:04:51.4065; frame size is 60 (003C hex) bytes.
DLC: Destination = Station Bridge011084, Art
DLC: Source   = Station U-B F5D800, Robert
DLC: Ethertype = 0800 (IP)
DLC:
IP: ——- IP Header ——-
IP:
IP: Version = 4, header length = 20 bytes
IP: Type of service = 00
IP: 000. .... = routine
IP: ...0 .... = normal delay
IP: .... 0... = normal throughput
IP: .... .0.. = normal reliability
IP: Total length = 44 bytes
IP: Identification = 2
IP: Flags = 0X
IP: .0.. .... = may fragment
IP: ..0. .... = last fragment
IP: Fragment offset = 0 bytes
IP: Time to live = 60 seconds/hops
IP: Protocol = 6 (TCP)
IP: Header checksum = 6DFE (correct)

IP: Source address = [XXX.YYY.200.85]
IP: Destination address = [XXX.YYY.200.99]
IP: No options
IP:
TCP: ──── TCP header ────
TCP:
TCP: Source port = 139
TCP: Destination port = 257
TCP: Sequence number = 257462
TCP: Acknowledgment number = 172328
TCP: Data offset = 20 bytes
TCP: Flags = 18
TCP: ..0. .... = (No urgent pointer)
TCP: ...1 .... = Acknowledgment
TCP: .... 1... = Push
TCP: .... .0.. = (No reset)
TCP: .... ..0. = (No SYN)
TCP: ....0 = (No FIN)
TCP: Window = 2074
TCP: Checksum = 8471 (correct)
TCP: No TCP options
TCP: [4 byte(s) of data]
TCP:
NETB: ──── NetBIOS Session protocol ────
NETB:
NETB: Type = 82 (Positive response)
NETB: Flags = 00
NETB: Total session packet length = 0
NETB:

Trace 6.9.6c. NetBIOS Session Request/Confirm

Sniffer Network Analyzer data 6-Nov at 11:04:32, TCPNETB.ENC, Pg 1

- - - - - - - - - - - - - - - Frame 13 - - - - - - - - - - - - - - - -

DLC: ──── DLC Header ────
DLC:
DLC: Frame 13 arrived at 11:04:51.4744; frame size is 114 (0072 hex) bytes.
DLC: Destination = Station U-B   F5D800, Robert
DLC: Source   = Station Bridge011084, Art
DLC: Ethertype = 0800 (IP)
DLC:
IP: ──── IP Header ────

```
IP:
IP:  Version = 4, header length = 20 bytes
IP:  Type of service = 00
IP:            000. .... = routine
IP:            ...0 .... = normal delay
IP:            .... 0... = normal throughput
IP:            .... .0.. = normal reliability
IP:  Total length = 100 bytes
IP:  Identification = 285
IP:  Flags = 0X
IP:  .0.. .... = may fragment
IP:  ..0. .... = last fragment
IP:  Fragment offset = 0 bytes
IP:  Time to live = 30 seconds/hops
IP:  Protocol = 6 (TCP)
IP:  Header checksum = 8AAB (correct)
IP:  Source address = [XXX.YYY.200.99]
IP:  Destination address = [XXX.YYY.200.85]
IP:  No options
IP:
TCP: ——- TCP header ——-
TCP:
TCP:  Source port = 257
TCP:  Destination port = 139
TCP:  Sequence number = 172391
TCP:  Acknowledgment number = 257507
TCP:  Data offset = 20 bytes
TCP:  Flags = 10
TCP:  ..0. .... = (No urgent pointer)
TCP:  ...1 .... = Acknowledgment
TCP:  .... 0... = (No push)
TCP:  .... .0.. = (No reset)
TCP:  .... ..0. = (No SYN)
TCP:  .... ...0 = (No FIN)
TCP:  Window = 979
TCP:  Checksum = D716 (correct)
TCP:  No TCP options
TCP:  [60 byte(s) of data]
TCP:
NETB: ——- NetBIOS Session protocol ——-
NETB:
NETB: Type = 00 (Session data)
NETB: Flags = 00
```

NETB: Total session packet length = 56
NETB:
SMB: —— SMB Tree Connect Command ——
SMB:
SMB: Function = 70 (Tree Connect)
SMB: Tree id   (TID) = 0000
SMB: Process id (PID) = 0000
SMB: File pathname = "\\ROBERT\DISK"
SMB: Password = ""
SMB: Device name = "A:"
SMB:

- - - - - - - - - - - - - - - - Frame 15 - - - - - - - - - - - - - - - - -

DLC: —— DLC Header ——
DLC:
DLC: Frame 15 arrived at 11:04:51.4870; frame size is 97 (0061 hex) bytes.
DLC: Destination = Station Bridge011084, Art
DLC: Source   = Station U-B F5D800, Robert
DLC: Ethertype = 0800 (IP)
DLC:
IP: —— IP Header ——
IP:
IP: Version = 4, header length = 20 bytes
IP: Type of service = 00
IP: 000. .... = routine
IP: ...0 .... = normal delay
IP: .... 0... = normal throughput
IP: .... .0.. = normal reliability
IP: Total length = 83 bytes
IP: Identification = 4
IP: Flags = 0X
IP: .0.. .... = may fragment
IP: ..0. .... = last fragment
IP: Fragment offset = 0 bytes
IP: Time to live = 60 seconds/hops
IP: Protocol = 6 (TCP)
IP: Header checksum = 6DD5 (correct)
IP: Source address = [XXX.YYY.200.85]
IP: Destination address = [XXX.YYY.200.99]
IP: No options
IP:
TCP: —— TCP header ——

```
TCP:
TCP:  Source port = 139
TCP:  Destination port = 257
TCP:  Sequence number = 257507
TCP:  Acknowledgment number = 172451
TCP:  Data offset = 20 bytes
TCP:  Flags = 10
TCP:  ..0. .... = (No urgent pointer)
TCP:  ...1 .... = Acknowledgment
TCP:  .... 0... = (No push)
TCP:  .... .0.. = (No reset)
TCP:  .... ..0. = (No SYN)
TCP:  .... ...0 = (No FIN)
TCP:  Window = 1951
TCP:  Checksum = 97A2 (correct)
TCP:  No TCP options
TCP:  [43 byte(s) of data]
TCP:
NETB: ——- NetBIOS Session protocol ——-
NETB:
NETB: Type = 00 (Session data)
NETB: Flags = 00
NETB: Total session packet length = 39
NETB:
SMB:  ——- SMB Tree Connect Response ——-
SMB:
SMB:  Function = 70 (Tree Connect)
SMB:  Tree id     (TID) = 0000
SMB:  Process id   (PID) = 0000
SMB:  Return code = 0,0 (OK)
SMB:  Maximum transmit size = 8240
SMB:  TID = 8F15
SMB:
```

Trace 6.9.6d. NetBIOS with Server Message Block Information

6.9.7 Implementing Multiple Protocol Stacks

Much has been said about workstation environments that allow the user to perform multiple operations simultaneously, such as printing while working on a spreadsheet. Such environments include IBM's OS/2 and Microsoft's Windows and LAN Manager. In any operating system, the user must be sure that the application is compatible with the environment. When multiple applications are involved, the scenario gets more complex. Let's look at what can happen in an environment that mixes DOS, OS/2, Windows, and a TCP/IP workstation package.

The internetwork in question contains two token rings in two separate locations. One ring contains an OS/2 Server and a number of workstations, and the other ring contains an SNA host. Routers connect the two rings (see Figure 6-14). The network administrator decides to experiment and combine multiple protocol stacks and operating systems on his workstation. For his experiment, he plans to use a TCP/IP workstation package to access the SNA host via the router. His workstation is running Windows, and the DOS-based TCP/IP workstation package resides on an OS/2 Server.

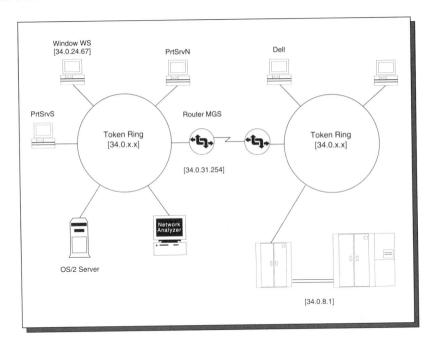

Figure 6-14. Multi-protocol Environment

Trace 6.9.7a begins with the Windows workstation (shown as Windows WS) entering the token ring. Frames 1 through 7 show the workstation transmitting two MAC Duplicate Address Test frames, reporting a change in its Stored Upstream Address (SUA) to the Configuration Report Server (CRS), and obtaining its initialization parameters from the Ring Parameter Server (RPS). Beginning in Frame 8, the Windows workstation begins to log into the OS/2 Server, known as ISCSWEST. NetBIOS Name Service messages verify the various names that Windows WS requires. A NetBIOS session is initialized in Frame 35 and confirmed in Frame 37. The protocol is then negotiated (Frames 39 and 43) and the SMB connection established (Frames 47 and 51). Subsequent Frames 52 through 470 (not shown) complete the login and establish a session with a print server, PrtSrv S. Beginning in Frame 471, a connection is made to a second print server, PrtSrv N. This connection follows a similar sequence of events: find the name (Frame 471), initialize the session (Frame 477), negotiate the protocol (Frame 481), and establish the connection (Frame 489). The workstation is then idle for a few seconds while the administrator ponders his next move.

The administrator starts Windows, shown in Frame 519. The TCP/IP workstation program that is required to access the remote SNA host is resident on the OS/2 Server. Since that program is DOS-based, the administrator opens a DOS Window and begins to load the file (shown as PFTP in Frame 582). The file opens properly (Frame 586), is read from the OS/2 Server (Frames 597 through 864, not shown in the trace), and closes (Frames 865 through 868). The Windows workstation is now ready to connect to the remote host using FTP. The workstation [34.0.24.67] broadcasts an ARP looking for the router that can connect it to the host [34.0.31.254]. It finds the router (Frame 874) and establishes a TCP connection (Frames 875 through 877) to Port = 5044. A second TCP connection to Port = 5054 is established (Frames 913 through 917), but is terminated shortly thereafter (Frames 922 through 924). The last indication of TCP-related protocol activity is in Frame 926; subsequent frames are NetBIOS Keep Alives (Frame 927), LLC Polls (Frames 928 through 934), and MAC-layer transmissions (Frame 935). It appears that the TCP/IP application is no longer active.

An indication that a problem exists comes in Frame 1001, a Report Soft Error frame (see Trace 6.9.7b). This frame is sent from the Windows workstation to the Ring Error Monitor (REM), indicating receiver congestion. In other words, the receiver of Windows workstation does not have sufficient buffer space for all the data that it is receiving. These MAC Report Soft Error frames continue to be transmitted, with no higher-layer processes active. Note that the remainder of the trace (Frames 1072 through 1093) shows no NetBIOS Session Alive messages and that the Windows workstation does not answer the polls from the OS/2 Server. The workstation has been reduced to its MAC-layer operation.

The problem was traced to an incompatibility between the DOS application, the DOS Window (under Microsoft Windows), and the OS/2 LAN Server. The problem was resolved by operating the TCP/IP workstation program from a DOS-based, rather than a Windows-based, workstation. Multi-layer incompatibilities can produce unusual behaviors!

Sniffer Network Analyzer data 30-May at 10:53:14, TCPWIN.TRC, Pg 1

SUMMARY		Delta T	Destination	Source	Summary
M	1		Windows WS	Windows WS	MAC Duplicate Address Test
	2	0.002	Windows WS	Windows WS	MAC Duplicate Address Test
	3	0.490	Config Srv	Windows WS	MAC Report SUA Change
	4	0.012	Broadcast	Windows WS	MAC Standby Monitor Present
	5	0.000	Param Server	Windows WS	MAC Request Initialization
	6	0.005	Windows WS	Station RPS.	MAC Initialize Ring Station
	7	0.000	Station RPS.	Windows WS	MAC Response
	8	0.010	NetBIOS	Windows WS	NETB Check name ISCW7166<00>
	9	0.990	NetBIOS	Windows WS	NETB Check name ISCW7166<00>
	10	0.499	NetBIOS	Windows WS	NETB Check name ISCW7166<00>
	11	0.500	NetBIOS	Windows WS	NETB Check name ISCW7166<00>
	12	0.499	NetBIOS	Windows WS	NETB Check name ISCW7166<00>
	13	0.499	NetBIOS	Windows WS	NETB Check name ISCW7166<00>
	14	0.500	NetBIOS	Windows WS	NETB Check group ISCDWEST<00>
	15	0.999	NetBIOS	Windows WS	NETB Check group ISCDWEST<00>
	16	0.499	NetBIOS	Windows WS	NETB Check group ISCDWEST<00>
	17	0.499	NetBIOS	Windows WS	NETB Check group ISCDWEST<00>
	18	0.499	NetBIOS	Windows WS	NETB Check group ISCDWEST<00>
	19	0.499	NetBIOS	Windows WS	NETB Check group ISCDWEST<00>
	20	0.486	Broadcast	Windows WS	MAC Standby Monitor Present
	21	6.373	NetBIOS	Windows WS	NETB Check name DATZ343
	22	0.624	Broadcast	Windows WS	MAC Standby Monitor Present
	23	0.013	NetBIOS	Windows WS	NETB Check name DATZ343 ISCDWES
	24	0.499	NetBIOS	Windows WS	NETB Check name DATZ343 ISCDWES
	25	0.500	NetBIOS	Windows WS	NETB Check name DATZ343 ISCDWES
	26	0.499	NetBIOS	Windows WS	NETB Check name DATZ343 ISCDWES
	27	0.499	NetBIOS	Windows WS	NETB Check name DATZ343 ISCDWES

28	0.529	NetBIOS	Windows WS	SMB C Transaction
				\MAILSLOT\NET\NETLOGON
29	0.144	NetBIOS	Windows WS	NETB Find name ISCSWEST
30	0.002	Windows WS	OS/2 Server	NETB Name ISCSWEST recognized
31	0.001	OS/2 Server	Windows WS	LLC C D=F0 S=F0 SABME P
32	0.001	Windows WS	OS/2 Server	LLC R D=F0 S=F0 UA F
33	0.000	OS/2 Server	Windows WS	LLC C D=F0 S=F0 RR NR=0 P
34	0.000	Windows WS	OS/2 Server	LLC R D=F0 S=F0 RR NR=0 F
35	0.000	OS/2 Server	Windows WS	NETB D=21 S=01 Session init
36	0.001	Windows WS	OS/2 Server	LLC R D=F0 S=F0 RR NR=1
37	0.000	Windows WS	OS/2 Server	NETB D=01 S=21 Session conf
38	0.000	OS/2 Server	Windows WS	LLC R D=F0 S=F0 RR NR=1
39	0.002	OS/2 Server	Windows WS	SMB C PC NET PGM 1.0 (more)
40	0.001	Windows WS	OS/2 Server	LLC R D=F0 S=F0 RR NR=2
41	0.000	Windows WS	OS/2 Server	NETB D=01 S=21 Data ACK
42	0.000	OS/2 Server	Windows WS	LLC R D=F0 S=F0 RR NR=2
43	0.009	Windows WS	OS/2 Server	SMB R Negotiated Protocol 4
44	0.000	OS/2 Server	Windows WS	LLC R D=F0 S=F0 RR NR=3
45	0.001	OS/2 Server	Windows WS	NETB D=21 S=01 Data ACK
46	0.001	Windows WS	OS/2 Server	LLC R D=F0 S=F0 RR NR=3
47	0.002	OS/2 Server	Windows WS	SMB C Setup account DATZ343
				SMB C Connect
				?????\\ISCSWEST\IPC$
48	0.001	Windows WS	OS/2 Server	LLC R D=F0 S=F0 RR NR=4
49	0.000	Windows WS	OS/2 Server	NETB D=01 S=21 Data ACK
50	0.000	OS/2 Server	Windows WS	LLC R D=F0 S=F0 RR NR=4
51	0.056	Windows WS	OS/2 Server	SMB R Setup
				SMB R IPC Connected
.				
.				
.				
471	0.004	NetBIOS	Windows WS	NETB Find name PRTSRVN
472	0.003	Windows WS	PrtSvrN	NETB Name PRTSRVN recognized
473	0.001	PrtSvrN	Windows WS	LLC C D=F0 S=F0 SABME P
474	0.001	Windows WS	PrtSvrN	LLC R D=F0 S=F0 UA F
475	0.000	PrtSvrN	Windows WS	LLC C D=F0 S=F0 RR NR=0 P
476	0.000	Windows WS	PrtSvrN	LLC R D=F0 S=F0 RR NR=0 F
477	0.000	PrtSvrN	Windows WS	NETB D=F6 S=04 Session init
478	0.001	Windows WS	PrtSvrN	LLC R D=F0 S=F0 RR NR=1
479	0.001	Windows WS	PrtSvrN	NETB D=04 S=F6 Session conf
480	0.000	PrtSvrN	Windows WS	LLC R D=F0 S=F0 RR NR=1
481	0.002	PrtSvrN	Windows WS	SMB C PC NET PGM 1.0 (more)

482	0.001	Windows WS	PrtSvrN	LLC R D=F0 S=F0 RR NR=2
483	0.001	Windows WS	PrtSvrN	NETB D=04 S=F6 Data ACK
484	0.000	PrtSvrN	Windows WS	LLC R D=F0 S=F0 RR NR=2
485	0.004	Windows WS	PrtSvrN	SMB R Negotiated Protocol 0
486	0.000	PrtSvrN	Windows WS	LLC R D=F0 S=F0 RR NR=3
487	0.001	PrtSvrN	Windows WS	NETB D=F6 S=04 Data ACK
488	0.001	Windows WS	PrtSvrN	LLC R D=F0 S=F0 RR NR=3
489	0.001	PrtSvrN	Windows WS	SMB C Connect
				LPT1:\\PRTSRVN\LASER3N
490	0.001	Windows WS	PrtSvrN	LLC R D=F0 S=F0 RR NR=4
491	0.001	Windows WS	PrtSvrN	NETB D=04 S=F6 Data ACK
492	0.000	PrtSvrN	Windows WS	LLC R D=F0 S=F0 RR NR=4
493	0.008	Windows WS	PrtSvrN	SMB R T=11D1 Connected
494	0.000	PrtSvrN	Windows WS	LLC R D=F0 S=F0 RR NR=5
495	0.001	PrtSvrN	Windows WS	NETB D=F6 S=04 Data ACK

.
.

.

519	0.727	OS/2 Server	Windows WS	SMB C Open \BIN\WINSTART.BAT
520	0.001	Windows WS	OS/2 Server	LLC R D=F0 S=F0 RR NR=87
521	0.000	Windows WS	OS/2 Server	NETB D=02 S=22 Data ACK
522	0.001	OS/2 Server	Windows WS	LLC R D=F0 S=F0 RR NR=92

.
.

.

582	1.248	OS/2 Server	Windows WS	SMB C Open \BIN\PFTP.EXE
583	0.001	Windows WS	OS/2 Server	LLC R D=F0 S=F0 RR NR=90
584	0.000	Windows WS	OS/2 Server	NETB D=02 S=22 Data ACK
585	0.002	OS/2 Server	Windows WS	LLC R D=F0 S=F0 RR NR=95
586	0.043	Windows WS	OS/2 Server	SMB R F=0016 Opened
587	0.001	OS/2 Server	Windows WS	LLC R D=F0 S=F0 RR NR=96
588	0.004	OS/2 Server	Windows WS	NETB D=22 S=02 Data ACK
589	0.000	Windows WS	OS/2 Server	LLC R D=F0 S=F0 RR NR=91
590	0.014	OS/2 Server	Windows WS	SMB C F=0016 Rd Bk Raw 64 at 0
591	0.002	Windows WS	OS/2 Server	NETB D=02 S=22 Data ACK
592	0.000	Windows WS	OS/2 Server	LLC R D=F0 S=F0 RR NR=92
593	0.001	Windows WS	OS/2 Server	NETB D=02 S=22 Data, 64 bytes
594	0.000	OS/2 Server	Windows WS	LLC R D=F0 S=F0 RR NR=97
595	0.001	OS/2 Server	Windows WS	LLC R D=F0 S=F0 RR NR=98
596	0.003	OS/2 Server	Windows WS	NETB D=22 S=02 Data ACK

.
.

.

865	0.007	OS/2 Server	Windows WS	SMB C F=0016 Close
866	0.001	Windows WS	OS/2 Server	LLC R D=F0 S=F0 RR NR=118
867	0.000	Windows WS	OS/2 Server	NETB D=02 S=22 Data ACK
868	0.003	Windows WS	OS/2 Server	SMB R Closed
869	0.000	OS/2 Server	Windows WS	LLC R D=F0 S=F0 RR NR=77
870	0.002	OS/2 Server	Windows WS	LLC R D=F0 S=F0 RR NR=78
871	0.004	OS/2 Server	Windows WS	NETB D=22 S=02 Data ACK
872	0.001	Windows WS	OS/2 Server	LLC R D=F0 S=F0 RR NR=119
873	0.124	Broadcast	Windows WS	ARP C PA=[34.0.31.254] PRO=IP
874	0.001	Windows WS	Router MGS	ARP R PA=[34.0.31.254]
				HA=00003000EF30 PRO=IP
875	0.014	Router MGS	Windows WS	TCP D=21 S=5044 SYN SEQ=0
				LEN=0 WIN=512
876	0.071	Windows WS	Router MGS	TCP D=5044 S=21 SYN ACK=1
				SEQ=76544276 LEN=0 WIN=8192
877	0.009	Router MGS	Windows WS	TCP D=21 S=5044
				ACK=76544277 WIN=512
878	0.066	Windows WS	Router MGS	FTP R PORT=5044
				220-FTPSERVE at ISCH00ARNA,
				11:01:08 on 05/30/91<0D>...
879	0.010	Router MGS	Windows WS	TCP D=21 S=5044
				ACK=76544387 WIN=511
880	0.585	PrtSvrS	Windows WS	LLC C D=F0 S=F0 RR NR=5 P
881	0.000	Windows WS	PrtSvrS	LLC R D=F0 S=F0 RR NR=6 F
882	2.006	Broadcast	Windows WS	MAC Standby Monitor Present
883	0.689	Broadcast	Windows WS	MAC Standby Monitor Present
884	0.301	OS/2 Server	Windows WS	LLC C D=F0 S=F0 RR NR=78 P
885	0.000	PrtSvrN	Windows WS	LLC C D=F0 S=F0 RR NR=6 P
886	0.000	Windows WS	OS/2 Server	LLC R D=F0 S=F0 RR NR=119 F
887	0.000	Windows WS	PrtSvrN	LLC R D=F0 S=F0 RR NR=6 F
888	0.106	Router MGS	Windows WS	FTP C PORT=5044 USER
				datz343<0D><0A>
889	0.080	Windows WS	Router MGS	TCP D=5044 S=21
				ACK=15 WIN=8178
890	0.015	Windows WS	Router MGS	FTP R PORT=5044 331 Send
				password please.<0D><0A>
891	0.008	Router MGS	Windows WS	TCP D=21 S=5044
				ACK=76544414 WIN=511
892	0.520	Windows WS	PrtSvrS	LLC C D=F0 S=F0 RR NR=6 P
893	0.000	PrtSvrS	Windows WS	LLC R D=F0 S=F0 RR NR=5 F
894	2.305	Router MGS	Windows WS	FTP C PORT=5044 PASS
				puffer<0D><0A>

895	0.036	Windows WS	Router MGS	TCP D=5044 S=21 ACK=28 WIN=8165
896	0.377	Windows WS	Router MGS	FTP R PORT=5044 230 DATZ343 is logged on<0D><0A>
897	0.007	Router MGS	Windows WS	TCP D=21 S=5044 ACK=76544441 WIN=511
898	0.538	PrtSvrS	Windows WS	LLC C D=F0 S=F0 RR NR=5 P
899	0.000	PrtSvrN	Windows WS	LLC C D=F0 S=F0 RR NR=6 P
900	0.000	OS/2 Server	Windows WS	LLC C D=F0 S=F0 RR NR=78 P
901	0.000	Windows WS	PrtSvrS	LLC R D=F0 S=F0 RR NR=6 F
902	0.000	Windows WS	PrtSvrN	LLC R D=F0 S=F0 RR NR=6 F
903	0.000	Windows WS	OS/2 Server	LLC R D=F0 S=F0 RR NR=119 F
904	2.554	Router MGS	Windows WS	FTP C PORT=5044 port 34,0,24,67, 19,190<0D><0A>
905	0.093	Windows WS	Router MGS	TCP D=5044 S=21 ACK=52 WIN=8141
906	0.012	Windows WS	Router MGS	FTP R PORT=5044 200 Port request OK.<0D><0A>
907	0.004	Broadcast	Windows WS	MAC Standby Monitor Present
908	0.004	Router MGS	Windows WS	TCP D=21 S=5044 ACK=76544463 WIN=511
909	0.039	Router MGS	Windows WS	FTP C PORT=5044 LIST<0D><0A>
910	0.048	Windows WS	Router MGS	TCP D=5044 S=21 ACK=58 WIN=8135
911	0.971	Windows WS	PrtSvrS	LLC C D=F0 S=F0 RR NR=6 P
912	0.000	PrtSvrS	Windows WS	LLC R D=F0 S=F0 RR NR=5 F
913	0.217	Windows WS	Router MGS	TCP D=5054 S=20 SYN SEQ=167535876 LEN=0 WIN=8192
914	0.007	Router MGS	Windows WS	TCP D=20 S=5054 SYN ACK=167535877 SEQ=0 LEN=0 WIN=512
915	0.004	Windows WS	Router MGS	FTP R PORT=5044 125 List started OK.<0D><0A>
916	0.008	Router MGS	Windows WS	TCP D=21 S=5044 ACK=76544485 WIN=511
917	0.025	Windows WS	Router MGS	TCP D=5054 S=20 ACK=1 WIN=8192
918	0.004	OS/2 Server	Windows WS	LLC C D=F0 S=F0 RR NR=78 P
919	0.000	PrtSvrN	Windows WS	LLC C D=F0 S=F0 RR NR=6 P
920	0.000	Windows WS	OS/2 Server	LLC R D=F0 S=F0 RR NR=119 F
921	0.000	Windows WS	PrtSvrN	LLC R D=F0 S=F0 RR NR=6 F

922	0.055	Windows WS	Router MGS	TCP D=5054 S=20 FIN ACK=1
				SEQ=167535877
				LEN=187 WIN=8192
923	0.008	Router MGS	Windows WS	TCP D=20 S=5054 FIN
				ACK=167536065 SEQ=1
				LEN=0 WIN=511
924	0.044	Windows WS	Router MGS	TCP D=5054 S=20
				ACK=2 WIN=8191
925	0.014	Windows WS	Router MGS	FTP R PORT=5044 250
				List completed
				successfully.<0D><0A>
926	0.166	Router MGS	Windows WS	TCP D=21 S=5044
				ACK=76544519 WIN=511
927	1.447	Windows WS	PrtSvrS	NETB Session alive
928	0.001	PrtSvrS	Windows WS	LLC R D=F0 S=F0 RR NR=6
929	2.259	PrtSvrN	Windows WS	LLC C D=F0 S=F0 RR NR=6 P
930	0.000	OS/2 Server	Windows WS	LLC C D=F0 S=F0 RR NR=78 P
931	0.000	Windows WS	PrtSvrN	LLC R D=F0 S=F0 RR NR=6 F
932	0.000	Windows WS	OS/2 Server	LLC R D=F0 S=F0 RR NR=119 F
933	0.998	PrtSvrS	Windows WS	LLC C D=F0 S=F0 RR NR=6 P
934	0.000	Windows WS	PrtSvrS	LLC R D=F0 S=F0 RR NR=6 F
935	0.667	Broadcast	Windows WS	MAC Standby Monitor Present
.				
.				
.				
996	0.215	Broadcast	Windows WS	MAC Standby Monitor Present
997	0.567	Windows WS	PrtSvrN	NETB Session alive
998	0.414	PrtSvrN	Windows WS	LLC C D=F0 S=F0 RR NR=6 P
999	0.000	Windows WS	PrtSvrN	LLC R D=F0 S=F0 RR NR=6 F
1000	0.670	Windows WS	PrtSvrN	LLC C D=F0 S=F0 RR NR=6 P
1001	0.328	Error Mon.	Windows WS	MAC Report Soft Error
.				
.				
.				
1071	0.678	Error Mon.	Windows WS	MAC Report Soft Error
1072	0.046	Windows WS	PrtSvrS	LLC C D=F0 S=F0 RR NR=6 P
1073	0.273	PrtSvrS	Windows WS	LLC C D=F0 S=F0 RR NR=6 P
1074	0.000	OS/2 Server	Windows WS	LLC C D=F0 S=F0 RR NR=78 P
1075	0.000	Windows WS	PrtSvrS	LLC R D=F0 S=F0 RR NR=6 F
1076	0.000	Windows WS	OS/2 Server	LLC R D=F0 S=F0 RR NR=119 F
1077	0.053	Windows WS	OS/2 Server	LLC C D=F0 S=F0 RR NR=119 P
1078	0.675	Windows WS	PrtSvrS	LLC R D=F0 S=F0 DM
1079	1.189	Error Mon.	Windows WS	MAC Report Soft Error

1080	0.087	Broadcast	Windows WS	MAC Standby Monitor Present
1081	1.047	Windows WS	OS/2 Server	LLC C D=F0 S=F0 RR NR=119 P
1082	1.904	Error Mon.	Windows WS	MAC Report Soft Error
1083	1.095	Windows WS	OS/2 Server	LLC C D=F0 S=F0 RR NR=119 P
1084	2.184	Error Mon.	Windows WS	MAC Report Soft Error
1085	0.777	Broadcast	Windows WS	MAC Standby Monitor Present
1086	0.037	Windows WS	OS/2 Server	LLC C D=F0 S=F0 RR NR=119 P
1087	2.183	Error Mon.	Windows WS	MAC Report Soft Error
1088	0.815	Windows WS	OS/2 Server	LLC C D=F0 S=F0 RR NR=119 P
1089	2.183	Error Mon.	Windows WS	MAC Report Soft Error
1090	0.815	Windows WS	OS/2 Server	LLC C D=F0 S=F0 RR NR=119 P
1091	0.961	Broadcast	Windows WS	MAC Standby Monitor Present
1092	1.221	Error Mon.	Windows WS	MAC Report Soft Error
1093	0.815	Windows WS	OS/2 Server	LLC C D=F0 S=F0 RR NR=119 P

Trace 6.9.7a.   TCP/IP Protocols Under Windows (Summary)

Sniffer Network Analyzer data 30-May at 10:53:14, TCPWIN.TRC, Pg 1

- - - - - - - - - - - - - Frame 1001 - - - - - - - - - - - - - - - - -

DLC: ——- DLC Header ——-
DLC:
DLC: Frame 1001 arrived at 10:56:07.766; frame size is 48 (0030 hex) bytes.
DLC: AC: Frame priority 0, Reservation priority 0, Monitor count 1
DLC: FC: MAC frame, PCF attention code: None
DLC: FS: Addr recognized indicators: 00, Frame copied indicators: 00
DLC: Destination = Functional address C00000000008, Error Mon.
DLC: Source   = Station IBM   6B95E7, Windows WS
DLC:
MAC: ——- MAC data ——-
MAC:
MAC: MAC Command: Report Soft Error
MAC: Source: Ring station, Destination: Ring Error Monitor
MAC: Subvector type: Isolating Error Counts
MAC: 0 line errors,   0 internal errors,   0 burst errors
MAC: 0 AC errors,   0 abort delimiters transmitted
MAC: Subvector type: Non-Isolating Error Counts
MAC: 0 lost frame errors, 3 receiver congestion, 0 FC errors
MAC: 0 frequency errors,   0 token errors
MAC: Subvector type: Physical Drop Number 00000000
MAC: Subvector type: Upstream Neighbor Address 400006020014
MAC:

Trace 6.9.7b. Windows Workstation Report Soft Error Details

In this chapter, we have completed our tour of the ARPA protocol stack as far as user applications are concerned. We have one more higher-layer topic to consider: the management of TCP/IP-based internetworks. We will study the Simple Network Management Protocol (SNMP) and Common Management Information Protocol (CMIP) in Chapter 7.

6.10 References

[6-1]   Stallings, William. *Handbook of Computer-Communications Standards*, Vol. 3, second edition. McMillan Publishing Company (Carmel, Indiana), 1990.

[6-2]   Braden, R. "Requirements for Internet Hosts: Application and Support." RFC 1123, October 1989.

[6-3]   Reynolds, J., and J. Postel. "Assigned Numbers." RFC 1700, October 1994.

[6-4]   Sollins, K. R. "The TFTP Protocol (Revision 2)." RFC 1350, July 1992.

[6-5]   Postel, J. "File Transfer Protocol." RFC 959, October 1985.

[6-6]   Romkey, John. "FTP's Tiresome Problems." *ConneXions* (September 1987): 9–11.

[6-7]   Sun Microsystems, Inc. "RPC: Remote Procedure Call Protocol Specification, Version 2." RFC 1057, June 1988.

[6-8]   Sun Microsystems, Inc. "XDR: External Data Representation Standard." RFC 1014, June 1987.

[6-9]   Sun Microsystems, Inc. "NFS: Network File System Protocol Specification." RFC 1094, March 1989.

[6-10] Peacock, Jeffrey. "Two Sound Technologies." *UNIX Review* (March 1991): 18-22.

[6-11] Sanderson, Don. "Distributed File Systems: Stepping Stone to Distributed Computing." *LAN Technology* (May 1991): 41–52.

[6-12] Gerber, Barry. "Distributing Files Unix Style: An NFS Primer." *Network Computing* (December 1991): 88–90.

[6-13] Alderson, Bill, and J. Scott Haugdahl. "NFS Woes Creating Work Nightmare." *Network Computing* (May 15, 1995): 111–112.

[6-14]   Malamud, Carl. *Analyzing Sun Networks*. Van Nostrand Reinhold (New York), 1992.

[6-15]   Postel, J., and J. Reynolds. "TELNET Protocol Specification." RFC 854, May 1983.

[6-16]   Postel, J., and J. Reynolds. "TELNET Option Specifications." RFC 855, May 1983.

[6-17]   Shein, Barry. "The TELNET Protocol." *ConneXions* (October 1989): 32–38.

[6-18]   Postel, J. "Simple Mail Transfer Protocol." RFC 821, August 1982.

[6-19]   Crocker, David H. "Standard for the Format of ARPA Internet Text Messages." RFC 822, August 1982.

[6-20]   Crocker, David. "Back to Basics: Internet Electronic Mail." *ConneXions* (January 1995): 8-17.

[6-21]   Steinke, Steve. "Priority E-Mail." *LAN Magazine* (July 1995): 46–52.

[6-22]   Borenstein, N. and N. Freed. "MIME (Multipurpose Internet Mail Extensions) Part One: Mechanisms for Specifying and Describing the Format of Internet Message Bodies." RFC 1521, September 1993.

[6-23]   Moore, K. "MIME (Multipurpose Internet Mail Extensions) Part Two: Message Header Extensions for Non-ASCII Text." RFC 1522, September 1993.

[6-24]   Robertson, Bruce. "MIME Speaks Volumes." *Network Computing* (November 1, 1994): 135-138.

[6-25]   Haugdahl, J. Scott. *Inside NetBIOS*, third edition. Architecture Technology Corporation (Minneapolis, Minn.), 1992.

[6-26]   NetBIOS Working Group. "Protocol Standard for a NetBIOS Service on TCP/UDP Transport: Concepts and Methods." RFC 1001, March 1987.

[6-27]   NetBIOS Working Group. "Protocol Standard for a NetBIOS Service on a TCP/UDP Transport: Detailed Specifications." RFC 1002, March 1987.

[6-28]   Enger, R., and J. Reynolds. "FYI on a Network Management Tool Catalog: Tools for Monitoring and Debugging TCP/IP Internets and Interconnected Devices." RFC 1470, June 1993.

[6-29]   VanBokkelen, J. "TELNET Terminal-Type Option." RFC 1091, February 1989.

[6-30]   Nasr, Alex. "TN3270: An Interoperability Option." *3TECH, The 3Com Technical Journal* (Winter 1992): 51–59.

[6-31]   Marsh, Bob. "How Important is TN3270 to You?" *Network Computing* (May 1993): 144–148.

Managing the Internet

The term *network management* means different things to different people. A corporate executive might consider the value of his or her internetwork—such as the data and time savings that come from internetworking—and the costs associated with downtime. A vendor sees potential sales opportunities; any incompatibilities between the network management system and the devices to be managed mean a potential opportunity to sell another product or service. Finally, the network manager—the person in the trenches, catching it from users, corporate managers, and vendors—sees "network management" as a dream; it's something he or she will be able to accomplish once all the fires are out and as long as no new fires erupt in the meantime.

So how can network managers find the time to design a plan to save time? Is that manager operating in a *reactive* or *proactive* mode? These issues have faced many managers of TCP/IP-related internetworks, and they undoubtedly gave rise to the development of the most popular protocol for internetwork management: the Simple Network Management Protocol (SNMP). In this chapter, we'll study the alternatives for managing TCP/IP-based internetworks; SNMP, plus other options from ISO and IEEE, both based upon ISO's Common Management Information Protocol, or CMIP.

Over the last few years, a major skirmish has been waged within the network management community regarding Internet (SNMP) vs. ISO (CMIP) network management solutions. (This skirmish is part of a bigger battle, however—the Internet vs. OSI protocol wars. The most famous combatants were TCP/IP and GOSIP (Government Open Systems Interconnection Profile), with TCP/IP being declared the clear winner [7-1].) While the CMIP solution has made some inroads, primarily with the telephone carriers and in Europe, SNMP has gathered extremely widespread support among internetworking vendors of hardware, software, and network management platform products.

We'll begin by discussing the issue of network management in general, and then we'll look at the various protocol alternatives individually. In response to the marketplace directives, however, we will invest the majority of our discussion time on the most popular solution—SNMP.

7.1 Managing Internetworks

All major players in the computing marketplace offer some type of network man-agement system. These vendors include Cabletron Systems, DEC, Hewlett-Packard, IBM, Novell, Intel, and a host of others. The requirement for network management systems undoubtedly grew out of the need to manage numerous terminals that were initially connected to mainframes and later to LANs. Today, network or internetwork management systems assist the human manager in understanding and dealing with the complexities of the internetwork.

Network management systems have many common threads, regardless of their size, shape, or manufacturer. ISO 7498-4 [7-2], which accompanies the Open Systems Interconnection Reference Model (OSI-RM), summarizes these similarities and offers a framework for network management. The standard divides the functions of network management into five Specific Management Functional Areas (SMFAs), shown in Figure 7-1. These include fault management, accounting management, configuration management, performance management, and security management. We'll look at each of these areas individually, although in practice there is some overlap between them.

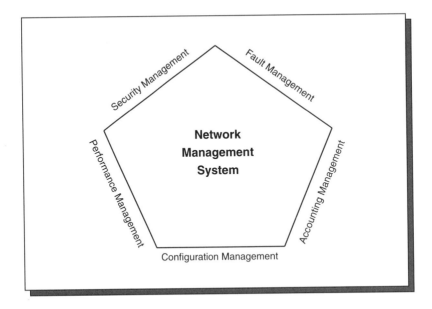

Figure 7-1. The OSI Specific Management Functional Areas

7.1.1 Fault Management

A fault within open systems is defined as something that causes those systems "to fail to meet their operational objectives." Three elements are involved in managing system faults: detection of the fault, isolation of the fault to a particular component, and correction of the fault. Fault management, therefore, may include the maintenance of error logs, error detection processes, and diagnostic testing procedures. For many managers, the term network management is synonymous with fault management.

7.1.2 Accounting Management

As businesses strive to more clearly identify their sources of revenue and expense, the practice of charging individual groups or organizations for their use of network resources is becoming more common. Accounting management provides mechanisms to identify costs, to inform the users of costs incurred, and to associate tariff information with resource use.

7.1.3 Configuration Management

Configuration management involves detailing parameters of network configuration, the current topology, and operational status of the network, as well as associating user names with devices. Also included is the ability to change the configuration of the system when necessary. Medium to large networks often find that the human resource costs necessary to move, add, and change network devices such as terminals (sometimes known as the MAC costs) can be very high.

7.1.4 Performance Management

Performance and fault management are difficult to separate. High performance usually implies a low incidence of faults. Performance management, however, goes beyond minimizing faults; it is responsible for gathering statistics on the operation of the network, maintaining and analyzing logs of the state of the system, and optimizing network operation.

7.1.5 Security Management

With recent news about viruses, worms, and hackers into the Internet, network security has become a new subindustry. The issue of security management includes the ability to create, delete, and control security services; to distribute security-related information; or to report security-related events. Other areas of responsibility include enforcing secure passwords for users; controlling access to subnets or hosts via bridges, routers, or gateways; and providing remote access to network elements for purposes of network diagnostics.

7.1.6 Managing TCP/IP-Based Internetworks

After our discussion about managing open systems, it's logical to ask if there's any difference between managing generic open systems and TCP/IP-based internetworks. Theoretically, the answer is no, since all internetworks are based on some type of layered architecture, be it OSI, ARPA, or SNA. Practically, however, there are big differences. First, there's a difference in perspective: TCP/IP-based internetworks are designed to be multivendor systems; systems built solely upon SNA or DECnet are single-vendor systems. Managers of multivendor systems start with different assumptions than those who purchase all their equipment from one supplier. If you know it's your job (not the vendor's) to integrate all of the subsystems, you'll look at management as an integral part of the internetwork, not an ancillary element.

A second difference lies in the implementation of network management systems and the protocols available for use. Within the Internet community, the Simple Network Management Protocol (SNMP) has gathered the most support from network management system vendors and from internetworking device manufacturers. A second standard, known as the Common Management Information Protocol (CMIP) has received international support from organizations such as the ISO, CCITT, and IEEE. A TCP/IP-based version of CMIP, known as CMOT (CMIP over TCP/IP), is also available as RFC 1189, but it has not gathered the widespread support of SNMP. Both SNMP and CMIP/CMOT are based on an Agent/Manager paradigm, which resembles the Client/Server paradigm with which we are all familiar. We'll study this model in the next section.

In RFC 1052, the Internet Architecture Board (IAB) declared support for the use of both SNMP and CMIP/CMOT; however, industry consensus in the last few years has overwhelmingly moved in favor of the SNMP solution. Various papers in two issues of *ConneXions, The Interoperability Report* provide practical information on the management of TCP/IP-based internetworks [7-3]. Marshall Rose's [7-4] and Uyless Black's

[7-5] books are also valuable references in the network management arena. A companion text, *Managing Internetworks with SNMP* [7-6], illustrates the use of SNMP with a number of protocol analyzer-based case studies.

7.2 The Agent/Manager Model

In the last few years, computing architectures have migrated from centralized, mainframe-based environments to distributed, minicomputer environments to today's popular client/server LAN environments. The architecture of network management systems has mirrored the migration path of computing architectures. They have moved from host-based systems to distributed systems to today's systems, which use a methodology called the Agent/Manager Model (shown in Figure 7-2) that resembles the Client/Server paradigm. (Agent/Manager is also called the Managed System/ Managing System.)

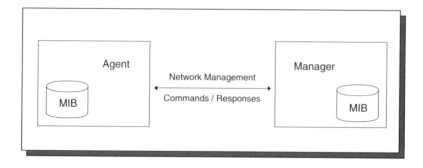

Figure 7-2. The Agent/Manager Model

To begin, the Agent/Manager system manages devices, which are called *objects*. ISO 7498-4 [7-2] defines four characteristics for each object: its attributes, its operations, the notifications it issues, and its relationships with other objects. Thus, the term object goes beyond a physical device to encompass the device's behaviors. The definition for each object is contained in the Management Information Base (MIB), which we will discuss in the next section.

The Agent resides in the object and reports the object's current status to the Manager. Most internetworking products, from the simplest bridge to the most complex ATM switch, come with an embedded SNMP agent.

The Manager is a console that maintains global knowledge of the internetwork in question. The console includes three functions: a Graphical User Interface (GUI), a database, and communications facilities. The GUI enables the human manager to visualize the internetwork. With most systems, the GUI draws a topological map that indicates the location and status (normal, abnormal, alarm, and so on) of each managed element and the links between elements. The console's database keeps track of the internetwork elements and the parameters for those elements. The console also includes a mechanism for communicating with the managed elements using a protocol such as SNMP or CMIP. These three functions enable the Manager to see what is happening on the internetwork, to communicate with the devices being managed to query or modify parameters, and to dynamically oversee the internetwork's operation. Two excellent articles that describe the Agent/Manager paradigm are [7-7] and [7-8].

Two protocols that employ this Agent/Manager paradigm are SNMP and CMIP/CMOT. Over the past few years, a controversy has raged in the internetworking industry over whether the SNMP or the CMIP/CMOT protocol will emerge as the predominant choice for network management. Both have a number of advantages and disadvantages. For example, SNMP is a proven technology, while CMIP is unproven. SNMP is relatively inexpensive in its implementation, while CMIP is not. On the other hand, CMIP is much more powerful than SNMP, although many current internetwork applications are satisfied with SNMP. CMIP is also an international (ISO) standard; SNMP is a de facto (Internet) standard. CMIP is connection-oriented, hence more reliable, while SNMP is connection-less. References [7-9] and [7-10] provide further details on the underlying philosophies of these two protocols; we will look at them individually in Sections 7.4 through 7.6. For a number of years, however, SNMP has been the preferred network management protocol, and for that reason we will concentrate our discussion on SNMP.

Once you've implemented the Agent/Manager paradigm and selected a way to communicate (i.e., SNMP or CMIP) between internetwork elements, you're almost ready to manage the internetwork. The final issue to consider is the type and amount of information you need to keep track of. We will discuss the nature of management information in the next section.

7.3 The SNMP Network Management Process

In the previous section, we discussed how the Agent/Manager model carries network management information between devices on a distributed, managed internetwork.

The type and amount of network management information transmitted over the internet determines the amount of processing and storage the Agent and the Manager will require, and it may also impact the choice of network management protocol—simple (SNMP) or more complex (CMIP/CMOT).

The information is contained within a management system that, because of the complexity of the information being managed, consists of multiple components: the Structure of Management Information (SMI), the Management Information Base (MIB), and the protocol (such as SNMP). The SMI identifies the structures that describe the management information, the MIB details the objects to be managed, and the protocol communicates between Agent and Manager.

In the next few sections, we will look at the SMI, the MIB and the protocol. Readers should be advised that the area of network management in general, and SNMP in particular, is a very dynamic subject, with new elements of the architectures added frequently. With SNMP, two versions of the protocol have been defined: SNMPv1 (1990) and SNMPv2 (1993), plus a revised SNMPv2, often called SNMPv2C, for Community-based SNMP (1996). The original Internet-standard Network Management Framework (SNMPv1) is defined in three documents: the SMI, RFC 1155 [7-11]; the MIB definitions, RFC 1212 [7-12]; and the protocol, RFC 1157 [7-13]. SNMPv2C (which obsoletes the 1993 version of SNMPv2) is defined in eight documents, RFCs 1901–1908, and is known as the SNMPv2 framework. The administrative infrastructure is discussed in RFC 1909, and a user-based security model is defined in RFC 1910.

As of this writing, the vast majority of the SNMP implementations within the internetworking industry have embraced SNMPv1, even though version 2 of the protocol contains significant improvements. These enhancements notwithstanding, we will concentrate our discussion on SNMPv1, but will also describe the improvements that SNMPv2C promises to bring to the network management process.

7.3.1 The Structure of Management Information

Since internetworks can be quite large and can maintain voluminous amounts of information about each device, network managers need a way to organize and manage that information. The SMI provides a mechanism to name and organize objects. The MIB stores the information about each managed object.

The SMI uses a conceptual tree, with various objects representing the leaves, to help users visualize the structure of the Internet. The objects are represented using the concepts from an ISO protocol, known as Abstract Syntax Notation - 1 (ASN.1) [7-14]. The SMI assigns each object a sequence of integers, known as an Object Identifier, to locate its position on the tree (see Figure 7-3).

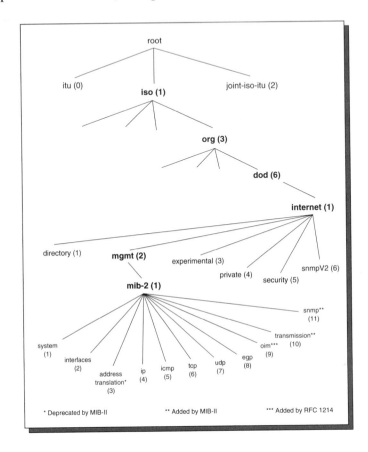

Figure 7-3. The Internet Management Information Base Tree

The root of the tree has no name, but it has three branches called children. Different standards bodies administer different branches: the ITU-T is in charge of Branch 0; ISO administers Branch 1; ITU-T and ISO jointly administer Branch 2.

ISO designates its branch for several organizations. For example, it has given Branch 3 to other international organizations. ISO gives Branch 1 to the U.S. Department of Defense (designated *dod*), which uses it for the Internet objects. So far in the Internet branch, all Object Identifiers begin with {1.3.6.1}, which means that their path from the root is *iso, org, dod, internet*. Historically, Object Identifiers have been enclosed in curly braces, so do designate them as such.

The Internet branch has six subbranches defined: *directory* (1), *mgmt* (2), *experimental* (3), *private* (4), *security* (5), and *SNMPV2* (6). *Directory* is planned for the OSI Directory; *mgmt* is used for objects defined in the Internet Activities Board (IAB)-approved documents; *experimental* is used for Internet experiments; *private* is used to define vendor-specific (or private MIB) objects; *security* is for management security; and *SNMPV2* contains SNMPv2-specific objects (defined as part of the SNMPv2 development, which will be discussed in Section 7.5).

The Internet Assigned Numbers Authority (IANA) administers the *experimental* and *private* branches and documents these administrations in the Assigned Numbers document (currently RFC 1700). IANA designates Branch 1 under the *private* branch for enterprises and assigns vendors an enterprise branch to identify their various devices. For example, an Object Identifier associated with the ABC Company would be designated {1.3.6.1.4.1.a}. The {1.3.6.1} designates the *internet* branch, 4.1 indicates a *private, enterprise* branch, and *a* is assigned to the ABC Company. The ABC Company could further assign identifiers for its bridges, routers, NICs, and so on—for example, {1.3.6.1.4.1.a.1.1}.

In addition to the Object Identifier, the SNMPv1 SMI defines six object (or data) types. These include the NetWorkAddress, IpAddress, Counter, Gauge, TimeTicks, and Opaque. For example, the IpAddress type represents a 32-bit Internet address. Further explanations about the syntax and usage of the types are given in RFC 1155. SNMPv2 defines additional data types, which will be discussed in Section 7.5.

7.3.2 Management Information Base

While the SMI defines the tree structure for the Object Identifiers, the MIB defines information about the actual objects being managed and/or controlled. For example, the MIB might store an IP routing table and its table entries.

Two versions of the Internet MIB for SNMPv1 have been published: MIB-I, RFC 1156 [7-15], and the enhanced MIB-II, RFC 1213 [7-16]. Within each MIB, the objects are divided into various groups. Grouping the objects accomplishes two objectives: it allows a more orderly assignment of Object Identifiers, and it defines the objects that the Agents must implement. The currently defined groups include:

Group	Object ID	Description
system	mib-2 1	Description of that entity.
interfaces	mib-2 2	Number of network interfaces that can send/receive IP datagrams.
at	mib-2 3	Tables of Network Address to Physical Address translations.
ip	mib-2 4	IP routing and datagram statistics.
icmp	mib-2 5	ICMP I/O statistics.
tcp	mib-2 6	TCP connection parameters and statistics.
udp	mib-2 7	UDP traffic statistics and datagram delivery problems.
egp	mib-2 8	EGP traffic, neighbors, and states.
transmission	mib-2 10	Transmission media information (future use).
snmp	mib-2 11	SNMP-related objects.

MIB-II has rendered the Address Translation (AT) group obsolete and has added the Transmission and SNMP groups. MIB-II has also added new values, variables, tables, columns, and so on to other groups. For example, the standard mentions a CMOT Object Identifier (mib-2 9), which is described in RFC 1214 on OSI Internet Management (OIM). Three excellent sources of information on MIBs include Dave Perkins' "How to Read and Use an SNMP MIB" [7-17], Bob Stewart's "Development and Integration of a Management Information Base" [7-18], and 3Com Corporation's Introduction to Simple Network Management Protocol: A Self-Study Guide [7-19].

A number of MIBs, both standard and vendor-specific (private), have been developed. One example is the RMON MIB, used for Remote Network Monitoring. Its functions include managing critical functions of remote networks, such as traffic thresholds, collisions on a particular segment, and alarms. Several RFCs define RMON functions: RMON for Ethernet networks, RFC 1757 [7-20]; RMON extensions to support token ring networks, RFC 1513 [7-21]. In addition, RMON functions supporting upper-layer protocol functions, known as RMON2 are currently under development [7-22]. References [7-23] and [7-24] are recent journal articles that discuss RMON applications.

Below is a representative list of available MIBs. For current information, see the (unofficial) index listed in the Simple Times newsletter [7-25].

RFC	Subject
1156	Management Information Base (MIB-I)
1212	Concise MIB Definitions
1213	Management Information Base (MIB-II)
1214	OSI Internet Management MIB (Historic)
1315	Frame Relay DTE Interface Type MIB
1406	DS1/E1 Interface Type MIB
1407	DS3/E3 Interface Type MIB
1493	Bridge MIB
1512	FDDI Interface Type MIB
1516	IEEE 802.3 Repeater MIB
1525	Source Routing Bridge MIB
1559	DECnet Phase IV MIB
1659	RS-232 Interface Type MIB
1660	Parallel Printer Interface Type MIB
1694	SMDS Interface Protocol (SIP) Interface Type MIB
1695	ATM MIB
1742	AppleTalk MIB
1748	IEEE 802.5 Token Ring Interface Type MIB
1757	Remote Network Monitoring (RMON) MIB
1759	Printer MIB
1850	OSPF version 2 MIB

7.4 Simple Network Management Protocol version 1 (SNMPv1)

So far, we've discussed two of the three elements of a network management system: the Structure of Management Information (SMI) and the Management Information Base (MIB). These elements provide management information and the mechanism for accessing that information. The third element is the protocol used between the Agent and the Manager.

The IAB determined the need for a network management protocol and reported it in RFC 1052 [7-26]. The IAB concluded at that time that SNMP should be used in the short term, with OSI-based management strategies as the long-term solution. Network managers, however, needed solutions that could be implemented immediately. Since

SNMP was available, it became the protocol of choice. Marketplace experience over the last few years has demonstrated the predominance of SNMP over OSI-based solutions, indicating that it has become more than just a short-term solution. Recent SNMP MIB developments, supporting broadband networking solutions, such as frame relay, SMDS and ATM, also testify to the firm foothold that SNMP has gathered within the network management community. Many analysts predict that it will be the favored long-term solution as well.

SNMP, which we will study in this section and in Section 7.5, is used predominantly with TCP/IP-based internets. CMIP/CMOT is intended for OSI-based internetworks and IEEE 802 LANs. We will discuss the OSI and IEEE strategies in Sections 7.6 and 7.7.

7.4.1 SNMPv1 Architecture

The Simple Network Management Protocol was based upon the Simple Gateway Monitoring Protocol (SGMP) described in RFC 1028. It was developed to be an efficient means of sending network management information over a UDP transport using Port numbers 161 (SNMP) and 162 (SNMPTRAP).

Although SNMP is an application, it is somewhat different from the other application protocols discussed in Chapter 6. As articulated by Case et al., "network management is an application fundamentally different in its requirements than any other application that makes use of the network" [7-27]. These differences include network management's needs for ubiquity, supporting instrumentation, and robustness that may not be necessary for other upper-layer processes.

In the SNMP architecture (see Figure 7-4) are several elements that we explored earlier in this chapter. SNMP offers a management system that includes the SNMP Manager. The managed system includes an SNMP Agent, resources to be managed, and the SNMP messages (such as the Get and the GetResponse) that communicate the management information. Note that the protocol implements only five messages—a testimony to the "simple" part of SNMP's name.

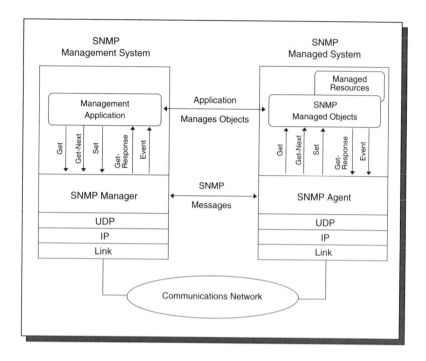

Figure 7-4. Simple Network Management Protocol Version 1 Architecture
(© 1990, IEEE)

7.4.2 SNMPv1 Messages

SNMP is a *polling* protocol in which the Manager asks a question (the poll) and the Agent responds. UDP transport transmits all SNMP messages, and all messages use Port number 161 except the Trap message, which uses Port number 162. The standard does not require SNMP implementations to accept messages that exceed 484 octets in length, although support for larger datagrams is recommended.

The SNMP message follows the UDP header and is placed within a transmission frame (see Figure 7-5). The message consists of a Version Identifier, an SNMP Community name, and the SNMP Protocol Data Units (PDUs). The Version Identifier ensures that both SNMP endpoints use the same version of the protocol. The Community name is encoded as a string of octets and is used for authentication; it ensures the proper relationship between the requesting SNMP Manager and the responding SNMP Agent. The combination of the Version Identifier and the Community name is sometimes called the Authentication header. This header is found in all SNMP messages.

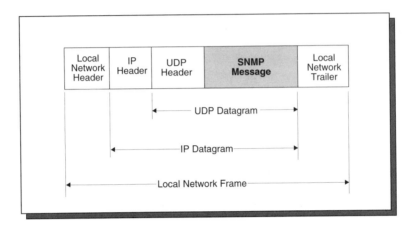

Figure 7-5. SNMP Message within a Transmission Frame

Five PDUs are defined for SNMP. These include GetRequest, GetResponse, GetNextRequest, SetRequest, and Trap. The GetRequest allows the SNMP Manager to access information stored in the Agent. The GetNextRequest is similar, but allows the Manager to obtain multiple values in the tree. SetRequest is used to change the value of a variable. GetResponse is a response to the GetRequest, GetNextRequest, or SetRequest, and also contains error and status information. Finally, the Trap PDU reports on an event that has occurred.

PDUs have two general structures, one for the Request/Response PDUs and another for the Trap (see Figures 7-6a and 7-6b, respectively). The Request/Response PDUs contain five fields that identify and transfer the management information in question. The first subfield is a PDU Type, which specifies which of the five PDUs is in use. The values are:

Value	PDU Type
0	GetRequest
1	GetNextRequest

2	GetResponse
3	SetRequest
4	Trap

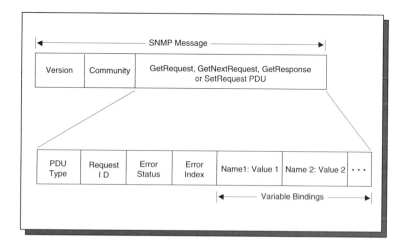

Figure 7-6a. SNMPv1 Get Request, GetNextRequest, GetResponse, and SetRequest PDU Structures

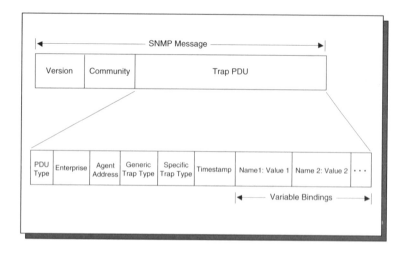

Figure 7-6b. SNMPv1 Trap PDU Structure

The Request ID field correlates the request from the SNMP Manager with the response from the SNMP Agent. The Error Status field indicates that some exception occurred while processing the request. Values for that field are:

Value	Error	Description
0	noError	No error
1	tooBig	Operation results are too big for a single SNMP message
2	noSuchName	Unknown variable name
3	badValue	Incorrect value or variable when using SetRequest
4	readOnly	SetRequest not allowed for read-only variable
5	genErr	Other error

The Error Index field points to the variable in the Variable Bindings field that caused the error. The first variable is given variable number 1, the second variable number 2, and so on. The last field is the Variable Bindings (VarBind) field, which contains the management information being requested. A VarBind pairs an object name with its value. An example of a VarBind would be a sysDescr (System Description) for object {1.3.6.1.2.1.1.1}, paired with a value that indicates the vendor-specified name for that system.

Because the Trap PDU reports on events rather than responding to the manager's query, it requires a different message structure. Seven fields follow the Trap PDU's Version and Community fields (review Figure 7-6b). The first field is the PDU Type, with the Trap assigned Type = 4. The second field is called Enterprise and contains the SNMP Agent's sysObjectID, which indicates the type of network management system located in that Agent. Next, the Agent Address field contains the IP address of the SNMP Agent that generated this trap. The Generic Trap Type specifies the exact type of message. There are seven possible values for this field:

Value	Trap	Description
0	coldStart	The sending protocol entity is reinitializing; the agent configuration or protocol entity implementation may be altered.
1	warmStart	The sending protocol entity is reinitializing; however, no alterations have been made.

2	linkDown	Communication link in the Agent has failed.
3	linkUp	Communication link in the Agent is now up.
4	Authentication Failure	The sending protocol entity has received an improperly authenticated message.
5	egpNeighborLoss	An EGP peer is down.
6	enterpriseSpecific	An enterprise-specific event has occurred, as defined in the Enterprise field that follows.

The Specific Trap Type elaborates on the type of trap indicated. The Timestamp field transmits the current value of the Agent's sysUpTime object, specifying when the indicated event occurred. As with the Request/Response PDUs, the Variable Bindings contain pairs of object names and values. Examples of the various SNMP PDUs will be explored in Section 7.10.

7.5 Simple Network Management Protocol version 2 (SNMPv2)

Despite its popularity, SNMP has some disadvantages. One obvious limitation is SNMP's use of a connectionless architecture based upon UDP transport. As discussed in Chapter 5, connectionless systems lack the reliability many applications may require. Second, it is cumbersome to retrieve SNMP information because the protocol offers no way to filter information. Thus, the SNMP Manager must obtain all the value(s) of the object(s), then determine whether they're of interest. (In contrast, CMIP allows conditional commands that query the value first, then determine whether the value should be transmitted.) Third, and associated with the information retrieval issue, polling of SNMP information (the GetRequest/GetResponse sequences) may consume precious internetwork bandwidth, especially if that polling is done over a WAN connection. Finally, the limited amount of security originally designed into the protocol (via the Community string) is not adequate for many internetwork applications.

As SNMP implementations became more widespread, the inadequacies of this "simple" protocol became more apparent. In 1992, the IETF began the process of formally addressing these issues, which fell into two major categories: protocol enhancements and security enhancements. The results from these two efforts were combined into what became known as SNMPv2, and were published as RFCs 1441–1452 in May 1993. References [7-28] through [7-30] detail the capabilities of SNMPv2.

Unfortunately, these enhancements, particularly in the area of security, were relatively complex. As a result, the marketplace, from both the perspective of the network management platform vendors (with their managers) and the internetworking hardware/software vendors (with their agents), did not readily embrace these enhancements [7-31].

As a result, the IETF went back to the drawing board and modified SNMPv2 to reflect more workable solutions. The results, published in January 1996 in RFCs 1901–1908 [7-32], document that work. The new version has been called SNMPv2C, where the "C" represents a *community-based* administrative framework. An SNMP community is defined in SNMPv1 (RFC 1157) as "a pairing of an SNMP agent with some arbitrary set of SNMP application entities." Further, each of these SNMP communities is named by a string of octets, called the community string. The community string occupies a field within the SNMPv1 that acts like a password, assuring a simple form of security between manager and agent.

In areas not relating to security, the revised version kept many of the original SNMPv2 enhancements. These include the availability of additional data types, the ability to retrieve large amounts of data with a single command (the GETBULK message), and the use of other transport protocols, such as AppleTalk, Novell's IPX, and the OSI Connectionless-mode Network Service (CLNS) and Connection-oriented Network Service (CONS) protocols. In essence, the complex security provisions from SNMPv2 were relaxed, with the other protocol enhancements left largely in place. At the time of this writing there are two proposed security frameworks: SNMPv2u, defined in RFC 1910; and SNMPv2*, currently defined in IETF draft documents. The IETF is continuing to study these security proposals. Another round of protocol enhancements that would finalize the security section is aticipated.

At this writing, however, it is premature to determine if the second pass at SNMPv2 will be more successful than the first, and will therefore provide a clear migration path from SNMPv1. Readers looking for more details on SNMPv2 are directed to RFCs 1901–1910, the *Simple Times* newsletter, (URLs: ftp://ftp.simple-times.org or http://www.simple-times.org) and the IETF mailing list for SNMP (subscribe by sending email to snmp-request@psi.com) or SNMPv2 (subscribe by sending email to snmpv2-request@tis.com).

7.6 Common Management Information Protocol (CMIP/CMOT)

The ISO defined a framework for network management, ISO 7498-4 (discussed in Section 7.1), and the five Specific Management Functional Areas (SMFAs) shown in Figure 7-1. CMIP/CMOT does not have the market acceptance of SNMP; however, for certain applications, such as those that require more rigorous error control, CMIP/CMOT has been used. For completeness in our discussion on network management alternatives, this section briefly describes the attributes of these protocols. Readers should keep in mind that this discussion is primarily for academic, not implementation, purposes.

ISO defines a Management Service interface that allows management applications to communicate within the OSI environment. This interface is the Common Management Information Service (CMIS), described in ISO/IEC 9595 [7-33]. The CMIS services provide for management operation, retrieval of information, and notification of network events. These services, along with the type of service, confirmed (C) or non-confirmed (NC), are listed below:

Service	Type	Description
M-GET	C	Information retrieval.
M-CANCEL-GET	C	Cancel outstanding M-GET.
M-SET	C/NC	Modify management information.
M-ACTION	C/NC	Perform an action.
M-CREATE	C	Create an instance of a managed object.
M-DELETE	C	Delete an instance of a managed object.
M-EVENT-REPORT	C/NC	Report of managed object event.

Mark Klerer's "The OSI Management Architecture: An Overview" [7-34] and Ian Sugarbroad's "An OSI-Based Interoperability Architecture for Managing Hybrid Networks" [7-35] put the OSI network management architectural issues into perspective.

The second half of ISO's network management protocol story is the Common Management Information Protocol (CMIP), defined in ISO/IEC 9596-1 [7-36]. CMIP communicates network management information between systems. This protocol is much more rigorous than SNMP for several reasons. First, it was designed for open systems rather than for a single implementation such as the Internet, which necessarily increases the complexity of the operation. Second, CMIP is an association-oriented protocol, which means that the two CMIP processes must establish an association before sending any management messages. (Recall that SNMP is connectionless.) This association is governed by two ISO Application Layer standards: the Remote Operation Service Element (ROSE) and the Association Control Service Element (ACSE).

The benefits of CMIP's rigor are seen in the services it can perform beyond those available with SNMP. One example is filtering, which allows you to make an operation (such as an M-SET) conditional upon the value of an object's attribute. A second example is scoping, which allows you to apply the management operation to a portion of the object class. These enhancements come with a price, however. The CMIP Agent consumes up to 400 Kbytes of memory, while its SNMP counterpart requires only 10 Kbytes [7-37].

As discussed earlier, the IAB, as reported in RFC 1109, intended to provide a migration path from SNMP to CMIP, allowing TCP/IP-based internetworks to migrate to OSI protocols. RFC 1189 [7-38] defined the protocol portion of this migration—the CMOT (CMIP over TCP/IP) protocol suite. (At the time of this writing, however, RFC 1189 has been classified as "historic", further substantiating the discussion at the beginning of this chapter about the strength of SNMP over CMIP solutions.)

The CMOT protocol suite (see Figure 7-7) uses the Internet protocols at the lower layers while incorporating the OSI management-related protocols, such as CMIP, at the higher layers. Either TCP or UDP may be used at the Transport Layer. Port numbers 163 (CMIP-Manager) and 164 (CMIP-Agent) are used for addressing at those layers. Lightweight Presentation Protocol (LPP), described in RFC 1085 [7-39], is defined for the Presentation Layer. LPP maps the ISO Management Service calls to or from TCP or UDP. Reference [7-40] provides further details on the design of CMOT.

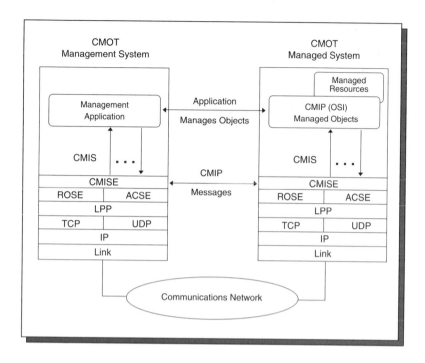

**Figure 7-7. Common Management Information Protocol (CMOT)
over TCP/IP Architecture**
(© 1990, IEEE)

In addition to using the CMIP protocol, the OSI-based network management scheme required modifications to the MIB. In Section 7.3.2, we discussed the Internet standards and private MIBs that support the SNMP and/or CMIP protocols. At one time, the developers attempted to devise an SMI/MIB for use with both SNMP and CMIP. But as the development process got underway, the developers discovered that independent standards would best serve the industry. As a result, they wrote a MIB specifically for OSI Internetwork Management, or OIM: RFC 1214 [7-41]. This MIB was designed as a companion to the Internet MIB-II (RFC 1213) to make the additions necessary to support CMIP. Like CMOT, the OIM MIB has also been designated as "historic."

One of the additions to MIB-II is a branch for OSI Internet Management (OIM). Reviewing Figure 7-3, note that under MIB (1), group number 9 is defined for OIM. This group number is reserved for OIM and has a branch of its own, defined in RFC 1214. The structure of that branch is:

Object	Identifier
cmotVersion:	oim 1
cmotACSEInfo:	oim 2
cmotSystemId:	oim 3
misc:	oim 4
objects:	oim 5
attributes:	oim 6
events:	oim 7
nameforms:	oim 8
actions:	oim 9

Other additions support ISO definitions, names, events, and name hierarchies as required by the OSI Structure of Management Information, designated ISO/IEC DIS 10165-1, 2, and 3. The OSI MIB itself is rather lengthy; readers contemplating a transition to OSI protocol stacks should study that document in its entirety.

Those network managers that plan a transition from TCP/IP and the Internet protocols to an OSI-based architecture may find themselves rather lonely, as the overwhelming choice of the industry has been to support SNMP, not CMIP/CMOT. To further amplify this point, the IETF has declared RFC 1214 "historic," meaning that few, if any, implementations are expected in the future.

7.7 IEEE LAN/MAN Management

The IEEE Project 802 LAN standards, such as 802.3 and 802.5, have been stable since the mid-1980s. With this basic architecture in place, the IEEE has been able to concentrate on the management of existing LANs and on emerging Metropolitan Area Network (MAN) architectures. The IEEE 802.1 standards, specifically 802.1B [7-42], are an outgrowth of those efforts.

The IEEE management structure is based on two other standards: the IEEE 802.2 Logical Link Control (LLC) and the ISO CMIP. It is sometimes referred to as CMOL (CMIP over LLC). The defined protocol uses the LLC connectionless service (called LLC Type 1), with the management information formatted according to the CMIP standard, ISO/IEC 9596-1 [7-36].

As a standards body, the IEEE has focused primarily on the Physical and Data Link Layers, with only a secondary interest in the rest of the OSI protocol stack. This focus extends to the functions it provides for LAN management. These functions are layered above the IEEE LAN/MAN Physical, Medium Access Control, and Logical Link Control Layers (see Figure 7-8).

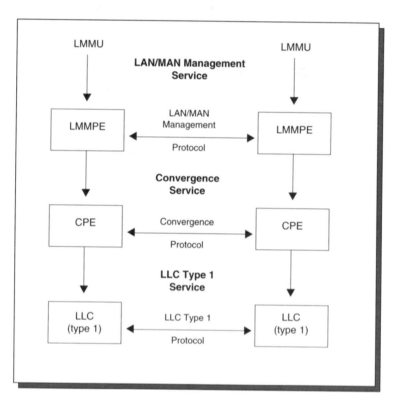

Figure 7-8. LAN/MAN Management Communication Architecture
(© 1992, IEEE)

Three elements are necessary to communicate management information between hosts: the Convergence Protocol Entity (CPE), the LAN/MAN Management Protocol Entity (LMMPE), and the LAN/MAN Management Service (LMMS). The CPE, which uses the Convergence Protocol, is the lowest-layer element. The convergence function allows the two CPEs to be aware of the existence of their peers (detecting reboots, etc.) and to determine whether the information coming from their peers is in sequence and without loss or duplication. The LMMPE uses the LAN/MAN management protocol, derived from CMIP. The LMMS is the management service available to the LAN/MAN Management User (LMMU). LMMS uses the ISO CMIS to define its service offerings. The LMMUs are the Manager and Agent processes.

Like their ISO relatives, the IEEE LAN/MAN management standards have not received wide acceptance in the marketplace, deferring, again, to the strength of SNMP.

7.8 Desktop Management Task Force

The Desktop Management Task Force (DMTF) was founded in 1992 by DEC, Hewlett-Packard, IBM, Intel, Microsoft, Novell, SunConnect (now known as SunSoft), and SynOptics Communications (now known as Bay Networks). The purpose of the DMTF is to develop a standard set of Application Programming Interfaces (APIs) that access and manage desktop systems, components, and related peripherals. At the present time, more than 300 organizations are members of the DMTF.

The Desktop Management Interface (DMI) technology is the management architecture developed by the DMTF (see Figure 7-9). The focus of the DMI is on desktop and LAN management, independent of the hardware system, software operating system, or network operating system in use. DMI is designed to be integrated with all network management protocols and consoles, such as SNMP and CMIP.

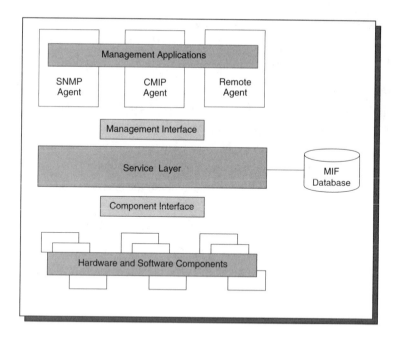

Figure 7-9. Desktop Management Interface
(Courtesy of the Desktop Management Task Force)

The DMI architecture is divided into three layers: the Management Applications Layer, which interfaces with various agents; the Service Layer, which includes the Management Information File (MIF) database; and the Hardware/Software Component Layer, which interfaces with the actual components being managed. Reference [7-43] is a brief tutorial on DMI, and reference [7-44] provides contact information for the DMTF.

7.9 Network Management Systems

At the beginning of this chapter, we mentioned that the network management marketplace is a rapidly growing industry, comprised of a virtual "who's who" of internetworking vendors. The players in this market fall into two general categories: minicomputer and/or mainframe manufacturers, and internetworking device manufacturers. These two types of vendors come to internetwork management from two different perspectives.

The minicomputer/mainframe manufacturers use a host-centric approach to their internetwork management systems. As a result, their systems tend to use proprietary protocols to communicate network management information. For example, IBM's

NetView is based on proprietary protocols and adds SNMP or CMIP/CMOT as required by the elements being managed. In contrast, both Hewlett-Packard and SunSoft base their platforms on the UNIX operating system, using TCP/IP and SNMP extensively.

The second group of players in the network management market are vendors of internetworking devices such as bridges and routers, network operating systems, workstations, protocol analyzers, and other hardware devices. These companies develop SNMP agents for their specific products, such as a LAN switch, but may also develop an application program or suite of programs that integrates with one of the network management platforms. These add-on applications enhance the manageability of the internetworking devices, going beyond the capabilities of SNMP to provide enhanced graphics and topological maps of the internetwork, advanced configuration tools, documentation aides, and other tools.

Survey articles and buyer's guides appear frequently in the journals to assist the network manager in finding the best product for their application. References [7-45] through [7-48] are recent examples of these surveys, while references [7-49] and [7-50] discuss some of the challenges of managing high-speed internetworks.

7.10 Case Study

Our final case study will consider the IEEE 802.3 network shown in Figure 7-10. The SNMP Manager is a PC-based network management application running on a PC. The SNMP Agent is a Xyplex, Inc. 10BASE-T hub card. In their respective specifications, both products claim to be compatible with MIB-I and MIB-II. Let's see if they are compatible with each other.

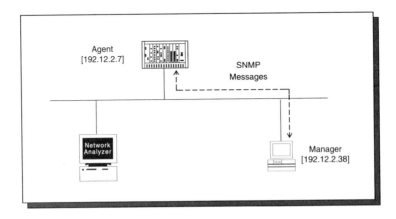

Figure 7-10. SNMP over Ethernet

To confirm compatibility, the network manager, Ross, instructs the SNMP Manager to query the System Group Objects (branch {1.3.6.1.2.1.1} in Figure 7-11). There are seven objects to be queried. The Manager issues requests for these objects in the order in which they appear in the subtree (see Trace 7.10a). The first request (Frame 31) asks for the sysDescr, the next for the sysObjectID and sysUpTime, and so on. Replies from the Agent begin in Frame 37. These identify the Xyplex 10BASE-T Hub, the system up time, the system contact, and so on.

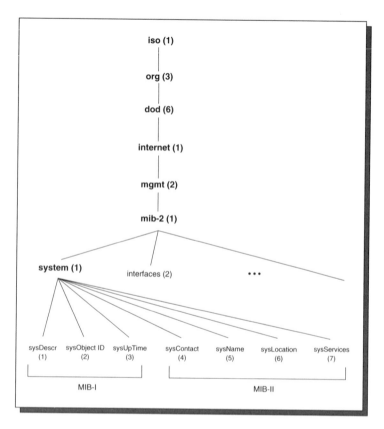

Figure 7-11. Internet MIB Tree for the System Group

Trace 7.10b shows the details of these Request/Response pairs. Note that for every GetRequest from the SNMP Manager, a corresponding GetResponse is returned. Frames 31 and 37 show the details of all protocol layers, which include the IP and UDP headers. Within the UDP header, the Destination port = 161 specifies the SNMP protocol. Also note that the GetNextRequest in Frame 31 uses a Request ID of 227475461. The corresponding response (Frame 37) uses the same number for identification. The next GetNextRequest (Frame 32) uses a different Request ID (227541001), which is repeated in the corresponding GetResponse (Frame 38). This pattern of Request/Response correlation continues through Frame 42.

Satisfied with these results, Ross decides to test the SetRequest PDU in Frame 43. The object that he elects to change is the sysContact, object {1.3.6.1.2.1.1.4.0}. The value of this object contains the name of the person responsible for the local network administration. Ross quickly realizes that he can accomplish two things with this one command: he can verify the compatibility of the two vendors' SNMP message sets, and he can change his own personal job responsibilities by putting someone else's name in this field. To do this, Ross enters the Community name for security purposes, the Object ID {1.3.6.1.2.1.1.4.0}, and the new value of that object (Bob Pjontek). The SNMP Agent on the hub responds in Frame 44 with the expected results. The SetRequest works, and Bob Pjontek is now the new network administrator. Ross wishes Bob well in his new responsibilities and moves on to the next test.

For his last compatibility check, Ross wishes to change the sysLocation object {1.3.6.1.2.1.1.6.0} using the SetRequest command in Frame 45. To Ross's surprise, the GetResponse returned by the hub in Frame 46 contains an Error Status = 3, indicating that a bad value was included in the SetRequest command. The Error index shows that the bad value is the second variable (Ottawa Demo Lab). Ross is perplexed as to why this SetRequest failed, while the previous command (Frames 43 and 44) succeeded. The only clue is an error code on the console that reads Object: Unknown.

A close examination of the two vendors' product manuals reveals the incompatibility. The hub manual shows that it does not allow a SetRequest for the sysLocation object for reasons of security. Since SNMP offers limited security (via the Authentication header), the hub vendor elected to allow a GetRequest to all objects, but a SetRequest to only some objects. This action does not violate the SNMP standard, but merely demonstrates the vendor's concern for internetwork security.

This experiment demonstrates another valuable lesson in today's "open systems" environments. The Internet protocols, being public domain standards, are about as open as you can get. Nevertheless, vendor-specific implementations must still be considered. This is another good example of why it's important to understand the vendor's implementation of the protocol as well as the protocol itself.

Sniffer Network Analyzer data 8-Sep at 00:07:34, file SNMPTEST.ENC, Pg 1

SUMMARY	Delta T	Destination	Source	Summary
31	22.2384	Agent	Manager	SNMP Next sysDescr =
32	0.0031	Agent	Manager	SNMP Next sysObjectID, sysUpTime
33	0.0023	Agent	Manager	SNMP Next system.4 =
34	0.0019	Agent	Manager	SNMP Next system.5 =
35	0.0020	Agent	Manager	SNMP Next system.6 =
36	0.0020	Agent	Manager	SNMP Next system.7 = 0
37	0.0094	Manager	Agent	SNMP Got sysDescr = MX-3610 Xyplex 10BASE-T Hub<0A> Xyplex hardware MX-3610 00.00.00 Rom 440000<0A>Xypl...
38	0.0110	Manager	Agent	SNMP Got sysObjectID, sysUpTime
39	0.0086	Manager	Agent	SNMP Got system.4.0 = Ross Dunthorne, LAA Inc., Ottawa, Ontario.
40	0.0085	Manager	Agent	SNMP Got system.5.0 = MX-3610
41	0.0084	Manager	Agent	SNMP Got system.6.0 =
42	0.0085	Manager	Agent	SNMP Got system.7.0 = 78
43	16.3451	Agent	Manager	SNMP Set system.4.0 = Bob Pjontek, LAA Inc., Ottawa, Ontario.
44	0.0118	Manager	Agent	SNMP Got system.4.0 = Bob Pjontek, LAA Inc., Ottawa, Ontario.
45	49.9424	Agent	Manager	SNMP Set system.6.0 = Ottawa Demo Lab
46	0.0105	Manager	Agent	SNMP Got Bad value system.6.0 = Ottawa Demo Lab

Trace 7.10a. SNMP Message Summary

Chapter 7: Managing the Internet

Sniffer Network Analyzer data 8-Sep at 00:07:34, file SNMPTEST.ENC, Pg 1

- - - - - - - - - - - - - - - - Frame 31 - - - - - - - - - - - - - - - - -

DLC: —— DLC Header ——-
DLC:
DLC: Frame 31 arrived at 00:08:24.5855; frame size is 84 (0054 hex) bytes.
DLC: Destination = Station Xyplex004DB7, Agent
DLC: Source   = Station NwkGnl0813FE, Manager
DLC: Ethertype = 0800 (IP)
DLC:
IP: —— IP Header ——-
IP:
IP: Version = 4, header length = 20 bytes
IP: Type of service = 00
IP: 000. .... = routine
IP: ...0 .... = normal delay
IP: .... 0... = normal throughput
IP: .... .0.. = normal reliability
IP: Total length = 70 bytes
IP: Identification = 3658
IP: Flags = 0X
IP: .0.. .... = may fragment
IP: ..0. .... = last fragment
IP: Fragment offset = 0 bytes
IP: Time to live = 255 seconds/hops
IP: Protocol = 17 (UDP)
IP: Header checksum = 2917 (correct)
IP: Source address = [192.12.2.38]
IP: Destination address = [192.12.2.7]
IP: No options
IP:
UDP: —— UDP Header ——-
UDP:
UDP: Source port = 9669 (SNMP)
UDP: Destination port = 161
UDP: Length = 50
UDP: Checksum = F42C (correct)
UDP:
SNMP: —— Simple Network Management Protocol ——
SNMP:
SNMP: Version = 0
SNMP: Community = public
SNMP: Command = Get next request

470

SNMP: Request ID = 227475461

SNMP: Error status = 0 (No error)

SNMP: Error index = 0

SNMP:

SNMP: Object = {1.3.6.1.2.1.1.1} (sysDescr)

SNMP: Value =

SNMP:

- - - - - - - - - - - - - - - - Frame 32 - - - - - - - - - - - - - - - - -

UDP: ——- UDP Header ——-

UDP:

UDP: Source port = 9669 (SNMP)

UDP: Destination port = 161

UDP: Length = 64

UDP: Checksum = 69A2 (correct)

UDP:

SNMP: ——- Simple Network Management Protocol ——-

SNMP:

SNMP: Version = 0

SNMP: Community = public

SNMP: Command = Get next request

SNMP: Request ID = 227541001

SNMP: Error status = 0 (No error)

SNMP: Error index = 0

SNMP:

SNMP: Object = {1.3.6.1.2.1.1.2} (sysObjectID)

SNMP: Value = }

SNMP:

SNMP: Object = {1.3.6.1.2.1.1.3} (sysUpTime)

SNMP: Value = 0 hundredths of a second

SNMP:

- - - - - - - - - - - - - - - - Frame 33 - - - - - - - - - - - - - - - - -

UDP: ——- UDP Header ——-

UDP:

UDP: Source port = 9669 (SNMP)

UDP: Destination port = 161

UDP: Length = 50

UDP: Checksum = DE29 (correct)

UDP:

SNMP: ——- Simple Network Management Protocol ——-

SNMP:

SNMP: Version = 0
SNMP: Community = public
SNMP: Command = Get next request
SNMP: Request ID = 227606553
SNMP: Error status = 0 (No error)
SNMP: Error index = 0
SNMP:
SNMP: Object = {1.3.6.1.2.1.1.4} (system.4)
SNMP: Value =
SNMP:

- - - - - - - - - - - - - - - - Frame 34 - - - - - - - - - - - - - - - - -

UDP: ——- UDP Header ——-
UDP:
UDP: Source port = 9669 (SNMP)
UDP: Destination port = 161
UDP: Length = 50
UDP: Checksum = D928 (correct)
UDP:
SNMP: ——- Simple Network Management Protocol ——-
SNMP:
SNMP: Version = 0
SNMP: Community = public
SNMP: Command = Get next request
SNMP: Request ID = 227672093
SNMP: Error status = 0 (No error)
SNMP: Error index = 0
SNMP:
SNMP: Object = {1.3.6.1.2.1.1.5} (system.5)
SNMP: Value =
SNMP:

- - - - - - - - - - - - - - - Frame 35 - - - - - - - - - - - - - - - - -

UDP: ——- UDP Header ——-
UDP:
UDP: Source port = 9669 (SNMP)
UDP: Destination port = 161
UDP: Length = 50
UDP: Checksum = D427 (correct)
UDP:
SNMP: ——- Simple Network Management Protocol ——-

SNMP:
SNMP: Version = 0
SNMP: Community = public
SNMP: Command = Get next request
SNMP: Request ID = 227737633
SNMP: Error status = 0 (No error)
SNMP: Error index = 0
SNMP:
SNMP: Object = {1.3.6.1.2.1.1.6} (system.6)
SNMP: Value =
SNMP:

- - - - - - - - - - - - - - - Frame 36 - - - - - - - - - - - - - - - - -

UDP: ——- UDP Header ——-
UDP:
UDP: Source port = 9669 (SNMP)
UDP: Destination port = 161
UDP: Length = 51
UDP: Checksum = CE22 (correct)
UDP:
SNMP: ——- Simple Network Management Protocol ——-
SNMP:
SNMP: Version = 0
SNMP: Community = public
SNMP: Command = Get next request
SNMP: Request ID = 227803173
SNMP: Error status = 0 (No error)
SNMP: Error index = 0
SNMP:
SNMP: Object = {1.3.6.1.2.1.1.7} (system.7)
SNMP: Value = 0
SNMP:

- - - - - - - - - - - - - - - Frame 37 - - - - - - - - - - - - - - - - -

DLC: ——- DLC Header ——-
DLC:
DLC: Frame 37 arrived at 00:08:24.6065; frame size is 186 (00BA hex) bytes.
DLC: Destination = Station NwkGnl0813FE, Manager
DLC: Source   = Station Xyplex004DB7, Agent
DLC: Ethertype = 0800 (IP)
DLC:

```
IP:  ——- IP Header ——-
IP:
IP:  Version = 4, header length = 20 bytes
IP:  Type of service = 00
IP:            000. .... = routine
IP:            ...0 .... = normal delay
IP:            .... 0... = normal throughput
IP:            .... .0.. = normal reliability
IP:  Total length = 172 bytes
IP:  Identification = 82
IP:  Flags = 0X
IP:  .0.. .... = may fragment
IP:  ..0. .... = last fragment
IP:  Fragment offset = 0 bytes
IP:  Time to live = 64 seconds/hops
IP:  Protocol = 17 (UDP)
IP:  Header checksum = F5A9 (correct)
IP:  Source address = [192.12.2.7]
IP:  Destination address = [192.12.2.38]
IP:  No options
IP:
UDP:  ——- UDP Header ——-
UDP:
UDP:  Source port = 161 (SNMP)
UDP:  Destination port = 9669
UDP:  Length = 152
UDP:  No checksum
UDP:
SNMP:  ——- Simple Network Management Protocol ——-
SNMP:
SNMP: Version = 0
SNMP: Community = public
SNMP: Command = Get response
SNMP: Request ID = 227475461
SNMP: Error status = 0 (No error)
SNMP: Error index = 0
SNMP:
SNMP: Object = {1.3.6.1.2.1.1.1.0} (sysDescr.0)
SNMP: Value  = MX-3610 - Xyplex 10BASE-T Hub<0A>Xyplex hardware MX-3610 00.00.00 Rom 440000<0A> ...
SNMP:
```

- - - - - - - - - - - - - - - - Frame 38 - - - - - - - - - - - - - - - - - -

UDP: —— UDP Header ——-
UDP:
UDP: Source port = 161 (SNMP)
UDP: Destination port = 9669
UDP: Length = 76
UDP: No checksum
UDP:
SNMP: —— Simple Network Management Protocol ——-
SNMP:
SNMP: Version = 0
SNMP: Community = public
SNMP: Command = Get response
SNMP: Request ID = 227541001
SNMP: Error status = 0 (No error)
SNMP: Error index = 0
SNMP:
SNMP: Object = {1.3.6.1.2.1.1.2.0} (sysObjectID.0)
SNMP: Value = {1.3.6.1.4.1.33.1.4}
SNMP:
SNMP: Object = {1.3.6.1.2.1.1.3.0} (sysUpTime.0)
SNMP: Value = 1058882 hundredths of a second
SNMP:

- - - - - - - - - - - - - - - - Frame 39 - - - - - - - - - - - - - - - - -

UDP: —— UDP Header ——-
UDP:
UDP: Source port = 161 (SNMP)
UDP: Destination port = 9669
UDP: Length = 93
UDP: No checksum
UDP:
SNMP: —— Simple Network Management Protocol ——-
SNMP:
SNMP: Version = 0
SNMP: Community = public
SNMP: Command = Get response
SNMP: Request ID = 227606553
SNMP: Error status = 0 (No error)
SNMP: Error index = 0

SNMP:
SNMP: Object = {1.3.6.1.2.1.1.4.0} (system.4.0)
SNMP: Value = Ross Dunthorne, LAA Inc., Ottawa, Ontario.
SNMP:

- - - - - - - - - - - - - - - Frame 40 - - - - - - - - - - - - - - - -

UDP: ——- UDP Header ——-
UDP:
UDP: Source port = 161 (SNMP)
UDP: Destination port = 9669
UDP: Length = 58
UDP: No checksum
UDP:
SNMP: ——- Simple Network Management Protocol ——-
SNMP:
SNMP: Version = 0
SNMP: Community = public
SNMP: Command = Get response
SNMP: Request ID = 227672093
SNMP: Error status = 0 (No error)
SNMP: Error index = 0
SNMP:
SNMP: Object = {1.3.6.1.2.1.1.5.0} (system.5.0)
SNMP: Value = MX-3610
SNMP:

- - - - - - - - - - - - - - - Frame 41 - - - - - - - - - - - - - - - -

UDP: ——- UDP Header ——-
UDP:
UDP: Source port = 161 (SNMP)
UDP: Destination port = 9669
UDP: Length = 51
UDP: No checksum
UDP:
SNMP: ——- Simple Network Management Protocol ——-
SNMP:
SNMP: Version = 0
SNMP: Community = public
SNMP: Command = Get response
SNMP: Request ID = 227737633
SNMP: Error status = 0 (No error)
SNMP: Error index = 0

SNMP:
SNMP: Object = {1.3.6.1.2.1.1.6.0} (system.6.0)
SNMP: Value =
SNMP:

- - - - - - - - - - - - - - - Frame 42 - - - - - - - - - - - - - - - - -

UDP: ——- UDP Header ——-
UDP:
UDP: Source port = 161 (SNMP)
UDP: Destination port = 9669
UDP: Length = 52
UDP: No checksum
UDP:
SNMP: ——- Simple Network Management Protocol ——-
SNMP:
SNMP: Version = 0
SNMP: Community = public
SNMP: Command = Get response
SNMP: Request ID = 227803173
SNMP: Error status = 0 (No error)
SNMP: Error index = 0
SNMP:
SNMP: Object = {1.3.6.1.2.1.1.7.0} (system.7.0)
SNMP: Value = 78
SNMP:

- - - - - - - - - - - - - - - Frame 43 - - - - - - - - - - - - - - - - -

UDP: ——- UDP Header ——-
UDP:
UDP: Source port = 9669 (SNMP)
UDP: Destination port = 161
UDP: Length = 68
UDP: Checksum = 1198 (correct)
UDP:
SNMP: ——- Simple Network Management Protocol ——-
SNMP:
SNMP: Version = 0
SNMP: Community = xyplex
SNMP: Command = Set request
SNMP: Request ID = 227868677
SNMP: Error status = 0 (No error)
SNMP: Error index = 0

SNMP:
SNMP: Object = {1.3.6.1.2.1.1.4.0} (system.4.0)
SNMP: Value = Bob Pjontek, LAA Inc., Ottawa, Ontario.
SNMP:

- - - - - - - - - - - - - - - - - Frame 44 - - - - - - - - - - - - - - - - -

UDP: ——- UDP Header ——-
UDP:
UDP: Source port = 161 (SNMP)
UDP: Destination port = 9669
UDP: Length = 68
UDP: No checksum
UDP:
SNMP: ——- Simple Network Management Protocol ——-
SNMP:
SNMP: Version = 0
SNMP: Community = xyplex
SNMP: Command = Get response
SNMP: Request ID = 227868677
SNMP: Error status = 0 (No error)
SNMP: Error index = 0
SNMP:
SNMP: Object = {1.3.6.1.2.1.1.4.0} (system.4.0)
SNMP: Value = Bob Pjontek, LAA Inc., Ottawa, Ontario.
SNMP:

- - - - - - - - - - - - - - - - Frame 45 - - - - - - - - - - - - - - - - -

UDP: ——- UDP Header ——-
UDP:
UDP: Source port = 9669 (SNMP)
UDP: Destination port = 161
UDP: Length = 66
UDP: Checksum = 2C01 (correct)
UDP:
SNMP: ——- Simple Network Management Protocol ——-
SNMP:
SNMP: Version = 0
SNMP: Community = xyplex
SNMP: Command = Set request
SNMP: Request ID = 227999749
SNMP: Error status = 0 (No error)
SNMP: Error index = 0
SNMP:

```
SNMP: Object = {1.3.6.1.2.1.1.6.0} (system.6.0)
SNMP: Value  = Ottawa Demo Lab
SNMP:


- - - - - - - - - - - - - - - Frame 46 - - - - - - - - - - - - - - - - -

UDP: ——— UDP Header ———-
UDP:
UDP:  Source port = 161 (SNMP)
UDP:  Destination port = 9669
UDP:  Length = 66
UDP:  No checksum
UDP:
SNMP: ——— Simple Network Management Protocol ———
SNMP:
SNMP: Version = 0
SNMP: Community = xyplex
SNMP: Command = Get response
SNMP: Request ID = 227999749
SNMP: Error status = 3 (Bad value)
SNMP: Error index = 2
SNMP:
SNMP: Object = {1.3.6.1.2.1.1.6.0} (system.6.0)
SNMP: Value  = Ottawa Demo Lab
SNMP:
```

Trace 7.10b. SNMP Message Details

In the previous seven chapters, we have concentrated on internetwork architectures that are based upon IP version 4. In our concluding chapter, we will study the next generation Internet Protocol, designated IPng or IP version 6 (IPv6).

7.11 References

[7-1]   Salus, Peter H. "Protocol Wars: Is OSI Finally Dead?" *ConneXions* (August 1995): 16–19.

[7-2]   International Organization for Standardization, *Information Processing Systems—Open Systems Interconnection—Basic Reference Model—Part 4: Management Framework*, ISO 7498-4-1989.

[7-3]   Special Issues: Network Management (March 1989); Network Management and Network Security (August 1990). *ConneXions.*

[7-4]   Rose, Marshall T. *The Simple Book: An Introduction to Management of TCP/IP-Based Internets*, second edition. Prentice-Hall (Englewood Cliffs, NJ), 1994.

[7-5]   Black, Uyless. *Network Management Standards*. McGraw-Hill (New York, NY), 1992.

[7-6]   Miller, Mark A. *Managing Internetworks with SNMP*. M&T Books, Inc. (New York, NY), 1993.

[7-7]   White, David W. "Internet Management—SNMP and CMOT: Two Ways to Do the Same Thing." *LAN Magazine* (July 1989): 147–150.

[7-8]   Thomas, Larry J. "The Distributed Management Choice." *LAN Technology* (April 1992): 53–70.

[7-9]   Ben-Artzi, Amatzia, et al. "Network Management of TCP/IP Networks: Present and Future." *IEEE Network Magazine* (July 1990): 35–43.

[7-10]   McGloghrie, K., and Marshall T. Rose. "Network Management of TCP/IP-Based Internets." *ConneXions* (March 1989): 3–9.

[7-11]   Rose, M., and K. McCloghrie. "Structure and Identification of Management Information for TCP/IP-Based Internets." RFC 1155, May 1990.

[7-12]   Rose, M., et al. "Concise MIB Definitions." RFC 1212, March 1991.

[7-13]   Case, J., et al. "A Simple Network Management Protocol (SNMP)." RFC 1157, May 1990.

[7-14]   International Organization for Standardization. *Information Processing Systems: Open Systems Interconnection, Specification of Abstract Syntax Notation One (ASN.1)*, ISO 8824, December 1987.

[7-15]   McCloghrie, K., et al. "Management Information Base for Network Management of TCP/IP-based Internets." RFC 1156, May 1990.

[7-16]   McCloghrie, K., and M. Rose. "Management Information Base for Network Management of TCP/IP-Based Internets: MIB-II." RFC 1213, March 1991.

[7-17]   Perkins, Dave. "How to Read and Use an SNMP MIB." *3TECH, The 3Com Technical Journal* (Spring 1991): 31–55.

[7-18]   Stewart, Bob. "Development and Integration of a Management Information Base." *ConneXions* (June 1991): 2–11.

[7-19]   3Com Corporation. *Introduction to Simple Network Management Protocol: A Self-Study Guide*. Document 8759-00, rev. A, August 1991.

[7-20]   Waldbusser, S. "Remote Network Monitoring Management Information Base." RFC 1757, February 1995.

[7-21]   Waldbusser, S. "Token Ring Extensions to the Remote Network Monitoring MIB." RFC 1513, September 1993.

[7-22]   Waldbusser, S. "Remote Network Monitoring Management Information Base.", Work in Progress, January 1996.

[7-23]   Tolly, Kevin. "RMON: A Ray of Hope for Token Ring Managers." *Data Communications* (October 1995): 72–80.

[7-24]   Carr, Jim. "RMON: The Enterprise Probe." *Internetwork* (October 1994): 24–32.

[7-25]   The *Simple Times* is an openly available quarterly newsletter devoted to SNMP Technology. For subscription information, send a message to:

   st-subscriptions@simple-times.org, with a subject line of *help*.

   Back issues are available at:

   http://www.simple-times.org
   ftp://ftp.simple-times.org

[7-26]   Cerf, V. "IAB Recommendations for the Development of Internet Network Management Standards." RFC 1052, April 1988.

[7-27]   Case, Jeffrey D., et al. "Network Management and the Design of SNMP." *ConneXions* (March 1989): 22–26.

[7-28]   Jander, Mary. "SNMP2: Coming Soon to a Network Near You." *Data Communications* (November 1992): 66–76.

[7-29]   Stallings, William. "SNMPv2: The New Direction in Network Management." *Network Computing* (July 1993): 140–143.

[7-30]   Higgins, Kelly Jackson. "Things Aren't So Simple with SNMPv2." *Communications Week* (October 13, 1993): 55–58.

[7-31]   Huntington-Lee, Jill. "SNMP Version 2 Update." ComNet 1996 Conference Session Notes, January 1996.

[7-32]   Case, J., et al. "Introduction to Community-Based SNMPv2." RFC 1901, January 1996.

[7-33]   International Organization for Standardization. *Information Processing Systems—Open Systems Interconnection—Common management information service definition*, ISO/IEC 9595, CCITT Recommendation X.710, IEEE 802.1-91/20, November 1990.

[7-34]   Klerer, Mark. "The OSI Management Architecture: an Overview." *IEEE Network Magazine* (March 1988): 20–29.

[7-35]   Sugarbroad, Ian. "An OSI-Based Interoperability Architecture for Managing Hybrid Networks." *IEEE Communications Magazine* (March 1990): 61–69.

[7-36]   International Organization for Standardization. *Information Processing Systems—Open Systems Interconnection—Common management information protocol specification*, ISO/IEC 9596-1, CCITT X.711, IEEE 802.1-91/21, November 1990.

[7-37]   Jander, Mary. "CMIP Gets a New Chance." *Data Communications* (September 1991): 51–56.

[7-38]   Warrier, U., et al. "The Common Management Information Services and Protocols for the Internet (CMOT and CMIP)." RFC 1189, October 1990.

[7-39]   Rose, M.T. "ISO Presentation Services on Top of TCP/IP-Based Internets." RFC 1085, December 1988.

[7-40]   Ben-Artzi, Amatzia. "The CMOT Network Management Architecture." *ConneXions* (March 1989): 14–19.

[7-41]   Labarre, L., Editor. "OSI Internet Management: Management Information Base." RFC 1214, April 1991.

[7-42]   Institute of Electrical and Electronics Engineers. "LAN/MAN Management." 802.1B, 1995.

[7-43]   McConnell, John. "DMTF: A Foundation for Systems Management?" *ConneXions* (September 1994): 22–27.

[7-44]   The Desktop Management Task Force may be contacted at:
Desktop Management Task Force
2111 SE 25th Avenue
Mailstop JF2-51
Hillsboro, OR 97124
Tel: (503) 264-9300 or (800) 556-3683
Fax: (503) 640-6963
Faxback: (800) 525-3019
URL: ftp://ftp.dmtf.org (login as user anonymous, password of email address)
URL: http://www.dmtf.org

[7-45]   Jander, Mary. "Management Frameworks—Moving Toward a Unified View of Distributed Networks." *Data Communications* (February 1994): 58–68.

[7-46]   Miller, Mark A. "Network Management Platforms on the Move." *Network World* (October 17, 1994): 55–68.

[7-47]   Mallory, Milt, et al. "Assembling the Network Management Puzzle." *Network Computing* (August 1, 1994): 60–70.

[7-48]   Miller, Mark A. "LAN Management: How Suite it Isn't." *Network World* (November 20, 1995): 45–48.

[7-49]   Herman, James. "The Challenge of Managing Broadband Networks." *Business Communications Review* (October 1995): 60–64.

[7-50]   Saunders, Steven. "How to Survive the Coming Crisis in Service and Support." *Data Communications* (December 1995): 58–67.

## CHAPTER 8

The Next Generation

In the late 1980s and the early 1990s, networks in particular, and networking in general experienced phenomenal growth. About that same time, the funding and usage policies that governed Internet traffic changed, moving the Internet from a government-sponsored network primarily focused on education and research to a widely available network that included commercial ventures as part of its *modus operandi*. The end result became more host connections, more users, and more traffic on the Internet.

But possibly more importantly, a shortage of IP addresses was anticipated, with the "Date of Doom" forecast for March 1994—the predicted time at which part of the current IP address space would be exhausted [8-1]. In response to these concerns, in July 1991, the Internet Engineering Task Force (IETF) began the process of researching the problem, soliciting proposals for solutions, and narrowing in on a conclusion, describing this preliminary process in RFC 1380 [8-2], published in November 1992. In addition, a new research area, called the IPng Area, was commissioned by the IETF to formally study these issues.

8.1 IPng Development

In December 1993, RFC 1550 was distributed, titled "IP: Next Generation (IPng) White Paper Solicitation" [8-3]. This RFC invited any interested party to submit their comments regarding any specific requirements for the IPng or any key factors that should be considered during the IPng selection process. Twenty-one responses were submitted that addressed a variety of topics, including: security (RFC 1675), a large corporate user's view (RFC 1687), a cellular industry view (RFC 1674), and a cable television industry view (RFC 1686). Many of these papers, plus a complete listing of the white paper responses are given in Scott Bradner and Allison Mankin's book *IPng—Internet Protocol Next Generation [8-4]*.

The IPng Area commissioned RFC 1726, "Technical Criteria for Choosing IP The Next Generation (IPng)" [8-5], to define a set of criteria that would be used in the IPng evaluation process. Seventeen criteria were noted:

- Scale—the IPng Protocol must scale to allow the identification and addressing of at least 10^{12} end systems and 10^9 individual networks.
- Topological Flexibility—the routing architecture and protocols of IPng must allow for many different network topologies.
- Performance—a state-of-the-art, commercial-grade router must be able to process and forward IPng traffic at speeds capable of fully utilizing common, commercially available, high-speed media at the time.
- Robust Service—the network service and its associated routing and control protocols must be robust.
- Transition—the protocol must have a straightforward transition plan from the current IPv4.
- Media Independence—the protocol must work across an internetwork of many different LAN, MAN, and WAN media, with individual link speeds ranging from a ones-of-bits per second to hundreds of gigabits per second.
- Unreliable Datagram Service—the protocol must support an unreliable datagram delivery service.
- Configuration, Administration and Operation—the protocol must permit easy and largely distributed configuration and operation. The automatic configuration of hosts and routers is required.
- Secure Operation—IPng must provide a secure network layer.
- Unique Naming—IPng must assign all IP-Layer objects global, ubiquitous, Internet unique names.
- Access and Documentation—the protocols that define IPng, its associated protocols, and the routing protocols, must be published in the standards track RFCs, be freely available, and be without licensing fees for implementation.
- Multicast—the protocol must support both unicast and multicast packet transmission.
- Extensibility—he protocol must be extensible; it must be able to evolve to meet the future service needs of the Internet.

- Network Service—the protocol must allow the network to associate packets with particular service classes, and must provide them with the services specified by those classes.

- Mobility—the protocol must support mobile hosts, networks, and internetworks.

- Control Protocol—the protocol must include elementary support for testing and debugging networks.

- Private Networks—IPng must allow users to build private internetworks on top of the basic Internet infrastructure.

Several proposals were evaluated vis-a-vis the above criteria. In January 1995, RFC 1752, "The Recommendation for the IP Next Generation Protocol," was issued [8-6]. This paper summarized the evaluations of three IPng proposals: Common Architecture for the Internet (CATNIP) [8-7] and [8-8], Simple Internet Protocol Plus (SIPP) [8-9] and [8-10], and the TCP/UDP Over CLNP-Addressed Networks (TUBA) [8-11] and [8-12].

8.1.1 Common Architecture for the Internet (CATNIP)

The objective of the CATNIP proposal is to provide some commonality between Internet, OSI, and Novell protocols. To accomplish this, CATNIP integrates a number of Network layer protocols, including the ISO Connectionless Network Protocol (CLNP), IP, and Novell's Internetwork Packet Exchange (IPX) protocol. In addition, the CATNIP design allows a number of Transport protocols, including the ISO Transport Protocol, class 4 (TP4), Connectionless Transport Protocol (CLTP), TCP, UDP, and Novell's Sequenced Packet Exchange (SPX), to run over any of the above Network layer protocols. According to the proposal, it would be possible for a single Transport layer protocol such as TCP, to operate over one Network layer protocol (such as IPv4) at one end of the connection, and over another Network layer protocol, (such as CLNP) at the other. As documented in RFC 1752, the reviewers felt that CATNIP met five of the key criteria, did not meet two of the criteria, and had mixed reviews or an unknown conclusion on the remaining criteria.

8.1.2 Simple Internet Protocol Plus (SIPP)

The objective of SIPP is to provide a new, evolutionary step from IPv4. As such, IPv4 functions which worked were retained, and functions which did not were removed.

In addition, SIPP installation is planned as a software upgrade and SIPP is inter operable with the existing IPv4. SIPP revises the IP header for more efficient processing and also increases the size of the IP addresses from 32 to 64 bits in length. As documented in RFC 1752, the reviewers felt that SIPP met ten of the key criteria, did not meet two of the criteria, and had mixed reviews or an unknown conclusion on the remaining criteria.

8.1.3 TCP/UDP Over CLNP-Addressed Networks (TUBA)

The key strategy behind TUBA is to replace the existing IPv4 Network layer with the ISO CLNP. There are two benefits to this: providing for increased address space, while allowing for TCP or UDP and related upper-layer applications to operate unchanged. The addresses defined for CLNP (and therefore in TUBA) are called Network Service Access Points, or NSAPs, which are variable length addresses. The use of CLNP at the Network layer would be supported by existing ISO routing protocols, including the Inter Domain Routing Protocol (IDRP), the Intermediate System-to-Intermediate System (IS-IS) protocol, and the End System-to-Intermediate System (ES-IS) protocol. As documented in RFC 1752, the reviewers felt that TUBA met five of the key criteria, did not meet one of the criteria, and had mixed reviews or an unknown conclusion on the remaining criteria.

As reported in RFC 1752, all three proposals exhibited significant problems, and CATNIP in particular was determined to be "too incomplete to be considered." As a result of these discussions, the SIPP proposal was revised, incorporating 128-bit addresses and dealing with other concerns. The final recommendation incorporated this revised SIPP proposal, coupled with the autoreconfiguration and transition elements of TUBA, the addressing work based upon the Classless Inter-Domain Routing, or CIDR (an intermediate solution to the address depletion problem [8-13] and [8-14]), plus routing header enhancements.

8.2 IPv6 Capabilities

Declaring a winner in athletic or political contests is a straightforward process; however, with protocol designs the process is not always as clear. As such there was no single "winner" of the IPv6 design contest, but actually a combination which drew on the individual strengths of several proposals. To quote from RFC 1752:

"This proposal represents a synthesis of multiple IETF efforts with much of the basic protocol coming from the SIPP effort, the autoconfiguration and transition portions influenced by TUBA, the addressing structure based on CIDR work and the routing header evolving out of the SDRP [Source Demand Routing Protocol] deliberations."

RFC 1752 goes on to describe the important features of IPng, formally designated IPv6. These capabilities include:

- Expanded addressing and routing—increasing the IP address field from 32 to 128 bits in length allows for a much greater number of addressable nodes, more levels of addressing hierarchy, defining new types of addresses, etc.
- Simplified header format—eliminating or making optional some of the IPv4 header fields to reduce the packet handling overhead, thus providing some compensation for the larger addresses. Even with the addresses, which are four times as long, the IPv6 header is only 40 octets in length, compared with 20 octets for IPv4.
- Extension headers and options—IPv6 options are placed in separate headers located after the core IPv6 header information, such that processing at every intermediate stop between source and destination may not be required.
- Authentication and privacy—required support in all implementations of IPv6 to authenticate the sender of a packet and to encrypt the contents of that packet, as required.
- Autoreconfiguration—support from node address assignments up to the use of the Dynamic Host Reconfiguration Protocol (DHCP).
- Source routes—support for a header that supports the Source Demand Routing Protocol (SDRP), such that a source-selected route may complement the route determined by the existing routing protocols.
- Simple and flexible transition—a transition plan with four basic requirements:
  - Incremental upgrade—allowing existing IPv4 hosts to be upgraded at any time without a dependency on other hosts or routers being upgraded.

- Incremental deployment—new IPv6 hosts and routers can be installed at any time without any prerequisites.
- Easy addressing—when existing installed IPv4 hosts or routers are upgraded to IPv6, they may continue to use their existing address, without needing a new assigned address.
- Low start-up costs—little or no preparation work is needed in order to upgrade existing IPv4 systems to IPv6, or to deploy new IPv6 systems.
- Quality of service capabilities—a new capability is added to enable the labeling of packets belonging to particular traffic "flows" for which the sender has requested special handling, such as non-default quality of service or "real-time" service.

8.3 IPv6 Documentation

The Internet Protocol—of any version— is the fundamental platform upon which the entire Internet Protocol suite is based. A revision to this protocol has a number of far-reaching effects, as illustrated by the following list of RFCs that have been published on the subject as of this writing:

RFC	Subject
1550	IPng White Paper Solicitation
1726	Technical Criteria for IPng
1752	Recommendation for IPng
1809	Using the Flow Label Field
1825	Security Architecture
1826	IP Authentication Header
1827	IP Encapsulating Security Payload (ESP)
1828	IP Authentication using Keyed MD5
1829	The ESP DES-CBC Transform
1883	IPv6 Specification
1884	IPv6 Addressing Architecture
1885	ICMPv6 for IPv6
1886	DNS Extensions to Support IPv6
1887	IPv6 Unicast Address Allocation
1924	Compact Representation of IPv6 Addresses
1933	Transition Mechanisms for IPv6 Hosts and Routers

In addition, there are a large number of Internet drafts that are currently in progress. Many of these documents will become RFCs in the future:

- Address autoconfiguration
- Additional address formats, such as unicast and experimental addresses
- Data Link Layer support, including Ethernet, token ring, FDDI, PPP, ATM, frame relay, and others
- Routing protocol extensions, including OSPF, RIP-II, and others
- Domain Name System (DNS) revisions
- Mobility Protocol
- Neighbor discovery
- Transition Guidelines

To keep abreast of these IPv6 developments, subscribe to the Internet's IPng mailing list by sending email to:

ipng-request@sunroof.eng.sun.com

8.4 IPv6 Specification

RFC 1883 [8-15], the IPv6 specification, summarizes the following changes from IPv4 to IPv6:

- Expanded Addressing Capabilities—increasing the address size from 32 bits to 128 bits, supporting more levels of address hierarchy, many more addressable nodes, scalable multicast addresses, plus the *anycast* address, which is used to send a packet to any one of a group of nodes.
- Header Format Simplification—eliminating or making optional some of the header fields, thus reducing the protocol processing overhead of the IPv6 header.
- Improved Support for Extensions and Options—including more efficient forwarding, less stringent limits on the length of options, and greater flexibility for future options.
- Flow Labeling Capability—a new function which enables packets which belong to a particular traffic "flow" to be labeled for special handling.
- Authentication and Privacy—extensions to support authentication, data integrity, and optional data confidentiality.

8.5 The IPv6 Header

The IPv6 header is 40 octets in length, with eight fields (see Figure 8-1).

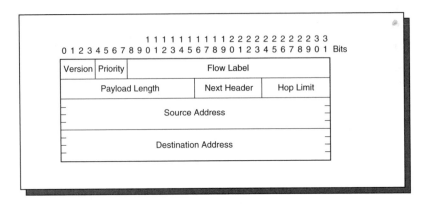

Figure 8-1. IPv6 Header Format

The Version field is four bits in length and identifies the version of the protocol. For IPv6, Version = 6.

The Priority field is four bits in length and enables a source to identify the desired delivery of its packets. The priority values are divided into two ranges:

0-7: source-provided congestion control
8-15: constant-rate, real-time packets

The Flow Label field is 24 bits in length and may be used by a host to request special handling for certain packets, such as those with a non-default quality of service.

The Payload Length field is a 16-bit unsigned integer which measures the length, given in octets, of the payload (i.e. the balance of the IPv6 packet). Payloads greater than 65,535 are allowed, and are called jumbo payloads. To indicate a jumbo payload, the value of the Payload Length is set to zero, and the actual payload length is carried in a Jumbo Payload hop-by-hop option.

The Next Header field is eight bits in length and identifies the header immediately following the IPv6 header. This field uses the same values as the IPv4 Protocol field. Examples are:

Value	Header
0	Hop-by-Hop Options
1	ICMPv4
4	IP in IP (encapsulation)
6	TCP
17	UDP
43	Routing
44	Fragment
50	Encapsulating Security Payload
51	Authentication
58	ICMPv6
59	None (no next header)
60	Destination Options

The Hop Limit field is eight bits in length and is decremented by one by each node that forwards the packet. When the Hop Limit equals zero, the packet is discarded and an error message is returned.

The Source Address is a 128-bit field that identifies the originator of the packet.

The Destination Address field is a 128-bit field that identifies the intended recipient of the packet, although possibly not the ultimate recipient of the packet, if a Routing header is present.

8.5.1 Extension Headers

The IPv6 design simplified the existing IPv4 header by placing many of the existing fields in optional headers. In this way, the processing of ordinary packets is not complicated by undue overhead, while the more complex conditions are still provided for. An IPv6 packet, which consists of an IPv6 packet plus its payload, may consist of zero, one, or more extension headers, as shown in Figure 8-2. Note the values of the Next Header fields in each example shown in the Figure. In the first case, no extension headers are required, the Next Header = TCP; and the TCP header and any upper layer protocol data follows. In the second case, a Routing header is required, therefore the IPv6 Next Header = Routing; in the Routing header, Next Header = TCP, and the TCP header and any upper layer protocol data follows. In the third case, both the Routing and Fragment headers are required, with the Next Header fields identified accordingly.

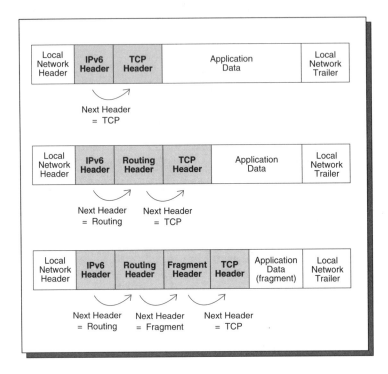

Figure 8-2. IPv6 Next Header Field Operation

The Hop-by-Hop Options header carries information that must be examined and processed by every node along a packet's delivery path, including the destination node. As a result, the Hop-by-Hop Options header, when present, must immediately follow the IPv6 header. The other extension headers are not examined or processed by any node along a packet's delivery path, until the packet reaches its intended destination(s). When processed, the operation is performed in the order in which the headers appear in the packet.

8.5.2 Extension Header Order

RFC 1883 recommends that the extension headers be placed in the IPv6 packet in a particular order:

- IPv6 header
- Hop-by-Hop Options header
- Destination Options header (for options to be processed by the first destination that appears in the IPv6 Destination Address field, plus any subsequent destinations listed in the Routing header)
- Routing header
- Fragment header
- Authentication header (as detailed in RFC 1827)
- Encapsulating Security Payload header (as detailed in RFC 1827)
- Destination Options header (for options to be processed by the final destination only)
- Upper Layer Protocol header (TCP, and so on)

Figure 8-3 illustrates the IPv6 and optional headers, with their suggested order.

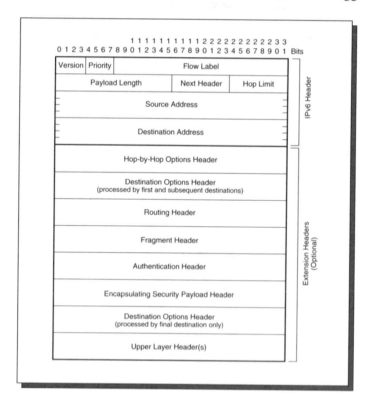

Figure 8-3. IPv6 Packet Format

8.5.3 Hop-by-Hop Options Header

The Hop-by-Hop Options header carries optional information that must be examined by every node along a packet's delivery path (see Figure 8-4). The presence of the Hop-by-Hop Options header is identified by a value of 0 in the Next Header field of the IPv6 header. This header contains two fields, plus options.

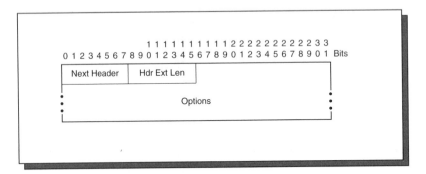

Figure 8-4. IPv6 Hop-by-Hop Options Header

The Next Header field is eight bits in length and identifies the header immediately following the Hop-by-Hop Options header. This field uses the same values as the IPv4 Protocol field.

The Header Extension Length (Hdr Ext Len) field is eight bits in length and measures the length of the Hop-by-Hop Options header in 8-octet units, not counting the first 8 octets.

The Options field is variable in length, as long as the complete Hop-by-Hop Options header is an integer multiple of eight octets in length. The options themselves are defined using a type-length-value (TLV) encoding format that is described in detail in RFC 1883. One option is defined in RFC 1883, the Jumbo Payload option, which is used to send IPv6 packets that are longer than 65,535 octets.

8.5.4 Destination Options Header

The Destination Options header carries optional information that need be examined only by a packet's destination node(s), as shown in Figure 8-5. The presence of the

496

Destination Options header is identified by a value of 60 in the preceding header's Next Header field. This header contains two fields, plus options.

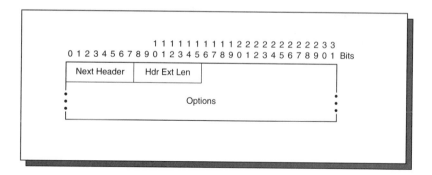

Figure 8-5. IPv6 Destination Options Header

The Next Header field is eight bits in length and identifies the header immediately following the Destination Options header. This field uses the same values as the IPv4 Protocol field.

The Header Extension Length (Hdr Ext Len) field is eight bits in length and measures the length of the Destination Options header in 8-octet units, not counting the first 8 octets.

The Options field is variable in length, such that the complete Destination Options header is an integer multiple of eight octets in length. The options themselves are defined using a type-length-value (TLV) encoding format that is described in detail in RFC 1883. Two options are defined in RFC 1883: the Pad1 option, used to insert one octet of padding into the Options area of a header; and PadN, used to insert two or more octets of padding into the Options area of a header.

8.5.5 Routing Header

The Routing Header lists one or more intermediate nodes that are "visited" on the path from the source to the destination (see Figure 8-6). The presence of the Routing header is identified by a value of 43 in the preceding header's Next Header field. This header contains four fields, plus type-specific data.

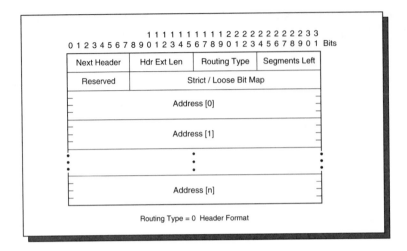

Figure 8-6. IPv6 Routing Header (Type = 0)

The Next Header field is eight bits in length and identifies the header immediately following the Routing header. This field uses the same values as the IPv4 Protocol field.

The Header Extension Length (Hdr Ext Len) field is eight bits in length and measures the length of the Routing header in 8-octet units, not counting the first 8 octets.

The Routing Type field is eight bits in length and identifies a particular Routing header variant. RFC 1883 defines one variant, Routing Type 0.

The Segments Left field is eight bits in length and indicates the number of route segments remaining, or in other words, the number of explicitly listed intermediate nodes still to be visited before reaching the final destination.

The Type-Specific field is variable in length, with a format defined by the particular Routing Type variant. For example, RFC 1883 defines the format for the Routing Type 0 header. This version of the Routing header includes a Strict/Loose Bit Map field which is 24 bits in length. This bit map indicates for each segment of the route whether the next destination must be a neighbor of the preceding address (S/L = 1) or whether it need not be a neighbor (S/L = 0). The 128-bit addresses would complete the Routing Header.

8.5.6 Fragment Header

The Fragment header is used by an IPv6 source to send packets that are larger than would fit in the path maximum transmission unit (MTU) to their destinations (see Figure 8-7). The presence of the Fragment header is identified by a value of 44 in the preceding header's Next Header field. Note that fragmentation for IPv6 is only done at the source node, not at intermediate routers along the packet's delivery path.

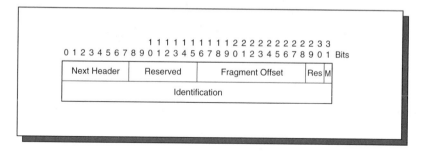

Figure 8-7. IPv6 Fragment Header

The Fragment header contains six fields. The Next Header field is eight bits in length and identifies the header immediately following the Fragment header. This field uses the same values as the IPv4 Protocol field.

The Reserved field is eight bits in length and is reserved for future use. This field is initialized to zero for transmission and is ignored on reception.

The Fragment Offset field is a 13-bit unsigned integer which measures the offset, in 8-octet units, of the data following this header, relative to the start of the fragmentable part of the original packet.

The Reserved field is two bits in length and is reserved for future use. This field is initialized to zero for transmission and is ignored on reception.

The M flag is one bit in length and determines if more fragments are coming (M = 1) or if this is the last fragment (M = 0).

The Identification field is 32 bits in length; it uniquely identifies the fragmented packet(s) during the reassembly process.

8.5.7 Authentication Header

Assuring secure data transmissions has become an increasingly important issue for network managers. The Internet community has addressed these issues in RFC 1825, "Security Architecture for the Internet Protocol" [8-16]. RFC 1825 contains several definitions which are important to the implementation of the accompanying protocols:

- Authentication: the property of knowing that the data received is the same as the data that was sent, and that the claimed sender is in fact the actual sender.
- Integrity: the property of ensuring that data is transmitted from source to destination without undetected alteration.
- Confidentiality: the property of communicating such that the intended recipients know what was being sent, but unintended parties cannot determine what was sent.
- Encryption: a mechanism commonly used to provide confidentiality.

Two headers are discussed in RFC 1825 to provide the IP security mechanisms. The Authentication header is defined in RFC 1826 [8-17], and the IP Encapsulating Security Payload (ESP) is defined in RFC 1827 [8-18].

The IP Authentication header provides integrity and authentication without confidentiality, and is illustrated in Figure 8-8. The presence of the Authentication header is identified by a value of 51 in the preceding header's Next Header field. This header contains five fields.

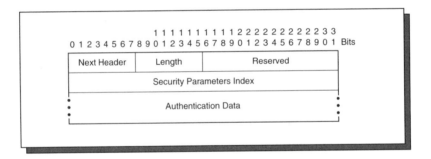

Figure 8-8. IPv6 Authentication Header

The Next Header field is eight bits in length and identifies the header immediately following the Fragment header. This field uses the same values as the IPv4 Protocol field.

The Length field is eight bits in length and provides the length of the Authentication field in 32-bit words. The minimum value is 0 words, which is only used in the case of a "null" authentication algorithm.

The Reserved field is sixteen bits in length and is reserved for future use. This field is initialized to zero for transmission. It is included in the Authentication Data calculation, but is otherwise ignored on reception.

The Security Parameters Index (SPI) field is a 32-bit pseudo-random value that identifies the security association for this datagram. The security association, as defined in RFC 1825, may include the Authentication algorithm, algorithm mode band key(s) being used with the IP Authentication header, the Encryption algorithm, algorithm mode and transform being used with the IP Encapsulating Security Payload, plus other security-related parameters. The value of SPI = 0 is reserved to indicate that "no security association exists." Other values, in the range of 1-255, are reserved for future use by the Internet Assigned Numbers Authority (IANA).

The Authentication Data is a variable-length field, containing an integral number of 32-bit words.

For additional details, refer to RFCs 1825 and 1826.

8.5.8 Encapsulating Security Payload Header

The Encapsulating Security Payload (ESP) Header is designed to provide integrity and confidentiality to IP datagrams; it may also provide authentication, depending on the algorithm used. The ESP header may also be used in conjunction with the Authentication header described above. The ESP process operates by encrypting the data to be protected and then placing that encrypted information in the data portion of the ESP payload. Depending upon the specific requirements, the mechanism may be used either to encrypt a Transport Layer segment, such as TCP or UDP data, or it may encrypt an entire IP datagram. The presence of the ESP header is identified by a value of 50 in the preceding header's Next Header field. This header is illustrated in Figure 8-9 and contains two fields.

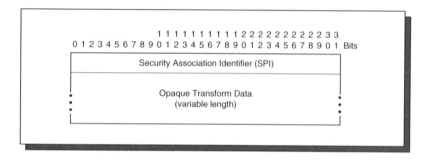

Figure 8-9. IPv6 Encapsulating Security Payload Header

The Security Parameter Association is a 32-bit pseudo-random value identifying the security association (as described above) for this datagram. If no security association exists, this field contains a value of zero. In addition, SPI values from 00000001 - 000000FFH are reserved by the IANA for future use.

The Opaque Transform Data is a variable-length field which contains the encrypted data, processed according to the encryption and authentication algorithm (called a *transform*) defined.

For additional details, refer to RFC 1827 [8-18].

8.5.9 No Next Header

The value of 59 in the Next Header field of an IPv6 packet or any of the extension headers indicates that nothing follows that header. As such, this is called a *No Next Header.*

8.6 IPv6 Addressing

As we discussed previously, one of the incentives behind the IPng effort which resulted in IPv6 was the limitations of the 32-bit IPv4 address structure. These new address formats are defined in RFC 1884, "IPv6 Addressing Architecture" [8-19], and RFC 1924, "Compact Representation of IPv6 Addresses."

8.6.1 IPv6 Address Types

RFC 1884 defines three different types of IPv6 addresses:

- Unicast—an identifier to a single interface. A packet sent to a unicast address is delivered to the interface identified by that address (see Figure 8-10a).

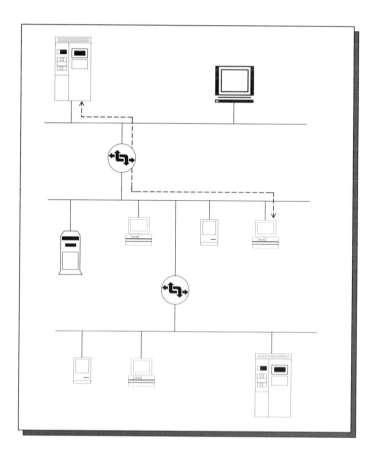

Figure 8-10a. Unicast Addressing

- Anycast—an identifier for a set of interfaces (typically belonging to different nodes). A packet sent to an anycast address is delivered to one of the interfaces identified by that address (the "nearest" one, according to the routing protocol's measure of distance), shown in Figure 8-10b.

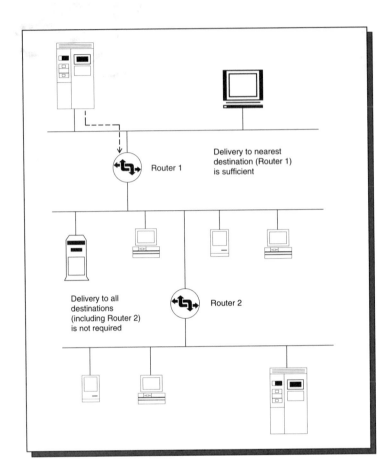

Figure 8-10b. Anycast Addressing

- Multicast—an identifier for a set of interfaces (typically belonging to different nodes). A packet sent to a multicast address is delivered to all interfaces identified by that address (see Figure 8-10c).

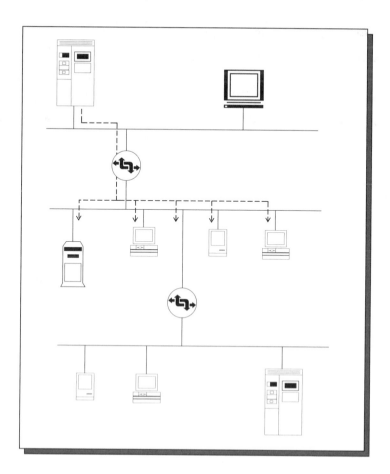

Figure 8-10c. Multicast Addressing

Note that the term *broadcast* does not appear, because the broadcast function is replaced by the multicast definition. In addition, IPv6 addresses of all types are assigned to interfaces, not nodes, such that one node (such as a router) may have multiple interfaces, and therefore multiple unicast addresses. In addition, a single interface may be assigned multiple addresses.

8.6.2 IPv6 Address Representation

IPv4 addresses are typically represented in dotted decimal notation. As such, a 32-bit address is divided into four 8-bit sections, and then each section is represented by a decimal number between 0 and 255, for example [129.144.52.38].

Since IPv6 addresses are 128 bits long, a different method of representation is required. As specified in RFC 1884, the preferred representation is:

x:x:x:x:x:x:x:x

where each "x" represents 16 bits, and each of those 16-bit sections is defined in hexadecimal. For example, an IPv6 address could be of the form:

FEDC:BA98:7654:3210:FEDC:BA98:7654:3210

Note that each of the 16-bit sections is separated by colons, and that four hexadecimal numbers are used to represent each 16-bit section. Should any one of the 16-bit sections contain leading zeros, those zeros are not required. For example:

1080:0000:0000:0000:0008:0800:200C:417A

may be simplified to:

1080:0:0:0:8:800:200C:417A

If long strings of zeros appear in an address, a double colon "::" may be used to indicate multiple groups of 16-bits of zeros, which further simplifies the example shown above:

1080::8:800:200C:417A

The use of the double colon is restricted to appear only once in an address, although it may be used to compress either the leading or trailing zeros in an address. For example, a loopback address of:

0:0:0:0:0:0:0:1

could be simplified as:

::1

For additional details, see RFCs 1884 and 1924.

8.6.3 IPv6 Address Prefixes

The 128-bit IPv6 address may be divided into a number of subfields to provide maximum flexibility for both current and future address representations. The leading bits, called the format prefix, define the specific type of IPv6 address. RFC 1884 defines a number of these prefixes, as shown in Figure 8-11. Note that address space has been allocated for NSAP, IPX, provider-based, and geographic-based addresses. Also note that multicast addresses begin with the binary value 11111111; any other prefix identifies a unicast address. Anycast addresses are part of the allocation for unicast addresses, and are not given a unique identifier.

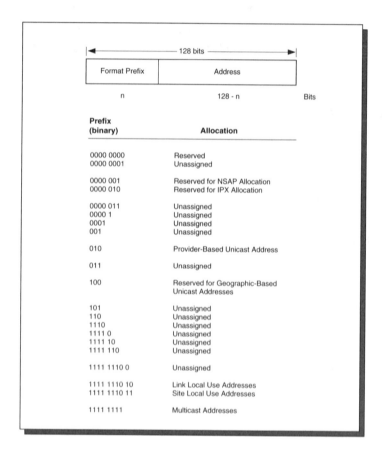

Figure 8-11. IPv6 Addressing Architecture

8.6.3.1 Unicast Addresses

A number of forms for unicast addresses have been defined for IPv6, some with more complex structures that provide for hierarchical address assignments. The most simple form would be a unicast address with no internal structure, in other words, with no address-defined hierarchy. The next possibility would be to specify a subnet prefix within the 128-bit address, thus dividing the address into a subnet prefix (with n bits) and an interface ID (with 128 - n bits). For environments with IEEE 802 LANs, this structure could be further expanded to include a subscriber prefix (n bits), a subnet ID (80 - n bits) and an interface ID (48 bits, as defined by the IEEE 802 MAC protocol in use). If the organization needed further hierarchy, a subscriber prefix (s bits), area ID (n bits), a subnet ID (m bits), and an interface ID (128 - s - n - m bits) could be defined. In summary, with a 128-bit address space available, a number of hierarchical formats are possible. RFC 1884 illustrates many of these.

8.6.3.2 Special Addresses

Two addresses have special meanings. The address 0:0:0:0:0:0:0:0 (also represented as 0::0) is defined as the unspecified address and indicates the absence of an address. This address might be used upon startup when a node has not yet had an address assigned. The unspecified address may never be assigned to any node.

The address 0:0:0:0:0:0:0:1 (also represented as 0::1) is defined as the loopback address. This address is used by a node to send a packet to itself. The loopback address may never be assigned to any interface.

8.6.3.3 Transition Addresses

Two special addresses have been defined for IPv4/IPv6 transition networks. The first such address is called an IPv4-Compatible IPv6 address. It is used when two IPv6 devices (such as hosts or routers) need to communicate via an IPv4 routing infra-structure. The devices at the edge of the IPv4 would use this special unicast address that carries an IPv4 address in the low order 32 bits. Note that the prefix is 96 bits of all zeros (see Figure 8-12).

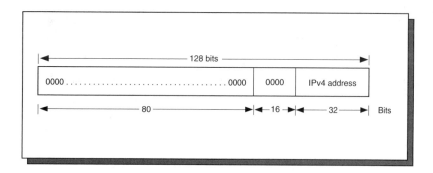

Figure 8-12. IPv4-Compatible IPv6 Address

The second type of transition address is called an IPv4-Mapped IPv6 address (see Figure 8-13). This address is used by IPv4-only nodes which do not support IPv6. For example, an IPv6 host would use an IPv4-Mapped IPv6 address to communicate with another host which only supported IPv4. Note that the prefix is 80 bits of zeros, followed by 16 bits of ones.

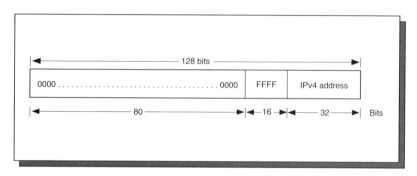

Figure 8-13. IPv4-Mapped IPv6 Address

8.7 ICMPv6 for IPv6

The Internet Control Message Protocol, version 6 (ICMPv6) [8-20], is a revised version of the ICMP defined in RFC 792, which incorporates a number of changes required to support IPv6. In addition, functions from the Internet Group Membership Protocol (IGMP), specified in RFC 1112 [8-21], have been incorporated into ICMPv6.

509

Note that like ICMP for IPv4, ICMPv6 is considered to be an integral part of IPv6, and must be implemented by every IPv6 node. The presence of the ICMPv6 header is identified by a value of 58 in the preceding header's Next Header field.

The ICMPv6 message format is very similar to its IPv4 counterpart. This message format is illustrated in Figure 8-14 and contains four fields:

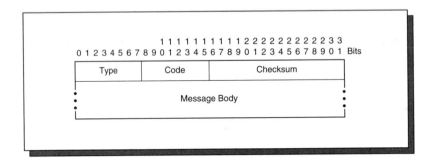

Figure 8-14. ICMPv6 Message Format

The Type field is eight bits in length and indicates the type of the message. The Type field values are divided into two groups: Error messages (Types 0-127) and Informational messages (Types 128-255). The Error messages include:

Type	Message
1	Destination unreachable
2	Packet too big
3	Time exceeded
4	Parameter problem

The Informational messages include:

Type	Message
128	Echo request
129	Echo reply
130	Group membership query
131	Group membership report
132	Group membership reduction

The Code field is eight bits in length and is used to create additional message information. For example, for the Destination Unreachable message, the following code values are defined:

Code	Meaning
0	No route to destination
1	Communication with destination administratively prohibited
2	Not a neighbor
3	Address unreachable
4	Port unreachable

Definitions for other message codes are contained in RFC 1885.

The Checksum is a 16-bit field that is used to detect data corruption in the ICMPv6 message and parts of the IPv6 header.

Specifics of the ICMPv6 message formats and their parameters can be found in RFC 1885.

8.8 The Great Transition: IPv4 to IPv6

The benefits derived from a new protocol must also be balanced by the costs associated with making a transition from the existing systems. These logistical and technical issues have been addressed in RFC 1933 "Transition Mechanisms for IPv6 Hosts and Routers," [8-22].

The developers of IPv6 recognized that not all systems would upgrade from IPv4 to IPv6 in the immediate future, and that for some systems, that upgrade may not be for years. To complicate matters, most internetworks are heterogeneous systems, with various routers, hosts, etc. manufactured by different vendors. If such a multivendor system were to be upgraded at one time, IPv6 capabilities would be required on all of the individual elements before the larger project could be attempted. Another (much larger) issue becomes the worldwide Internet, which operates across 24 different time zones. Upgrading this system in a single process would be even more difficult.

Given the above constraints, it therefore becomes necessary to develop strategies for IPv4 and IPv6 to coexist, until such time as IPv6 becomes the preferred option. At the time of this writing, two mechanisms for this coexistence have been proposed:

a dual IP layer and IPv6 over IPv4 tunneling. These two alternatives will be discussed in the following sections.

8.8.1 Dual IP Layers

The simplest mechanism for IPv4 and IPv6 coexistence is for both of the protocol stacks to be implemented on the same device. That device, which could be either a host or a router, is then referred to as an IPv6/IPv4 node. The IPv6/IPv4 node has the capability to send and receive both IPv4 and IPv6 packets, and can therefore inter-operate with an IPv4 device using IPv4 packets and with an IPv6 device using IPv6 packets (see Figure 8-15). The IPv6/IPv4 node would be configured with addresses that support both protocols, and those addresses might or might not be related to each other. Other address-related functions, such as the Dynamic Host Configuration Protocol (DHCP), the Bootstrap Protocol (BOOTP), and the Domain Name System (DNS), may also be involved in this process.

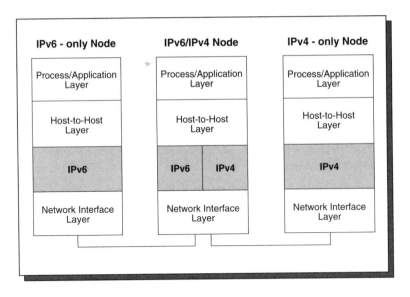

Figure 8-15. Dual IP Layer Architecutre

8.8.2 Tunneling

Tunneling is a process whereby information from one protocol is encapsulated inside the frame or packet of another architecture, thus enabling the original data to be carried over that second architecture. The tunneling scenarios for IPv6/IPv4 are designed to enable an existing IPv4 infrastructure to carry IPv6 packets by encapsulating the IPv6 information inside IPv4 packets.

The encapsulation process is illustrated in Figure 8-16. Note that the resulting IPv4 packet contains both an IPv4 header and an IPv6 header, plus all of the upper-layer information, such as the TCP header, application data, and so on. The tunneling process involves three distinct steps: encapsulation, decapsulation, and tunnel management. At the encapsulating node (or tunnel entry point), the IPv4 header is created, and the encapsulated packet is transmitted. At the decapsulating node (or tunnel exit point), the IPv4 header is removed and the IPv6 packet is processed. In addition, the encapsulating node may maintain configuration information regarding the tunnels that are established, such as the maximum transfer unit (MTU) size that is supported in that tunnel.

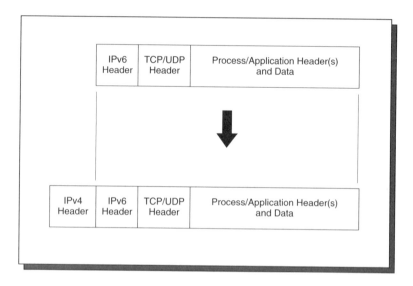

Figure 8-16. Encapsulating IPv6 in IPv4

RFC 1933 defines four possible tunnel configurations that could be established between routers and hosts:

- Router-to-Router: IPv6/IPv4 routers that are separated by an IPv4 infrastructure tunnel IPv6 packets between themselves. In this case, the tunnel would span one segment of the packet's end-to-end path.

- Host-to-Router: an IPv6/IPv4 host tunnels IPv6 packets to an IPv6/IPv4 router that is reachable via an IPv4 infrastructure. In this case, the tunnel would span the first segment of the packet's end-to-end path.
- Host-to-Host: IPv6/IPv4 hosts that are interconnected by an IPv4 infrastructure can tunnel IPv6 packets across the IPv4 infrastructure. In this case, the tunnel spans the packet's entire end-to-end path.
- Router-to-Host: IPv6/IPv4 routers can tunnel IPv6 packets to an IPv6/IPv4 host which is the final destination. In this case, the tunnel would span only the final segment of the packet's end-to-end path.

For a tunnel to operate, addresses of both the tunnel endpoint and the packet's destination must be known, and these two addresses are not necessarily the same. The manner in which the tunnel endpoint address is determined defines one of two types of tunnels: an automatic tunnel or a configured tunnel. These alternatives will be explored below.

From the above four tunneling scenarios, the first two terminate on a router, which then decapsulates the information and forwards the IPv6 packet to its final destination. Note that the tunnel endpoint address is different from the final destination endpoint address. This requires the node performing the tunneling to determine the tunnel endpoint from some configuration information. For this reason, this type of tunneling is called *configured tunneling*.

In the last two tunneling scenarios, the termination point of the tunnel and the final destination of the IPv6 packet are the same—both end at a host. In this case, the tunnel endpoint address and the IPv6 packet endpoint address both identify the same device. But note that the tunnel endpoint address is an IPv4 address, while the host address is an IPv6 address. If the IPv4 and IPv6 addresses can be correlated, the tunneling process is considerably simplified. For this reason, this type of tunneling is called *automatic tunneling*. This is, in fact, the purpose of the IPv4-compatible IPv6 address (review Figure 8-12). Note from the figure that the 32-bit IPv4 address occupies the lower 32 bits of the IPv6 address, and that the balance of the address is filled with all zeros.

For further details on tunneling and associated functions, see RFC 1933.

As expected, IPv6 has generated a great deal of interest among users, vendors, and network managers. References [8-23] through [8-31] are examples of recent journal articles that discuss various aspects of the protocol, and references [8-32] and [8-33] are recent books that discuss the new protocol and implementation strategies.

8.9 References

[8-1]   Mankin, Allison. "The Trillion Node Internet: An Update on IPv6." ComNet 1996 Conference Proceedings, January 1996.

[8-2]   Gross, P., and P. Almquist. "IESG Deliberations on Routing and Addressing." RFC 1380, November 1992.

[8-3]   Bradner, S., and A. Mankin. "IP: Next Generation (IPng) White Paper Solicitation." RFC 1550, December 1993.

[8-4]   Bradner, Scott O., and Allison Mankin, Editors. *IPng —Internet Protocol Next Generation.* Addison-Wesley Publishing Company, (Reading, MA), 1996.

[8-5]   Partridge, C., and F. Kastenholz. "Technical Criteria for Choosing IP The Next Generation (IPng)." RFC 1726, December 1994.

[8-6]   Bradner, S., and A. Mankin. "The Recommendation for the IP Next Generation Protocol." RFC 1752, January 1995.

[8-7]   McGovern, M., and R. Ullman. "CATNIP: Common Architecture for the Internet." RFC 1707, October 1994.

[8-8]   McGovern, Michael, and Robert Ullmann. "The CATNIP: Purrposed Common Architecture for the Internet." *ConneXions* (May 1994): 18-27.

[8-9]   Hinden, R. "Simple Internet Protocol Plus White Paper." RFC 1710, October 1994.

[8-10] Hinden, Robert M. "Simple Internet Protocol Plus (SIPP) Overview." *ConneXions* (May 1994): 34-48.

[8-11] Callon, R. "TCP and UDP with Bigger Addresses (TUBA)." RFC 1347, June 1992.

[8-12] Ford, Peter S., et al. "TUBA: CLNP as IPng." *ConneXions* (May 1994): 28-33.

[8-13] Fuller, V., et al. "Classless Inter-Domain Routing (CIDR): An Address Assignment and Aggregation Strategy." RFC 1519, 1993.

[8-14] Solensky, Frank. "CIDR Effects: Getting More Out of IPv4." *ConneXions* (May 1994): 14-17.

[8-15] Deering, S., and R. Hinden. "Internet Protocol, Version 6 (IPv6) Specification." RFC 1883, December 1995.

[8-16] Atkinson, R. "Security Architecture for the Internet Protocol." RFC 1825, August 1995.

[8-17] Atkinson, R. "IP Authentication Header." RFC 1826, August 1995.

[8-18] Atkinson, R. "IP Encapsulating Security Payload (ESP)." RFC 1827, August 1995.

[8-19] Hinden, R., and S. Deering, Editors. "IP Version 6 Addressing Architecture." RFC 1884, December 1995.

[8-20] Conta, A., and S. Deering. "Internet Control Message Protocol (ICMPv6) for the Internet Protocol Version 6 (IPv6) Specification." RFC 1885, December 1995.

[8-21] Deering, S. "Host Extensions for IP Multicasting." RFC 1112, August 1989.

[8-22] Gilligan, Robert E. and Erik Nordmark. RFC 1933, "Transition Mechanisms for IPv6 Hosts and Routers." April 1996.

[8-23] Special Issue: IP—The Next Generation. *ConneXions* (May 1994).

[8-24] Britton, E. G., et al. "TCP/IP: The next generation." *IBM Systems Journal* (Volume 34, number 3, 1995): 452-471.

[8-25] Dixon, Tim. "IPng—What it Means for OSI." *ConneXions* (March 1995): 19-23.

[8-26] Hinden, Robert M. "IP Next Generation Overview." *ConneXions* (March 1995): 2-18.

[8-27] Moskowitz, Robert G. "Plan Now for the New Internet Protocol." *Network Computing* (May 1, 1995): 144-150.

[8-28] Callon, Ross. "Migrate to IPng or Retrofit IP?" *Network World* (June 5, 1995): 41.

[8-29]   Cooney, Michael. "Is IP at a Fork In the Road?" *Network World* (October 23, 1995): 24.

[8-30]   Gilligan, Robert E., and Ross Callon. "IPv6 Transitions Mechanisms Overview." *ConneXions* (October 1995): 2-17.

[8-31]   Hinden, Robert M. "IP Next Generation Overview." (May 14, 1995): 1-21. Available via the Internet at URL:http://playground.sun.com/pub/ipng/html/INET-IPng-Paper.html.

[8-32]   Huitema, Christian. *IPv6: The New Internet Protocol*. Prentice-Hall, Inc., (Upper Saddle River, NJ) 1996.

[8-33]   Murphy, Eamon, et. al. *TCP/IP Tutorial and Technical Overview*. Prentice Hall PTR (Upper Saddle River, NJ), 1995.

Addresses of Standards Organizations

ANSI STANDARDS

American National Standards Institute
1430 Broadway
New York, NY 10018
Tel: (212) 354-3300
Sales Department (212) 642-4900
URL: http://www.ansi.org

ATIS PUBLICATIONS

Alliance for Telecommunications Industry Solutions
(formerly the Exchange Carriers Standards Association)
1200 G St. N.W., Suite 500
Washington, DC 20005
Tel: (202) 628-6380
Fax: (202) 393-5453
URL: http://www.atis.org

AT&T PUBLICATIONS

Lucent Technologies
P.O. Box 19901
Indianapolis, IN 46219
Tel: (317) 322-6557 or (800) 432-6600
Fax: (800) 566-9568
URL: http://ciccatii.attdocs.com

BELLCORE STANDARDS

Bell Communications Research
Information Management Services
8 Corporate Place, Suite 3A-184
Piscataway, NJ 08854-4196
Tel: (908) 699-5800 or (800) 521-2673
Fax: (908) 336-2559
URL: http://www.bellcore.com

CSA STANDARDS

Canadian Standards Association
178 Rexdale Boulevard
Etobicoke, ONT M9W 1R9
Canada
Tel: (416) 747-4363
Fax: (416) 747-2473

DDN STANDARDS

DDN Network Information Center Government Systems, Inc.
14200 Park Meadow Drive
Suite 200
Chantilly, VA 22021
Tel: (703) 802-4535 or (800) 365-3642

DISA STANDARDS

Defense Information Systems Agency
URL: http://www.itsi.disa.mil

ECMA STANDARDS

**European Computer
Manufacturers Association**
114 Rue de Rhone
CH-1204 Geneva
Switzerland
Tel: 41 22 849 60 00
Fax: 41 22 849 60 01
Email: helpdesk@ecma.ch
URL: http://www.ecma.ch

EIA STANDARDS

Electronic Industries Association
2500 Wilson Blvd.
Arlington, VA 22201
Tel: (703) 907-7500
Fax: (703) 907-7501
URL: http://www.eia.org

ETSI STANDARDS

**European Telecommunications
Standards Institute**
ETSI Publications Office
06921 Sophia Antipolis Cedex
France
Tel: 33 92 94 42 41
Fax: 33 93 95 81 33
Email: anja.mulder@etsi.fr
URL: http://www.etsi.fr

FEDERAL INFORMATION PROCESSING STANDARDS (FIPS)

U.S. Department of Commerce
National Technical Information Service
5285 Port Royal Road
Springfield, VA 22161
Tel: (703) 487-4650

FEDERAL STANDARDS SALE

General Service Administration
GSA Specification Unit (WFSIS) Room 6039
7th & D Streets SW
Washington, DC 20407
Tel: (202) 472-2205

IEC STANDARDS

International Electrotechnical Commission
IEC Central Office
3, rue de Verenbe
P.O. Box 131
1211 Geneva 20
Switzerland
Tel: 41 22 919 02 11
Fax: 41 22 919 03 00
Email: dn@iec.ch
URL: http://www.hike.te.chibau.ac.jp/ikeda/IEC

IEEE STANDARDS

**Institute of Electrical and
Electronics Engineers**
445 Hoes Lane
Piscataway, NJ 08855-1331
Tel: (908) 981-1393 or (800) 678-IEEE
Fax: (908) 562-1571
URL: http://www.ieee.org

INTERNET STANDARDS

Internet Society International
12020 Sunrise Valley Drive
Suite 210
Reston, VA 22019
Tel: (703) 648-9888
Fax: (703) 648-9887
Email: isoc@isoc.org
URL: http://www.isoc.org
(See Appendix D for further information.)

ISO STANDARDS

**International Organization
for Standardization**
1, Rue de Varembé
Case postale 56
CH-1211 Geneva 20
Switzerland
Tel: 41 22 749-0111
Fax: 41 22 733-3430
Email: central@isocs.iso.ch
URL: http://www.iso.ch

ITU STANDARDS

International Telecommunications Union
Information Services Department
Place des Nations
1211 Geneva 20
Switzerland
Tel: 41 22 730-5111
Fax: 41 22 733-7256
Email: helpdesk@itu.ch
URL: http://www.itu.ch

MILITARY STANDARDS

Naval Publications and Forms Center
Commanding Officer
NPFC 43
5801 Tabor Avenue
Philadelphia, PA 19120
Tel: (215) 697-3321

NISI STANDARDS

**National Institute of Standards
and Technology**
Technology Building 820, NIST N
Room B-562
Gaithersburg, MD 20899
Tel: (301) 975-2816
Fax: (301) 948 6213
URL: http://www.ncsl.nist.gov

WWW STANDARDS

World Wide Web Consortium
Massachusetts Institute of Technology
Laboratory for Computer Science
545 Technology Square
Cambridge, MA 02139
Tel: (617) 253-2613
Fax: (617) 258-8682
Email: www-request@w3.org
URL: http://www.w3.org
URL: ftp://ftp.w3.org

OBTAINING STANDARDS

Many of the above standards may be purchased from:

Global Engineering Documents
15 Inverness Way East
Englewood, CO 80112
Tel: (303) 397-2715 or (800) 854-7179
Fax: (303) 397-2740
URL: http://www.ihs.com

Phillips Business Information, Inc.
1201 Seven Locks Road
Potomac, MD 20854
Tel: (301) 424 3338 or (800) 777-5006
Fax: (301) 309-3847
Email: clientservices.pbi@phillips.com

Broadband Technology Forums

ATM Forum
Worldwide Headquarters
303 Vintage Park Dr.
Foster City, CA 94404
Tel: (415) 949-6700
Fax: (415) 525-0182
Faxback: (415) 688-4318
Email: info@atmforum.com
URL: http://www.atmforum.com

ATM Forum
European Office
10, rue Thierry Le Luron
92593 Levallois-Perret Cedex, France
Tel: 33 1 46 39 56 56
Fax: 33 1 46 39 56 99

Frame Relay Forum
North American Office
303 Vintage Park Drive
Foster City, CA 94404-1138
Tel: (415) 578-6980
Fax: (415) 525-0182
Faxback: (415) 688-4317
Email: frf@interop.com
URL: ftp://frame-relay.indiana.edu
/pub/frame-relay
URL: http://frame-relay.indiana.edu

Frame Relay Forum
Pacific Office
c/o Interlink Communications
Unit #4 14 Aquatic Drive
Frenchs Forest, NSW 2086 Australia
Tel: 61 2 975 2577
Fax: 61 2 452 5397

Frame Relay Forum
European Office
c/o OST, BP 158
Z1 Sud Est rue du bas Village
35510 Cesson Sevigne cedex, France
Tel: 33 99 51 76 55
Fax: 33 99 41 71 75

Frame Relay Forum
Japanese Office
c/o FPT, Nisso No. 22 Building, 5th Floor
1-11-10, Azabudai
Minato-ku Tokyo, 106, Japan
Tel: 81 3 3583 5811
Fax: 81 3 3583 5813

SMDS Interest Group
303 Vintage Park Drive
Foster City, CA 94404
Tel: (415) 578-6979
Fax: (415) 525-0182
Faxback: (415) 688-4314
Email: sig@interop.com
URL: ftp://ftp.acc.com/pub/protocols/smds

Selected Manufacturers of TCP/IP-Related Internetworking Products

Accton Technology Corp.
1962 Zanker Rd.
San Jose, CA 95112
(408) 452-8900
(800) 926-9288
Fax: (408) 452-8988

ADAX, Inc.
614 Bancroft Way
Berkeley, CA 94710
(415) 548-7047
Fax: (415) 548-5526

ADC Kentrox
P.O. Box 10704
Portland, OR 97210
(503) 643-1681
(800) 733-5511
Fax: (503) 641-3341

ADI Systems
2115 Ringwood Ave.
San Jose, CA 95131
(408) 944-0100
(800) 228-0530
Fax: (408) 944-0300

Advanced Computer Communications (ACC)
340 Storke Road
Santa Barbara, CA 93117
(805) 685-4455
(800) 444-7854
Fax: (805) 685-4465

Advanced Logic Research
9401 Jeronimo
Irvine, CA 92718
(714) 581-6770
(800) 444-4257
Fax: (714) 581-9240

AGE Netmanage
12651 High Bluff Drive
San Diego, CA 92130
(619) 755-1000
Fax: (619) 755-3998

The AG Group
2540 Camino Diablo #202
Walnut Creek, CA 94596
(510) 937-7900
Fax: (510) 937-2479

Alcatel Network Systems
2912 Wake Forest Road
Raleigh, NC 27609
(919) 850-6000
Fax: (919) 850-6171

Alisa Systems, Inc.
221 E. Walnut, Suite 175
Pasadena, CA 91101
(818) 792-9474
(800) 992-5472
Fax: (818) 792-4068

Allied Telesis, Inc.
950 Kifer Road
Sunnyvale, CA 94086
(408) 730-0950
Fax: (408) 736-0100

Alta Group of Cadence Design
Systems, Inc.
555 N. Mathilda Avenue
Sunnyvale, CA 94086
(408) 733-1595
(408) 523-4601

Andrew Corporation
23610 Telo Ave
Torrance, CA 90505
(310) 784-8000
(800) 328-2696
Fax: (310) 784-8090

Andyne Computing Ltd.
544 Princess St., Suite 202
Kingston, Ontario
K7L 1C7, CANADA

Anixter Brothers, Inc.
6602 Owens Drive, Suite 300
Pleasanton, CA 94588
(415) 463-1223
Fax: (415) 463-1255

Apertus Technologies
7275 Flying Cloud Drive
Eden Prairie, MN 55344
(612) 828-0300
(800) 321-0454
Fax: (612) 828-0299

Apertus Technologies
5775 Wayzata Boulevard
Minneapolis, MN 55416
(800) 826-0313

Apple Computer, Inc.
20525 Mariani Avenue
Cupertino, CA 95014
(408) 996-1010
(800) 776-2333
Fax: (408) 974-6726

APT Communications, Inc.
9607 Dr. Perry Rd.
Ijamsville, MD 21754
(301) 831-1182
(800) 842-0626
Fax: (301) 874-5255

Armon Networking
314 E. Carrillo Street, Suite 3
Santa Barbara, CA 93101
(805) 965-0859
(800) 499-7666
Fax: (805) 965-5689

Artisoft
2202 N. Forbes Blvd.
Tucson, AZ 85745
(520) 670-7100
Fax: (520) 670-7101

Asante Technologies
821 Fox Lane
San Jose, CA 95131
(408) 435-8388
(800) 662-9686

526

ascom/IN-NET
15150 Avenue of Science #100
San Diego, CA 92128
(800) 283-3334
Fax: (619) 487-3697

ascom Timeplex Inc.
400 Chestnut Ridge Road
Woodcliff Lake, NJ 07675
(201) 391-1111
(800) 755-8526
Fax: (201) 573-6470

AT&T Computer Systems
Gatehall Drive
Parsippany, NJ 07054
(201) 397-4800
Fax: (201) 397-4918

AT&T EasyLink Services
400 Interpace Pkwy.
Parsippany, NJ 07054
(201) 331-4000
(800) 242-6005

Attachmate Corp.
3617 131st Avenue SE
Bellevue, WA 98006
(206) 644-4010
(800) 426-6283
Fax: (206) 747-9924

Aurora Technologies
176 Second Avenue
Waltham, MA 02154
(617) 290-4800
Fax: (617) 290-4844

Auspex Systems Inc.
5200 Great America Parkway
Santa Clara, CA 95054
(408) 986-2000
Fax: (408) 986-2020

Autotrol Technology
12500 N. Washington
Denver, CO 80241
(303) 452-4919
Fax: (303) 252-2249

Axis Communications
4 Constitution Way
Woburn, MA 01801
(617) 938-1188
(800) 444-2947
Fax: (617) 938-6161

AXON Networks
199 Wells Avenue
Newton, MA 02159
(617) 630-9600
Fax: (617) 630-9604

**Aydin Computer &
Monitor Systems**
700 Dresher Rd.
Horsham, PA 19044
(215) 657-7510
Fax: (215) 657-5470

Banyan Systems, Inc.
120 Flanders Road #5
Westboro, MA 01581
(508) 898-1000
(800) 828-2404
Fax: (508) 836-1810

Barr Systems
4131 NW 28 Lane
Gainesville, FL 32614-7015
(352) 491-3100
(800) 227-7797
Fax: (352) 491-3141

Bay Networks
P.O. Box 58185
4401 Great America Parkway
Santa Clara, CA 95052-8185

BBN Communications Corp.
150 Cambridge Park Drive
Cambridge, MA 02140
(617) 873-2000
Fax: (617) 491-0921

Bellcore
331 Newman Springs Road
Red Bank, NJ 07701-7030
(908) 758-2032
Fax: (908) 758-4369

Berkeley Software Design
5575 Tech Center Drive #110
Colorado Springs, CO 80918
(719) 593-9445
(800) 487-2738
Fax: (719) 593-2082

BGL Technology Corporation
455 W 115 Avenue
Northglenn, CO 80233
(303) 451-5005
Fax: (303) 451-5227

Black Box Corporation
1000 Park Drive
P.O. Box 12800
Pittsburgh, PA 15241
(412) 746-5500
Fax: (412) 746-0746

BLAST, INC.
P.O. Box 808
Pittsboro, NC 27312
(919) 542-3007
(800) 242-5278
Fax: (919) 542-0161

Border Network Technologies
20 Toronto Street, Suite 1400
Toronto, Ontario, Canada M5C 2B8
(416) 368-7157
(800) 334-8195
Fax: (416) 368-7789

BRIO Technology Inc.
650 Castro St., Suite 650
Mountain View, CA 94041
(415) 961-4110
(800) 486-2746
Fax: (415) 961-4572

BSDI
5575 Tech Center Drive
Colorado Springs, CO 80918
(719) 593-9445
(800) 800-4273
Fax: (719) 598-4238

Bull HN Information Systems
Technology Park
2 Wall Street
Billerica, MA 01821
(508) 294-6000
Fax: (508) 294-6440

Bytex
4 Technology Dr.
Westborough, MA 01581-1760
(508) 366-8000
(800) 227-1145
Fax: (508) 366-7970

Cabletron Systems, Inc.
P.O. Box 5005
Rochester, NH 03867-0505
(603) 332-9400
Fax: (603) 332-4616

CACI Products
3333 N. Torey Pines Ct.
La Jolla, CA 92037
(619) 457-9681
Fax: (619) 457-1184

Cactus Computer, Inc.
1120 Metrocrest Dr., Suite 103
Carrollton, TX 75006
(214) 416-0525
Fax: (214) 416-7151

California Microwave
650 N. Mary Avenue
Sunnyvale, CA 94086
(408) 732-4000
(800) 831-3104
Fax: (408) 720-6290

California Software
2121 E. Pacific Coast Highway
Suite 120A
Corona Del Mar, CA 92625
(714) 729-4222
(800) 830-3311
Fax: (714) 729-2272

Castelle
3255-3 Scott Boulevard
Santa Clara, CA 95054
(408) 496-0474
Fax: (408) 496-0502

Castle Rock Computing
20863 Stevens Creek Boulevard
Suite 530
Cupertino, CA 95014
(408) 366-6540
Fax: (408) 252-2379

Cayman Systems, Inc.
100 Maple Street
Stoneham, MA 02180
(617) 279-1101
(800) 473-4776
Fax: (617) 438-4680

C.D. Connection
5805 State Bridge Road
Suite #G 303
Duluth, GA 30155
(770) 446-1332
Fax: (770) 446-9164

CE Software
1801 Industrial Circle
West Des Moines, IA 50265
(515) 221-1801
(800) 523-7638
Fax: (515) 221-1806

Century Software
5284 Commerce Drive, Suite C-134
Salt Lake City, UT 84107
(801) 268-3088
(800) 329-2384
Fax: (801) 268-2772

CERFnet
Box 85608
San Diego, CA 92186
(619) 455-3900
(800) 876-2373
Fax: (619) 455-3990

CHI
31200 Carter Street
Solon, OH 44139
(216) 349-8605
(800) 828-0599
Fax: (216) 349-8609

Chipcom Corporation
118 Turnpike Rd.
Southborough, MA 01772
(508) 460-8900
(800) 228-9930
Fax: (508) 460-8950

Chorus Systems
1999 S. Bascom Avenue, Suite 400
Campbell, CA 95008
(408) 879-4100
(800) 972-4678
Fax: 879-4102

Cisco Systems Inc.
170 W Tasman Drive
San Jose, CA 95134
(408) 526-4000
(800) 553-6387
Fax: (408) 526-4100

Citrix Systems
210 University Drive, Suite 700
Coral Springs, FL 33071
(305) 755-0559
(800) 437-7503
Fax: (305) 341-6880

Claflin & Clayton, Inc.
203 Southwest Cutoff
Northboro, MA 01532
(508) 393-7979
Fax: (508) 393-8788

Clearpoint Enterprises
25 Birch St., Unit #B 41
Milford, MA 01757
(508) 473-6111
(800) 253-2778
Fax: (508) 473-0112

CNet Technology
2199 Zanker Road
San Jose, CA 95131
(408) 954-8000
(800) 486-2638
Fax: (408) 954-8866

CNT/Brixton Systems
125 Cambridge Park Drive
Cambridge, MA 02140
(617) 498-2300
(800) 274-9866
Fax: (617) 498-2480

Codenoll Technology
1086 N. Broadway
Yonkers, NY 10701
(914) 965-6300
Fax: (914) 965-9811

Comlink, Inc.
601 Commerce Drive, Suite 130
Roseville, CA 95678
(916) 783-8885
(800) 433-3892
Fax: (916) 783-2076

CommTouch Software
1206 W. Hillsdale Boulevard
Suite C
San Mateo, CA 94403
(415) 578-6580
Fax: (415) 578-8580

COMPAQ Computer Corporation
P.O. Box 692000
Houston, TX 77269
(713) 370-0670
(800) 345-1518
Fax: (713) 514-1740

Compatible Systems Corporation
P.O. Drawer 17220
Boulder, CO 80308
(303) 444-9532
(800) 356-0283
Fax: (303) 444-9595

Compression Technologies
7141 77 Avenue
Edmonton, Alberta, Canada T6BOU5
(403) 463-5310
(800) 661-9277
Fax: (403) 465-2113

Computer Associates
575 Herndon Parkway
Herndon, VA 22070
(703) 708-3000
Fax: (703) 708-3025

Computerm
111 Wood Street
Pittsburgh, PA 15222
(412) 391-7804
Fax: (412) 391-1964

Computer Network Technology
125 Cambridge Park Drive
Cambridge, MA 02140
(617) 661-6262
Fax: (617) 498-2480

Computer Network Technology
6500 Wedgwood Rd.
Maple Grove, MN 55311
(612) 550-8000
Fax: (612) 550-8800

Compuware Corporation
983 University Avenue
Los Gatos, CA 95030
(408) 395-1800
Fax: (408) 399-1392

Concord Communications Inc.
33 Boston Post Road
Marlborough, MA 01752
(508) 460-4646
Fax: (508) 481-9772

Concurrent Computer Corporation
One Robbins Road
Westford, MA 01886
(508) 692-6200

Connectware
1301 E. Arapaho Road
Richardson, TX 75081
(214) 907-1093
(800) 282-2535
Fax: (214) 907-1594

Control Data Systems, Inc.
4201 N. Lexington Avenue
Arden Hills, MN 55126
(612) 482-2100
Fax: (612) 482-2791

Cray Communications
9020 Junction Drive
Annapolis, MD 20701
(301) 317-7710
(800) 359-7710
Fax: (301) 317-7220

Cray Research, Inc.
655 Lone Oak Drive
Egan, MN 55121
(612) 683-7100
Fax: (612) 683-7199

CrossComm Corporation
450 Donald Lynch Boulevard
Marlboro, MA 01752
(508) 481-4060
(800) 388-1200
Fax: (508) 229-5535

CrossWind Technologies
1505 Ocean Street
Santa Cruz, CA 95060
(408) 469-1780
Fax: (408) 469-1750

Crystal Point, Inc.
22232 17th Avenue SE #301
Bothell, WA 98021
(206) 487-3656
Fax: (206) 487-3773

CyberCorp
P.O. Box 1985
Kennesaw, GA 30144
(770) 424-6240
Fax: (770) 424-8995

D-Link Systems
5 Musick
Irvine, CA 92718
(714) 455-1688
(800) 326-1688
Fax: (714) 455-2521

Dart Communications
61 Albany Street
P.O. Box 618
Cazenovia, NY 13035
(315) 655-1024
Fax: (315) 655-1025

Data General Corporation
4400 Computer Drive
Westboro, MA 01580
(508) 366-8911
(800) 328-2436
Fax: (508) 366-1744

Data Interface Systems, Corp.
11130 Jollyville Road, Suite 300
Austin, TX 78759
(512) 346-5641
(800) 351-4244
Fax: (512) 346-4035

Datapoint Corporation
8400 Datapoint Drive
San Antonio, TX 78229-8500
(512) 593-7900
(800) 733-1500
Fax: (512) 593-7472

Datastorm Technologies
P.O. Box 1471
Columbia, MO 65205
(314) 443-3282
Fax: (314) 875-0595

Dayna Communications
50 S. Main St., 5th Fl.
Salt Lake City, UT 84144
(801) 531-0203
Fax: (801) 359-9135

Daystar Digital, Inc.
5556 Atlanta Hwy.
Flowery Branch, GA 30542
(770) 967-2077
(800) 962-2077
Fax: (770) 967-3018

DeskTalk Systems
19401 S. Vermont Avenue
Suite F100
Torrance, CA 90502
(310) 323-5998
Fax: (310) 323-6197

Dickens Data Systems
1175 North Meadow Park, Suite 150
Roswell, GA 30076
(770) 475-8860
Fax: (770) 442-7525

Digi International
1299 Orleans Drive
Sunnyvale, CA 94089
(408) 744-2770
(800) 466-4576
Fax: (408) 744-2790

Digilog
2360 Maryland Road
Willow Grove, PA 19090
(215) 830-9400
(800) 344-4564
Fax: (215) 830-9444

**Digital Equipment
Corporation (DEC)**
111 Powdermill Road
Maynard, MA 01754
(508) 493-5111
(800) 344-4825
Fax: (508) 493-8787

Digital Link
217 Humboldt Ct.
Sunnyvale, CA 94089
(408) 745-6200
(800) 441-1142
Fax: (408) 745-6250

Digital Pathways
201 Ravendale Drive
Mountain View, CA 94043
(415) 964-0707
(800) 344-7284
Fax: (415) 961-7487

Digital Products
411 Waverly Oaks Road
Waltham, MA 02154
(617) 647-1234
(800) 243-2333
Fax: (617) 647-4474

Digital Technology
2300 Edwin C. Moses Blvd.
Dayton, OH 45408
(513) 443-0412
(800) 852-1252
Fax: (513) 226-0511

Distinct Corporation
P.O. Box 3410
Saratoga, CA 95070
(408) 366-8933
Fax: (408) 366-0153

Diversified Computer Systems
3775 Iris Avenue, Suite 1B
Boulder, CO 80301
(303) 447-9251
Fax: (303) 447-1406

Eicon Technology Incorporated
14755 Preston Road, Suite 620
Dallas, TX 75240
(214) 239-3270
(800) 803-4266
Fax: (214) 239-3304

Emerging Technologies Inc.
900 Walt Whitman Rd.
Melville, NY 11747
(516) 271-4525
Fax: (516) 271-4814

Emulex Corporation
3535 Harbor Blvd.
Costa Mesa, CA 92626
(714) 662-5600
(800) 854-7112
Fax: (714) 241-0792

Encore Computer Corporation
6901 W. Sunrise Boulevard
Plantation, FL 33313
(305) 587-2900
(800) 726-2230
Fax: (954) 797-5592

Enterprise Solutions Ltd.
2900 Townsgate Road, Suite 210
Westlake Village, CA 91361
(805) 449-4181
Fax: (805) 449-4186

Epilogue Technology
10501 Montgomery NE, Suite 250
Albuquerque, NM 87111
(505) 271-9933
Fax: (505) 271-9798

Equinox Systems
1 Equinox Way
Sunrise, FL 33351
(954) 746-9000
(800) 275-3500
Fax: (954) 746-9101

Esker
350 Sansome St., Suite 210
San Francisco, CA 96104
(415) 675-7777
(800) 883-7537
Fax: 675-7775

Essex Systems Inc.
One Essex Green Drive
Peabody, MA 01960
(508) 750-6200
Fax: (508) 531-5541

European MicroGraf
269 Mount Hermon Road
Suite 100
Scotts Valley, CA 95066
(408) 461-6061
Fax: (408) 461-6056

Farallon Computing
2470 Mariner Square Loop
Alameda, CA 94501
(510) 814-5000
Fax: (510) 814-5020

FEL Computing
10 Main Street
P.O. Box 72
Williamsville, VT 05362
(802) 348-7171
(800) 639-4110
Fax: (802) 348-7124

Fibermux Corporation
21415 Plummer Street
Chatsworth, CA 91311
(818) 709-6000
(800) 800-4624
Fax: (818) 725-2525

Fibronics International Inc.
16 Esquire Road
North Billerica, MA 01862
(508) 671-9440
(800) 327-9526
Fax: (508) 667-7262

Firefox
2099 Gateway Place, 7th Floor
San Jose, CA 95710-1017
(408) 467-1100
(800) 230-6090
Fax: (408) 467-1105

Forest Computer
1749 Hamilton Road
Okemos, MI 48864
(517) 349-4700
Fax: (517) 349-2947

Frederick Engineering Inc.
10200 Old Columbia Road
Columbia, MD 21046
(410) 290-9000
Fax: (410) 381-7180

Frontier Software Development Inc.
1501 Main St., Suite 40
Tewksbury, MA 01876
(508) 244-4000
Fax: (508) 851-6956

Frontier Technologies Corp.
10201 N. Port Washington Rd. 13 West
Mequon, WI 53092
(414) 241-4555
Fax: (414) 241-7084

FTP Software, Inc.
2 High Street
North Andover, MA 01845
(508) 685-4000
Fax: (508) 794-4477

FutureSoft
12012 Wickchester Lane, Suite 600
Houston, TX 77079
(713) 496-9400
(800) 989-8908
Fax: (713) 496-1090

Gandalf Data Inc.
130 Colonnade Road
Nepean, Ontario, Canada K2E 7M4
(708) 517-3600
(800) 426-3253
Fax: (708) 517-3627

General DataCom, Inc.
1579 Straits Turnpike
Middlebury, CT 06762-1299
(203) 574-1118
Fax: (203) 758-8507

Glasgal Communications Inc.
151 Veterans Drive
Northvale, NJ 07647
(201) 768-8082
Fax: (201) 768-2947

Gradient Technologies
5 Mt. Royal Avenue #2
Marlboro, MA 01752
(508) 624-9600
(800) 525-4343
Fax: (508) 229-0338

Gupta Technologies
1040 Marsh Rd.
Menlo Park, CA 94025
(415) 321-9500
(800) 876-3267
Fax: (415) 321-5471

Harris Computer Systems Division
2101 W. Cypress Creek Road
Fort Lauderdale, FL 33309
(305) 974-1700
(800) 666-4544
Fax: (305) 977-5580

Hayes Microcomputer Products, Inc.
5835 Peachtree Corners E
Norcross, GA 30092
(770) 840-9200
Fax: (770) 447-0178

Hewlett-Packard Company
3000 Hanover St.
Palo Alto, CA 94304
(415) 857-1501
(800) 752-0900
Fax: (415) 857-5518

Hewlett-Packard
Colorado Telecommunications Division
5070 Centennial Blvd.
Colorado Springs, CO 80919
(719) 531-4000
Fax: (719) 531-4505

Honeywell Information Systems
Federal Systems Divisions
7900 West Park Drive
McLean, VA 22102
(703) 827-3894
Fax: (703) 827-3729

Hummingbird Communications
706 Hillsboro Street
Raleigh, NC 27603
(919) 831-8989
Fax: (919) 831-8990

Hummingbird Communications Ltd.
1 Sparks Avenue
North York, Ontario, Canada M2H 2W1
(416) 496-2200
Fax: (416) 496-2207

IBM
Old Orchard Road
Armonk, NY 10504
(914) 765-1900
(800) 426-3333
Fax: (800) 232-9426

IDEAssociates Inc.
7 Oak Park
Bedford, MA 01730
(617) 275-2800
Fax: (617) 533-0500

IMC Networks
16931 Milliken Avenue
Irvine, CA 92714
(714) 724-1070
(800) 624-1070
Fax: (714) 720-1020

Information Presentation Technologies
994 Mill Street, Suite 200
San Luis Obispo, CA 93401
(805) 541-3000
Fax: (805) 541-3037

Informix Software, Inc.
16011 College Blvd.
Lenexa, KS 66219
(913) 599-7100
(800) 331-1763
Fax: (913) 599-8590

Innosoft International
1050 E. Garvey Avenue South
West Covina, CA 91790
(818) 919-3600
(800) 552-5444
Fax: (818) 919-3614

Insignia Solutions
1300 Charleston Road
Mountain View, CA 94043
(415) 335-7100
(800) 848-7677
Fax: (415) 335-7105

InterCon Systems Corporation
950 Herndon Pkwy., Suite. 420
Herndon, VA 22070
(703) 709-9890
Fax: (703) 709-5555

InterConnections Incorporated
14711 N.E. 29th Place
Bellevue, WA 98007
(206) 881-5773
(800) 881-5774
Fax: (206) 867-5022

Interface Systems, Inc.
5855 Interface Drive
Ann Arbor, MI 48103
(313) 769-5900
(800) 544-4072
Fax: (313) 769-1047

Intergraph
One Madison Industrial Park
Huntsville, AL 35894
(205) 730-2700
(800) 414-8991
Fax: (205) 730-4136

Interlink Computer Sciences, Inc.
47370 Freemont Blvd.
Freemont, CA 94538
(510) 657-9800
(800) 422-3711
Fax: (510) 659-6381

Interphase
13800 Senlac
Dallas, TX 75234
(214) 654-5000
Fax: (214) 654-5500

I/O Concepts
Bellewood Six, Suite 303
2125 112th Avenue NE
Bellevue, WA 98004-2948
(206) 450-0650
Fax: (206) 622-0058

Ipswitch
81 Hartwell Avenue
Lexington, MA 02173
(617) 676-5700
Fax: (617) 676-5710

ISICAD
1920 W. Corporate Way
Anaheim, CA 92801
(714) 533-8910
(800) 634-1223
Fax: (714) 533-8642

ISOCOR
3240 Ocean Park Boulevard, Suite 2010
Santa Monica, CA 90405
(310) 581-8100
Fax: (310) 581-3111

James River Group
125 N. First Street
Minneapolis, MN 55401
(612) 339-2521
Fax: (612) 339-4445

J & L Information Systems
9600 Topenga Canyon Boulevard
Chatsworth, CA 91311
(818) 709-1778
Fax: (818) 882-1424

JSB
108 Whispering Pines Drive, Suite 115
Scotts Valley, CA 95066
(408) 438-8300
(800) 572-8649
Fax: (408) 438-8360

LANcity Corporation
100 Brickstone Square
Andover, MA 01810
(508)475-4050
(800) 526-2489
Fax: (508) 475-0550

LANshark Systems
784 Morrison Road
Columbus, OH 43230
(614) 751-1111
Fax: (614) 751-1112

Lanwan Technologies
1566 La Pradera Drive
Campbell, CA 95008
(408) 374-8190
Fax: (408) 741-0152

LANworks Technologies
2425 Skymark Drive
Mississauga, Ontario, Canada L4W 4Y6
(905) 238-5528
(800) 808-3000
Fax: (905) 238-9407

Lars Com
4600 Patrick Henry Drive
Santa Clara, CA 95054
(408) 988-6600
Fax: (408) 986-8690

Levi, Ray & Shoup
2401 W. Monroe Street
Springfield, IL 62704
(217) 793-3800
Fax: (217) 787-3286

Lightspeed Software
1800 19th Street
Bakersfield, CA 93301
(805) 324-4291
Fax: (805) 324-1437

Litton-FiberCom
3353 Orange Avenue N.E.
Roanoke, VA 24012
(540) 342-6700
(800) 423-1183
Fax: (540) 342-5961

Livingston Enterprises, Inc.
6920 Koll Center Pkwy, Suite 220
Pleasanton, CA 94566
(415) 426-0770
Fax: (415) 426-8951

Locus Computing
9800 La Cienega Boulevard
Inglewood, CA 90301-4440
(310) 337-5995
(800) 955-6287
Fax: (310) 670-2980

Loral Command & Control
9970 Federal Drive
Colorado Springs, CO 80921
(719) 594-1000
Fax: (719) 594-1305

Lotus Development
640 Lee Road #200
Wayne, PA 19087
(610) 640-9600
Fax: (610) 251-3550

Madge Networks, Inc.
2310 N 1st Street
San Jose, CA 95131
(408) 955-0700
(800) 876-2343
Fax: (408) 955-0970

McData Corporation
310 Interlocken Pkwy.
Broomfield, CO 80021
(303) 460-9200
(800) 752-0388
Fax: (303) 465-4996

MCI Communications Corp.
8003 W. Park Drive
McLean, VA 22102
(800) 888-0800
Fax: (703) 260-7099

Meridian Technology
11 McBride Corporate Drive, Suite 250
Chesterfield, MO 63005-1407
(314) 532-7708
Fax: (314) 532-3242

Mesa Graphics Inc.
P.O. Box 600
Los Alamos, NM 87544
(505) 672-1998

Metrix Corporation
13595 Dullis Technology Drive
Herndon, VA 22071-3424
(703) 742-6000
(800) 366-4665
Fax: (703) 713-3805

Micom Communications Corp.
4100 Los Angeles Ave.
Simi Valley, CA 93063
(805) 583-8600
(800) 642-6687
Fax: (805) 583-1997

Microcom, Inc.
500 River Ridge Drive
Norwood, MA 02062-5028
(617) 551-1000
(800) 822-8224
Fax: (617) 551-1006

Micro Computer Systems
2300 Valley View, Suite 800
Irving, TX 75062
(214) 659-1514
Fax: (214) 659-1624

Microdyne Corporation
3601 Eisenhower Avenue, Suite 300
Alexandria, VA 22304
(703) 329-3700
(800) 255-3967
Fax: (703) 329-3722

Micro Integration
1 Science Park
Frostburg, MD 215322
(301) 777-3307
(800) 642-5888
Fax: (301) 689-0808

Microplex Systems
8525 Commerce Court
Burnaby, British Columbia, Canada V5A 4N3
(604) 444-4232
(800) 665-7798
Fax: (604) 444-4239

Microsoft Corporation
One Microsoft Way
Redmond, WA 98052-6399
(206) 882-8080
(800) 227-4679
Fax: (206) 936-7329

Microsystems Engineering Company
2500 Highland Avenue, Suite 350
Lombard, IL 60148
(708) 261-0111
(800) 775-8790
Fax: (708) 261-9520

Micro Technology
4905 E. La Palma Avenue
Anaheim, CA 92807
(714) 970-0300
(800) 999-9684
Fax: (714) 970-5413

Microtest, Inc.
4747 N. 22nd Street
Phoenix, AZ 85016
(602) 971-6464
(800) 526-9675
Fax: (602) 971-6963

Midnight Networks
200 Fifth Avenue
Waltham, MA 02154
(617) 890-1001
Fax: (617) 890-0028

Milkyway Networks
2650 Queensview Drive, Suite 255
Ottawa, Ontario, Canada K2B 8H6
(613) 596-5549
(800) 499-2530
Fax: (613) 596-5615

Miramar Systems
121 Gray Avenue #200B
Santa Barbara, CA 93101
(805) 966-2432
Fax: (805) 965-1824

Mitsubishi
201 Broadway
Cambridge, MA 02139
(617) 621-7500
Fax: (617) 621-7550

Momentum Software Corp.
401 S. Van Brunt St.
Englewood, NJ 07631
(800) 767-1462
(201) 871-0077
Fax: (201) 871-0807

Morning Star Technologies, Inc.
3518 Riverside Drive, Suite 101
Columbus, OH 43221
(614) 451-1883
Fax: (614) 459-5054

Motorola Codex
20 Cabot Blvd.
Mansfield, MA 02048
(508) 261-4000
(800) 544-0062
Fax: (508) 261-7118

Mt. Xinu, Inc.
2560 9th Street, Suite 312
Berkeley, CA 94710
(510) 644-0146
Fax: (510) 644-2680

Multi-Tech Systems
2205 Woodale Dr.
Mounds View, MN 55112
(612) 785-3500
(800) 328-9717
Fax: (612) 785-9874

National Semiconductor
2900 Semiconductor Dr.
Santa Clara, CA 95052
(408) 721-5000
(800) 272-9959
Fax: (408) 739-9803

NCD Software Corporation
101 Rowland Way, Suite 300
Novato, CA 94945
(415) 898-8649
Fax: (415) 898-8299

NCR Corporation
1700 S. Patterson Blvd.
Dayton, OH 45479
(513) 445-5000
(800) 225-5627
Fax: (513) 445-1847

NEC America
10 Rio Robles
San Jose, CA 95134
(408) 433-1200
(800) 222-4632
Fax: (408) 433-1239

Neon Software, Inc.
3685 Mt. Diablo Boulevard
Lafayette, CA 94549
(510) 283-9771
Fax: (510) 283-6507

**Netcom On-Line
Communication Services**
3031 Tisch Way, Suite 200
San Jose, CA 95128
(408) 983-5950
(800) 353-6600
Fax: (408) 984-6879

NetFrame Systems
1545 Barber Lane
Milpitas, CA 95035
(408) 944-0600
(800) 852-3726
Fax: (408) 434-4190

Netlink
1881 Worcester Road
Framingham, MA 01701
(508) 879-6306
(800) 638-5465
Fax: (508) 872-8136

NetManage, Inc.
10725 N. De Anza Boulevard
Cupertino, CA 95014
(408) 973-7171
Fax: (408) 257-6405

Netscape Communications
501 East Middlefield Road
Mountain View, CA 94043
(415) 254-1900
(800) 638-7483
Fax: (415) 528-4124

NetSoft
31 Technology Drive, 2nd Floor
Irvine, CA 92718
(714) 753-0800
Fax: (714) 753-0810

Netwise
2477 55th St.
Boulder, CO 80301
(303) 442-8280
(800) 733-7722
Fax: (303) 442-3798

Network Design and Analysis
60 Gough Road, 2nd Floor
Markham, Ontario, Canada L3R 8X7
(905) 477-9534
(800) 387-4234
Fax: (905) 477-9572

Network Equipment Technologies Inc.
800 Saginaw Dr.
Redwood City, CA 94063
(415) 366-4400
(800) 234-4638
Fax: (415) 366-5675

Network General Corporation
4200 Bohannon Drive
Menlo Park, CA 94025
(415) 688-2700
(800) 395-3151
Fax: (415) 321-0855

541

Network Systems Corporation
7600 Boone Ave. N.
Minneapolis, MN 55428
(612) 424-4888
(800) 248-8777
Fax: (612) 424-1661

Network TeleSystems
550 Del Ray Avenue
Sunnyvale, CA 94086
(408) 523-8100
Fax: (408) 523-8118

Network Translation
2464 Embarcadero Way
Palo Alto, CA 94303
(415) 494-6387
Fax: (415) 424-9110

Networth, Inc.
8404 Esters Boulevard
Irving, TX 75063
(214) 929-1700
(800) 544-5255
Fax: (214) 929-1720

Newbridge Networks
593 Herndon Pkwy.
Herndon, VA 22070-5241
(703) 834-3600
(800) 332-1080
Fax: (703) 471-7080

NHC Communications
5450 Cole de Liesse
Mount Royal, Quebec, Canada H4P 1A5
(514) 735-2741
(800) 361-1965
Fax: (514) 735-8057

NobleNet
337 Turnpike Road
Southboro, MA 01772
(508) 460-8222
(800) 809-8988
Fax: (508) 460-3456

Novell, Inc.
122 East 1700 South
Provo, UT 84606
(801) 429-7000
(800) 638-9273
Fax: (801) 429-5155

Novell, Inc.
2180 Fortune Drive
San Jose, CA 95131
(408) 434-2300
(800) 243-8526
Fax: (408) 435-1706

Nynex Information Solutions Group Inc.
Four W. Red Oak Lane
White Plains, NY 10604
(914) 644-7800

ONSTREAM Networks
3393 Octavious Drive
Santa Clara, CA 95054
(408) 727-4545
(800) 477-7050
Fax: (408) 727-5151

ON Technology
1 Cambridge Center
Cambridge, MA 02142
(617) 374-1400
(800) 767-6683
Fax: (617) 374-1433

OpenConnect Systems
2711 LBJ Freeway, Suite 800
Dallas, TX 75234
(214) 484-5200
Fax: (214) 484-6100

Optical Data Systems (ODS)
1101 E. Arapaho Road
Richardson, TX 75081
(214) 234-6400
Fax: (214) 234-4059

Oracle Corp.
500 Oracle Pkwy.
Redwood Shores, CA 94065
(415) 506-7000
(800) 392-2999
Fax: (415) 506-7255

Pacific Data Products
9855 Scranton Road
San Diego, CA 92121
(619) 552-0880
Fax: (619) 552-0889

Pacific Softworks
4000 Via Pescador
Camarillo, CA 93012
(805) 484-2128
(800) 541-9508
Fax: (805) 484-3929

Peer Networks
1190 Saratoga Avenue, Suite 130
San Jose, CA 95129-3443
(408) 556-0723
Fax: (408) 556-0735

Penril Datability Networks
1300 Quince Orchard Blvd.
Gaithersburg, MD 20878
(301) 921-8600
(800) 473-6745
Fax: (301) 921-8376

Peregrine Systems
12670 High Bluff Drive
San Diego, CA 92130
(619) 481-5000
(800) 638-5231
Fax: (619) 481-1751

Performance Systems International
510 Huntmar Park Drive
Herndon, VA 22070
(703) 904-4100
(800) 774-0852
Fax: (703) 904-4200

Performance Technology
800 Lincoln Center
7800 IH-10 West, Ste. 800
San Antonio, TX 78230
(210) 979-2000
(800) 327-8526
Fax: (210) 979-2002

PeriCom
Golden Crest Corp. Center, Suite 106
2271 Highway 33
Hamilton, NJ 08690
(609) 588-5300
(800) 233-2206
Fax: (609) 588-8906

Persoft Inc.
465 Science Dr.
Madison, WI 53711
(608) 273-6000
(800) 368-5283
Fax: (608) 273-8227

Piiceon
1996 Lundy Avenue
San Jose, CA 95131
(408) 432-0292
(800) 366-2983
Fax: (408) 943-1309

Plexcom
2255 Agate Court
Simi Valley, CA 93065
(805) 522-3333
Fax (805) 583-4764

Premenos
1000 Burnett Avenue, 2nd Floor
Concord, CA 94520
(510) 602-2000
Fax: (510) 602-2133

Process Software Corporation
959 Concord Street
Framingham, MA 01701
(508) 879-6994
Fax: (508) 879-0042

Proteon, Inc.
9 Technology Drive
Westborough, MA 01581
(508) 898-2800
(800) 545-7464
Fax: (508) 366-8901

PureData
180 W. Beaver Creek Rd.
Richmond Hill, Ontario, Canada L4B 1B4
(905) 731-6444
Fax: (905) 731-7017

QNF
2650 San Tomas Expressway
Santa Clara, CA 95051
(408) 986-9400
Fax: (408) 727-3725

Quadritek Systems
10 Valley Stream Parkway, Suite 240
Malvern, PA 19355
(610) 725-8535
(800) 367-7835
Fax: (610) 725-8559

Qualcomm
6455 Lusk Boulevard
San Diego, CA 92121
(619) 658-1291
Fax: (619) 452-9096

Quarterdeck
13160 Mindanal, 3rd Floor
Marina Del Rey, CA 90292
(310) 309-3700
Fax: (310) 309-2217

Racal-Interlan, Inc.
60 Codman Hill Road
Boxborough, MA 01719
(508) 263-9929
(800) 526-8255
Fax: (508) 263-8655

Racal Data Communications
1601 N. Harrison Pkwy.
Sunrise, FL 33323-2899
(305) 846-1601
(800) 722-2555
Fax: (305) 846-5510

Racore Computer Products
170 Knowles Dr. #206
Los Gatos, CA 95030
(408) 374-8290
(800) 635-1274
Fax: (408) 374-6653

Raptor Systems
69 Hickory Drive
Waltham, MA 02154
(617) 487-7700
(800) 932-4536

Remedy
1505 Salado Drive
Mountain View, CA 94043
(415) 903-5200
Fax: (415) 903-9001

Research Triangle Institute
3040 Cornwallis Road
P.O. Box 12194
Research Triangle Park, NC 27709-2194
(919) 541-6000
Fax: (919) 541-5985

Retix
2401 Colorado Avenue, Suite 200
Santa Monica, CA 90404
(310) 828-3400
(800) 255-2333
Fax: (310) 828-2255

Rexon
1900 Pike Road, Suite E
Longmont, CO 80501
(303) 682-3700
(800) 422-2587
Fax: (303) 776-7706

RFI Communications & Security
360 Turtle Creek Court
San Jose, CA 95125-1389
(408) 298-5400
Fax: (408) 275-0156

Rockwell Network Systems
7402 Hollister Avenue
Santa Barbara, CA 93117
(805) 968-4262
(800) 262-8023
Fax: (805) 968-6478

RSA Data Security
100 Marine Parkway, Suite 500
Redwood City, CA 94065-1031
(415) 595-8782
Fax: (415) 595-1873

Santa Cruz Operation (SCO)
400 Encinal Street
P.O. Box 1900
Santa Cruz, CA 95061
(408) 425-7222
(800) 726-8649
Fax: (408) 461-3182

SBE, Inc.
4550 North Canyon Road
San Ramon, CA 94583-1369
(510) 355-2000
(800) 925-2660

Seagate EMS
19925 Stevens Creek Boulevard
Cupertino, CA 95014
(408) 342-4500
(800) 961-8860
Fax: (408) 342-4600

Shiva Corporation
Northwest Park
63 Third Avenue
Burlington, MA 01803
(617) 270-8300
(800) 458-3550
Fax: (617) 788-1539

Siemens Stromberg-Carlson
900 Broken Sound Pkwy.
Boca Raton, FL 33487
(407) 955-5000
Fax: (407) 955-6538

Simpact Associates, Inc.
9210 Sky Park Court
San Diego, CA 92123
(619) 565-1865
Fax: (619) 560-2836

Simware Inc.
2 Gurdwara Road
Ottawa, Ontario, Canada K2E 1A2
(613) 727-1779
(800) 267-9991
Fax: (613) 727-8797

Siren Software
505 Hamilton Avenue
Palo Alto, CA 94301
(415) 322-0600
Fax: (415) 617-1313

Sirius Systems, Inc.
Box 2202
Petersburg, VA 23804
(804) 733-7944
Fax (804) 861-0358

SMC
3 Arkay Drive
Hauppauge, NY 11788
(516) 435-6000
(800) 992-4762
Fax: (516) 435-6973

SNMP Research
3001 Kimberlin Heights Road
Knoxville, TN 37920
(615) 573-1434
Fax: (615) 573-9197

Softronics
5085 List Drive
Colorado Springs, CO 80919
(719) 593-9540
(800) 225-8590
Fax: (719) 548-1878

Software AG of North America, Inc.
11190 Sunrise Valley Drive
Reston, VA 22091
(703) 860-5050
(800) 525-7859
Fax: (703) 391-6731

The Software Group Ltd.
642 Welham Road
Barrie, Ontario, Canada L4M 6E7
(705) 725-9999
Fax: (705) 725-9666

Software Kinetics Ltd.
65 Iber Road
Stittsville, Ontario, Canada K2S 1E7
(613) 831-0888
Fax: (613) 831-1836

Software Moguls
12301 Whitewater Drive, Suite 160
Minnetonka, MN 55343
(612) 932-6738
Fax: (612) 932-6736

Software Ventures
2907 Claremont Avenue
Berkeley, CA 94705
(510) 644-3232
Fax: (510) 848-0885

SONY Corporation
3300 Zanker Road
San Jose, CA 95134
(408) 432-1600AN
Fax: (408) 432-1874

Spartacus Technologies
239 Littleton Road, Suite 1B
Westford, MA 01886
(508) 392-3400
Fax: (508) 392-3417

Spider Island Software
4790 Irvine Boulevard, Suite 105-347
Irvine, CA 92720
(714) 453-8095

Spider Software
Spider Park, Stanwell Street
Edinburgh, Scotland, EH6 5NG
44 167 252 1122
(800) 282-9260
Fax: 44 161 252 1133

Spyglass
1230 E. Diehl Road, Suite 304
Naperville, IL 60563
(708) 505-1010
(800) 647-8901
Fax: (708) 505-4944

StarNine Technologies, Inc.
2550 Ninth Street, Suite 112
Berkeley, CA 94710
(510) 548-0391
Fax: (510) 548-0393

StarWare
2150 Shattuck Avenue, Suite 204
Berkeley, CA 94704
(510) 704-2000
(800) 763-0050
Fax: (510) 704-2001

Sterling Software
1800 Alexander Bell Drive
Reston, VA 22091
(703) 264-8000
(800) 533-5128
Fax: (703) 260-0063

Sterling Software Inc.
200 W. Lowe Street
Fairfield, IA 52556
(515) 472-7077
(800) 522-4252
Fax: (515) 472-7198

SunConnect Inc.
2550 Garcia Ave.
Mountain View, CA 94043-1100
(415) 960-1300
(800) 786-7638
Fax: (415) 962-1952

Sun Microsystems, Inc.
2550 Garcia Avenue
Mountain View, CA 94043
(415) 960-1300
(800) 872-4786
Fax: (415) 336-3475

SunSoft
2550 Garcia Avenue
Mountain View, CA 94043
(800) 643-8300

Sybase
3035 Center Green Drive
Boulder, CO 80301
(303) 413-4000
Fax: (303) 413-4001

Sybase Inc.
6475 Christie Ave.
Emeryville, CA 94608
(510) 596-3500
Fax: (510) 658-9441

Symantec Corporation
445 Broad Hollow Road #200
Melville, NY 11747
(516) 465-2400
Fax: (516) 465-2401

Synergy Software
2457 Perkiomen Avenue
Reading, PA 19606
(610) 779-0522
Fax: (610) 370-0548

Tangent Computer Inc.
1197 Airport Blvd.
Burlingame, CA 94010
(415) 342-9388
(800) 223-6677
Fax: (415) 342-9380

Tangram Enterprise Solutions Inc.
5511 Capital Center Drive
Raleigh, NC 27606
(919) 851-6000
(800) 722-2482
Fax: (919) 851-6004

TechGnosis
One Van De Graaff Drive
Burlington, MA 01803
(617) 229-6100
(800) 443-1601

Technically Elite Concepts Inc.
1686 Dell Avenue
Campbell, CA 95008
(408) 370-4300
(800) 474-7888
Fax: (408) 370-4222

Tekelec
26580 W. Agoura Rd.
Calabasas, CA 91302
(818) 880-5656
(800) 835-3532
Fax: (818) 880-6993

TEKnique
911 N. Plum Grove Road
Schaumburg, IL 60173
(708) 706-9700
Fax: (708) 706-9735

Tektronix, Inc.
P.O. Box 1197
Redmond, OR 97756
(503) 923-0333
(800) 833-9200
Fax: (503) 923-4434

Telebit Corporation
1315 Chesapeake Terrace
Sunnyvale, CA 94089
(408) 745-3086
Fax: (408) 734-4333

Telecommunications Techniques Corp.
20410 Observation Dr.
Germantown, MD 20876
(301) 353-1550
(800) 638-2049
Fax: (301) 353-0731

Telematics International, Inc.
1201 W. Cypress Creek Road
Ft. Lauderdale, FL 33309
(305) 772-3070
Fax: (305) 351-4405

Telos
460 Herndon Parkway
Herndon, VA 22070
(703) 471-6000
(800) 999-9987
Fax: (703) 318-1883

Tenon Intersystems
1123 Chapala Street
Santa Barbara, CA 93101
(805) 963-6983
Fax: (805) 962-8202

Teubner & Associates
7th and Main
P.O. Box 1994
Stillwater, OK 74074
(405) 624-2254
Fax: (405) 624-3010

TGV, Inc.
101 Cooper Street
Santa Cruz, CA 95060
(408) 427-4365
Fax: (408) 457-5208

Themis Computer
3185 Laurel View
Fremont, CA 94538
(510) 252-0870
Fax: (510) 490-5529

The Mitre Corporation
7525 Colshire Drive
McLean, VA 22102
(703) 883-6728
Fax: (703) 883-3315

The Santa Cruz Operation
400 Encinal Street P.O. Box 1900
Santa Cruz, CA 95061-1900
(408) 425-7222
Fax: (408) 458-4227

3Com Corporation
5400 Bayfront Plaza
Santa Clara, CA 95052
(408) 764-5000
(800) 638-3266
Fax: (408) 764-5001

Thursby Software Systems
5840 W. Interstate 20, Suite 100
Arlington, TX 76017
(817) 478-5070
(800) 283-5070
Fax: (817) 561-2313

Tone Software
1735 S. Brookhurst Street
Anaheim, CA 92804-6491
(714) 991-9460
(800) 833-8663
Fax: (714) 991-1831

Touch Communications
250 E. Hacienda Ave.
Campbell, CA 95008
(408) 374-2500
Fax: (408) 374-1680

Transition Networks
6475 City West Parkway
Minneapolis, MN 55344
(612) 941-7600
(800) 325-2725
Fax: (612) 941-2322

Triticom
11800 Singletree Lane
Eden Prairie, MN 55344
(612) 937-0772
Fax: (612) 937-1998

Tsoft
P.O. Box 14897
Berkeley, CA 94712
(510) 843-8763
Fax: (510) 704-9781

TTC/LP Com
270 Santa Ana Ct.
Sunnyvale, CA 94086
(408) 749-8008
Fax: (408) 736-1951

UB Networks
3900 Freedom Circle
Santa Clara, CA 95052-8030
(408) 496-0111
(800) 873-6381
Fax: (408) 970-7386

UDS Motorola, Inc.
5000 Bradford Drive
Huntsville, AL 35805-1993
(205) 430-8000
(800) 451-2369
Fax: (205) 430-7265

Unisys
P.O. Box 500
Blue Bell, PA 19424
(215) 986-4011
Fax: (215) 986-6850

U.S. Robotics Software
8100 N. McCormick Blvd.
Skokie, IL 60076-2920
(504) 923-0888
(800) 292-2988

Verilink Corp.
145 Baytech Drive
San Jose, CA 95134
(408) 945-1199
(800) 543-1008
Fax: (408) 946-5124

Walker Richer and Quinn, Inc.
1500 Dexter Avenue N.
Seattle, WA 98109-3032
(206) 217-7500
(800) 872-2829
Fax: (206) 217-0293

Wall Data, Inc.
11332 NE 122 Way
Kirkland, WA 98034
(206) 814-9255
(800) 755-9255
Fax: (206) 814-4305

Wandel and Goltermann
1030 Swabia Court
Research Triangle Park, NC 27709
(919) 941-5730
(800) 346-6332
Fax: (919) 941-9226

Wang Laboratories
600 Technology Park Drive
Billerica, MA 01821
(508) 967-5000
(800) 225-0654
Fax: (508) 967-7020

Webster Computer Corporation
2109 O'Toole Ave., Suite J
San Jose, CA 95131
(408) 954-8054
(800) 457-0903
Fax: (408) 954-1832

Western Digital Corporation
8105 Irvine Center Drive
Irvine, CA 92718
(714) 932-5000
Fax: (714) 932-6098

White Pine Software, Inc.
40 Simon St., Suite 201
Nashua, NH 03060-3043
(603) 886-9050
(800) 241-7463
Fax: (603) 886-9051

White Pine Software
1485 Saratoga Avenue
San Jose, CA 95129
(408) 446-1919
(800) 426-2230
Fax: (408) 446-0666

Whittaker Communications
2200 Lawson Lane
Santa Clara, CA 95054
(408) 565-6000
(800) 395-5267
Fax: (408) 565-6001

Wilcom Products
Rt. 3 Daniel Webster Hwy.
Laconia, NH 03246
(603) 524-2622
Fax: (603) 528-3804

Wingra Technologies Inc.
450 Science Drive 1 West
Madison, WI 53711
(608) 238-8637
Fax: (608) 238-8986

The Wollongong Group, Inc.
1129 San Antonio Road
Palo Alto, CA 94303
(415) 962-7100
(800) 872-8649
Fax: (415) 969-5547

XCd
3002 Dow Avenue, Suite 110
Tustin, CA 92680
(714) 573-7055
Fax: (714) 573-7084

Xerox Corporation
100 Clinton Ave. S., 5-B
Rochester, NY 14644
(716) 423-5090
Fax: (716) 423-5733

Xinetron Inc.
3022 Scott Boulevard
Santa Clara, CA 95054
(408) 727-5509
(800) 345-4415
Fax: (408) 727-6499

Xircom
26025 Mureau Road
Calabasas, CA 91302
(800) 874-7875
(818) 878-7600
Fax: (818) 878-7630

XLink Technology
1546 Centre Pointe Drive
Milpitas, CA 95035
(408) 263-8201
Fax: (408) 263-8203

Xyplex, Inc.
330 Codman Hill Rd.
Boxborough, MA 01719
(508) 264-9900
(800) 338-5316
Fax: (508) 264-9930

Zenith Electronics Corporation
Communication Products Division
1000 Milwaukee Avenue
Glenview, IL 60025
(708) 391-8000
(800) 788-7244
Fax: (708) 391-8919

Sources of Internet Information

Much of the adminstration functions for the Internet are handled by the InterNIC. Directory and Database services are handled by AT&T, while Registration Services are handled by Network Solutions, Inc. Addresses for these organizations are listed below.

Internet Directory and Database Services

AT&T
Tel: (800) 862-0677 or (908) 668-6587
Fax: (908) 668-3763
Email: admin@ds.internic.net
URL: ftp://ds.internic.net

Registration Services

Network Solutions, Inc.
Attn.: InterNIC Registration Services
505 Huntmar Park Drive
Herndon, VA 22070
Tel: (703) 742-4777
Email: admin@rs.internic.net

Internet Organizations

A number of groups contribute to the management, operation, and proliferation of the Internet. These include (in alphabetical order):

CommerceNet
URL: http://www.commerce.net
Email: info@commerce.net

Commercial Internet Exchange Association
URL: http://www.cix.org
Email: helpdesk@cix.org

Internet Architectures Board
URL: http://www.iab.org
Email: iab-contact@isi.edu

Internet Assigned Numbers Authority
URL: http://www.iana.org
Email: iana@isi.edu

Internet Engineering Task Force
URL: http://www.ietf.cnri.reston.va.us
Email: ietf-web@cnri.reston.va.us

Internet Society
URL: http://www.isoc.org
Email: isoc@isoc.org

World Wide Web Consortium
URL: http://www.w3.org
Email: www-request@w3.org

Obtaining RFCs

The following is an excerpt from the file *rfc-retrieval.txt*, which is available from many of the RFC repositories listed below. This information is subject to change; obtain the current version of the rfc-retrieval file if problems occur. Also note that each RFC site may have instructions for file retrieval (such as a particular subdirectory) that are unique to that location.

RFCs may be obtained via Email or FTP from many RFC Repositories. The Primary Repositories will have the RFC available when it is first announced, as will many Secondary Repositories. Some Secondary Repositories may take a few days to make available the most recent RFCs.

Many of these repositories also now have World Wide Web servers. Try the following URL as a starting point:

http://www.isi.edu/rfc-editor/

Primary Repositories:

RFCs can be obtained via FTP from DS.INTERNIC.NET, NIS.NSF.NET, NISC.JVNC.NET, FTP.ISI.EDU, WUARCHIVE.WUSTL.EDU, SRC.DOC.IC.AC.UK, FTP.NCREN.NET, FTP.SESQUI.NET, or NIS.GARR.IT.

1. DS.INTERNIC.NET—InterNIC Directory and Database Services
   RFC's may be obtained from DS.INTERNIC.NET via FTP, WAIS, and electronic mail. Through FTP, RFC's are stored as rfc/rfcnnnn.txt or rfc/rfcnnnn.ps, where "nnnn" is the RFC number. Log in as "anonymous" and provide your e-mail address as the password. Through WAIS, you may use either your local WAIS client or telnet to DS.INTERNIC.NET and log in as "wais" (no password required) to access a WAIS client. Help information and a tutorial for using WAIS are available online. The WAIS database to search is "rfcs".

   Directory and Database Services also provides a mail server interface. Send a mail message to mailserv@ds.internic.net and include any of the following commands in the message body:

document-by-name rfcnnnn	where "nnnn" is the RFC number. The text version is sent.
file /ftp/rfc/rfcnnnn.yyy	where "nnnn" is the RFC number and "yyy" is "txt" or "ps".
help	to get information on how to use the mailserver.

   The InterNIC Directory and Database Services Collection of Resource Listings, Internet Documents such as RFCs, FYIs, STDs, and Internet

Drafts, and Publicly Accessible Databases are also now available via Gopher. All our collections are wais-indexed and can be searched from the Gopher menu.

To access the InterNIC Gopher Servers, please connect to "internic.net" port 70.

Contact: admin@ds.internic.net

2. NIS.NSF.NET—To obtain RFCs from NIS.NSF.NET via FTP, log in with username "anonymous" and password "guest"; then connect to the directory of RFCs with cd /internet/documents/rfc. The file name is of the form rfcnnnn.txt (where "nnnn" refers to the RFC number).

   For sites without FTP capability, electronic mail query is available from NIS.NSF.NET. Address the request to NIS-INFO@NIS.NSF.NET and leave the subject field of the message blank. The first text line of the message must be "send rfcnnnn.txt" with nnnn the RFC number.

   Contact: rfc-mgr@merit.edu

3. NISC.JVNC.NET—RFCs can also be obtained via FTP from NISC.JVNC.NET, with the pathname rfc/rfcNNNN.txt (where "NNNN" refers to the number of the RFC). An index can be obtained with the pathname rfc/rfc-index.txt.

   JvNCnet also provides a mail service for those sites which cannot use FTP. Address the request to "SENDRFC@NISC.JVNC.NET" and in the "Subject:" field of the message indicate the RFC number, as in "Subject: rfcNNNN" (where NNNN is the RFC number). Please note that RFCs whose numbers are less than 1000 need not place a leading "0". For example, RFC932 is fine.) For a complete index to the RFC library, enter "rfc-index" in the "Subject:" field, as in "Subject: rfc-index". No text in the body of the message is needed.

   Contact: rfc-admin@nisc.jvnc.net

4. FTP.ISI.EDU—RFCs can be obtained via FTP from FTP.ISI.EDU, with the pathname in-notes/rfcnnnn.txt (where "nnnn" refers to the number of the RFC). Log in with FTP username "anonymous" and password "guest".

RFCs can also be obtained via electronic mail from ISI.EDU by using the RFC-INFO service. Address the request to "rfc-info@isi.edu" with a message body of:

Retrieve: RFC

Doc-ID: RFCnnnn

(Where "nnnn" refers to the number of the RFC [always use 4 digits—the DOC-ID of RFC 822 is "RFC0822"]). The RFC-INFO@ISI.EDU server provides other ways of selecting RFCs based on keywords and such; for more information send a message to "rfc-info@isi.edu" with the message body "help: help".

Contact: RFC-Manager@ISI.EDU

5. WUARCHIVE.WUSTL.EDU—RFCs can also be obtained via FTP from WUARCHIVE.WUSTL.EDU, with the pathname info/rfc/rfcnnnn.txt.Z (where "nnnn" refers to the number of the RFC and "Z" indicates that the document is in compressed form).

    At WUARCHIVE.WUSTL.EDU the RFCs are in an "archive" file system and various archives can be mounted as part of an NFS file system.Please contact Chris Myers (chris@wugate.wustl.edu) if you want to mount this file system in your NFS.

    Contact: chris@wugate.wustl.edu

6. SRC.DOC.IC.AC.UK—RFCs can be obtained via FTP from SRC.DOC.IC.AC.UK with the pathname rfc/rfcnnnn.txt.Z or rfc/rfcnnnn.ps.Z (where "nnnn" refers to the number of the RFC). Log in with FTP username "anonymous" and password"your-email-address". To obtain the RFC Index, use the pathname rfc/rfc-index.txt.Z. (The trailing .Z indicates that the document is in compressed form.)

    SRC.DOC.IC.AC.UK also provides an automatic mail service for those sites in the UK which cannot use FTP. Address the request to info-server@doc.ic.ac.uk with a Subject: line of "wanted" and a message body of:

    request sources

    topic path rfc/rfcnnnn.txt.Z

    request end

(Where "nnnn" refers to the number of the RFC.) Multiple requests may be included in the same message by giving multiple "topic path" commands on separate lines. To request the RFC Index, the command should read: topic path rfc/rfc-index.txt.Z

The archive is also available using NIFTP and the ISO FTAM system.

Contact: ukuug-soft@doc.ic.ac.uk

7. FTP.NCREN.NET—To obtain RFCs from FTP.NCREN.NET via FTP, log in with username "anonymous" and your internet e-mail address as password. The RFCs can be found in the directory /rfc, with file names of the form: rfcNNNN.txt or rfcNNNN.ps, where NNNN refers to the RFC number.

This repository is also accessible via WAIS and the Internet Gopher.

Contact: rfc-mgr@ncren.net

8. FTP.SESQUI.NET   RFCs can be obtained via FTP from FTP.SESQUI.NET, with the pathname pub/rfc/rfcnnnn.xxx (where "nnnn" refers to the number of the RFC and xxx indicates the document form: txt for ASCII and ps for Postscript).

At FTP.SESQUI.NET the RFCs are in an "archive" file system and various archives can be mounted as part of an NFS file system.Please contact RFC-maintainer (rfc-maint@sesqui.net) if you want to mount this file system in your NFS.

Contact: rfc-maint@sesqui.net

9. NIS.GARR.IT—RFCs can be obtained from NIS.GARR.IT FTP archive with the pathname mirrors/RFC/rfcnnnn.txt (where "nnnn" refers to the number of the RFC). Login with FTP, username "anonymous" and password "guest".

Summary of ways to get RFC from GARR-NIS ftp archive:

Via ftp: ftp.nis.garr.it directory mirrors/RFC
Via gopher: gopher.nis.garr.it folders
               GARR-NIS anonymous FTP
               "ftp.nis.garr.it"
               mirrors

	RFC
Via WWW:	ftp://ftp.nis.garr.it/mirrors/RFC
Via e-mail:	send a mail to dbserv@nis.garr.it whose body contains "get mirrors/RFC/rfc<number>.[txt,ps]".

To get via electronic mail a file in the ftp archive, put the get <fullpathname> command either in the subject or as a mail body line of a mail message sent to dbserv@nis.garr.it. <fullpathname> must be the concatenation of two strings, the directory path and the filename. Remember: use uppercase and lowercase exactly! The directory path is listed at the beginning of each block of files.

Example: to get RFC1004... the command should be:
get mirrors/RFC/rfc1004.txt.

Secondary Repositories:

Sweden

Host:	sunic.sunet.se
Directory:	rfc
Host:	chalmers.se
Directory:	rfc

Germany

Site:	EUnet Germany
Host:	ftp.Germany.EU.net
Directory:	pub/documents/rfc

France

Site:	Institut National de la Recherche en Informatique et Automatique (INRIA)
Address:	info-server@inria.fr
Notes:	RFCs are available via email to the above address. Info Server manager is Mireille Yamajako (yamajako@inria.fr).

Netherlands

Site:	EUnet
Host:	mcsun.eu.net
Directory:	rfc
Notes:	RFCs in compressed format.

France

Site:	Centre d'Informatique Scientifique et Medicale (CISM)
Contact:	ftpmaint@univ-lyon1.fr
Host:	ftp.univ-lyon1.fr
Directories:	pub/rfc/* Classified by hundreds pub/mirrors/rfc Mirror of Internic
Notes:	Files compressed with gzip. Online decompression done by the FTP server.

Finland

Site:	FUNET
Host:	nic.funet.fi
Directory:	index/RFC
Directory:	/pub/doc/networking/documents/rfc
Notes:	RFCs in compressed format. Also provides email access by sending mail to archive-server@nic.funet.fi.

Norway

Host:	ugle.unit.no
Directory:	pub/rfc

Denmark

Site:	University of Copenhagen
Host:	ftp.denet.dk
Directory:rfc	

Australia and Pacific Rim

Site:	munnari
Contact:	Robert Elz <kre@cs.mu.OZ.AU>

Host: munnari.oz.au

Directory: rfc

Notes: rfc's in compressed format rfcNNNN.Z postscript rfc's rfcNNNN.ps.Z

Site: The Programmers' Society
University of Technology, Sydney

Contact: ftp@progsoc.uts.edu.au

Host: ftp.progsoc.uts.edu.au

Directory: rfc (or std). Both are stored uncompressed.

South Africa

Site: The Internet Solution

Contact: ftp-admin@is.co.za

Host: ftp.is.co.za

Directory: internet/in-notes/rfc

United States

Site: cerfnet

Contact: help@cerf.net

Host: nic.cerf.net

Directory: netinfo/rfc

Site: NASA NAIC

Contact: rfc-updates@naic.nasa.gov

Host: naic.nasa.gov

Directory: files/rfc

Site: NIC.DDN.MIL (DOD users only)

Contact: NIC@nic.ddn.mil

Host: NIC.DDN.MIL

Directory: rfc/rfcnnnn.txt

Note: DOD users only may obtain RFC's via FTP from NIC.DDN.MIL. Internet users should NOT use this source due to inadequate connectivity.

Site:	uunet
Contact:	James Revell <revell@uunet.uu.net>
Host:	ftp.uu.net
Directory:	inet/rfc

The RFC-Info Service

The following describes the RFC-Info Service, which is an Internet document and information retrieval service. The text that follows describes in detail the service, which was obtained by using "Help:Help" as discussed below.

RFC-Info is an e-mail based service to help in locating and retrieving RFCs, FYIs, STDs, and IMRs. Users can ask for "lists" of all RFCs, FYIs, STDs, and IMRs having certain attributes such as their ID number, keywords, title, author, issuing organization, and date.

To use the service send e-mail to RFC-INFO@ISI.EDU with your requests in the body of the message. Feel free to put anything in the SUBJECT, the system ignores it. The body of the message is processed with case independence.

To get started you may send a message to RFC-INFO@ISI.EDU with requests such as in the following examples (without the explanation between []):

`Help: Help`	[to get this information page]
`List: FYI`	[list the FYI notes]
`List: RFC` `keywords: window`	[list RFCs with window as keyword or in title]
`List: FYI` `Keywords: window`	[list FYIs about windows]
`List: *` `Author: Cooper`	[list all documents by Cooper]
`List: RFC` `title: ARPA*NET`	[list RFCs about ARPANET, ARPA NETWORK, etc.]

`List: RFC`
`Organization: MITRE`
`Dated-after: Jul-01-1991`
`Dated-before: Aug-31-1991`
	[list RFCs issued by MITRE, dated 7+8/1991]

562

List: RFC	[list RFCs obsoleting a given RFC]
Obsoletes: RFC0010	
List: RFC	[list RFCs by authors starting with "Bracken"]
Author: Bracken*	[* is a wild card matching all endings]
List: IMR	[list the IMRs for the first 6 months of 92]
Dated-after:	Dec-31-1991
Dated-before:	Jul-01-1992
Retrieve: RFC	[retrieve RFC 822]
Doc-ID: RFC082	[note, always 4 digits in RFC#]
Retrieve: FYI	[retrieve FYI 4]
Doc-ID: FYI0004	[note, always 4 digits in FYI#]
Retrieve: STD	[retrieve STD 1]
Doc-ID: STD0001	[note, always 4 digits in STD#]
Retrieve: IMR	[retrieve May 1992 Internet Monthly Report]
Doc-ID: IMR9205	[note, always 4 digits = YYMM]
Help: Manual	[to retrieve the long user manual, 30+ pages]
Help: List	[how to use the LIST request]
Help: Retrieve	[how to use the RETRIEVE request]
Help: Topics	[list topics for which help is available]
Help: Dates	["Dates" is such a topic]
List: keywords	[list the keywords in use]
List: organizations	[list the organizations known to the system]

A useful way to test this service is to retrieve the file "Where and how to get new RFCs" (which is also the file *rfc-retrieval.txt* noted above in the section *Obtaining RFCs*). Place the following in the message body:

```
Help: ways_to_get_rfcs
```

Internet Mailing Lists

A number of mailing lists are maintained on the Internet for the purposes of soliciting information and discussions on specific subjects. In addition, a number of the Internet Engineering Task Force (IETF) working groups maintain a list for the exchange of information that is specific to that group.

For example, the IETF maintains two lists: the IETF General Discussion list and the IETF Announcement list. To join the IETF Announcement list, send a request to:

    Email: ietf-announce-request@cnri.reston.va.us

To join the IETF General Discussion, send a request to:

    Email: ietf-request@cnri.reston.va.us

A number of other mailing lists are available. To join a mailing list, send a message to the associated request list:

    Email: listname-request@listhost

A complete listing of the current IETF working groups and their respective mailing lists is available at:

    URL: http://www.ietf.cnri.reston.va.us/mailinglists.html

RFC Index

This Appendix lists RFC 1000 (August 1987) through RFC 1936 (April 1996) in reverse numerical order. This is an excerpt from the file *rfc-index.txt*, which can be obtained in its entirety as shown in the instructions below for retrieving RFC documents (see the last line before the first RFC listing).

RFC citations appear in this format:

> NUM STD   Author 1, ... Author 5., "Title of RFC", Issue date.
> (Pages=##) (Format=.txt or .ps) (FYI ##) (STD ##) (RTR ##)
> (Obsoletes RFC####) (Updates RFC####)

Key to citations:

is the RFC number; ## p. is the total number of pages.

The format and byte information follows the page information in parenthesies. The format, either ASCII text (TXT) or PostScript (PS) or both, is noted, followed by an equals sign and the number of bytes for that version (PostScript is a registered trademark of Adobe Systems Incorporated). The example (Format: PS=xxx TXT=zzz bytes) shows that the PostScript version of the RFC is xxx bytes and the ASCII text version is zzz bytes.

The (Also FYI ##) phrase gives the equivalent FYI number if the RFC was also issued as an FYI document.

"Obsoletes xxx" refers to other RFCs that this one replaces; "Obsoleted by xxx" refers to RFCs that have replaced this one. "Updates xxx" refers to other RFCs that this one merely updates (but does not replace); "Updated by xxx" refers to RFCs that have been updated by this one (but not replaced). Only immediately succeeding and/or preceding RFCs are indicated, not the entire history of each earlier or later RFC in a related series.

For example:

1129   D. Mills, "Internet time synchronization: The Network TimeProtocol",
10/01/1989. (Pages=29) (Format=.ps)

Many RFCs are available online; if not, this is indicated by (Not online).

Online copies are available via FTP from the InterNIC Directory and Database Services server, ds.internic.net, as rfc/rfc####.txt or rfc/rfc####.ps (#### is the RFC number without leading zeroes).

RFCs may be requested through electronic mail from the InterNIC Directory and Database Services automated mail server by sending a message to mailserv@ds.internic.net.In the body of the message, include the following command:

      document-by-name rfcNNNN

where NNNN is the number of the RFC. For PostScript RFCs, specify the extension, e.g. "document-by-name rfcNNNN.ps". Multiple requests can be sent in a single message by specifying each document in a comma-separated list (e.g. "document-by-name rfcNNNN, rfcYYYY"), or by including multiple "document-by-name" commands on separate lines.

The RFC Index can be requested by typing "document-by-name rfc-index".

1936	I	J. Touch, B. Parham, "Implementing the Internet Checksum in Hardware", 04/10/1996. (Pages=21) (Format=.txt)
1935	I	J. Quarterman, S. Carl-Mitchell, "What is the Internet, Anyway?", 04/10/1996. (Pages=11) (Format=.txt)
1934	I	K. Smith, "Ascend's Multilink Protocol Plus (MP+)", 04/08/1996. (Pages=47) (Format=.txt)
1933	PS	R. Gilligan, E. Nordmark, "Transition Mechanisms for IPv6 Hosts and Routers", 04/08/1996. (Pages=22) (Format=.txt)
1932	I	R. Cole, D. Shur, C. Villamizar, "IP over ATM: A Framework Document", 04/08/1996. (Pages=31) (Format=.txt)
1931	I	D. Brownell, "Dynamic RARP Extensions and Administrative Support for Automatic Network Address Allocation", 04/03/1996. (Pages=11) (Format=.txt)
1930		J. Hawkinson, T. Bates, "Guidelines for creation, selection, and registration of an Autonomous System (AS)", 04/03/1996. (Pages=10) (Format=.txt)

1929	PS	M. Leech, "Username/Password Authentication for SOCKS V5", 04/03/1996. (Pages=2) (Format=.txt)
1928	PS	M. Leech, M. Ganis, Y. Lee, R. Kuris, D. Koblas, L. Jones, "SOCKS Protocol Version 5", 04/03/1996. (Pages=9) (Format=.txt)
1927	I	C. Rogers, "Suggested Additional MIME Types for Associating Documents", 04/01/1996. (Pages=3) (Format=.txt)
1926	I	J. Eriksson, "An Experimental Encapsulation of IP Datagrams on Top of ATM", 04/01/1996. (Pages=2) (Format=.txt)
1925	I	R. Callon, "The Twelve Networking Truths", 04/01/1996. (Pages=3) (Format=.txt)
1924	I	R. Elz, "A Compact Representation of IPv6 Addresses", 04/01/1996. (Pages=6) (Format=.txt)
1923	I	J. Halpern, S. Bradner, "RIPv1 Applicability Statement for Historic Status", 03/25/1996. (Pages=3) (Format=.txt)
1922	I	H. Zhu, D. Hu, Z. Wang, T. Kao, W. Chang, M. Crispin, "Chinese Character Encoding for Internet Messages", 03/26/1996. (Pages=27) (Format=.txt)
1921	I	J. Dujonc, "TNVIP protocol", 03/25/1996. (Pages=30) (Format=.txt)
1920	S	J. Postel, "INTERNET OFFICIAL PROTOCOL STANDARDS", 03/22/1996. (Pages=40) (Format=.txt) (Obsoletes RFC1880) (STD 1)
1919	I	M. Chatel, "Classical versus Transparent IP Proxies", 03/28/1996. (Pages=35) (Format=.txt)
1918		Y. Rekhter, R. Moskowitz, D. Karrenberg, G. de Groot, E. Lear, "Address Allocation for Private Internets", 02/29/1996. (Pages=9) (Format=.txt) (Obsoletes RFC1627)
1917		P. Nesser, "An Appeal to the Internet Community to Return Unused IP Networks (Prefixes) to the IANA", 02/29/1996. (Pages=10) (Format=.txt)
1916	I	H. Berkowitz, P. Ferguson, W. Leland, P. Nesser, "Enterprise Renumbering: Experience and Information Solicitation", 02/28/1996. (Pages=8) (Format=.txt)
1915		F. Kastenholz, "Variance for The PPP Connection Control Protocol and The PPP Encryption Control Protocol", 02/28/1996. (Pages=7) (Format=.txt)
1914	PS	P. Faltstrom, R. Schoultz, C. Weider, "How to interact with a Whois++ mesh", 02/28/1996. (Pages=10) (Format=.txt)

1913   PS   C. Weider, J. Fullton, S. Spero, "Architecture of the Whois++ Index Service", 02/28/1996. (Pages=16) (Format=.txt)

1912   I   D. Barr, "Common DNS Operational and Configuration Errors", 02/28/1996. (Pages=16) (Format=.txt)

1911   E   G. Vaudreuil, "Voice Profile for Internet Mail", 02/19/1996. (Pages=22) (Format=.txt)

1910   E   G. Waters, "User-based Security Model for SNMPv2", 02/28/1996. (Pages=44) (Format=.txt)

1909   E   K. McCloghrie, "An Administrative Infrastructure for SNMPv2", 02/28/1996. (Pages=19) (Format=.txt)

1908   DS   J. Case, K. McCloghrie, M. Rose, S. Waldbusser, "Coexistence between Version 1 and Version 2 of the Internet-standard Network Management Framework", 01/22/1996. (Pages=10) (Format=.txt) (Obsoletes RFC1452)

1907   DS   J. Case, K. McCloghrie, M. Rose, S. Waldbusser, "Management Information Base for Version 2 of the Simple Network Management Protocol (SNMPv2)", 01/22/1996. (Pages=20) (Format=.txt) (Obsoletes RFC1450)

1906   DS   J. Case, K. McCloghrie, M. Rose, S. Waldbusser, "Transport Mappings for Version 2 of the Simple Network Management Protocol (SNMPv2)", 01/22/1996. (Pages=13) (Format=.txt) (Obsoletes RFC1449)

1905   DS   J. Case, K. McCloghrie, M. Rose, S. Waldbusser, "Protocol Operations for Version 2 of the Simple Network Management Protocol (SNMPv2)", 01/22/1996. (Pages=24) (Format=.txt) (Obsoletes RFC1448)

1904   DS   J. Case, K. McCloghrie, M. Rose, S. Waldbusser, "Conformance Statements for Version 2 of the Simple Network Management Protocol (SNMPv2)", 01/22/1996. (Pages=24) (Format=.txt) (Obsoletes RFC1444)

1903   DS   J. Case, K. McCloghrie, M. Rose, S. Waldbusser, "Textual Conventions for Version 2 of the Simple Network Management Protocol (SNMPv2)", 01/22/1996. (Pages=23) (Format=.txt) (Obsoletes RFC1443)

1902   DS   J. Case, K. McCloghrie, M. Rose, S. Waldbusser, "Structure of Management Information for Version 2 of the Simple Network Management Protocol (SNMPv2)", 01/22/1996. (Pages=40) (Format=.txt) (Obsoletes RFC1442)

1901   E   J. Case, K. McCloghrie, M. Rose, S. Waldbusser, "Introduction to Community-based SNMPv2", 01/22/1996. (Pages=8) (Format=.txt)

1900   I   B. Carpenter, Y. Rekhter, "Renumbering Needs Work", 02/28/1996. (Pages=4) (Format=.txt)

1898   I   D. Eastlake, B. Boesch, S. Crocker, M. Yesil, "CyberCash Credit Card Protocol Version 0.8", 02/19/1996. (Pages=52) (Format=.txt)

1897   E   R. Hinden, J. Postel, "IPv6 Testing Address Allocation", 01/25/1996. (Pages=4) (Format=.txt)

1896   I   P. Resnick, A. Walker, "The text/enriched MIME Content-type", 02/19/1996. (Pages=21) (Format=.txt) (Obsoletes RFC1563)

1895   I   E. Levinson, "The Application/CALS-1840 Content-type", 02/15/1996. (Pages=6) (Format=.txt)

1894   PS   K. Moore, G. Vaudreuil, "An Extensible Message Format for Delivery Status Notifications", 01/15/1996. (Pages=31) (Format=.txt)

1893   PS   G. Vaudreuil, "Enhanced Mail System Status Codes", 01/15/1996. (Pages=15) (Format=.txt)

1892   PS   G. Vaudreuil, "The Multipart/Report Content Type for the Reporting of Mail System Administrative Messages", 01/15/1996. (Pages=4) (Format=.txt)

1891   PS   K. Moore, "SMTP Service Extension for Delivery Status Notifications", 01/15/1996. (Pages=31) (Format=.txt)

1890   PS   H. Schulzrinne, "RTP Profile for Audio and Video Conferences with Minimal Control", 01/25/1996. (Pages=18) (Format=.txt)

1889   PS   H. Schulzrinne, S. Casner, R. Frederick, V. Jacobson, "RTP: A Transport Protocol for Real-Time Applications", 01/25/1996. (Pages=75) (Format=.txt)

1887   I   Y. Rekhter, T. Li, "An Architecture for IPv6 Unicast Address Allocation", 01/04/1996. (Pages=25) (Format=.txt)

1886   PS   S. Thomson, C. Huitema, "DNS Extensions to support IP version 6", 01/04/1996. (Pages=5) (Format=.txt)

1885   PS   A. Conta, S. Deering, "Internet Control Message Protocol (ICMPv6) for the Internet Protocol Version 6 (IPv6)", 01/04/1996. (Pages=20) (Format=.txt)

1884   PS   R. Hinden, S. Deering, "IP Version 6 Addressing Architecture", 01/04/1996. (Pages=18) (Format=.txt)

1883   PS   S. Deering, R. Hinden, "Internet Protocol, Version 6 (IPv6) Specification", 01/04/1996. (Pages=37) (Format=.txt)

1882   I   B. Hancock, "The 12-Days of Technology Before Christmas", 12/26/1995. (Pages=5) (Format=.txt)

1881   I   I. IESG, "IPv6 Address Allocation Management", 12/26/1995. (Pages=2) (Format=.txt)

1880   S   J. Postel, "INTERNET OFFICIAL PROTOCOL STANDARDS", 11/29/1995. (Pages=38) (Format=.txt) (Obsoletes RFC1800) (STD 1)

1879   I   B. Manning, "Class A Subnet Experiment Results and Recommendations", 01/15/1996. (Pages=6) (Format=.txt)

1878   I   T. Pummill, B. Manning, "Variable Length Subnet Table For IPv4", 12/26/1995. (Pages=8) (Format=.txt) (Obsoletes RFC1860)

1877   I   S. Cobb, "PPP Internet Protocol Control Protocol Extensions for Name Server Addresses", 12/26/1995. (Pages=6) (Format=.txt)

1876   E   C. Davis, P. Vixie, T. Goodwin, I. Dickinson, "A Means for Expressing Location Information in the Domain Name System", 01/15/1996. (Pages=18) (Format=.txt) (Updates RFC1034)

1875   I   N. Berge, "UNINETT PCA Policy Statements", 12/26/1995. (Pages=10) (Format=.txt)

1874   E   E. Levinson, "SGML Media Types", 12/26/1995. (Pages=6) (Format=.txt)

1873   E   E. Levinson, J. Clark, "Message/External-Body Content-ID Access Type", 12/26/1995. (Pages=4) (Format=.txt)

1872   E   E. Levinson, "The MIME Multipart/Related Content-type", 12/26/1995. (Pages=8) (Format=.txt)

1871   J. Postel, "Addendum to RFC 1602—Variance Procedure", 11/29/1995. (Pages=4) (Format=.txt) (Updates RFC1602)

1870   S   J. Klensin, N. Freed, K. Moore, "SMTP Service Extension for Message Size Declaration", 11/06/1995. (Pages=9) (Format=.txt) (Obsoletes RFC1653) (STD 10)

1869   S   J. Klensin, N. Freed, M. Rose, E. Stefferud, D. Crocker, "SMTP Service Extensions", 11/06/1995. (Pages=11) (Format=.txt) (Obsoletes RFC1651) (STD 10)

1868   E   G. Malkin, "ARP Extension—UNARP", 11/06/1995. (Pages=4) (Format=.txt)

1867   E   E. Nebel, L. Masinter, "Form-based File Upload in HTML", 11/07/1995. (Pages=13) (Format=.txt)

1866   PS   T. Berners-Lee, D. Connolly, "Hypertext Markup Language—2.0", 11/03/1995. (Pages=77) (Format=.txt)

1865   I   W. Houser, J. Griffin, C. Hage, "EDI Meets the Internet: Frequently Asked Questions about Electronic Data Interchange (EDI) on the Internet", 01/04/1996. (Pages=42) (Format=.txt)

1864	DS	J. Myers, M. Rose, "The Content-MD5 Header Field", 10/24/1995. (Pages=4) (Format=.txt) (Obsoletes RFC1544)
1863	E	D. Haskin, "A BGP/IDRP Route Server alternative to a full mesh routing", 10/20/1995. (Pages=16) (Format=.txt)
1862	I	M. McCahill, J., M. Schwartz, K. Sollins, T. Verschuren, C.Weider, "Report of the IAB Workshop on Internet Information Infrastructure, October 12-14, 1994", 11/03/1995. (Pages=27) (Format=.txt)
1861	I	A. Gwinn, "Simple Network Paging Protocol - Version 3 - Two-Way Enhanced", 10/19/1995. (Pages=23) (Format=.txt)
1860	I	T. Pummill, B. Manning, "Variable Length Subnet Table For IPv4", 10/20/1995. (Pages=3) (Format=.txt) (Obsoleted by RFC1878)
1859	I	Y. Pouffary, "ISO Transport Class 2 Non-use of Explicit Flow Control over TCP RFC1006 extension", 10/20/1995. (Pages=8) (Format=.txt)
1858	I	P. Ziemba, D. Reed, P. Traina, "Security Considerations for IP Fragment Filtering", 10/25/1995. (Pages=10) (Format=.txt)
1857	I	M. Lambert, "A Model for Common Operational Statistics", 10/20/1995. (Pages=27) (Format=.txt) (Updates RFC1404)
1856	I	H. Clark, "The Opstat Client-Server Model for Statistics Retrieval", 10/20/1995. (Pages=21) (Format=.txt)
1855	I	S. Hambridge, "Netiquette Guidelines", 10/20/1995. (Pages=21) (Format=.txt) (FYI 28)
1854	PS	N. Freed, A. Cargille, "SMTP Service Extension for Command Pipelining", 10/04/1995. (Pages=7) (Format=.txt)
1853	I	W. Simpson, "IP in IP Tunneling", 10/04/1995. (Pages=8) (Format=.txt)
1852	E	P. Metzger, W. Simpson, "IP Authentication using Keyed SHA", 10/02/1995. (Pages=6) (Format=.txt)
1851	E	P. Metzger, P. Karn, W. Simpson, "The ESP Triple DES-CBC Transform", 10/02/1995. (Pages=9) (Format=.txt)
1850	DS	F. Baker, R. Coltun, "OSPF Version 2 Management Information Base", 11/03/1995. (Pages=80) (Format=.txt) (Obsoletes RFC1253)
1848	PS	S. Crocker, N. Freed, J. Galvin, S. Murphy, "MIME Object Security Services", 10/03/1995. (Pages=48) (Format=.txt)

1847	PS	J. Galvin, S. Murphy, S. Crocker, N. Freed, "Security Multiparts for MIME: Multipart/Signed and Multipart/Encrypted", 10/03/1995. (Pages=11) (Format=.txt)
1846	E	A. Durand, F. Dupont, "SMTP 521 reply code", 10/02/1995. (Pages=4)(Format=.txt)
1845	E	D. Crocker, N. Freed, A. Cargille, "SMTP Service Extension for Checkpoint/Restart", 10/02/1995. (Pages=8) (Format=.txt)
1844	I	E. Huizer, "Multimedia E-mail (MIME) User Agent checklist", 08/24/1995. (Pages=8) (Format=.txt) (Obsoletes RFC1820)
1843	I	F. Lee, "HZ—A Data Format for Exchanging Files of Arbitrarily Mixed Chinese and ASCII characters", 08/24/1995. (Pages=5) (Format=.txt)
1842	I	Y. Wei, Y. Zhang, J. Li, J. Ding, Y. Jiang, "ASCII Printable Characters-Based Chinese Character Encoding for Internet Messages", 08/24/1995. (Pages=5) (Format=.txt)
1841	I	J. Chapman, D. Coli, A. Harvey, B. Jensen, K. Rowett, "PPP Network Control Protocol for LAN Extension", 09/29/1995. (Pages=66) (Format=.txt)
1838	E	S. Kille, "Use of the X.500 Directory to support mapping between X.400 and RFC 822 Addresses", 08/22/1995. (Pages=8) (Format=.txt)
1837	E	S. Kille, "Representing Tables and Subtrees in the X.500 Directory", 08/22/1995. (Pages=7) (Format=.txt)
1836	E	S. Kille, "Representing the O/R Address hierarchy in the X.500 Directory Information Tree", 08/22/1995. (Pages=11) (Format=.txt)
1835	PS	P. Deutsch, R. Schoultz, P. Faltstrom, C. Weider, "Architecture of the WHOIS++ service", 08/16/1995. (Pages=41) (Format=.txt)
1834	I	J. Gargano, K. Weiss, "Whois and Network Information Lookup Service Whois++", 08/16/1995. (Pages=7) (Format=.txt)
1833	PS	R. Srinivasan, "Binding Protocols for ONC RPC Version 2", 08/09/1995. (Pages=14) (Format=.txt)
1832	PS	R. Srinivasan, "XDR: External Data Representation Standard", 08/09/1995. (Pages=24) (Format=.txt)
1831	PS	R. Srinivasan, "RPC: Remote Procedure Call Protocol Specification Version 2", 08/09/1995. (Pages=18) (Format=.txt)
1830	E	G. Vaudreuil, "SMTP Service Extensions for Transmission of Large and Binary MIME Messages", 08/16/1995. (Pages=8) (Format=.txt)

1829	PS	P. Metzger, P. Karn, W. Simpson, "The ESP DES-CBC Transform", 08/09/1995. (Pages=10) (Format=.txt)
1828	PS	P. Metzger, W. Simpson, "IP Authentication using Keyed MD5", 08/09/1995. (Pages=5) (Format=.txt)
1827	PS	R. Atkinson, "IP Encapsulating Security Payload (ESP)", 08/09/1995. (Pages=12) (Format=.txt)
1826	PS	R. Atkinson, "IP Authentication Header", 08/09/1995. (Pages=13) (Format=.txt)
1825	PS	R. Atkinson, "Security Architecture for the Internet Protocol", 08/09/1995. (Pages=22) (Format=.txt)
1824	I	H. Danisch, "The Exponential Security System TESS: An Identity-Based Cryptographic Protocol for Authenticated Key-Exchange (E.I.S.S.-Report 1995/4)", 08/11/1995. (Pages=21) (Format=.txt)
1823	I	T. Howes, M. Smith, "The LDAP Application Program Interface", 08/09/1995. (Pages=22) (Format=.txt)
1822	I	J. Lowe, "A Grant of Rights to Use a Specific IBM patent with Photuris", 08/14/1995. (Pages=2) (Format=.txt)
1821	I	M. Borden, E. Crawley, B. Davie, S. Batsell, "Integration of Real-time Services in an IP-ATM Network Architecture", 08/11/1995. (Pages=24) (Format=.txt)
1820	I	E. Huizer, "Multimedia E-mail (MIME) User Agent Checklist", 08/22/1995. (Pages=8) (Format=.txt) (Obsoleted by RFC1844)
1819	E	L. Delgrossi, L. Berger, "Internet Stream Protocol Version 2 (ST2) Protocol Specification—Version ST2+", 08/11/1995. (Pages=109) (Format=.txt) (Obsoletes RFC1190)
1818	S	J. Postel, T. Li, Y. Rekhter, "Best Current Practices", 08/04/1995. (Pages=3) (Format=.txt)
1817	I	Y. Rekhter, "CIDR and Classful Routing", 08/04/1995. (Pages=2) (Format=.txt)
1816	I	F. Networking Council (FNC), "U.S. Government Internet Domain Names", 08/03/1995. (Pages=8) (Format=.txt) (Obsoletes RFC1811)
1815	I	M. Ohta, "Character Sets ISO-10646 and ISO-10646-J-1", 08/01/1995. (Pages=6) (Format=.txt)
1814	I	E. Gerich, "Unique Addresses are Good", 06/22/1995. (Pages=3) (Format=.txt)

1813   I   B. Callaghan, B. Pawlowski, P. Staubach, "NFS Version 3 Protocol Specification", 06/21/1995. (Pages=126) (Format=.txt)

1812   PS   F. Baker, "Requirements for IP Version 4 Routers", 06/22/1995. (Pages=175) (Format=.txt) (Obsoletes RFC1716)

1811   I   F. Networking Council, "U.S. Government Internet Domain Names", 06/21/1995. (Pages=3) (Format=.txt) (Obsoleted by RFC1816)

1810   I   J. Touch, "Report on MD5 Performance", 06/21/1995. (Pages=7) (Format=.txt)

1809   I   C. Partridge, "Using the Flow Label Field in IPv6", 06/14/1995. (Pages=6) (Format=.txt)

1808   PS   R. Fielding, "Relative Uniform Resource Locators", 06/14/1995. (Pages=16) (Format=.txt)

1807   I   R. Lasher, D. Cohen, "A Format for Bibliographic Records", 06/21/1995. (Pages=16) (Format=.txt)

1806   E   R. Troost, S. Dorner, "Communicating Presentation Information in Internet Messages: The Content-Disposition Header", 06/07/1995. (Pages=8) (Format=.txt)

1805   I   A. Rubin, "Location-Independent Data/Software Integrity Protocol", 06/07/1995. (Pages=6) (Format=.txt)

1804   E   G. Mansfield, P. Rajeev, S. Raghavan, T. Howes, "Schema Publishing in X.500 Directory", 06/09/1995. (Pages=10) (Format=.txt)

1803   I   R. Wright, A. Getchell, T. Howes, S. Sataluri, P. Yee, W. Yeong, "Recommendations for an X.500 Production Directory Service", 06/07/1995. (Pages=8) (Format=.txt)

1802   I   H. Alvestrand, K. Jordan, S. Langlois, J. Romaguera, "Introducing Project Long Bud: Internet Pilot Project for the Deployment of X.500 Directory Information in Support of X.400 Routing", 06/12/1995. (Pages=11) (Format=.txt)

1801   E   S. Kille, "MHS Use of the X.500 Directory to support MHS Routing", 06/09/1995. (Pages=73) (Format=.txt)

1800   S   J. Postel, "INTERNET OFFICIAL PROTOCOL STANDARDS", 07/11/1995. (Pages=36) (Format=.txt) (Obsoletes RFC1780) (STD 1) (Obsoleted by RFC1880)

1798   PS   A. Young, "Connection-less Lightweight Directory Access Protocol", 06/07/1995. (Pages=9) (Format=.txt)

1797	E	I. Assigned Numbers Authority, (IANA), "Class A Subnet Experiment", 04/25/1995. (Pages=4) (Format=.txt)
1796	I	C. Huitema, J. Postel, S. Crocker, "Not All RFCs are Standards", 04/25/1995. (Pages=4) (Format=.txt)
1795	I	L. Wells, A. Bartky, "Data Link Switching: Switch-to-Switch Protocol AIW DLSw RIG: DLSw Closed Pages, DLSw Standard Version 1.0", 04/25/1995. (Pages=91) (Format=.txt)
1794	I	T. Brisco, "DNS Support for Load Balancing", 04/20/1995. (Pages=7) (Format=.txt)
1793	PS	J. Moy, "Extending OSPF to Support Demand Circuits", 04/19/1995. (Pages=31) (Format=.txt)
1792	E	T. Sung, "TCP/IPX Connection Mib Specification", 04/18/1995. (Pages=9) (Format=.txt)
1791	E	T. Sung, "TCP And UDP Over IPX Networks With Fixed Path MTU", 04/18/1995. (Pages=12) (Format=.txt)
1790	I	V. Cerf, "An Agreement between the Internet Society and Sun Microsystems, Inc. in the Matter of ONC RPC and XDR Protocols", 04/17/1995. (Pages=6) (Format=.txt)
1789	I	C. Yang, "INETPhone: Telephone Services and Servers on Internet", 04/17/1995. (Pages=6) (Format=.txt)
1788	E	W. Simpson, "ICMP Domain Name Messages", 04/14/1995. (Pages=7) (Format=.txt)
1787	I	Y. Rekhter, "Routing in a Multi-provider Internet", 04/14/1995. (Pages=8) (Format=.txt)
1786	I	T. Bates, E. Gerich, L. Joncheray, J. Jouanigot, and others, "Representation of IP Routing Policies in a Routing Registry (ripe-81++)", 03/28/1995. (Pages=83) (Format=.txt)
1785	I	G. Malkin, A. Harkin, "TFTP Option Negotiation Analysis", 03/28/1995. (Pages=2) (Format=.txt) (Updates RFC1350)
1784	PS	G. Malkin, A. Harkin, "TFTP Timeout Interval and Transfer Size Options", 03/28/1995. (Pages=5) (Format=.txt) (Updates RFC1350)
1783	PS	G. Malkin, A. Harkin, "TFTP Blocksize Option", 03/28/1995. (Pages=5) (Format=.txt) (Updates RFC1350)
1782	PS	G. Malkin, A. Harkin, "TFTP Option Extension", 03/28/1995. (Pages=6) (Format=.txt) (Updates RFC1350)

1781   PS   S. Kille, "Using the OSI Directory to Achieve User Friendly Naming", 03/28/1995. (Pages=26) (Format=.txt) (Obsoletes RFC1484)

1780   S   J. Postel, "INTERNET OFFICIAL PROTOCOL STANDARDS", 03/28/1995. (Pages=39) (Format=.txt) (Obsoletes RFC1720) (STD 1) (Obsoleted by RFC1800)

1779   DS   S. Kille, "A String Representation of Distinguished Names", 03/28/1995. (Pages=8) (Format=.txt) (Obsoletes RFC1485)

1778   DS   T. Howes, S. Kille, W. Yeong, C. Robbins, "The String Representation of Standard Attribute Syntaxes", 03/28/1995. (Pages=12) (Format=.txt) (Obsoletes RFC1488)

1777   DS   W. Yeong, T. Howes, S. Kille, "Lightweight Directory Access Protocol", 03/28/1995. (Pages=22) (Format=.txt) (Obsoletes RFC1487)

1776   I   S. Crocker, "The Address is the Message", 04/01/1995. (Pages=2) (Format=.txt)

1775   I   D. Crocker, "To Be 'On' the Internet", 03/17/1995. (Pages=4) (Format=.txt)

1774   I   P. Traina, "BGP-4 Protocol Analysis", 03/21/1995. (Pages=10) (Format=.txt)

1773   I   P. Traina, "Experience with the BGP-4 protocol", 03/21/1995. (Pages=9) (Format=.txt) (Obsoletes RFC1656)

1772   DS   Y. Rekhter, P. Gross, "Application of the Border Gateway Protocol in the Internet", 03/21/1995. (Pages=19) (Format=.txt) (Obsoletes RFC1655)

1771   DS   Y. Rekhter, T. Li, "A Border Gateway Protocol 4 (BGP-4)", 03/21/1995. (Pages=57) (Format=.txt) (Obsoletes RFC1654)

1770   I   C. Graff, "IPv4 Option for Sender Directed Multi-Destination Delivery", 03/28/1995. (Pages=6) (Format=.txt)

1769   I   D. Mills, "Simple Network Time Protocol (SNTP)", 03/17/1995. (Pages=14) (Format=.txt)

1768   E   D. Marlow, "Host Group Extensions for CLNP Multicasting", 03/03/1995. (Pages=42) (Format=.txt)

1767   PS   D. Crocker, "MIME Encapsulation of EDI Objects", 03/02/1995. (Pages=7) (Format=.txt)

1766   PS   H. Alvestrand, "Tags for the Identification of Languages", 03/02/1995. (Pages=9) (Format=.txt)

1765   E   J. Moy, "OSPF Database Overflow", 03/02/1995. (Pages=9) (Format=.txt)

1764   PS   S. Senum, "The PPP XNS IDP Control Protocol (XNSCP)", 03/01/1995. (Pages=5) (Format=.txt)

1763   PS   S. Senum, "The PPP Banyan Vines Control Protocol (BVCP)", 03/01/1995. (Pages=10) (Format=.txt)

1762   DS   S. Senum, "The PPP DECnet Phase IV Control Protocol (DNCP)", 03/01/1995. (Pages=7) (Format=.txt) (Obsoletes RFC1376)

1761   I   B. Callaghan, R. Gilligan, "Snoop Version 2 Packet Capture File Format", 02/09/1995. (Pages=6) (Format=.txt)

1760   I   N. Haller, "The S/KEY One-Time Password System", 02/15/1995. (Pages=12) (Format=.txt)

1759   PS   R. Smith, F. Wright, T. Hastings, S. Zilles, J. Gyllenskog, "Printer MIB", 03/28/1995. (Pages=113) (Format=.txt)

1758   I   T. American Directory Forum, "NADF Standing Documents: A Brief Overview", 02/09/1995. (Pages=4) (Format=.txt)

1757   DS   S. Waldbusser, "Remote Network Monitoring Management Information Base", 02/10/1995. (Pages=91) (Format=.txt) (Obsoletes RFC1271)

1756   E   T. Rinne, "REMOTE WRITE PROTOCOL—VERSION 1.0", 01/19/1995. (Pages=11) (Format=.txt)

1755   PS   M. Perez, F. A. Mankin, E. Hoffman, G. Grossman, A. Malis, "ATM Signaling Support for IP over ATM", 02/17/1995. (Pages=32) (Format=.txt)

1754   I   M. Laubach, "IP over ATM Working Group's Recommendations for the ATM Forum's Multiprotocol BOF Version 1", 01/19/1995. (Pages=7) (Format=.txt)

1753   I   J. Chiappa, "IPng Technical Requirements Of the Nimrod Routing and Addressing Architecture", 01/05/1995. (Pages=18) (Format=.txt)

1752   PS   S. Bradner, A. Mankin, "The Recommendation for the IP Next Generation Protocol", 01/18/1995. (Pages=52) (Format=.txt)

1751   I   D. McDonald, "A Convention for Human-Readable 128-bit Keys", 12/29/1994. (Pages=15) (Format=.txt)

1750   I   D. Eastlake, S. Crocker, J. Schiller, "Randomness Recommendations for Security", 12/29/1994. (Pages=25) (Format=.txt)

1749   PS   K. McCloghrie, F. Baker, E. Decker, "IEEE 802.5 Station Source Routing MIB using SMIv2", 12/29/1994. (Pages=10) (Format=.txt) (Updates RFC1748)

1748   DS   K. McCloghrie, E. Decker, "IEEE 802.5 MIB using SMIv2", 12/29/1994. (Pages=25) (Format=.txt) (Updated by RFC1749)

1747   PS   J. Hilgeman, S. Nix, A. Bartky, W. Clark, "Definitions of Managed Objects for SNA Data Link Control: SDLC", 01/11/1995. (Pages=67) (Format=.txt)

1746   I   B. Manning, D. Perkins, "Ways to Define User Expectations", 12/30/1994. (Pages=18) (Format=.txt)

1745   PS   K. Varadhan, S. Hares, Y. Rekhter, "BGP4/IDRP for IP—OSPF Interaction", 12/27/1994. (Pages=19) (Format=.txt)

1744   I   G. Huston, "Observations on the Management of the Internet Address Space", 12/23/1994. (Pages=12) (Format=.txt)

1743   DS   K. McCloghrie, E. Decker, "IEEE 802.5 MIB using SMIv2", 12/27/1994. (Pages=25) (Format=.txt) (Obsoletes RFC1231)

1742   PS   S. Waldbusser, K. Frisa, "AppleTalk Management Information Base II", 01/05/1995. (Pages=84) (Format=.txt) (Obsoletes RFC1243)

1741   I   P. Faltstrom, D. Crocker, E. Fair, "MIME Content Type for BinHex Encoded Files", 12/22/1994. (Pages=6) (Format=.txt)

1740   PS   P. Faltstrom, D. Crocker, E. Fair, "MIME Encapsulation of Macintosh files - MacMIME", 12/22/1994. (Pages=16) (Format=.txt)

1739   I   G. Kessler, S. Shepard, "A Primer On Internet and TCP/IP Tools", 12/22/1994. (Pages=32) (Format=.txt)

1738   PS   T. Berners-Lee, L. Masinter, M. McCahill, "Uniform Resource Locators (URL)", 12/20/1994. (Pages=25) (Format=.txt)

1737   I   K. Sollins, L. Masinter, "Functional Requirements for Uniform Resource Names", 12/20/1994. (Pages=7) (Format=.txt)

1736   I   J. Kunze, "Functional Requirements for Internet Resource Locators", 02/09/1995. (Pages=10) (Format=.txt)

1735   E   J. Heinanen, R. Govindan, "NBMA Address Resolution Protocol (NARP)", 12/15/1994. (Pages=11) (Format=.txt)

1734   PS   J. Myers, "POP3 AUTHentication command", 12/20/1994. (Pages=5) (Format=.txt)

1733   I   M. Crispin, "DISTRIBUTED ELECTRONIC MAIL MODELS IN IMAP4", 12/20/1994. (Pages=3) (Format=.txt)

1732   I   M. Crispin, "IMAP4 COMPATIBILITY WITH IMAP2 AND IMAP2BIS", 12/20/1994. (Pages=5) (Format=.txt)

1731   PS   J. Myers, "IMAP4 Authentication mechanisms", 12/20/1994. (Pages=6) (Format=.txt)

1730   PS   M. Crispin, "INTERNET MESSAGE ACCESS PROTOCOL—VERSION 4", 12/20/1994. (Pages=77) (Format=.txt)

1729   I   C. Lynch, "Using the Z39.50 Information Retrieval Protocol in the Internet Environment", 12/16/1994. (Pages=8) (Format=.txt)

1728   I   C. Weider, "Resource Transponders", 12/16/1994. (Pages=6) (Format=.txt)

1727   I   C. Weider, P. Deutsch, "A Vision of an Integrated Internet Information Service", 12/16/1994. (Pages=11) (Format=.txt)

1726   I   F. Kastenholz, C. Partridge, "Technical Criteria for Choosing IP: The Next Generation (IPng)", 12/20/1994. (Pages=31) (Format=.txt)

1725   DS   J. Myers, M. Rose, "Post Office Protocol—Version 3", 11/23/1994. (Pages=18) (Format=.txt) (Obsoletes RFC1460)

1724   DS   G. Malkin, F. Baker, "RIP Version 2 MIB Extension", 11/15/1994. (Pages=18) (Format=.txt) (Obsoletes RFC1389)

1723   DS   G. Malkin, "RIP Version 2 Carrying Additional Information", 11/15/1994. (Pages=9) (Format=.txt) (Updates RFC1058) (Obsoletes RFC1388)

1722   DS   G. Malkin, "RIP Version 2 Protocol Applicability Statement", 11/15/1994. (Pages=5) (Format=.txt)

1721   I   G. Malkin, "RIP Version 2 Protocol Analysis", 11/15/1994. (Pages=4) (Format=.txt) (Obsoletes RFC1387)

1720   S   J. Postel, I. Architecture Board (IAB), "INTERNET OFFICIAL PROTOCOL STANDARDS", 11/23/1994. (Pages=41) (Format=.txt) (Obsoletes RFC1610) (STD 1) (Obsoleted by RFC1780)

1719   I   P. Gross, "A Direction for IPng", 12/16/1994. (Pages=5) (Format=.txt)

1718   I   T. IETF Secretariat, G. Malkin, "The Tao of IETF—A Guide for New Attendees of the Internet Engineering Task Force", 11/23/1994. (Pages=23) (Format=.txt) (FYI 17) (Obsoletes RFC1539)

1717   PS   K. Sklower, B. Lloyd, G. McGregor, D. Carr, "The PPP Multilink Protocol (MP)", 11/21/1994. (Pages=21) (Format=.txt)

1716   I   P. Almquist, F. Kastenholz, "Towards Requirements for IP Routers", 11/04/1994. (Pages=186) (Format=.txt) (Obsoletes RFC1009) (Obsoleted by RFC1812)

1715	I	C. Huitema, "The H Ratio for Address Assignment Efficiency", 11/03/1994. (Pages=4) (Format=.txt)
1714	I	S. Williamson, M. Kosters, "Referral Whois Protocol (RWhois)", 12/15/1994. (Pages=46) (Format=.txt, .ps)
1713	I	A. Romao, "Tools for DNS debugging", 11/03/1994. (Pages=13) (Format=.txt) (FYI 27)
1712	E	C. Farrell, M. Schulze, S. Pleitner, D. Baldoni, "DNS Encoding of Geographical Location", 11/01/1994. (Pages=7) (Format=.txt)
1711	I	J. Houttuin, "Classifications in E-mail Routing", 10/26/1994. (Pages=19) (Format=.txt)
1710	I	R. Hinden, "Simple Internet Protocol Plus White Paper", 10/26/1994. (Pages=23) (Format=.txt)
1709	I	J. Gargano, D. Wasley, "K-12 Internetworking Guidelines", 12/23/1994. (Pages=26) (Format=.txt, .ps) (FYI 26)
1708	I	D. Gowin, "NTP PICS PROFORMA For the Network Time Protocol Version 3", 10/26/1994. (Pages=13) (Format=.txt)
1707	I	M. McGovern, R. Ullmann, "CATNIP: Common Architecture for the Internet", 11/02/1994. (Pages=16) (Format=.txt)
1706	I	B. Manning, R. Colella, "DNS NSAP Resource Records", 10/26/1994. (Pages=10) (Format=.txt) (Obsoletes RFC1637)
1705	I	R. Carlson, D. Ficarella, "Six Virtual Inches to the Left: The Problem with IPng", 10/26/1994. (Pages=23) (Format=.txt)
1704	I	N. Haller, R. Atkinson, "On Internet Authentication", 10/26/1994. (Pages=17) (Format=.txt)
1703	I	M. Rose, "Principles of Operation for the TPC.INT Subdomain: Radio Paging —Technical Procedures", 10/26/1994. (Pages=9) (Format=.txt)
1702	I	S. Hanks, T. Li, D. Farinacci, P. Traina, "Generic Routing Encapsulation over IPv4 networks", 10/21/1994. (Pages=4) (Format=.txt)
1701	I	S. Hanks, T. Li, D. Farinacci, P. Traina, "Generic Routing Encapsulation (GRE)", 10/21/1994. (Pages=8) (Format=.txt)
1700	S	J. Reynolds, J. Postel, "ASSIGNED NUMBERS", 10/20/1994. (Pages=230) (Format=.txt) (Obsoletes RFC1340) (STD 2)
1698	I	P. Furniss, "Octet Sequences for Upper-Layer OSI to Support Basic Communications Applications", 10/26/1994. (Pages=29) (Format=.txt)

1697	PS	D. Brower, R. Purvy, A. Daniel, M. Sinykin, J. Smith, "Relational Database Management System (RDBMS) Management Information Base (MIB) using SMIv2", 08/23/1994. (Pages=38) (Format=.txt)
1696	PS	J. Barnes, L. Brown, R. Royston, S. Waldbusser, "Modem Management Information Base (MIB) using SMIv2", 08/25/1994. (Pages=31) (Format=.txt)
1695	PS	M. Ahmed, K. Tesink, "Definitions of Managed Objects for ATM Management Version 8.0 using SMIv2", 08/25/1994. (Pages=73) (Format=.txt)
1694	DS	T. Brown, K. Tesink, "Definitions of Managed Objects for SMDS Interfaces using SMIv2", 08/23/1994. (Pages=35) (Format=.txt) (Obsoletes RFC1304)
1693	E	T. Connolly, P. Amer, P. Conrad, "An Extension to TCP : Partial Order Service", 11/01/1994. (Pages=36) (Format=.txt)
1692	PS	P. Cameron, D. Crocker, D. Cohen, J. Postel, "Transport Multiplexing Protocol (TMux)", 08/17/1994. (Pages=12) (Format=.txt)
1691	I	W. Turner, "The Document Architecture for the Cornell Digital Library", 08/17/1994. (Pages=10) (Format=.txt)
1690	I	G. Huston, "Introducing the Internet Engineering and Planning Group (IEPG)", 08/17/1994. (Pages=2) (Format=.txt)
1689	I	J. Foster, "A Status Report on Networked Information Retrieval: Tools and Groups", 08/17/1994. (Pages=204) (Format=.txt) (FYI 25) (RTR 13)
1688	I	W. Simpson, "IPng Mobility Considerations", 08/11/1994. (Pages=9) (Format=.txt)
1687	I	E. Fleischman, "A Large Corporate User's View of IPng", 08/11/1994. (Pages=13) (Format=.txt)
1686	I	M. Vecchi, "IPng Requirements: A Cable Television Industry Viewpoint", 08/11/1994. (Pages=14) (Format=.txt)
1685	I	H. Alvestrand, "Writing X.400 O/R Names", 08/11/1994. (Pages=11) (Format=.txt) (RTR 12)
1684	I	P. Jurg, "Introduction to White Pages Services Based on X.500", 08/11/1994. (Pages=10) (Format=.txt)
1683	I	R. Clark, M. Ammar, K. Calvert, "Multiprotocol Interoperability In IPng", 08/11/1994. (Pages=12) (Format=.txt)

1682   I   J. Bound, "IPng BSD Host Implementation Analysis", 08/11/1994. (Pages=10) (Format=.txt)

1681   I   S. Bellovin, "On Many Addresses per Host", 08/08/1994. (Pages=5) (Format=.txt)

1680   I   C. Brazdziunas, "IPng Support for ATM Services", 08/08/1994. (Pages=7) (Format=.txt)

1679   I   D. Green, P. Irey, D. Marlow, K. O'Donoghue, "HPN Working Group Input to the IPng Requirements Solicitation", 08/08/1994. (Pages=10) (Format=.txt)

1678   I   E. Britton, J. Tavs, "IPng Requirements of Large Corporate Networks", 08/08/1994. (Pages=8) (Format=.txt)

1677   I   B. Adamson, "Tactical Radio Frequency Communication Requirements for IPng", 08/08/1994. (Pages=9) (Format=.txt)

1676   I   A. Ghiselli, D. Salomoni, C. Vistoli, "INFN Requirements for an IPng", 08/11/1994. (Pages=4) (Format=.txt)

1675   I   S. Bellovin, "Security Concerns for IPng", 08/08/1994. (Pages=4) (Format=.txt)

1674   I   M. Taylor, "A Cellular Industry View of IPng", 08/08/1994. (Pages=3) (Format=.txt)

1673   I   R. Skelton, "Electric Power Research Institute Comments on IPng", 08/08/1994. (Pages=4) (Format=.txt)

1672   I   J. Brownlee, "Accounting Requirements for IPng", 08/08/1994. (Pages=2) (Format=.txt)

1671   I   B. Carpenter, "IPng White Paper on Transition and Other Considerations", 08/08/1994. (Pages=8) (Format=.txt)

1670   I   D. Heagerty, "Input to IPng Engineering Considerations", 08/08/1994. (Pages=3) (Format=.txt)

1669   I   J. Curran, "Market Viability as an IPng Criteria", 08/08/1994. (Pages=4) (Format=.txt)

1668   I   D. Estrin, T. Li, Y. Rekhter, "Unified Routing Requirements for IPng", 08/08/1994. (Pages=3) (Format=.txt)

1667   I   S. Symington, D. Wood, J. Pullen, "Modeling and Simulation Requirements for IPng", 08/08/1994. (Pages=7) (Format=.txt)

1666   PS   Z. Kielczewski, D. Kostick, K. Shih, "Definitions of Managed Objects for SNA NAUs using SMIv2", 08/11/1994. (Pages=68) (Format=.txt)

1665   PS   Z. Kielczewski, D. Kostick, K. Shih, "Definitions of Managed Objects for SNA NAUs using SMIv2", 07/22/1994. (Pages=67) (Format=.txt)

1664   E   C. Allocchio, A. Bonito, B. Cole, S. Giordano, R. Hagens, "Using the Internet DNS to Distribute RFC1327 Mail Address MappingTables", 08/11/1994. (Pages=23) (Format=.txt)

1663   PS   D. Rand, "PPP Reliable Transmission", 07/21/1994. (Pages=7) (Format=.txt)

1662   S   W. Simpson, "PPP in HDLC-like Framing", 07/21/1994. (Pages=27) (Format=.txt) (Obsoletes RFC1549) (STD 51)

1661   S   W. Simpson, "The Point-to-Point Protocol (PPP)", 07/21/1994. (Pages=54) (Format=.txt) (Obsoletes RFC1548) (STD 51)

1660   DS   B. Stewart, "Definitions of Managed Objects for Parallel-printer-like Hardware Devices using SMIv2", 07/20/1994. (Pages=10) (Format=.txt) (Obsoletes RFC1318)

1659   DS   B. Stewart, "Definitions of Managed Objects for RS-232-like Hardware Devices using SMIv2", 07/20/1994. (Pages=21) (Format=.txt) (Obsoletes RFC1317)

1658   DS   B. Stewart, "Definitions of Managed Objects for Character Stream Devices using SMIv2", 07/20/1994. (Pages=18) (Format=.txt) (Obsoletes RFC1316)

1657   PS   S. Willis, J. Burruss, J. Chu, "Definitions of Managed Objects for the Fourth Version of the Border Gateway Protocol (BGP-4) using SMIv2", 07/21/1994. (Pages=21) (Format=.txt)

1656   I   P. Traina, "BGP-4 Protocol Document Roadmap and Implementation Experience", 07/21/1994. (Pages=4) (Format=.txt) (Obsoleted by RFC1773)

1655   PS   Y. Rekhter, P. Gross, "Application of the Border Gateway Protocol in the Internet", 07/21/1994. (Pages=19) (Format=.txt) (Obsoletes RFC1268) (Obsoleted by RFC1772)

1654   PS   Y. Rekhter, T. Li, "A Border Gateway Protocol 4 (BGP-4)", 07/21/1994. (Pages=56) (Format=.txt) (Obsoleted by RFC1771)

1653   DS   J. Klensin, N. Freed, K. Moore, "SMTP Service Extension for Message Size Declaration", 07/18/1994. (Pages=8) (Format=.txt) (Obsoletes RFC1427) (Obsoleted by RFC1870)

1652   DS   J. Klensin, N. Freed, M. Rose, E. Stefferud, D. Crocker, "SMTP Service Extension for 8bit-MIMEtransport", 07/18/1994. (Pages=6) (Format=.txt) (Obsoletes RFC1426)

1651   DS   J. Klensin, N. Freed, M. Rose, E. Stefferud, D. Crocker, "SMTP Service Extensions", 07/18/1994. (Pages=11) (Format=.txt) (Obsoletes RFC1425) (Obsoleted by RFC1869)

1650   PS   F. Kastenholz, "Definitions of Managed Objects for the Ethernet-like Interface Types using SMIv2", 08/23/1994. (Pages=20) (Format=.txt)

1649   I   R. Hagens, A. Hansen, "Operational Requirements for X.400 Management Domains in the GO-MHS Community", 07/18/1994. (Pages=14) (Format=.txt)

1648   PS   C. Cargille, "Postmaster Convention for X.400 Operations", 07/18/1994. (Pages=4) (Format=.txt)

1647   PS   B. Kelly, "TN3270 Enhancements", 07/15/1994. (Pages=33) (Format=.txt)

1646   I   C. Graves, T. Butts, M. Angel, "TN3270 Extensions for LUname and Printer Selection", 07/14/1994. (Pages=13) (Format=.txt)

1645   I   A. Gwinn, "Simple Network Paging Protocol—Version 2", 07/14/1994. (Pages=15) (Format=.txt) (Obsoletes RFC1568)

1644   E   R. Braden, "T/TCP—TCP Extensions for Transactions Functional Specification", 07/13/1994. (Pages=38) (Format=.txt)

1643   S   F. Kastenholz, "Definitions of Managed Objects for the Ethernet-like Interface Types", 07/13/1994. (Pages=19) (Format=.txt) (Obsoletes RFC1623) (STD 50)

1642   E   D. Goldsmith, M. Davis, "UTF-7—A Mail-Safe Transformation Format of Unicode", 07/13/1994. (Pages=14) (Format=.txt, .ps)

1641   E   D. Goldsmith, M. Davis, "Using Unicode with MIME", 07/13/1994. (Pages=6) (Format=.txt, .ps)

1640   I   S. Crocker, "The Process for Organization of Internet Standards Working Group (POISED)", 06/09/1994. (Pages=10) (Format=.txt)

1639   E   D. Piscitello, "FTP Operation Over Big Address Records (FOOBAR)", 06/09/1994. (Pages=5) (Format=.txt) (Obsoletes RFC1545)

1638   PS   F. Baker, R. Bowen, "PPP Bridging Control Protocol (BCP)", 06/09/1994. (Pages=28) (Format=.txt) (Obsoletes RFC1220)

1637   E   B. Manning, R. Colella, "DNS NSAP Resource Records", 06/09/1994. (Pages=11) (Format=.txt) (Obsoletes RFC1348) (Obsoleted by RFC1706)

1636   I   I. Architecture Board, R. Braden, D. Clark, S. Crocker, C. Huitema, "Report of IAB Workshop on Security in the Internet Architecture—February 8-10, 1994", 06/09/1994. (Pages=52) (Format=.txt)

1635   I   P. Deutsch, A. Emtage, A. Marine, "How to Use Anonymous FTP", 05/25/1994. (Pages=13) (Format=.txt) (FYI 24)

1634   I   M. Allen, "Novell IPX Over Various WAN Media (IPXWAN)", 05/24/1994. (Pages=23) (Format=.txt) (Obsoletes RFC1551)

1633   I   R. Braden, D. Clark, S. Shenker, "Integrated Services in the Internet Architecture: An Overview", 06/09/1994. (Pages=33) (Format=.txt, .ps)

1632   I   A. Getchell, S. Sataluri, "A Revised Catalog of Available X.500 Implementations", 05/20/1994. (Pages=94) (Format=.txt) (FYI 11) (Obsoletes RFC1292)

1631   I   P. Francis, K. Egevang, "The IP Network Address Translator (Nat)", 05/20/1994. (Pages=10) (Format=.txt)

1630   I   T. Berners-Lee, "Universal Resource Identifiers in WWW: A Unifying Syntax for the Expression of Names and Addresses of Objects on the Network as used in the World-Wide Web", 06/09/1994. (Pages=28) (Format=.txt)

1629   DS   R. Colella, R. Callon, E. Gardner, Y. Rekhter, "Guidelines for OSI NSAP Allocation in the Internet", 05/19/1994. (Pages=52) (Format=.txt) (Obsoletes RFC1237)

1628   PS   J. Case, "UPS Management Information Base", 05/19/1994. (Pages=45) (Format=.txt)

1627   I   E. Lear, E. Fair, D. Crocker, T. Kessler, "Network 10 Considered Harmful (Some Practices Shouldn't be Codified)", 07/01/1994. (Pages=8) (Format=.txt) (Obsoleted by RFC1918)

1626   PS   R. Atkinson, "Default IP MTU for use over ATM AAL5", 05/19/1994. (Pages=5) (Format=.txt)

1625   I   M. J. Fullton, K. J. Goldman, B. J. Kunze, H. Morris, F. Schiettecatte, "WAIS over Z39.50-1988", 06/09/1994. (Pages=7) (Format=.txt)

1624   I   A. Rijsinghani, "Computation of the Internet Checksum via Incremental Update", 05/20/1994. (Pages=6) (Format=.txt) (Updates RFC1071)

1623   S   F. Kastenholz, "Definitions of Managed Objects for the Ethernet-like Interface Types", 05/24/1994. (Pages=23) (Format=.txt) (Obsoletes RFC1398) (STD 50) (Obsoleted by RFC1643)

1622   I   P. Francis, "Pip Header Processing", 05/20/1994. (Pages=16) (Format=.txt)

1621   I   P. Francis, "Pip Near-term Architecture", 05/20/1994. (Pages=51) (Format=.txt)

1620   I   R. Braden, J. Postel, Y. Rekhter, "Internet Architecture Extensions for Shared Media", 05/20/1994. (Pages=19) (Format=.txt)

1619   PS   W. Simpson, "PPP over SONET/SDH", 05/13/1994. (Pages=5) (Format=.txt)

1618   PS   W. Simpson, "PPP over ISDN", 05/13/1994. (Pages=7) (Format=.txt)

1617   I   P. Barker, S. Kille, T. Lenggenhager, "Naming and Structuring Guidelines for X.500 Directory Pilots", 05/20/1994. (Pages=28) (Format=.txt) (RTR 11) (Obsoletes RFC1384)

1616   I   E. Huizer, J. Romaguera, RARE WG-MSG Task Force 88, "X.400(1988) for the Academic and Research Community in Europe", 05/19/1994. (Pages=44) (Format=.txt) (RTR 10)

1615   I   J. Houttuin, J. Craigie, "Migrating from X.400(84) to X.400(88)", 05/19/1994. (Pages=17) (Format=.txt) (RTR 9)

1614   I   C. Adie, "Network Access to Multimedia Information", 05/20/1994. (Pages=79) (Format=.txt) (RTR 8)

1613   I   J. Forster, G. Satz, G. Glick, R. Day, "cisco Systems X.25 over TCP (XOT)", 05/13/1994. (Pages=13) (Format=.txt)

1612   PS   R. Austein, J. Saperia, "DNS Resolver MIB Extensions", 05/17/1994. (Pages=36) (Format=.txt)

1611   PS   R. Austein, J. Saperia, "DNS Server MIB Extensions", 05/17/1994. (Pages=32) (Format=.txt)

1610   S   J. Postel, I. Architecture Board (IAB), "INTERNET OFFICIAL PROTOCOL STANDARDS", 07/08/1994. (Pages=37) (Format=.txt) (Obsoletes RFC1600) (STD 1) (Obsoleted by RFC1720)

1609   E   G. Mansfield, T. Johannsen, M. Knopper, "Charting Networks in the X.500 Directory", 03/25/1994. (Pages=15) (Format=.txt)

1608   E   T. Johannsen, G. Mansfield, M. Kosters, S. Sataluri, "Representing IP Information in the X.500 Directory", 03/25/1994. (Pages=20) (Format=.txt)

1607   I   V. Cerf, "A VIEW FROM THE 21ST CENTURY", 04/01/1994. (Pages=13) (Format=.txt)

1606   I   J. Onions, "A Historical Perspective On The Usage Of IP Version 9", 04/01/1994. (Pages=4) (Format=.txt)

1605   I   W. Shakespeare, "SONET to Sonnet Translation", 04/01/1994. (Pages=3) (Format=.txt)

1604   PS   T. Brown, "Definitions of Managed Objects for Frame Relay Service", 03/25/1994. (Pages=46) (Format=.txt) (Obsoletes RFC1596)

1603   I   E. Huizer, D. Crocker, "IETF Working Group Guidelines and Procedures", 03/24/1994. (Pages=29) (Format=.txt)

1602   I   I. Architecture Board, I. Engineering Steer, C. Huitema, P. Gross, "The Internet Standards Process—Revision 2", 03/24/1994. (Pages=37) (Format=.txt) (Obsoletes RFC1310) (Updated by RFC1871)

1601   I   C. Huitema, I. Architecture Board (IAB), "Charter of the Internet Architecture Board (IAB)", 03/22/1994. (Pages=6) (Format=.txt) (Obsoletes RFC1358)

1600   S   J. Postel, "INTERNET OFFICIAL PROTOCOL STANDARDS", 03/14/1994. (Pages=36) (Format=.txt) (Obsoletes RFC1540) (STD 1) (Obsoleted by RFC1610)

1598   PS   W. Simpson, "PPP in X.25", 03/17/1994. (Pages=8) (Format=.txt)

1597   I   Y. Rekhter, R. Moskowitz, D. Karrenberg, G. de Groot, "Address Allocation for Private Internets", 03/17/1994. (Pages=8) (Format=.txt)

1596   PS   T. Brown, "Definitions of Managed Objects for Frame Relay Service", 03/17/1994. (Pages=46) (Format=.txt) (Obsoleted by RFC1604)

1595   PS   T. Brown, K. Tesink, "Definitions of Managed Objects for the SONET/SDH Interface Type", 03/11/1994. (Pages=59) (Format=.txt)

1594   I   A. Marine, J. Reynolds, G. Malkin, "FYI on Questions and Answers: Answers to Commonly asked 'New Internet User' Questions", 03/11/1994. (Pages=44) (Format=.txt) (FYI 4) (Obsoletes RFC1325)

1593   I   W. McKenzie, J. Cheng, "SNA APPN Node MIB", 03/10/1994. (Pages=120) (Format=.txt)

1592   E   B. Wijnen, G. Carpenter, K. Curran, A. Sehgal, G. Waters, "Simple Network Management Protocol Distributed Protocol Interface Version 2.0", 03/03/1994. (Pages=54) (Format=.txt) (Obsoletes RFC1228)

1591   I   J. Postel, "Domain Name System Structure and Delegation", 03/03/1994. (Pages=7) (Format=.txt)

1590   I   J. Postel, "Media Type Registration Procedure", 03/02/1994. (Pages=7) (Format=.txt) (Updates RFC1521)

1589   I   D. Mills, "A Kernel Model for Precision Timekeeping", 03/03/1994. (Pages=37) (Format=.txt)

1588   I   J. Postel, C. Anderson, "WHITE PAGES MEETING REPORT", 02/25/1994. (Pages=35) (Format=.txt)

1587   PS   R. Coltun, V. Fuller, "The OSPF NSSA Option", 03/24/1994. (Pages=17) (Format=.txt)

1586   I   O. deSouza, M. Rodrigues, "Guidelines for Running OSPF Over Frame Relay Networks", 03/24/1994. (Pages=6) (Format=.txt)

1585   I   J. Moy, "MOSPF: Analysis and Experience", 03/24/1994. (Pages=13) (Format=.txt)

1584   PS   J. Moy, "Multicast Extensions to OSPF", 03/24/1994. (Pages=102) (Format=.txt, .ps)

1583   DS   J. Moy, "OSPF Version 2", 03/23/1994. (Pages=212) (Format=.txt, .ps) (Obsoletes RFC1247)

1582   PS   G. Meyer, "Extensions to RIP to Support Demand Circuits", 02/18/1994. (Pages=32) (Format=.txt)

1581   I   G. Meyer, "Protocol Analysis for Extensions to RIP to Support Demand Circuits", 02/18/1994. (Pages=5) (Format=.txt)

1580   I   E. EARN Staff, "Guide to Network Resource Tools", 03/22/1994. (Pages=107) (Format=.txt) (FYI 23)

1579   I   S. Bellovin, "Firewall-Friendly FTP", 02/18/1994. (Pages=4) (Format=.txt)

1578   I   J. Sellers, "FYI on Questions and Answers: Answers to Commonly Asked 'Primary and Secondary School Internet User' Questions", 02/18/1994. (Pages=53) (Format=.txt) (FYI 22)

1577   PS   M. Laubach, "Classical IP and ARP over ATM", 01/20/1994. (Pages=17) (Format=.txt)

1576   I   J. Penner, "TN3270 Current Practices", 01/20/1994. (Pages=10) (Format=.txt)

1575   DS   S. Hares, C. Wittbrodt, "An Echo Function for CLNP (ISO 8473)", 02/18/1994. (Pages=10) (Format=.txt) (Obsoletes RFC1139)

1574   I   S. Hares, C. Wittbrodt, "Essential Tools for the OSI Internet", 02/18/1994. (Pages=14) (Format=.txt) (Obsoletes RFC1139)

1573   PS   K. McCloghrie, F. Kastenholz, "Evolution of the Interfaces Group of MIB-II", 01/20/1994. (Pages=55) (Format=.txt) (Obsoletes RFC1229)

1572   PS   S. Alexander, "Telnet Environment Option", 01/14/1994. (Pages=7) (Format=.txt)

1571   I   D. Borman, "Telnet Environment Option Interoperability Issues", 01/14/1994. (Pages=4) (Format=.txt) (Updates RFC1408)

1570   PS   W. Simpson, "PPP LCP Extensions", 01/11/1994. (Pages=22) (Format=.txt) (Updates RFC1548)

1569   I   M. Rose, "Principles of Operation for the TPC.INT Subdomain: Radio Paging —Technical Procedures", 01/07/1994. (Pages=6) Format=.txt)

1568   I   A. Gwinn, "Simple Network Paging Protocol—Version 1(b)", 01/07/1994. (Pages=4) (Format=.txt) (Obsoleted by RFC1645)

1567   PS   G. Mansfield, S. Kille, "X.500 Directory Monitoring MIB", 01/11/1994. (Pages=19) (Format=.txt)

1566   PS   N. Freed, S. Kille, "Mail Monitoring MIB", 01/11/1994. (Pages=21) (Format=.txt)

1565   PS   N. Freed, S. Kille, "Network Services Monitoring MIB", 01/11/1994. (Pages=18) (Format=.txt)

1564   I   P. Barker, R. Hedberg, "DSA Metrics (OSI-DS 34 (v3))",01/14/1994. (Pages=20) (Format=.txt)

1563   I   N. Borenstein, "The text/enriched MIME Content-type", 01/10/1994. (Pages=16) (Format=.txt, .ps) (Obsoletes RFC1523) (Obsoleted by RFC1896)

1562   I   G. Michaelson, M. Prior, "Naming Guidelines for the AARNet X.500 Directory Service", 12/29/1993. (Pages=4) (Format=.txt)

1561   E   D. Piscitello, "Use of ISO CLNP in TUBA Environments", 12/23/1993. (Pages=25) (Format=.txt)

1560   I   B. Leiner, Y. Rekhter, "The MultiProtocol Internet", 12/23/1993. (Pages=5) (Format=.txt)

1559   DS   J. Saperia, "DECnet Phase IV MIB Extensions", 12/27/1993. (Pages=69) (Format=.txt) (Obsoletes RFC1289)

1558   I   T. Howes, "A String Representation of LDAP Search Filters", 12/23/1993. (Pages=3) (Format=.txt)

1557   I   K. Chon, H. Je Park, U. Choi, "Korean Character Encoding for Internet Messages", 12/27/1993. (Pages=5) (Format=.txt)

1556   I   H. Nussbacher, "Handling of Bi-directional Texts in MIME", 12/23/1993. (Pages=3) (Format=.txt)

1555   I   H. Nussbacher, Y. Bourvine, "Hebrew Character Encoding for Internet Messages", 12/23/1993. (Pages=5) (Format=.txt)

1554	I	M. Ohta, K. Handa, "ISO-2022-JP-2: Multilingual Extension of ISO-2022-JP", 12/23/1993. (Pages=6) (Format=.txt)
1553	PS	S. Mathur, M. Lewis, "Compressing IPX Headers Over WAN Media (CIPX)", 12/09/1993. (Pages=27) (Format=.txt)
1552	PS	W. Simpson, "The PPP Internetwork Packet Exchange Control Protocol (IPXCP)", 12/09/1993. (Pages=19) (Format=.txt)
1551	I	M. Allen, "Novell IPX Over Various WAN Media (IPXWAN)", 12/09/1993. (Pages=22) (Format=.txt) (Obsoletes RFC1362) (Obsoleted by RFC1634)
1550	I	S. Bradner, A. Mankin, "IP: Next Generation (IPng) White Paper Solicitation", 12/16/1993. (Pages=6) (Format=.txt)
1549	DS	W. Simpson, "PPP in HDLC Framing", 12/09/1993. (Pages=20) (Format=.txt) (Obsoleted by RFC1662)
1548	DS	W. Simpson, "The Point-to-Point Protocol (PPP)", 12/09/1993. (Pages=62) (Format=.txt) (Obsoletes RFC1331) (Obsoleted by RFC1661) (Updated by RFC1570)
1547	I	D. Perkins, "Requirements for an Internet Standard Point-to-Point Protocol", 12/09/1993. (Pages=21) (Format=.txt)
1546	I	C. Partridge, T. Mendez, W. Milliken, "Host Anycasting Service", 11/16/1993. (Pages=9) (Format=.txt)
1545	E	D. Piscitello, "FTP Operation Over Big Address Records (FOOBAR)", 11/16/1993. (Pages=5) (Format=.txt) (Obsoleted by RFC1639)
1544	PS	M. Rose, "The Content-MD5 Header Field", 11/16/1993. (Pages=3) (Format=.txt) (Obsoleted by RFC1864)
1543	I	J. Postel, "Instructions to RFC Authors", 10/28/1993. (Pages=16) (Format=.txt) (Obsoletes RFC1111)
1542	PS	W. Wimer, "Clarifications and Extensions for the Bootstrap Protocol", 10/27/1993. (Pages=23) (Format=.txt) (Obsoletes RFC1532)
1541	PS	R. Droms, "Dynamic Host Configuration Protocol", 10/27/1993. (Pages=39) (Format=.txt) (Obsoletes RFC1531)
1540	S	J. Postel, "INTERNET OFFICIAL PROTOCOL STANDARDS", 10/22/1993. (Pages=34) (Format=.txt) (Obsoletes RFC1500) (STD 1) (Obsoleted by RFC1600)
1539	I	G. Malkin, "The Tao of IETF—A Guide for New Attendees of the Internet Engineering Task Force", 10/07/1993. (Pages=22) (Format=.txt) (FYI 17) (Obsoletes RFC1391) (Obsoleted by RFC1718)

1538	I	W. Behl, B. Sterling, W. Teskey, "Advanced SNA/IP: A Simple SNA Transport Protocol", 10/06/1993. (Pages=10) (Format=.txt)
1537	I	P. Beertema, "Common DNS Data File Configuration Error", 10/06/1993. (Pages=9) (Format=.txt)
1536	I	A. Kumar, J. Postel, C. Neuman, P. Danzig, S. Miller, "Common DNS Implementation Errors and Suggested Fixes", 10/06/1993. (Pages=12) (Format=.txt)
1535	I	E. Gavron, "A Security Problem and Proposed Correction With Widely Deployed DNS Software", 10/06/1993. (Pages=5) (Format=.txt)
1534	PS	R. Droms, "Interoperation Between DHCP and BOOTP", 10/08/1993. (Pages=4) (Format=.txt)
1533	PS	S. Alexander, R. Droms, "DHCP Options and BOOTP Vendor Extensions", 10/08/1993. (Pages=30) (Format=.txt) (Obsoletes RFC1497)
1532	PS	W. Wimer, "Clarifications and Extensions for the Bootstrap Protocol", 10/08/1993. (Pages=22) (Format=.txt) (Updates RFC0951) (Obsoleted by RFC1542)
1531	PS	R. Droms, "Dynamic Host Configuration Protocol", 10/07/1993. (Pages=39) (Format=.txt) (Obsoleted by RFC1541)
1530	I	C. Malamud, M. Rose, "Principles of Operation for the TPC.INT Subdomain: General Principles and Policy", 10/06/1993. (Pages=7) (Format=.txt)
1529	I	C. Malamud, M. Rose, "Principles of Operation for the TPC.INT Subdomain: Remote Printing—Administrative Policies", 10/06/1993. (Pages=5) (Format=.txt) (Obsoletes RFC1486)
1528	E	C. Malamud, M. Rose, "Principles of Operation for the TPC.INT Subdomain: Remote Printing—Technical Procedures", 10/06/1993. (Pages=12) (Format=.txt) (Obsoletes RFC1486)
1527	I	G. Cook, "What Should We Plan Given the Dilemma of the Network?", 09/30/1993. (Pages=17) (Format=.txt)
1526	I	D. Piscitello, "Assignment of System Identifiers for TUBA/CLNP Hosts", 09/30/1993. (Pages=8) (Format=.txt)
1525	PS	E. Decker, K. McCloghrie, P. Langille, A. Rijsinghani, "Definitions of Managed Objects for Source Routing Bridges", 09/30/1993. (Pages=18) (Format=.txt) (Obsoletes RFC1286)
1524	I	N. Borenstein, "A User Agent Configuration Mechanism For Multimedia Mail Format Information", 09/23/1993. (Pages=12) (Format=.txt)

1523   I   N. Borenstein, "The text/enriched MIME Content-type", 09/23/1993. (Pages=15) (Format=.txt) (Obsoleted by RFC1563)

1522   DS   K. Moore, "MIME (Multipurpose Internet Mail Extensions) Part Two: Message Header Extensions for Non-ASCII Text", 09/23/1993. (Pages=10) (Format=.txt) (Obsoletes RFC1342)

1521   DS   N. Borenstein, N. Freed, "MIME (Multipurpose Internet Mail Extensions) Part One: Mechanisms for Specifying and Describing the Format of Internet Message Bodies", 09/23/1993. (Pages=81) (Format=.txt, .ps) (Obsoletes RFC1341) (Updated by RFC1590)

1520   I   Y. Rekhter, C. Topolcic, "Exchanging Routing Information Across Provider Boundaries in the CIDR Environment", 09/24/1993. (Pages=9) (Format=.txt)

1519   PS   V. Fuller, T. Li, J. Yu, K. Varadhan, "Classless Inter-Domain Routing (CIDR): an Address Assignment and Aggregation Strategy", 09/24/1993. (Pages=24) (Format=.txt) (Obsoletes RFC1338)

1518   PS   Y. Rekhter, T. Li, "An Architecture for IP Address Allocation with CIDR", 09/24/1993. (Pages=27) (Format=.txt)

1517   PS   R. Hinden, "Applicability Statement for the Implementation of Classless Inter-Domain Routing (CIDR)", 09/24/1993. (Pages=4) (Format=.txt)

1516   DS   D. McMaster, K. McCloghrie, "Definitions of Managed Objects for IEEE 802.3 Repeater Devices", 09/10/1993. (Pages=40) (Format=.txt) (Obsoletes RFC1368)

1515   PS   D. McMaster, K. McCloghrie, S. Roberts, "Definitions of Managed Objects for IEEE 802.3 Medium Attachment Units (MAUs)", 09/10/1993. (Pages=25) (Format=.txt)

1514   PS   P. Grillo, S. Waldbusser, "Host Resources MIB", 09/23/1993. (Pages=33) (Format=.txt)

1513   PS   S. Waldbusser, "Token Ring Extensions to the Remote Network Monitoring MIB", 09/23/1993. (Pages=55) (Format=.txt) (Updates RFC1271)

1512   PS   J. Case, A. Rijsinghani, "FDDI Management Information Base", 09/10/1993. (Pages=51) (Format=.txt) (Updates RFC1285)

1511   I   J. Linn, "Common Authentication Technology Overview", 09/10/1993. (Pages=2) (Format=.txt)

1510   PS   J. Kohl, B. Neuman, "The Kerberos Network Authentication Service (V5)", 09/10/1993. (Pages=112) (Format=.txt)

1509   PS   J. Wray, "Generic Security Service API: C-bindings", 09/10/1993. (Pages=48) (Format=.txt)

1508   PS   J. Linn, "Generic Security Service Application Program Interface", 09/10/1993. (Pages=49) (Format=.txt)

1507   E   C. Kaufman, "DASS—Distributed Authentication Security Service", 09/10/1993. (Pages=119) (Format=.txt)

1506   I   J. Houttuin, "A Tutorial on Gatewaying Between X.400 and Internet Mail", 09/23/1993. (Pages=39) (Format=.txt) (RTR 6)

1505   E   A. Costanzo, D. Robinson, R. Ullmann, "Encoding Header Field for Internet Messages", 08/27/1993. (Pages=36) (Format=.txt) (Obsoletes RFC1154)

1504   I   A. Oppenheimer, "Appletalk Update-Based Routing Protocol: Enhanced Appletalk Routing", 08/27/1993. (Pages=82) (Format=.txt)

1503   I   K. McCloghrie, M. Rose, "Algorithms for Automating Administration in SNMPv2 Managers", 08/26/1993. (Pages=19) (Format=.txt)

1502   PS   H. Alvestrand, "X.400 Use of Extended Character Sets", 08/26/1993. (Pages=16) (Format=.txt)

1501   I   E. Brunsen, "OS/2 User Group", 08/06/1993. (Pages=2) (Format=.txt)
1500 S   J. Postel, "INTERNET OFFICIAL PROTOCOL STANDARDS", 08/30/1993. (Pages=36) (Format=.txt) (Obsoletes RFC1410) (STD 1) (Obsoleted by RFC1540)

1498   I   J. Saltzer, "On the Naming and Binding of Network Destinations", 08/04/1993. (Pages=10) (Format=.txt)

1497   DS   J. Reynolds, "BOOTP Vendor Information Extensions", 08/04/1993. (Pages=8) (Format=.txt) (Updates RFC0951) (Obsoletes RFC1395) (Obsoleted by RFC1533)

1496   PS   H. Alvestrand, J. Romaguera, K. Jordan, "Rules for downgrading messages from X.400/88 to X.400/84 when MIME content-types are present in the messages", 08/26/1993. (Pages=7) (Format=.txt) (Updates RFC1328)

1495   PS   H. Alvestrand, S. Kille, R. Miles, M. Rose, S. Thompson, "Mapping between X.400 and RFC-822 Message Bodies", 08/26/1993. (Pages=15) (Format=.txt) (Updates RFC1327)

1494   PS   H. Alvestrand, S. Thompson, "Equivalences between 1988 X.400 and RFC-822 Message Bodies", 08/26/1993. (Pages=26) (Format=.txt)

1493   DS   E. Decker, P. Langille, A. Rijsinghani, K. McCloghrie, "Definitions of Managed Objects for Bridges", 07/28/1993. (Pages=34) (Format=.txt) (Obsoletes RFC1286)

1492   I   C. Finseth, "An Access Control Protocol, Sometimes Called TACACS", 07/23/1993. (Pages=21) (Format=.txt)

1491   I   C. Weider, R. Wright, "A Survey of Advanced Usages of X.500", 07/26/1993. (Pages=18) (Format=.txt) (FYI 21)

1490   DS   T. Bradley, C. Brown, A. Malis, "Multiprotocol Interconnect over Frame Relay", 07/26/1993. (Pages=35) (Format=.txt) (Obsoletes RFC1294)

1489   I   A. Chernov, "Registration of a Cyrillic Character Set", 07/23/1993. (Pages=5) (Format=.txt)

1488   PS   T. Howes, S. Hardcastle-Kille, W. Yeong, C. Robbins, "The X.500 String Representation of Standard Attribute Syntaxes", 07/29/1993. (Pages=11) (Format=.txt) (Obsoleted by RFC1778)

1487   PS   W. Yeong, T. Howes, S. Hardcastle-Kille, "X.500 Lightweight Directory Access Protocol", 07/29/1993. (Pages=21) (Format=.txt) (Obsoleted by RFC1777)

1486   E   M. Rose, C. Malamud, "An Experiment in Remote Printing", 07/30/1993. (Pages=14) (Format=.txt) (Obsoleted by RFC1529, RFC1528)

1485   PS   S. Hardcastle-Kille, "A String Representation of Distinguished Names (OSI-DS 23 (v5))", 07/28/1993. (Pages=7) (Format=.txt) (Obsoleted by RFC1779)

1484   E   S. Hardcastle-Kille, "Using the OSI Directory to Achieve User Friendly Naming (OSI-DS 24 (v1.2))", 07/28/1993. (Pages=25) (Format=.txt) (Obsoleted by RFC1781)

1483   PS   J. Heinanen, "Multiprotocol Encapsulation over ATM Adaptation Layer 5", 07/20/1993. (Pages=16) (Format=.txt)

1482   I   M. Knopper, "Aggregation Support in the NSFNET Policy Routing Database", 07/20/1993. (Pages=7) (Format=.txt)

1481   I   C. Huitema, I. Architecture Board, "IAB Recommendation for an Intermediate Strategy to Address the Issue of Scaling", 07/02/1993. (Pages=2) (Format=.txt)

1480   I   A. Cooper, J. Postel, "The US Domain", 06/28/1993. (Pages=47) (Format=.txt) (Obsoletes RFC1386)

1479   PS   M. Steenstrup, "Inter-Domain Policy Routing Protocol Specification: Version 1", 07/26/1993. (Pages=108) (Format=.txt)

1478 PS M. Lepp, M. Steenstrup, "An Architecture for Inter-Domain Policy Routing", 07/26/1993. (Pages=35) (Format=.txt)

1477 I M. Steenstrup, "IDPR as a Proposed Standard", 07/26/1993. (Pages=13) (Format=.txt)

1476 E R. Ullmann, "RAP: Internet Route Access Protocol", 06/17/1993. (Pages=20) (Format=.txt)

1475 E R. Ullmann, "TP/IX: The Next Internet", 06/17/1993. (Pages=35) (Format=.txt)

1474 PS F. Kastenholz, "The Definitions of Managed Objects for the Bridge Network Control Protocol of the Point-to-Point Protocol", 06/08/1993. (Pages=15) (Format=.txt)

1473 PS F. Kastenholz, "The Definitions of Managed Objects for the IP Network Control Protocol of the Point-to-Point Protocol", 06/08/1993. (Pages=9) (Format=.txt)

1472 PS F. Kastenholz, "The Definitions of Managed Objects for the Security Protocols of the Point-to-Point Protocol", 06/08/1993. (Pages=11) (Format=.txt)

1471 PS F. Kastenholz, "The Definitions of Managed Objects for the Link Control Protocol of the Point-to-Point Protocol", 06/08/1993. (Pages=25) (Format=.txt)

1470 I R. Enger, J. Reynolds, "FYI on a Network Management Tool Catalog: Tools for Monitoring and Debugging TCP/IP Internets and Interconnected Devices", 06/25/1993. (Pages=216) (Format=.txt) (FYI 2) (Obsoletes RFC1147)

1469 PS T. Pusateri, "IP Multicast over Token-Ring Local Area Networks", 06/17/1993. (Pages=4) (Format=.txt)

1468 I J. Murai, M. Crispin, E. van der Poel, "Japanese Character Encoding for Internet Messages", 06/04/1993. (Pages=6) (Format=.txt)

1467 I C. Topolcic, "Status of CIDR Deployment in the Internet", 08/06/1993. (Pages=9) (Format=.txt) (Obsoletes RFC1367)

1466 I E. Gerich, "Guidelines for Management of IP Address Space", 05/26/1993. (Pages=10) (Format=.txt) (Obsoletes RFC1366)

1465 E D. Eppenberger, "Routing coordination for X.400 MHS services within a multi protocol / multi network environment Table Format V3 for static routing", 05/26/1993. (Pages=31) (Format=.txt)

1464 E R. Rosenbaum, "Using the Domain Name System To Store Arbitrary String Attributes", 05/27/1993. (Pages=4) (Format=.txt)

1463	I	E. Hoffman, L. Jackson, "FYI on Introducing the Internet—A Short Bibliography of Introductory Internetworking Readings for the Network Novice", 05/27/1993. (Pages=4) (Format=.txt) (FYI 19)
1462	I	E. Krol, E. Hoffman, "FYI on 'What is the Internet?'", 05/27/1993. (Pages=11) (Format=.txt) (FYI 20)
1461	PS	D. Throop, "SNMP MIB extension for MultiProtocol Interconnect over X.25", 05/27/1993. (Pages=30) (Format=.txt)
1460	DS	M. Rose, "Post Office Protocol—Version 3", 06/16/1993. (Pages=19) (Format=.txt) (Obsoletes RFC1225) (Obsoleted by RFC1725)
1459	E	J. Oikarinen, D. Reed, "Internet Relay Chat Protocol", 05/26/1993. (Pages=65) (Format=.txt)
1458	I	R. Braudes, S. Zabele, "Requirements for Multicast Protocols", 05/26/1993. (Pages=19) (Format=.txt)
1457	I	R. Housley, "Security Label Framework for the Internet", 05/26/1993. (Pages=14) (Format=.txt)
1456	I	C. Nguyen, H. Ngo, C. Bui, T. van Nguyen, "Conventions for Encoding the Vietnamese Language VISCII: VIetnamese Standard Code for Information Interchange VIQR: VIetnamese Quoted-Readable Specification", 05/08/1993. (Pages=7) (Format=.txt)
1455	E	D. Eastlake, III, "Physical Link Security Type of Service", 05/26/1993. (Pages=6) (Format=.txt)
1454	I	T. Dixon, "Comparison of Proposals for Next Version of IP", 05/08/1993. (Pages=15) (Format=.txt)
1453	I	W. Chimiak, "A Comment on Packet Video Remote Conferencing and the Transport/Network Layers", 04/15/1993. (Pages=10) (Format=.txt)
1452	PS	J. Case, K. McCloghrie, M. Rose, S. Waldbusser, "Coexistence between version 1 and version 2 of the Internet-standard Network Management Framework", 05/03/1993. (Pages=17) (Format=.txt) (Obsoleted by RFC1908)
1451	PS	J. Case, K. McCloghrie, M. Rose, S. Waldbusser, "Manager to Manager Management Information Base", 05/03/1993. (Pages=36) (Format=.txt)
1450	PS	J. Case, K. McCloghrie, M. Rose, S. Waldbusser, "Management Information Base for version 2 of the Simple Network Management Protocol (SNMPv2)", 05/03/1993. (Pages=27) (Format=.txt) (Obsoleted by RFC1907)

1449   PS   J. Case, K. McCloghrie, M. Rose, S. Waldbusser, "Transport Mappings for version 2 of the Simple Network Management Protocol (SNMPv2)", 05/03/1993. (Pages=24) (Format=.txt) (Obsoleted by RFC1906)

1448   PS   J. Case, K. McCloghrie, M. Rose, S. Waldbusser, "Protocol Operations for version 2 of the Simple Network Management Protocol (SNMPv2)", 05/03/1993. (Pages=36) (Format=.txt) (Obsoleted by RFC1905)

1447   PS   K. McCloghrie, J. Galvin, "Party MIB for version 2 of the Simple Network Management Protocol (SNMPv2)", 05/03/1993. (Pages=50) (Format=.txt)

1446   PS   J. Galvin, K. McCloghrie, "Security Protocols for version 2 of the Simple Network Management Protocol (SNMPv2)", 05/03/1993. (Pages=51) (Format=.txt)

1445   PS   J. Davin, K. McCloghie, "Administrative Model for version 2 of the Simple Network Management Protocol (SNMPv2)", 05/03/1993. (Pages=47) (Format=.txt)

1444   PS   J. Case, K. McCloghrie, M. Rose, S. Waldbusser, "Conformance Statements for version 2 of the Simple Network Management Protocol (SNMPv2)", 05/03/1993. (Pages=33) (Format=.txt) (Obsoleted by RFC1904)

1443   PS   J. Case, K. McCloghrie, M. Rose, S. Waldbusser, "Textual Conventions for version 2 of the Simple Network Management Protocol (SNMPv2)", 05/03/1993. (Pages=31) (Format=.txt) (Obsoleted by RFC1903)

1442   PS   J. Case, K. McCloghrie, M. Rose, S. Waldbusser, "Structure of Management Information for version 2 of the Simple Network Management Protocol (SNMPv2)", 05/03/1993. (Pages=55) (Format=.txt) (Obsoleted by RFC1902)

1441   PS   J. Case, K. McCloghrie, M. Rose, S. Waldbusser, "Introduction to version 2 of the Internet-standard Network Management Framework", 05/03/1993. (Pages=13) (Format=.txt)

1440   E   R. Troth, "SIFT/UFT: Sender-Initiated/Unsolicited File Transfer", 07/23/1993. (Pages=9) (Format=.txt)

1439   I   C. Finseth, "The Uniqueness of Unique Identifiers", 03/25/1993. (Pages=11) (Format=.txt)

1438   I   A. Chapin, C. Huitema, "Internet Engineering Task Force Statements Of Boredom (SOBs)", 03/31/1993. (Pages=2) (Format=.txt)

1437   I   N. Borenstein, M. Linimon, "The Extension of MIME Content-Types to a New Medium", 04/01/1993. (Pages=6) (Format=.txt)

1436 I F. Anklesaria, M. McCahill, P. Lindner, D. Johnson, D. John, D. Torrey, B. Alberti, "The Internet Gopher Protocol (a distributed document search and retrieval protocol)", 03/18/1993. (Pages=16) (Format=.txt)

1435 I S. Knowles, "IESG Advice from Experience with Path MTU Discovery", 03/17/1993. (Pages=2) (Format=.txt)

1434 I R. Dixon, D. Kushi, "Data Link Switching: Switch-to-Switch Protocol", 03/17/1993. (Pages=33) (Format=.txt, .ps)

1433 E J. Garrett, J. Hagan, J. Wong, "Directed ARP", 03/05/1993. (Pages=17) (Format=.txt)

1432 I J. Quarterman, "Recent Internet Books", 03/03/1993. (Pages=15) (Format=.txt)

1431 I P. Barker, "DUA Metrics", 02/26/1993. (Pages=19) (Format=.txt)

1430 I S. Kille, E. Huizer, V. Cerf, R. Hobby, S. Kent, "A Strategic Plan for Deploying an Internet X.500 Directory Service", 02/26/1993. (Pages=20) (Format=.txt)

1429 I E. Thomas, "Listserv Distribute Protocol", 02/24/1993. (Pages=8) (Format=.txt)

1428 I G. Vaudreuil, "Transition of Internet Mail from Just-Send-8 to 8Bit-SMTP/MIME", 02/10/1993. (Pages=6) (Format=.txt)

1427 PS K. Moore, N. Freed, J. Klensin, "SMTP Service Extension for Message Size Declaration", 02/10/1993. (Pages=8) (Format=.txt) (Obsoleted by RFC1653)

1426 PS J. Klensin, N. Freed, M. Rose, E. Stefferud, D. Crocker, "SMTP Service Extension for 8bit-MIMEtransport", 02/10/1993. (Pages=6) (Format=.txt) (Obsoleted by RFC1652)

1425 PS J. Klensin, N. Freed, M. Rose, E. Stefferud, D. Crocker, "SMTP Service Extensions", 02/10/1993. (Pages=10) (Format=.txt) (Obsoleted by RFC1651)

1424 PS B. Kaliski, "Privacy Enhancement for Internet Electronic Mail: Part IV: Key Certification and Related Services", 02/10/1993. (Pages=9) (Format=.txt)

1423 PS D. Balenson, "Privacy Enhancement for Internet Electronic Mail: Part III: Algorithms, Modes, and Identifiers", 02/10/1993. (Pages=14) (Format=.txt) (Obsoletes RFC1115)

1422 PS S. Kent, "Privacy Enhancement for Internet Electronic Mail: Part II: Certificate-Based Key Management", 02/10/1993. (Pages=32) (Format=.txt) (Obsoletes RFC1114)

1421   PS   J. Linn, "Privacy Enhancement for Internet Electronic Mail: Part I:
              Message Encryption and Authentication Procedures", 02/10/1993.
              (Pages=42) (Format=.txt) (Obsoletes RFC1113)

1420   PS   S. Bostock, "SNMP over IPX", 03/03/1993. (Pages=4) (Format=.txt)
              (Obsoletes RFC1298)

1419   PS   G. Minshall, M. Ritter, "SNMP over AppleTalk", 03/03/1993. (Pages=7)
              (Format=.txt)

1418   PS   M. Rose, "SNMP over OSI", 03/03/1993. (Pages=4) (Format=.txt)
              (Obsoletes RFC1283)

1417   I   T. Myer, NADF, "NADF Standing Documents: A Brief Overview",
              02/04/1993. (Pages=4) (Format=.txt) (Obsoletes RFC1295)

1416   E   D. Borman, "Telnet Authentication Option", 02/01/1993. (Pages=7)
              (Format=.txt) (Obsoletes RFC1409)

1415   PS   J. Mindel, R. Slaski, "FTP-FTAM Gateway Specification", 01/27/1993.
              (Pages=58) (Format=.txt)

1414   PS   M. St. Johns, M. Rose, "Ident MIB", 02/04/1993. (Pages=13) (Format=.txt)

1413   PS   M. St. Johns, "Identification Protocol", 02/04/1993. (Pages=10)
              (Format=.txt) (Obsoletes RFC0931)

1412   E   K. Alagappan, "Telnet Authentication: SPX", 01/27/1993. (Pages=4)
              (Format=.txt)

1411   E   D. Borman, "Telnet Authentication: Kerberos Version 4", 01/26/1993.
              (Pages=4) (Format=.txt)

1410   S   Internet Architecture Board, L. Chapin, "IAB OFFICIAL PROTOCOL
              STANDARDS", 03/24/1993. (Pages=35) (Format=.txt) (Obsoletes
              RFC1360) (STD 1) (Obsoleted by RFC1500)

1409   E   D. Borman, "Telnet Authentication Option", 01/26/1993. (Pages=7)
              (Format=.txt) (Obsoleted by RFC1416)

1408   H   D. Borman, "Telnet Environment Option", 01/26/1993. (Pages=7)
              (Format=.txt) (Updated by RFC1571)

1407   PS   T. Cox, K. Tesink, "Definitions of Managed Objects for the DS3/E3
              Interface Type", 01/26/1993. (Pages=55) (Format=.txt) (Obsoletes
              RFC1233)

1406   PS   F. Baker, J. Watt, "Definitions of Managed Objects for the DS1 and E1
              Interface Types", 01/26/1993. (Pages=50) (Format=.txt) (Obsoletes
              RFC1232)

1405   E   C. Allocchio, "Mapping between X.400(1984/1988) and Mail-11 (DECnet mail)", 01/20/1993. (Pages=19) (Format=.txt)

1404   I   B. Stockman, "A Model for Common Operational Statistics", 01/20/1993. (Pages=27) (Format=.txt) (Updated by RFC1857)

1403   PS   K. Varadhan, "BGP OSPF Interaction", 01/14/1993. (Pages=17) (Format=.txt) (Obsoletes RFC1364)

1402   I   J. Martin, "There's Gold in them thar Networks! Searching for Treasure in all the Wrong Places", 01/14/1993. (Pages=39) (Format=.txt) (FYI 10) (Obsoletes RFC1290)

1401   I   Internet Architecture Board, L. Chapin, "Correspondence between the IAB and DISA on the use of DNS throughout the Internet", 01/13/1993. (Pages=8) (Format=.txt)

1400   I   A. Williamson, "Transition and Modernization of the Internet Registration Service", 03/25/1993. (Pages=7) (Format=.txt)

1398   DS   F. Kastenholz, "Definitions of Managed Objects for the Ethernet-like Interface Types", 01/14/1993. (Pages=24) (Format=.txt) (Obsoletes RFC1284) (Obsoleted by RFC1623)

1397   PS   D. Haskin, "Default Route Advertisement in BGP2 and BGP3 Versions of the Border Gateway Protocol", 01/13/1993. (Pages=2) (Format=.txt)

1396   I   S. Crocker, "The Process for Organization of Internet Standards Working Group (POISED)", 01/11/1993. (Pages=10) (Format=.txt)

1395   DS   J. Reynolds, "BOOTP Vendor Information Extensions", 01/11/1993. (Pages=8) (Format=.txt) (Updates RFC0951) (Obsoletes RFC1084) (Obsoleted by RFC1497)

1394   I   P. Robinson, "Relationship of Telex Answerback Codes to Internet Domains", 01/08/1993. (Pages=15) (Format=.txt)

1393   E   G. Malkin, "Traceroute Using an IP Option", 01/11/1993. (Pages=7) (Format=.txt)

1392   I   G. Malkin, T. Parker, "Internet Users' Glossary", 01/12/1993. (Pages=53) (Format=.txt) (FYI 18)

1391   I   G. Malkin, "The Tao of IETF: A Guide for New Attendees of the Internet Engineering Task Force", 01/06/1993. (Pages=19) (Format=.txt) (FYI 17) (Obsoleted by RFC1539)

1390   S   D. Katz, "Transmission of IP and ARP over FDDI Networks", 01/05/1993. (Pages=12) (Format=.txt) (Obsoletes RFC1188) (STD 36)

1389   PS   G. Malkin, F. Baker, "RIP Version 2 MIB Extension", 01/06/1993.
              (Pages=13) (Format=.txt) (Obsoleted by RFC1724)

1388   PS   G. Malkin, "RIP Version 2 Carrying Additional Information", 01/06/1993.
              (Pages=7) (Format=.txt) (Updates RFC1058) (Obsoleted by RFC1723)

1387   I   G. Malkin, "RIP Version 2 Protocol Analysis", 01/06/1993. (Pages=3)
              (Format=.txt) (Obsoleted by RFC1721)

1386   I   A. Cooper, J. Postel, "The US Domain", 12/28/1992. (Pages=31)
              (Format=.txt) (Obsoleted by RFC1480)

1385   I   Z. Wang, "EIP: The Extended Internet Protocol A Framework for
              Maintaining Backward Compatibility", 11/13/1992. (Pages=17)
              (Format=.txt)

1384   I   P. Barker, S. Hardcastle-Kille, "Naming Guidelines for Directory Pilots",
              02/11/1993. (Pages=12) (Format=.txt, .ps) (Obsoleted by RFC1617)

1383   I   C. Huitema, "An Experiment in DNS Based IP Routing", 12/28/1992.
              (Pages=14) (Format=.txt)

1382   PS   D. Throop, "SNMP MIB Extension for the X.25 Packet Layer", 11/10/1992.
              (Pages=69) (Format=.txt)

1381   PS   D. Throop, F. Baker, "SNMP MIB Extension for X.25 LAPB", 11/10/1992.
              (Pages=33) (Format=.txt)

1380   I   P. Gross, P. Almquist, "IESG Deliberations on Routing and Addressing",
              11/09/1992. (Pages=22) (Format=.txt)

1379   I   R. Braden, "Extending TCP for Transactions —Concepts", 11/05/1992.
              (Pages=38) (Format=.txt)

1378   PS   B. Parker, "The PPP AppleTalk Control Protocol (ATCP)", 11/05/1992.
              (Pages=16) (Format=.txt)

1377   PS   D. Katz, "The PPP OSI Network Layer Control Protocol (OSINLCP)",
              11/05/1992. (Pages=10) (Format=.txt)

1376   PS   S. Senum, "The PPP DECnet Phase IV Control Protocol (DNCP)",
              11/05/1992. (Pages=6) (Format=.txt) (Obsoleted by RFC1762)

1375   I   P. Robinson, "Suggestion for New Classes of IP Addresses", 11/03/1992.
              (Pages=7) (Format=.txt)

1374   PS   J. Renwick, A. Nicholson, "IP and ARP on HIPPI", 11/02/1992.
              (Pages=43) (Format=.txt)

1373   I   T. Tignor, "PORTABLE DUAs", 10/27/1992. (Pages=12) (Format=.txt)

1372	PS	D. Borman, C. Hedrick, "Telnet Remote Flow Control Option", 10/23/1992. (Pages=6) (Format=.txt) (Obsoletes RFC1080)
1371	I	P. Gross, "Choosing a 'Common IGP' for the IP Internet (The IESG's Recommendation to the IAB)", 10/23/1992. (Pages=9) (Format=.txt)
1370	PS	Internet Architecture Board, "Applicability Statement for OSPF", 10/23/1992. (Pages=2) (Format=.txt)
1369	I	F. Kastenholz, "Implementation Notes and Experience for The Internet Ethernet MIB", 10/23/1992. (Pages=7) (Format=.txt)
1368	PS	D. McMaster, K. McCloghrie, "Definitions of Managed Objects for IEEE 802.3 Repeater Devices", 10/26/1992. (Pages=40) (Format=.txt) (Obsoleted by RFC1516)
1367	I	C. Topolcic, "Schedule for IP Address Space Management Guidelines", 10/22/1992. (Pages=3) (Format=.txt) (Obsoleted by RFC1467)
1366	I	E. Gerich, "Guidelines for Management of IP Address Space", 10/22/1992. (Pages=8) (Format=.txt) (Obsoleted by RFC1466)
1365	I	K. Siyan, "An IP Address Extension Proposal", 09/10/1992. (Pages=6) (Format=.txt)
1364	PS	K. Varadhan, "BGP OSPF Interaction", 09/11/1992. (Pages=14) (Format=.txt) (Obsoleted by RFC1403)
1363	E	C. Partridge, "A Proposed Flow Specification", 09/10/1992. (Pages=20) (Format=.txt)
1362	I	M. Allen, "Novell IPX Over Various WAN Media (IPXWAN)", 09/10/1992. (Pages=13) (Format=.txt) (Obsoleted by RFC1551)
1361	I	D. Mills, "Simple Network Time Protocol (SNTP)", 08/10/1992. (Pages=10) (Format=.txt)
1360	S	Internet Architecture Board, A. Chapin, "IAB OFFICIAL PROTOCOL STANDARDS", 09/09/1992. (Pages=33) (Format=.txt) (Obsoletes RFC1280) (STD 1) (Obsoleted by RFC1410)
1359	I	ACM SIGUCCS, "Connecting to the Internet What Connecting Institutions Should Anticipate", 08/14/1992. (Pages=25) (Format=.txt) (FYI 16)
1358	I	L. Chapin, "Charter of the Internet Architecture Board (IAB)", 08/07/1992. (Pages=5) (Format=.txt) (Obsoleted by RFC1601)
1357	I	D. Cohen, "A Format for E-mailing Bibliographic Records", 07/10/1992. (Pages=13) (Format=.txt)

1356   PS   A. Malis, D. Robinson, R. Ullmann, "Multiprotocol Interconnect on X.25 and ISDN in the Packet Mode", 08/06/1992. (Pages=14) (Format=.txt) (Obsoletes RFC0877)

1355   I   J. Curran, A. Marine, "Privacy and Accuracy Issues in Network Information Center Databases", 08/04/1992. (Pages=4) (Format=.txt) (FYI 15)

1354   PS   F. Baker, "IP Forwarding Table MIB", 07/06/1992. (Pages=12) (Format=.txt)

1353   H   K. McCloghrie, J. Davin, J. Galvin, "Definitions of Managed Objects for Administration of SNMP Parties", 07/06/1992. (Pages=26) (Format=.txt)

1352   H   J. Davin, J. Galvin, K. McCloghrie, "SNMP Security Protocols", 07/06/1992. (Pages=41) (Format=.txt)

1351   H   J. Davin, J. Galvin, K. McCloghrie, "SNMP Administrative Model", 07/06/1992. (Pages=35) (Format=.txt)

1350   S   K. Sollins, "THE TFTP PROTOCOL (REVISION 2)", 07/10/1992. (Pages=11) (Format=.txt) (Obsoletes RFC0783) (STD 33) (Updated by RFC1782, RFC1784, RFC1783, RFC1785)

1349   PS   P. Almquist, "Type of Service in the Internet Protocol Suite", 07/06/1992. (Pages=28) (Format=.txt) (Updates RFC1248)

1348   E   B. Manning, "DNS NSAP RRs", 07/01/1992. (Pages=4) (Format=.txt) (Updates RFC1035) (Obsoleted by RFC1637)

1347   I   R. Callon, "TCP and UDP with Bigger Addresses (TUBA), A Simple Proposal for Internet Addressing and Routing", 06/19/1992. (Pages=9) (Format=.txt, .ps)

1346   I   P. Jones, "Resource Allocation, Control, and Accounting for the Use of Network Resources", 06/19/1992. (Pages=6) (Format=.txt)

1345   I   K. Simonsen, "Character Mnemonics & Character Sets", 06/11/1992. (Pages=103) (Format=.txt)

1344   I   N. Borenstein, "Implications of MIME for Internet Mail Gateways", 06/11/1992. (Pages=9) (Format=.txt, .ps)

1343   I   N. Borenstein, "A User Agent Configuration Mechanism For Multimedia Mail Format Information", 06/11/1992. (Pages=10)(Format=.txt, .ps)

1342   PS   K. Moore, "Representation of Non-ASCII Text in Internet Message Headers", 06/11/1992. (Pages=7) (Format=.txt) (Obsoleted by RFC1522)

1341   PS   N. Borenstein, N. Freed, "MIME (Multipurpose Internet Mail Extensions): Mechanisms for Specifying and Describing the Format of Internet Message Bodies", 06/11/1992. (Pages=80) (Format=.txt, .ps) (Obsoleted by RFC1521)

1340   S   J. Reynolds, J. Postel, "ASSIGNED NUMBERS", 07/10/1992. (Pages=139) (Format=.txt) (Obsoletes RFC1060) (STD 2) (Obsoleted by RFC1700)

1339   E   S. Dorner, P. Resnick, "Remote Mail Checking Protocol", 06/29/1992. (Pages=5) (Format=.txt)

1338   I   V. Fuller, T. Li, K. Varadhan, J. Yu, "Supernetting: an Address Assignment and Aggregation Strategy", 06/26/1992. (Pages=20) (Format=.txt) (Obsoleted by RFC1519)

1337   I   R. Braden, "TIME-WAIT Assassination Hazards in TCP", 05/27/1992. (Pages=11) (Format=.txt)

1336   I   G. Malkin, "Who's Who in the Internet Biographies of IAB, IESG and IRSG Members", 05/27/1992. (Pages=33) (Format=.txt) (FYI 9) (Obsoletes RFC1251)

1335   Z. Wang, J. Crowcroft, "A Two-Tier Address Structure for the Internet: A Solution to the Problem of Address Space Exhaustion", 05/26/1992. (Pages=7) (Format=.txt)

1334   PS   B. Lloyd, W. Simpson, "PPP Authentication Protocols", 10/20/1992. (Pages=16) (Format=.txt)

1333   PS   W. Simpson, "PPP Link Quality Monitoring", 05/26/1992. (Pages=17) (Format=.txt)

1332   PS   G. McGregor, "The PPP Internet Protocol Control Protocol (IPCP)", 05/26/1992. (Pages=14) (Format=.txt) (Obsoletes RFC1172)

1331   PS   W. Simpson, "The Point-to-Point Protocol (PPP) for the Transmission of Multi-protocol Datagrams over Point-to-Point Links", 05/26/1992. (Pages=69) (Format=.txt) (Obsoletes RFC1171) (Obsoleted by RFC1548)

1330   I   ESCC X.500/X.400 Task Force, "Recommendations for the Phase I Deployment of OSI Directory Services (X.500) and OSI Message Handling Services (X.400) within the ESnet Community", 05/22/1992. (Pages=87) (Format=.txt)

1329   I   P. Kuehn, "Thoughts on Address Resolution for Dual MAC FDDI Networks", 05/19/1992. (Pages=28) (Format=.txt)

1328   PS   S. Hardcastle-Kille, "X.400 1988 to 1984 downgrading", 05/18/1992. (Pages=5) (Format=.txt) (Updated by RFC1496)

1327   PS   S. Hardcastle-Kille, "Mapping between X.400(1988) / ISO 10021 and RFC 822", 05/18/1992. (Pages=113) (Format=.txt) (Updates RFC0822) (Obsoletes RFC1148) (Updated by RFC1495)

1326   I   P. Tsuchiya, "Mutual Encapsulation Considered Dangerous", 05/15/1992. (Pages=5) (Format=.txt)

1325   I   G. Malkin, A. Marine, "FYI on Questions and Answers: Answers to Commonly asked 'New Internet User' Questions", 05/15/1992. (Pages=42) (Format=.txt) (FYI 4) (Obsoletes RFC1206) (Obsoleted by RFC1594)

1324   I   D. Reed, "A Discussion on Computer Network Conferencing", 05/13/1992. (Pages=11) (Format=.txt)

1323   PS   D. Borman, R. Braden, V. Jacobson, "TCP Extensions for High Performance", 05/13/1992. (Pages=37) (Format=.txt) (Obsoletes RFC1185)

1322   I   D. Estrin, S. Hotz, Y. Rekhter, "A Unified Approach to Inter-Domain Routing", 05/11/1992. (Pages=38) (Format=.txt)

1321   I   R. Rivest, "The MD5 Message-Digest Algorithm", 04/16/1992. (Pages=21) (Format=.txt)

1320   I   R. Rivest, "The MD4 Message-Digest Algorithm", 04/16/1992. (Pages=20) (Format=.txt) (Obsoletes RFC1186)

1319   I   B. Kaliski, "The MD2 Message-Digest Algorithm", 04/16/1992. (Pages=17) (Format=.txt) (Updates RFC1115)

1318   PS   B. Stewart, "Definitions of Managed Objects for Parallel-printer-like Hardware Devices", 04/16/1992. (Pages=11) (Format=.txt) (Obsoleted by RFC1660)

1317   PS   B. Stewart, "Definitions of Managed Objects for RS-232-like Hardware Devices", 04/16/1992. (Pages=17) (Format=.txt) (Obsoleted by RFC1659)

1316   PS   B. Stewart, "Definitions of Managed Objects for Character Stream Devices", 04/16/1992. (Pages=17) (Format=.txt) (Obsoleted by RFC1658)

1315   PS   C. Brown, F. Baker, C. Carvalho, "Management Information Base for Frame Relay DTEs", 04/09/1992. (Pages=19) (Format=.txt)

1314   PS   D. Cohen, A. Katz, "A File Format for the Exchange of Images in the Internet", 04/10/1992. (Pages=23) (Format=.txt)

1313   I   C. Partridge, "Today's Programming for KRFC AM 1313 Internet Talk Radio", 04/01/1992. (Pages=3) (Format=.txt)

1312	E	R. Nelson, G. Arnold, "Message Send Protocol", 04/01/1992. (Pages=8) (Format=.txt) (Obsoletes RFC1159)
1311	I	Internet Activities Board, A. Chapin, "Introduction to the STD Notes", 03/14/1992. (Pages=5) (Format=.txt)
1310	I	Internet Activities Board, A. Chapin, "The Internet Standards Process", 03/14/1992. (Pages=23) (Format=.txt) (Obsoleted by RFC1602)
1309	I	S. Heker, J. Reynolds, C. Weider, "Technical Overview of Directory Services Using the X.500 Protocol", 03/12/1992. (Pages=16) (Format=.txt) (FYI 14)
1308	I	J. Reynolds, C. Weider, "Executive Introduction to Directory Services Using the X.500 Protocol", 03/12/1992. (Pages=4) (Format=.txt) (FYI 13)
1307	E	A. Nicholson, J. Young, "Dynamically Switched Link Control Protocol", 03/12/1992. (Pages=13) (Format=.txt)
1306	I	A. Nicholson, J. Young, "Experiences Supporting By-Request Circuit-Switched T3 Networks", 03/12/1992. (Pages=10) (Format=.txt)
1305	PS	D. Mills, "Network Time Protocol (v3)", 04/09/1992. (Pages=120) (Format=.txt) (Obsoletes RFC1119)
1304	PS	T. Cox, K. Tesink, "Definitions of Managed Objects for the SIP Interface Type", 02/28/1992. (Pages=25) (Format=.txt) (Obsoleted by RFC1694)
1303	I	K. McCloghrie, M. Rose, "A Convention for Describing SNMP-based Agents", 02/26/1992. (Pages=12) (Format=.txt)
1302	I	D. Sitzler, P. Smith, A. Marine, "Building a Network Information Services Infrastructure", 02/25/1992. (Pages=13) (Format=.txt) (FYI 12)
1301	I	S. Armstrong, A. Freier, K. Marzullo, "Multicast Transport Protocol", 02/19/1992. (Pages=38) (Format=.txt)
1300	I	S. Greenfield, "Remembrances of Things Past", 02/07/1992. (Pages=4) (Format=.txt)
1298	I	R. Wormley, S. Bostock, "SNMP over IPX", 02/07/1992. (Pages=5) (Format=.txt) (Obsoleted by RFC1420)
1297	I	D. Johnson, "NOC Internal Integrated Trouble Ticket System Functional Specification Wishlist ('NOC TT REQUIREMENTS')", 01/31/1992. (Pages=12) (Format=.txt)
1296	I	M. Lottor, "Internet Growth (1981-1991)", 01/29/1992. (Pages=9) (Format=.txt)

1295　I　NADF, "User Bill of Rights for Entries and Listings in the Public Directory", 01/29/1992. (Pages=2) (Format=.txt) (Obsoleted by RFC1417)

1294　PS　T. Bradley, C. Brown, A. Malis, "Multiprotocol Interconnect over Frame Relay", 01/17/1992. (Pages=28) (Format=.txt) (Obsoleted by RFC1490)

1293　PS　T. Bradley, C. Brown, "Inverse Address Resolution Protocol", 01/17/1992. (Pages=6) (Format=.txt)

1292　I　R. Lang, R. Wright, "A Catalog of Available X.500 Implementations", 01/03/1992. (Pages=103) (Format=.txt) (FYI 11) (Obsoleted by RFC1632)

1291　I　V. Aggarwal, "Mid-Level Networks: Potential Technical Services", 12/30/1991. (Pages=10) (Format=.txt, .ps)

1290　I　J. Martin, "There's Gold in them thar Networks! or Searching for Treasure in All the Wrong Places", 12/31/1991. (Pages=27) (Format=.txt) (FYI 10) (Obsoleted by RFC1402)

1289　PS　J. Saperia, "DECnet Phase IV MIB Extensions", 12/20/1991. (Pages=64) (Format=.txt) (Obsoleted by RFC1559)

1288　DS　D. Zimmerman, "The Finger User Information Protocol", 12/19/1991. (Pages=12) (Format=.txt) (Obsoletes RFC1196)

1287　I　R. Braden, V. Cerf, L. Chapin, D. Clark, R. Hobby, "Towards the Future Internet Architecture", 12/12/1991. (Pages=29) (Format=.txt)

1286　PS　K. McCloghrie, E. Decker, P. Langille, A. Rijsinghani, "Definitions of Managed Objects for Bridges", 12/11/1991. (Pages=40) (Format=.txt) (Obsoleted by RFC1493, RFC1525)

1285　PS　J. Case, "FDDI Management Information Base", 01/24/1992. (Pages=46) (Format=.txt) (Updated by RFC1512)

1284　PS　J. Cook, "Definitions of Managed Objects for the Ethernet-like Interface Types", 12/04/1991. (Pages=21) (Format=.txt) (Obsoleted by RFC1398)

1283　E　M. Rose, "SNMP over OSI", 12/06/1991. (Pages=8) (Format=.txt) (Obsoletes RFC1161) (Obsoleted by RFC1418)

1282　I　B. Kantor, "BSD Rlogin", 12/04/1991. (Pages=5) (Format=.txt) (Obsoletes RFC1258)

1281　I　S. Crocker, B. Fraser, R. Pethia, "Guidelines for the Secure Operation of the Internet", 11/27/1991. (Pages=10) (Format=.txt)

1280　S　Internet Activities Board, A. Chapin, "IAB OFFICIAL PROTOCOL STANDARDS", 03/14/1992. (Pages=32) (Format=.txt) (Obsoletes RFC1250) (STD 1) (Obsoleted by RFC1360)

1263   I   L. Peterson, S. O'Malley, "TCP Extensions Considered Harmful", 10/22/1991. (Pages=19) (Format=.txt)

1262   Internet Activities Board, "Guidelines for Internet Measurement Activities", 10/15/1991. (Pages=3) (Format=.txt)

1261   I   S. Williamson, L. Nobile, "Transition of NIC Services", 09/19/1991. (Pages=3) (Format=.txt)

1259   I   M. Kapor, "Building The Open Road: The NREN As Test-Bed For The National Public Network", 09/17/1991. (Pages=23) (Format=.txt)

1258   I   B. Kantor, "BSD Rlogin", 09/11/1991. (Pages=5) (Format=.txt) (Obsoleted by RFC1282)

1257   I   C. Partridge, "Isochronous Applications Do Not Require Jitter-Controlled Networks", 09/09/1991. (Pages=4) (Format=.txt)

1256   PS   S. Deering, "ICMP Router Discovery Messages", 09/05/1991. (Pages=19) (Format=.txt)

1255   I   T. Directory Forum, "A Naming Scheme for c=US", 09/05/1991. (Pages=25) (Format=.txt) (Obsoletes RFC1218)

1254   I   A. Mankin, K. Ramakrishnan, "Gateway Congestion Control Survey", 08/30/1991. (Pages=25) (Format=.txt)

1253   PS   F. Baker, R. Coltun, "OSPF Version 2 Management Information Base", 08/30/1991. (Pages=42) (Format=.txt) (Obsoletes RFC1252) (Obsoleted by RFC1850)

1252   PS   F. Baker, R. Coltun, "OSPF Version 2 Management Information Base", 08/21/1991. (Pages=42) (Format=.txt) (Obsoletes RFC1248) (Obsoleted by RFC1253)

1251   G. Malkin, "Who's Who in the Internet: Biographies of IAB, IESG and IRSG Members", 08/19/1991. (Pages=26) (Format=.txt) (FYI 9) (Obsoleted by RFC1336)

1250   S   J. Postel, "IAB Official Protocol Standards", 08/26/1991. (Pages=28) (Format=.txt) (Obsoletes RFC1200) (STD 1) (Obsoleted by RFC1280)

1249   I   T. Howes, M. Smith, B. Beecher, "DIXIE Protocol Specification", 08/09/1991. (Pages=10) (Format=.txt)

1248   PS   F. Baker, R. Coltun, "OSPF Version 2 Management Information Base", 08/08/1991. (Pages=42) (Format=.txt) (Obsoleted by RFC1252) (Updated by RFC1349)

1247   DS   J. Moy, "OSPF Version 2", 08/08/1991. (Pages=189) (Format=.txt, .ps)
              (Obsoletes RFC1131) (Obsoleted by RFC1583)

1246   I   J. Moy, "Experience with the OSPF Protocol", 08/08/1991. (Pages=31)
              (Format=.txt, .ps)

1245   I   J. Moy, "OSPF Protocol Analysis", 08/08/1991. (Pages=12) (Format=.txt, .ps)

1244   I   P. Holbrook, J. Reynolds, "Site Security Handbook", 07/23/1991.
              (Pages=101) (Format=.txt) (FYI 8)

1243   PS   S. Waldbusser, "AppleTalk Management Information Base", 07/08/1991.
              (Pages=29) (Format=.txt) (Obsoleted by RFC1742)

1242   S. Bradner, "Benchmarking Terminology for Network Interconnection
              Devices", 07/02/1991. (Pages=12) (Format=.txt)

1241   E   D. Mills, R. Woodburn, "A Scheme for an Internet Encapsulation Protocol:
              Version 1", 07/02/1991. (Pages=15) (Format=.txt, .ps)

1240   PS   K. Dobbins, W. Haggerty, C. Shue, "OSI Connectionless Transport
              Services on Top of UDP—Version: 1", 06/26/1991. (Pages=8)
              (Format=.txt)

1239   PS   J. Reynolds, "Reassignment of Experimental MIBs to Standard MIBs",
              06/25/1991. (Pages=2) (Format=.txt) (Updates RFC1233)

1238   E   G. Satz, "CLNS MIB—for Use with Connectionless Network Protocol (ISO
              8473) and End System to Intermediate System (ISO 9542)", 06/25/1991.
              (Pages=32) (Format=.txt) (Obsoletes RFC1162)

1237   PS   R. Colella, E. Gardner, R. Callon, "Guidelines for OSI NSAP Allocation in
              the Internet", 07/23/1991. (Pages=49) (Format=.txt, .ps) (Obsoleted by
              RFC1629)

1236   L. Morales, P. Hasse, "IP to X.121 Address Mapping for DDN",
              06/25/1991. (Pages=7) (Format=.txt)

1235   E   J. Ioannidis, G. Maguire, Jr., "The Coherent File Distribution Protocol",
              06/20/1991. (Pages=12) (Format=.txt)

1234   PS   D. Provan, "Tunneling IPX Traffic through IP Networks", 06/20/1991.
              (Pages=6) (Format=.txt)

1233   H   T. Cox, K. Tesink, "Definitions of Managed Objects for the DS3 Interface
              Type", 05/23/1991. (Pages=23) (Format=.txt) (Obsoleted by RFC1407)
              (Updated by RFC1239)

1232   H   F. Baker, C. Kolb, "Definitions of Managed Objects for the DS1 Interface
              Type", 05/23/1991. (Pages=28) (Format=.txt) (Obsoleted by RFC1406)

1231	DS	E. Decker, R. Fox, K. McCloghrie, "IEEE 802.5 Token Ring MIB", 02/11/1993. (Pages=23) (Format=.txt) (Obsoleted by RFC1743)
1230	H	R. Fox, K. McCloghrie, "IEEE 802.4 Token Bus MIB", 05/23/1991. (Pages=23) (Format=.txt)
1229	DS	K. McCloghrie, "Extensions to the Generic-Interface MIB", 08/03/1992. (Pages=16) (Format=.txt) (Obsoleted by RFC1573)
1228	E	G. Carpenter, B. Wijnen, "SNMP-DPI—Simple Network Management Protocol Distributed Program Interface", 05/23/1991. (Pages=50) (Format=.txt) (Obsoleted by RFC1592)
1227	E	M. Rose, "SNMP MUX Protocol and MIB", 05/23/1991. (Pages=13) (Format=.txt)
1226	E	B. Kantor, "Internet Protocol Encapsulation of AX.25 Frames", 05/13/1991. (Pages=2) (Format=.txt)
1225	DS	M. Rose, "Post Office Protocol—Version 3", 05/14/1991. (Pages=16) (Format=.txt) (Obsoletes RFC1081) (Obsoleted by RFC1460)
1224	E	L. Steinberg, "Techniques for Managing Asynchronously Generated Alerts", 05/10/1991. (Pages=22) (Format=.txt)
1223		J. Halpern, "OSI CLNS and LLC1 Protocols on Network Systems HYPERchannel", 05/09/1991. (Pages=12) (Format=.txt)
1222		H. Braun, Y. Rekhter, "Advancing the NSFNET Routing Architecture", 05/08/1991. (Pages=6) (Format=.txt)
1221		W. Edmond, "Host Access Protocol (HAP) Specification—Version 2", 04/16/1991. (Pages=68) (Format=.txt) (Updates RFC0907)
1220	PS	F. Baker, "Point-to-Point Protocol Extensions for Bridging", 04/17/1991. (Pages=18) (Format=.txt) (Obsoleted by RFC1638)
1219		P. Tsuchiya, "On the Assignment of Subnet Numbers", 04/16/1991. (Pages=13) (Format=.txt)
1218		N. Directory Forum, "A Naming Scheme for c=US", 04/03/1991. (Pages=23) (Format=.txt) (Obsoleted by RFC1255)
1217		V. Cerf, "Memo from the Consortium for Slow Commotion Research (CSCR)", 04/01/1991. (Pages=5) (Format=.txt)
1216		P. Kunikos, P. Richard, "Gigabit Network Economics and Paradigm Shifts", 03/30/1991. (Pages=4) (Format=.txt)
1215	I	M. Rose, "A Convention for Defining Traps for use with the SNMP", 03/27/1991. (Pages=9) (Format=.txt)

1214   H   L. Labarre, "OSI Internet Management: Management Information Base", 04/05/1991. (Pages=83) (Format=.txt)

1213   S   K. McCloghrie, M. Rose, "Management Information Base for Network Management of TCP/IP-based Internets: MIB-II", 03/26/1991. (Pages=70) (Format=.txt) (Obsoletes RFC1158) (STD 17)

1212   S   K. McCloghrie, M. Rose, "Concise MIB Definitions", 03/26/1991. (Pages=19) (Format=.txt) (STD 16)

1211   A. Westine, J. Postel, "Problems with the Maintenance of Large Mailing Lists", 03/22/1991. (Pages=54) (Format=.txt)

1210   V. Cerf, P. Kirstein, B. Randell, "Network and Infrastructure User Requirements for Transatlantic Research Collaboration—Brussels, July 16-18, and Washington July 24-25, 1990", 03/21/1991. (Pages=36) (Format=.txt)

1209   DS   J. Lawrence, D. Piscitello, "The Transmission of IP Datagrams over the SMDS Service", 03/06/1991. (Pages=11) (Format=.txt)

1208   O. Jacobsen, D. Lynch, "A Glossary of Networking Terms", 03/04/1991. (Pages=18) (Format=.txt)

1207   G. Malkin, A. Marine, J. Reynolds, "Answers to Commonly asked 'Experienced Internet User' Questions", 02/28/1991. (Pages=15) (Format=.txt) (FYI 7)

1206   G. Malkin, A. Marine, "FYI on Questions and Answers—Answers to Commonly asked 'New Internet User' Questions", 02/26/1991. (Pages=32) (Format=.txt) (FYI 4) (Obsoletes RFC1177) (Obsoleted by RFC1325)

1205   P. Chmielewski, "5250 Telnet Interface", 02/21/1991. (Pages=12) (Format=.txt)

1204   E   D. Lee, S. Yeh, "Message Posting Protocol (MPP)", 02/15/1991. (Pages=6) (Format=.txt)

1203   H   J. Rice, "Interactive Mail Access Protocol—Version 3", 02/08/1991. (Pages=49) (Format=.txt) (Obsoletes RFC1064)

1202   I   M. Rose, "Directory Assistance Service", 02/07/1991. (Pages=11) (Format=.txt)

1201   H   D. Provan, "Transmitting IP Traffic over ARCNET Networks", 02/01/1991. (Pages=7) (Format=.txt) (Obsoletes RFC1051)

1200   S   J. Postel, "IAB Official Protocol Standards", 04/01/1991. (Pages=31) (Format=.txt) (Obsoletes RFC1140) (STD 1) (Obsoleted by RFC1250)

1199   I   J. Reynolds, "Request for Comments Summary RFC Numbers 1100-1199", 12/31/1991. (Pages=22) (Format=.txt)

1198   I   B. Scheifler, "FYI on the X Window System", 01/01/1991. (Pages=3) (Format=.txt)

1197   I   M. Sherman, "Using ODA for Translating Multimedia Information", 12/31/1990. (Pages=2) (Format=.txt)

1196   DS   D. Zimmerman, "The Finger User Information Protocol", 12/26/1990. (Pages=12) (Format=.txt) (Obsoletes RFC1194) (Obsoleted by RFC1288)

1195   PS   R. Callon, "Use of OSI IS-IS for Routing in TCP/IP and Dual Environments", 12/19/1990. (Pages=68) (Format=.txt, .ps)

1194   DS   D. Zimmerman, "The Finger User Information Protocol", 11/21/1990. (Pages=12) (Format=.txt) (Obsoletes RFC0742) (Obsoleted by RFC1196)

1193   D. Ferrari, "Client Requirements for Real-Time Communication Services", 11/15/1990. (Pages=24) (Format=.txt)

1192   B. Kahin, "Commercialization of the Internet Summary Report", 11/12/1990. (Pages=13) (Format=.txt)

1191   DS   J. Mogul, S. Deering, "Path MTU Discovery", 11/16/1990. (Pages=19) (Format=.txt)

1190   E   C. Topolcic, "Experimental Internet Stream Protocol, Version 2 (ST-II)", 10/30/1990. (Pages=148) (Format=.txt) (Obsoleted by RFC1819)

1189   H   L. Besaw, B. Handspicker, L. LaBarre, U. Warrier, "The Common Management Information Services and Protocols for the Internet", 10/26/1990. (Pages=15) (Format=.txt) (Obsoletes RFC1095)

1188   DS   D. Katz, "A Proposed Standard for the Transmission of IP Datagrams over FDDI Networks", 10/30/1990. (Pages=10) (Format=.txt) (Obsoletes RFC1103) (Obsoleted by RFC1390)

1187   E   J. Davin, K. McCloghrie, M. Rose, "Bulk Table Retrieval with the SNMP", 10/18/1990. (Pages=12) (Format=.txt)

1186   I   R. Rivest, "The MD4 Message Digest Algorithm", 10/18/1990. (Pages=18) (Format=.txt) (Obsoleted by RFC1320)

1185   E   R. Braden, V. Jacobson, L. Zhang, "TCP Extension for High-Speed Paths", 10/15/1990. (Pages=21) (Format=.txt) (Obsoleted by RFC1323)

1184   DS   D. Borman, "Telnet Linemode Option", 10/15/1990. (Pages=23) (Format=.txt) (Obsoletes RFC1116)

1183	E	R. Ullman, P. Mockapetris, L. Mamakos, C. Everhart, "New DNS RR Definitions", 10/08/1990. (Pages=11) (Format=.txt)
1181		R. Blokzijl, "RIPE Terms of Reference", 09/26/1990. (Pages=2) (Format=.txt)
1180		T. Socolofsky, C. Kale, "A TCP/IP Tutorial", 01/15/1991. (Pages=28) (Format=.txt)
1179	I	L. McLaughlin, III, "Line Printer Daemon Protocol", 09/04/1990. (Pages=14) (Format=.txt)
1178		D. Libes, "Choosing a Name for Your Computer", 09/04/1990. (Pages=8) (Format=.txt) (FYI 5)
1177		G. Malkin, A. Marine, J. Reynolds, "FYI on Questions and Answers— Answers to Commonly Asked 'New Internet User' Questions", 09/04/1990. (Pages=24) (Format=.txt) (FYI 4) (Obsoleted by RFC1206)
1176	E	M. Crispin, "Interactive Mail Access Protocol—Version 2", 08/20/1990. (Pages=30) (Format=.txt) (Obsoletes RFC1064)
1175		M. A. Yuan, J. K. Roubicek, K. T. LaQuey, "FYI on Where to Start - A Bibliography of Internetworking Information", 08/16/1990. (Pages=43) (Format=.txt) (FYI 3)
1174	I	V. Cerf, "IAB Recommended Policy on Distributing Internet Identifier Assignment and IAB Recommended Policy Change to Internet 'Connected' Status", 08/09/1990. (Pages=9) (Format=.txt)
1173		J. Van Bokkelen, "Responsibilities of Host and Network Managers A Summary of the 'Oral Tradition' of the Internet", 08/07/1990. (Pages=5) (Format=.txt)
1172	PS	R. Hobby, D. Perkins, "The Point-to-Point Protocol (PPP) Initial Configuration Options", 07/24/1990. (Pages=40) (Format=.txt) (Obsoleted by RFC1332)
1171	DS	D. Perkins, "The Point-to-Point Protocol for the Transmission of Multi-Protocol Datagrams Over Point-to-Point Links", 07/24/1990. (Pages=48) (Format=.txt) (Obsoletes RFC1134) (Obsoleted by RFC1331)
1170	I	R. Fougner, "Public Key Standards and Licenses", 01/11/1991. (Pages=2) (Format=.txt)
1169		K. Mills, V. Cerf, "Explaining the Role of GOSIP", 08/09/1990. (Pages=15) (Format=.txt)
1168		Ward, J. Postel, DeSchon, A. Westine, "Intermail and Commercial Mail Relay Services", 07/17/1990. (Pages=23) (Format=.txt, .ps)

1167		V. Cerf, "Thoughts on the National Research and Education Network", 07/12/1990. (Pages=8) (Format=.txt)
1166		S. Kirkpatrick, M. Recker, "Internet Numbers", 07/11/1990. (Pages=182) (Format=.txt)
1165	E	J. Crowcroft, J. Onions, "Network Time Protocol (NTP) over the OSI Remote Operations Service", 06/25/1990. (Pages=9) (Format=.txt)
1164	PS	J. Honig, D. Katz, M. Mathis, Y. Rekhter, J. Yu, "Application of the Border Gateway Protocol in the Internet", 06/20/1990. (Pages=23) (Format=.txt) (Obsoleted by RFC1268)
1163	PS	K. Lougheed, Y. Rekhter, "A Border Gateway Protocol (BGP)", 06/20/1990. (Pages=29) (Format=.txt) (Obsoletes RFC1105) (Obsoleted by RFC1267)
1162		G. Satz, "Connectionless Network Protocol (ISO 8473) and End System to Intermediate System (ISO 9542) Management Information Base", 06/05/1990. (Pages=70) (Format=.txt) (Obsoleted by RFC1238)
1161	E	M. Rose, "SNMP over OSI", 06/05/1990. (Pages=8) (Format=.txt) (Obsoleted by RFC1283)
1160		V. Cerf, "The Internet Activities Board", 05/25/1990. (Pages=11) (Format=.txt) (Updates RFC1120)
1159	E	R. Nelson, "Message Send Protocol", 06/25/1990. (Pages=2) (Format=.txt) (Obsoleted by RFC1312)
1158	PS	M. Rose, "Management Information Base for Network Management of TCP/IP-based Internets: MIB-II", 05/23/1990. (Pages=133) (Format=.txt) (Obsoletes RFC1156) (Obsoleted by RFC1213)
1157	S	M. Schoffstall, M. Fedor, J. Davin, J. Case, "A Simple Network Management Protocol (SNMP)", 05/10/1990. (Pages=36) (Format=.txt) (Updates RFC1098) (STD 15)
1156	S	K. McCloghrie, M. Rose, "Management Information Base for Network Management of TCP/IP-based internets", 05/10/1990. (Pages=91) (Format=.txt) (Updates RFC1066) (Obsoleted by RFC1158)
1155	S	K. McCloghrie, M. Rose, "Structure and Identification of Management Information for TCP/IP-based Internets", 05/10/1990. (Pages=22) (Format=.txt) (Updates RFC1065) (STD 17)
1154	E	R. Ullmann, D. Robinson, "Encoding Header Field for Internet Messages", 04/16/1990. (Pages=7) (Format=.txt) (Updates RFC1049) (Obsoleted by RFC1505)

Appendix E: RFC Index

1153	E	F. Wancho, "Digest Message Format", 04/01/1990. (Pages=4) (Format=.txt)
1152		C. Partridge, "Workshop Report: Internet Research Steering Group Workshop on Very-High-Speed Networks", 04/06/1990. (Pages=23) (Format=.txt)
1151	E	R. Hinden, C. Partridge, "Version 2 of the Reliable Data Protocol (RDP)", 04/05/1990. (Pages=4) (Format=.txt) (Updates RFC0908)
1150	I	G. Malkin, J. Reynolds, "F.Y.I. on F.Y.I.: Introduction to the F.Y.I. Notes", 03/01/1990. (Pages=4) (Format=.txt) (FYI 1)
1149		D. Waitzman, "A Standard for the Transmission of IP Datagrams on Avian Carriers", 04/01/1990. (Pages=2) (Format=.txt)
1148	E	B. Kantor, S. Kille, P. Lapsley, "Mapping between X.400 (1988) / ISO 10021 and RFC 822", 03/01/1990. (Pages=94) (Format=.txt) (Obsoletes RFC0987) (Obsoleted by RFC1327)
1147	I	R. Stine, "FYI on a Network Management Tool Catalog: Tools for Monitoring and Debugging TCP/IP Internets and Interconnected Devices",04/04/1990. (Pages=126) (Format=.txt, .ps) (FYI 2)(Obsoleted by RFC1470)
1146	E	J. Zweig, C. Partridge, "TCP Alternate Checksum Options",03/01/1991. (Pages=5) (Format=.txt) (Obsoletes RFC1145)
1145	E	J. Zweig, C. Partridge, "TCP Alternate Checksum Options", 02/01/1990. (Pages=5) (Format=.txt) (Obsoleted by RFC1146)
1144	PS	V. Jacobson, "Compressing TCP/IP headers for low-speed serial links", 02/01/1990. (Pages=43) (Format=.txt, .ps)
1143		D. Bernstein, "The Q Method of Implementing TELNET Option Negotiation", 02/01/1990. (Pages=10) (Format=.txt)
1142	I	D. Oran, "OSI IS-IS Intra-domain Routing Protocol", 12/30/1991. (Pages=117) (Format=.txt, .ps)
1141		T. Mallory, A. Kullberg, "Incremental Updating of the Internet Checksum", 01/01/1990. (Pages=2) (Format=.txt) (Updates RFC1071)
1140	S	J. Postel, "IAB Official Protocol Standards", 05/11/1990. (Pages=27) (Format=.txt) (Obsoletes RFC1130) (STD 1) (Obsoleted by RFC1200)
1139	PS	R. Hagens, "Echo function for ISO 8473", 01/30/1990. (Pages=6) (Format=.txt) (Obsoleted by RFC1574, RFC1575)
1138	I	S. Kille, "Mapping between X.400(1988) / ISO 10021 and RFC 822", 12/01/1989. (Pages=92) (Format=.txt) (Updates RFC1026)

1137 E S. Kille, "Mapping between full RFC 822 and RFC 822 with restricted encoding", 12/01/1989. (Pages=3) (Format=.txt) (Updates RFC0976)

1136 S. Hares, D. Katz, "Administrative Domains and Routing Domains: A model for routing in the Internet", 12/01/1989. (Pages=10) (Format=.txt)

1135 J. Reynolds, "Helminthiasis of the Internet", 12/01/1989. (Pages=33) (Format=.txt)

1134 PS D. Perkins, "Point-to-Point Protocol: A proposal for multi-protocol transmission of datagrams over Point-to-Point links", 11/01/1989. (Pages=38) (Format=.txt) (Obsoleted by RFC1171)

1133 J. Yu, H. Braun, "Routing between the NSFNET and the DDN", 11/01/1989. (Pages=10) (Format=.txt)

1132 S L. McLaughlin, "Standard for the transmission of 802.2 packets over IPX networks", 11/01/1989. (Pages=4) (Format=.txt)

1131 PS J. Moy, "OSPF specification", 10/01/1989. (Pages=107) (Format=.txt, .ps) (Obsoleted by RFC1247)

1130 S Internet Activities Board, Defense Advanced Resarch Projects Agency, "IAB official protocol standards", 10/01/1989. (Pages=17) (Format=.txt) (Obsoletes RFC1100) (STD 1) (Obsoleted by RFC1140)

1129 D. Mills, "Internet time synchronization: The Network Time Protocol", 10/01/1989. (Pages=29) (Format=.txt, .ps)

1128 D. Mills, "Measured performance of the Network Time Protocol in the Internet system", 10/01/1989. (Pages=20) (Format=.txt, .ps)

1127 R. Braden, "Perspective on the Host Requirements RFCs", 10/01/1989. (Pages=20) (Format=.txt)

1126 M. Little, "Goals and functional requirements for inter-autonomous system routing", 10/01/1989. (Pages=25) (Format=.txt)

1125 D. Estrin, "Policy requirements for inter Administrative Domain routing", 11/01/1989. (Pages=18) (Format=.txt, .ps)

1124 B. Leiner, "Policy issues in interconnecting networks", 09/01/1989. (Pages=54) (Format=.txt, .ps)

1123 S R. Braden, "Requirements for Internet hosts—application and support", 10/01/1989. (Pages=98) (Format=.txt) (STD 3)

1122 S R. Braden, "Requirements for Internet hosts—communication layers", 10/01/1989. (Pages=116) (Format=.txt) (STD 3)

1121   J. Postel, L. Kleinrock, V. Cerf, B. Boehm, "Act one—the poems",
               09/01/1989. (Pages=6) (Format=.txt)

1120   V. Cerf, "Internet Activities Board", 09/01/1989. (Pages=11) (Format=.txt)
               (Updated by RFC1160)

1119   S   D. Mills, "Network Time Protocol version 2 specification and
               implementation", 09/01/1989. (Pages=64) (Format=.txt, .ps) (Obsoletes
               RFC1059) (STD 12) (Obsoleted by RFC1305)

1118   E. Krol, "Hitchhikers guide to the Internet", 09/01/1989. (Pages=24)
               (Format=.txt)

1117   M. Stahl, S. Romano, M. Recker, "Internet numbers", 08/01/1989.
               (Pages=109) (Format=.txt) (Obsoletes RFC1062)

1116   PS   D. Borman, "Telnet Linemode option", 08/01/1989. (Pages=21)
               (Format=.txt) (Obsoleted by RFC1184)

1115   H   J. Linn, "Privacy enhancement for Internet electronic mail: Part III—
               algorithms, modes, and identifiers [Draft]", 08/01/1989. (Pages=8)
               (Format=.txt) (Obsoleted by RFC1423) (Updated by RFC1319)

1114   H   S. Kent, J. Linn, "Privacy enhancement for Internet electronic mail: Part
               II—certificate-based key management [Draft]", 08/01/1989. (Pages=25)
               (Format=.txt) (Obsoleted by RFC1422)

1113   H   J. Linn, "Privacy enhancement for Internet electronic mail: Part I —
               message enciphermenand authentication procedures [Draft]", 08/01/1989.
               (Pages=34) (Format=.txt) (Obsoletes RFC0989) (Obsoleted by RFC1421)

1112   S   S. Deering, "Host extensions for IP multicasting", 08/01/1989. (Pages=17)
               (Format=.txt) (Obsoletes RFC0988) (STD 5)

1111   J. Postel, "Request for comments on Request for Comments: Instructions
               to RFC authors", 08/01/1989. (Pages=6) (Format=.txt) (Obsoletes
               RFC0825) (Obsoleted by RFC1543)

1110   A. McKenzie, "Problem with the TCP big window option", 08/01/1989.
               (Pages=3) (Format=.txt)

1109   V. Cerf, "Report of the second Ad Hoc Network Management Review
               Group", 08/01/1989. (Pages=8) (Format=.txt)

1108   PS   S. Kent, "U.S. Department of Defense Security Options for the Internet
               Protocol", 11/27/1991. (Pages=17) (Format=.txt) (Obsoletes RFC1038)

1107   K. Sollins, "Plan for Internet directory services", 07/01/1989. (Pages=19)
               (Format=.txt)

1106   R. Fox, "TCP big window and NAK options", 06/01/1989. (Pages=13) (Format=.txt)

1105   E   K. Lougheed, Y. Rekhter, "Border Gateway Protocol BGP", 06/01/1989. (Pages=17) (Format=.txt) (Obsoleted by RFC1163)

1104   H. Braun, "Models of policy based routing", 06/01/1989. (Pages=10) (Format=.txt)

1103   PS   D. Katz, "Proposed standard for the transmission of IP datagrams over FDDI Networks", 06/01/1989. (Pages=9) (Format=.txt) (Obsoleted by RFC1188)

1102   D. Clark, "Policy routing in Internet protocols", 05/01/1989. (Pages=22) (Format=.txt)

1101   P. Mockapetris, "DNS encoding of network names and other types", 04/01/1989. (Pages=14) (Format=.txt) (Updates RFC1034)

1100   S   Defense Advanced Research Projects Agency, Internet Activities Board, "IAB official protocol standards", 04/01/1989. (Pages=14) (Format=.txt) (Obsoletes RFC1083) (STD 1) (Obsoleted by RFC1130)

1099   I   J. Reynolds, "Request for Comments Summary RFC Numbers 1000-1099", 12/19/1991. (Pages=22) (Format=.txt)

1098   J. Case, C. Davin, M. Fedor, "Simple Network Management Protocol SNMP", 04/01/1989. (Pages=34) (Format=.txt) (Obsoletes RFC1067) (Updated by RFC1157)

1097   B. Miller, "Telnet subliminal-message option", 04/01/1989.(Pages=3) (Format=.txt)

1096   G. Marcy, "Telnet X display location option", 03/01/1989.(Pages=3) (Format=.txt)

1095   DS   U. Warrier, L. Besaw, "Common Management Information Services and Protocol over TCP/IP CMOT", 04/01/1989. (Pages=67) (Format=.txt)(Obsoleted by RFC1189)

1094   H   Sun Microsystems, Inc, "NFS: Network File System Protocol specification", 03/01/1989. (Pages=27) (Format=.txt)

1093   H. Braun, "NSFNET routing architecture", 02/01/1989. (Pages=9) (Format=.txt)

1092   J. Rekhter, "EGP and policy based routing in the new NSFNET backbone", 02/01/1989. (Pages=5) (Format=.txt)

1091		J. VanBokkelen, "Telnet terminal-type option", 02/01/1989.(Pages=7) (Format=.txt) (Obsoletes RFC0930)
1090		R. Ullmann, "SMTP on X.25", 02/01/1989. (Pages=4) (Format=.txt)
1089		M. Schoffstall, C. Davin, M. Fedor, J. Case, "SNMP over Ethernet", 02/01/1989. (Pages=3) (Format=.txt)
1088	S	L. McLaughlin, "Standard for the transmission of IP datagrams over NetBIOS networks", 02/01/1989. (Pages=3) (Format=.txt)
1087		Defense Advanced Research Projects Agency, Internet Activities Board, "Ethics and the Internet", 01/01/1989.(Pages=2) (Format=.txt)
1086		J. Onions, M. Rose, "ISO-TP0 bridge between TCP and X.25", 12/01/1988. (Pages=9) (Format=.txt)
1085		M. Rose, "ISO presentation services on top of TCP/IP based internets", 12/01/1988. (Pages=32) (Format=.txt)
1084	DS	J. Reynolds, "BOOTP vendor information extensions", 12/01/1988. (Pages=8) (Format=.txt) (Obsoletes RFC1048) (Obsoleted by RFC1395)
1083	S	Defense Advanced Research Projects Agency, Internet Activities Board, "IAB official protocol standards", 12/01/1988. (Pages=12) (Format=.txt) (STD 1) (Obsoleted by RFC1100)
1082	H	M. Rose, "Post Office Protocol—version 3: Extended service offerings", 11/01/1988. (Pages=11) (Format=.txt)
1081	PS	M. Rose, "Post Office Protocol—version 3", 11/01/1988. (Pages=16) (Format=.txt) (Obsoleted by RFC1225)
1080		C. Hedrick, "Telnet remote flow control option", 11/01/1988. (Pages=4) (Format=.txt) (Obsoleted by RFC1372)
1079		C. Hedrick, "Telnet terminal speed option", 12/01/1988. (Pages=3) (Format=.txt)
1078		M. Lottor, "TCP port service Multiplexer TCPMUX", 11/01/1988. (Pages=2) (Format=.txt)
1077		B. Leiner, "Critical issues in high bandwidth networking", 11/01/1988. (Pages=46) (Format=.txt)
1076		G. Trewitt, C. Partridge, "HEMS monitoring and control language", 11/01/1988. (Pages=42) (Format=.txt) (Obsoletes RFC1023)
1075	E	S. Deering, C. Partridge, D. Waitzman, "Distance Vector Multicast Routing Protocol", 11/01/1988. (Pages=24) (Format=.txt)

1074   J. Rekhter, "NSFNET backbone SPF based Interior Gateway Protocol",
            10/01/1988. (Pages=5) (Format=.txt)

1073   D. Waitzman, "Telnet window size option", 10/01/1988. (Pages=4)
            (Format=.txt)

1072   E   R. Braden, V. Jacobson, "TCP extensions for long-delay paths",
            10/01/1988. (Pages=16) (Format=.txt)

1071   R. Braden, D. Borman, C. Partridge, "Computing the Internet checksum",
            09/01/1988. (Pages=24) (Format=.txt)(Updated by RFC1141, RFC1624)

1070   R. Hagens, N. Hall, M. Rose, "Use of the Internet as a subnetwork for
            experimentation with the OSI network layer", 02/01/1989.(Pages=17)
            (Format=.txt)

1069   R. Callon, H. Braun, "Guidelines for the use of Internet-IP addresses in the
            ISO Connectionless-Mode Network Protocol",02/01/1989. (Pages=10)
            (Format=.txt) (Obsoletes RFC0986)

1068   A. DeSchon, R. Braden, "Background File Transfer Program BFTP",
            08/01/1988. (Pages=27) (Format=.txt)

1067   J. Case, M. Fedor, M. Schoffstall, J. Davin, "Simple Network Management
            Protocol", 08/01/1988. (Pages=33) (Format=.txt) (Obsoleted by RFC1098)

1066   H   K. McCloghrie, M. Rose, "Management Information Base for network
            management of TCP/IP-based internets", 08/01/1988.
            (Pages=90)(Format=.txt) (Updated by RFC1156)

1065   H   K. McCloghrie, M. Rose, "Structure and identification of management
            information for TCP/IP-based internets", 08/01/1988.
            (Pages=21)(Format=.txt) (Updated by RFC1155)

1064   H   M. Crispin, "Interactive Mail Access Protocol: Version 2", 07/01/1988.
            (Pages=26) (Format=.txt) (Obsoleted by RFC1203, RFC1176)

1063   C. Kent, K. McCloghrie, J. Mogul, C. Partridge, "IP MTU Discovery
            options", 07/01/1988. (Pages=11) (Format=.txt)

1062   S. Romano, M. Stahl, M. Recker, "Internet numbers", 08/01/1988.
            (Pages=65) (Format=.txt) (Obsoletes RFC1020) (Obsoleted by RFC1117)

1061   "Not Issued". (Pages=0) (Format=)

1060   S   J. Postel, J. Reynolds, "ASSIGNED NUMBERS", 03/20/1990. (Pages=86)
            (Format=.txt) (Obsoletes RFC1010) (STD 2) (Obsoleted by RFC1340)

1059		D. Mills, "Network Time Protocol version 1 specification and implementation", 07/01/1988. (Pages=58) (Format=.txt)(Obsoletes RFC0958) (Obsoleted by RFC1119)
1058	S	C. Hedrick, "Routing Information Protocol", 06/01/1988.(Pages=33) (Format=.txt) (STD 34) (Updated by RFC1723, RFC1388)
1057	I	Sun Microsystems, Inc, "RPC: Remote Procedure Call Protocol specification version 2", 06/01/1988. (Pages=25) (Format=.txt)(Obsoletes RFC1050)
1056	I	M. Lambert, "PCMAIL: A distributed mail system for personal computers", 06/01/1988. (Pages=38) (Format=.txt)(Obsoletes RFC0993)
1055	S	J. Romkey, "Nonstandard for transmission of IP datagrams over serial lines: SLIP", 06/01/1988. (Pages=6) (Format=.txt)
1054		S. Deering, "Host extensions for IP multicasting", 05/01/1988. (Pages=19) (Format=.txt) (Obsoletes RFC0988)
1053		S. Levy, T. Jacobson, "Telnet X.3 PAD option", 04/01/1988. (Pages=21) (Format=.txt)
1052		V. Cerf, "IAB recommendations for the development of Internet network management standards", 04/01/1988. (Pages=14)(Format=.txt)
1051	S	P. Prindeville, "Standard for the transmission of IP datagrams and ARP packets over ARCNET networks", 03/01/1988. (Pages=4)(Format=.txt) (Obsoleted by RFC1201)
1050	H	Sun Microsystems, Inc, "RPC: Remote Procedure Call Protocol specification", 04/01/1988. (Pages=24) (Format=.txt)(Obsoleted by RFC1057)
1049	S	M. Sirbu, "Content-type header field for Internet messages", 03/01/1988. (Pages=8) (Format=.txt) (STD 11) (Updated by RFC1154)
1048	DS	P. Prindeville, "BOOTP vendor information extensions", 02/01/1988. (Pages=7) (Format=.txt) (Obsoleted by RFC1084)
1047		C. Partridge, "Duplicate messages and SMTP", 02/01/1988. (Pages=3) (Format=.txt)
1046		W. Prue, J. Postel, "Queuing algorithm to provide type-of-service for IP links", 02/01/1988. (Pages=11) (Format=.txt)
1045	E	D. Cheriton, "VMTP: Versatile Message Transaction Protocol: Protocol specification", 02/01/1988. (Pages=123) (Format=.txt)

1044   S   K. Hardwick, J. Lekashman, "Internet Protocol on Network System's HYPERchannel: Protocol specification", 02/01/1988. (Pages=43) (Format=.txt)

1043   A. Yasuda, T. Thompson, "Telnet Data Entry Terminal option: DODIIS implementation", 02/01/1988. (Pages=26) (Format=.txt)(Updates RFC0732)

1042   S   J. Postel, J. Reynolds, "Standard for the transmission of IP datagrams over IEEE 802 networks", 02/01/1988. (Pages=15) (Format=.txt) (Obsoletes RFC0948)

1041   Y. Rekhter, "Telnet 3270 regime option", 01/01/1988. (Pages=6) (Format=.txt)

1040   J. Linn, "Privacy enhancement for Internet electronic mail: Part I: Message encipherment and authentication procedures", 01/01/1988. (Pages=29) (Format=.txt) (Obsoletes RFC0989)

1039   D. Latham, "DoD statement on Open Systems Interconnection protocols", 01/01/1988. (Pages=3) (Format=.txt) (Obsoletes RFC0945)

1038   M. St. Johns, "Draft revised IP security option", 01/01/1988.(Pages=7) (Format=.txt) (Obsoleted by RFC1108)

1037   H   B. Greenberg, S. Keene, "NFILE—a file access protocol", 12/01/1987. (Pages=86) (Format=.txt)

1036   M. Horton, R. Adams, "Standard for interchange of USENET messages", 12/01/1987. (Pages=19) (Format=.txt) (Obsoletes RFC0850)

1035   S   P. Mockapetris, "Domain names—implementation and specification", 11/01/1987. (Pages=55) (Format=.txt) (Obsoletes RFC0973) (STD 13) (Updated by RFC1348)

1034   S   P. Mockapetris, "Domain names—concepts and facilities", 11/01/1987. (Pages=55) (Format=.txt) (Obsoletes RFC0973) (STD 13)(Updated by RFC1101, RFC1876)

1033   M. Lottor, "Domain administrators operations guide", 11/01/1987. (Pages=22) (Format=.txt)

1032   M. Stahl, "Domain administrators guide", 11/01/1987. (Pages=14) (Format=.txt)

1031   W. Lazear, "MILNET name domain transition", 11/01/1987. (Pages=10) (Format=.txt)

1030		M. Lambert, "On testing the NETBLT Protocol over divers networks", 11/01/1987. (Pages=16) (Format=.txt)
1029		G. Parr, "More fault tolerant approach to address resolution for a Multi-LAN system of Ethernets", 05/01/1988. (Pages=17) (Format=.txt)
1028	H	J. Case, J. Davin, M. Fedor, M. Schoffstall, "Simple Gateway Monitoring Protocol", 11/01/1987. (Pages=38) (Format=.txt)
1027		S. Carl-Mitchell, J. Quarterman, "Using ARP to implement transparent subnet gateways", 10/01/1987. (Pages=8) (Format=.txt)
1026	PS	S. Kille, "Addendum to RFC 987: Mapping between X.400 and RFC-822", 09/01/1987. (Pages=4) (Format=.txt) (Updates RFC0987) (Updated by RFC1138)
1025		J. Postel, "TCP and IP bake off", 09/01/1987. (Pages=6) (Format=.txt)
1024		C. Partridge, G. Trewitt, "HEMS variable definitions", 10/01/1987. (Pages=74) (Format=.txt)
1023		G. Trewitt, C. Partridge, "HEMS monitoring and control language", 10/01/1987. (Pages=17) (Format=.txt) (Obsoleted by RFC1076)
1022		C. Partridge, G. Trewitt, "High-level Entity Management Protocol HEMP", 10/01/1987. (Pages=12) (Format=.txt)
1021	H	C. Partridge, G. Trewitt, "High-level Entity Management System HEMS", 10/01/1987. (Pages=5) (Format=.txt)
1020		S. Romano, M. Stahl, "Internet numbers", 11/01/1987. (Pages=51) (Format=.txt) (Obsoletes RFC0997) (Obsoleted by RFC1062)
1019		D. Arnon, "Report of the Workshop on Environments for Computational Mathematics", 09/01/1987. (Pages=8) (Format=.txt)
1018		A. McKenzie, "Some comments on SQuID", 08/01/1987. (Pages=3) (Format=.txt)
1017		B. Leiner, "Network requirements for scientific research: Internet task force on scientific computing", 08/01/1987. (Pages=19) (Format=.txt)
1016		W. Prue, J. Postel, "Something a host could do with source quench: The Source Quench Introduced Delay SQuID", 07/01/1987. (Pages=18) (Format=.txt)
1015		B. Leiner, "Implementation plan for interagency research Internet", 07/01/1987. (Pages=24) (Format=.txt)

1014		Sun Microsystems, Inc, "XDR: External Data Representation standard", 06/01/1987. (Pages=20) (Format=.txt)
1013		R. Scheifler, "X Window System Protocol, version 11: Alpha update April 1987", 06/01/1987. (Pages=101) (Format=.txt)
1012		J. Reynolds, J. Postel, "Bibliography of Request For Comments 1 through 999", 06/01/1987. (Pages=64) (Format=.txt)
1011	S	J. Postel, J. Reynolds, "Official Internet protocols", 05/01/1987. (Pages=52) (Format=.txt) (Obsoletes RFC0991) (STD 1)
1010	S	J. Postel, J. Reynolds, "Assigned numbers", 05/01/1987. (Pages=44) (Format=.txt) (Obsoletes RFC0990) (STD 2) (Obsoleted by RFC1060)
1009	H	R. Braden, J. Postel, "Requirements for Internet gateways", 06/01/1987. (Pages=55) (Format=.txt) (Obsoletes RFC0985) (STD 4) (Obsoleted by RFC1716)
1008		W. McCoy, "Implementation guide for the ISO Transport Protocol", 06/01/1987. (Pages=73) (Format=.txt)
1007		W. McCoy, "Military supplement to the ISO Transport Protocol", 06/01/1987. (Pages=23) (Format=.txt)
1006	S	D. Cass, M. Rose, "ISO transport services on top of the TCP: Version: 3", 05/01/1987. (Pages=17) (Format=.txt) (Obsoletes RFC0983) (STD 35)
1005		A. Khanna, A. Malis, "ARPANET AHIP-E Host Access Protocol enhanced AHIP", 05/01/1987. (Pages=31) (Format=.txt)
1004	E	D. Mills, "Distributed-protocol authentication scheme", 04/01/1987. (Pages=8) (Format=.txt)
1003		A. Katz, "Issues in defining an equations representation standard", 03/01/1987. (Pages=7) (Format=.txt)
1002	S	Defense Advanced Research Projects Agency, End-to-End Services Task Force, Internet Activities Board, a TCP/UDP transport: Detailed specifications", 03/01/1987.(Pages=85) (Format=.txt) (STD 19)
1001	S	Defense Advanced Research Projects Agency, End-to-End Services Task Force, Internet Activities Board, NetBIOS Working Group, "Protocol standard for a NetBIOS service on a TCP/UDP transport: Concepts and methods", 03/01/1987. (Pages=68) (Format=.txt) (STD 19)
1000		J. Postel, J. Reynolds, "Request For Comments reference guide", 08/01/1987. (Pages=149) (Format=.txt) (Obsoletes RFC0999)

APPENDIX F

Internet Parameters

This appendix is an excerpt from RFC 1700, "Assigned Numbers" by J. Reynolds and J. Postel, October 1994. RFC 1700 is maintained by the Internet Assigned Numbers Authority (IANA) at USC-Information Sciences Institute (ISI). This excerpt shows addresses, port numbers, and parameters that assist in the troubleshooting and analysis of TCP/IP-based internetworks. For complete information, obtain RFC 1700 as shown in Appendix D. This excerpt includes:

- Introduction
- Data Notations
- Transmission Order of Bytes
- Significance of Bits
- Special Addresses
- Version Numbers
- Protocol Numbers
- Well-Known Port Numbers
- Registered Port Numbers
- Internet Multicast Addresses
- IP Parameters
    - IP Option Numbers
    - IP Time to Live Parameters
    - IP TOS Parameters
- ICMP Type Numbers
- TCP Parameters
    - TCP Option Numbers
    - TCP Alternate Checksum Numbers
- TELNET Parameters
    - TELNET Options

TELNET Authentication Types

- Domain System Parameters
- BOOTP and DHCP Parameters
- Address Family Numbers
- OSPF Authentication Codes
- Network Management Parameters
- Address Resolution Protocol Parameters

  Reverse Address Resolution Protocol Operation Codes

  Dynamic Reverse ARP

  Inverse Address Resolution Protocol

  Protocol Type
- IEEE Numbers of Interest
- Ethernet Numbers

  EtherTypes

  IANA Ethernet Address Block

  Ethernet Vendor Address Components

  Ethernet Multicast Addresses
- X.25 Type Numbers
- Public Data Network Numbers
- XNS Protocol Types
- Point to Point Protocol Parameters
- Protocol and Service Names

Introduction

The files in the following directory document the currently assigned values for several series of numbers used in network protocol implementations:

```
ftp://ftp.isi.edu/in-notes/iana/assignments
```

The Internet Assigned Numbers Authority (IANA) is the central coordinator for the assignment of unique parameter values for Internet protocols. The IANA is chartered by the Internet Society (ISOC) and the Federal Network Council (FNC) to act as the clearinghouse to assign and coordinate the use of numerous Internet protocol parameters.

The Internet protocol suite, as defined by the Internet Engineering Task Force (IETF) and its steering group (the IESG), contains numerous parameters, such as internet addresses, domain names, autonomous system numbers (used in some routing protocols), protocol numbers, port numbers, management information base object identifiers, including private enterprise numbers, and many others.

The common use of the Internet protocols by the Internet community requires that the particular values used in these parameter fields be assigned uniquely. It is the task of the IANA to make those unique assignments as requested and to maintain a registry of the currently assigned values.

Requests for parameter assignments (protocols, ports, etc.) should be sent to <iana@isi.edu>.

Requests for SNMP network management private enterprise number assignments should be sent to <iana-mib@isi.edu>.

The IANA is located at and operated by the Information Sciences Institute (ISI) of the University of Southern California (USC).

If you are developing a protocol or application that will require the use of a link, socket, port, protocol, etc., please contact the IANA to receive a number assignment.

Joyce K. Reynolds
Internet Assigned Numbers Authority
USC — Information Sciences Institute
4676 Admiralty Way
Marina del Rey, California 90292-6695

Electronic mail: IANA@ISI.EDU
Phone: +1 310-822-1511

Most of the protocols are documented in the RFC series of notes. Some of the items listed are undocumented. Further information on protocols can be found in the memo, "Internet Official Protocol Standards" (STD 1).

Data Notations

The convention in the documentation of Internet Protocols is to express numbers in decimal and to picture data in "big-endian" order. That is, fields are described left to right, with the most significant octet on the left and the least significant octet on the right.

The order of transmission of the header and data described in this document is resolved to the octet level. Whenever a diagram shows a group of octets, the order of transmission of those octets is the normal order in which they are read in English. For example, in the following diagram the octets are transmitted in the order they are numbered.

```
 0                   1                   2                   3
 0 1 2 3 4 5 6 7 8 9 0 1 2 3 4 5 6 7 8 9 0 1 2 3 4 5 6 7 8 9 0 1
+-+-+-+-+-+-+-+-+-+-+-+-+-+-+-+-+-+-+-+-+-+-+-+-+-+-+-+-+-+-+-+-+
|       1       |       2       |       3       |       4       |
+-+-+-+-+-+-+-+-+-+-+-+-+-+-+-+-+-+-+-+-+-+-+-+-+-+-+-+-+-+-+-+-+
|       5       |       6       |       7       |       8       |
+-+-+-+-+-+-+-+-+-+-+-+-+-+-+-+-+-+-+-+-+-+-+-+-+-+-+-+-+-+-+-+-+
|       9       |      10       |      11       |      12       |
+-+-+-+-+-+-+-+-+-+-+-+-+-+-+-+-+-+-+-+-+-+-+-+-+-+-+-+-+-+-+-+-+
```

Transmission Order of Bytes

Whenever an octet represents a numeric quantity, the left-most bit in the diagram is the high order or most significant bit. That is, the bit labeled 0 is the most significant bit. For example, the following diagram represents the value 170 (decimal).

```
 0 1 2 3 4 5 6 7
+-+-+-+-+-+-+-+-+
|1 0 1 0 1 0 1 0|
+-+-+-+-+-+-+-+-+
```

Significance of Bits

Similarly, whenever a multi-octet field represents a numeric quantity, the left-most bit of the whole field is the most significant bit. When a multi-octet quantity is transmitted, the most significant octet is transmitted first.

Special Addresses

There are five classes of IP addresses: Class A through Class E. Of these, Classes A, B, and C are used for unicast addresses, Class D is used for multicast addresses, and Class E addresses are reserved for future use.

With the advent of classless addressing, the network-number part of an address may be of any length, and the whole notion of address classes becomes less important.

There are certain special cases for IP addresses. These special cases can be concisely summarized using the earlier notation for an IP address:

```
IP-address ::=  { <Network-number>, <Host-number> }
```

or

```
IP-address ::=  { <Network-number>, <Subnet-number>,

                                      <Host-number>

}
```

if we also use the notation "-1" to mean the field contains all 1 bits. Some common special cases are as follows:

(a) {0, 0}

This host on this network. Can only be used as a source address (see note later).

(b) {0, <Host-number>}

Specified host on this network. Can only be used as a source address.

(c) {-1, -1}

Limited broadcast. Can only be used as a destination address, and a datagram with this address must never be forwarded outside the (sub-)net of the source.

(d) {<Network-number>, -1}

Directed broadcast to specified network. Can only be used as a destination address.

(e) {<Network-number>, <Subnet-number>, -1}

Directed broadcast to specified subnet. Can only be used as a destination address.

(f) {<Network-number>, -1, -1}

Directed broadcast to all subnets of specified subnetted network. Can only be used as a destination address.

```
(g) {127, <any>}
```

Internal host loopback address. Should never appear outside a host.

```
URL = ftp://ftp.isi.edu/in-notes/iana/assignments/introduction
```

Version Numbers

In the Internet Protocol-IP (RFC 791) there is a field to identify the version of the internetwork general protocol. This field is 4 bits in size.

Assigned Internet Version Numbers

Decimal	Keyword	Version
0		Reserved
1–3		Unassigned
4	IP	Internet Protocol
5	ST	ST Datagram Mode
6	SIP	Simple Internet Protocol
7	TP/IX	TP/IX: The Next Internet
8	PIP	The P Internet Protocol
9	TUBA	TUBA
10–14	Unassigned	
15	Reserved	

```
URL = ftp://ftp.isi.edu/in-notes/iana/assignments/version-numbers
```

Protocol Numbers

In the Internet Protocol-IP (RFC 791) there is a field, called Protocol, to identify the next level protocol. This is an 8 bit field.

Table F-1. Assigned Internet Protocol Numbers

Decimal	Keyword	Protocol
0	Reserved	
1	ICMP	Internet Control Message
2	IGMP	Internet Group Management
3	GGP	Gateway-to-Gateway
4	IP	IP in IP (encapsulation)
5	ST	Stream
6	TCP	Transmission Control
7	UCL	UCL
8	EGP	Exterior Gateway Protocol
9	IGP	any private interior gateway
10	BBN-RCC-MON	BBN RCC Monitoring
11	NVP-II	Network Voice Protocol
12	PUP	PUP
13	ARGUS	ARGUS
14	EMCON	EMCON
15	XNET	Cross Net Debugger
16	CHAOS	Chaos
17	UDP	User Datagram
18	MUX	Multiplexing
19	DCN-MEAS	DCN Measurement Subsystems
20	HMP	Host Monitoring
21	PRM	Packet Radio Measurement
22	XNS-IDP	XEROX NS IDP
23	TRUNK-1	Trunk-1
24	TRUNK-2	Trunk-2
25	LEAF-1	Leaf-1
26	LEAF-2	Leaf-2
27	RDP	Reliable Data Protocol
28	IRTP	Internet Reliable Transaction
29	ISO-TP4	ISO Transport Protocol Class 4

30	NETBLT	Bulk Data Transfer Protocol
31	MFE-NSP	MFE Network Services Protocol
32	MERIT-INP	MERIT Internodal Protocol
33	SEP	Sequential Exchange Protocol
34	3PC	Third Party Connect Protocol
35	IDPR	Inter-Domain Policy Routing Protocol
36	XTP	XTP
37	DDP	Datagram Delivery Protocol
38	IDPR-CMTP	IDPR Control Message Transport Protocol
39	TP++	TP++ Transport Protocol
40	IL	IL Transport Protocol
41	SIP	Simple Internet Protocol
42	SDRP	Source Demand Routing Protocol
43	SIP-SR	SIP Source Route
44	SIP-FRAG	SIP Fragment
45	IDRP	Inter-Domain Routing Protocol
46	RSVP	Reservation Protocol
47	GRE	General Routing Encapsulation
48	MHRP	Mobile Host Routing Protocol
49	BNA	BNA
50	SIPP-ESP	SIPP Encap Security Payload
51	SIPP-AH	SIPP Authentication Header
52	I-NLSP	Integrated Net Layer Security TUBA
53	SWIPE	IP with Encryption
54	NHRP	NBMA Next Hop Resolution Protocol
55–60		Unassigned
61		any host internal protocol
62	CFTP	CFTP
63	any local network	
64	SAT-EXPAK	SATNET and Backroom EXPAK
65	KRYPTOLAN	Kryptolan
66	RVD	MIT Remote Virtual Disk Protocol
67	IPPC	Internet Pluribus Packet Core

68		any distributed file system
69	SAT-MON	SATNET Monitoring
70	VISA	VISA Protocol
71	IPCV	Internet Packet Core Utility
72	CPNX	Computer Protocol Network Executive
73	CPHB	Computer Protocol Heart Beat
74	WSN	Wang Span Network
75	PVP	Packet Video Protocol
76	BR-SAT-MON	Backroom SATNET Monitoring
77	SUN-ND	SUN ND PROTOCOL-Temporary
78	WB-MON	WIDEBAND Monitoring
79	WB-EXPAK	WIDEBAND EXPAK
80	ISO-IP	ISO Internet Protocol
81	VMTP	VMTP
82	SECURE-VMTP	SECURE-VMTP
83	VINES	VINES
84	TTP	TTP
85	NSFNET-IGP	NSFNET-IGP
86	DGP	Dissimilar Gateway Protocol
87	TCF	TCF
88	IGRP	IGRP
89	OSPFIGP	OSPFIGP
90	Sprite-RPC	Sprite RPC Protocol
91	LARP	Locus Address Resolution Protocol
92	MTP	Multicast Transport Protocol
93	AX.25	AX.25 Frames
94	IPIP	IP-within-IP Encapsulation Protocol
95	MICP	Mobile Internetworking Control Pro.
96	SCC-SP	Semaphore Communications Sec. Pro.
97	ETHERIP	Ethernet-within-IP Encapsulation
98	ENCAP	Encapsulation Header
99		any private encryption scheme
100	GMTP	GMTP

101–254	Unassigned	
255	Reserved	

```
URL = ftp://ftp.isi.edu/in-notes/iana/assignments/protocol-numbers
```

Well-Known Port Numbers

The Well-Known Ports are controlled and assigned by the IANA and on most systems can only be used by system (or root) processes or by programs executed by privileged users.

Ports are used in the TCP (RFC 793) to name the ends of logical connections which carry long term conversations. For the purpose of providing services to unknown callers, a service contact port is defined. This list specifies the port used by the server process as its contact port. The contact port is sometimes called the "well-known port".

To the extent possible, these same port assignments are used with the UDP (RFC 768).

The assigned ports use a small portion of the possible port numbers. For many years the assigned ports were in the range 0-255. Recently, the range for assigned ports managed by the IANA has been expanded to the range 0-1023.

Table F-2. Port Assignments

Keyword	Decimal	Description
	0/tcp	Reserved
	0/udp	Reserved
#		Jon Postel <postel@isi.edu>
tcpmux	1/tcp	TCP Port Service Multiplexer
tcpmux	1/udp	TCP Port Service Multiplexer
#		Mark Lottor <MKL@nisc.sri.com>
compressnet	2/tcp	Management Utility
compressnet	2/udp	Management Utility
compressnet	3/tcp	Compression Process
compressnet	3/udp	Compression Process

#		Bernie Volz <VOLZ@PROCESS.COM>
#		Unassigned
rje	5/tcp	Remote Job Entry
rje	5/udp	Remote Job Entry
#		Jon Postel <postel@isi.edu>
#	6/tcp	Unassigned
#	6/udp	Unassigned
echo	7/tcp	Echo
echo	7/udp	Echo
#		Jon Postel <postel@isi.edu>
#	8/tcp	Unassigned
#	8/udp	Unassigned
discard	9/tcp	Discard
discard	9/udp	Discard
#		Jon Postel <postel@isi.edu>
#	10/tcp	Unassigned
#	10/udp	Unassigned
systat	11/tcp	Active Users
systat	11/udp	Active Users
#		Jon Postel <postel@isi.edu>
#	12/tcp	Unassigned
#	12/udp	Unassigned
daytime	13/tcp	Daytime
daytime	13/udp	Daytime
#		Jon Postel <postel@isi.edu>
#	14/tcp	Unassigned
#	14/udp	Unassigned
#	15/tcp	Unassigned [was netstat]
#	15/udp	Unassigned
#	16/tcp	Unassigned
#	16/udp	Unassigned
qotd	17/tcp	Quote of the Day
qotd	17/udp	Quote of the Day
#		Jon Postel <postel@isi.edu>

msp	18/tcp	Message Send Protocol
msp	18/udp	Message Send Protocol
#		Rina Nethaniel <—-none—->
chargen	19/tcp	Character Generator
chargen	19/udp	Character Generator
ftp-data	20/tcp	File Transfer [Default Data]
ftp-data	20/udp	File Transfer [Default Data]
ftp	21/tcp	File Transfer [Control]
ftp	21/udp	File Transfer [Control]
#		Jon Postel <postel@isi.edu>
#	22/tcp	Unassigned
#	22/udp	Unassigned
telnet	23/tcp	Telnet
telnet	23/udp	Telnet
#		Jon Postel <postel@isi.edu>
	24/tcp	any private mail system
	24/udp	any private mail system
#		Rick Adam <rick@UUNET.UU.NET>
smtp	25/tcp	Simple Mail Transfer
smtp	25/udp	Simple Mail Transfer
#		Jon Postel <postel@isi.edu>
#	26/tcp	Unassigned
#	26/udp	Unassigned
nsw-fe	27/tcp	NSW User System FE
nsw-fe	27/udp	NSW User System FE
#		Robert Thomas <BThomas@F.BBN.COM>
#	28/tcp	Unassigned
#	28/udp	Unassigned
msg-icp	29/tcp	MSG ICP
msg-icp	29/udp	MSG ICP
#		Robert Thomas <BThomas@F.BBN.COM>
#	30/tcp	Unassigned
#	30/udp	Unassigned
msg-auth	31/tcp	MSG Authentication

msg-auth	31/udp	MSG Authentication
#		Robert Thomas <BThomas@F.BBN.COM>
#	32/tcp	Unassigned
#	32/udp	Unassigned
dsp	33/tcp	Display Support Protocol
dsp	33/udp	Display Support Protocol
#		Ed Cain <cain@edn-unix.dca.mil>
#	34/tcp	Unassigned
#	34/udp	Unassigned
	35/tcp	any private printer server
	35/udp	any private printer server
#		Jon Postel <postel@isi.edu>
#	36/tcp	Unassigned
#	36/udp	Unassigned
time	37/tcp	Time
time	37/udp	Time
#		Jon Postel <postel@isi.edu>
rap	38/tcp	Route Access Protocol
rap	38/udp	Route Access Protocol
#		Robert Ullmann <ariel@world.std.com>
rlp	39/tcp	Resource Location Protocol
rlp	39/udp	Resource Location Protocol
#		Mike Accetta <MIKE.ACCETTA@CMU-CS-A.EDU>
#	40/tcp	Unassigned
#	40/udp	Unassigned
graphics	41/tcp	Graphics
graphics	41/udp	Graphics
nameserver	42/tcp	Host Name Server
nameserver	42/udp	Host Name Server
nicname	43/tcp	Who Is
nicname	43/udp	Who Is
mpm-flags	44/tcp	MPM FLAGS Protocol
mpm-flags	44/udp	MPM FLAGS Protocol
mpm	45/tcp	Message Processing Module [recv]

mpm	45/udp	Message Processing Module [recv]
mpm-snd	46/tcp	MPM [default send]
mpm-snd	46/udp	MPM [default send]
#		Jon Postel <postel@isi.edu>
ni-ftp	47/tcp	NI FTP
ni-ftp	47/udp	NI FTP
#		Steve Kille <S.Kille@isode.com>
auditd	48/tcp	Digital Audit Daemon
auditd	48/udp	Digital Audit Daemon
#		Larry Scott <scott@zk3.dec.com>
login	49/tcp	Login Host Protocol
login	49/udp	Login Host Protocol
#		Pieter Ditmars <pditmars@BBN.COM>
re-mail-ck	50/tcp	Remote Mail Checking Protocol
re-mail-ck	50/udp	Remote Mail Checking Protocol
#		Steve Dorner <s-dorner@UIUC.EDU>
la-maint	51/tcp	IMP Logical Address Maintenance
la-maint	51/udp	IMP Logical Address Maintenance
#		Andy Malis <malis_a@timeplex.com>
xns-time	52/tcp	XNS Time Protocol
xns-time	52/udp	XNS Time Protocol
#		Susie Armstrong <Armstrong.wbst128@XEROX>
domain	53/tcp	Domain Name Server
domain	53/udp	Domain Name Server
#		Paul Mockapetris <PVM@ISI.EDU>
xns-ch	54/tcp	XNS Clearinghouse
xns-ch	54/udp	XNS Clearinghouse
#		Susie Armstrong <Armstrong.wbst128@XEROX>
isi-gl	55/tcp	ISI Graphics Language
isi-gl	55/udp	ISI Graphics Language
xns-auth	56/tcp	XNS Authentication
xns-auth	56/udp	XNS Authentication
#		Susie Armstrong <Armstrong.wbst128@XEROX>
	57/tcp	any private terminal access

	57/udp	any private terminal access
#		Jon Postel <postel@isi.edu>
xns-mail	58/tcp	XNS Mail
xns-mail	58/udp	XNS Mail
#		Susie Armstrong <Armstrong.wbst128@XEROX>
	59/tcp	any private file service
	59/udp	any private file service
#		Jon Postel <postel@isi.edu>
	60/tcp	Unassigned
	60/udp	Unassigned
ni-mail	61/tcp	NI MAIL
ni-mail	61/udp	NI MAIL
#		Steve Kille <S.Kille@isode.com>
acas	62/tcp	ACA Services
acas	62/udp	ACA Services
#		E. Wald <ewald@via.enet.dec.com>
#		63/tcp Unassigned
#		63/udp Unassigned
covia	64/tcp	Communications Integrator (CI)
covia	64/udp	Communications Integrator (CI)
#		"Tundra" Tim Daneliuk
#		<tundraix!tundra@clout.chi.il.us>
tacacs-ds	65/tcp	TACACS-Database Service
tacacs-ds	65/udp	TACACS-Database Service
#		Kathy Huber <khuber@bbn.com>
sql*net	66/tcp	Oracle SQL*NET
sql*net	66/udp	Oracle SQL*NET
#		Jack Haverty <jhaverty@ORACLE.COM>
bootps	67/tcp	Bootstrap Protocol Server
bootps	67/udp	Bootstrap Protocol Server
bootpc	68/tcp	Bootstrap Protocol Client
bootpc	68/udp	Bootstrap Protocol Client
#		Bill Croft <Croft@SUMEX-AIM.STANFORD.EDU>
tftp	69/tcp	Trivial File Transfer

tftp	69/udp	Trivial File Transfer
#		David Clark <ddc@LCS.MIT.EDU>
gopher	70/tcp	Gopher
gopher	70/udp	Gopher
#		Mark McCahill <mpm@boombox.micro.umn.edu>
netrjs-1	71/tcp	Remote Job Service
netrjs-1	71/udp	Remote Job Service
netrjs-2	72/tcp	Remote Job Service
netrjs-2	72/udp	Remote Job Service
netrjs-3	73/tcp	Remote Job Service
netrjs-3	73/udp	Remote Job Service
netrjs-4	74/tcp	Remote Job Service
netrjs-4	74/udp	Remote Job Service
#		Bob Braden <Braden@ISI.EDU>
	75/tcp	any private dial out service
	75/udp	any private dial out service
#		Jon Postel <postel@isi.edu>
deos	76/tcp	Distributed External Object Store
deos	76/udp	Distributed External Object Store
#		Robert Ullmann <ariel@world.std.com>
	77/tcp	any private RJE service
	77/udp	any private RJE service
#		Jon Postel <postel@isi.edu>
vettcp	78/tcp	vettcp
vettcp	78/udp	vettcp
#		Christopher Leong <leong@kolmod.mlo.dec.com>
finger	79/tcp	Finger
finger	79/udp	Finger
#		David Zimmerman <dpz@RUTGERS.EDU>
www-http	80/tcp	World Wide Web HTTP
www-http	80/udp	World Wide Web HTTP
#		Tim Berners-Lee <timbl@nxoc01.cern.ch>
hosts2-ns	81/tcp	HOSTS2 Name Server
hosts2-ns	81/udp	HOSTS2 Name Server

#		Earl Killian <EAK@MORDOR.S1.GOV>
xfer	82/tcp	XFER Utility
xfer	82/udp	XFER Utility
#		Thomas M. Smith <tmsmith@esc.syr.ge.com>
mit-ml-dev	83/tcp	MIT ML Device
mit-ml-dev	83/udp	MIT ML Device
#		David Reed <—none—>
ctf	84/tcp	Common Trace Facility
ctf	84/udp	Common Trace Facility
#		Hugh Thomas <thomas@oils.enet.dec.com>
mit-ml-dev	85/tcp	MIT ML Device
mit-ml-dev	85/udp	MIT ML Device
#		David Reed <—none—>
mfcobol	86/tcp	Micro Focus Cobol
mfcobol	86/udp	Micro Focus Cobol
#		Simon Edwards <—none—>
	87/tcp	any private terminal link
	87/udp	any private terminal link
#		Jon Postel <postel@isi.edu>
kerberos	88/tcp	Kerberos
kerberos	88/udp	Kerberos
#		B. Clifford Neuman <bcn@isi.edu>
su-mit-tg	89/tcp	SU/MIT Telnet Gateway
su-mit-tg	89/udp	SU/MIT Telnet Gateway
#		Mark Crispin <MRC@PANDA.COM>
dnsix	90/tcp	DNSIX Securit Attribute Token Map
dnsix	90/udp	DNSIX Securit Attribute Token Map
#		Charles Watt <watt@sware.com>
mit-dov	91/tcp	MIT Dover Spooler
mit-dov	91/udp	MIT Dover Spooler
#		Eliot Moss <EBM@XX.LCS.MIT.EDU>
npp	92/tcp	Network Printing Protocol
npp	92/udp	Network Printing Protocol
#		Louis Mamakos <louie@sayshell.umd.edu>

dcp	93/tcp	Device Control Protocol
dcp	93/udp	Device Control Protocol
#		Daniel Tappan <Tappan@BBN.COM>
objcall	94/tcp	Tivoli Object Dispatcher
objcall	94/udp	Tivoli Object Dispatcher
#		Tom Bereiter <—none—->
supdup	95/tcp	SUPDUP
supdup	95/udp	SUPDUP
#		Mark Crispin <MRC@PANDA.COM>
dixie	96/tcp	DIXIE Protocol Specification
dixie	96/udp	DIXIE Protocol Specification
#		Tim Howes <Tim.Howes@terminator.cc.umich.edu>
swift-rvf	97/tcp	Swift Remote Vitural File Protocol
swift-rvf	97/udp	Swift Remote Vitural File Protocol
#		Maurice R. Turcotte
#		<mailrus!uflorida!rm1!dnmrt%rmatl@uunet.UU.NET>
tacnews	98/tcp	TAC News
tacnews	98/udp	TAC News
#		Jon Postel <postel@isi.edu>
metagram	99/tcp	Metagram Relay
metagram	99/udp	Metagram Relay
#		Geoff Goodfellow <Geoff@FERNWOOD.MPK.CA.U>
newacct	100/tcp	[unauthorized use]
hostname	101/tcp	NIC Host Name Server
hostname	101/udp	NIC Host Name Server
#		Jon Postel <postel@isi.edu>
iso-tsap	102/tcp	ISO-TSAP
iso-tsap	102/udp	ISO-TSAP
#		Marshall Rose <mrose@dbc.mtview.ca.us>
gppitnp	103/tcp	Genesis Point-to-Point Trans Net
gppitnp	103/udp	Genesis Point-to-Point Trans Net
acr-nema	104/tcp	ACR-NEMA Digital Imag. & Comm. 300
acr-nema	104/udp	ACR-NEMA Digital Imag. & Comm. 300
#		Patrick McNamee <—none—->

csnet-ns	105/tcp	Mailbox Name Nameserver
csnet-ns	105/udp	Mailbox Name Nameserver
#		Marvin Solomon <solomon@CS.WISC.EDU>
3com-tsmux	106/tcp	3COM-TSMUX
3com-tsmux	106/udp	3COM-TSMUX
#		Jeremy Siegel <jzs@NSD.3Com.COM>
rtelnet	107/tcp	Remote Telnet Service
rtelnet	107/udp	Remote Telnet Service
#		Jon Postel <postel@isi.edu>
snagas	108/tcp	SNA Gateway Access Server
snagas	108/udp	SNA Gateway Access Server
#		Kevin Murphy <murphy@sevens.lkg.dec.com>
pop2	109/tcp	Post Office Protocol—Version 2
pop2	109/udp	Post Office Protocol—Version 2
#		Joyce K. Reynolds <jkrey@isi.edu>
pop3	110/tcp	Post Office Protocol—Version 3
pop3	110/udp	Post Office Protocol—Version 3
#		Marshall Rose <mrose@dbc.mtview.ca.us>
sunrpc	111/tcp	SUN Remote Procedure Call
sunrpc	111/udp	SUN Remote Procedure Call
#		Chuck McManis <cmcmanis@sun.com>
mcidas	112/tcp	McIDAS Data Transmission Protocol
mcidas	112/udp	McIDAS Data Transmission Protocol
#		Glenn Davis <davis@unidata.ucar.edu>
auth	113/tcp	Authentication Service
auth	113/udp	Authentication Service
#		Mike St. Johns <stjohns@arpa.mil>
audionews	114/tcp	Audio News Multicast
audionews	114/udp	Audio News Multicast
#		Martin Forssen <maf@dtek.chalmers.se>
sftp	115/tcp	Simple File Transfer Protocol
sftp	115/udp	Simple File Transfer Protocol
#		Mark Lottor <MKL@nisc.sri.com>
ansanotify116/tcp		ANSA REX Notify

ansanotify116/udp		ANSA REX Notify
#		Nicola J. Howarth <njh@ansa.co.uk>
uucp-path	117/tcp	UUCP Path Service
uucp-path	117/udp	UUCP Path Service
sqlserv	118/tcp	SQL Services
sqlserv	118/udp	SQL Services
#		Larry Barnes <barnes@broke.enet.dec.com>
nntp	119/tcp	Network News Transfer Protocol
nntp	119/udp	Network News Transfer Protocol
#		Phil Lapsley <phil@UCBARPA.BERKELEY.EDU>
cfdptkt	120/tcp	CFDPTKT
cfdptkt	120/udp	CFDPTKT
#		John Ioannidis <ji@close.cs.columbia.ed>
erpc	121/tcp	Encore Expedited Remote Pro.Call
erpc	121/udp	Encore Expedited Remote Pro.Call
#		Jack O'Neil <—-none—->
smakynet	122/tcp	SMAKYNET
smakynet	122/udp	SMAKYNET
#		Mike O'Dowd <odowd@ltisun8.epfl.ch>
ntp	123/tcp	Network Time Protocol
ntp	123/udp	Network Time Protocol
#		Dave Mills <Mills@HUEY.UDEL.EDU>
ansatrader	124/tcp	ANSA REX Trader
ansatrader	124/udp	ANSA REX Trader
#		Nicola J. Howarth <njh@ansa.co.uk>
locus-map	125/tcp	Locus PC-Interface Net Map Ser
locus-map	125/udp	Locus PC-Interface Net Map Ser
#		Eric Peterson <lcc.eric@SEAS.UCLA.EDU>
unitary	126/tcp	Unisys Unitary Login
unitary	126/udp	Unisys Unitary Login
#		<feil@kronos.nisd.cam.unisys.com>
locus-con	127/tcp	Locus PC-Interface Conn Server
locus-con	127/udp	Locus PC-Interface Conn Server
#		Eric Peterson <lcc.eric@SEAS.UCLA.EDU>

646

gss-xlicen	128/tcp	GSS X License Verification
gss-xlicen	128/udp	GSS X License Verification
#		John Light <johnl@gssc.gss.com>
pwdgen	129/tcp	Password Generator Protocol
pwdgen	129/udp	Password Generator Protocol
#		Frank J. Wacho
		<WANCHO@WSMR-SIMTEL20.ARMY.MIL>
cisco-fna	130/tcp	cisco FNATIVE
cisco-fna	130/udp	cisco FNATIVE
cisco-tna	131/tcp	cisco TNATIVE
cisco-tna	131/udp	cisco TNATIVE
cisco-sys	132/tcp	cisco SYSMAINT
cisco-sys	132/udp	cisco SYSMAINT
statsrv	133/tcp	Statistics Service
statsrv	133/udp	Statistics Service
#		Dave Mills <Mills@HUEY.UDEL.EDU>
ingres-net	134/tcp	INGRES-NET Service
ingres-net	134/udp	INGRES-NET Service
#		Mike Berrow <—-none—->
loc-srv	135/tcp	Location Service
loc-srv	135/udp	Location Service
#		Joe Pato <apollo!pato@EDDIE.MIT.EDU>
profile	136/tcp	PROFILE Naming System
profile	136/udp	PROFILE Naming System
#		Larry Peterson <llp@ARIZONA.EDU>
netbios-ns	137/tcp	NETBIOS Name Service
netbios-ns	137/udp	NETBIOS Name Service
netbios-dgm	138/tcp	NETBIOS Datagram Service
netbios-dgm	138/udp	NETBIOS Datagram Service
netbios-ssn	139/tcp	NETBIOS Session Service
netbios-ssn	139/udp	NETBIOS Session Service
#		Jon Postel <postel@isi.edu>
emfis-data	140/tcp	EMFIS Data Service
emfis-data	140/udp	MFIS Data Service

emfis-cntl	141/tcp	EMFIS Control Service
emfis-cntl	141/udp	EMFIS Control Service
#		Gerd Beling <GBELING@ISI.EDU>
bl-idm	142/tcp	Britton-Lee IDM
bl-idm	142/udp	Britton-Lee IDM
#		Susie Snitzer <—-none—->
imap2	143/tcp	Interim Mail Access Protocol v2
imap2	143/udp	Interim Mail Access Protocol v2
#		Mark Crispin <MRC@PANDA.COM>
news	144/tcp	NewS
news	144/udp	NewS
#		James Gosling <JAG@SUN.COM>
uaac	145/tcp	UAAC Protocol
uaac	145/udp	UAAC Protocol
#		David A. Gomberg <gomberg@GATEWAY.MITRE.ORG>
iso-tp0	146/tcp	ISO-IP0
iso-tp0	146/udp	ISO-IP0
iso-ip	147/tcp	ISO-IP
iso-ip	147/udp	ISO-IP
#		Marshall Rose <mrose@dbc.mtview.ca.us>
cronus	148/tcp	CRONUS-SUPPORT
cronus	148/udp	CRONUS-SUPPORT
#		Jeffrey Buffun <jbuffum@APOLLO.COM>
aed-512	149/tcp	AED 512 Emulation Service
aed-512	149/udp	AED 512 Emulation Service
#		Albert G. Broscius <broscius@DSL.CIS.UPENN.EDU>
sql-net	150/tcp	SQL-NET
sql-net	150/udp	SQL-NET
#		Martin Picard <<—-none—->
hems	151/tcp	HEMS
hems	151/udp	HEMS
#		Christopher Tengi <tengi@Princeton.EDU>
bftp	152/tcp	Background File Transfer Program

bftp	152/udp	Background File Transfer Program
#		Annette DeSchon <DESCHON@ISI.EDU>
sgmp	153/tcp	SGMP
sgmp	153/udp	SGMP
#		Marty Schoffstahl <schoff@NISC.NYSER.NET>
netsc-prod	154/tcp	NETSC
netsc-prod	154/udp	NETSC
netsc-dev	155/tcp	NETSC
netsc-dev	155/udp	NETSC
#		Sergio Heker <heker@JVNCC.CSC.ORG>
sqlsrv	156/tcp	SQL Service
sqlsrv	156/udp	SQL Service
#		Craig Rogers <Rogers@ISI.EDU>
knet-cmp	157/tcp	KNET/VM Command/Message Protocol
knet-cmp	157/udp	KNET/VM Command/Message Protocol
#		Gary S. Malkin <GMALKIN@XYLOGICS.COM>
pcmail-srv	158/tcp	PCMail Server
pcmail-srv	158/udp	PCMail Server
#		Mark L. Lambert <markl@PTT.LCS.MIT.EDU>
nss-routing	159/tcp	NSS-Routing
nss-routing	159/udp	NSS-Routing
#		Yakov Rekhter <Yakov@IBM.COM>
sgmp-traps	160/tcp	SGMP-TRAPS
sgmp-traps	160/udp	SGMP-TRAPS
#		Marty Schoffstahl <schoff@NISC.NYSER.NET>
snmp	161/tcp	SNMP
snmp	161/udp	SNMP
snmptrap	162/tcp	SNMPTRAP
snmptrap	162/udp	SNMPTRAP
#		Marshall Rose <mrose@dbc.mtview.ca.us>
cmip-man	163/tcp	CMIP/TCP Manager
cmip-man	163/udp	CMIP/TCP Manager
cmip-agent	164/tcp	CMIP/TCP Agent
smip-agent	164/udp	CMIP/TCP Agent

#		Amatzia Ben-Artzi <—-none—->
xns-courier	165/tcp	Xerox
xns-courier	165/udp	Xerox
#		Susie Armstrong <Armstrong.wbst128@XEROX.COM>
s-net	166/tcp	Sirius Systems
s-net	166/udp	Sirius Systems
#		Brian Lloyd <—-none—->
namp	167/tcp	NAMP
namp	167/udp	NAMP
#		Marty Schoffstahl <schoff@NISC.NYSER.NET>
rsvd	168/tcp	RSVD
rsvd	168/udp	RSVD
#		Neil Todd <mcvax!ist.co.uk!neil@UUNET.UU.NET>
send	169/tcp	SEND
send	169/udp	SEND
#		William D. Wisner <wisner@HAYES.FAI.ALASKA.EDU>
print-srv	170/tcp	Network PostScript
print-srv	170/udp	Network PostScript
#		Brian Reid <reid@DECWRL.DEC.COM>
multiplex	171/tcp	Network Innovations Multiplex
multiplex	171/udp	Network Innovations Multiplex
cl/1	172/tcp	Network Innovations CL/1
cl/1	172/udp	Network Innovations CL/1
#		Kevin DeVault <<—-none—->
xyplex-mux	173/tcp	Xyplex
xyplex-mux	173/udp	Xyplex
#		Bob Stewart <STEWART@XYPLEX.COM>
mailq	174/tcp	MAILQ
mailq	174/udp	MAILQ
#		Rayan Zachariassen <rayan@AI.TORONTO.EDU>
vmnet	175/tcp	VMNET
vmnet	175/udp	VMNET
#		Christopher Tengi <tengi@Princeton.EDU>

genrad-mux	176/tcp	GENRAD-MUX
genrad-mux	176/udp	GENRAD-MUX
#		Ron Thornton <thornton@qm7501.genrad.com>
xdmcp	177/tcp	X Display Manager Control Protocol
xdmcp	177/udp	X Display Manager Control Protocol
#		Robert W. Scheifler <RWS@XX.LCS.MIT.EDU>
nextstep	178/tcp	NextStep Window Server
NextStep	178/udp	NextStep Window Server
#		Leo Hourvitz <leo@NEXT.COM>
bgp	179/tcp	Border Gateway Protocol
bgp	179/udp	Border Gateway Protocol
#		Kirk Lougheed <LOUGHEED@MATHOM.CISCO.COM>
ris	180/tcp	Intergraph
ris	180/udp	Intergraph
#		Dave Buehmann <ingr!daveb@UUNET.UU.NET>
unify	181/tcp	Unify
unify	181/udp	Unify
#		Vinod Singh <—none—>
audit	182/tcp	Unisys Audit SITP
audit	182/udp	Unisys Audit SITP
#		Gil Greenbaum <gcole@nisd.cam.unisys.com>
ocbinder	183/tcp	OCBinder
ocbinder	183/udp	OCBinder
ocserver	184/tcp	OCServer
ocserver	184/udp	OCServer
#		Jerrilynn Okamura <—none—>
remote-kis	185/tcp	Remote-KIS
remote-kis	185/udp	Remote-KIS
kis	186/tcp	KIS Protocol
kis	186/udp	KIS Protocol
#		Ralph Droms <rdroms@NRI.RESTON.VA.US>
aci	187/tcp	Application Communication Interface
aci	187/udp	Application Communication Interface

#		Rick Carlos <rick.ticipa.csc.ti.com>
mumps	188/tcp	Plus Five's MUMPS
mumps	188/udp	Plus Five's MUMPS
#		Hokey Stenn <hokey@PLUS5.COM>
qft	189/tcp	Queued File Transport
qft	189/udp	Queued File Transport
#		Wayne Schroeder <schroeder@SDS.SDSC.EDU>
gacp	190/tcp	Gateway Access Control Protocol
cacp	190/udp	Gateway Access Control Protocol
#		C. Philip Wood <cpw@LANL.GOV>
prospero	191/tcp	Prospero Directory Service
prospero	191/udp	Prospero Directory Service
#		B. Clifford Neuman <bcn@isi.edu>
osu-nms	192/tcp	OSU Network Monitoring System
osu-nms	192/udp	OSU Network Monitoring System
#		Doug Karl <KARL-D@OSU-20.IRCC.OHIO-STATE.EDU>
srmp	193/tcp	Spider Remote Monitoring Protocol
srmp	193/udp	Spider Remote Monitoring Protocol
#		Ted J. Socolofsky <Teds@SPIDER.CO.UK>
irc	194/tcp	Internet Relay Chat Protocol
irc	194/udp	Internet Relay Chat Protocol
#		Jarkko Oikarinen <jto@TOLSUN.OULU.FI>
dn6-nlm-aud	195/tcp	DNSIX Network Level Module Audit
dn6-nlm-aud	195/udp	DNSIX Network Level Module Audit
dn6-smm-red	196/tcp	DNSIX Session Mgt Module Audit Redir
dn6-smm-red	196/udp	DNSIX Session Mgt Module Audit Redir
#		Lawrence Lebahn <DIA3@PAXRV-NES.NAVY.MIL>
dls	197/tcp	Directory Location Service
dls	197/udp	Directory Location Service
dls-mon	198/tcp	Directory Location Service Monitor
dls-mon	198/udp	Directory Location Service Monitor
#		Scott Bellew <smb@cs.purdue.edu>
smux	199/tcp	SMUX

smux	199/udp	SMUX
#		Marshall Rose <mrose@dbc.mtview.ca.us>
src	200/tcp	IBM System Resource Controller
src	200/udp	IBM System Resource Controller
#		Gerald McBrearty <—-none—->
at-rtmp	201/tcp	AppleTalk Routing Maintenance
at-rtmp	201/udp	AppleTalk Routing Maintenance
at-nbp	202/tcp	AppleTalk Name Binding
at-nbp	202/udp	AppleTalk Name Binding
at-3	203/tcp	AppleTalk Unused
at-3	203/udp	AppleTalk Unused
at-echo	204/tcp	AppleTalk Echo
at-echo	204/udp	AppleTalk Echo
at-5	205/tcp	AppleTalk Unused
at-5	205/udp	AppleTalk Unused
at-zis	206/tcp	AppleTalk Zone Information
at-zis	206/udp	AppleTalk Zone Information
at-7	207/tcp	AppleTalk Unused
at-7	207/udp	AppleTalk Unused
at-8	208/tcp	AppleTalk Unused
at-8	208/udp	AppleTalk Unused
#		Rob Chandhok <chandhok@gnome.cs.cmu.edu>
tam	209/tcp	Trivial Authenticated Mail Protocol
tam	209/udp	Trivial Authenticated Mail Protocol
#		Dan Bernstein <brnstnd@stealth.acf.nyu.edu>
z39.50	210/tcp	ANSI Z39.50
z39.50	210/udp	ANSI Z39.50
#		Mark Needleman
#		<mhnur%uccmvsa.bitnet@cornell.cit.cornell.edu>
914c/g	211/tcp	Texas Instruments 914C/G Terminal
914c/g	211/udp	Texas Instruments 914C/G Terminal
#		Bill Harrell <—-none—->
anet	212/tcp	ATEXSSTR
anet	212/udp	ATEXSSTR

#		Jim Taylor <taylor@heart.epps.kodak.com>
ipx	213/tcp	IPX
ipx	213/udp	IPX
#		Don Provan <donp@xlnvax.novell.com>
vmpwscs	214/tcp	VM PWSCS
vmpwscs	214/udp	VM PWSCS
#		Dan Shia <dset!shia@uunet.UU.NET>
softpc	215/tcp	Insignia Solutions
softpc	215/udp	Insignia Solutions
#		Martyn Thomas <—-none—->
atls	216/tcp	Access Technology License Server
atls	216/udp	Access Technology License Server
#		Larry DeLuca <henrik@EDDIE.MIT.EDU>
dbase	217/tcp	dBASE Unix
dbase	217/udp	dBASE Unix
#		Don Gibson
#		<sequent!aero!twinsun!ashtate.A-T.COM!dong @uunet.UU.NET>
mpp	218/tcp	Netix Message Posting Protocol
mpp	218/udp	Netix Message Posting Protocol
#		Shannon Yeh <yeh@netix.com>
uarps	219/tcp	Unisys ARPs
uarps	219/udp	Unisys ARPs
#		Ashok Marwaha <—-none—->
imap3	220/tcp	Interactive Mail Access Protocol v3
imap3	220/udp	Interactive Mail Access Protocol v3
#		James Rice <RICE@SUMEX-AIM.STANFORD.EDU>
fln-spx	221/tcp	Berkeley rlogind with SPX auth
fln-spx	221/udp	Berkeley rlogind with SPX auth
rsh-spx	222/tcp	Berkeley rshd with SPX auth
rsh-spx	222/udp	Berkeley rshd with SPX auth
cdc	223/tcp	Certificate Distribution Center
cdc	223/udp	Certificate Distribution Center
#		Kannan Alagappan <kannan@sejour.enet.dec.com>

#	224-241	Reserved
#		Jon Postel <postel@isi.edu>
#	242/tcp	Unassigned
#	242/udp	Unassigned
sur-meas	243/tcp	Survey Measurement
sur-meas	243/udp	Survey Measurement
#		Dave Clark <ddc@LCS.MIT.EDU>
#	244/tcp	Unassigned
#	244/udp	Unassigned
link	245/tcp	LINK
link	245/udp	LINK
dsp3270	246/tcp	Display Systems Protocol
dsp3270	246/udp	Display Systems Protocol
#		Weldon J. Showalter <Gamma@MINTAKA.DCA.MIL>
#	247-255	Reserved
#		Jon Postel <postel@isi.edu>
#	256-343	Unassigned
pdap	344/tcp	Prospero Data Access Protocol
pdap	344/udp	Prospero Data Access Protocol
#		B. Clifford Neuman <bcn@isi.edu>
pawserv	345/tcp	Perf Analysis Workbench
pawserv	345/udp	Perf Analysis Workbench
zserv	346/tcp	Zebra server
zserv	346/udp	Zebra server
fatserv	347/tcp	Fatmen Server
fatserv	347/udp	Fatmen Server
csi-sgwp	348/tcp	Cabletron Management Protocol
csi-sgwp	348/udp	Cabletron Management Protocol
#	349-370	Unassigned
clearcase	371/tcp	Clearcase
clearcase	371/udp	Clearcase
#		Dave LeBlang <leglang@atria.com>
ulistserv	372/tcp	Unix Listserv
ulistserv	372/udp	Unix Listserv

#		Anastasios Kotsikonas <tasos@cs.bu.edu>
legent-1	373/tcp	Legent Corporation
legent-1	373/udp	Legent Corporation
legent-2	374/tcp	Legent Corporation
legent-2	374/udp	Legent Corporation
#		Keith Boyce <—-none—->
hassle	375/tcp	Hassle
hassle	375/udp	Hassle
#		Reinhard Doelz <doelz@comp.bioz.unibas.ch>
nip	376/tcp	Amiga Envoy Network Inquiry Proto
nip	376/udp	Amiga Envoy Network Inquiry Proto
#		Kenneth Dyke <kcd@cbmvax.cbm.commodore.com>
tnETOS	377/tcp	NEC Corporation
tnETOS	377/udp	NEC Corporation
dsETOS	378/tcp	NEC Corporation
dsETOS	378/udp	NEC Corporation
#		Tomoo Fujita <tf@arc.bs1.fc.nec.co.jp>
is99c	379/tcp	TIA/EIA/IS-99 modem client
is99c	379/udp	TIA/EIA/IS-99 modem client
is99s	380/tcp	TIA/EIA/IS-99 modem server
is99s	380/udp	TIA/EIA/IS-99 modem server
#		Frank Quick <fquick@qualcomm.com>
hp-collector	381/tcp	hp performance data collector
hp-collector	381/udp	hp performance data collector
hp-managed-node		382/tcp hp performance data managed node
hp-managed-node		382/udp hp performance data managed node
hp-alarm-mgr	383/tcp	hp performance data alarm manager
hp-alarm-mgr	383/udp	hp performance data alarm manager
#		Frank Blakely <frankb@hpptc16.rose.hp.com>
arns	384/tcp	A Remote Network Server System
arns	384/udp	A Remote Network Server System
#		David Hornsby <djh@munnari.OZ.AU>
ibm-app	385/tcp	IBM Application
ibm-app	385/tcp	IBM Application

#		Lisa Tomita <—-none—->
asa	386/tcp	ASA Message Router Object Def.
asa	386/udp	ASA Message Router Object Def.
#		Steve Laitinen <laitinen@brutus.aa.ab.com>
aurp	387/tcp	Appletalk Update-Based Routing Pro.
aurp	387/udp	Appletalk Update-Based Routing Pro.
#		Chris Ranch <cranch@novell.com>
unidata-ldm	388/tcp	Unidata LDM Version 4
unidata-ldm	388/udp	Unidata LDM Version 4
#		Glenn Davis <davis@unidata.ucar.edu>
ldap	389/tcp	Lightweight Directory Access Protocol
ldap	389/udp	Lightweight Directory Access Protocol
#		Tim Howes <Tim.Howes@terminator.cc.umich.edu>
uis	390/tcp	UIS
uis	390/udp	UIS
#		Ed Barron <—-none—->
synotics-relay	391/tcp	SynOptics SNMP Relay Port
synotics-relay	391/udp	SynOptics SNMP Relay Port
synotics-broker	392/tcp	SynOptics Port Broker Port
synotics-broker	392/udp	SynOptics Port Broker Port
#		Illan Raab <iraab@synoptics.com>
dis		393/tcp Data Interpretation System
dis		393/udp Data Interpretation System
#		Paul Stevens <pstevens@chinacat.Metaphor.COM>
embl-ndt	394/tcp	EMBL Nucleic Data Transfer
embl-ndt	394/udp	EMBL Nucleic Data Transfer
#		Peter Gad <peter@bmc.uu.se>
netcp	395/tcp	NETscout Control Protocol
netcp	395/udp	NETscout Control Protocol
#		Anil Singhal <—-none—->
netware-ip	396/tcp	Novell Netware over IP
netware-ip	396/udp	Novell Netware over IP
mptn	397/tcp	Multi Protocol Trans. Net.
mptn	397/udp	Multi Protocol Trans. Net.

#		Soumitra Sarkar <sarkar@vnet.ibm.com>
kryptolan	398/tcp	Kryptolan
kryptolan	398/udp	Kryptolan
#		Peter de Laval <pdl@sectra.se>
#	399/tcp	Unassigned
#	399/udp	Unassigned
work-sol	400/tcp	Workstation Solutions
work-sol	400/udp	Workstation Solutions
#		Jim Ward <jimw@worksta.com>
ups	401/tcp	Uninterruptible Power Supply
ups	401/udp	Uninterruptible Power Supply
#		Guenther Seybold <gs@hrz.th-darmstadt.de>
genie	402/tcp	Genie Protocol
genie	402/udp	Genie Protocol
#		Mark Hankin <—-none—->
decap	403/tcp	decap
decap	403/udp	decap
nced	404/tcp	nced
nced	404/udp	nced
ncld	405/tcp	ncld
ncld	405/udp	ncld
#		Richard Jones <—-none—->
imsp	406/tcp	Interactive Mail Support Protocol
imsp	406/udp	Interactive Mail Support Protocol
#		John Myers <jgm+@cmu.edu>
timbuktu	407/tcp	Timbuktu
timbuktu	407/udp	Timbuktu
#		Marc Epard <marc@waygate.farallon.com>
prm-sm	408/tcp	Prospero Resource Manager Sys. Man.
prm-sm	408/udp	Prospero Resource Manager Sys. Man.
prm-nm	409/tcp	Prospero Resource Manager Node Man.
prm-nm	409/udp	Prospero Resource Manager Node Man.
#		B. Clifford Neuman <bcn@isi.edu>
decladebug	410/tcp	DECLadebug Remote Debug Protocol

decladebug	410/udp	DECLadebug Remote Debug Protocol
#		Anthony Berent <berent@rdgeng.enet.dec.com>
rmt	411/tcp	Remote MT Protocol
rmt	411/udp	Remote MT Protocol
#		Peter Eriksson <pen@lysator.liu.se>
synoptics-trap	412/tcp	Trap Convention Port
synoptics-trap	412/udp	Trap Convention Port
#		Illan Raab <iraab@synoptics.com>
smsp	413/tcp	SMSP
smsp	413/udp	SMSP
infoseek	414/tcp	InfoSeek
infoseek	414/udp	InfoSeek
#		Steve Kirsch <stk@frame.com>
bnet	415/tcp	BNet
bnet	415/udp	BNet
#		Jim Mertz <JMertz+RV09@rvdc.unisys.com>
silverplatter	416/tcp	Silverplatter
silverplatter	416/udp	Silverplatter
#		Peter Ciuffetti <petec@silverplatter.com>
onmux	417/tcp	Onmux
onmux	417/udp	Onmux
#		Stephen Hanna <hanna@world.std.com>
hyper-g	418/tcp	Hyper-G
hyper-g	418/udp	Hyper-G
#		Frank Kappe <fkappe@iicm.tu-graz.ac.at>
ariel1	419/tcp	Ariel
ariel1	419/udp	Ariel
#		Jonathan Lavigne <BL.JPL@RLG.Stanford.EDU>
smpte	420/tcp	SMPTE
smpte	420/udp	SMPTE
#		Si Becker <71362.22@CompuServe.COM>
ariel2	421/tcp	Ariel
ariel2	421/udp	Ariel
ariel3	422/tcp	Ariel

ariel3	422/udp	Ariel
#		Jonathan Lavigne <BL.JPL@RLG.Stanford.EDU>
opc-job-start	423/tcp	IBM Operations Planning and Control Start
opc-job-start	423/udp	IBM Operations Planning and Control Start
opc-job-track	424/tcp	IBM Operations Planning and Control Track
opc-job-track	424/udp	IBM Operations Planning and Control Track
#		Conny Larsson <cocke@VNET.IBM.COM>
icad-el	425/tcp	ICAD
icad-el	425/udp	ICAD
#		Larry Stone <lcs@icad.com>
smartsdp	426/tcp	smartsdp
smartsdp	426/udp	smartsdp
#		Alexander Dupuy <dupuy@smarts.com>
svrloc	427/tcp	Server Location
svrloc	427/udp	Server Location
#		<veizades@ftp.com>
ocs_cmu	428/tcp	OCS_CMU
ocs_cmu	428/udp	OCS_CMU
ocs_amu	429/tcp	OCS_AMU
ocs_amu	429/udp	OCS_AMU
#		Florence Wyman <wyman@peabody.plk.af.mil>
utmpsd	430/tcp	UTMPSD
utmpsd	430/udp	UTMPSD
utmpcd	431/tcp	UTMPCD
utmpcd	431/udp	UTMPCD
iasd	432/tcp	IASD
iasd	432/udp	IASD
#		Nir Baroz <nbaroz@encore.com>
nnsp	433/tcp	NNSP
nnsp	433/udp	NNSP
#		Rob Robertson <rob@gangrene.berkeley.edu>
mobileip-agent	434/tcp	MobileIP-Agent
mobileip-agent	434/udp	MobileIP-Agent
mobilip-mn	435/tcp	MobilIP-MN

mobilip-mn	435/udp	MobilIP-MN
#		Kannan Alagappan <kannan@sejour.lkg.dec.com>
dna-cml	436/tcp	DNA-CML
dna-cml	436/udp	DNA-CML
#		Dan Flowers <flowers@smaug.lkg.dec.com>
comscm	437/tcp	comscm
comscm	437/udp	comscm
#		Jim Teague <teague@zso.dec.com>
dsfgw	438/tcp	dsfgw
dsfgw	438/udp	dsfgw
#		Andy McKeen <mckeen@osf.org>
dasp	39/tcp	dasp Thomas Obermair
dasp	439/udp	dasp tommy@inlab.m.eunet.de
#		Thomas Obermair <tommy@inlab.m.eunet.de>
sgcp	440/tcp	sgcp
sgcp	440/udp	sgcp
#		Marshall Rose <mrose@dbc.mtview.ca.us>
decvms-sysmgt	441/tcp	decvms-sysmgt
decvms-sysmgt	441/udp	decvms-sysmgt
#		Lee Barton <barton@star.enet.dec.com>
cvc_hostd	442/tcp	cvc_hostd
cvc_hostd	442/udp	cvc_hostd
#		Bill Davidson <billd@equalizer.cray.com>
https	443/tcp	https MCom
https	443/udp	https MCom
#		Kipp E.B. Hickman <kipp@mcom.com>
snpp	444/tcp	Simple Network Paging Protocol
snpp	444/udp	Simple Network Paging Protocol
#		[RFC1568]
microsoft-ds	445/tcp	Microsoft-DS
microsoft-ds	445/udp	Microsoft-DS
#		Arnold Miller <arnoldm@microsoft.com>
ddm-rdb	446/tcp	DDM-RDB
ddm-rdb	446/udp	DDM-RDB

ddm-dfm	447/tcp	DDM-RFM
ddm-dfm	447/udp	DDM-RFM
ddm-byte	448/tcp	DDM-BYTE
ddm-byte	448/udp	DDM-BYTE
#		Jan David Fisher <jdfisher@VNET.IBM.COM>
as-servermap	449/tcp	AS Server Mapper
as-servermap	449/udp	AS Server Mapper
#		Barbara Foss <BGFOSS@rchvmv.vnet.ibm.com>
tserver	450/tcp	TServer
tserver	450/udp	TServer
#		Harvey S. Schultz <hss@mtgzfs3.mt.att.com>
#	451-511	Unassigned
exec	512/tcp	remote process execution;
#		authentication performed using
#		passwords and UNIX loppgin names
biff	512/udp	used by mail system to notify users
#		of new mail received; currently
#		receives messages only from
#		processes on the same machine
login	513/tcp	remote login a la telnet;
#		automatic authentication performed
#		based on privileged port numbers
#		and distributed data bases which
#		identify "authentication domains"
who	513/udp	maintains data bases showing who's
#		logged in to machines on a local
#		net and the load average of the
#		machine
cmd	514/tcp	like exec, but automatic
#		authentication is performed as for
#		login server
syslog	514/udp	
printer	515/tcp	spooler
printer	515/udp	spooler

#	516/tcp	Unassigned
#	516/udp	Unassigned
talk	517/tcp	like tenex link, but across
#		machine — unfortunately, doesn't
#		use link protocol (this is actually
#		just a rendezvous port from which a
#		tcp connection is established)
talk	517/udp	like tenex link, but across
#		machine — unfortunately, doesn't
#		use link protocol (this is actually
#		just a rendezvous port from which a
		tcp connection is established)
ntalk	518/tcp	
ntalk	518/udp	
utime	519/tcp	unixtime
utime	519/udp	unixtime
efs	520/tcp	extended file name server
router	520/udp	local routing process (on site);
#		uses variant of Xerox NS routing
#		information protocol
#	521-524	Unassigned
timed	525/tcp	timeserver
timed	525/udp	timeserver
tempo	526/tcp	newdate
tempo	526/udp	newdate
#	527-529	Unassigned
courier	530/tcp	rpc
courier	530/udp	rpc
conference	531/tcp	chat
conference	531/udp	chat
netnews	532/tcp	readnews
netnews	532/udp	readnews
netwall	533/tcp	for emergency broadcasts
netwall	533/udp	for emergency broadcasts

#	534-538	Unassigned
apertus-ldp	539/tcp	Apertus Technologies Load Determination
apertus-ldp	539/udp	Apertus Technologies Load Determination
uucp	540/tcp	uucpd
uucp	540/udp	uucpd
uucp-rlogin	541/tcp	uucp-rlogin Stuart Lynne
uucp-rlogin	541/udp	uucp-rlogin sl@wimsey.com
#	542/tcp	Unassigned
#	542/udp	Unassigned
klogin	543/tcp	
klogin	543/udp	
kshell	544/tcp	krcmd
kshell	544/udp	krcmd
#	545-549	Unassigned
new-rwho	550/tcp	new-who
new-rwho	550/udp	new-who
#	551-555	Unassigned
dsf	555/tcp	
dsf	555/udp	
remotefs	556/tcp	rfs server
remotefs	556/udp	rfs server
#	557-559	Unassigned
rmonitor	560/tcp	rmonitord
rmonitor	560/udp	rmonitord
monitor	561/tcp	
monitor	561/udp	
chshell	562/tcp	chcmd
chshell	562/udp	chcmd
#	563/tcp	Unassigned
#	563/udp	Unassigned
9pfs	564/tcp	plan 9 file service
9pfs	564/udp	plan 9 file service
whoami	565/tcp	whoami
whoami	565/udp	whoami

#	566-569	Unassigned
meter	570/tcp	demon
meter	570/udp	demon
meter	571/tcp	udemon
meter	571/udp	udemon
#	572-599	Unassigned
ipcserver	600/tcp	Sun IPC server
ipcserver	600/udp	Sun IPC server
nqs	607/tcp	nqs
nqs	607/udp	nqs
urm	606/tcp	Cray Unified Resource Manager
urm	606/udp	Cray Unified Resource Manager
#		Bill Schiefelbein <schief@aspen.cray.com>
sift-uft	608/tcp	Sender-Initiated/Unsolicited File Transfer
sift-uft	608/udp	Sender-Initiated/Unsolicited File Transfer
#		Rick Troth <troth@rice.edu>
npmp-trap	609/tcp	npmp-trap
npmp-trap	609/udp	npmp-trap
npmp-local	610/tcp	npmp-local
npmp-local	610/udp	npmp-local
npmp-gui	611/tcp	npmp-gui
npmp-gui	611/udp	npmp-gui
#		John Barnes <jbarnes@crl.com>
ginad	634/tcp	ginad
ginad	634/udp	ginad
#		Mark Crother <mark@eis.calstate.edu>
mdqs	666/tcp	
mdqs	666/udp	
doom	666/tcp	doom Id Software
doom	666/tcp	doom Id Software
#		<ddt@idcube.idsoftware.com>
elcsd	704/tcp	errlog copy/server daemon
elcsd	704/udp	errlog copy/server daemon
entrustmanager	709/tcp	EntrustManager

entrustmanager	709/udp	EntrustManager
#		Peter Whittaker <pww@bnr.ca>
netviewdm1	729/tcp	IBM NetView DM/6000 Server/Client
netviewdm1	729/udp	IBM NetView DM/6000 Server/Client
netviewdm2	730/tcp	IBM NetView DM/6000 send/tcp
netviewdm2	730/udp	IBM NetView DM/6000 send/tcp
netviewdm3	731/tcp	IBM NetView DM/6000 receive/tcp
netviewdm3	731/udp	IBM NetView DM/6000 receive/tcp
#		Philippe Binet (phbinet@vnet.IBM.COM)
netgw	741/tcp	netGW
netgw	741/udp	netGW
netrcs	742/tcp	Network based Rev. Cont. Sys.
netrcs	742/udp	Network based Rev. Cont. Sys.
#		Gordon C. Galligher <gorpong@ping.chi.il.us>
flexlm	744/tcp	Flexible License Manager
flexlm	44/udp	Flexible License Manager
#		Matt Christiano
#		<globes@matt@oliveb.atc.olivetti.com>
fujitsu-dev	747/tcp	Fujitsu Device Control
fujitsu-dev	747/udp	Fujitsu Device Control
ris-cm	748/tcp	Russell Info Sci Calendar Manager
ris-cm	748/udp	Russell Info Sci Calendar Manager
kerberos-adm	749/tcp	kerberos administration
kerberos-adm	749/udp	kerberos administration
rfile	750/tcp	
loadav	750/udp	
pump	751/tcp	
pump	751/udp	
qrh	752/tcp	
qrh	752/udp	
rrh	753/tcp	
rrh	753/udp	
tell	754/tcp	send
tell	754/udp	send

nlogin	758/tcp
nlogin	758/udp
con	759/tcp
con	759/udp
ns	760/tcp
ns	760/udp
rxe	761/tcp
rxe	761/udp
quotad	762/tcp
quotad	762/udp
cycleserv	763/tcp
cycleserv	763/udp
omserv	764/tcp
omserv	764/udp
webster	765/tcp
webster	765/udp
phonebook	767/tcp phone
phonebook	767/udp phone
vid	769/tcp
vid	769/udp
cadlock	770/tcp
cadlock	770/udp
rtip	771/tcp
rtip	771/udp
cycleserv2	772/tcp
cycleserv2	772/udp
submit	773/tcp
notify	773/udp
rpasswd	774/tcp
acmaint_dbd	774/udp
entomb	775/tcp
acmaint_transd	775/udp
wpages	776/tcp
wpages	776/udp

wpgs	780/tcp	
wpgs	780/udp	
concert	786/tcp	Concert
concert	786/udp	Concert
#		Josyula R. Rao <jrrao@watson.ibm.com>
mdbs_daemon	800/tcp	
mdbs_daemon	800/udp	
device	801/tcp	
device	801/udp	
xtreelic	996/tcp	Central Point Software
xtreelic	996/udp	Central Point Software
#		Dale Cabell <dacabell@smtp.xtree.com>
maitrd	997/tcp	
maitrd	997/udp	
busboy	998/tcp	
puparp	998/udp	
garcon	999/tcp	
applix	999/udp	Applix ac
puprouter	999/tcp	
puprouter	999/udp	
cadlock	1000/tcp	
ock	1000/udp	
	1023/tcp	Reserved
	1024/udp	Reserved
#		IANA <iana@isi.edu>

Registered Port Numbers

The Registered Ports are not controlled by the IANA and on most systems can be used by ordinary user processes or programs executed by ordinary users.

Ports are used in the TCP (RFC793) to name the ends of logical connections which carry long term conversations. For the purpose of providing services to unknown callers, a service contact port is defined. This list specifies the port used by the server process as its contact port. While the IANA can not control uses of these ports it does register or list uses of these ports as a convienence to the community.

To the extent possible, these same port assignments are used with the UDP (RFC768).

The Registered Ports are in the range 1024–65535, and are listed in RFC 1700.

```
URL = ftp://ftp.isi.edu/in-notes/iana/assignments/port-numbers
```

Internet Multicast Addresses

Host Extensions for IP Multicasting specifies the extensions required of a host implementation of the Internet Protocol (IP) to support multicasting. Current addresses are listed below.

Table F-3. Internet Multicast Addresses

Addresses	Description
224.0.0.0	Base Address (Reserved)
224.0.0.1	All Systems on this Subnet
224.0.0.2	All Routers on this Subnet
224.0.0.3	Unassigned
224.0.0.4	DVMRP Routers
224.0.0.5	OSPFIGP OSPFIGP All Routers
224.0.0.6	OSPFIGP OSPFIGP Designated Routers
224.0.0.7	ST Routers
224.0.0.8	ST Hosts
224.0.0.9	RIP2 Routers
224.0.0.10	IGRP Routers
224.0.0.11	Mobile-Agents
224.0.0.12- 224.0.0.255	Unassigned
224.0.1.0	VMTP Managers Group
224.0.1.1	NTP Network Time Protocol
224.0.1.2	SGI-Dogfight
224.0.1.3	Rwhod

224.0.1.4	VNP
224.0.1.5	Artificial Horizons - Aviator
224.0.1.6	NSS - Name Service Server
224.0.1.7	AUDIONEWS - Audio News Multicast
224.0.1.8	SUN NIS+ Information Service
224.0.1.9	MTP Multicast Transport Protocol
224.0.1.10	IETF-1-LOW-AUDIO
224.0.1.11	IETF-1-AUDIO
224.0.1.12	IETF-1-VIDEO
224.0.1.13	IETF-2-LOW-AUDIO
224.0.1.14	IETF-2-AUDIO
224.0.1.15	IETF-2-VIDEO
224.0.1.16	MUSIC-SERVICE
224.0.1.17	SEANET-TELEMETRY
224.0.1.18	SEANET-IMAGE
224.0.1.19	MLOADD
224.0.1.20	any private experiment
224.0.1.21	DVMRP on MOSPF
224.0.1.22	SVRLOC
224.0.1.23	XINGTV
224.0.1.24	microsoft-ds
224.0.1.25	nbc-pro
224.0.1.26	nbc-pfn
224.0.1.27- 224.0.1.255	Unassigned
224.0.2.1	"rwho" Group (BSD) (unofficial)
224.0.2.2	SUN RPC PMAPPROC_CALLIT
224.0.3.000- 224.0.3.255	RFE Generic Service
224.0.4.000- 224.0.4.255	RFE Individual Conferences
224.0.5.000- 224.0.5.127	CDPD Groups
224.0.5.128- 224.0.5.255	Unassigned

224.0.6.000- 224.0.6.127	Cornell ISIS Project
224.0.6.128- 224.0.6.255	Unassigned
224.1.0.0- 224.1.255.255	ST Multicast Groups
224.2.0.0- 224.2.255.255	Multimedia Conference Calls
224.252.0.0- 224.255.255.255	DIS transient groups
232.0.0.0- 232.255.255.255	VMTP transient groups

These addresses are listed in the Domain Name Service under MCAST.NET and 224.IN-ADDR.ARPA.

Note that when used on an Ethernet or IEEE 802 network, the 23 low-order bits of the IP Multicast address are placed in the low-order 23 bits of the Ethernet or IEEE 802 net multicast address 1.0.94.0.0.0. See the section on "IANA Ethernet Address Block".

```
URL = ftp://ftp.isi.edu/in-notes/iana/assignments/multicast-addresses
```

IP Parameters

IP Option Numbers

The Internet Protocol (IP) has provision for optional header fields identified by an option type field. Options 0 and 1 are exactly one octet, which is their type field. All other options have their one-octet type field, followed by a one-octet length field, followed by length-2 octets of option data. The option type field is subdivided into a one-bit copied flag, a two-bit class field, and a five-bit option number. These taken together form an eight-bit value for the option type field. IP options are commonly referred to by this value.

Table F-4. IP Option Numbers

Copy	Class	Number	Value	Name
0	0	0	0 EOOL	- End of Options List
0	0	1	1 NOP	- No Operation
1	0	2	130 SEC	- Security
1	0	3	131 LSR	- Loose Source Route
0	2	4	68 TS	- Time Stamp
1	0	5	133 E-SEC	- Extended Security
1	0	6	134 CIPSO	- Commercial Security
0	0	7	7 RR	- Record Route
1	0	8	136 SID	- Stream ID
1	0	9	137 SSR	- Strict Source Route
0	0	10	10 ZSU	- Experimental Measurement
0	0	11	11 MTUP	- MTU Probe
0	0	12	12 MTUR	- MTU Reply
1	2	13	205 FINN	- Experimental Flow Control
1	0	14	142 VISA	- Expermental Access Control
0	0	15	15 ENCODE	- ???
1	0	16	144 IMITD	- IMI Traffic Descriptor
1	0	17	145 EIP	- ???
0	2	18	82 TR	- Traceroute
1	0	19	147 ADDEXT	- Address Extension

IP Time to Live Parameter

The current recommended default time to live (TTL) for the Internet Protocol (IP) is 64.

IP TOS Parameters

This documents the default Type-of-Service values that are currently recommended for the most important Internet protocols.

TOS Value	Description
0000	Default
0001	Minimize Monetary Cost
0010	Maximize Reliability
0100	Maximize Throughput
1000	Minimize Delay
1111	Maximize Security

The TOS value is used to indicate "better". Only one TOS value or property can be requested in any one IP datagram.

Generally, protocols which are involved in direct interaction with a human should select low delay, while data transfers which may involve large blocks of data need high throughput. Finally, high reliability is most important for datagram-based Internet management functions.

Application protocols not included in these tables should be able to make appropriate choice of low delay (8 decimal, 1000 binary) or high throughput (4 decimal, 0100 binary).

The following are recommended values for TOS:

Protocol	TOS Value	Type-of-Service Value
TELNET (1)	1000	(minimize delay)
FTP		
Control	1000	(minimize delay)
Data (2)	0100	(maximize throughput)
TFTP	1000	(minimize delay)
SMTP (3)		
Command phase	1000	(minimize delay)
DATA phase	0100	(maximize throughput)
Domain Name Service		
UDP Query	1000	(minimize delay)
TCP Query	0000	
Zone Transfer	0100	(maximize throughput)

NNTP	0001	(minimize monetary cost)
ICMP		
Errors	0000	
Requests	0000 (4)	
Responses	<same as request> (4)	
Any IGP	0010	(maximize reliability)
EGP	0000	
SNMP	0010	(maximize reliability)
BOOTP	0000	

Notes:

1. Includes all interactive user protocols (e.g., rlogin).
2. Includes all bulk data transfer protocols (e.g., rcp).
3. If the implementation does not support changing the TOS during the lifetime of the connection, then the recommended TOS on opening the connection is the default TOS (0000).
4. Although ICMP request messages are normally sent with the default TOS, there are sometimes good reasons why they would be sent with some other TOS value. An ICMP response always uses the same TOS value as was used in the corresponding ICMP request message.

An application may (at the request of the user) substitute 0001 (minimize monetary cost) for any of the above values.

```
URL = ftp://ftp.isi.edu/in-notes/iana/assignments/ip-parameters
```

ICMP Type Numbers

The Internet Control Message Protocol (ICMP) has many messages that are identified by a "type" field.

Table F-5. ICMP Type Numbers

Type	Name
0	Echo Reply
1	Unassigned
2	Unassigned
3	Destination Unreachable
4	Source Quench
5	Redirect
6	Alternate Host Address
7	Unassigned
8	Echo
9	Router Advertisement
10	Router Selection
11	Time Exceeded
12	Parameter Problem
13	Timestamp
14	Timestamp Reply
15	Information Request
16	Information Reply
17	Address Mask Request
18	Address Mask Reply
19	Reserved (for Security)
20–29	Reserved (for Robustness Experiment)
30	Traceroute
31	Datagram Conversion Error
32	Mobile Host Redirect
33	IPv6 Where-Are-You
34	IPv6 I-Am-Here
35	Mobile Registration Request
36	Mobile Registration Reply
37–255	Reserved

Many of these ICMP types have a "code" field. Here we list the types again with their assigned code fields.

Table F-6. ICMP Code Field Assignments

Type	Name
0	Echo Reply
	Codes
	0 No Code
1	Unassigned
2	Unassigned
3	Destination Unreachable
	Codes
	0 Net Unreachable
	1 Host Unreachable
	2 Protocol Unreachable
	3 Port Unreachable
	4 Fragmentation Needed and Don't Fragment was Set
	5 Source Route Failed
	6 Destination Network Unknown
	7 Destination Host Unknown
	8 Source Host Isolated
	9 Communication with Destination Network is Administratively Prohibited
	10 Communication with Destination Host is Administratively Prohibited
	11 Destination Network Unreachable for Type of Service
	12 Destination Host Unreachable for Type of Service
4	Source Quench
	Codes
	0 No Code
5	Redirect
	Codes
	0 Redirect Datagram for the Network (or subnet)
	1 Redirect Datagram for the Host
	2 Redirect Datagram for the Type of Service and Network
	3 Redirect Datagram for the Type of Service and Host

6	Alternate Host Address
	Codes
	0 Alternate Address for Host
7	Unassigned
8	Echo
	Codes
	0 No Code
9	Router Advertisement
	Codes
	0 No Code
10	Router Selection
	Codes
	0 No Code
11	Time Exceeded
	Codes
	0 Time to Live exceeded in Transit
	1 Fragment Reassembly Time Exceeded
12	Parameter Problem
	Codes
	0 Pointer indicates the error
	1 Missing a Required Option
	2 Bad Length
13	Timestamp
	Codes
	0 No Code
14	Timestamp Reply
	Codes
	0 No Code
15	Information Request
	Codes
	0 No Code
16	Information Reply
	Codes
	0 No Code

17	Address Mask Request
	Codes
	0 No Code
18	Address Mask Reply
	Codes
	0 No Code
19	Reserved (for Security)
20–29	Reserved (for Robustness Experiment)
30	Traceroute
31	Datagram Conversion Error
32	Mobile Host Redirect
33	IPv6 Where-Are-You
34	IPv6 I-Am-Here
35	Mobile Registration Request
36	Mobile Registration Reply

```
URL = ftp://ftp.isi.edu/in-notes/iana/assignments/icmp-parameters
```

TCP Parameters

TCP Option Numbers

The Transmission Control Protocol (TCP) has provision for optional header fields identified by an option kind field. Options 0 and 1 are exactly one octet, which is their kind field. All other options have their one-octet kind field, followed by a one-octet length field, followed by length-2 octets of option data.

Table F-7. TCP Option Numbers

Kind	Length	Meaning
0	-	End of Option List
1	-	No-Operation
2	4	Maximum Segment Lifetime
3	3	WSOPT - Window Scale

4	2	SACK Permitted
5	N	SACK
6	6	Echo (obsoleted by option 8)
7	6	Echo Reply (obsoleted by option 8)
8	10	TSOPT - Time Stamp Option
9	2	Partial Order Connection Permitted
10	5	Partial Order Service Profile
11		CC
12		CC.NEW
13		CC.ECHO
14	3	TCP Alternate Checksum Request
15	N	TCP Alternate Checksum Data
16		Skeeter
17		Bubba
18	3	Trailer Checksum Option

TCP Alternate Checksum Numbers

Number	Description
0	TCP Checksum
1	8-bit Fletchers's algorithm
2	16-bit Fletchers's algorithm
3	Redundant Checksum Avoidance

```
URL = ftp://ftp.isi.edu/in-notes/iana/assignments/tcp-parameters
```

TELNET Parameters

TELNET Options

The Telnet Protocol has a number of options that may be negotiated. These options are listed here. "Internet Official Protocol Standards" (STD 1) provides more detailed information.

Table F-8. TELNET Options

Options	Name
0	Binary Transmission
1	Echo
2	Reconnection
3	Suppress Go Ahead
4	Approx Message Size Negotiation
5	Status
6	Timing Mark
7	Remote Controlled Trans and Echo
8	Output Line Width
9	Output Page Size
10	Output Carriage-Return Disposition
11	Output Horizontal Tab Stops
12	Output Horizontal Tab Disposition
13	Output Formfeed Disposition
14	Output Vertical Tabstops
15	Output Vertical Tab Disposition
16	Output Linefeed Disposition
17	Extended ASCII
18	Logout
19	Byte Macro
20	Data Entry Terminal
22	SUPDUP
22	SUPDUP Output
23	Send Location
24	Terminal Type
25	End of Record
26	TACACS User Identification
27	Output Marking
28	Terminal Location Number

680

29	Telnet 3270 Regime
30	X.3 PAD
31	Negotiate About Window Size
32	Terminal Speed
33	Remote Flow Control
34	Linemode
35	X Display Location
36	Environment Option
37	Authentication Option
38	Encryption Option
39	New Environment Option
40	TN3270E
255	Extended-Options-List

TELNET Authentication Types

In RFC1409, a list of authentication types is introduced. Additions to the list are registered by the IANA and documented here.

Type	Description
0	NULL
1	KERBEROS_V4
2	KERBEROS_V5
3	SPX
4–5	Unassigned
6	RSA
7–9	Unassigned
10	LOKI
11	SSA

```
URL = ftp://ftp.isi.edu/in-notes/iana/assignments/telnet-options
```

Domain Name System Parameters

The Internet Domain Naming System (DOMAIN) includes several parameters. These are documented in RFC1034 and RFC1035. The CLASS parameter is listed here. The per CLASS parameters are defined in separate RFCs as indicated.

Domain System Parameters:

Decimal	Name
0	Reserved
1	Internet (IN)
2	Unassigned
3	Chaos (CH)
4	Hessoid (HS)
5–65534	Unassigned
65535	Reserved

In the Internet (IN) class the following TYPEs and QTYPEs are defined:

Table F-9. DNS Internet Class Type Definitions

TYPE	Value and Meaning
A	1 a host address
NS	2 an authoritative name server
MD	3 a mail destination (Obsolete - use MX)
MF	4 a mail forwarder (Obsolete - use MX)
CNAME	5 the canonical name for an alias
SOA	6 marks the start of a zone of authority
MB	7 a mailbox domain name (EXPERIMENTAL)
MG	8 a mail group member (EXPERIMENTAL)
MR	9 a mail rename domain name (EXPERIMENTAL)
NULL	10 a null RR (EXPERIMENTAL)
WKS	11 a well known service description
PTR	12 a domain name pointer
HINFO	13 host information

MINFO	14 mailbox or mail list information
MX	15 mail exchange
TXT	16 text strings
RP	17 for Responsible Person
AFSDB	18 for AFS Data Base location
X25	19 for X.25 PSDN address
ISDN	20 for ISDN address
RT	21 for Route Through
NSAP	22 for NSAP address, NSAP style A record
NSAP-PTR	23 for domain name pointer, NSAP style
SIG	24 for security signature
KEY	25 for security key
PX	26 X.400 mail mapping information
GPOS	27 Geographical Position
AAAA	28 IP6 Address
AXFR	252 transfer of an entire zone
MAILB	253 mailbox-related RRs (MB, MG or MR)
MAILA	254 mail agent RRs (Obsolete - see MX)
*	255 A request for all records

URL = ftp://ftp.isi.edu/in-notes/iana/assignments/dns-parameters

BOOTP and DHCP Parameters

The Bootstrap Protocol-BOOTP (RFC951) describes an IP/UDP bootstrap protocol (BOOTP) which allows a diskless client machine to discover its own IP address, the address of a server host, and the name of a file to be loaded into memory and executed. The Dynamic Host Configuration Protocol-DHCP (RFC1531) provides a framework for automatic configuration of IP hosts. The "DHCP Options and BOOTP Vendor Information Extensions" (RFC1533) describes the additions to the Bootstrap Protocol (BOOTP) which can also be used as options with the Dynamic Host Configuration Protocol (DHCP).

Table F-10. BOOTP Vendor Extensions and DHCP Options

Tag	Name	Data Length	Meaning
0	Pad	0	None
1	Subnet Mask	4	Subnet Mask Value
2	Time Offset	4	Time Offset in Seconds from UTC
3	Gateways	N	N/4 Gateway addresses
4	Time Server	N	N/4 Timeserver addresses
5	Name Server	N	N/4 IEN-116 Server addresses
6	Domain Server	N	N/4 DNS Server addresses
7	Log Server	N	N/4 Logging Server addresses
8	Quotes Server	N	N/4 Quotes Server addresses
9	LPR Server	N	N/4 Printer Server addresses
10	Impress Server	N	N/4 Impress Server addresses
11	RLP Server	N	N/4 RLP Server addresses
12	Hostname	N	Hostname string
13	Boot File Size	2	Size of boot file in 512 byte chunks
14	Merit Dump File		Client to dump and name the file to dump it to
15	Domain Name	N	The DNS domain name of the client
16	Swap Server	N	Swap Server addeess
17	Root Path	N	Path name for root disk
18	Extension File	N	Path name for more BOOTP info
19	Forward On/Off	1	Enable/Disable IP Forwarding
20	SrcRte On/Off	1	Enable/Disable Source Routing
21	Policy Filter	N	Routing Policy Filters
22	Max DG Assembly	2	Max Datagram Reassembly Size
23	Default IP TTL	1	Default IP Time to Live
24	MTU Timeout	4	Path MTU Aging Timeout
25	MTU Plateau	N	Path MTU Plateau Table
26	MTU Interface	2	Interface MTU Size
27	MTU Subnet	1	All Subnets are Local
28	Broadcast Address	4	Broadcast Address
29	Mask Discovery	1	Perform Mask Discovery

30	Mask Supplier	1	Provide Mask to Others
31	Router Discovery	1	Perform Router Discovery
32	Router Request	4	Router Solicitation Address
34	Trailers	1	Trailer Encapsulation
35	ARP Timeout	4	ARP Cache Timeout
36	Ethernet	1	Ethernet Encapsulation
37	Default TCP TTL	1	Default TCP Time to Live
38	Keepalive Time	4	TCP Keepalive Interval
39	Keepalive Data	1	TCP Keepalive Garbage
40	NIS Domain	N	NIS Domain Name
41	NIS Servers	N	NIS Server Addresses
42	NTP Servers	N	NTP Server Addresses
43	Vendor Specific	N	Vendor Specific Information
44	NETBIOS Name Srv	N	NETBIOS Name Servers
45	NETBIOS Dist Srv	N	NETBIOS Datagram Distribution
46	NETBIOS Note Type	1	NETBIOS Note Type
47	NETBIOS Scope	N	NETBIOS Scope
48	X Window Font	N	X Window Font Server
49	X Window Manmager	N	X Window Display Manager
50	Address Request	4	Requested IP Address
51	Address Time	4	IP Address Lease Time
52	Overload	1	Overloaf "sname" or "file"
53	DHCP Msg Type	1	DHCP Message Type
54	DHCP Server Id	4	DHCP Server Identification
55	Parameter List	N	Parameter Request List
56	DHCP Message	N	DHCP Error Message
57	DHCP Max Msg Size	2	DHCP Maximum Message Size
58	Renewal Time	4	DHCP Renewal (T1) Time
59	Rebinding Time	4	DHCP Rebinding (T2) Time
60	Class Id	N	Class Identifier
61	Client Id	N	Client Identifier
62	Netware/IP Domain	N	Netware/IP Domain Name
63	Netware/IP Option	N	Netware/IP sub Options

685

64–127			Unassigned
128–54			Reserved
255	End	0	None

URL = ftp://ftp.isi.edu/in-notes/iana/assignments/bootp-and-dhcp-parameters

Address Family Numbers

Several protocols deal with multiple address families. The 16-bit assignments are listed here.

Number	Description
0	Reserved
1	IP (IP version 4)
2	IP6 (IP version 6)
3	NSAP
4	HDLC (8-bit multidrop)
5	BBN 1822
6	802 (includes all 802 media plus Ethernet "canonical format")
7	E.163
8	E.164 (SMDS, Frame Relay, ATM)
9	F.69 (Telex)
10	X.121 (X.25, Frame Relay)
11	IPX
12	Appletalk
13	Decnet IV
14	Banyan Vines
65535	Reserved

URL = ftp://ftp.isi.edu/in-notes/iana/assignments/address-family-numbers

OSPF Authentication Codes

The Open Shortest Path First (OSPF) protocols have a provision for authentication, and the type of authentication can be indicated by a code number. The following are the registered authentication codes.

Code	Authentication Method
0	No Authentication
1	Simple Password Authentication
2–65535	Reserved

URL = ftp://ftp.isi.edu/in-notes/iana/assignments/ospf-authentication-codes

Network Management Parameters

For the management of hosts and gateways on the Internet a data structure for the information has been defined. This data structure should be used with any of several possible management protocols, such as the "Simple Network Management Protocol"—SNMP (RFC1157), or the "Common Management Information Protocol over TCP"—CMOT (RFC1095).

The data structure is the "Structure and Indentification of Management Information for TCP/IP-based Internets"—SMI (RFC1155), and the "Management Information Base for Network Management of TCP/IP-based Internets"—MIB-II (RFC1213).

The SMI includes the provision for parameters or codes to indicate experimental or private data structures. These parameter assignments are listed here.

The older "Simple Gateway Monitoring Protocol"—SGMP (RFC1028) also defined a data structure. The parameter assignments used with SGMP are included here for historical completeness.

The network management object identifiers are under the iso (1), org (3), dod (6), internet (1), or 1.3.6.1, branch of the name space.

The major branches are:

1	iso
1.3	org
1.3.6	dod
1.3.6.1	internet
1.3.6.1.1	directory
1.3.6.1.2	mgmt
1.3.6.1.2.1	mib-2
1.3.6.1.2.1.2.2.1.3	ifType
1.3.6.1.2.1.10	transmission
1.3.6.1.2.1.10.23	transmission.ppp
1.3.6.1.2.1.27	application
1.3.6.1.2.1.28	mta
1.3.6.1.3	experimental
1.3.6.1.4	private
1.3.6.1.4.1	enterprise
1.3.6.1.5	security
1.3.6.1.6	SNMPv2
1.3.6.1.7	mail

SMI Network Management Directory Codes

Prefix: iso.org.dod.internet.directory {1.3.6.1.1.}

Decimal	Name	Description
all	Reserved	Reserved for future use

SMI Network Management MGMT Codes

Prefix: iso.org.dod.internet.mgmt {1.3.6.1.2.}

Decimal	Name	Description
0	Reserved	
1	MIB	

Table F-11. SMI Network Management MIB-2 Codes

Prefix: `iso.org.dod.internet.mgmt.mib-2 {1.3.6.1.2.1}`

Decimal	Name	Description
0	Reserved	Reserved
1	system	System
2	interfaces	Interfaces
3	at	Address Translation
4	ip	Internet Protocol
5	icmp	Internet Control Message
6	tcp	Transmission Control Protocol
7	udp	User Datagram Protocol
8	egp	Exterior Gateway Protocol
9	cmot	CMIP over TCP
10	transmission	Transmission
11	snmp	Simple Network Management
12	GenericIF	Generic Interface Extensions
13	Appletalk	Appletalk Networking
14	ospf	Open Shortest Path First
15	bgp	Border Gateway Protocol
16	rmon	Remote Network Monitoring
17	bridge	Bridge Objects
18	DecnetP4	Decnet Phase 4
19	Character	Character Streams
20	snmpParties	SNMP Parties
21	snmpSecrets	SNMP Secrets
22	snmpDot3RptrMgt	
23	rip-2	Routing Information Protocol
24	ident	Identification Protocol
25	host	Host Resources
26	snmpDot3MauMgt	802.3 Medium Attachment Units
27	application	Network Services Monitoring
28	mta	Mail Monitoring

29	dsa	X.500 Directory Monitoring
30	IANAifType	Interface Types
31	ifMIB	Interface Types
32	dns	Domain Name System
33	upsMIB	Uninterruptible Power Supplies
34	sannauMIB	SNA NAU MIB
35	etherMIB	Ethernet-like generic objects
36	sipMIB	SMDS inteface objects
37	atmMIB	ATM objects
38	mdmMIB	Dial-up modem objects
39	rdbmsMIB	relational database objects

Table F-12. ifType Definitions

Prefix: iso.org.dod.internet.mgmt.mib-2.interface {1.3.6.1.2.1.2}

ifTable.ifEntry.ifType {1.3.6.1.2.1.2.2.1.3}

Decimal	Name	Description
1	other	none of the following
2	regular1822	BBN Report 1822
3	hdh1822	BBN Report 1822
4	ddn-x25	BBN Report 1822
5	x25	X.25
6	ethernet-csmacd	
7	IEEE802.3	CSMACD-like Objects
8	IEEE802.4	Token Bus-like Objects
9	IEEE802.5	Token Ring-like Objects
10	iso88026-man	
11	starLan	
12	proteon-10Mbit	
13	proteon-80Mbit	
14	hyperchannel	
15	FDDI	FDDI Objects
16	lapb	LAP B

17	sdlc	
18	ds1	T1/E1 Carrier Objects
19	e1	obsolete
20	basicISDN	
21	primaryISDN	
22	propPointToPointSerial	
23	ppp	Point-to-Point Protocol
24	softwareLoopback	
25	eon	
26	ethernet-3Mbit	
27	nsip	
28	slip	
29	ultra	
30	ds3	DS3/E3 Interface Objects
31	sip	SMDS Interface Objects
32	frame-relay	Frame Relay Objects
33	RS-232	RS-232 Objects
34	Parallel	Parallel Printer Objects
35	arcnet	ARC network
36	arcnet-plus	ARC network plus
37	atm	ATM
38	MIOX25	MIOX25
39	SONET	SONET or SDH
40	x25ple	X.25 packet level
41	iso88022llc	802.2 LLC
42	localTalk	
43	smds-dxi	SMDS DXI
44	frameRelayService	Frame Relay DCE
45	v35	V.35
46	hssi	HSSI
47	hippi	HIPPI
48	modem	generic modem
49	aal5	AAL5 over ATM
50	sonetPath	

51	sonetVT	
52	smds-icip	SMDS Inter-Carrier Interface Protocol
53	propVirtual	proprietary vitural/internal interface
54	propMultiLink	proprietary multi-link multiplexing
55	IEEE802.12	100BaseVG
56	fibre-channel	Fibre Channel

Table F-13. Transmission Group Definitions

Prefix: `iso.org.dod.internet.mgmt.mib-2.transmission {1.3.6.1.2.1.10}`

Decimal	Name	Description
5	x25	X.25
7	IEEE802.3	CSMACD-like Objects
8	IEEE802.4	Token Bus-like Objects
9	IEEE802.5	Token Ring-like Objects
15	FDDI	FDDI Objects
16	lapb	LAP B
18	ds1	T1 Carrier Objects
19	e1	E1 Carrier Objects
23	ppp	Point-to-Point Protocol
30	ds3	DS3/E3 Interface Objects
31	sip	SMDS Interface Objects
32	frame-relay	Frame Relay Objects
33	RS-232	RS-232 Objects
34	Parallel	Parallel Printer Objects
35	arcnet	ARC network
36	arcnet-plus	ARC network plus
37	atm	ATM
38	MIOX25	MIOX25
39	sonetMIB	SONET MIB
44	frnetservMIB	Frame Relay Service MIB for DCE

PPP Definitions

Prefix: `iso.org.dod.internet.mgmt.mib-2.transmission {1.3.6.1.2.1.10}`

PPP `{1.3.6.1.2.1.10.23}`

Decimal	Name	Description
1	pppLcp	ppp link control
2	pppSecurity	ppp security
3	ppplp	ppp IP network control
4	pppBridge	ppp bridge network control

Table F-14. SMI Network Management Experimental Codes

Prefix: `iso.org.dod.internet.experimental {1.3.6.1.3.}`

Decimal	Name	Description
0	Reserved	
1	CLNS	ISO CLNS Objects
* 2	T1-Carrier	T1 Carrier Objects
* 3	IEEE802.3	Ethernet-like Objects
* 4	IEEE802.5	Token Ring-like Objects
* 5	DECNet-PHIV	DECNet Phase IV
* 6	Interface	Generic Interface Objects
* 7	IEEE802.4	Token Bus-like Objects
* 8	FDDI	FDDI Objects
9	LANMGR-1	LAN Manager V1 Objects
10	LANMGR-TRAPS	LAN Manager Trap Objects
11	Views	SNMP View Objects
12	SNMP-AUTH	SNMP Authentication Objects
* 13	BGP	Border Gateway Protocol
* 14	Bridge	Bridge MIB
* 15	DS3	DS3 Interface Type
* 16	SIP	SMDS Interface Protocol
* 17	Appletalk	Appletalk Networking

* 18	PPP	PPP Objects
* 19	Character MIB	Character MIB
* 20	RS-232 MIB	RS-232 MIB
* 21	Parallel MIB	Parallel MIB
22	atsign-proxy	Proxy via Community
* 23	OSPF	OSPF MIB
24	Alert-Man	Alert-Man
25	FDDI-Synoptics	FDDI-Synoptics
* 26	Frame Relay	Frame Relay MIB
* 27	rmon	Remote Network Management MIB
28	IDPR	IDPR MIB
29	HUBMIB	IEEE 802.3 Hub MIB
30	IPFWDTBLMIB	IP Forwarding Table MIB
31	LATM MIB	
32	SONET MIB	
33	IDENT	
34	MIME-MHS	
35	MAUMIB	IEEE 802.3 Mau MIB
36	Host Resources	Host Resources MIB
37	ISIS-MIB	Integrated ISIS protocol MIB
38	Chassis	Chassis MIB
39	ups	ups
40	App-Mon	Application Monitoring MIB
41	ATM UNI	ATM
42	FC	Fibre Channel
* 43	DNS	Domain Name Service
44	X.25	X.25 MIB
45	Frame Relay Serv.	Frame Relay Service MIB
46	Madman-Applications	
47	Madman-MTA	
48	Madman-DSA	
49	Modem	
50	SNA NAU	
51	SDLC	SDLC

52	DNS	Domain Name Service
53	network-objects	IP info ix X.500
54	printmib	
55	rdbmsmib	
56	sipMIB	
57	stllmib	ST-II protocol MIB
58	802.5 SSR MIB	802.5 Station Source Routing MIB

* = obsoleted

SMI Private Codes

Prefix: `iso.org.dod.internet.private {1.3.6.1.4}`

Decimal	Name	Description
0	Reserved	
1	enterprise	private enterprises

SMI Private Enterprise Codes

Prefix: `iso.org.dod.internet.private.enterprise {1.3.6.1.4.1}`

See the file "enterprise-numbers".

SMI Security Codes

Prefix: `iso.org.dod.internet.security {1.3.6.1.5}`

Decimal	Name	Description
0	Reserved	
1	kerberosV4	Kerberos version 4 objects
2	kerberosV5	Kerberos version 5 objects

SMI SNMPv2 Codes

Prefix: `iso.org.dod.internet.snmpv2 {1.3.6.1.6}`

SMI Mail Codes

Prefix: iso.org.dod.internet.mail {1.3.6.1.7}

1	mime-mhs

URL = ftp://ftp.isi.edu/in-notes/iana/assignments/smi-numbers

Private Enterprise Numbers

SMI Network Management Private Enterprise Codes

Prefix: iso.org.dod.internet.private.enterprise {1.3.6.1.4.1}

This file is:

ftp://ftp.isi.edu/in-notes/iana/assignments/enterprise-numbers

Address Resolution Protocol Parameters

The Address Resolution Protocol (ARP) specified in RFC826 has several parameters. The assigned values for these parameters are listed here.

Reverse Address Resolution Protocol Operation Codes

The Reverse Address Resolution Protocol (RARP) specified in RFC903 uses the
"Reverse" codes below.

Dynamic Reverse ARP

The Dynamic Reverse Address Resolution Protocol (DRARP) uses the "DRARP"
codes below. For further information, contact: David Brownell
(suneast!helium!db@Sun.COM).

Inverse Address Resolution Protocol

The Inverse Address Resolution Protocol (IARP) specified in RFC1293 uses the "InARP" codes below.

Table F-15. InARP Assignments

Number	Operation Code (op)
1	REQUEST
2	REPLY
3	request Reverse
4	reply Reverse
5	DRARP-Request
6	DRARP-Reply
7	DRARP-Error
8	InARP-Request
9	InARP-Reply
10	ARP-NAK

Number	Hardware Type (hrd)
1	Ethernet (10Mb)
2	Experimental Ethernet (3Mb)
3	Amateur Radio AX.25
4	Proteon ProNET Token Ring
5	Chaos
6	IEEE 802 Networks
7	ARCNET
8	Hyperchannel
9	Lanstar
10	Autonet Short Address
11	LocalTalk
12	LocalNet (IBM PCNet or SYTEK LocalNET)

13	Ultra link
14	SMDS
15	Frame Relay
16	Asynchronous Transmission Mode (ATM)
17	HDLC
18	Fibre Channel
19	Asynchronous Transmission Mode (ATM)
20	Serial Line
21	Asynchronous Transmission Mode (ATM)

Protocol Type (pro)

Use the same codes as listed in the section called "Ethernet Numbers" (all hardware types use this code set for the protocol type).

```
URL = ftp://ftp.isi.edu/in-notes/iana/assignments/arp-parameters
```

IEEE 802 Numbers of Interest

Some of the networks of all classes are IEEE 802 Networks. These systems may use a Link Service Access Point (LSAP) field in much the same way as the MILNET uses the "link" field. Further, there is an extension of the LSAP header called the Sub-Network Access Protocol (SNAP).

The IEEE likes to describe numbers in binary in bit transmission order, which is the opposite of the big-endian order used throughout the Internet protocol documentation.

Table F-16. IEEE LSAP Assignments

Link Service Access Point		Description	
IEEE		Internet	
binary		binary	decimal
00000000 00000000	0	Null LSAP	
01000000 00000010	2	Indiv LLC Sublayer Mgt	
11000000 00000011	3	Group LLC Sublayer Mgt	

00100000 00000100	4	SNA Path Control
01100000 00000110	6	Reserved (DOD IP)
01110000 00001110	14	PROWAY-LAN
01110010 01001110	78	EIA-RS 511
01111010 01011110	94	ISI IP
01110001 10001110	142	PROWAY-LAN
01010101 10101010	170	SNAP
01111111 11111110	254	ISO CLNS IS 8473
11111111 11111111	255	Global DSAP

These numbers (and others) are assigned by the IEEE Standards Office. The address is:

> IEEE Registration Authority
> c/o Iris Ringel
> IEEE Standards Dept
> 445 Hoes Lane, P.O. Box 1331
> Piscataway, NJ 08855-1331
> Phone: +1 908 562 3813
> Fax: +1 908 562 1571

The fee is $1000 and it takes 10 working days after receipt of the request form and fee. They will not do anything via fax or phone.

At an ad hoc special session on "IEEE 802 Networks and ARP," held during the TCP Vendors Workshop (August 1986), an approach to a consistent way to send DoD-IP datagrams and other IP related protocols (such as the Address Resolution Protocol (ARP)) on 802 networks was developed, using the SNAP extension (see RFC1042).

```
URL = ftp://ftp.isi.edu/in-notes/iana/assignments/ieee-802-numbers
```

Ethernet Numbers

EtherTypes

Many of the networks of all classes are Ethernets (10Mb) or Experimental Ethernets (3Mb). These systems use a message "type" field in much the same way the ARPANET uses the "link" field.

If you need an EtherType, contact:

Xerox Systems Institute
3400 Hillview Ave.
PO Box 10034
Palo Alto, CA 94303
Phone: 415-813-7164
Contact: Fonda Lix Pallone

The following list of EtherTypes is contributed unverified information from various sources.

Table F-17. EtherType Assignments

Ethernet		Exp. Ethernet		Description
decimal	Hex	decimal	octal	
000	0000-05DC	-	-	IEEE802.3 Length Field
257	0101-01FF	-	-	Experimental
512	0200	512	1000	XEROX PUP (see 0A00)
513	0201	-	-	PUP Addr Trans (see 0A01)
	0400			Nixdorf
1536	0600	1536	3000	XEROX NS IDP
	0660			DLOG
	0661			DLOG
2048	0800	513	1001	Internet IP (IPv4)
2049	0801	-	-	X.75 Internet
2050	0802	-	-	NBS Internet
2051	0803	-	-	ECMA Internet
2052	0804	-	-	Chaosnet
2053	0805	-	-	X.25 Level 3
2054	0806	-	-	ARP
2055	0807	-	-	XNS Compatability
2076	081C	-	-	Symbolics Private
2184	0888-088A	-	-	Xyplex
2304	0900	-	-	Ungermann-Bass net debugr

2560	0A00	-	-	Xerox IEEE802.3 PUP
2561	0A01	-	-	PUP Addr Trans
2989	0BAD	-	-	Banyan Systems
4096	1000	-	-	Berkeley Trailer nego
4097	1001-100F	-	-	Berkeley Trailer encap/IP
5632	1600	-	-	Valid Systems
16962	4242	-	-	PCS Basic Block Protocol
21000	5208	-	-	BBN Simnet
24576	6000	-	-	DEC Unassigned (Exp.)
24577	6001	-	-	DEC MOP Dump/Load
24578	6002	-	-	DEC MOP Remote Console
24579	6003	-	-	DEC DECNET Phase IV Route
24580	6004	-	-	DEC LAT
24581	6005	-	-	DEC Diagnostic Protocol
24582	6006	-	-	DEC Customer Protocol
24583	6007	-	-	DEC LAVC, SCA
24584	6008-6009	-	-	DEC Unassigned
24586	6010-6014	-	-	3Com Corporation
28672	7000	-	-	Ungermann-Bass download
28674	7002	-	-	Ungermann-Bass dia/loop
28704	7020-7029	-	-	LRT
28720	7030	-	-	Proteon
28724	7034	-	-	Cabletron
32771	8003	-	-	Cronus VLN
32772	8004	-	-	Cronus Direct
32773	8005	-	-	HP Probe
32774	8006	-	-	Nestar
32776	8008	-	-	AT&T
32784	8010	-	-	Excelan
32787	8013	-	-	SGI diagnostics
32788	8014	-	-	SGI network games
32789	8015	-	-	SGI reserved
32790	8016	-	-	SGI bounce server
32793	8019	-	-	Apollo Computers

32815	802E	-	-	Tymshare
32816	802F	-	-	Tigan, Inc.
32821	8035	-	-	Reverse ARP
32822	8036	-	-	Aeonic Systems
32824	8038	-	-	DEC LANBridge
32825	8039-803C	-	-	DEC Unassigned
32829	803D	-	-	DEC Ethernet Encryption
32830	803E	-	-	DEC Unassigned
32831	803F	-	-	DEC LAN Traffic Monitor
32832	8040-8042	-	-	DEC Unassigned
32836	8044	-	-	Planning Research Corp.
32838	8046	-	-	AT&T
32839	8047	-	-	AT&T
32841	8049	-	-	ExperData
32859	805B	-	-	Stanford V Kernel exp.
32860	805C	-	-	Stanford V Kernel prod.
32861	805D	-	-	Evans & Sutherland
32864	8060	-	-	Little Machines
32866	8062	-	-	Counterpoint Computers
32869	8065	-	-	Univ. of Mass. @ Amherst
32870	8066	-	-	Univ. of Mass. @ Amherst
32871	8067	-	-	Veeco Integrated Auto.
32872	8068	-	-	General Dynamics
32873	8069	-	-	AT&T
32874	806A	-	-	Autophon
32876	806C	-	-	ComDesign
32877	806D	-	-	Computgraphic Corp.
32878	806E-8077	-	-	Landmark Graphics Corp.
32890	807A	-	-	Matra
32891	807B	-	-	Dansk Data Elektronik
32892	807C	-	-	Merit Internodal
32893	807D-807F	-	-	Vitalink Communications
32896	8080	-	-	Vitalink TransLAN III
32897	8081-8083	-	-	Counterpoint Computers

32923	809B	-	-	Appletalk
32924	809C-809E	-	-	Datability
32927	809F	-	-	Spider Systems Ltd.
32931	80A3	-	-	Nixdorf Computers
32932	80A4-80B3	-	-	Siemens Gammasonics Inc.
32960	80C0-80C3	-	-	DCA Data Exchange Cluster
	80C4			Banyan Systems
	80C5			Banyan Systems
32966	80C6	-	-	Pacer Software
32967	80C7	-	-	Applitek Corporation
32968	80C8-80CC	-	-	Intergraph Corporation
32973	80CD-80CE	-	-	Harris Corporation
32975	80CF-80D2	-	-	Taylor Instrument
32979	80D3-80D4	-	-	Rosemount Corporation
32981	80D5	-	-	IBM SNA Service on Ether
32989	80DD	-	-	Varian Associates
32990	80DE-80DF	-	-	Integrated Solutions TRFS
32992	80E0-80E3	-	-	Allen-Bradley
32996	80E4-80F0	-	-	Datability
33010	80F2	-	-	Retix
33011	80F3	-	-	AppleTalk AARP (Kinetics)
33012	80F4-80F5	-	-	Kinetics
33015	80F7	-	-	Apollo Computer
33023	80FF-8103	-	-	Wellfleet Communications
33031	8107-8109	-	-	Symbolics Private
33072	8130	-	-	Hayes Microcomputers
33073	8131	-	-	VG Laboratory Systems
	8132-8136			Bridge Communications
33079	8137-8138	-	-	Novell, Inc.
33081	8139-813D	-	-	KTI
	8148			Logicraft
	8149			Network Computing Devices
	814A			Alpha Micro
33100	814C	-	-	SNMP

	814D			BIIN
	814E			BIIN
	814F			Technically Elite Concept
	8150			Rational Corp
	8151-8153			Qualcomm
	815C-815E			Computer Protocol Pty Ltd
	8164-8166			Charles River Data System
	817D-818C			Protocol Engines
	818D			Motorola Computer
	819A-81A3			Qualcomm
	81A4			ARAI Bunkichi
	81A5-81AE			RAD Network Devices
	81B7-81B9			Xyplex
	81CC-81D5			Apricot Computers
	81D6-81DD			Artisoft
	81E6-81EF			Polygon
	81F0-81F2			Comsat Labs
	81F3-81F5			SAIC
	81F6-81F8			VG Analytical
	8203-8205			Quantum Software
	8221-8222			Ascom Banking Systems
	823E-8240			Advanced Encryption Syste
	827F-8282			Athena Programming
	8263-826A			Charles River Data System
	829A-829B			Inst Ind Info Tech
	829C-82AB			Taurus Controls
	82AC-8693			Walker Richer & Quinn
	8694-869D			Idea Courier
	869E-86A1			Computer Network Tech
	86A3-86AC			Gateway Communications
	86DB			SECTRA
	86DE			Delta Controls
34543	86DF	-	-	ATOMIC

	86E0-86EF			Landis & Gyr Powers
	8700-8710			Motorola
	8A96-8A97			Invisible Software
36864	9000	-	-	Loopback
36865	9001	-	-	3Com(Bridge) XNS Sys Mgmt
36866	9002	-	-	3Com(Bridge) TCP-IP Sys
36867	9003	-	-	3Com(Bridge) loop detect
65280	FF00	-	-	BBN VITAL-LanBridge cache
	FF00-FF0F			ISC Bunker Ramo

The standard for transmission of IP datagrams over Ethernets and Experimental Ethernets is specified in RFC894 and RFC895 respectively.

NOTE: Ethernet 48-bit address blocks are assigned by the IEEE.

> IEEE Registration Authority
> c/o Iris Ringel
> IEEE Standards Department
> 445 Hoes Lane, P.O. Box 1331
> Piscataway, NJ 08855-1331
> Phone: +1 908 562 3813
> Fax: +1 908 562 1571

IANA Ethernet Address Block

The IANA owns an Ethernet address block which may be used for multicast address asignments or other special purposes.

The address block in IEEE binary is: 0000 0000 0000 0000 0111 1010

In the normal Internet dotted decimal notation this is 0.0.94 since the bytes are transmitted higher order first and bits within bytes are transmitted lower order first (see "Data Notations" in the Introduction).

IEEE CSMA/CD and Token Bus bit transmission order: 00 00 5E

IEEE Token Ring bit transmission order: 00 00 7A

Appearance on the wire (bits transmitted from left to right):

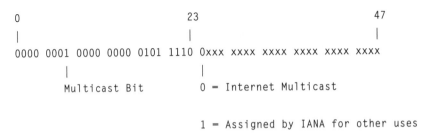

```
0                               23                              47
|                               |                               |
1000 0000 0000 0000 0111 1010 xxxx xxx0 xxxx xxxx xxxx xxxx
|                                        |
Multicast Bit                            0 - Internet Multicast
                                         1 - Assigned by IANA for
                                               other uses
```

Appearance in memory (bits transmitted right-to-left within octets, octets transmitted left-to-right):

```
0                               23                              47
|                               |                               |
0000 0001 0000 0000 0101 1110 0xxx xxxx xxxx xxxx xxxx xxxx
          |                     |
          Multicast Bit         0 - Internet Multicast

                                1 = Assigned by IANA for other uses
```

The latter representation corresponds to the Internet standard bit-order, and is the format that most programmers have to deal with. Using this representation, the range of Internet Multicast addresses is:

```
01-00-5E-00-00-00  to  01-00-5E-7F-FF-FF  in hex, or

1.0.94.0.0.0  to  1.0.94.127.255.255  in dotted decimal
```

Ethernet Vendor Address Components

Ethernet hardware addresses are 48 bits, expressed as 12 hexadecimal digits (0–9, plus A–F, capitalized). These 12 hex digits consist of the first/left 6 digits (which should match the vendor of the Ethernet interface within the station) and the last/right 6 digits which specify the interface serial number for that interface vendor.

Ethernet addresses might be written unhyphenated (e.g., 123456789ABC), or with one hyphen (e.g., 123456-789ABC), but should be written hyphenated by octets (e.g., 12-34-56-78-9A-BC).

These addresses are physical station addresses, not multicast or broadcast, so the second hex digit (reading from the left) will be even, not odd.

At present, it is not clear how the IEEE assigns Ethernet block addresses, whether in blocks of 2**24 or 2**25, and whether multicasts are assigned with that block or separately. A portion of the vendor block address is reportedly assigned serially, with the other portion intentionally assigned randomly. If there is a global algorithm for which addresses are designated to be physical (in a chipset) versus logical (assigned in software), or globally assigned versus locally assigned addresses, some of the known addresses do not follow the scheme (e.g., AA0003; 02xxxx).

Table F-18. Ethernet Vendor Addresses

Address	Vendor
00000C	Cisco
00000E	Fujitsu
00000F	NeXT
000010	Sytek
00001D	Cabletron
000020	DIAB (Data Intdustrier AB)
000022	Visual Technology
00002A	TRW
000032	GPT Limited (reassigned from GEC Computers Ltd)
00005A	S & Koch
00005E	IANA
000065	Network General
00006B	MIPS
000077	MIPS
00007A	Ardent
000089	Cayman Systems Gatorbox
000093	Proteon
00009F	Ameristar Technology
0000A2	Wellfleet
0000A3	Network Application Technology
0000A6	Network General (internal assignment, not for products)

0000A7	NCD	X-terminals
0000A9	Network Systems	
0000AA	Xerox	Xerox machines
0000B3	CIMLinc	
0000B7	Dove	Fastnet
0000BC	Allen-Bradley	
0000C0	Western Digital	
0000C5	Farallon phone net card	
0000C6	HP Intelligent Networks Operation (formerly Eon Systems)	
0000C8	Altos	
0000C9	Emulex	Terminal Servers
0000D7	Dartmouth College (NED Router)	
0000D8	3Com? Novell?	PS/2
0000DD	Gould	
0000DE	Unigraph	
0000E2	Acer Counterpoint	
0000EF	Alantec	
0000FD	High Level Hardvare (Orion, UK)	
000102	BBN	BBN internal usage (not registered)
0020AF	3COM ???	
001700	Kabel	
008064	Wyse Technology / Link Technologies	
00802B	IMAC ???	
00802D	Xylogics, Inc.	Annex terminal servers
00808C	Frontier Software Development	
0080C2	IEEE 802.1 Committee	
0080D3	Shiva	
00AA00	Intel	
00DD00	Ungermann-Bass	
00DD01	Ungermann-Bass	
020701	Racal InterLan	
020406	BBN	BBN internal usage (not registered)
026086	Satelcom MegaPac (UK)	
02608C	3Com	IBM PC; Imagen; Valid; Cisco

02CF1F	CMC	Masscomp; Silicon Graphics; Prime EXL
080002	3Com (Formerly Bridge)	
080003	ACC (Advanced Computer Communications)	
080005	Symbolics	Symbolics LISP machines
080008	BBN	
080009	Hewlett-Packard	
08000A	Nestar Systems	
08000B	Unisys	
080011	Tektronix, Inc.	
080014	Excelan	BBN Butterfly, Masscomp, Silicon Graphics
080017	NSC	
08001A	Data General	
08001B	Data General	
08001E	Apollo	
080020	Sun	Sun machines
080022	NBI	
080025	CDC	
080026	Norsk Data (Nord)	
080027	PCS Computer Systems GmbH	
080028	TI	Explorer
08002B	DEC	
08002E	Metaphor	
08002F	Prime Computer Prime 50-Series LHC300	
080036	Intergraph CAE stations	
080037	Fujitsu-Xerox	
080038	Bull	
080039	Spider Systems	
080041	DCA Digital Comm. Assoc.	
080045	???? (maybe Xylogics, but they claim not to know this number)	
080046	Sony	
080047	Sequent	
080049	Univation	
08004C	Encore	
08004E	BICC	

080056	Stanford University	
080058	???	DECsystem-20
08005A	IBM	
080067	Comdesign	
080068	Ridge	
080069	Silicon Graphics	
08006E	Concurrent	Masscomp
080075	DDE (Danish Data Elektronik A/S)	
08007C	Vitalink	TransLAN III
080080	XIOS	
080086	Imagen/QMS	
080087	Xyplex	terminal servers
080089	Kinetics	AppleTalk-Ethernet interface
08008B	Pyramid	
08008D	XyVision	XyVision machines
080090	Retix Inc	Bridges
484453	HDS ???	
800010	AT&T	
AA0000	DEC	obsolete
AA0001	DEC	obsolete
AA0002	DEC	obsolete
AA0003 machines	DEC	Global physical address for some DEC
AA0004	DEC	Local logical address for systems running
		DECNET

Ethernet Multicast Addresses

An Ethernet multicast address consists of the multicast bit, the 23-bit vendor component, and the 24-bit group identifier assigned by the vendor. For example, DEC is assigned the vendor component 08-00-2B, so multicast addresses assigned by DEC have the first 24-bits 09-00-2B (since the multicast bit is the low-order bit of the first byte, which is "the first bit on the wire").

Table F-19. Ethernet Multicast Addresses

Ethernet Address	Type Field	Usage
Multicast Addresses:		
01-00-5E-00-00-00-	0800	Internet Multicast
01-00-5E-7F-FF-FF		
01-00-5E-80-00-00-	????	Internet reserved by IANA
01-00-5E-FF-FF-FF		
01-80-C2-00-00-00	-802-	Spanning tree (for bridges)
09-00-02-04-00-01?	8080?	Vitalink printer
09-00-02-04-00-02?	8080?	Vitalink management
09-00-09-00-00-01	8005	HP Probe
09-00-09-00-00-01	-802-	HP Probe
09-00-09-00-00-04	8005?	HP DTC
09-00-1E-00-00-00	8019?	Apollo DOMAIN
09-00-2B-00-00-00	6009?	DEC MUMPS?
09-00-2B-00-00-01	8039?	DEC DSM/DTP?
09-00-2B-00-00-02	803B?	DEC VAXELN?
09-00-2B-00-00-03	8038	DEC Lanbridge Traffic Monitor (LTM)
09-00-2B-00-00-04	????	DEC MAP End System Hello
09-00-2B-00-00-05	????	DEC MAP Intermediate System Hello
09-00-2B-00-00-06	803D?	DEC CSMA/CD Encryption?
09-00-2B-00-00-07	8040?	DEC NetBios Emulator?
09-00-2B-00-00-0F	6004	DEC Local Area Transport (LAT)
09-00-2B-00-00-1x	????	DEC Experimental
09-00-2B-01-00-00	8038	DEC LanBridge Copy packets
		(All bridges)
09-00-2B-01-00-01	8038	DEC LanBridge Hello packets
		(All local bridges)
		1 packet per second, sent by the
		designated LanBridge
09-00-2B-02-00-00	????	DEC DNA Lev. 2 Routing Layer routers?

09-00-2B-02-01-00	803C?	DEC DNA Naming Service Advertisement?
09-00-2B-02-01-01	803C?	DEC DNA Naming Service Solicitation?
09-00-2B-02-01-02	803E?	DEC DNA Time Service?
09-00-2B-03-xx-xx	????	DEC default filtering by bridges?
09-00-2B-04-00-00	8041?	DEC Local Area Sys. Transport (LAST)?
09-00-2B-23-00-00	803A?	DEC Argonaut Console?
09-00-4E-00-00-02?	8137?	Novell IPX
09-00-56-00-00-00-	????	Stanford reserved
09-00-56-FE-FF-FF		
09-00-56-FF-00-00-	805C	Stanford V Kernel, version 6.0
09-00-56-FF-FF-FF		
09-00-77-00-00-01	????	Retix spanning tree bridges
09-00-7C-02-00-05	8080?	Vitalink diagnostics
09-00-7C-05-00-01	8080?	Vitalink gateway?
0D-1E-15-BA-DD-06	????	HP
AB-00-00-01-00-00	6001	DEC Maintenance Operation Protocol
		(MOP) Dump/Load Assistance
AB-00-00-02-00-00	6002	DEC Maintenance Operation Protocol
		(MOP) Remote Console
		1 System ID packet every 8-10 minutes,
		by every:
		DEC LanBridge
		DEC DEUNA interface
		DEC DELUA interface
		DEC DEQNA interface
		(in a certain mode)
AB-00-00-03-00-00	6003	DECNET Phase IV end node Hello
		packets 1 packet every 15 seconds, sent by
		each DECNET host
AB-00-00-04-00-00	6003	DECNET Phase IV Router Hello packets
		1 packet every 15 seconds, sent by the
		DECNET router
AB-00-00-05-00-00	????	Reserved DEC through AB-00-03-FF-FF-FF
AB-00-03-00-00-00	6004	DEC Local Area Transport (LAT) - old

AB-00-04-00-xx-xx	????	Reserved DEC customer private use
AB-00-04-01-xx-yy	6007	DEC Local Area VAX Cluster groups
		Sys. Communication Architecture (SCA)
CF-00-00-00-00-00	9000	Ethernet Configuration Test protocol
		(Loopback)

Broadcast Address:

FF-FF-FF-FF-FF-FF	0600	XNS packets, Hello or gateway search?
		6 packets every 15 seconds, per XNS station
FF-FF-FF-FF-FF-FF	0800	IP (e.g. RWHOD via UDP) as needed
FF-FF-FF-FF-FF-FF	0804	CHAOS
FF-FF-FF-FF-FF-FF	0806	ARP (for IP and CHAOS) as needed
FF-FF-FF-FF-FF-FF	0BAD	Banyan
FF-FF-FF-FF-FF-FF	1600	VALID packets, Hello or gateway search?
		1 packet every 30 seconds, per VALID station
FF-FF-FF-FF-FF-FF	8035	Reverse ARP
FF-FF-FF-FF-FF-FF	807C	Merit Internodal (INP)
FF-FF-FF-FF-FF-FF	809B	EtherTalk

```
URL = ftp://ftp.isi.edu/in-notes/iana/assignments/ethernet-numbers
```

X.25 Type Numbers

ITU-T defines the high order two bits of the first octet of call user data as follows:

00-	Used for other CCITT recomendations (such as X.29)
01-	Reserved for use by "national" administrative authorities
10-	Reserved for use by international administrative authorities
11-	Reserved for arbitrary use between consenting DTEs

Call User Data (hex)	Protocol
01	PAD
C5	Blacker front-end descr dev

CC	IP
CD	ISO-IP
CF	PPP
DD	Network Monitoring

*NOTE: ISO SC6/WG2 approved assignment net in ISO 9577 (January 1990).

```
URL = ftp://ftp.isi.edu/in-notes/iana/assignments/x25-type-numbers
```

Public Data Network Numbers

One of the Internet Class A Networks is the international system of Public Data Networks. This section lists the mapping between the Internet Addresses and the Public Data Network Addresses (X.121).

Table F-20. Public Data Network Assignments

Internet	Public Data Net	Description
014.000.000.000		Reserved
014.000.000.001	3110-317-00035 00	PURDUE-TN
014.000.000.002	3110-608-00027 00	UWISC-TN
014.000.000.003	3110-302-00024 00	UDEL-TN
014.000.000.004	2342-192-00149 23	UCL-VTEST
014.000.000.005	2342-192-00300 23	UCL-TG
014.000.000.006	2342-192-00300 25	UK-SATNET
014.000.000.007	3110-608-00024 00	UWISC-IBM
014.000.000.008	3110-213-00045 00	RAND-TN
014.000.000.009	2342-192-00300 23	UCL-CS
014.000.000.010	3110-617-00025 00	BBN-VAN-GW
014.000.000.011	2405-015-50300 00	CHALMERS
014.000.000.012	3110-713-00165 00	RICE
014.000.000.013	3110-415-00261 00	DECWRL
014.000.000.014	3110-408-00051 00	IBM-SJ
014.000.000.015	2041-117-01000 00	SHAPE
014.000.000.016	2628-153-90075 00	DFVLR4-X25

014.000.000.017	3110-213-00032 00	ISI-VAN-GW
014.000.000.018	2624-522-80900 52	FGAN-SIEMENS-X25
014.000.000.019	2041-170-10000 00	SHAPE-X25
014.000.000.020	5052-737-20000 50	UQNET
014.000.000.021	3020-801-00057 50	DMC-CRC1
014.000.000.022	2624-522-80329 02	FGAN-FGANFFMVAX-X25
014.000.000.023	2624-589-00908 01	ECRC-X25
014.000.000.024	2342-905-24242 83	UK-MOD-RSRE
014.000.000.025	2342-905-24242 82	UK-VAN-RSRE
014.000.000.026	2624-522-80329 05	DFVLRSUN-X25
014.000.000.027	2624-457-11015 90	SELETFMSUN-X25
014.000.000.028	3110-408-00146 00	CDC-SVL
014.000.000.029	2222-551-04400 00	SUN-CNUCE
014.000.000.030	2222-551-04500 00	ICNUCEVM-CNUCE
014.000.000.031	2222-551-04600 00	SPARE-CNUCE
014.000.000.032	2222-551-04700 00	ICNUCEVX-CNUCE
014.000.000.033	2222-551-04524 00	CISCO-CNUCE
014.000.000.034	2342-313-00260 90	SPIDER-GW
014.000.000.035	2342-313-00260 91	SPIDER-EXP
014.000.000.036	2342-225-00101 22	PRAXIS-X25A
014.000.000.037	2342-225-00101 23	PRAXIS-X25B
014.000.000.038	2403-712-30250 00	DIAB-TABY-GW
014.000.000.039	2403-715-30100 00	DIAB-LKP-GW
014.000.000.040	2401-881-24038 00	DIAB-TABY1-GW
014.000.000.041	2041-170-10060 00	STC
014.000.000.042	2222-551-00652 60	CNUCE
014.000.000.043	2422-510-05900 00	Tollpost-Globe AS
014.000.000.044	2422-670-08900 00	Tollpost-Globe AS
014.000.000.045	2422-516-01000 00	Tollpost-Globe AS
014.000.000.046	2422-450-00800 00	Tollpost-Globe AS
014.000.000.047	2422-610-00200 00	Tollpost-Globe AS
014.000.000.048	2422-310-00300 00	Tollpost-Globe AS
014.000.000.049	2422-470-08800 00	Tollpost-Globe AS
014.000.000.050	2422-210-04600 00	Tollpost-Globe AS

014.000.000.051	2422-130-28900 00	Tollpost-Globe AS
014.000.000.052	2422-310-27200 00	Tollpost-Globe AS
014.000.000.053	2422-250-05800 00	Tollpost-Globe AS
014.000.000.054	2422-634-05900 00	Tollpost-Globe AS
014.000.000.055	2422-670-08800 00	Tollpost-Globe AS
014.000.000.056	2422-430-07400 00	Tollpost-Globe AS
014.000.000.057	2422-674-07800 00	Tollpost-Globe AS
014.000.000.058	2422-230-16900 00	Tollpost-Globe AS
014.000.000.059	2422-518-02900 00	Tollpost-Globe AS
014.000.000.060	2422-370-03100 00	Tollpost-Globe AS
014.000.000.061	2422-516-03400 00	Tollpost-Globe AS
014.000.000.062	2422-616-04400 00	Tollpost-Globe AS
014.000.000.063	2422-650-23500 00	Tollpost-Globe AS
014.000.000.064	2422-330-02500 00	Tollpost-Globe AS
014.000.000.065	2422-350-01900 00	Tollpost-Globe AS
014.000.000.066	2422-410-00700 00	Tollpost-Globe AS
014.000.000.067	2422-539-06200 00	Tollpost-Globe AS
014.000.000.068	2422-630-07200 00	Tollpost-Globe AS
014.000.000.069	2422-470-12300 00	Tollpost-Globe AS
014.000.000.070	2422-470-13000 00	Tollpost-Globe AS
014.000.000.071	2422-170-04600 00	Tollpost-Globe AS
014.000.000.072	2422-516-04300 00	Tollpost-Globe AS
014.000.000.073	2422-530-00700 00	Tollpost-Globe AS
014.000.000.074	2422-650-18800 00	Tollpost-Globe AS
014.000.000.075	2422-450-24500 00	Tollpost-Globe AS
014.000.000.076	2062-243-15631 00	DPT-BXL-DDC
014.000.000.077	2062-243-15651 00	DPT-BXL-DDC2
014.000.000.078	3110-312-00431 00	DPT-CHI
014.000.000.079	3110-512-00135 00	DPT-SAT-ENG
014.000.000.080	2080-941-90550 00	DPT-PAR
014.000.000.081	4545-511-30600 00	DPT-PBSC
014.000.000.082	4545-513-30900 00	DPT-HONGKONG
014.000.000.083	4872-203-55000 00	UECI-TAIPEI
014.000.000.084	2624-551-10400 20	DPT-HANOVR

014.000.000.085	2624-569-00401 99	DPT-FNKFRT
014.000.000.086	3110-512-00134 00	DPT-SAT-SUPT
014.000.000.087	4602-3010-0103 20	DU-X25A
014.000.000.088	4602-3010-0103 21	FDU-X25B
014.000.000.089	2422-150-33700 00	Tollpost-Globe AS
014.000.000.090	2422-271-07100 00	Tollpost-Globe AS
014.000.000.091	2422-516-00100 00	Tollpost-Globe AS
014.000.000.092	2422-650-18800 00	Norsk Informas.
014.000.000.093	2422-250-30400 00	Tollpost-Globe AS
014.000.000.094		Leissner Data AB
014.000.000.095		Leissner Data AB
014.000.000.096		Leissner Data AB
014.000.000.097		Leissner Data AB
014.000.000.098		Leissner Data AB
014.000.000.099		Leissner Data AB
014.000.000.100		Leissner Data AB
014.000.000.101		Leissner Data AB
014.000.000.102		Leissner Data AB
014.000.000.103		Leissner Data AB
014.000.000.104		Leissner Data AB
014.000.000.105		Leissner Data AB
014.000.000.106		Leissner Data AB
014.000.000.107		Leissner Data AB
014.000.000.108		Leissner Data AB
014.000.000.109		Leissner Data AB
014.000.000.110		Leissner Data AB
014.000.000.111		Leissner Data AB
014.000.000.112		Leissner Data AB
014.000.000.113		Leissner Data AB
014.000.000.114		Leissner Data AB
014.000.000.115		Leissner Data AB
014.000.000.116		Leissner Data AB
014.000.000.117		Leissner Data AB
014.000.000.118		Leissner Data AB

014.000.000.119		Leissner Data AB
014.000.000.120		Leissner Data AB
014.000.000.121		Leissner Data AB
014.000.000.122		Leissner Data AB
014.000.000.123		Leissner Data AB
014.000.000.124		Leissner Data AB
014.000.000.125		Leissner Data AB
014.000.000.126		Leissner Data AB
014.000.000.127		Leissner Data AB
014.000.000.128		Leissner Data AB
014.000.000.129	2422-150-17900 00	Tollpost-Globe A
014.000.000.130	2422-150-42700 00	Tollpost-Globe AS
014.000.000.131	2422-190-41900 00	T-G Airfreight AS
014.000.000.132	2422-616-16100 00	Tollpost-Globe AS
014.000.000.133	2422-150-50700-00	Tollpost-Globe Int.
014.000.000.134	2422-190-28100-00	Intersped AS
014.000.000.135- 014.255.255.254		Unassigned
014.255.255.255		Reserved

The standard for transmission of IP datagrams over the Public Data Network is specified in RFC1356.

```
URL = ftp://ftp.isi.edu/in-notes/iana/assignments/public-data-network- numbers
```

XNS Protocol Types

Assigned well-known socket numbers	
Routing Information	1
Echo	2
Router Error	3
Experimental	40–77

Assigned internet packet types

Routing Information	1
Echo	2
Error	3
Packet Exchange	4
Sequenced Packet	5
PUP	12
DoD IP	13
Experimental	20–37

```
URL = ftp://ftp.isi.edu/in-notes/iana/assignments/xns-protocol-types
```

Point to Point Protocol Parameters

PPP DLL Protocol Numbers

The Point-to-Point Protocol (PPP) Data Link Layer contains a 16-bit Protocol field to identify the encapsulated protocol. The Protocol field is consistent with the ISO 3309 (HDLC) extension mechanism for Address fields. All Protocols MUST be assigned such that the least significant bit of the most significant octet equals "0", and the least significant bit of the least significant octet equals "1".

Table F-21. Assigned PPP DLL Protocol Numbers

Value (in hex)	Protocol Name
0001	Padding Protocol
0003 to 001f	reserved (transparency inefficient)
0021	Internet Protocol
0023	OSI Network Layer
0025	Xerox NS IDP
0027	DECnet Phase IV
0029	Appletalk
002b	Novell IPX

002d	Van Jacobson Compressed TCP/IP
002f	Van Jacobson Uncompressed TCP/IP
0031	Bridging PDU
0033	Stream Protocol (ST-II)
0035	Banyan Vines
0037	reserved (until 1993)
0039	AppleTalk EDDP
003b	AppleTalk SmartBuffered
003d	Multi-Link
003f	NETBIOS Framing
0041	Cisco Systems
0043	Ascom Timeplex
0045	Fujitsu Link Backup and Load Balancing (LBLB)
0047	DCA Remote Lan
0049	Serial Data Transport Protocol (PPP-SDTP)
004b	SNA over 802.2
004d	SNA
004f	IP6 Header Compression
006f	Stampede Bridging
007d	reserved (Control Escape)
007f	reserved (compression inefficient)
00cf	reserved (PPP NLPID)
00fb	compression on single link in multilink group
00fd	1st choice compression
00ff	reserved (compression inefficient)
0201	802.1d Hello Packets
0203	IBM Source Routing BPDU
0205	DEC LANBridge100 Spanning Tree
0231	Luxcom
0233	Sigma Network Systems
8001–801f	Not Used —reserved
8021	Internet Protocol Control Protocol
8023	OSI Network Layer Control Protocol
8025	Xerox NS IDP Control Protocol

8027	DECnet Phase IV Control Protocol
8029	Appletalk Control Protocol
802b	Novell IPX Control Protocol
802d	reserved
802f	reserved
8031	Bridging NCP
8033	Stream Protocol Control Protocol
8035	Banyan Vines Control Protocol
8037	reserved till 1993
8039	reserved
803b	reserved
803d	Multi-Link Control Protocol
803f	NETBIOS Framing Control Protocol
807d	Not Used —reserved
8041	Cisco Systems Control Protocol
8043	Ascom Timeplex
8045	Fujitsu LBLB Control Protocol
8047	DCA Remote Lan Network Control Protocol (RLNCP)
8049	Serial Data Control Protocol (PPP-SDCP)
804b	SNA over 802.2 Control Protocol
804d	SNA Control Protocol
804f	IP6 Header Compression Control Protocol
006f	Stampede Bridging Control Protocol
80cf	Not Used — reserved
80fb	compression on single link in multilink group control
80fd	Compression Control Protocol
80ff	Not Used —reserved
c021	Link Control Protocol
c023	Password Authentication Protocol
c025	Link Quality Report
c027	Shiva Password Authentication Protocol
c029	CallBack Control Protocol (CBCP)
c081	Container Control Protocol
c223	Challenge Handshake Authentication Protocol

c281	Proprietary Authentication Protocol
c26f	Stampede Bridging Authorization Protocol
c481	Proprietary Node ID Authentication Protocol

Protocol field values in the "0xxx" to "3xxx" range identify the network-layer protocol of specific datagrams, and values in the "8xxx" to "Bxxx" range identify datagrams belonging to the associated Network Control Protocol (NCP), if any.

It is recommended that values in the "02xx" to "1Exx" and "xx01" to "xx1F" ranges not be assigned, as they are compression inefficient.

Protocol field values in the "4xxx" to "7xxx" range are used for protocols with low volume traffic which have no associated NCP.

Protocol field values in the "Cxxx" to "Exxx" range identify datagrams as Control Protocols (such as LCP).

PPP LCP and IPCP Codes

The Point-to-Point Protocol (PPP) Link Control Protocol (LCP), the Compression Control Protocol (CCP), Internet Protocol Control Protocol (IPCP), and other control protocols, contain an 8 bit Code field which identifies the type of packet. These Codes are assigned as follows:

Table F-22. PPP LCP and IPCP Codes

Code	Packet Type
1	Configure-Request
2	Configure-Ack
3	Configure-Nak
4	Configure-Reject
5	Terminate-Request
6	Terminate-Ack
7	Code-Reject
8	* Protocol-Reject
9	* Echo-Request
10	* Echo-Reply
11	* Discard-Request

12	* Identification
13	* Time-Remaining
14	+ Reset-Request
15	+ Reset-Reply

* LCP Only

+ CCP Only

PPP LCP Configuration Option Types

The Point-to-Point Protocol (PPP) Link Control Protocol (LCP) specifies a number of Configuration Options which are distinguished by an 8-bit Type field. These Types are assigned as follows:

Table F-23. PPP LCP and IPCP Configuration Option Types

Type	Configuration Option
1	Maximum-Receive-Unit
2	Async-Control-Character-Map
3	Authentication-Protocol
4	Quality-Protocol
5	Magic-Number
6	RESERVED
7	Protocol-Field-Compression
8	Address-and-Control-Field-Compression
9	FCS-Alternatives
10	Self-Describing-Pad
11	Numbered-Mode
12	Multi-Link-Procedure
13	Callback
14	Connect-Time
15	Compound-Frames
16	Nominal-Data-Encapsulation
17	Multilink-MRRU
18	Multilink-Short-Sequence-Number-Header-Format

19	Multilink-Endpoint-Discriminator
20	Proprietary
21	DCE-Identifier

The Point-to-Point Protocol (PPP) Link Control Protocol (LCP) FCS-Alternatives Configuration Option contains an 8-bit Options field which identifies the FCS used. These are assigned as follows:

Bit	FCS
1	Null FCS
2	CCITT 16-Bit FCS
4	CCITT 32-bit FCS

PPP LCP Callback Operation Fields

The Point-to-Point Protocol (PPP) Link Control Protocol (LCP) Callback Configuration Option contains an 8-bit Operations field which identifies the format of the Message. These are assigned as follows:

Operation	Description
0	Location determined by user authentication
1	Dialing string
2	Location identifier
3	E.164 number
4	X.500 distinguished name
5	unassigned
6	Location is determined during CBCP negotiation

PPP IPCP Configuration Option Types

The Point-to-Point Protocol (PPP) Internet Protocol Control Protocol (IPCP) specifies a number of Configuration Options which are distinguished by an 8-bit Type field. These Types are assigned as follows:

Type	Configuration Option
1	IP-Addresses (deprecated)
2	IP-Compression-Protocol
3	IP-Address

PPP ATCP Configuration Option Types

The Point-to-Point Protocol (PPP) Apple Talk Control Protocol (ATCP) specifies a number of Configuration Options (RFC1378) which are distinguished by an 8-bit Type field. These Types are assigned as follows:

Type	Configuration Option
1	AppleTalk-Address
2	Routing-Protocol
3	Suppress-Broadcasts
4	AT-Compression-Protocol
5	Reserved
6	Server-information
7	Zone-information
8	Default-Router-Address

PPP OSINLCP Configuration Option Types

The Point-to-Point Protocol (PPP) OSI Network Layer Control Protocol (OSINLCP) specifies a number of Configuration Options (RFC1377) which are distinguished by an 8-bit Type field. These Types are assigned as follows:

Type	Configuration Option
1	Align-NPDU

PPP Bridging Configuration Option Types

The Point-to-Point Protocol (PPP) Bridging Control Protocol (BCP) specifies a number of Configuration Options which are distinguished by an 8 bit Type field. These Types are assigned as follows:

Type	Configuration Option
1	Bridge-Identification
2	Line-Identification
3	MAC-Support
4	Tinygram-Compression
5	LAN-Identification
6	MAC-Address
7	Spanning-Tree-Protocol

PPP Bridging MAC Types

The Point-to-Point Protocol (PPP) Bridging Control Protocol (BCP) contains an 8-bit MAC Type field which identifies the MAC encapsulated. These Types are assigned as follows:

Type	MAC	
0	Reserved	
1	IEEE 802.3/Ethernet	with canonical addresses
2	IEEE 802.4	with canonical addresses
3	IEEE 802.5	with non-canonical addresses
4	FDDI	with non-canonical addresses
5–10	reserved	
11	IEEE 802.5	with canonical addresses
12	FDDI	with canonical addresses

PPP Bridging Spanning Tree

The Point-to-Point Protocol (PPP) Bridging Control Protocol (BCP) Spanning Tree Configuration Option contains an 8-bit Protocol field which identifies the spanning tree used. These are assigned as follows:

Protocol	Spanning Tree
0	Null —no spanning tree protocol supported
1	IEEE 802.1D spanning tree protocol
2	IEEE 802.1G extended spanning tree protocol
3	IBM source route spanning tree protocol
4	DEC LANbridge 100 spanning tree protocol

URL = ftp://ftp.isi.edu/in-notes/iana/assignments/ppp-numbers

Protocol and Service Names

These are the Official Protocol Names as they appear in the Domain Name System WKS records and the NIC Host Table. Their use is described in RFC952.

A protocol or service may be up to 40 characters taken from the set of uppercase letters, digits, and the punctuation character hyphen. It must start with a letter, and end with a letter or digit.

Table F-24. Official Protocol Names

Acronym	Stands for
ARGUS	ARGUS Protocol
ARP	Address Resolution Protocol
AUTH	Authentication Service
BBN-RCC-MON	BBN RCC Monitoring
BL-IDM	Britton Lee Intelligent Database Machine
BOOTP	Bootstrap Protocol
BOOTPC	Bootstrap Protocol Client
BOOTPS	Bootstrap Protocol Server
BR-SAT-MON	Backroom SATNET Monitoring
CFTP	CFTP
CHAOS	CHAOS Protocol
CHARGEN	Character Generator Protocol
CISCO-FNA	CISCO FNATIVE

CISCO-TNA	CISCO TNATIVE
CISCO-SYS	CISCO SYSMAINT
CLOCK	DCNET Time Server Protocol
CMOT	Common Mgmnt Info Ser and Prot over TCP/IP
COOKIE-JAR	Authentication Scheme
CSNET-NS	CSNET Mailbox Nameserver Protocol
DAYTIME	Daytime Protocol
DCN-MEAS	DCN Measurement Subsystems Protocol
DCP	Device Control Protocol
DGP	Dissimilar Gateway Protocol
DISCARD	Discard Protocol
DMF-MAIL	Digest Message Format for Mail
DOMAIN	Domain Name System
ECHO	Echo Protocol
EGP	Exterior Gateway Protocol
EHF-MAIL	Encoding Header Field for Mail
EMCON	Emission Control Protocol
EMFIS-CNTL	EMFIS Control Service
EMFIS-DATA	EMFIS Data Service
FCONFIG	Fujitsu Config Protocol
FINGER	Finger Protocol
FTP	File Transfer Protocol
FTP-DATA	File Transfer Protocol Data
GGP	Gateway Gateway Protocol
GRAPHICS	Graphics Protocol
HMP	Host Monitoring Protocol
HOST2-NS	Host2 Name Server
HOSTNAME	Hostname Protocol
ICMP	Internet Control Message Protocol
IGMP	Internet Group Management Protocol
IGP	Interior Gateway Protocol
IMAP2	Interim Mail Access Protocol version 2
INGRES-NET	INGRES-NET Service
IP	Internet Protocol

IPCU	Internet Packet Core Utility
IPPC	Internet Pluribus Packet Core
IP-ARC	Internet Protocol on ARCNET
IP-ARPA	Internet Protocol on ARPANET
IP-CMPRS	Compressing TCP/IP Headers
IP-DC	Internet Protocol on DC Networks
IP-DVMRP	Distance Vector Multicast Routing Protocol
IP-E	Internet Protocol on Ethernet Networks
IP-EE	Internet Protocol on Exp. Ethernet Nets
IP-FDDI	Transmission of IP over FDDI
IP-HC	Internet Protocol on Hyperchannnel
IP-IEEE	Internet Protocol on IEEE 802
IP-IPX	Transmission of 802.2 over IPX Networks
IP-MTU	IP MTU Discovery Options
IP-NETBIOS	Internet Protocol over NetBIOS Networks
IP-SLIP	Transmission of IP over Serial Lines
IP-WB	Internet Protocol on Wideband Network
IP-X25	Internet Protocol on X.25 Networks
IRTP	Internet Reliable Transaction Protocol
ISI-GL	ISI Graphics Language Protocol
ISO-TP4	ISO Transport Protocol Class 4
ISO-TSAP	ISO TSAP
LA-MAINT	IMP Logical Address Maintenance
LARP	Locus Address Resolution Protocol
LDP	Loader Debugger Protocol
LEAF-1	Leaf-1 Protocol
LEAF-2	Leaf-2 Protocol
LINK	Link Protocol
LOC-SRV	Location Service
LOGIN	Login Host Protocol
MAIL	Format of Electronic Mail Messages
MERIT-INP	MERIT Internodal Protocol
METAGRAM	Metagram Relay
MIB	Management Information Base

MIT-ML-DEV	MIT ML Device
MFE-NSP	MFE Network Services Protocol
MIT-SUBNET	MIT Subnet Support
MIT-DOV	MIT Dover Spooler
MPM	Internet Message Protocol (Multimedia Mail)
MPM-FLAGS	MPM Flags Protocol
MPM-SND	MPM Send Protocol
MSG-AUTH	MSG Authentication Protocol
MSG-ICP	MSG ICP Protocol
MUX	Multiplexing Protocol
NAMESERVER	Host Name Server
NETBIOS-DGM	NETBIOS Datagram Service
NETBIOS-NS	NETBIOS Name Service
NETBIOS-SSN	NETBIOS Session Service
NETBLT	Bulk Data Transfer Protocol
NETED	Network Standard Text Editor
NETRJS	Remote Job Service
NI-FTP	NI File Transfer Protocol
NI-MAIL	NI Mail Protocol
NICNAME	Who Is Protocol
NFILE	A File Access Protocol
NNTP	Network News Transfer Protocol
NSW-FE	NSW User System Front End
NTP	Network Time Protocol
NVP-II	Network Voice Protocol
OSPF	Open Shortest Path First Interior GW Protocol
PCMAIL	Pcmail Transport Protocol
POP2	Post Office Protocol—Version 2
POP3	Post Office Protocol—Version 3
PPP	Point-to-Point Protocol
PRM	Packet Radio Measurement
PUP	PUP Protocol
PWDGEN	Password Generator Protocol
QUOTE	Quote of the Day Protocol

RARP	A Reverse Address Resolution Protocol
RATP	Reliable Asynchronous Transfer Protocol
RE-MAIL-CK	Remote Mail Checking Protocol
RDP	Reliable Data Protocol
RIP	Routing Information Protocol
RJE	Remote Job Entry
RLP	Resource Location Protocol
RTELNET	Remote Telnet Service
RVD	Remote Virtual Disk Protocol
SAT-EXPAK	Satnet and Backroom EXPAK
SAT-MON	SATNET Monitoring
SEP	Sequential Exchange Protocol
SFTP	Simple File Transfer Protocol
SGMP	Simple Gateway Monitoring Protocol
SNMP	Simple Network Management Protocol
SMI	Structure of Management Information
SMTP	Simple Mail Transfer Protocol
SQLSRV	SQL Service
ST	Stream Protocol
STATSRV	Statistics Service
SU-MIT-TG	SU/MIT Telnet Gateway Protocol
SUN-RPC	SUN Remote Procedure Call
SUPDUP	SUPDUP Protocol
SUR-MEAS	Survey Measurement
SWIFT-RVF	Remote Virtual File Protocol
TACACS-DS	TACACS-Database Service
TACNEWS	TAC News
TCP	Transmission Control Protocol
TCP-ACO	TCP Alternate Checksum Option
TELNET	Telnet Protocol
TFTP	Trivial File Transfer Protocol
THINWIRE	Thinwire Protocol
TIME	Time Server Protocol
TP-TCP	ISO Transport Service on top of the TCP

TRUNK-1	Trunk-1 Protocol
TRUNK-2	Trunk-2 Protocol
UCL	University College London Protocol
UDP	User Datagram Protocol
NNTP	Network News Transfer Protocol
USERS	Active Users Protocol
UUCP-PATH	UUCP Path Service
VIA-FTP	VIA Systems-File Transfer Protocol
VISA	VISA Protocol
VMTP	Versatile Message Transaction Protocol
WB-EXPAK	Wideband EXPAK
WB-MON	Wideband Monitoring
XNET	Cross Net Debugger
XNS-IDP	Xerox NS IDP

```
URL = ftp://ftp.isi.edu/in-notes/iana/assignments/service-names
```

Acronyms and Abbreviations

A

A	Ampere
AA	Administrative Authority
AAL	ATM Adaption Layer
AARP	AppleTalk Address Resolution Protocol
ABM	Asynchronous Balanced Mode (of HDLC)
ABP	Alternate Bipolar
ACF	Access Control Field
ACK	Acknowledgement
ACS	Asynchronous Communication Server
ACSE	Association Control Service Element
ACTLU	Activate Logical Unit
ACTPU	Activate Physical Unit
ADPCM	Adaptive Differential Pulse Code Modulation
ADSP	AppleTalk Data Stream Protocol
AEP	AppleTalk Echo Protocol
AFI	Authority and Format Identifier
AFP	AppleTalk Filing Protocol

AFRP	ARCNET Fragmentation Protocol
AGS	Asynchronous Gateway Server
AI	Artificial Intelligence
AIN	Advanced Intelligent Network
AIS	Alarm Indication Signal
AIX	Advanced Interactive Executive
AL	Alignment
AM	Active Monitor
AMI	Alternate Mark Inversion
AMT	Address Mapping Table
ANSI	American National Standards Institute
API	Applications Program Interface
APPC	Advanced Program-to-Program Communication
ARE	All Routes Explorer
AREA	Area Identifier
ARI	Address Recognized Indicator Bit
ARM	Asynchronous Response Mode
ARP	Address Resolution Protocol
ARPA	Advanced Research Projects Agency
ARPANET	Advanced Research Projects Agency Network
ASCII	American Standard Code for Information Interchange
ASN.1	Abstract Syntax Notation One
ASP	AppleTalk Session Protocol
ATIS	Alliance for Telecommunications Industry Solutions
ATM	Asynchronous Transfer Mode
ATM DXI	ATM Data Exchange Interface
ATM UNI	ATM User-Network Interface
ATP	AppleTalk Transaction Protocol
AU	Access Unit

B

B	B Channel
B	Broadband
B8ZS	Bipolar with 8 ZERO Substitution
BAPI	Bridge Application Program Interface
BAsize	Buffer Allocation size
BC	Block Check
BC	Bearer Capability
Bc	Committed Burst
BCD	Binary Coded Decimal
BCN	Backward Congestion Notification
Be	Excess Burst
BECN	Backward Explicit Congestion Notification
BER	Basic Encoding Rules
BER	Bit Error Ratio
BEtag	Beginning-End tag
B-ICI	Broadband Inter Carrier Interface
BIF	Bus Indentification Field
BIOS	Basic Input/Output System
BIP	Bit Interleaved Parity
BIP-n	Bit Interleaved Parity-n
B-ISDN	Broadband Integrated Services Digital Network
B-ISSI	Broadband Inter-Switching System Interface
BITNET	Because It's Time NETwork
BIU	Basic Information Unit
B-NT1	Network Termination 1 for B-ISDN
B-NT2	Network Termination 2 for B-ISDN
BOC	Bell Operating Company
BOM	Beginning-of-message

BOOTP   Bootstrap Protocol

BPDU   Bridge Protocol Data Unit

bps   Bits Per Second

BPV   Bipolar Violations

BRI   Basic Rate Interface

BSC   Binary Synchronous Communication

BSD   Berkeley Software Distribution

BSS   Broadband Switching System

B-TE   B-ISDN Terminal Equipment

B-TE1   Terminal Equipment 1 for B-ISDN

B-TE2   Terminal Equipment 2 for B-ISDN

B-TA   Terminal Adapter for B-ISDN

BTag   Begin Tag

BTU   Basic Transmission Unit

C

CAD/CAM   Computer-Aided Design and Manufacturing

CBR   Constant Bit Rate

CC   Configuration Control

CCIS   Common Channel Interoffice Signaling

CCR   Commitment, Concurrency, and Recovery

CDV   Cell Delay Variance

CHAP   Challenge Handshake Authentication Protocol

CI   Congestion Indication

CICS   Customer Information Communication System

CIR   Committed Information Rate

CLNP   Connectionless Network Protocol

CLNS   Connectionless-mode Network Services

CLP   Cell Loss Priority

CLS	Connectionless Service
CLTP	Connectionless Transport Protocol
CMIP	Common Management Information Protocol
CMIS	Common Management Information Service
CMOL	CMIP on IEEE 802.2 Logical Link Control
CMOT	Common Management Information Protocol Over TCP/IP
COM	Continuation of Message
CONS	Connection-mode Network Services
COS	Corporation for Open Systems
CP	Common Part
CPCS	Common Part Convergence Sublayer
CPE	Customer Premises Equipment
CPI	Common Part Indicator
C/R	Command/Response bit
CRC	Cyclic Redundancy Check
CREN	The Corporation for Research and Educational Networking
CRS	Cell Relay Service
CS	Convergence Sublayer
CSI	Convergence Sublayer Indicator
CSMA/CD	Carrier Sense Multiple Access with Collision Detection
CSNET	Computer+Science Network
CSPDN	Circuit Switched Public Data Network
CSU	Channel Service Unit
CTERM	Command Terminal Protocol
CTS	Common Transport Semantics

D

D	D Channel
DA	Destination Address

DAP	Data Access Protocol
DARPA	Defense Advanced Research Projects Agency
DAT	Duplicate Address Test
DCA	Defense Communications Agency
DCC	Data Country Code
DCE	Data Circuit-Terminating Equipment
DCN	Data Communications Network
DCS n/n	Digital Cross connect System at Level n
DDCMP	Digital Data Communications Message Protocol
DDI	Direct Dialing In
DDN	Defense Data Network
DDP	Datagram Delivery Protocol
DDS	Digital Data Service
DE	Discard Eligible
DECmcc	DEC Management Control Center
DEMPR	DEC Multiport Repeater
DFI	DSP Format Identifier (see DSP)
DH	DMPDU Header
DHCP	Dynamic Host Configuration Protocol
DIX	DEC, Intel, and Xerox
DL	Data Link
DLC	Data Link Control
DLCI	Data Link Connection Identifier
DMA	Direct Memory Access
DMDD	Distributed Multiplexing Distributed Demultiplexing
DMPDU	Derived MAC Protocol Data Unit
DNIC	Data Network Identification Code
DNS	Domain Name System
DOD	Department of Defense
DPA	Demand Protocol Architecture

DQDB	Distributed Queue Dual Bus
DQSM	Distributed Queue State Machine
DRP	DECnet Routing Protocol
DSAP	Destination Service Access Point
DSG	Default Slot Generator
DSGS	Default Slot Generator Subfield
DS0	Digital Signal Level 0 (64 kbps)
DS1	Digital Signal Level 1 (1.544 Mbps)
DS3	Digital Signal Level 3 (44.736 Mbps)
DSP	Domain Specific Part
DSS	Domain SAP Server
DSU	Data Service Unit
DSU/CSU	Data Service Unit/Channel Service Unit
DSX-n	Digital Signal Cross Connect Level n
DT	DMPDU Trailer (see DMPDU)
DTE	Data Terminal Equipment
DTR	Data Terminal Ready
DXC	Digital Cross-Connect
DXI	Data Exchange Interface

E

EA	Extended Address
EBCDIC	Extended Binary Coded Decimal Interchange Code
ECL	End Communication Layer
ECSA	Exchange Carriers Standards Association
ED	End Delimiter
EDI	Electronic Data Interchange
EFCN	Explicit Forward Congestion Notification
EGA	Enhanced Graphics Array

EGP	Exterior Gateway Protocol
EIA	Electronic Industries Association
ELAP	EtherTalk Link Access Protocol
EOM	End-of-Message
EOT	End of Transmission
ES	Errored Second
ESF	Extended Superframe Format
ESI	End System Identifier
ESIG	European SMDS Interest Group
ES-IS	End System to Intermediate System Protocol
ET	Exchange Termination
ETS	External Timing Source
ETag	End Tag
ETSS	External Timing Source Subfield
ETSI	European Telecommunications Standards Institute
EXOS	Excelan Open System
Ext	Extension

F

FAL	File Access Listener
FAT	File Access Table
FCC	Federal Communications Commission
FCI	Frame Copied Indicator Bit
FCN	Forward Congestion Notification
FCS	Frame Check Sequence
FDDI	Fiber Distributed Data Interface
FDM	Frequency Division Multiplexing
FEBE	Far End Block Error
FEC	Forward Error Correction

FECN	Forward Error Congestion Notification
FERF	Far End Receive Failure
FFS	For Further Study
FH	Frame Handler
FID	Format Identifer
FIFO	First-in First-out
FIPS	Federal Information Processing Standard
FM	Function Management
FMD	Function Management Data
FMIF	Frame Mode Information Field
FNC	Federal Network Council
FOTS	Fiber Optic Transport System
FR	Frame Relay
FRS	Frame Relay Service
FR-UNI	Frame Relay User Network Interface
FRAD	Frame Relay Assembler/Disassembler
FRND	Frame Relay Network Device
FR-SSCS	Frame Relay Service Specific Convergence Sublayer
FT1	Fractional T1
FTAM	File Transfer Access and Management
FTP	File Transfer Protocol

G

G	Giga-
GB	Gigabyte
GFC	Generic Flow Control
GFI	General Format ID
GHz	Gigahertz
GOSIP	Government OSI Profile
GUI	Graphical User Interface

H

H	Hexadecimal
HA	Hardware Address
HCS	Header Check Sequence
HDLC	High Level Data Link Control
Hdr	Header
HEC	Header Error Control
HEL	Header Extension Length
HEMS	High-level Entity Management System
HLC	High Layer Compatibility
HLEN	Hardware Length
HLLAPI	High Level Language API
HLPI	Higher Layer Protocol Identifier
HOB	Head-of-Bus
HOB_A	Head of Bus A
HOB_B	Head of Bus B
HOBS	Head of Bus Subfield
HSSI	High Speed Serial Interface
Hz	Hertz

I

I	Information
IA5	International Alphabet No. 5
IAB	Internet Architecture Board
IAC	Interpret as Command
IANA	Internet Assigned Numbers Authority
ICD	International Code Designator
ICF	Isochronous Convergence Function

ICI	Interexchange Carrier Interface
ICIP	Inter Carrier Interface Protocol
ICMP	Internet Control Message Protocol
ICP	Internet Control Protocol
IDI	Initial Domain Identifier
IDP	Internetwork Datagram Protocol
IDU	Interface Data Unit
IE	Information Element
IEC	International Electrotechnical Commission
IEEE	Institute of Electrical and Electronics Engineers
IESG	Internet Engineering Steering Group
IETF	Internet Engineering Task Force
I/G	Individual/Group
IGMP	Internet Group Management Protocol
IGP	Interior Gateway Protocol
IGRP	Internet Gateway Routing Protocol
ILMI	Interim Local Management Interface
IMPDU	Initial MAC Protocol Data Unit
IMPS	Interface Message Processors
I/O	Input/Output
IOC	Inter-Office Channel
IP	Internet Protocol
IPC	Interprocess Communications Protocol
IPX	Internetwork Packet Exchange
IR	Internet Router
IRTF	Internet Research Task Force
ISA	Industry Standard Architecture
ISDN	Integrated Services Digital Network
ISDU	Isochronous Service Data Unit
IS-IS	Intermediate System to Intermediate System Protocol

ISO	International Organization for Standardization
ISOC	Internet Society
ISODE	ISO Development Environment
ISSI	Inter-Switching System Interface
ISSIP_CLS	Inter-Switching System Interface ProtocolConnectionless Service
ISU	Isochronous Service User
IT	Information Type
ITU	International Telecommunication Union
ITU-T	ITU Telecommunication Standardization Sector (formerly CCITT)
IVDLAN	Integrated Voice/Data Local Area Network
IWF	Interworking Function
IWU	Interworking Unit
IXC	Inter-Exchange Carrier

K

Kbps	Kilo Bits per Second
KHz	Kilohertz

L

LAA	Locally Administered Address
LAN	Local Area Network
LAP	Link Access Procedure
LAPB	Link Access Procedure Balanced
LAPD	Link Access Procedure D Channel
LAPF	Link Access Procedures to Frame Mode Bearer Services
LAT	Local Area Transport
LATA	Local Access Transport Area
LAVC	Local Area VAX Cluster

LCN	Logical Channel Number
LCP	Link Control Protocol
LE	Local Exchange
LEC	Local Exchange Carrier
LEN	Length
LF	Largest Frame
LFC	Local Function Capabilities
LGN	Logical Channel Group Number
LI	Link Identifier
LI	Length Indicator
LIPC	Logical Inter-Process Communication
LIS	Logical IP Subnetwork
LL	Logical Link
LLAP	LocalTalk Link Access Protocol
LLC	Logical Link Control
LLI	Logical Link Identifier
LME	Layer Management Entity
LMI	Local Management Interface
LMI	Layer Management Interface
LMMP	LAN/MAN Management Protocol
LMMPE	LAN/MAN Management Protocol Entity
LMMS	LAN/MAN Management Service
LMMU	LAN/MAN Management User
LMM	LAN/WAN Management User
LOC	Loss of Cell
LOF	Loss of Frame
LOH	Line Overhead
LOP	Loss of Pointer
LOS	Loss of Signal
LPP	Lightweight Presentation Protocol

LSA	Link State Algorithm
LSB	Least Significant Bit
LSL	Link Support Layer
LSS	Link Status Signal
LT	Line Termination
LTE	Line Terminating Equipment

M

MAC	Medium Access Control
MAN	Metropolitan Area Network
MAP	Management Application Protocol
Mbps	Mega Bits Per Second
MCF	MAC Convergence Function (see MAC)
MCP	MAC Convergence Protocol (see MAC)
MHS	Message Handling Service
MHz	Megahertz
MIB	Management Information Base
MID	Message IDentifier
MID	Multiplexing Identifier
MILNET	MILitary NETwork
MIPS	Millions Instructions Per Second
MIS	Management Information Systems
MLID	Multiple Link Interface Driver
MMF	Multi Mode Fiber
MNP	Microcom Networking Protocol
M/O	Mandatory/Optional
MOP	Maintenance Operations Protocol
ms	Milliseconds
MSAP	MAC Service Access Point

MSAU	Multistation Access Unit
MSB	Most Significant Bit
MSDU	MAC Service Data Unit (see MAC)
MSN	Monitoring Cell Sequence Number
MSS	MAN Switching System
MTA	Message Transfer Agent
MTBF	Mean Time Between Failure
MTTR	Mean Time To Repair
MTU	Maximum Transmission Unit
MUX	Multiplex, Multiplexor

N

NACS	NetWare Asynchronous Communications Server
NAK	Negative Acknowledgement
NASI	Netware Asynchronous Service Interface
NAU	Network Addressable Unit
NAUN	Nearest Active Upstream Neighbor
NBP	Name Binding Protocol
NCP	Network Control Program
NCP	NetWare Core Protocol
NCSI	Network Communications Services Interface
NDIS	Network Driver Interface Standard
NetBEUI	NetBIOS Extended User Interface (see NetBIOS)
NetBIOS	Network Basic Input/Output System
NFS	Network File System
NIC	Network Information Center
NIC	Network Interface Card
NIC	Network Independent Clock
NICE	Network Information and Control Exchange

NIS	Names Information Socket
NIST	National Institute of Standards and Technology
NLM	NetWare Loadable Module
NMP	Network Management Process
NMS	Network Management Station
NNI	Network-Network Interface
NNI	Network-Node Interface
NOC	Network Operations Center
NOS	Network Operating System
NPC	Network Parameter Control
NRM	Normal Response Mode
NRZ	Non-Return to Zero
NSF	National Science Foundation
NSAP	Network Service Access Point
NSP	Network Services Protocol
NT	Network Termination
NT1	Network Termination of type 1
NT2	Network Termination of type 2

O

OAM	Operations Administration and Maintenance
OC-1	Optical Carrier, Level 1 (51.84 Mbps)
OC-3	Optical Carrier, Level 3 (155.52 Mbps)
OC-n	Optical Carrier, Level n
ODA	Office Document Architecture
ODI	Open Data Link Interface
OID	Object Identifier
OIM	OSI Internet Management
OOF	Out of Frame

OS	Operating System
OSF	Open Software Foundation
OSI	Open Systems Interconnection
OSI-RM	Open Systems Interconnection Reference Model
OSPF	Open Shortest Path First
OUI	Organizationally Unique Identifier

P

PA	Protocol Address
PABX	Private Automatic Branch Exchange
PAD	Packet Assembler and Disassembler
PAD	Padding
PAP	Password Authentication Protocol
PAP	Printer Access Protocol
PAR	Positive Acknowledgement with Retransmission
PBX	Private Branch Exchange
PC	Personal Computer
PCI	Protocol Control Information
PCM	Pulse Code Modulation
PCSM	Page Counter State Machine
PDN	Public Data Network
PDU	Protocol Data Unit
PEP	Packet Exchange Protocol
PH	Packet Handler
Ph-SAP	Physical layer Service Access Point
PHY	Physical Layer Protocol
PI	Protocol Identification
PID	Protocol Identifier
PL	PAD Length

PL	Physical Layer
PLEN	Protocol Length
PLCP	Physical Layer Convergence Protocol
PLCSM	Physical Layer Connection State Machine
PLP	Packet Layer Protocol
PM	Physical Medium
POH	Path Overhead
POI	Path Overhead Identifier
POP	Point of Presence
POP	Post Office Protocol
POSIX	Portable Operating System Interface—UNIX
POTS	Plain Old Telephone Service
PPP	Point-to-Point Protocol
PRSIG	Pacific Rim SMDS Interest Group
PSN	Packet Switch Node
PSP	Presentation Services Process
PSPDN	Packet Switched Public Data Network
PSR	Previous Segment Received
PSTN	Public Switched Telephone Network
PT	Payload Type
PTN	Personal Telecommunications Number
PTP	Point-to-Point
PUC	Public Utility Commission
PVC	Permanent Virtual Circuit
PVC	Permanent Virtual Connection

Q

QA	Queued Arbitrated
QOS	Quality of Service

R

RARP	Reverse Address Resolution Protocol
RBOC	Regional Bell Operating Company
RC	Routing Control
RD	Route Descriptor
RD	Routing Domain Identifier
RDT	Remote Digital Terminal
RDTD	Restricted Differential Time Delay
REM	Ring Error Monitor
REQ	Request
RFC	Request for Comments
RFH	Remote Frame Handler
RFS	Remote File System
RH	Request/Response Header
RI	Routing Information
RII	Route Information Indicator
RIP	Routing Information Protocol
RJE	Remote Job Entry
ROSE	Remote Operations Service Element
RMON	Remote Monitoring
RPC	Remote Procedure Call
RPS	Ring Parameter Service
RQ	Request Counter
RQM	Request Queue Machine
RSM	Reassembly State Machine
RSX	Realtime resource-Sharing eXecutive
RT	Routing Type
RU	Request/Response Unit
RUIP	Remote User Information Program
RX	Receive

S

SA	Source Address
SABME	Set Asynchronous Balanced Mode Extended
SAP	Service Access Point
SAP	Service Advertising Protocol
SAPI	Service Access Point Identifier
SAR	Segmentation and Reassembly
SAT	Subscriber Access Termination
SCS	System Communication Services
SDH	Synchronous Digital Hierarchy
SDL	Functional Specification and Description Language
SDLC	Synchronous Data Link Control
SDN	Software Defined Network
SDSU	SMDS Data Service Unit
SDU	Service Data Unit
SEL	NSAP Selector
SEQ	Sequence
SET	Switching System (SS) Exchange Termination
SG_1	Slot Generator type 1 function
SG_2	Slot Generator type 2 function
SG_D	Default Slot Generator function
SGMP	Simple Gateway Management Protocol
SIG	SMDS Interest Group (see SMDS)
SIP	SMDS Interface Protocol (see SMDS)
SIP_CLS	SIP Connectionless Service (see SIP)
SIR	Sustained Information Rate
SIU	Subscriber Interface Unit
SLIP	Serial Line IP (see IP)
SM	Standby Monitor

SMAE	System Management Application Entity
SMB	Server Message Block
SMDS	Switched Multimegabit Data Service
SMF	Single Mode Fiber
SMFA	Specific Management Functional Area
SMI	Structure of Management Information
SMT	Station Management
SMTP	Simple Mail Transfer Protocol
SN	Sequence Number
SNA	System Network Architecture
SNADS	Systems Network Architecture Distribution Services
SNAP	Sub-Network Access Protocol
SNCF	Sub-Network Configuration Field
SNI	Subscriber-Network Interface
SNMP	Simple Network Management Protocol
SOH	Start of Header
SOH	Section Overhead
SONET	Synchronous Optical Network
SPA	Sender Protocol Address
SPE	Synchronous Payload Envelope
SPN	Subscriber Premises Network
SPP	Sequenced Packet Protocol
SPX	Sequenced Packet Exchange
SR	Source Routing
SRF	Specifically Routed Frame
SRI	Stanford Research Institute
SRI	SIP Relay Interface (see SIP)
SRT	Source Routing Transparent
SS	Switching System
SSAP	Source Service Access Point

SSCS	Service Specific Convergence Sublayer
SSCF	Service Specific Coordination Function
SSCOP	Service Specific Connection Oriented Protocol
SSM	Single Segment Message
SS7	Common Channel Signalling System No. 7
SSTL	Sender ATM Subaddress (see ATM)
ST	Segment Type
STE	Spanning Tree Explorer
STE	Section Terminating Equipment
STM	Synchronous Tranfer Mode
STS-N	Synchronous Transport Signal level-N
SUA	Stored Upstream Address
SVC	Switched Virtual Connection
SVC	Switched Virtual Circuit

T

TA	Technical Advisory
TA	Terminal Adapter
TAG	Technology Advisory Group
TB	Terabyte
TC	Transmission Convergence
TCB	Transmission Control Block
TCP	Transmission Control Protocol
TDI	Transport Driver Interface
TDM	Time Division Multiplexing
TE	Terminal Equipment
TE1	Terminal Equipment of type 1
TE2	Terminal Equipment of type 2
TEI	Terminal Endpoint Identifier

TID	Terminal Identifier
TR	Technical Reference
TCP	Transmission Control Protocol
TCP/IP	Transmission Control Protocol/Internet Protocol
TDM	Time Division Multiplexing
TELNET	Telecommunications Network
TFTP	Trivial File Transfer Protocol
TH	Transmission Header
TLAP	TokenTalk Link Access Protocol
TLI	Transport Layer Interface
TLV	Type-Length-Value Encoding
TP	Transport Protocol
TR	Technical Reference
TS	Time Stamp
TSR	Terminate-and-Stay Resident
TSTL	Target ATM Subaddress (see ATM)
TTL	Time-to-Live
TUC	Total User Cell Number
TX	Transmit

U

UA	Unnumbered Acknowledgement
UA	User Agent
UAS	Unavailable Seconds
UDI	Unrestricted Digital Information
UDI-TA	Unrestricted Digital Information with Tones/Announcements
UDP	User Datagram Protocol
UI	Unnumbered Information Frame
U/L	Universal/Local

ULP	Upper Layer Protocols
UNI	User Network Interface
UNMA	Unified Network Management Architecture
UPC	Usage Parameter Control
USID	User Service Identificator
UT	Universal Time
UTP	Unshielded Twisted Pair
UU	User-to-User
UUCP	UNIX to UNIX Copy Program

V

V	Volt
VAN	Value Added Network
VAP	Value Added Process
VARP	VINES Address Resolution Protocol
VBR	Variable Bit Rate
VC	Virtual Channel
VCC	Virtual Channel Connection
VCI	Virtual Channel Identifier
VDD	Virtual Device Driver
VF	Voice Frequency Services
VFRP	VINES Fragmentation Protocol
VGA	Video Graphics Array
VICP	VINES Internet Control Protocol
VINES	Virtual Networking System
VIP	VINES Internet Protocol
VIPC	VINES Interprocess Communications
VLSI	Very Large Scale Integration
VMS	Virtual Memory System

VP	Virtual Path
VPC	Virtual Path Connection
VPI	Virtual Path Identifier
VRTP	VINES Routing Update Protocol
VSPP	VINES Sequenced Packet Protocol
VT	Virtual Terminal
VT	Virtual Tributary

W

WAN	Wide Area Network
WDM	Wavelength Division Multiplexing
WIN	Window
WINS	Windows Internet Name Service

X

X	Unassigned Bit
XA-SMDS	Exchange Access SMDS
XDR	External Data Representation
XID	Exchange Identification
XMP	X/Open Management Protocol
XNS	Xerox Network System

Z

ZIP	Zone Information Protocol
ZIS	Zone Information Socket
ZIT	Zone Information Table

TRADEMARKS

- PostScript is a trademark of Adobe Systems.

- Apple, the Apple logo, AppleShare, AppleTalk, Apple IIGS, EtherTalk, LaserWriter, LocalTalk, Macintosh, and TokenTalk are registered trademarks; and APDA, Finder, Image Writer, and Quickdraw are trademarks of Apple Computer, Inc.

- Banyan, the Banyan logo, and VINES are registered trademarks of Banyan Systems Inc.; and StreetTalk, VANGuard and NetRPC are trademarks of Banyan Systems, Inc.

- COMPAQ is a trademark of COMPAQ Computer Corporation.

- DEC, DECnet, LanWORKS, LAT, LAVC, Mailbus, Message Router, Micro-VAX, MOP, Rdb, ThinWire, Ultrix, VAX, VAX Cluster, and VMS Mail are trademarks, and Ethernet is a registered trademark of Digital Equipment Corporation.

- OnNet is a trademark of, and PC/TCP and FTP Software are registered trademarks of FTP Software, Inc.

- HP is a trademark of the Hewlett-Packard Company.

- Intel and Ethernet are registered trademarks of Intel Corporation.

- Dispatcher/SMTP and WatchTower are trademarks of Intercon Systems Corporation.

- AS/400, DISOSS, IBM PC LAN, PC/AT, PC/XT, PROFS, SNA, SNADS, System/370, System/38, 3270 Display Station, DB2, ESCON, MicroChannel, VMS/ESA, MVS/SP, MVS/XA, Netbios, SAA, System View, VM/ESA, VM/XA, VSE/ESA, and VTAM are trademarks of International Business Machines Corporation; and AIX, AT, IBM, NetView, OS/2, OS/400, and PS/2 are registered trademarks of International Business Machines Corporation.

- X and X Window System are trademarks of the Massachusetts Institute of Technology.

- Microsoft, MS-DOS, and LAN Manager are registered trademarks of, and Windows NT is a trademark of Microsoft Corporation.

- Network General and Sniffer Analyzer are trademarks of Network General Corporation.

INDEX

Index

Index

Index

Windows
    Internet support and, 31-36
    NT, 49-53
Wollongong Group, Inc., 26, 32, 36
Workstations, Internet support with Macintosh,
        36-39
Write Request (WRQ), 334

X

X.25, 28, 85-87
    Link Access Procedure Balanced (LAPD),
        85-86
    protocol, 127-37
Xerox, 70

This CD contains a collection of public domain Internet documents, from the Internet Architecture Board (IAB), Internet Engineering Task Force (IETF), Internet Research Group (IRG), and other Internet-related organizations. Each document category is placed in a separate subdirectory identified by document type. These include:

- BCP - the Best Current Practices documents
- FYI - the For Your Information documents
- IMR - the Internet Monthly Report documents, starting with January 1994
- RFC - the Request for Comments documents, starting with RFC 700, and in subdirectories by hundreds (e.g. RFC 1800 is in subdirectory RFC18XX)
- RTR - the RARE Technical Report documents
- STD - the Internet Standard documents

In addition there are two other subdirectories which include:

- INDEX - index files for the FYIs, RFCs and STDs
- RETRIEVE - retrieval instructions for the above files

Files on this CD are either in ASCII text (.txt) or PostScript (.ps) formats.